PAGES PACKED WITH ESSENTIAL INFORMATION

"Value-packed, unbeatable, accurate, and comprehensive."

—The Los Angeles Times

"The guides are aimed not only at young budget travelers but at the independent traveler; a sort of streetwise cookbook for traveling alone."

—The New York Times

"Unbeatable; good sight-seeing advice; up-to-date info on restaurants, hotels, and inns; a commitment to money-saving travel; and a wry style that brightens nearly every page."

—The Washington Post

THE BEST TRAVEL BARGAINS IN YOUR BUDGET

"All the dirt, dirt cheap."

—People

"Let's Go follows the creed that you don't have to toss your life's savings to the wind to travel—unless you want to."

—The Salt Lake Tribune

REAL ADVICE FOR REAL EXPERIENCES

"The writers seem to have experienced every rooster-packed bus and lunar-surfaced mattress about which they write."

—The New York Times

"[Let's Go's] devoted updaters really walk the walk (and thumb the ride, and trek the trail). Learn how to fish, haggle, find work—anywhere."

—Food & Wine

"A world-wise traveling companion—always ready with friendly advice and helpful hints, all sprinkled with a bit of wit."

—The Philadelphia Inquirer

A GUIDE WITH A SPIRIT AND A SOCIAL CONSCIENCE

"Lighthearted and sophisticated, informative and fun to read. [Let's Go] helps the novice traveler navigate like a knowledgeable old hand."

—Atlanta Journal-Constitution

"The serious mission at the book's core reveals itself in exhortations to respect the culture and the environment—and, if possible, to visit as a volunteer, a student, or a teacher rather than a tourist."

—San Francisco Chronicle

Berlin Overview

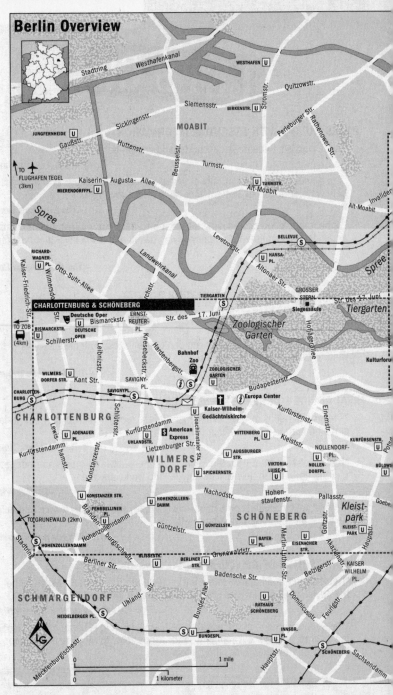

TO FLUGHAFEN TEGEL (3km)

TO ZOB (4km)

TO GRUNEWALD (2km)

MOABIT

Stadtring
Westhafenkanal
WESTHAFEN Ⓤ
Quitzowstr.
Siemensstr.
BIRKENSTR. Ⓤ
Stromstr.
Perleburger Str.
Rathenower Str.
JUNGFERNHEIDE Ⓤ
Gaußstr.
Sickingenstr.
Huttenstr.
Beusselstr.
Turmstr.
Kaiserin- Augusta- Allee
MIERENDORFFPL. Ⓤ
Ⓤ TURMSTR.
Alt-Moabit
Alt-Moabit
Invalider
Spree
Landwehrkanal
Levetzowstr.
BELLEVUE Ⓢ
Spree
Ⓤ HANSA- PL.
Altonaer Str.
GROSSER STERN
Str. des 17. Juni
RICHARD-WAGNER-PL. Ⓤ
Otto-Suhr-Allee
Wilmersdo...str.
TIERGARTEN
Ⓢ
CHARLOTTENBURG & SCHÖNEBERG
Deutsche Oper Ⓤ
Bismarckstr.
ERNST-REUTER-PL.
Str. des 17. Juni
Siegessäule
Zoologischer Garten
Tiergarten
BISMARCKSTR. Ⓤ
DEUTSCHE OPER
Schillerstr.
Leibnizstr.
Knesebeckstr.
Hardenbergstr.
Bahnhof Zoo
ZOOLOGISCHER GARTEN Ⓤ
Hofjägeralle
Kulturforu
WILMERS-DORFER STR. Ⓤ
Kant Str.
SAVIGNY-PL.
ⓘ Ⓢ
Budapesterstr.
CHARLOTTEN-BURG Ⓢ
Schlüterstr.
SAVIGNYPL. Ⓢ
✉
Ⓤ
Kaiser-Wilhelm-Gedächtniskirche
ⓘ Europa Center
Kurfürstenstr.
Einemstr.
CHARLOTTENBURG
Lewis-...hamstr.
ADENAUER PL. Ⓤ
Kurfürstendamm
Konstanzerstr.
UHLANDSTR. Ⓤ
American Express
Lietzenburger Str.
Joachimstaler Str.
WITTENBERG PL. Ⓤ
Kleiststr.
NOLLENDORF-PL.
KURFÜRSTENSTR. Ⓤ
Pots...
Kurfürstendamm
Ⓤ AUGSBURGER STR.
Ⓤ NOLLEN-DORFPL.
BÜLOWS Ⓤ
WILMERS-DORF
Ⓤ SPICHERNSTR.
VIKTORIA-LUISE-PL. Ⓤ
KONSTANZER STR. Ⓤ
HOHENZOLLERN-DAMM Ⓤ
Nachodstr.
Hohen-staufenstr.
Pallasstr.
Goebe...
Kleist-park
FEHRBELLINER PL. Ⓤ
Brande...burgischestr.
GÜNTZELSTR. Ⓤ
Güntzelstr.
SCHÖNEBERG
Goltzstr.
KLEIST-PARK Ⓤ
Hauptstr.
Hohenzollernstr. Ⓢ
Hohenzollerndamm
BAYER-PL. Ⓤ
Martin-Luther-Str.
EISENACHER STR. Ⓤ
Akazienstr.
Belziger...str.
KAISER WILHELM PL.
BLISSESTR. Ⓤ
Berliner Str.
BERLINER STR. Ⓤ
Grunewaldstr.
Badensche Str.
SCHMARGENDORF
HEIDELBERGER PL. Ⓢ
Uhland- str.
Bundes Allee
RATHAUS SCHÖNEBERG Ⓤ
Dominicusstr.
Feurigstr.
Stadtring
BUNDESPL. Ⓢ
INNSBR. Ⓤ
SCHÖNEBERG Ⓢ
Sachsendamm
Mecklenburgischestr.
Hauptstr.

Kaiser-Friedrich-Str.

0 _____ 1 mile
0 _____ 1 kilometer

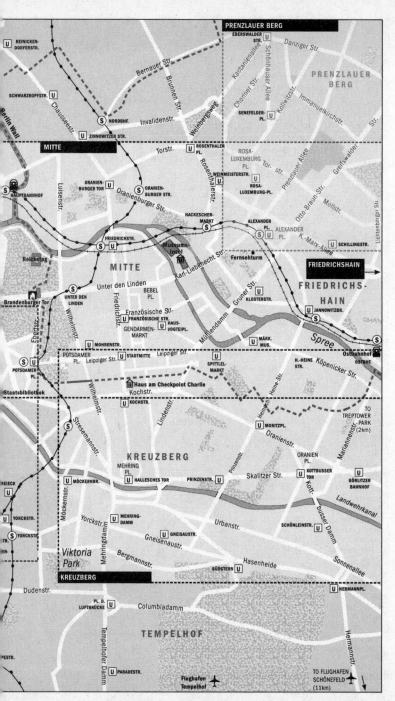

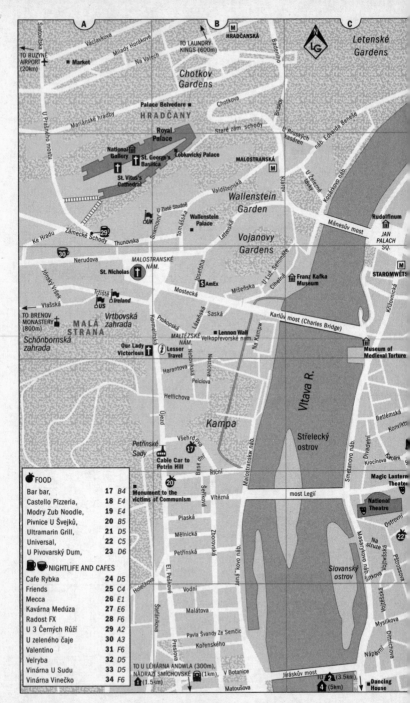

A Václavkova · Milady Horákové · Na Valech
Siatonska
B TO LAUNDRY KINGS (600m) · HRADČANSKÁ M
C Letenské Gardens

TO RUZYNĚ AIRPORT (20km) · ■ Market
U Prašného mostu

Chotkov Gardens

Palace Belvedere ■ · Chotkova · Badeniho
Mariánské hradby · **HRADČANY**
Staré zám. schody · U Bruských kasáren · náb. Edvarda Beneše
Royal Palace
National Gallery · St. George's Basilica · Lobkovický Palace · **MALOSTRANSKÁ** M
St. Vitus's Cathedral · Klárov · U Železné lávky · Kosárkovo náb.

Valdštejnská · *Wallenstein Garden* · **Rudolfinum** 🏛 · JAN PALACH SQ.
U Zlaté Studně · DUK · Tomášská · Wallenstein Palace · Letenská · Mánesův most

Ke Hradu · Zámecké Schody · Thunovská · Sněmovní
29 · *Vojanovy Gardens* · **STAROMĚSTS** M
30 · Nerudova · **MALOSTRANSKÉ NÁM.** · Josefská · Křižovnická
Jánský Vršek · St. Nicholas 🏛 · U Luž. semináře
Vlašská · Tržiště · Ireland 🍀 · Mostecká · Míšeňská · Cihelná · Franz Kafka Museum
US ⚑ · Saská · Karlův most (Charles Bridge)
TO BRENOV MONASTERY (800m) ← · **MALÁ STRANA** · *Vrtbovská zahrada* · AmEx ✉ · Lázeňská · Prokopská · Dražického nám.
Schönbornská zahrada · Karmelitská · **MALTÉZSKÉ NÁM.** · Velkopřevorské nám. · ● Lennon Wall · Na Kampě
Our Lady Victorious 🏛 · ℹ Lesser Travel · Nosticova · **Museum of Medieval Torture** 🏛
Harantova · Pelclova
Hellichova
Kampa · *Vltava R.*
Petřínské Sady · Všehrdova
17 · Cable Car to Petrin Hill · Besední · Říční · *Střelecký ostrov* · **Magic Lantern Theatre**
20 · Monument to the victims of Communism · Šeříková · Vítězná · most Legií · **National Theatre**
Plaská · Malostranské náb. · Smetanovo náb. · Divadelní · Ostrovní
Mělnická · Zborovská · Masarykovo náb. · Na struze · Pštrossova · 22
Petřínská · *Slovanský ostrov* · Šítkova
Holečkova · El. Peškové · Vodní · Myslíkova
Janáčkovo náb. · Dittrichova
Malátova · Náplavní
Štefánikova · Pavla Švandy Ze Semčíc · Kořenského
Preslova · TO U LÉKÁRNA ANDWLA (300m), NÁDRAŽÍ SMÍCHOVSKÉ (1km) 🚂 (1.5km) · V Botanice · Jiráskův most · TO 2 (3.5km), 4 (5km) · ■ Dancing House
Matoušova

🍎 **FOOD**

Bar bar,	**17**	*B4*
Castello Pizzeria,	**18**	*E4*
Modry Zub Noodle,	**19**	*E4*
Pivnice U Švejků,	**20**	*B5*
Ultramarin Grill,	**21**	*D5*
Universal,	**22**	*C5*
U Pivovarský Dum,	**23**	*D6*

🍸 **NIGHTLIFE AND CAFES**

Cafe Rybka	**24**	*D5*
Friends	**25**	*C4*
Mecca	**26**	*E1*
Kavárna Medúza	**27**	*E6*
Radost FX	**28**	*F6*
U 3 Černých Růží	**29**	*A2*
U zeleného čaje	**30**	*A3*
Valentino	**31**	*F6*
Velryba	**32**	*D5*
Vinárna U Sudu	**33**	*D5*
Vinárna Vinečko	**34**	*F6*

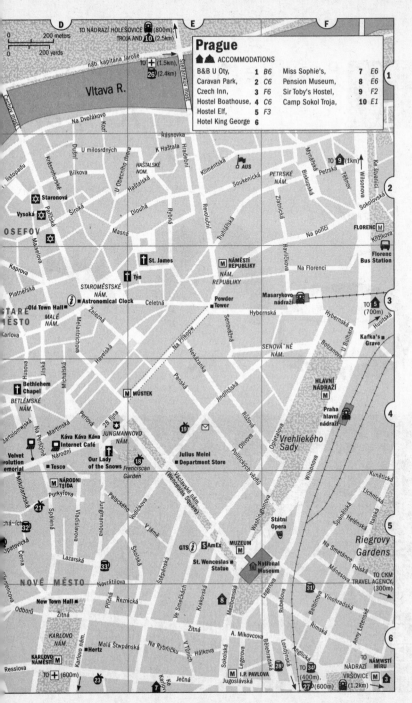

Prague

🔺🔺 ACCOMMODATIONS

B&B U Oty,	**1**	B6	Miss Sophie's,	**7**	E6
Caravan Park,	**2**	C6	Pension Museum,	**8**	E6
Czech Inn,	**3**	F6	Sir Toby's Hostel,	**9**	F2
Hostel Boathouse,	**4**	C6	Camp Sokol Troja,	**10**	E1
Hostel Elf,	**5**	F3			
Hotel King George	**6**				

TO NÁDRAŽÍ HOLEŠOVICE (800m),
TROJA AND 10 (2.5km)

náb. kapitána Jaroše

TO ✚ (1.5km)
26 (2.4km)

TO 9 (1km)

TO 5 (700m)

TO CKM TRAVEL AGENCY, (300m)

TO NÁDRAŽÍ (400m),
27 (600m)

NÁMWSTÍ MIRU

VRŠOVICE (1.2km)

TO 34

TO ✚ (600m)

Vltava R.

Na Dvořákovo

Rásnovka

listopadu

Dušní

U milosrdných

K Haštala   Hradební

Krásnohorské

Bílkova

HAŠTALSKÉ
NOM.

Klimentská

🚩 AUS

PETRSKÉ
NÁM.

Mynářská

Petrská   Petrská   Ke živanici

Wilsonova

Staronová

Siroká

Haštalská

Soukenická

Zlatnická

Biskupská

Sokolovská

Vysoká

Pořičská

Dlouhá

Rybná

Revoluční

Masná

OSEFOV

Maselova

✡

Kaprova

Platnéřská

Masná

Truhlářská

Na poříčí

Na Florenci

FLORENC Ⓜ
Křižíkova

Florenc
Bus Station

🏛 St. James

STAROMĚSTSKÉ
NÁM.

Týn

Ⓜ NÁMĚSTÍ
REPUBLIKY
NÁM.
REPUBLIKY

Na Florenci

Masarykovo
nádraží

TARÉ   ℹ Old Town Hall ■ Astronomical Clock
MĚSTO   MALÉ
NÁM.

Celetná

Powder
Tower

Hybernská

Hybernská

TO 5
(700m)

Husitská

Karlova

Melantrichova

Železná

Na Příkopě

Senovážná

SENOVÁ NÉ
NÁM.

Bolzanova

U Bulhara

Kafka's ■
Grave

Husova

Jilská

Michalská

Haveiská

Na Příkopě

Panská

HLAVNÍ
NÁDRAŽÍ

Bethlehem
Chapel

BETLÉMSKÉ
NÁM.

Ⓜ MÚSTEK

Jindřišská

Růžová

Praha ■
hlavní
nádraží

artolomwská

Na Perštýně

Martinská

Perlová

28 října 🌼
JUNGMANNOVO
NÁM.

19

Olivova

Opletalova

Politických vězňů

Vrehlieekého
Sady

Velvet
evolution
emorial

Káva Káva Káva
■ Internet Café

Národní

Our Lady
of the Snows

ℹ

18

Julius Meinl
■ Department Store

Franciscan
Garden

Václavské nám.
(Wenceslas Square)

Washingtonova

Wilsonova

Kunětická

Lichnická

Ⓜ NÁRODNÍ
TŘÍDA

Purkyňova

Palackého

Jungmannova

Vodičkova

Státní
Opera

Španělská   Helénská   Italská

Riegrovy
Gardens

21

Spálená

Vladislavova

V jámě

Školská

Štěpánská

GTS ℹ $ AmEx

MUZEUM
Ⓜ

St. Wenceslas
Statue

🏛 National
Museum

Na Smetance

Polská

Mánesova

TO CKM
TRAVEL AGENCY,
(300m)

32

chá–ích

Lazarská

33

Krakovská

Mezibranská

Legerova

Rubešova

31

Balbínova

Vinohradská

Anny Letenské

NOVÉ MĚSTO

Opatovická

Černá

renecnová

Odborů

New Town Hall ■

Žitná

KARLOVO
NÁM.

Navrátilova

Příčná   Řeznická

8

Žitná

A. Mikovcova

 Římská

6

Malá Štwpánská   ■ Hertz

Na Rybníčku

Hálkova

Sokolská

Legerova

Bělehradská

Londýnská

Angličká

KARLOVO
NÁMESTÍ Ⓜ

Karlovo nám.

V Tůních

Ⓜ I.P. PAVLOVA

28

TO 34

NÁMWSTÍ
MIRU

Resslova

TO ✚ (600m)

23

7

Ke
Karlovu

Ječná

Jugoslávská

27 (600m)

VRŠOVICE (1.2km)

Ⓜ 3

V

BERLIN, PRAGUE
& BUDAPEST

RESEARCHERS
JUSTIN KEENAN   **RACHEL NOLAN**

MARY POTTER MANAGING EDITOR
DAVID ANDERSSON RESEARCH MANAGER, PRAGUE & BUDAPEST
SARA S. O'ROURKE RESEARCH MANAGER, BERLIN

EDITORS

COURTNEY A. FISKE   **SARA PLANA**
RUSSELL FORD RENNIE   **CHARLIE E. RIGGS**
OLGA I. ZHULINA

LET'S GO PUBLICATIONS

TRAVEL GUIDES

Australia
Austria & Switzerland
Brazil
Britain
California
Central America
Chile
China
Costa Rica
Costa Rica, Nicaragua & Panama
Eastern Europe
Ecuador
Egypt
Europe
France
Germany
Greece
Guatemala & Belize
Hawaii
India & Nepal
Ireland
Israel
Italy
Japan
Mexico
New Zealand
Peru
Puerto Rico
Southeast Asia
Spain & Portugal with Morocco
Thailand
USA
Vietnam
Western Europe
Yucatan Peninsula

ROADTRIP GUIDE

Roadtripping USA

ADVENTURE GUIDES

Alaska
Pacific Northwest
Southwest USA

CITY GUIDES

Amsterdam
Barcelona
Berlin, Prague & Budapest
Boston
Buenos Aires
Florence
London
London, Oxford, Cambridge & Edinburgh
New York City
Paris
Rome
San Francisco
Washington, DC

POCKET CITY GUIDES

Amsterdam
Berlin
Boston
Chicago
London
New York City
Paris
San Francisco
Venice
Washington, DC

ABOUT LET'S GO

THE STUDENT TRAVEL GUIDE
Let's Go publishes the world's favorite student travel guides, written entirely by
Harvard students. Armed with pens, notebooks, and a few changes of clothes
stuffed into their backpacks, our student researchers go across continents,
through time zones, and above expectations to seek out invaluable travel experiences for our readers. Because we are a completely student-run company,
we have a unique perspective on how students travel, where they want to go,
and what they're looking to do when they get there. If your dream is to grab a
machete and forge through the jungles of Costa Rica, we can take you there. If
you'd rather bask in the Riviera sun at a beachside cafe, we'll set you a table. In
short, we write for readers who know that there's more to travel than tour buses.
To keep up, visit our website, www.letsgo.com, where you can sign up to blog,
post photos from your trips, and connect with the Let's Go community.

TRAVELING BEYOND TOURISM
We're on a mission to provide our readers with sharp, fresh coverage packed
with socially responsible opportunities to go beyond tourism. Each guide's
Beyond Tourism chapter shares ideas about responsible travel, study abroad,
and how to give back to the places you visit while on the road. To help you
gain a deeper connection with the places you travel, our fearless researchers
scour the globe to give you the heads-up on both world-renowned and off-the-
beaten-track opportunities. We've also opened our pages to respected writers
and scholars to hear their takes on the countries and regions we cover, and
asked travelers who have worked, studied, or volunteered abroad to contribute
first-person accounts of their experiences.

FIFTY YEARS OF WISDOM
Let's Go has been on the road for 50 years and counting. We've grown a
lot since publishing our first 20-page pamphlet to Europe in 1960, but five
decades and 54 titles later our witty, candid guides are still researched and
written entirely by students on shoestring budgets who know that train
strikes, stolen luggage, food poisoning, and marriage proposals are all part of
a day's work. This year, for our 50th anniversary, we're publishing 26 titles—
including 6 brand new guides—brimming with editorial honesty, a commitment to students, and our irreverent style. Here's to the next 50!

THE LET'S GO COMMUNITY
More than just a travel guide company, Let's Go is a community that reaches
from our headquarters in Cambridge, MA all across the globe. Our small
staff of dedicated student editors, writers, and tech nerds comes together
because of our shared passion for travel and our desire to help other travelers get the most out of their experience. We love it when our readers
become part of the Let's Go community as well—when you travel, drop us a
postcard (67 Mt. Auburn St., Cambridge, MA 02138, USA), send us an e-mail
(feedback@letsgo.com), or sign up on our website (www.letsgo.com) to tell
us about your adventures and discoveries.

**For more information, updated travel coverage, and news from our researcher team,
visit us online at www.letsgo.com.**

CONTENTS

RESEARCHERS

Rachel Nolan *Berlin*

There is perhaps no one more qualified than RaNo to write about Germany's capital city. A Let's Go legend and freelance journalist by trade, Rachel spent the months after graduation and between researching living in Berlin. She took the city by storm—and bike—getting lost in (and rediscovering) its quirks and blazing a trail of impeccable prose. With an instinctive ability to differentiate trendy-and-hip from trying-too-hard, and hot-new-thing from old-and-boring, Rachel successfully captured not only Berlin's spirit, but rather, its zeitgeist.

Justin Keenan *Prague and Budapest*

Justin Keenan's approach to travel writing has often been labeled as Naturalist, his research as Modernist, and his subdued cultural commentary as proto-Industrialist; in fact, his summer séance reached such pinnacles of sublimity that his transcendence could be called post-Transcendentalist. His work bursts with a lyricism that echoes Lord Byron and a voice so his own that it could be called neo-Joycean. At the end of the day, his readers will agree that the only thing Pre-Raphaelite about Justin's writing is the paper it's printed on! Justin Keenan is a senior concentrating in English.

STAFF WRITERS

Dan Barbero	Kyle Bean
Sanders Bernstein	Julia Cain
Nick Charyk	Anna Kendrick
Meg Popkin	Madeleine Schwartz

CONTRIBUTING WRITER

Maryana Pinchuk earned a Bachelor of Arts from Tulane University in New Orleans, where she studied English, Russian, and French literature. Now at Harvard, she continues to pursue her interest in art and revolution—and deliver the odd lecture on 1960s rock—in a PhD program in Slavic Languages and Literature.

ACKNOWLEDGMENTS

DAVID THANKS: Justin, primarily for forcing me to ask the higher-ups how many times I could print "motherf***er" in the guide (count it!). Mary cuz she rocks. Sean Kingston cuz he makes Mary rock. Mary's dad, for liking my jokes. Abby & Sarah, for the advice. My vegan roomies, for the War Room couch. Andrew, for you know, whatever. SPlana & the Ed pod. RM happy hours. Hasty Pudding. Metro Station. Communism. Hey, Mom, what's up?

SARA THANKS: RaNo for being a pro and MPMP for watching over me. LGHQ for caffeine, A/C, couches, baked goods, all-nighters, and other fond memories. Dad for hilarity, Ken for proper perspective, Nelly for the definition of fun, Gram for endless support, Mike for wisdom, Mom for all the rest.

THE EDITORS THANK: First and foremost our lord (Jay-C) and savior (Starbucks, Terry's Chocolate Orange). We also owe gratitude to Barack Obama (peace be upon Him), the Oxford comma, the water cooler, bagel/payday Fridays, the HSA "SummerFun" team for being so inclusive, Rotio (wherefore art thou Rotio?), the real Robinson Crusoe, the Cambridge weather and defective umbrellas, Bolt-Bus, Henry Louis Gates, Jr. (sorry 'bout the phone call), the office blog, gratuitous nudity, the 20-20-20 rule and bananas (no more eye twitches), the Portuguese flag, trips to the beach (ha!), sunbathing recently married Mormon final club alums, non-existent free food in the square, dog-star puns, and last but not least, America. The local time in Tehran is 1:21am. But seriously, the MEs and RMs, our researchers (and all their wisdom on tablecloths and hipsters), LGHQ, HSA, our significant others (future, Canadian, and otherwise), and families (thanks Mom).

Managing Editor
Mary Potter
Research Managers
David Andersson, Sara S. O'Rourke
Editors
Courtney A. Fiske, Sara Plana, Russell Ford Rennie, Charlie E. Riggs, Olga I. Zhulina
Typesetter
C. Alexander Tremblay

Publishing Director
Laura M. Gordon
Editorial Director
Dwight Livingstone Curtis
Publicity and Marketing Director
Vanessa J. Dube
Production and Design Director
Rebecca Lieberman
Cartography Director
Anthony Rotio
Website Director
Lukáš Tóth
Managing Editors
Ashley Laporte, Iya Megre, Mary Potter, Nathaniel Rakich
Technology Project Manager
C. Alexander Tremblay
Director of IT
David Fulton-Howard
Financial Associates
Catherine Humphreville, Jun Li

President
Daniel Lee
General Manager
Jim McKellar

PRICE RANGES

① ② ③ ④ ⑤ BERLIN, PRAGUE, AND BUDAPEST

Our researchers list establishments in order of value from best to worst, honoring our favorites with the Let's Go thumbpick (🖒). We have also incorporated a system of price ranges based on a rough expectation of what you will spend. For **accommodations,** we base our range on the cheapest price for which a single traveler can stay for one night. For **restaurants,** we estimate the average amount one traveler will spend in one sitting. The table below tells you what you'll *typically* find at the corresponding price range, but keep in mind that no system can allow for the quirks of individual establishments.

ACCOMMODATIONS	BERLIN	PRAGUE	BUDAPEST	WHAT YOU'RE *LIKELY* TO FIND
❶	under €15	under 440KČ	under 3000Ft	Campgrounds, hostels, and university dorms. Expect bunk beds, concrete and a communal bath.
❷	€15-23	440-650KČ	3000-4000Ft	Upper-end hostels or lower-end hotels.
❸	€24-30	651-800KČ	4001-5700Ft	A small room with a private bath. Should have decent amenities, such as a phone and TV. Breakfast may be included.
❹	€31-35	801-1100KČ	5701-9000Ft	Should have bigger rooms than a ❸, but with more amenities or in a more convenient location.
❺	over €35	over 1100KČ	over 9000Ft	Large hotels or upscale chains. If it's a ❺ and doesn't have the perks you want, you've paid too much.

FOOD	BERLIN	PRAGUE	BUDAPEST	WHAT YOU'RE *LIKELY* TO FIND
❶	under €4	under 110KČ	under 1200Ft	Street food, kebab and shawarma, bakeries, some cafes, and university cafeterias.
❷	€4-8	110-220KČ	1200-1800Ft	Pizza, sandwiches, unpretentious piles of meat, and deep-fried local cuisine. Likely a sit-down meal.
❸	€9-12	221-340KČ	1801-2400Ft	Mid-priced entrees, pub fare, seafood, and a wine list. Since, you'll have a waiter, tip will set you back a little extra.
❹	€13-20	341-450KČ	2401-3500Ft	A somewhat fancy restaurant. Entrees tend to be heartier or more elaborate, but you're really paying for ambience.
❺	over €20	over 450KČ	over 3500Ft	Your meal may cost more than your room, but there's a reason—duckling, venison medallions, aquatic birds, wildfowl, and *foie gras*. French words on the menu and a decent wine list.

DISCOVER BERLIN, PRAGUE, AND BUDAPEST

The cities of Berlin, Prague, and Budapest are known for their alternative art, electrifying nightlife, and political progressive youth; but it hasn't always been this way. The citizens of these cities have been confronting the problems of history head-on for centuries, but over the course of the 1900s the problems accelerated and intensified. The boulevards of Beaux Arts apartment buildings in West Berlin, the eerie grandeur of Prague's ancient bridges stretching over the mighty Vltava, and the elegant facades of Budapest's Imperial past all do their part to conceal the trauma of two world wars, multiple totalitarian regimes, and a genocide that murdered an estimated 11 million. More recently, Berlin was partitioned by a 30 mi. wall; East Berlin languished under a secret police system that kept tabs on some six million of its citizens while West Berlin, still under Allied control following WWII, became a haven for artists, punks, left-wing activists, and those looking to avoid military conscription. Save for a couple of short-lived thaws, citizens of Hungary and Czechoslovakia waited in lines that snaked around blocks to buy bread, while artists and intellectuals suffered persecution at the hands of a brutal Soviet regime. For years it looked like there was no end in sight, until the relatively peaceful Revolutions of 1989 hurtled East Germany, Czechoslovakia, and Hungary full-speed toward capitalism. Look a little closer at these resilient (and beautiful) cities and you'll find signs of a tumultuous twentieth century everywhere you cast your eye.

Moving forward into the 21st century, Berlin, Prague, and Budapest are no longer weighed down by their turbulent past: it's now been over 20 years since the Wall fell, which means that the youngest generation has grown up with little or no memory of what life was like under Communism. The cities themselves have come of age as well: for the first time in decades, young people are eager to live in and visit Prague and Budapest in particular. In most neighborhoods in Berlin, Prague, and Budapest you can barely walk half a block without being bombarded by hip bars, clubs, cafes, cool galleries, secondhand clothing stores, and young people just hanging out with beers on the sidewalk. Two decades of transformation have left their mark on these cities, and young artists, writers, and intellectuals have tried to puzzle through the confusion and contradictions in multimedia installations in Berlin, over pints or black coffee at Prague's pubs, or on the roofs of squatter clubs in Budapest. So join the fray: whether you're here for a week or a semester, prepare for a brush with the edge of avant-garde art, film, theater, and music. Dust off your Doc Martens, button up your skinny jeans, and forget everything you've learned about secondhand smoke: Berlin, Prague, and Budapest welcome you.

 IN THE END, ALL WE REALLY WANT TO KNOW IS: Would you be *Hungary* for *Turkey* in *Greece* if you could pay for it with a *Czech*?

WHEN TO GO

Tourists visit these three cities year-round. The summer months (May-September) offer the best weather and the highest concentration of tourists. The

DISCOVER

Central Europe

WARSAW

BERLIN

GERMANY

POLAND

PRAGUE

KRAKÓW

MUNICH

CZECH REPUBLIC

ZURICH

SLOVAKIA

VIENNA

AUSTRIA

HUNGARY

SWITZERLAND

BUDAPEST

SLOVENIA

LJUBLJANA

summer is the most difficult time to find cheap accommodations, but it also brings the most entertainment: bars and clubs will be hopping, many sights and attractions will stay open later, and festivals (many of them free) will be off the Richter. To avoid the crowds, spring and autumn are better bets; spring has calmer and more consistent weather. The winter can be bitterly cold and precipitous in Berlin, Prague, and Budapest; if you must visit then, be sure to pack your *Mitte*-ns.

WHAT TO DO

READING RAINBOWS

Berlin, Prague, and Budapest are literary cities. When you're there, you'll inevitably find yourself on a grassy knoll poring through Milan Kundera's *The Unbearable Lightness of Being*. You just won't be able to help it. It's in the water or something. Speaking of which, these cities are also prone to flash thunderstorms, so your sunny knoll may quickly turn into a flooded mudpit. Never fear! You'll soon discover that these cities are also flooded with tiny streetside coffeeshops for your (dry) reading pleasure.

DISCOVER

LET THE SUN SHINE IN	LET IT RAIN
BERLIN: TIERGARTEN (p. 95). Stretching from Bahnhof Zoo in the west to the Brandenburg Gate in the east, this vast landscaped park was once used by Prussian monarchs as a hunting and parade ground.	**BERLIN: CAFE BILDERBUCH (p. 83)**. Settle into a velvety couch and order a brunch basket (they're served all day). With its oak bookcases and fringed lamps, this Schöneberg cafe feels more like a Venetian library.
BERLIN: PFAUENINSEL PEACOCK ISLAND, (p. 100). It just *sounds* wonderful and park-like, doesn't it? Friedrich Wilhelm II constructed a "ruined" castle here and romped around it with his mistress; today, a flock of its namesake fowl roam the manicured orchards and trails.	**BERLIN: SWHARZES CAFE (p. 83)**. Schwarzes has become the most popular boho cafe in Charlottenburg for a reason: absinthe all night in the dimly lit, frescoed space, followed by a delicious breakfast when the sun comes up.
BERLIN: GÖRLITZER PARK (p. 100). Get your hipster barbecue on at this park in Kreuzberg, which was built on the ruins of a deserted train station. If you can't quite bring yourself to do the grilling, stop in at **Das Edelweiß**, the park's cafe.	**BERLIN: TADSHICKISCHE TEESTUBE (p. 84)**. Dating back to Soviet days, this Tajik teahouse has served tea in samovars and tasty sour-cream-covered meat pierogi. Take off your shoes and settle cross-legged with your copy of *Berlin Alexanderplatz*.
PRAGUE: LETNÁ PARK (p. 189). Perhaps the only reason to go to Holešovice, this park is a nice escape from the bustle of Prague proper. The view from the park's Metronome is one of the best in the city.	**PRAGUE: ČAJOVNA POD STROMEM ČAJOVÝM (p. 174)**. Check your e-mail in the no-shoes area of this vaguely Near Eastern-themed teahouse. Peruse a (non-English) menu of over 100 varieties of tea.
PRAGUE: CHARLES UNIVERSITY BOTANICAL GARDENS (p. 178). Relax on a bench surrounded by thousands of varieties of flowers and trees, but be prepared to hike up a steep slope to get there.	**PRAGUE: GLOBE BOOKSTORE AND CAFE (p. 164)**. Owner of the largest collection of English-language books in Central Europe, the Globe is a favorite place for Anglophone expats to congregate.
PRAGUE: PETŘÍN HILL (p. 183). If you visit in spring or summer, don't miss the hundreds of beautiful rose varieties that blossom in the Rose Garden at the top of the Petřín hill.	**PRAGUE: KAVÁRNA V SEDMÉM NEBI (p. 171)**. This bustling, central cafe has a neighborhood feel and is a popular hangout for artists, intellectuals, and those who just like the smell of cloves.
BUDAPEST: THE VÁROSLIGET (p. 250). Budapest's massive city park is dominated by an artificial pond and is home to the Frankenstein-esque Vajdahunyad Castle.	**BUDAPEST: CAFE MARVELOSA (p. 244)**. Students and intellectuals gather to read or work on their laptops while genteely enjoying dishes named for 19th-century artists and poets.
BUDAPEST: ERZSÉBET TÉR (p. 246). One of the city's best-loved parks, it is home to open green spaces, a long staircase dotted with tables and chairs, and a reflecting pool.	**BUDAPEST: 1000 TEA (p. 232)**. One thousand teas may be stretching it, though the menu is certainly impressive, containing every tea you could imagine, as well as some unique blends.
BUDAPEST: MARGARET ISLAND (p. 211). The island provides Budapest's residents with just about every kind of recreational activity available, and there is also plenty of green space for relaxing.	**BUDAPEST: BAR LADINO (p. 236)**. During the day, the cafe is home to various young people and a few dedicated elderly card players. At night, the cafe transforms into a popular but not overcrowded bar.

🏛 ARTSY FARTSY

These three cities offer plenty of opportunities to prance among famous cubist paintings and abstract sculptures and pretend that you know what the hell you're talking about. In addition to oodles of galleries and museums, we've listed the best spots to refuel after a long day of pontificating.

THE GOODS	THE GOULASH
BERLIN: GEMÄLDEGALERIE (p. 106) This is the place to come in Berlin—and arguably in Germany—to see paintings.	**BERLIN: MAROUSH (p. 87)**. This Lebanese joint in Kreuzberg is cosier and cheaper than the competition, and its chicken shawarma can't be beat.
BERLIN: HAMBURGER BAHNHOF: MUSEUM FÜR GEGENWART (MUSEUM FOR THE PRESENT) (p. 107). If you like your art a little more contemporary, you can't do much better than the Museum for the Present.	**BERLIN: MONSIEUR VUONG (p. 84)** In case you couldn't get enough of those gallerists in the other column, you'll probably find a few more chowing down on delicious Vietnamese food at this trendy restaurant in Mitte.
BERLIN: KUNST-WERKE BERLIN (INSTITUTE OF CONTEMPORARY ART) (p. 107). Okay, the Institute of Contemporary Art ain't half bad, either.	**BERLIN: HANS WURST** (p. 85) When you just can't take any more heavy German cuisine, hop on over to this organic, vegan cafe in Prenzlauer Berg.

DISCOVER

THE GOODS	THE GOULASH
PRAGUE: VELETRŽNI PALACE (p. 190) There's no better way to spend a rainy Prague afternoon than getting lost in the flagship (and largest) collection of Prague's dispersed National Gallery.	**PRAGUE: BAR BAR** (p. 169) Expect the unexpected at this eatery/drinkery with surprising food combinations on the menu. Don't ignore the television set sculptures: they're part of the ambience.
PRAGUE: MUSEUM OF CZECH CUBISM (p. 190) Demonstrates how Czech Cubism permeated all spheres of the fine arts during its heyday (including some that it shouldn't have, like home furniture).	**PRAGUE: FRAKTAL** (p. 174) Come for the big portions of delicious American and Mexican food; stay for the odd but enjoyable seating arrangements. Tree-stump tables reserved for hobbits only.
PRAGUE: MUCHA MUSEUM (p. 190) The highlights of this museum, which is devoted to the work of Alfons Mucha, are his many posters featuring "la divine" Sarah Bernhardt.	**PRAGUE: DYNAMO (p. 161)** Enjoy an award-winning meal of duck or pork (or even some veggie options) after exploring the many shops and bookstores in the area.
BUDAPEST: ART HALL (p. 260) Designed primarily for young people and students, this museum attempts to engage viewers with an array of hyper-contemporary media art and installation exhibits.	**BUDAPEST: HUMMUS BAR** (p. 235). Cross your legs and lounge on the floor cushions at this pita paradise. If you're vegetarian or vegan, this place will knock your socks off.
BUDAPEST: LUDWIG MUSEUM (p. 259) Focuses on 20th- and 21st-century Hungarian painting and sculpture. You will also see appearances from international masters and American pop artists.	**BUDAPEST: GIERO** (p. 237) If you're getting homesick, go on an expedition to this hidden gem. If you manage to find it, you'll be made right at home and fed like you're one of the family.
BUDAPEST: MUSEUM OF APPLIED ARTS (p. 259) The most exciting exhibits are this museum's oddities, which range from an array of Tiffany glass objects to an astronomical clock once owned by Emperor Maximilian II.	**BUDAPEST: RING CAFE AND BAR** (p. 238) Like shiny things? This cafe is the best place to stare at people out the window, and at yourself in the reflective interior. The food's great, too.

IN HIGH SPIRITS

Let's cut to the chase, if not the chaser: a lot of people come to Berlin, Prague, and Budapest to party, and for good reason. The alcohol is potent and cheap, and the nightlife famously vibrant. There's a reason they call it Booty-pest, after all. Just don't let it keep you in bed all the next day; these cities also offer an astounding range of religious spectacles to help you transcend your hangover.

GOD IS GOOD	GOOD GOD, I'M DRUNK
BERLIN: KAISER-WILHELM-GEDÄCHTNISKIRCH (p. 89) This neo-Romanesque church took quite a hit during WWII. Check out the beautiful mosaics inside, and be sure to visit the small exhibit with horrific photos of the city in the wake of WWII.	**BERLIN: MONARCH BAR** (p. 120) Your local priest probably wouldn't approve of the cheap beer (or the dingy stairwell leading up to it), but what your local priest don't know won't hurt him.
BERLIN: BERLINER DOM (p. 93). This elegantly bulky, multiple-domed cathedral proves once and for all that Protestants churches can be every bit as dramatic as Catholic ones.	**BERLIN: BERGHAIN/PANORAMA BAR** (p. 119). The granddaddy of Berlin's "it" clubs deserves its reputation as a must-visit, so paint yourself dayglow and brush up on your techtonic dancing.
BERLIN: NEUE SYNAGOGUE (p. 94). Now a museum of the history of Berlin's Jewish community, this impressive synagogue was built in the 1850s and is modeled after the Alhambra in Spain.	**BERLIN: ROSE'S** (p. 122). This popular gay and lesbian club in Kreuzberg is an intense—and somewhat claustrophobic—night out. Brace yourself for decor filled with hearts, glowing lips, furry ceilings, feathers, and glitter.
PRAGUE: BONE CHAPEL AT KUTNA HORA (p. 205) After the plague left the village's graveyard with a surplus of corpses, a monk (and later an artist) decided to do a little decorating.	**PRAGUE: CROSS CLUB** (p. 203). A bar with a bizarre mix of aesthetics. Don't miss the crowded techno-industrial lower level, lit by all manner of glowing, flashing, and spinning contraptions.
PRAGUE: PINKAS SYNAGOGUE (p. 183) The most dramatic of all the Prague-agogues, it has the names of Prague's Holocaust victims inscribed on its walls and is a grand finale of the Josefov synagogue tour.	**PRAGUE: HAPU (p. 201)**. Something of a bartender's bar, this inconspicuous little Žižkov haunt serves some of the most creative and best-mixed cocktails in Prague.

DISCOVER

GOD IS GOOD	GOOD GOD, I'M DRUNK
PRAGUE: SAINT VITUS'S CATHEDRAL (p. 186) This centerpiece of the castle complex is an architectural masterpiece complete with magnificent towers and more flying buttresses than it knows what to do with.	**PRAGUE: BLIND EYE (p. 201)** Named after the one-eyed Jan Žižka, who also lends his name to Žižkov itself, it serves a wide assortment of inappropriately-named drinks. "Sex with the Bartender," anyone?
BUDAPEST: SAINT STEPHEN'S BASILICA (p. 248) Its Panorama Tower offers an amazing 360° view of the city. A mere 100Ft will buy you 2min. of viewing time of St. Stephen's mummified right hand.	**BUDAPEST: CORVINTETŐ (p. 269)** Don't be misled by the graffiti-covered tile stairs—this club situated on top of a former state-owned department store is one of the most stylish places to party in Budapest.
BUDAPEST: GREAT SYNAGOGUE (p. 248) The largest synagogue in Europe and the second largest in the world. Its interior is richly adorned with geometric patterns and chandeliers.	**BUDAPEST: SZIMPLA KERT (p. 266)** Budapest's original and perhaps best-loved ruin pub is also one of the largest. Enjoy the open-air courtyard where old bathtubs and sedans serve as choice seating.
BUDAPEST: BASILICA AT ESZTERGOM (p. 273) Inside, find one of the largest church organs in Hungary and the skull of St. Stephen. The view from the cupola is one of the best you'll ever see.	**BUDAPEST: MUMUS (p. 266)** Instead of loud music and dancing you'll find students, artists, and backpackers relaxing at tables made from old oil drums while enjoying some of the cheapest drinks in town.

LET'S GET SOME SHOES

1989 gave Berlin, Prague, and Budapest many things, among them an end to Soviet repression and the dissolution of a brutal secret police force. But it also brought shopping! That, and a seemingly endless supply of Soviet-throwback kitsch. (DDR-themed bars in Berlin, the Museum of Communism in Prague, or a Soviet-era sculpture park in Budapest, anyone?) The table below has all you need to shop your way through Berlin, Prague, and Budapest, without missing out on any awkward relics from the Soviet era.

THE WONDERS OF SOCIALISM	THE GLORY OF THE FREE MARKET
BERLIN: BERLINER MAUER DOKUMENTATIONZENTRUM (BERLIN WALL DOCUMENTATION CENTER, (p. 97) If you really want to learn about the DDR, skip out on the overpriced and overcrowded Checkpoint Charlie and visit this museum.	**BERLIN: KADEWE** (p. 122). This 7-story Kaufhaus des Westens (Shopping Mall of the West) is the largest department store on the continent. Better stock up before you head farther east; you never know when you'll next find a Missoni bathing suit.
BERLIN: KLUB DER REPUBLIC (KDR BAR, (p. 117) Berlin is full of DDR-themed bars and clubs (yeah, it's just a thing... we don't really know either), but this is the real thing: a DDR-era ballroom turned neighborhood watering hole.	**BERLIN: ST. GEORGE'S BOOKSTORE** (p. 123). This store has the largest selection of secondhand books in all of Berlin. It also offers many free readings, concerts, movie nights, and other events—stop by and ask the English-speaking staff when the fun is.
BERLIN: MARX ENGELS FORUM (p. 93) Don't miss out on the opportunity to hop on Marx's lap for a photo shoot. Your Facebook friends will thank you.	**BERLIN: MAUERPARK** (p. 122). One of Berlin's best flea markets takes over Mauerpark in Prenzlauer Berg every Sunday, selling everything from food to furniture to bicycles.
PRAGUE: LETNÁ PARK (p. 189) On a plateau overlooking the Vltava, Letná has been home to an enormous Stalin statue, a pirate radio station, and an underground rock club. Those days are over; all that remains is some graffiti and a large metronome.	**PRAGUE: PRAŽSKÁ TRŽNICE V HOLEŠOVICÍCH** (PRAGUE MARKET AT HOLEŠOVICE) This flea market on the outskirts of town is a one-stop shop for clothing, produce, crafts, and even electronic equipment.
PRAGUE: ŽIŽKA STATUE AND MAUSOLEUM (p. 188) This mausoleum holds the remains of Klement Gottwald, Communist Czechoslovakia's first president, and other infamous Party leaders. A museum is slated to open on the site in the fall of 2009.	**PRAGUE: TRŽNICE PANKRÁC** (PANKRÁC MARKET). This small market yields some of the best thrift-store style finds in the city.
PRAGUE: MUSEUM OF COMMUNISM (p. 192) This museum explores life in Communist Czechoslovakia. If the exhibit halls get you down, head over to the gift shop, which has a much better sense of humor.	**PRAGUE: OLD TOWN SQUARE** (p. 180) If you're in the market for marionettes and Czech Garnets (or any souvenir, for that matter), the vendors at the Old Town Square have got you covered.

DISCOVER

THE WONDERS OF SOCIALISM	THE GLORY OF THE FREE MARKET
BUDAPEST: MEMENTO PARK (p. 257) Tired of hiking all around these cities to catch every last vestige of Soviet-era statuary? Lovers of grim monuments rejoice! To eliminate the hassle of running back and forth, the citizens of Budapest have moved all of their Communist monuments out to Memento Park.	**BUDAPEST: GREAT MARKET HALL** (p. 246) The building itself is worth the trip: inside, you'll find beautiful arched windows and a colorfully tiled roof. You'll also find row after row of produce stalls as well as food stands and vendors hawking all manner of kitschy trinkets.
BUDAPEST: LIBERTY MONUMENT (p. 254) Once a tribute to "Soviet heroes," Liberty Monument was reclaimed after 1989 and dedicated to those throughout history who have fought for Hungary's freedom.	**BUDAPEST: VÁCI UTCA** (p. 208). Váci utca is *the* place to be when the time rolls around for souvenirs: you're bound to find something for everyone on your list, whether it's that designer leather bag for mom or an "I Love Hungary" mug for dad.
BUDAPEST: CORVIN DEPARTMENT STORE AND CORVINTETŐ (p. 269) During the Communist years, this was Budapest's state-run department store. Today, it's one of the most stylish places to party in the whole city. When you tire of dancing, climb up to the roof and for a stunning view of the sunrise.	**BUDAPEST: MAMMUT MALL** (p. 231). About as Western as Central European shopping malls get: complete with brand names and classy cafes. A little slice of the American suburbs, right in Budapest.

ESSENTIALS

PLANNING YOUR TRIP

ENTRANCE REQUIREMENTS
Passport (p. 10). Required for all non-EU travelers and must be valid for at least 90 days after end of stay. Citizens of most EU states may use their national identity cards.
Visa (p. 11). Required for most foreign nationals. Not required for most citizens of EU states or for citizens of Australia, Canada, New Zealand, or the US for stays under 90 days.
Work Permit (p. 11). Required for all foreigners planning to work in Germany, the Czech Republic, or Hungary.

EMBASSIES AND CONSULATES

CONSULAR SERVICES AT HOME

GERMAN

Australia: Embassy, 119 Empire Circuit, Yarralumla, ACT 2600 (☎02 6270 1911; www.canberra.diplo.de). Consulates in Melbourne, 480 Punt Rd., South Yarra, VIC 3141 (☎03 9864 6888); Sydney, 13 Trelawney St., Woollahra, NSW 2025 (☎02 9328 7733).

Canada: Embassy, Ottawa, 1 Waverly St., Ottawa ON, K2P 0T8 (☎613-232-1101; www.ottawa.diplo.de). Consulates in Montreal, Edifice Marathon, 1250 Blvd. René-Lévesque Oueste Ste. 4315, Québec, H3B 4W8 (☎514-931-2277; www.montreal.diplo.de); Toronto, 77 Bloor St. West Ste. 1702, ON, M5S 2T1 (☎416 925 2813; www.toronto.diplo.de); Vancouver, World Trade Centre Ste. 704, 999 Canada Pl., BC, V6C 3E1 (☎604-684-8377; www.vancouver.diplo.de).

Ireland: Embassy, Dublin, 31 Trimleston Ave., Booterstown, Blackrock (☎01 269 3011; www.dublin.diplo.de).

New Zealand: Embassy, Wellington, 90-92 Hobson St., Thorndon 6011 (☎04 473 6063; www.wellington.diplo.de).

UK: Embassy, London, 23 Belgrave Sq. SW1X 8PZ (☎020 7824 1300; www.london.diplo.de). Consulate in Edinburgh.

US: Embassy, Washington, DC, 4645 Reservoir Rd., N.W. 20007 (☎202-298-4000; www.germany.info). Consulates in Atlanta, Boston, Chicago, Houston, Miami, New York, and San Francisco (see embassy website for contact information).

CZECH

Australia: Canberra, Culgoa Circuit, O'Malley, ACT 2606 (☎02 6290 1386; www.mzv.cz/canberra). Consulates in Adelaide, Melbourne, Perth, and Sydney.

Canada: Ottawa, 251 Cooper St., ON K2P 0G2 (☎613-562-3875; http://old.mzv.cz/ wwwo/?amb=58). Consulates in Calgary, Montreal, Toronto, Vancouver, and Winnipeg.

Ireland: Dublin, 57 Northumberland Rd., Ballsbridge (☎016 681 135; www.mzv.cz/dublin).

New Zealand: Consulate-General, Auckland, Level 3, BMW Mini Centre, 11-15 Great South Road and corner of Margot Street, Newmarket (☎9 522 8736; auckland@honorary.mvz.cz).

UK: London, 6-30 Kensington Palace Gardens, Kensington, W8 4QY (☎020 7243 1115; www.mzv.cz/london). Consulates in Belfast, Cardiff, and Edinburgh.

US: Washington, DC, 3900 Spring of Freedom St. NW, (☎202-274-9100; www.mzv.cz/ washington). Consulates in cities all over the US.

HUNGARIAN

Australia: Canberra, 17 Beale Crescent, Deakin, ACT 2600 (☎62 82 3226; hungcbr@ ozemail.com.au). Consulate in Sydney.

Canada: Ottawa, 299 Waverley St., ON K2P 0V9 (☎613-230-2717; sysadmin@huem-bott.org). Consulates in Montreal and Toronto.

Ireland: 2 Fitzwilliam Pl., Dublin (☎661 2902; titkarsag2@huembrom.it).

New Zealand: Consulate-General, 37 Abbott St., Wellington 6004 (☎973 7507; www. hungarianconsulate.co.nz).

UK: London, 35 Eaton Pl., London SW1X 8BY (☎20 7235 5218; www.mfa.gov.hu/ kulkepviselet/UK).

US: Washington, D.C., 3910 Shoemaker St., NW (☎202-362-6730; www.huembwas.org).

CONSULAR SERVICES ABROAD

BERLIN

Australia: Wallstr. 76-79 (☎30 880 088; www.germany.embassy.gov.au). Open M-Th 8:30am-5pm and F 8:30am-4:15pm.

Canada: Leipziger Platz 17 (☎30 20 3120; www.germany.gc.ca). Open M-F 9am-noon and by appointment 2-4pm.

Ireland: Friedrichstr. 200 (☎30 220 720; www.embassyofireland.de). Open M-F 9:30am-12:30pm and 2:30-4:45pm.

New Zealand: Atrium Friedrichstr. (☎30 20 621; nzembassy.berlin@t-online.de). Open M-Th 9am-1pm and 2-5:30pm, F 9am-1pm and 2-4:30pm.

UK: Wilhlemstr. 70-71 (☎30 20 457; www.britischebotschaft.de/en). Open M-F 9am-noon and 2-4pm.

US: Neustadtische Kirchstr. 4-5 (☎30 238 5174; http://germany.usembassy.gov). Open M-F 8:30am-noon.

PRAGUE

Australia: Consulate-General, 6th fl. Solitaire Building, Klimentská ul. 10 (☎296 578 350). Open M-Th 8:30am-5pm, F 8:30am-2pm. Citizens should contact the UK embassy in an emergency.

Canada: Muchova 6, 160 00 Prague 6 (☎272 101 800; www.czechrepublic.gc.ca). Open M-F 9:30am-12:30pm and 1:30-4:30pm. Consular office open only in the morning.

Ireland: Velvyslanectv Irska, Tržiště 13 (☎254 530 061; www.embassyofireland.cz). Ⓜ A: Malostranská. Open M-F 9:30am-12:30pm and 2:30-4:30pm.

New Zealand: Consulate-General, Dykova 19, 101 00 Prague 10 (☎222 514 672). Citizens should contact the UK embassy in an emergency.

UK: Thunovská 14, 118 00 Prague 1 (☎257 402 111). Ⓜ A: Malostranská. Open M-F 9am-noon.

US: Tržiště 15, 118 01 Prague 1 (☎257 530 663; www.usembassy.cz). Ⓜ A: Malostranská. Open M-F 9am-noon.

BUDAPEST

Australia: Kiralyhago ter 8-9, (☎457 9777; www.hungary.embassy.gov.au).

Canada: 1027 Ganz utca 12-14 (☎392 3360; www.hungary.gc.ca).

Ireland: Bank Center, Granit Tower, 5th fl., Szabadsag ter 7 (☎301 4960; www.embassyofireland.hu).

New Zealand: Teréz krt. 38 (☎331 4908).

UK: Harmincad utca 6, 1051 (☎266 2888; www.britnagykovetseg.hu).

TOURIST OFFICES

BERLIN

The **German National Tourist Office** (**GNTO**; www.germany-tourism.de) is an umbrella organization that supervises Germany's international tourist infrastructure and provides trip-planning information. The website is a goldmine for quick references. It also runs offices abroad:

Australia: Sydney, P.O. Box 1461, N.S.W. 2001 (☎02 8296 0488; gnto@germany.org.au).

Canada: Toronto, 480 University Ave. Ste. 1500, ON M5G 1V2 (☎416 968 1685; info@gnto.ca).

UK: London, P.O. Box 2695, W1A 3TN (☎09001 600100; www.germany-tourism.co.uk).

US: New York, 122 E. 42nd St., New York, NY 10168 (☎212-661-7200; www.cometogermany.com). Los Angeles, 1334 Parkview Ave Ste. 300, Manhattan Beach, CA 90266 (☎310-545-1350; gntolax@aol.com). Chicago, P.O. Box 59594, Chicago, IL 60659 (☎773-539-6303; gntoch@aol.com).

PRAGUE

Green "i"s mark tourist offices in Prague. The **Pražská Informační Služba** (**PIS**; www.pis.cz) provides info on sights and events, distributes lists of hostels and hotels, and often books rooms. **CzechTourism** is the state-run tourism agency. Be aware, however, that their Prague offices are often crowded.

BUDAPEST

Tourinform (www.tourinform.hu) is a useful first-stop service and has three Budapest offices. Tourinform doesn't make accommodation reservations but will find vacancies, especially in university dorms and private *panzió* (pensions). Offices stock maps and provide local information; employees generally speak English and German. The state-owned travel agency **IBUSZ** (www.ibusz.hu) will book private rooms, exchange money, and sell train tickets. Pick up *Tourist Information: Hungary and Budapest in Your Pocket* and the monthly entertainment guide *Programme in Hungary* (both free and in English).

ESSENTIALS

DOCUMENTS AND FORMALITIES

PASSPORTS

REQUIREMENTS

Citizens of Australia, Canada, Ireland, New Zealand, the UK, and the US need valid passports to enter the **Schengen area;** see box below) and to re-enter their home countries. You will not be permitted to enter if your passport expires in under six months; returning home with an expired passport is illegal and may result in a fine.

NEW PASSPORTS

Citizens of Australia, Canada, Ireland, New Zealand, the UK, and the US can apply for a passport at any passport office or at selected post offices and courts of law. Citizens of these countries may also download passport applications from the official website of their country's government or passport office. Any new passport or renewal applications must be filed in advance of the departure date, though most passport offices offer rush services for a steep fee. Note, however, that "rushed" passports still take up to two weeks to arrive.

 ONE EUROPE. European unity has come a long way since 1957, when the European Economic Community (EEC) was created to promote European solidarity and cooperation. Since then, the EEC has become the European Union (EU), a mighty political, legal, and economic institution. On May 1, 2004, 10 South, Central, and Eastern European countries—Cyprus, the Czech Republic, Estonia, Hungary, Latvia, Lithuania, Malta, Poland, Slovakia, and Slovenia—were admitted into the EU, joining 15 other member states: Austria, Belgium, Denmark, Finland, France, Germany, Greece, Ireland, Italy, Luxembourg, the Netherlands, Portugal, Spain, Sweden, and the UK. On January 1, 2007, two others, Bulgaria and Romania, came into the fold, bringing the tally of member states to 27.

What does this have to do with the average non-EU tourist? The EU's policy of freedom of movement means that most border controls have been abolished and visa policies harmonized. Under this treaty, formally known as the Schengen Agreement, you're still required to carry a passport (or government-issued ID card for EU citizens) when crossing an internal border, but, once you've been admitted into one country, you're free to travel to other participating states. Most EU states are already members of Schengen (excluding Cyprus), as are Iceland and Norway. EU newcomers Bulgaria and Romania are still in the process of implementing the free travel agreement. The UK and Ireland have opted out of the agreement, but have created their own Common Travel Area, whose regulations match those of Schengen.

PASSPORT MAINTENANCE

Photocopy the page of your passport with your photo as well as your visas, traveler's check serial numbers, and any other important documents. Carry one set of copies in a safe place, apart from the originals, and leave another set at home.

If you lose your passport, immediately notify the local police and your home country's nearest embassy or consulate. To expedite its replacement, you must show ID and proof of citizenship; it also helps to know all information previously recorded in the passport. In some cases, a replacement may take weeks to process, and it may be valid only for a limited time. Any visas stamped in your old passport will be lost forever. In an emergency, ask for immediate temporary traveling papers that will permit you to re-enter your home country.

VISAS AND WORK PERMITS

EU citizens do not need a visa. Citizens of Australia, Canada, New Zealand, and the US do not need a visa for stays of up to 90 days, but this three-month period begins upon entry into any of the countries that belong to the EU's **freedom of movement** zone. Those staying longer than 90 days may purchase a visa at their local embassy or consulate. Double-check entrance requirements at the nearest embassy or consulate of your destination country (listed on (p. 7) for up-to-date information before departure. US citizens can also consult http://travel.state.gov.

Entering Germany, Hungary, or the Czech Republic to study requires a special visa. For more information, see the **Beyond Tourism** chapter (p. 36). Admittance to a country as a traveler does not include the right to work, which is authorized only by a work permit.

IDENTIFICATION

When you travel, always carry at least two forms of identification on your person, including a photo ID. A passport and a driver's license will usually suffice. Never carry all of your IDs together; instead, split them up in case of theft or loss and keep photocopies in your luggage and at home.

STUDENT AND YOUTH IDENTIFICATION

The **International Student Identity Card (ISIC),** the most widely accepted form of student ID, provides discounts on some sights, accommodations, food, and transportation, access to a 24hr. emergency help line, and insurance benefits for US cardholders. ISIC cardholders, for example, get reduced admission to a number of Berlin museums, the Old Town Hall in Prague, and the Royal Palace in Budapest (p. 252). Applicants must be full-time secondary or post-secondary school students at least 12 years old. Because of the proliferation of fake ISICs, some services (particularly airlines) require additional proof of student identity. For travelers who are under 26 years old but are not students, the **International Youth Travel Card (IYTC)** offers many of the same benefits as the ISIC.

Each of these identity cards costs US$22. ISICs and IYTCs are valid for one year from the date of issue. To learn more about ISICs and IYTCs, visit www. myisic.com. Many student travel agencies (p. 20) issue the cards; for a list of issuing agencies or more information, see the **International Student Travel Confederation (ISTC)** website (www.istc.org).

The **International Student Exchange Card (ISE Card)** is a similar identification card available to students, faculty, and children aged 12 to 26. The card provides discounts, medical benefits, access to a 24hr. emergency help line, and the ability to purchase student airfares. An ISE Card costs US$25; visit www.isecard.com for more info.

CUSTOMS

Upon entering Germany, the Czech Republic, or Hungary, you must declare certain items from abroad and pay a duty on the value of those articles if they exceed the allowance established by the customs service. Upon returning home, you must likewise declare all articles acquired abroad and pay a duty on the value of articles in excess of your home country's allowance. Jot down a list of any valuables brought from home and register them with customs before traveling abroad. It's a good idea to keep receipts for all goods acquired abroad.

 CUSTOMS IN THE EU. As well as freedom of movement of people travelers in the European Union can also take advantage of the freedom of movement of goods. This means that there are no customs controls at internal EU borders and travelers are free to transport whatever legal substances they like as long as it is for their own personal (non-commercial) use.

ESSENTIALS

MONEY

CURRENCY AND EXCHANGE

Germany is on the **euro**. The Czech Republic is expected to adopt the euro for itself some time in the next five years, but its economy currently still runs on the **koruna** (Kč; crown), plural koruny. Hungary uses the **forint** (Ft) and has no immediate plans to join the eurozone. One forint is divided into 100 fillérs, which have disappeared almost entirely from circulation.

The currency charts below are based on August 2009 exchange rates. Check the currency converter on websites like www.xe.com or www.bloomberg.com for the latest exchange rates.

EURO (€)			
AUS$1 = €0.58		1€ = AUS$1.72	
CDN$1 = €0.65		1€ = CDN$1.55	
NZ$1 = €0.47		1€ = NZ$2.14	
UK£1 = €1.18		1€ = UK£0.85	
US$1 = €0.70		1€ = US$1.44	

KORUNY (Kč)			
AUS$1 = 15.15Kč		10Kč = AUS$0.66	
CDN$1 = 16.80Kč		10Kč = CDN$0.60	
EUR€1 = 26Kč		10Kč = EUR€0.39	
NZ$1 = 12.15Kč		10Kč = NZ$0.82	
UK£1 = 30.67Kč		10Kč = UK£0.33	
US$1 = 18.08Kč		10Kč = US$0.55	

FORINTS (Ft)			
AUS$1 = 155.96Ft		1000Ft = AUS$6.40	
CDN$1 = 173.29Ft		1000Ft = CDN$5.76	
EUR€1 = 267.73Ft		1000Ft = EUR€3.73	
NZ$1 = 125.19Ft		1000Ft = NZ$7.98	
UK£1 = 315.90Ft		1000Ft = UK£3.16	
US$1 = 186.36Ft		1000Ft = US$5.36	

As a general rule, it's cheaper to convert money abroad than at home. While currency exchange will probably be available in your arrival airport, it's wise to bring enough foreign currency to last for at least 24-72hr.

When changing money abroad, try banks or currency exchanges that have at most a **5% margin** between their buy and sell prices. Since you lose money with every transaction, it makes sense to convert large sums at one time. Travelers in Prague and Budapest should be vigilant about **currency exchange scams;** the maximum legal commission for cash-to-cash exchange is 1%. Some exchanges will advertise deceptively good rates for "selling" local currency, but actually charge high rates for "buying" it. Other exchanges have confusing signs or conceal real rates in the fine print. Make sure to ask what the actual rate is before changing money. The exchange near Old Town Square in Prague has good rates and a low commission. Never change money on the streets.

If you use traveler's checks or bills, carry some in small denominations (the equivalent of US$50 or less) for times when you are forced to exchange money at poor rates, but bring a range of denominations since charges may be applied per check cashed. Store your money in a variety of forms; ideally, at any given time you will be carrying some cash, some traveler's checks, and an ATM or credit card. In Prague, tellers rarely keep large amounts of change on hand, so paying in large bills may be a problem.

TRAVELER'S CHECKS

Traveler's checks are one of the safest and most convenient means of carrying funds and are readily accepted in Berlin, Prague, and Budapest; **American Express** and **Visa** are the best-recognized brands. Many banks and agencies sell them for a small commission. Check issuers provide refunds if the checks are lost or stolen, and many provide additional services, such as toll-free refund hotlines abroad, emergency message services, and assistance with lost and stolen credit cards or passports. In Budapest, banks like **OTP** and **Raiffensen** offer the best exhchange rates. Ask about toll-free refund hotlines and the location of refund centers when purchasing checks. Remember: always carry emergency cash.

American Express: Checks available with commission at AmEx offices and select banks (www.americanexpress.com). AmEx cardholders can also purchase checks by phone (☎+1-800-528-4800). Cheques for Two can be signed by either of 2 people traveling together. For purchase locations or more information, contact AmEx's service centers: in Australia ☎2 9271 8666, in Canada and the US 800-528-4800, in New Zealand 9 583 8300, in the UK 1273 571 600, in Germany 069 9797, in the Czech Republic 955 512 241, in Hungary 1235 4300.

Visa: Checks available at banks worldwide. For the location of the nearest office, call the Visa Travelers Cheque Global Refund and Assistance Center: in the UK ☎800 895 078, in the US 800-227-6811; elsewhere, call the UK collect at 2079 378 091.

CREDIT, DEBIT, AND ATM CARDS

Where they are accepted, credit cards often offer superior exchange rates—up to 5% better than the retail rate used by banks and other currency-exchange establishments. Credit cards may also offer services such as insurance or emergency help and are sometimes required to reserve hotel rooms or rental cars. **MasterCard** and **Visa** are the most frequently accepted; **American Express** cards work at some ATMs and at AmEx offices and major airports. **Eurocard** is also extremely common in Germany.

The use of ATM cards is widespread in Berlin, Prague, and Budapest. Depending on the system that your bank at home uses, you can most likely access your personal bank account from abroad. ATMs get the same wholesale exchange rate as credit cards, but there is often a limit on the amount of money you can withdraw per day (usually around US$500). There is also typically a surcharge of US$1-5 per withdrawal, so it pays to be efficient.

Debit cards are as convenient as credit cards but withdraw money directly from the holder's checking account. A debit card can be used wherever its associated credit card company (usually MasterCard or Visa) is accepted.

The two major international money networks are **MasterCard/Maestro/Cirrus** (for ATM locations call ☎+1-800-424-7787 or visit www.mastercard.com) and **Visa/PLUS** (for ATM locations visit http://visa.via.infonow.net/locator/global/). Most ATMs charge a transaction fee that is paid to the bank that owns the ATM. It is a good idea to contact your bank or credit-card company before going abroad; frequent charges in a foreign country can sometimes prompt a fraud alert, which will freeze your account.

PINS AND ATMS. To use a cash or credit card to withdraw money from a cash machine (ATM) in Europe, you must have a four-digit Personal Identification Number (PIN). If your PIN is longer than four digits, ask your bank whether you can just use the first four or whether you'll need a new one. Credit cards don't usually come with PINs, so, if you intend to hit up ATMs in Europe with a credit card, call your credit card company before leaving to request one.

Travelers with alphabetic rather than numerical PINs may also be thrown off by the absence of letters on European cash machines. Here are the corresponding numbers to use: 1 = QZ; 2 = ABC; 3 = DEF; 4 = GHI; 5 = JKL; 6 = MNO; 7 = PRS; 8 = TUV; 9 = WXY. Note that if you mistakenly punch the wrong code into the machine multiple (often three) times, it can swallow your card for good.

GETTING MONEY FROM HOME

If you run out of money while traveling, the easiest and cheapest solution is to have someone back home make a deposit to your bank account. Otherwise, consider one of the options below.

WIRING MONEY

It is possible to arrange a **bank money transfer,** which means asking a bank back home to wire money to a bank in Berlin, Prague, or Budapest. This is the cheapest way to transfer cash, but it's also the slowest, usually taking several days or more. Note that some banks may only release your funds in local currency, potentially sticking you with a poor exchange rate; inquire about this in advance. Money transfer services like **Western Union** are faster and more convenient than bank transfers—but also much pricier. Western Union has many locations worldwide. To find one, visit www.westernunion.com or call the appropriate number: in Australia ☎1800 173 833, in Canada and the US 800-325-6000, in the UK 0800 735 1815, in Germany 018 018 181 23, in the Czech Republic 0224 948 252, or in Hungary 145 66 030. To wire money using a credit card: in Canada and the US call ☎800-CALL-CASH, in the UK 0800 833 833. German, Czech, and Hungarian banks do not issue personal checks to their customers, and therefore won't cash them unless you have an account with the bank (and even then only for a high fee).

US STATE DEPARTMENT (US CITIZENS ONLY)

In serious emergencies only, the US State Department will forward money within hours to the nearest consular office, which will then disburse it according to instructions for a US$30 fee. If you wish to use this service, you must

contact the Overseas Citizens Services division of the US State Department
(☎+1-202-501-4444, from US 888-407-4747).

COSTS

The cost of your trip will vary considerably depending on where you visit, how
you travel, and where you stay. The most significant expenses will probably be
your round-trip (return) airfare (see **Getting There: By Plane,** (p. 20) and a railpass
or bus pass (see **Getting Around: By Train,** (p. 23).

To give you a general idea, a bare-bones day in Berlin or Prague (sleeping in
hostels/guesthouses, buying food at supermarkets) would cost about US$40
(€28 or 722Kč); the same day in Budapest would cost about $30 (5588Ft). A
slightly more comfortable day in Berlin or Prague (sleeping in hostels/guest-
houses and the occasional budget hotel, eating one meal per day at a restaurant, going out at night) would cost US$65 (€45 or 1173Kč); the same day in
Budapest would cost about $50 (9315Ft). For a luxurious day, the sky's the
limit. Don't forget to factor in emergency reserve funds (at least US$200) when
planning how much money you'll need.

Some simpler ways to save money on your trip include looking for free entertainment, splitting accommodation and food costs with trustworthy fellow
travelers, and buying food in supermarkets rather than eating out. Bring a **sleep-
sack** (folding a large sheet in half length-wise and sewing the seam will work)
to avoid charges for linens in hostels and do your **laundry** in the sink (unless
you're explicitly prohibited from doing so). Museums often have certain days
once a month or once a week when admission is free; plan accordingly. If you
are eligible, consider getting an ISIC or an IYTC; many sights and museums
offer reduced admission to students and youths. For getting around quickly,
bikes are the most economical option. Renting a bike is cheaper than renting
a moped or scooter. Drinking at bars and clubs quickly becomes expensive.
It's cheaper to buy alcohol at a supermarket and imbibe before going out. That
said, don't go overboard. Though staying within your budget is important, don't
do so at the expense of your health or safety.

TIPPING

BERLIN

Most Germans only round up a euro or two in restaurants and bars as tips,
no matter the bill, and may give a small tip when getting a service, like a taxi
ride. Tips in Germany are not left on the table, but handed directly to the
server. If you don't want any change, say *Das steht so* (dahs SHTAYT zo) or
Das stimmt so (dahs SHTIMT zo).

PRAGUE

Tipping in Prague is casual and not mandatory. Aim for around 5-10% if you're
satisfied with your service. Touristy restaurants in the center of town will
expect a 15-20% tip, but it's best to avoid those places anyway.

BUDAPEST

Tipping is pretty simple in Budapest. Just round up when paying the bill or aim for
around 10%. Give your tip directly to your waiter; don't leave it on the table. Don't
bother bargaining with cabbies, but make sure to set a price before getting in.

ESSENTIALS

CONVERTERS AND ADAPTERS. Electricity in Berlin, Prague, and Budapest is 230 volts AC, enough to fry any 120V North American appliance. Americans and Canadians should buy an **adapter** (which changes the shape of the plug; US$5) and a **converter** (which changes the voltage; US$10-30). Don't make the mistake of using only an adapter (unless appliance instructions explicitly state otherwise). Australians, Brits, and New Zealanders (who use 230V at home) won't need a converter but will need a set of adapters to use anything electrical. For more on all things adaptable, check out http://kropla.com/electric.htm.

SAFETY AND HEALTH

GENERAL ADVICE

In any type of crisis, the most important thing to do is **stay calm.** Your country's embassy abroad (p. 7) is usually your best resource in an emergency; registering with that embassy upon arrival in the country is a good idea. The government offices listed in the **Travel Advisories** box can provide information on the services they offer their citizens in case of emergencies abroad.

LOCAL LAWS AND POLICE

The police in Berlin, Prague, and Budapest all have highly visible presences, and you should not hesitate to contact them if you are the victim of a crime. In all three cities, ☎112 is the number for emergency assistance. Berlin probably has the most respected and reputable police force, although travelers there may find certain regulations harsh and unusual—a keenness for ticketing jaywalkers, for instance. Be sure to carry a valid passport, as police have the right to ask for identification. Police in Prague and Budapest can sometimes be unhelpful if you are the victim of a currency exchange scam; in that case, you might be better off seeking advice from your embassy or consulate.

DRUGS AND ALCOHOL

If you carry insulin, syringes, or any prescription drugs in these cities, you must carry a copy of the prescriptions and a doctor's note. Avoid public drunkenness: it will jeopardize your safety and earn you the disdain of locals. The drinking age in Germany is 16 for beer and wine and 18 for spirits. In Hungary and the Czech Republic, drinking is permitted at age 18. Recreational drugs like marijuana are illegal and best avoided altogether. Embassies may be unwilling to help those arrested on drug charges.

SPECIFIC CONCERNS

PETTY CRIME AND SCAMS

Scams and petty theft are unhappily common in these cities, particularly Prague and Budapest. An especially common scam in bars and nightclubs involves a local woman inviting a traveler to buy her drinks, which end up costing exorbitant prices; the proprietors of the establishment (in cahoots with the scam artist) may then use force to ensure that the bill is paid.

Travelers should always check the prices of drinks before ordering. Another common scam involves a team of con artists posing as metro clerks and demanding that you pay large fines because your ticket is invalid. Credit card fraud is also common Eastern Europe. Travelers who have lost credit cards or fear that the security of their accounts has been compromised should contact their credit card companies immediately.

Con artists often work in groups and may involve children. Beware of certain classics: sob stories that require money, rolls of bills "found" on the street, mustard spilled (or saliva spit) onto your shoulder to distract you while they snatch your bag. **Never let your passport or your bags out of your sight.** Hostel workers will sometimes stand at bus and train arrival points to recruit tired and disoriented travelers to their hostel; never believe strangers who tell you that theirs is the only hostel open. Beware of **pickpockets** in city crowds, especially on public transportation. Also, be alert in public telephone booths. If you must say your calling-card number, do so very quietly; if you punch it in, make sure no one can look over your shoulder.

Visitors to Berlin, Prague, and Budapest should never enter a taxicab containing anyone in addition to the driver and should never split a cab ride with strangers. While traveling by train, it may be preferable to travel in cheaper "cattle-car" type seating arrangements; the large number of witnesses makes such carriages safer than seating in individual compartments. Travelers should avoid riding on night buses or trains, where the risk of robbery or assault is particularly high. Let's Go discourages hitchhiking and picking up hitchhikers.

> **TRAVEL ADVISORIES.** The following government offices provide travel information and advisories by telephone, by fax, or via the web:
>
> **Australian Department of Foreign Affairs and Trade:** ☎2 6261 1111; www.dfat.gov.au.
>
> **Canadian Department of Foreign Affairs and International Trade (DFAIT):** ☎800-267-8376; www.dfait-maeci.gc.ca.
>
> **New Zealand Ministry of Foreign Affairs:** ☎4 439 8000; www.mfat.govt.nz.
>
> **United Kingdom Foreign and Commonwealth Office:** ☎20 7008 1500; www.fco.gov.uk.
>
> **US Department of State:** ☎888-407-4747, +1-202-501-4444 from abroad; http://travel.state.gov.

PERSONAL SAFETY

EXPLORING AND TRAVELING

To avoid unwanted attention, try to blend in as much as possible. Respecting local customs (in many cases, dressing more conservatively than you would at home) may ward off would-be hecklers. Familiarize yourself with your surroundings before setting out and carry yourself with confidence. Check maps in shops and restaurants rather than on the street. If you are traveling alone, be sure someone at home knows your itinerary and never tell anyone you meet that you're by yourself. When walking at night, stick to busy, well-lit streets and avoid dark alleyways. If you ever feel uncomfortable, leave the area as quickly and directly as you can. There is no sure-fire way to avoid all the threatening situations that you might encounter while traveling, but a good **self-defense course** will give you concrete ways to react to unwanted advances.

Impact, Prepare, and **Model Mugging** (www.modelmugging.org) can refer you to local self-defense courses in Australia, Canada, and the US.

POSSESSIONS AND VALUABLES

Never leave your belongings unattended; crime can occur in even the safest-looking hostel or hotel. Bring your own padlock for hostel lockers and don't ever use lockers to store valuables. Be particularly careful on **buses** and **trains;** horror stories abound about determined thieves who wait for travelers to fall asleep. Carry your bag or purse in front of you where you can see it. When traveling with others, sleep in alternate shifts. When alone, be careful in selecting a train compartment: never stay in an empty one and always use a lock to secure your pack to the luggage rack.

There are a few steps you can take to minimize the financial risk associated with traveling. First, **bring as little with you as possible.** Second, buy a few combination **padlocks** to secure your belongings either in your pack or in a hostel or train-station locker. Third, **carry as little cash as possible.** Keep your traveler's checks and ATM/credit cards in a **money belt** (not a "fanny pack," hipster) along with your passport and ID cards. Fourth, **keep a small cash reserve separate from your primary stash.** This should be about US$50 (US dollars or euro are best) sewn into or stored in the depths of your pack, along with your traveler's check numbers and photocopies of your important documents.

For information see currency exchange scams p. 16.

PRE-DEPARTURE HEALTH

In your passport, write the names of any people you wish to be contacted in case of a medical emergency and list any allergies or medical conditions. Matching a prescription to a foreign equivalent is not always easy, safe, or possible, so, if you take **prescription drugs,** carry up-to-date prescriptions or a statement from your doctor stating the medications' trade names, manufacturers, chemical names, and dosages. While traveling, be sure to keep all medication with you in your carry-on luggage.

Common drugs such as aspirin, acetaminophen, and antihistamines (allergy medicines) are readily available in most pharmacies in Berlin, Prague, and Budapest. The German word for pharmacy is *apotheke;* in Hungarian it is *gyógyszertár;* in Czech it is *lekarna* and they are marked by green crosses. Certain drugs like Sudafed, some cough syrups, and Benadryl are not available at all, so you should plan accordingly.

USEFUL ORGANIZATIONS AND PUBLICATIONS

The American **Centers for Disease Control and Prevention** (**CDC;** ☎+1-800-CDC-INFO/232-4636; www.cdc.gov/travel) maintains an international travelers' hotline and an informative website. Consult the appropriate government agency of your home country for consular information sheets on health, entry requirements, and other issues for various countries. For quick information on health and other travel warnings, call the **Overseas Citizens Services** (☎+1-202-647-5225) or contact a passport agency, embassy, or consulate abroad.

STAYING HEALTHY

Common sense is the simplest prescription for good health while you travel. Drink lots of fluids to prevent dehydration and constipation and wear sturdy, broken-in shoes and clean socks.

ONCE IN BERLIN, PRAGUE, OR BUDAPEST

TICK-BORNE DISEASES

Ticks—which can carry Lyme and other diseases—are more common in forested or rural areas than in cities, but they can also be found in Prague's and Budapest's public parks.

Lyme disease: A bacterial infection carried by ticks and marked by a circular bull's-eye rash of 2 in. or more. Later symptoms include fever, headache, fatigue, and aches and pains. Antibiotics are effective if administered early. Left untreated, Lyme can cause problems in joints, the heart, and the nervous system. If you find a tick attached to your skin, grasp the head with tweezers as close to your skin as possible and apply slow, steady traction. Removing a tick within 24hr. greatly reduces the risk of infection. Do not try to remove ticks with petroleum jelly, nail polish remover, or a hot match. Ticks usually inhabit moist, shaded environments and heavily wooded areas. If you are going to be hiking in these areas, wear long clothes and DEET.

Tick-borne encephalitis: A viral infection of the central nervous system transmitted during the summer by tick bites (primarily in wooded areas) or by consumption of unpasteurized dairy products. The risk of contracting the disease is relatively low, especially if precautions are taken against tick bites.

OTHER HEALTH CONCERNS

MEDICAL CARE ON THE ROAD

Berlin, Prague, and Budapest all have relatively high-quality, inexpensive hospitals and health care systems, although the Czech Republic's and Hungary's are weaker than Germany's. Travelers are more likely to find English-speaking doctors on staff at a Berlin hospital, but they are more likely to have credit cards accepted at a Prague or Budapest hospital. Ambulance services in Prague can be slow and unreliable, and they sometimes demand payment on delivery.

If you are concerned about obtaining medical assistance while traveling, you may wish to employ special support services. The **International Association for Medical Assistance to Travelers (IAMAT;** US ☎+1-716-754-4883, Canada +1-416-652-0137; www.iamat.org) has free membership, lists English-speaking doctors worldwide, and offers details on immunization requirements and sanitation.

Those with medical conditions (such as diabetes, allergies to antibiotics, epilepsy, or heart conditions) may want to obtain a **MedicAlert** membership (US$40 per year), which includes, among other things, a stainless-steel ID tag and a 24hr. collect-call number. Contact the MedicAlert Foundation International (from US ☎888-633-4298, outside US +1-209-668-3333; www.medicalert.org).

ESSENTIALS

GETTING TO BERLIN, PRAGUE, AND BUDAPEST

BY PLANE

When it comes to airfare, a little effort can save you a bundle. The key is to hunt around, be flexible, and ask about discounts. Students, seniors, and those under 26 should never have to pay full price for a ticket.

AIRFARES

Airfares to Berlin, Prague, and Budapest peak between June and September; holidays are also expensive. Midweek (M-Th morning) round-trip flights run cheaper than weekend flights, but they are generally more crowded and less likely to permit frequent-flier upgrades. Not fixing a return date ("open return") or arriving in and departing from different cities ("open-jaw") can be pricier than round-trip flights. Patching one-way flights together is the most expensive way to travel. Fortunately for visitors to any of these popular cities, flights between capitals or regional hubs tend to be cheaper.

If Berlin, Prague, or Budapest are stops on a more extensive globe-hop, consider a round-the-world (RTW) ticket. Tickets usually include at least five stops and are valid for about a year; prices range US$3000-8000. Try the airline consortiums **Oneworld** (www.oneworld.com), **Skyteam** (www.skyteam.com), and **Star Alliance** (www.staralliance.com).

High-season (June-September) fares for round-trip flights to Berlin from the US or Canadian east coast cost somewhere in the vicinity of US$500-700; from the US or Canadian west coast US$600-800; from the UK UK£30-150; from Australia AUS$1500-2000; from New Zealand NZ$2500-3500. Round-trip tickets to Prague or Budapest from the American or Canadian east coast cost around US$700-1000; from the west coast US$800-1100; from the UK UK£30-150; from Australia AUS$1500-2000; from New Zealand NZ$2500-3500. Prices drop US$200-500 during the low season (October-May).

BUDGET AND STUDENT TRAVEL AGENCIES

While knowledgeable agents specializing in flights to Central and Eastern Europe can make your life easy, they may not spend the time to find you the lowest possible fare—they get paid on commission. Travelers holding ISICs and IYTCs (p. 11) qualify for big discounts from student travel agencies. Most flights from budget agencies are on major airlines.

The Adventure Travel Company, 124 MacDougal St., New York City, NY 10021, USA (☎+1-212-674-2887; www.theadventuretravelcompany.com). Offices across Canada and the US including New York City, San Diego, San Francisco, and Seattle.

STA Travel, 2871 Broadway, New York City, NY 10025, USA (24hr. reservations and info ☎+1-800-781-4040; www.statravel.com). A student and youth travel organization with offices worldwide, including US offices in Los Angeles, New York City, Seattle, Washington, DC, and a number of other college towns. Ticket booking, travel insurance, railpasses, and more. Walk-in offices are located throughout Australia (☎134 782), New Zealand (☎474 400), and the UK (☎8712 230 0040).

FLIGHT PLANNING ON THE INTERNET. The internet may be the budget traveler's dream when it comes to finding and booking bargain fares, but the array of options can be overwhelming. Many airline sites offer special last-minute deals on the web.

STA (www.statravel.com) and **StudentUniverse** (www.studentuniverse. com) provide quotes on student tickets, while **Orbitz** (www.orbitz.com), **Expedia** (www.expedia.com), and **Travelocity** (www.travelocity.com) offer full travel services. **Priceline** (www.priceline.com) lets you specify a price and obligates you to buy any ticket that meets or beats it; **Hotwire** (www.hotwire. com) offers bargain fares but won't reveal the airline or flight times until you buy. Other sites that compile deals include www.bestfares.com, www.flights. com, www.lowestfare.com, www.onetravel.com, and www.travelzoo.com.

Cheapflights (www.cheapflights.co.uk) is a useful search engine for finding—you guessed it—cheap flights. **Booking Buddy** (www.bookingbuddy.com), **Kayak** (www.kayak.com), and **SideStep** (www.sidestep.com) are online tools that let you enter your trip information and search multiple sites at once. *Let's Go* does not endorse any of these websites. As always, be cautious and research companies before you hand over your credit card number.

COMMERCIAL AIRLINES

TRAVELING FROM NORTH AMERICA

Crossing the pond? Standard commercial carriers like **American** (☎+1-800-433-7300; www.aa.com), **United** (☎+1-800-538-2929; www.ual.com), and **Northwest** (☎+1-800-225-2525; www.nwa.com) will probably offer the most convenient flights, but they may not be the cheapest. Check **Air France** (☎+1-800-237-2747; www.airfrance.us), **Alitalia** (☎+1-800-223-5730; www.alitaliausa.com), **British Airways** (☎+1-800-247-9297; www.britishairways.com), and **Lufthansa** (☎+1-800-399-5838; www.lufthansa.com) for cheap tickets from destinations throughout the US to all over Europe. You might find an even better deal on one of the following airlines, if any of their limited departure points is convenient for you.

Finnair: ☎+358 600 140 140; www.finnair.com. Cheap round-trips from Chicago, Los Angeles, and New York City to Helsinki; connections to Berlin, Budapest, and Prague.

Icelandair: ☎+1-800-223-5500; www.icelandair.com. Departs from Boston, Minneapolis, New York City, Orlando, and Seattle with stopovers in Iceland.

Martinair: ☎+1-800-223-5500; www.icelandair.com. Fly from Miami to Amsterdam and connect to Berlin, Budapest, or Prague.

TRAVELING FROM IRELAND AND THE UK

Aer Lingus: ☎+1-800-474-7424; www.aerlingus.ie. Affordable flights to Berlin, Budapest, and Prague from Dublin and Cork.

KLM: ☎+44 8712 227 474; www.klmuk.com. Cheap tickets to Berlin, Prague, and Budapest from London, Dublin, and elsewhere in the British Isles.

TRAVELING FROM AUSTRALIA AND NEW ZEALAND

Qantas Air: from Australia ☎13 13 13, from New Zealand ☎800 808 767; www.qantas.com.au. Flights from Australia and New Zealand to Berlin, Prague, or Budapest for around AUS$2500.

Thai Airways: from Australia ☎1300 65 19 60, from New Zealand ☎9 256 8518; www. thaiair.com. Auckland, Melbourne, Perth, and Sydney to Frankfurt and Berlin.

BUDGET AIRLINES

For travelers who don't place a premium on convenience or sustainability, we recommend ▓budget airlines as the best way to jet around Europe. Travelers can often snag these tickets for illogically low prices (i.e., less than the price of a meal in the airport food court), but you get what you pay for: namely, minimalist service and no frills. In addition, many budget airlines fly out of smaller regional airports several kilometers out of town. You'll have to buy shuttle tickets to reach the airports of many of these airlines, so plan on adding an hour or so to your travel time. After round-trip shuttle tickets and fees for services that might come standard on other airlines, that €1 sale fare can suddenly jump to €20-100. Still, it's possible save money even if you live outside the continent by hopping a cheap flight to anywhere in Europe and using budget airlines to reach your final destination. Prices vary dramatically; shop around, book months ahead, pack light, and stay flexible to nab the best fares. For a more detailed list of these airlines by country, check out www.whichbudget.com.

berlinair: ☎+49 01 805 737 800; www.airberlin.com. Flights to Berlin from London, New York, and Los Angeles.

bmibaby: from the UK ☎9111 545 454, elsewhere +44 870 126 6726; www.bmibaby. com. Departures from throughout the UK. Manchester to Prague (UK£20).

easyJet: ☎+44 871 244 2366; www.easyjet.com. London to Berlin (UK£30), Prague (UK£30), and Budapest (UK£50).

Germanwings: ☎+49 020 7365 4997; www.germanwings.com. German subsidiary of Eurowings with flights across Europe. London to Berlin (€30).

Ryanair: from Ireland ☎0818 30 30 30, UK 0871 246 0000; www.ryanair.com. To Prague from Dublin and Birmingham; to Budapest from Dublin and Bristol; to Berlin from Dublin, Edinburgh, and London.

SkyEurope: from the UK ☎0906 680 0065, elsewhere +352 27 00 27 28; www.skyeurope.com. Destinations in 19 countries around Europe. London to Prague (UK£40).

TUIfly: ☎01805 757 510; www.tuifly.com. Hanover-based travel agency with affiliates throughout Europe and the Mediterranean. Flights from the UK starting at €15.

Wizz Air: from the UK ☎0904 475 9500, Ireland 1550 475 970; www.wizzair.com. London to Prague (UK£40) and Budapest (£60).

BY TRAIN

One cheap option for visiting Berlin, Prague, or Budapest may be to fly into a Western European capital and then take the train from there. Unless you're visiting as part of a larger European trip, this strategy probably makes less since for Berlin than it does for Prague or Budapest, since Berlin is already an international destination for most major airlines. Travelers to Prague and Budapest often fly into Vienna. For information on European trains, see p. 23

If you plan on passing through other countries en route to your final destination, be sure to check the **transit visa** requirements for those countries.

GETTING AROUND CENTRAL EUROPE

BY TRAIN

Trains in this region of the world are comfortable, convenient, and reasonably swift. Trains, however, are not always safe; for safety tips, see p. 16. Make sure you are on the correct car, as trains sometimes split at crossroads. Towns listed in parentheses on European train schedules require a train switch at the town listed immediately before the parentheses.

You can either buy a **railpass,** which allows you unlimited travel within a particular region for a given period of time, or rely on buying individual **point-to-point** tickets as you go. Almost all countries give students or those under 26 direct discounts on regular domestic rail tickets, and many also sell a student or youth card that provides 20-50% off all fares for up to a year.

RESERVATIONS. While seat reservations are required only for selected trains (usually on major lines), you are not guaranteed a seat without one. You should make reservations in advance during peak holiday and tourist seasons (at the very latest, a few hours ahead).

OVERNIGHT TRAINS. On night trains, you won't waste valuable daylight hours traveling and you can avoid the hassle and expense of staying at a hotel. However, drawbacks include discomfort, sleepless nights, the lack of scenery, and, most importantly, safety concerns. **Sleeping accommodations** on trains differ from country to country, but typically you can either sleep upright in your seat or pay for a separate space. **Couchettes** (berths) typically have from four to six seats per compartment; **sleepers** (beds) in private sleeping cars offer more privacy and comfort but are considerably more expensive. If you are using a railpass valid only for a restricted number of days, inspect train schedules to maximize the use of your pass: an overnight train or boat journey often uses up one of your travel days if it departs after 7pm.

SHOULD YOU BUY A RAILPASS? Railpasses were conceived to allow you to jump on any train in Europe, go wherever you want whenever you want, and change your plans at will. In practice, it's not so simple. You still must stand in line to validate your pass, pay for supplements, and fork over cash for seat and couchette reservations. More importantly, railpasses don't always pay off. If you plan to spend extensive time on trains hopping between big cities, a railpass will probably be worth it. But in many cases, especially if you are under 26, point-to-point tickets may prove a cheaper option.

MULTINATIONAL RAILPASSES

EURAIL PASSES. Eurail is **valid** in much of Europe: Austria, Belgium, Bulgaria, Croatia, the Czech Republic, Denmark, Finland, France, Germany, Greece, Hungary, Ireland, Italy, Luxembourg, Montenegro, the Netherlands, Norway, Poland, Portugal, Romania, Serbia, Slovenia, Spain, Sweden, and Switzerland. **Eurail Global Passes,** valid for a given number of consecutive days, are best for those planning on spending extensive time on trains every few days. Global passes valid for 10+ predetermined (not necessarily consecutive) days within a certain period are more cost-effective for those traveling longer distances less frequently. Prices start at $687 (1st class, 15 days). **Eurail Flexi Passes** offer the same service as Global Passes but with flexible dates within a given period (starting at $811 for 10 travel days in a 2-month period). **Eurail Saver Passes** provide first-class travel for travelers in groups of two to five (starting at $582 per person for 15 days). **Eurail Youth Passes** provides parallel second-class perks for those under 26, starting at $446 for 15 days. Check online for complete rates and discounts (www.raileurope.com).

Passholders receive a timetable for major routes and a map with details on possible rental, hotel, and museum discounts. Passholders often also receive reduced fares or free passage on many boat, bus, and private railroad lines.

The **Eurail Select Pass** is a slimmed-down version of the Eurail Pass: it allows five, six, eight, 10, or 15 days of unlimited travel in any two-month period within three, four, or five bordering countries of 23 European nations. **Eurail Select Passes** (for individuals) and **Eurail Select Saver Passes** (for people traveling in groups of 2 to 5) range from $435/370 per person (5 days, 3 countries) to $962/818 (15 days, 5 countries). The **Eurail Select Youth Pass** (2nd class) costs $284-626. You are entitled to the same freebies afforded by the Eurail Pass, but only when they are within or between countries that you have purchased.

SHOPPING AROUND FOR A EURAIL. Eurail Passes are designed by the EU itself and can be bought only by non-Europeans almost exclusively from non-European distributors. These passes must be sold at uniform prices determined by the EU. However, some travel agents tack on a handling fee, and others offer certain bonuses with purchase, so shop around. Also, keep in mind that pass prices usually go up each year, so, if you're planning to travel early in the year, you can save cash by purchasing before January 1 (you have 6 months from the purchase date to validate your pass in Europe).

It is best to buy your pass before leaving; only a few places in major European cities sell them, and at a marked-up price. You can get a replacement for a lost pass only if you have purchased insurance on it under the Pass Security Plan (€10). Eurail Passes are available through travel agents, student travel agencies like STA (p. 20), and **Rail Europe** (Canada ☎800-361-7245, US +1-800-622-8600; www.raileurope.com) or **Flight Centre** (☎866-967-5351; www.flightcentre.com). It is also possible to buy directly from Eurail's website, www.eurail.com.

OTHER MULTINATIONAL PASSES. If your travels will be limited to one area, regional passes are often good values. Eurail sells passes that cover Germany and the Czech Republic (5 days within 2 months €200) or Austria and Hungary (€134). For those who have lived for at least six months in one of the European countries where **InterRail Passes** are valid, they prove an economical option. The InterRail Pass allows travel within 30 European countries (excluding the passholder's country of residence). The **Global Pass** is valid for a given number of days (not necessarily consecutive) within a 10-day to one-month period. (5 days within 10 days adult 1st class €329, adult 2nd class €249, youth 2nd class €159; 10 days within 22 days €489/359/239; 22 days continuous €629/469/309; 1 month continuous €809/599/399.) The **One Country Pass** limits travel within one European country. Passholders receive free admission to many museums as well as **discounts** on accommodations, food, and some ferries. Passes are available at www.interrailnet.com as well as from travel agents, at major train stations throughout Europe, and through online vendors (such as www.railpassdirect.co.uk).

DOMESTIC TRAINS

GERMANY

German trains are famously reliable and fast. **Deutsche Bahn (DB)** is the major rail provider. Their trains include speedy **InterCityExpress (ICE)** trains, which leave every hour and shuttle between major German cities; **InterCity (IC)** and **Eurocity (EC)** trains, which follow similar routes at a slower speed; and local trains, which run in an extensive, country-wide network that includes IRE, RE, RB, and S-Bahn service.

Deutsche Bahn offers some terrific discounts. Groups of at least six can save up to 70% by reserving in advance, and children under 14 ride free with a guardian. The **Deutsche Bahn Pass** is designed for tourists and allows unlimited travel for four to 10 days within one month. Non-Europeans can purchase Deutsche Bahn passes in their home countries and—with a passport—in major German train stations. A second-class railpass costs €160 for four days of unlimited travel and €20 per extra day. The **German Rail Youth Pass,** for tourists under 26, costs €130 for four days and €10 per extra day.

CZECH REPUBLIC

Most Czech trains are run by **České Dráhy** (Czech Railways). The fastest international trains in the Czech Republic are **EuroCity** and **InterCity** (*expresní;* marked in blue on schedules). *Rychlík* trains are fast domestic trains (*zrychlený vlak;* marked in red on schedules). Avoid slow *osobní* trains, marked in white. *Odjezdy* (departures) are printed on yellow posters; *příjezdy* (arrivals) are printed on white. Seat reservations (*mistenka,* 10Kč) are recommended on express and international trains and for first-class seating.

HUNGARY

Although Hungary is modernizing its rail network, expect trains to run a little bit slower than their Czech or German counterparts. **IMagyar Allamvasutak (MAV)** is the biggest Hungarian provider. Check international and domestic schedules and fares at ▨www.elvira.hu.

Személyvonat trains have many local stops and are excruciatingly slow; *gyorsvonat* trains, listed in red on schedules, move much faster for the same price. Large towns are connected by blue express lines; these air-conditioned **InterCity** trains are the fastest. A *pótjegy* (seat reservation) is required on trains labeled "R," and violators face a hefty fine. Departures *(indulás)* are listed on white posters while arrivals *(érkezés)* are shown on yellow ones.

A basic vocabulary can help you navigate the train system: *vágány* (track) and *állomás* or *pályaudvar* (station, abbreviated *pu*) are useful words. The *peron* (platform) is rarely indicated until the train approaches the station and will sometimes be announced in Hungarian; look closely out the window as you approach. Many stations are not marked; ask the conductor what time the train will arrive (or simply point to your watch and say the town's name).

FURTHER RESOURCES FOR TRAIN TRAVEL
Info on rail travel and railpasses: www.raileurope.com.
Point-to-point fares and schedules: www.raileurope.com/us/rail/fares_ schedules/index.htm. Allows you to calculate whether buying a railpass would save you money.
Railsaver: www.railsaver.com. Uses your itinerary to calculate the best railpass for your trip.
European Railway Server: www.railfaneurope.net. Links to rail servers throughout Europe.

BY BUS

Though European trains and railpasses are extremely popular, in some cases buses prove a better option. Often cheaper than railpasses, **international bus passes** allow unlimited travel on a hop-on, hop-off basis between major European cities. The prices below are based on high-season travel.

Arriva (☎+44 0191 520 4000; www.arriva.co.uk). UK-based bus company with service throughout much of Central and Eastern Europe.

Busabout (☎+44 8450 267 514; www.busabout.com). Offers 3 interconnecting bus circuits covering 29 of Europe's best bus hubs. Prices start at $579 (students $549) for 1 circuit.

CSAD (☎487 823 215; www.dpuk.cz). Runs national and international bus lines through the Czech Republic.

Eurolines (Germany ☎18 0579 0303, Czech Republic 245 005 245, Hungary 1 382 0888; www.eurolines.com). The largest operator of Europe-wide coach services. Offers unlimited 15- and 30-day passes to 41 major European cities (high season 15-day pass €345, 30-day pass €455, under 26 €290/375; mid-season €240/330, under 26 €205/270; low season €205/310, under 26 €175/240).

Volánbusz (☎061 382 0888; www.volanbusz.hu/en). Hungary's largest bus line.

BY CAR

Cars offer freedom, access to the countryside, and an escape from the town-to-town mentality of trains. In Germany, they also offer terrifying speed. Although a single traveler won't save by renting a car, four usually will. If you can't decide between train and car travel, you may benefit from a combination of the two; Rail Europe and other railpass vendors offer rail-and-drive packages (p. 23). Fly-and-drive packages are also often available from travel agents or airline/rental agency partnerships and may offer up to a week of free or discounted rental.

Before setting off, know the laws of the countries in which you'll be driving (see below). For an informal primer on European road signs and conventions, check out www.travlang.com/signs. The **Association for Safe International Road Travel** (ASIRT; ☎+1-301-983-5252; www.asirt.org) can provide more specific information about road conditions.

GERMANY

With the exception of a few older, rural roads in the east, most German roads are in good shape. Drivers should be extremely cautious on the **Autobahn**—Germany's integrated highway network—which has no general speed limit, only a recommendation of 130km per hr. (81 mph). Watch for signs indicating right-of-way (usually designated by a yellow triangle). The Autobahn is indicated by "A" on signs; secondary highways, where the speed limit is usually 100km per hr. (62 mph), are noted as "B" on signs. In cities and towns, speeds hover around 30-60km per hr. (19-37 mph). Passing on the right is illegal in Germany, as is talking on a cell phone while driving. The legal maximum for blood alcohol level is 0.08%.

The **Allgemeiner Deutscher Automobil Club (ADAC;** ☎0180 222 2222; www.adac.de) is Europe's largest automobile association, offering support to motorists all over Germany. Members of worldwide partner organizations (including the American AAA) can contact the ADAC for assistance.

CZECH REPUBLIC

Although the Czech Republic's highways are generally safe and well-maintained, drivers there can be somewhat reckless, and the country has one of the highest road fatality rates in Europe. Smaller, rural roads can have potholes and confusing signs or lane markings.

Speed limits are generally around 50km per hr. (56 mph) in towns, 90km per hr. on rural roads, and 130km per hr. (81 mph) on highways. Driving legally on major Czech highways requires a road usage **tax sticker,** available at gasoline stations. Passing on the right, driving while talking on a cell phone, and driving under the influence of alcohol is illegal; penalties for the latter can be extremely harsh.

HUNGARY

Hungary's roads and highways are in good condition—for the most part. Roads in Budapest are safe, but drivers there may occasionally run into construction areas that are not marked or blockaded. In the countryside, there are a number of dimly lit, narrow, and uneven roads, which may at times be blocked by farm animals or agricultural equipment.

Speed limits are generally 130km per hr. (81 mph) on highways, 110km per hr. (68 mph), and 50km per hr. (31 mph) in town. Many motorists drive well above the speed limit, however. Hungary has a harsh policy against drunk driving: those found on the road and under the influence face steep fines or even jail time. Around Budapest police have become especially vigilant in doing roadside checks. Other illegal offenses in Hungary include driving while talking on a cell phone, turning right on a red light, and failing to wear a seat belt. For 24hr. English assistance, contact the **Magyar Autóklub (MAK;** in Budapest, ☎345 18000).

DRIVING PERMITS AND CAR INSURANCE

If you plan to drive a car while in Germany, the Czech Republic, or Hungary, you must be over 18 and have a valid driver's license from home and an **International Driving Permit (IDP).** Your IDP, valid for one year, must be issued in your own country before you depart. An application for an IDP usually requires one or two photos, a current local license, an additional form of identification, and a fee. To apply, contact your home country's automobile association. Be vigilant when purchasing an IDP online. Many vendors sell permits of questionable legitimacy for higher prices.

Most credit cards cover standard insurance. If you rent, lease, or borrow a car, you will need a **green card,** or **International Insurance Certificate,** to certify that you have liability insurance and that it applies abroad. Green cards can be obtained at car-rental agencies, car dealers (for those leasing cars), some travel agents, and some border crossings. Rental agencies may require you to purchase theft insurance in countries that they consider to have a high risk of auto theft.

RENTING A CAR

You can rent a car from a US-based firm (Alamo, Avis, Budget, or Hertz) with European offices, from a European-based company with local representatives (Europcar), or from a tour operator (Auto Europe, Europe By Car, and Kemwel Holiday Autos) that will arrange a rental for you from a European company at its own rates. Multinationals offer greater flexibility, but tour operators often strike better deals. It is always significantly less expensive to reserve a car from the US than from Europe. Expect to pay US$80-400 per week plus tax for a tiny car. Reserve ahead and pay in advance if at all possible. The minimum rental age in Germany, the Czech Republic, and Hungary is usually 25, although some agencies will rent to 21-year-olds with a fee. At most agencies, all that's needed to rent a car is a license from home and proof that you've had it for a year.

Car rental is available through the following agencies:

Alamo (US ☎+1-877-222-9075, Berlin Airport ☎405 540 3285, Prague Airport 220 114 554, Budapest Airport 061 421 8373; www.alamo.com).

Auto Europe (☎North America +1-888-223-5555, Europe ☎800 22 355 555; www.autoeurope.com).

Avis (Berlin Airport ☎030 60 915 710, Prague Airport 235 362 420, Budapest Airport 061 296 6421; www.avis.com).

Budget (US ☎+1-800-527-0700, outside US ☎+1-800-472-3325; www.budgetrentacar.com).

Europcar International (Berlin Airport ☎634 9160, Prague Airport 235 364 531, Budapest Airport 421 8370; www.europcar.com).

Europe by Car (☎+1-800-223-1516; www.europebycar.com).

Hertz (US ☎+1-800-654-3131, outside US ☎+1-800-654-3001; www.hertz.com).

Kemwel (☎+1-800-678-0678, reservations ☎+1-877-820-0668; www.kemwel.com).

BY THUMB

LET'S NOT GO. *Let's Go* strongly urges you to consider the risks before you choose to hitch. We do not recommend hitching as a safe means of transportation, and none of the information presented here is intended to do so.

No one should hitchhike without careful consideration of the risks involved. Hitching means entrusting your life to a random person who happens to stop beside you on the road, and hitchers always risk theft, assault, sexual harassment, and unsafe driving. Some travelers report that hitchhiking allows them to meet local people and travel in areas where public transportation is sketchy. The choice, however, remains yours.

Hitchhiking at night can be particularly dangerous; experienced hitchers stand in well-lit places. For women traveling alone, hitching is just too dangerous. A man and a woman are a safer combination, two men will have a harder time, and three will go nowhere. Experienced hitchers pick a spot outside of built-up areas where drivers can stop, return to the road without causing an accident, and look over potential passengers as they approach. Hitching (or even standing) on highways is usually illegal: one may only thumb at rest stops or at the entrance ramps to highways. Finally, success will depend on appearance. Drivers prefer hitchers who are neat and wholesome-looking.

Germany does have a very popular rideshare service known as the **Verband der Deutschen Mitfahrzentralen** (www.mitfahrzentrale.de), which pairs drivers with riders. The fee varies according to the destination. Some hitchhikers in Germany report that they have more success asking people for rides at rest stops than than standing on highways; if you know the license plate code of for your destination, it might be useful to check the plates of prospective rides. Hitchers in the Czech Republic should be sure to give an emphatic thumbs-up when gesturing for a ride. A thumb pointed down could be taken as a solicitation for prostitution. Hitchhiking is more common in Hungary and the Czech Republic than it is in much of western Europe.

KEEPING IN TOUCH

BY EMAIL AND INTERNET

Internet access is readily available throughout Berlin, Prague, and Budapest. Most Internet cafes in Berlin charge around €1-2 per hour, in Prague 80-100kč per hour, in Budapest 500-600Ft per hour. Free internet access is often available at hostels. Hungarian and Czech keyboards can be tricky, but there should be options to change to the English setting.

Although in some places it's possible to forge a remote link with your home server, in most cases this is a much slower (and thus more expensive) option than taking advantage of free **web-based email accounts** (e.g., www.gmail.com).

WARY WI-FI. Wireless hot spots make internet access possible in public and remote places. Unfortunately, they also pose **security risks.** Hot spots are public, open networks that use unencrypted, unsecured connections. They are susceptible to hacks and "packet sniffing"—the theft of passwords and other private information. To prevent problems, disable "ad hoc" mode, turn off file sharing and network discovery, encrypt your email, turn on your firewall, beware of phony networks, and watch for over-the-shoulder creeps.

BY TELEPHONE

CALLING HOME FROM ABROAD

Prepaid phone cards are a common and relatively inexpensive means of calling abroad. Each one comes with a Personal Identification Number (PIN) and a toll-free access number. To purchase prepaid phone cards, check online for the best rates; www.callingcards.com is a good place to start. Online providers generally send your access number and PIN via email, with no actual "card" involved. You can also call home with prepaid phone cards purchased in Berlin, Prague, or Budapest (see **Calling Within One Country,** p. 30).

PLACING INTERNATIONAL CALLS. To call abroad from home or to call home from abroad, dial:

1. The **international dialing prefix.** To call from **Australia,** dial ☎0011; **Canada** or the US, ☎011; **Ireland, New Zealand,** the **UK, Germany, Hungary,** or the **Czech Republic** ☎00.
2. The **country code** of the country you want to call. To call **Australia,** dial ☎61; **Canada** or the **US,** ☎1; **Ireland,** ☎353; **New Zealand,** ☎64; the **UK,** ☎44; **Germany,** ☎49; the **Czech Republic** ☎420; **Hungary** ☎36.
3. The **city/area code.** *Let's Go* lists city codes in boxes near the beginning of the seperate chapters of this book and only includes a city code next to an individual phone number when that code is different from that of the rest of the city. Berlin's city code is ☎030; Budapest's is 061. In Germany, if the first digit is a zero (e.g., ☎030 for Berlin), omit the zero when calling from abroad (e.g., dial ☎30 from the U.S. to reach Berlin). In Hungary, if the first two digits are 06, omit the 06 when calling from abroad (e.g. ☎1 for Budapest). The Czech Republic does not use city codes, and there is no need to dial a zero before the first digit.
4. The **local number.**

Another option is to purchase a **calling card,** linked to a major national telecommunications service in your home country. Calls are billed collect or to your account. Cards generally come with instructions for dialing both domestically and internationally.

Placing a collect call through an international operator can be expensive but may be necessary in case of an emergency. You can frequently call collect without even possessing a company's calling card just by calling its access number and following the instructions.

CALLING WITHIN ONE COUNTRY

Remember that all city codes begin with a zero in Germany and that city codes are not used at all in the Czech Republic. Dial ☎06 before Hungarian domestic calls, unless you see it already listed in the number.

Old-fashioned, coin-operated telephone booths are disappearing in Berlin, Prague, and Budapest, although some do still exist. Especially in Prague and Budapest, callers will have an easier time finding booths that take pre-paid telephone cards. Don't call the numbers posted in many booths for credit card calling; most charge exorbitant rates. In Budapest, international calls require red or blue phones, the latter of which tend to end calls after 3-9min. In all three cities, phone rates typically tend to be highest in the morning, lower in the evening, and lowest on Sundays and late at night.

CELLULAR PHONES

The international standard for cell phones is **Global System for Mobile Communication (GSM).** To make and receive calls in Germany, the Czech Republic, or Hungary, you will need a GSM-compatible phone and a **SIM (Subscriber Identity Module) card,** a country-specific, thumbnail-size chip that gives you a local phone number and plugs you into the local network. Many SIM cards are pre-paid, and incoming calls are frequently free. You can buy additional cards or vouchers (usually available at convenience stores) to "top up" your phone. For more information on GSM phones, check out www.telestial.com. Companies like **Cellular Abroad** (www.cellularabroad.com) rent cell phones that work in a variety of destinations around the world.

 GSM PHONES. Just having a GSM phone doesn't mean you're necessarily good to go when you travel abroad. The majority of GSM phones sold in the US operate on a different frequency (1900) than international phones (900/1800) and will not work abroad. Tri-band phones work on all three frequencies (900/1800/1900) and will operate through most of the world. Additionally, some GSM phones are SIM-locked and will only accept SIM cards from a single carrier. You'll need a SIM-unlocked phone to use a SIM card from a local carrier when you travel.

TIME DIFFERENCES

Germany, the Czech Republic, and Hungary are all 1hr. ahead of Greenwich Mean Time (GMT) and all observe Daylight Saving Time.

BY MAIL

SENDING MAIL HOME

Airmail is the best way to send mail home from Berlin, Prague, or Budapest. **Aerogrammes,** printed sheets that fold into envelopes and travel via airmail, are available at post offices. Write "airmail" or *"par avion"* on the front. Most post offices will charge exorbitant fees or simply refuse to send aerogrammes with enclosures. Surface mail is by far the cheapest and slowest way to send mail. It takes one to two months to cross the Atlantic and one to three to cross the Pacific—good for heavy items you won't need for a while, like souvenirs that you've acquired along the way.

SENDING MAIL ABROAD

To ensure timely delivery, mark envelopes "airmail," *"par avion," "letecky"* (in the Czech Republic), or *"légiposta"* (in Hungary). In addition to the standard postage system, **Federal Express** (☎+1-800-463-3339; www.fedex.com) handles most express mail services. Sending letters (up to 50g) domestically in Germany requires €0.55, in the Czech Republic 10kč, in Hungary 33Ft.

There are several ways to arrange pickup of letters sent to you while you are abroad. Mail can be sent via **Poste Restante** (General Delivery) to almost any city or town with a post office. Address Poste Restante letters like so:

Václav HAVEL
Poste Restante
Prague, Czech Republic.

The mail will go to a special desk in the central post office, unless you specify a post office by street address or postal code. It's best to use the largest post office, since mail may be sent there regardless. Bring your passport (or other photo ID) for pickup; there may be a small fee. If the clerks insist that there is nothing for you, ask them to check under your first name as well. *Let's Go* lists post offices in **Practical Information.**

ACCOMMODATIONS

HOSTELS

Many hostels are laid out dorm-style, often with large single-sex rooms and bunk beds, although private rooms that sleep from two to four are becoming more common. They sometimes have kitchens and utensils for your use, breakfast and other meals, storage areas, laundry facilities, internet, transportation to airports, and bike or moped rentals. However, there can be drawbacks: some hostels impose a maximum stay, close during certain daytime "lockout" hours, have a curfew, don't accept reservations, or, less frequently, require that you do chores. A dorm bed in a hostel will average around €15 in Berlin, around 440Kč in Prague, and about 3000Ft in Budapest. A private room costs €20 in Berlin, 500kč in Prague, and 400Ft in Budapest.

ESSENTIALS

ESSENTIALS

> **A HOSTELER'S BILL OF RIGHTS.** There are certain standard fea-
> tures that we do not include in our hostel listings. Unless we state otherwise,
> you can expect that every hostel has no lockout, no curfew, free hot showers,
> some system of secure luggage storage, and no key deposit.

HOSTELLING INTERNATIONAL

Joining the youth hostel association in your own country (listed below) auto-
matically grants you membership privileges in **Hostelling International (HI)**, a fed-
eration of national hosteling associations. Non-HI members may be allowed
to stay in some hostels, but they will have to pay extra to do so. HI hostels
are scattered throughout Berlin, Prague, and Budapest and offer discounts to
members. HI's umbrella organization's website (www.hihostels.com), which
lists the web addresses and phone numbers of all national associations, can be
a great place to begin researching hosteling in a specific region. Other hosteling
websites include www.hostels.com and www.hostelplanet.com.

Most HI hostels also honor **guest memberships**—you'll get a blank card with
space for six validation stamps. Each night you'll pay a nonmember supplement and earn one guest stamp; six stamps make you a member. This system
works well most of the time, but in some cases you may need to remind the
hostel reception. Most student travel agencies (p. 20) sell HI cards, as do all of
the national hosteling organizations listed below.

Australian Youth Hostels Association (AYHA), 422 Kent St., Sydney, NSW 2000
(☎2 9261 1111; www.yha.com.au). AUS$42, under 26 AUS$32.

Hostelling International-Canada (HI-C), 205 Catherine St., Ste. 400, Ottawa, ON K2P
1C3 (☎613-237-7884; www.hihostels.ca). CDN$35, under 18 free.

Hostelling International Northern Ireland (HINI), 22-32 Donegall Rd., Belfast BT12
5JN (☎28 9032 4733; www.hini.org.uk). UK£15, under 25 UK£10.

Youth Hostels Association (England and Wales), Trevelyan House, Dimple Rd., Matlock,
Derbyshire DE4 3YH (☎1629 592 600 ; www.yha.org.uk). UK£16, under 26 UK£10.

Youth Hostels Association of New Zealand Inc. (YHANZ), Level 1, 166 Moorhouse Ave.,
P.O. Box 436, Christchurch (☎+64 3 379 9970, in NZ 0800 278 299; www.yha.org.nz).
NZ$40, under 18 free.

Hostelling International-USA, 8401 Colesville Rd., Ste. 600, Silver Spring, MD 20910
(☎301-495-1240; www.hiayh.org). US$28, under 18 free.

OTHER TYPES OF ACCOMMODATIONS

HOTELS

Hotel singles cost from around €35 per night in Berlin, 1000Kč in Prague,
5700Ft in Budapest. If you make reservations in writing, indicate your night
of arrival and the number of nights you plan to stay. The hotel will send you a
confirmation and may request payment for the first night.

LONG-TERM ACCOMMODATIONS

Travelers planning to stay in Berlin, Prague, or Budapest for extended periods
of time may find it most cost-effective to rent an apartment. A basic one-bed-
room (or studio) apartment in Berlin will range €400-500 per month, in Prague

1300-1600Kč, in Budapest 90,000-150,000Ft. Besides the rent itself, prospective tenants are usually also required to front a security deposit (frequently 1 month's rent) and the last month's rent.

Shared houses in Germany, called **Wohngemeinschaften (WGs),** are a popular option for students and young professionals. German-language listings can be found online at a few sites including www.studenten-wg.de, www.wg-gesucht.de, and www.kijiji.de. Foreign visitors often find it easier to rent through **Mitwohnzentralen** (homeshare companies), which find rooms for individuals in shared apartments. These companies charge a percentage of each month's rent as commission. Shop around to find the best rates.

SPECIFIC CONCERNS

WOMEN TRAVELERS

Women exploring on their own inevitably face some additional safety concerns. Single women can consider staying in hostels that offer single rooms that lock from the inside or in religious organizations with single-sex rooms. It's a good idea to stick to centrally located accommodations and to avoid solitary late-night treks or metro rides. Always carry extra cash for a phone call, bus, or taxi. **Hitchhiking** is never safe for lone women or even for two women traveling together. Look as if you know where you're going and approach older women or couples for directions if you're lost or feeling uncomfortable in your surroundings. Generally, the less you look like a tourist, the better off you'll be. Dress conservatively, especially in rural areas. Wearing a conspicuous **wedding band** sometimes helps to prevent unwanted advances.

Your best answer to verbal harassment is no answer at all; feigning deafness, sitting motionless, and staring straight ahead at nothing in particular will usually do the trick. Don't hesitate to seek out a police officer or a passerby if you are being harassed. Memorize the emergency numbers in places you visit and consider carrying a whistle on your keychain. A self-defense course will both prepare you for a potential attack and raise your level of awareness of your surroundings (see **Personal Safety,** p. 17).

GLBT TRAVELERS

Attitudes toward gay, lesbian, bisexual, and transgendered (GLBT) travelers are generally progressive and accepting in Berlin, Prague, and Budapest, although public displays of affection may be frowned upon in some neighborhoods in the latter two cities. Each of these cities has a thriving GLBT nightlife scene. Listed below are contact organizations, mail-order catalogs, and publishers that offer materials addressing some specific concerns. **Out and About** (www.planetout.com) offers a comprehensive website and a weekly newsletter addressing gay travel concerns.

> **Gay's the Word,** 66 Marchmont St., London WC1N 1AB, UK (☎+44 20 7278 7654; http://freespace.virgin.net/gays.theword). The largest gay and lesbian bookshop in the UK, with both fiction and nonfiction titles. Mail-order service available.

> **Giovanni's Room,** 345 S. 12th St., Philadelphia, PA 19107, USA (☎+1-215-923-2960; www.giovannisroom.com). An international lesbian and gay bookstore with mail-order service (carries many of the publications listed below).

International Lesbian and Gay Association (ILGA), 17 Rue de la Charité, 1210 Brussels, Belgium (☎+32 2 502 2471; www.ilga.org). Provides political information, such as homosexuality laws of individual countries.

ADDITIONAL GLBT RESOURCES

Damron Men's Travel Guide, Damron Women's Traveller, Damron Accommodations Guide, Damron City Guide, and *Damron Women's Traveller.* Published annually by Damron Travel Guides. For info, call ☎+1-415-255-0404 or visit www.damron.com.

The Gay Vacation Guide: The Best Trips and How to Plan Them, by Mark Chesnut. Kensington Books.

Gayellow Pages USA/Canada, by Frances Green. Gayellow Pages. Also publishes regional editions. Visit Gayellow pages online at http://gayellowpages.com.

Spartacus International Gay Guide 2009, by Bruno Gmunder Verlag.

TRAVELERS WITH DISABILITIES

Berlin is an extremely accessible to disabled travelers: 51 underground and 118 suburban train stations can be reached by elevator or ramp, and many buses and trams are equipped with special ramps that allow wheelchair-bound travelers to board. **Mobidat,** an online database (www.mobidat.net; only available in German) rates museums, sights, and theaters on their accessibility to disabled travelers. Prague and Budapest—both of which have cobbled, uneven streets—are less accessible, although Prague has made an effort to revamp its public transportation system in the last several years. Travelers should inform airlines and hotels of their disabilities when making reservations, as some time may be needed to prepare special accommodations. Call ahead to restaurants, museums, and other facilities to find out if they are wheelchair accessible. Guide-dog owners should inquire as to the quarantine policies of each destination country.

For disabled travelers on a larger Central European trip, rail is probably the most convenient form of transport: many stations have ramps, and some trains have wheelchair lifts, special seating areas, and specially equipped toilets. All Eurostar, some InterCity (IC), and some EuroCity (EC) trains are wheelchair-accessible, as are most ICE, EC, IC, and IR trains in Germany. Local trains in Hungary and the Czech republic have limited resources for wheelchair-accessibility. For those who wish to rent cars, some major car-rental agencies (e.g., Hertz) offer hand-controlled vehicles.

Accessible Journeys, 35 W. Sellers Ave., Ridley Park, PA 19078, USA (☎+1-800-846-4537; www.disabilitytravel.com). Designs tours for wheelchair users and slow walkers. The site has tips and forums for all travelers.

Flying Wheels Travel, 143 W. Bridge St., Owatonna, MN 55060, USA (☎+1-877-451-5006; www.flyingwheelstravel.com). Specializes in escorted trips to Europe for people with physical disabilities; plans custom trips worldwide.

Mobility International USA (MIUSA), 132 E. Broadway, Ste. 343, Eugene, OR 97401, USA (☎+1-541-343-1284; www.miusa.org). Provides a variety of books and other publications containing information for travelers with disabilities.

Society for Accessible Travel and Hospitality (SATH), 347 5th Ave., Ste. 605, New York City, NY 10016, USA (☎+1-212-447-7284; www.sath.org). An advocacy group that publishes free online travel information. Annual membership US$49, students and seniors US$29.

DIETARY CONCERNS

The travel section of **The Vegetarian Resource Group's** website, at www.vrg.org/travel, has a comprehensive list of organizations and websites that are geared toward helping vegetarians and vegans traveling abroad. *Vegetarian Europe*, edited by Alex Bourke, lists vegetarian restaurants in 23 countries. For more information, visit your local bookstore or health-food store. Vegetarians will also find numerous resources on the web; try www.vegdining.com, www.happycow.net, and www.vegetariansabroad.com, for starters.

Travelers who keep **kosher** should contact synagogues in larger cities for information on kosher restaurants. Synagogue or college Hillels should have access to lists of Jewish institutions across the nation. If you are strict in your observance, you may have to prepare your own food on the road. Travelers looking for **halal** restaurants may find www.zabihah.com a useful resource.

LET'S GO ONLINE. Plan your next trip on our newly redesigned website, **www.letsgo.com.** It features the latest travel info on your favorite destinations as well as tons of interactive features: make your own itinerary, read blogs from our trusty Researchers, browse our photo library, watch exclusive videos, check out our newsletter, find travel deals, and buy new guides. We're always updating and adding new features, so check back often!

ESSENTIALS

BEYOND TOURISM

A PHILOSOPHY FOR TRAVELERS

HIGHLIGHTS OF BEYOND TOURISM IN BERLIN, PRAGUE, AND BUDAPEST

BE A MENTOR to schoolchildren in the city of Berlin (p. 38).
TILL THE FIELDS of an organic farm outside of Budapest (p. 38).

As a tourist, you are always a foreigner. Sure, hostel-hopping and sightseeing can be great fun, but connecting with a foreign country through studying, volunteering, or working can extend your travels beyond tourist traps. We usually don't like to brag, but we're going to for a moment: this is what's different about a *Let's Go* traveler. Instead of feeling like a stranger in a strange land, you can understand Berlin, Prague, or Budapest like a local. Instead of being that tourist asking for directions, you can be the one who gives them (and correctly!). All the while, you get the satisfaction of leaving one of these countries in better shape than you found it. It's not wishful thinking—it's Beyond Tourism.

As a **volunteer** in one of these cities, you can roll up your sleeves, cinch down your Captain Planet belt, and get your hands dirty doing anything from working on a farm to taking care of soldiers' children. This chapter is chock-full of ideas on how to get involved, whether you're looking to pitch in for a day or run away from home for a whole new life in German activism.

We here at Let's Go are big fans of **studying** abroad. When we find ourselves reading Kafka in his favorite cafe (see **Cafe Louvre**, p. 165), it actually makes us feel sorry for those poor tourists who don't get to do homework while they're in Prague. That said, we here at the Go are huge nerds. Therefore, we've also provided a few fun alternatives to traditional study, where your homework might consist of practicing your brewing skills.

Working abroad is one of the best ways to immerse yourself in a new culture, meet locals, and learn to appreciate a non-US currency. Yes, we know you're on vacation, but we're not talking about normal desk jobs—we're talking about teaching English, doing science research, or being an au pair, all in the name of funding another month of globe-trotting.

SHARE YOUR EXPERIENCE. Have you had a particularly enjoyable volunteer, study, or work experience that you'd like to share with other travelers? Post it to our website, www.letsgo.com!

VOLUNTEERING

Got an itch to save the world? We here at Let's Go get all types of itches, so we can commiserate. Volunteering can be a powerful and fulfilling experience, especially when combined with the thrill of traveling in a new place. Hungary and the Czech Republic, with their stunning natural beauty, diverse populations, and history of political unrest, pose unique and important challenges that are ripe fodder for volunteer organizations. Berlin in particular is a city known for social activism and community building organizations. Researching a program before committing is your best bet to find the volunteer opportunity that is right for you. If you can, talk to people who have participated in the program, and find out what you're getting into, as living and working conditions can vary greatly from one organization to another.

Most people who volunteer in Berlin, Prague, and Budapest do so on a short-term basis at organizations that make use of drop-in or once-a-week volunteers. The best way to find opportunities that match your interests and schedule may be to check with local or national volunteer centers. As always, read up before heading out.

Those looking for longer, more intensive volunteer opportunities usually choose to go through a parent organization that takes care of logistical details and often provides a group environment and support system—for a fee. There are two main types of organizations—religious and secular—although there are rarely restrictions on participation for either. Websites like **www.volunteerabroad.com, www.idealist.org,** and **www.servenet.org** allow you to search for volunteer openings both in your country and abroad.

> **I HAVE TO PAY TO VOLUNTEER?** Many volunteers are surprised to learn that some organizations require large fees or "donations," but don't go calling them scams just yet. While such fees may seem ridiculous at first, they often keep the organization afloat, covering airfare, room, board, and administrative expenses for the volunteers. (Other organizations must rely on private donations and government subsidies.) If you're concerned about how a program spends its fees, request an annual report or finance account. A reputable organization won't refuse to inform you of how volunteer money is spent. Pay-to-volunteer programs might be a good idea for young travelers who are looking for more support and structure (such as pre-arranged transportation and housing) or anyone who would rather not deal with the uncertainty of creating a volunteer experience from scratch.

GENERAL RESOURCES

Action Without Borders, (www.idealist.org). An extensive internet bulletin board listing over 46,000 volunteer organizations and with a versatile search engine.

Coordinating Committee for International Voluntary Service, UNESCO House, 31 r. François Bonvin, 75732 Paris Cedex 15, France (☎33 14 56 84 936; www.unesco.org/ccivs). This umbrella organization links over 140 NGOs worldwide. The "Members" section on the website includes a list of volunteer branches throughout Central and Eastern Europe with contact information.

GoAbroad.com (www.goabroad.com) maintains an extensive directory of study, work, and volunteer opportunities around the globe.

Transitions Abroad, P.O. Box 745, Bennington, VT 05201, USA (☎+1-802-442-4827; www.transitionsabroad.com). This preeminent "beyond tourism" magazine also publishes a number of books and hosts an extensive list of online resources including opportunities to volunteer, work, or study abroad.

Working Abroad, P.O. Box 454, Flat 1, Brighton, East Sussex BN1 3ZS, UK (www.workingabroad.com). An online network of voluntary and professional work organizations. For a US$52 fee, they provide a personalized listing of overseas opportunities based on one's capabilities and interests.

ENVIRONMENTAL CONSERVATION

You may have to hop a bus or a train out to the country if you really want to get down and dirty with organic farming and ecotourism, but don't let that stop you. Check out one of these organizations, grab a ticket, and go wild in the wilderness.

Agriventure, Lerchenborg Gods, 4400 Kalunborg, DNK (☎45 59 51 15 25; www.iaea.de or www.agriventure.com). Organizes agricultural exchanges and homestays at farms throughout Europe, including in Germany. Prices vary by program.

Bund Jugend, Am Köllnischer Park 1A, 10179 Berlin (☎030 27 58 65 84; www.bundjugend.de). This eco-friendly group provides information and organizes events for youth in Germany, including volunteer and internship opportunities.

Earthwatch, 3 Clocktower Pl. Ste. 100, Box 75, Maynard, MA 01754, USA (☎+1-800-776-0188 or 978-461-0081; www.earthwatch.org). Arranges 1- to 3-week programs in Germany and the Czech Republic to promote conservation of natural resources. Fees vary based on location and duration; costs average US$1700 plus airfare.

INEX - Association of Voluntary Service, Senovázné námĕstí 24, 116 47 Prague 1 (☎420 234 621 527; www.inexsda.cz/eng). Ecological and historical preservation efforts as well as construction projects in the Czech Republic.

World Wide Opportunities on Organic Farms (WWOOF), Postfach 210259, 01263 Dresden, DEU (www.wwoof.de). The granddaddy of Beyond Tourism. Membership (€20) in WWOOF offers room and board at a variety of organic farms in Germany, the Czech Republic, and Hungary in exchange for work.

YOUTH AND HEALTH OUTREACH

Let's Go officially endorses both youth and health. The following groups can help arrange anything from volunteering in a medical clinic to leading fieldtrips to the Berlin Zoo.

Big Friends for Youngsters, Tempelhofer Ufer 11, D-10963 Berlin (☎030 25 76 76 12; www.biffy.de). The German arm of Big Brothers Big Sisters; provides mentoring for children on a longer term basis.

Doctors Without Borders, 333 7th Ave., 2nd fl., New York, NY 10001, USA (☎+1-212-679-6800; www.doctorswithoutborders.org/volunteer). Medical and non-medical volunteer assignments wherever there is need.

UNICEF (United Nations Children's Fund), Prague Office: E. Peskove 17/741, 150 00 Prague 5 (☎2 5732 0244; www.unicef.cz); Budapest office: II LH VI.1, 1027 (☎1 201 4923; www.unicef.hu). UN organization, with offices in Prague and Budapest, as well as in Koeln, Germany. Accepts volunteers for teaching and healthcare projects. Undergraduate degree and work experience required.

Camp Adventure Youth Services, 1223 W. 22nd Street, Cedar Falls, IA 50614, USA (☎+1-319-273-5960; www.uni.edu/campadv). Sends college students to 118 camps in 16 countries (including Germany) to serve as counselors for children of US military. Airfare, housing, travel, food stipend, and 12 units of undergraduate credit provided. Participation fee of about US$285.

COMMUNITY DEVELOPMENT

Weeks of solo travel got you down? In the mood to develop a little community? Need a project? We're not talking about getting a bunch of your newly found hostel buddies together for a game of foosball in the common room (though that's great, too). We're talking about grassroots organizing, working with the elderly, and helping out with events at local community centers.

AFS Interkulturelle Begegnungen e.V. (AFS Intercultural Programs), Postfach 50 01 42, 22701 Hamburg, DEU (☎040 399 2220; www.afs.de). In the US, 71 West 23rd St., New York, NY 10010 (☎+1-212-807-8686; www.afs.org). 6- to 12-month volunteer opportunities to serve local communities available for 18+ travelers. Student exchanges available for high schoolers over the summer and during the school year.

Canadian Alliance for Development Initiatives and Projects, 129-1271 Howe St., Vancouver, BC V62 1R3, CAN (☎+1-604-628-7400; www. cadip.org). Offers diverse 2- to 3-week programs in Germany, with the aims of peace, tolerance, and community. Program fee roughly US$280, including accommodations and food.

Freunde der Erziehungskunst Rudolf Steiners e.V. (Friends of Waldorf Education), Neisser Str. 10, D-76139 Karlsruhe, DEU (☎0721 35 48 06 17; www.freunde-waldorf.de/en/voluntary-services/in-germany). 75 placements for 7-12 months and 1-2 years to volunteer with disabled or elderly people. Group housing included. Stipend of €150 per month. Must be over 18 and have basic German language skills.

Habitat for Humanity International, 121 Habitat St., Americus, GA 31709, USA (☎+1-800-422-4828; www.habitat.org). Volunteers build houses in over 83 countries, including Germany and Hungary. Periods of involvement range from 2 weeks to 3 years. Volunteers must pay for all living costs and airfare.

Service Civil International Voluntary Service (SCI-IVS), SCI Deutscher Zweig e.V., Blücherstr. 14, D-53115 Bonn, DEU (☎0228 21 20 86; www.sci-d.de). In the US, **SCI USA,** 5474 Walnut Level Rd., Crozet, VA 22932 (☎+1-206-350-6585; www.sci-ivs.org). Arranges work experience in German civil service camps from 2 weeks to 12 months for individuals over 18. Program fee US$250.

United Planet, 11 Arlington St., Boston, MA 02116 USA (☎+1-617-267-7763; www.unitedplanet.org). Sends volunteers aged 18-30 to perform a wide range of community service work. Short-term (up to 12 weeks) and long-term (6-12 months) for individuals and groups. 6 months US$4695; 1 year US$7195.

Volunteers for Peace, 1034 Tiffany Rd., Belmont, VT 05730, USA (☎+1-802-259-2759; www.vpf.org). Grassroots organization arranges 1-12 week or 3-12 month programs for individuals or groups to volunteer in low-income housing, environmental projects, social services, and historic preservation. Registration fee US$250. Typically 18+.

SOCIAL AND POLITICAL ACTIVISM

This category has a lot of overlap; for instance, political parties often do work relating to (and hopefully helping) the environment or providing aid to health organizations. Although we like to think that our blessing is the political holy grail, it is important to remember that Let's Go does not endorse any of the organizations listed here.

Amnesty International, Prague Office: Provaznicka 3, Prague 1, 110 00 (☎420 2 24 243 600; www.amnesty.cz); Budapest Office: Rózsa u. 44. II/4, Budapest, 1064 (☎36 1 321 4799; www.amnesty.hu). International human rights organization with various internship and volunteer positions available in Central and Eastern Europe. German office is located in Bonn.

Internationale Begegnung in Gemeinschartsdiensten, e.V., Schlossertstr. 28, 70819 Stuttgart, DEU (☎0711 649 0263; www.ibg-workcamps.org). Brings together Germans and foreigners to promote mutual understanding while working on projects to serve local communities. 30hr. of volunteer work per week. Application fee about US$88.

ICJA Freiwilligenaustausch weltweit, e.V., Stralauer Allee 20E, 10245 Berlin (☎030 21 23 82 52; www.icja.de). Non-profit that promotes sociopolitical commitment by organizing practical peace work for volunteers for 2-12 months.

Service Civil International (SCI), Blücherstr. 14, 53115 Bonn, DEU (☎0228 21 20 86; www.sci-d.de). Non-profit, international organization sends volunteers to work for peace, nonviolent conflict resolution, social justice, lasting development, and intercultural exchange in Germany. There are over 35 national branches on 5 continents. SCI also cooperates with approximately 80 partner organizations.

Mobility International USA, 132 E. Broadway St., Ste. 343, Eugene, OR 97401, USA (☎+1-541-343-1284; www.miusa.org). Joins people with and without disabilities to staff international community service projects and to champion disability rights.

STUDYING

A growing number of students report that studying abroad is the highlight of their learning careers. It's difficult to dread the first day of school when fairytale Prague is your campus and your meal plan consists of exotic restaurants and sunny beer gardens. Study-abroad programs range from basic language and culture courses to university-level classes, often for college credit. In order to choose a program that best fits your needs, research as much as you can before making your decision—determine costs and duration as well as what kinds of students participate in the program and what sorts of accommodations are provided.

In programs that have large groups of students who speak English, there is a trade-off. You may feel more comfortable in the community, but you will not have the same opportunity to practice a foreign language or to befriend other international students. For accommodations, dorm life provides a better opportunity to mingle with fellow students, but there is less of a chance to experience the local culture. If you live with a host family, you could potentially build lifelong friendships with natives and experience day-to-day life in more depth, but you might also get stuck sharing a room with their pet tarantula.

VISA AND PERMITS FOR STUDY. In most Eastern European countries, studying requires a special student visa. In Germany, **residence permits** are necessary for all foreign citizens to study. Applying for such a visa or permit usually requires proof of admission to a university or program abroad. Contact your local consulate or embassy (see **Consulates and Embassies, p. 7**) for more info.

UNIVERSITIES

Most university-level study-abroad programs are conducted in the home language of the country in which you are studying, although many programs offer classes in English as well as lower-level language courses. Savvy linguists may find it cheaper to enroll directly in a university abroad, although this may make getting college credit more difficult. You can search **www. studyabroad.com** for various semester-abroad programs that meet your criteria. If you're a college student, your friendly neighborhood study-abroad office is often the best place to start.

AMERICAN PROGRAMS

American Field Service (AFS), 71 W. 23rd St., 17th fl., New York, NY 10010, USA (☎+1-212-807-8686; www.afs.org), with branches in over 50 countries. Offers summer-, semester-, and year-long homestay exchanges in Germany, the Czech Republic, and Hungary for high school students and graduating seniors. Community service programs also offered for young adults 18+. Teaching programs available for current and retired teachers. Financial aid available.

American Institute for Foreign Study (AIFS), River Plaza, 9 W. Broad St., Stamford, CT 06902, USA (☎+1-866-906-2437; www.aifs.com). Organizes programs for high-school and college study in universities in Germany, the Czech Republic, and Hungary. Provides volunteer opportunities for its students in Prague.

College Consortium for International Studies (CCIS), 2000 P St. NW, Ste. 503, Washington, DC 20036, USA (☎+1-800-453-6956 or 202-223-0330; www.ccisstudyabroad.org). This organization offers varied academic programs to 2nd- through 4th-year university students. Semester programs in Berlin and Prague, and a summer program in Prague. Some programs include internships.

Congress-Bundestag Youth Exchange for Young Professionals, 81 United Nations Plaza, New York, NY 10017, USA (☎+1-212-497-3500; www.cdsintl.org/cbyx/cbyxfromusa.htm). Co-sponsored by the German and US governments, this year-long cultural exchange is geared toward 18-24 year-old young professionals. 75 people are chosen to participate in language immersion, classes, and an internship in Germany; airfare and accommodations are provided. Application deadline is Dec. 1.

Council on International Educational Exchange (CIEE), 300 Fore St., Portland, ME 04101, USA (☎+1-207-553-4000 or 800-40-STUDY/407-8839; www.ciee.org). One of the most comprehensive resources for work, academic, and internship programs around the world, including Prague and Budapest.

Cultural Experiences Abroad (CEA), 2005 W. 14th Street, Ste. 113, Tempe, AZ 85281-6977, USA (☎+1-800-266-4441 or 480-557-7900; www.ccisstudyabroad.org). Offers academic study in many cities around the world, including Prague. Courses offered in Czech or English.

Deutscher Akademischer Austauschdienst (DAAD), 871 United Nations Plaza, New York, NY 10017, USA (☎ 212-758-3223; www.daad.org). In Germany, Kennedyallee 50, 53175 Bonn; mailing address Postfach 200404, 53134 Bonn. Info on language instruction, exchanges, and scholarships for study in Germany. Processes foreign enrollment in German universities. Also distributes applications and informational brochures.

Institute for the International Education of Students (IES), 33 N. LaSalle Street, 15th fl., Chicago, IL 60602-2602, USA (☎+1-312-944-1750 or 800-995-2300; www.iesabroad.org). A non-profit organization that has academic and internship programs in many international cities, including Berlin.

International Association for the Exchange of Students for Technical Experience (IAESTE), 10400 Little Patuxent Pkwy., Ste. 250, Columbia, MD 21044, USA (☎+1-410-997-3068; www.iaeste.org). Offers 8- to 12-week internships in Germany, the Czech Republic, and Hungary for college students who have completed 2 years of technical study.

International Studies Abroad (ISA), 1640-B E. 2nd St., Ste. 200, Austin, TX 78702, USA (☎+1-800-580-8826 or 512-480-8522; www.studiesabroad.com). Semester and summer programs in Prague that include Czech language courses.

NYU Study Abroad, 7 E. 12th Street, 6th fl., New York, NY 10003, USA (☎+1-212-998-4433; www.nyu.edu/studyabroad). Offers a semester or year of liberal arts undergraduate study at the NYU Center in Prague, near Charles University.

NYU, Tisch School of the Arts, 721 Broadway, 12th fl., New York, NY 10003, USA (☎+1-212-998-1500; www.specialprograms.tisch.nyu.edu). Study filmmaking in Prague.

School for International Training (SIT) Study Abroad, 1 Kipling Rd., P.O. Box 676, Brattleboro, VT 05302, USA (☎+1-888-272-7881 or 802-258-3212; www.sit.edu/studyabroad). Semester-long programs in Prague run approximately US$18,000. Also runs **The Experiment in International Living** (☎+1-800-345-2929; www.experimentinternational.org), 3- to 5-week summer programs that offer high-school students cross-cultural homestays, community service, ecological adventure, and language training in Germany (with some excursions to the Czech Republic). US$6000.

University Study Abroad Consortium, USAC/323, Reno, NV 89557, USA (☎+1-775-784-6569; www.usac.unr.edu). Offers summer-, semester-, and year-long programs in Czech language and culture in Prague. From US$3480.

Youth for Understanding USA (YFU), 6400 Goldsboro Rd., Ste. 100, Bethesda, MD 20817, USA (☎+1-866-493-8872 or 1-240-235-2100; www.yfu.org). Places US high school students for a year, semester, or summer in various countries, including Germany and Hungary. US$75 application fee plus $500 enrollment deposit.

CITY-SPECIFIC PROGRAMS

Central European University, Nádor utca 9, Budapest 1051 (☎36 13 27 30 09; www.ceu.hu). Affiliated with the Open Society Institute-Budapest. Offers international students the opportunity to take graduate-level courses in Budapest. Financial aid available. Joins with Bard College for the **CEU Professional Internship Program**, which offers internships and further academic study to US college students.

Charles University, Vratislavova 10/29, 128 00 Prague 2 (www.ujop.cuni.cz). Central Europe's oldest university offers courses in Czech culture, language, and history for durations ranging from 6 weeks to 10 months.

LANGUAGE SCHOOLS

Old lady making snarky comments to you in the plaza? Rude cashier at the strudel shop? Cute moped dude that is totally into you? As renowned novelist Gustave Flaubert always said, "Language is a cracked kettle on which we beat out tunes for bears to dance to." While we here at Let's Go have absolutely no clue what he is talking about, we do know that without the local language in your toolbelt, you're up a creek without *ein paddel*. Fear not! Language schools are here to help.

Though language school courses rarely count for college credit, they do offer a unique way to get acquainted with the culture of the country you're visiting. Schools can be independently run or university-affiliated, local or international, youth-oriented or full of old people—the options are endless. Berlin is home to many a German program; local language programs are newer to and fewer in Prague and Budapest. The programs below are a good place to start:

PROGRAMS IN BERLIN

BWS Germalingua, Bayerstr. 13, 80335 Munich, DEU (☎089 59 98 92 00; www.germalingua.com). Full- and part-time language classes in Munich and Berlin for up to 1 year. 6-week courses from about US$1450 (standard) and US$1650 (intensive) with a single room in a dorm or a homestay for about an additional US$200 per week. Individual lessons also available from US$580 per week.

DID Deutsch-Institut, Hauptstr. 26, 63811 Stockstadt/Main, DEU (☎49 602 741 770; www.did.de). German language classes in Berlin and other cities for up to 48 weeks. 6-week courses from about US$1530 (standard) and US$1810 (intensive) with a single room in a dorm or a homestay for about an additional US$210 per week. Specific language programs (e.g. business German) and other activities also available.

Eurocentres, 56 Eccleston Sq., London SW1V 1PH, UK (☎+44 20 7963 8450; www.eurocentres.com). Language programs for beginning to advanced students with homestays in Berlin for 2-12 weeks. Must be 16+. Prices begin at roughly US$520 for 2 weeks.

German Language School (GLS), Kastanienallee 82, 10435 Berlin (☎030 78 00 89 11; www.gls-berlin.de). This Berlin-based language school offers a variety of language courses with on-site accommodation or homestays, internships, high school exchanges, and summer camps in Berlin and Munich for 18+. Standard 5-week course roughly US$740, 5-week accommodation roughly US$1950.

Goethe-Institut Berlin, Neue Schönhauser Str. 20, D-10178 Berlin (☎49 30 259 063, toll-free from North America 1-888-446-3843; www.goethe.de). Look on the web, contact your local branch, or write to the main office. Runs German language programs in Berlin. Goethe also conducts language and high school exchange programs in 13 other German cities and abroad. 8-week intensive summer course about US$2800, with room about US$4000.

Sprachenatelier Berlin, Frankfurter Allee 40, 10247 Berlin (☎49 030 27 58 98 55; www.sprachenatelier-berlin.com). Part-time intensive German language classes in Berlin for up to 16 weeks. 8-week morning or afternoon courses from about US$750.

PROGRAMS IN PRAGUE AND BUDAPEST

AMOS Czech for Foreigners, Dukelských hrdinů 21 (Strossmayerovo náměstí), 170 00, Prague 7 (☎420 606 112 220; www.czechforforeigners.cz). Offers several inexpensive Czech language courses. 5-week intensive course for US$33 (plus textbook costs).

International Language Centers, I, Markovits Iván utca 4, I/5, Budapest (☎36 01 202 3337; www.hungarianlanguage.net). 4-week (US$597), semester-long (US$1075), and summer-long (US$537) Hungarian courses as well as private lessons (US$7-18 per hr.).

Languages Abroad, 413 Ontario St., Toronto, ON M5A 2V9, CAN (☎+1-800-219-9924 or 416-925-2112; www.languagesabroad.com). 1- to 6-week language programs (from US$1650) in the Czech Republic and Hungary as well as volunteer and internship opportunities (18+), and language programs for corporate executives (26+) and young multilinguals (10+).

Language Corps, 53 Whispering Way, Stow, MA 01775, USA (☎+1-877-216-3267; www.languagecorps.com), has 4-week TESOL certification programs in Budapest (US$18950) and Prague (US$1995).

BOOZE SCHOOL

Berlin, Prague, and Budapest have several things in common; one of them is a love of alcohol. We recognize that this may appeal to a reader or two, so, budding brewmasters, check out the organization below:

VLB Berlin, Seestr. 13, 13353, Berlin (☎49 30 45 08 02 67 or 49 30 45 08 02 98; www.vlb-berlin.org). For more than 120 years VLB has been working in the field of research, development and training for the brewing industry. It offers various types of brewing courses. 6-day course for novice brewers US$1765. 5-month full-time "Certified Brewmaster" course US$18,200. Materials (and lunch!) included for both.

WORKING

We haven't yet found money growing on trees, but we do have a team of dedicated Researchers looking high and low. In the meantime, Central Europe is filled with great opportunities to earn a living and travel at the same time. As with volunteering, work opportunities tend to fall into two categories. Some travelers want long-term jobs that allow them to integrate into a community, while others seek out short-term jobs to finance the next leg of their travels. **Transitions Abroad** (www.transitionsabroad.com) offers updated online listings for work over any time period.

The recruitment of non-EU workers is strictly regulated in Germany and much of Central and Eastern Europe; consult federally run employment offices for information on legal formalities. In Germany, these fall under the umbrella of **Bundesanstalt für Arbeit** (Federal Employment Service; www.arbeitsagentur. de), through which you can find local agencies. The best tips on jobs for foreigners often come from other travelers or resources at hostels and tourist offices; English-language newspaper and web listings are another place to start. Online search engines are also increasingly useful. While big job sites like **Monster** (www.monster.de) and **JobSafari** (www.jobsafari.de) have loads of listings, travelers might have more luck with local, user-driven sites like the popular **Kijiji** (www.kijiji.de) or local classifieds like the **Prague Post** (www.praguepost.com) or the **Budapest Sun** (www.budapestsun.com).

VISAS AND PERMITS FOR WORK. Already suffering from rampant unemployment, many Central and Eastern European countries make it very difficult for foreigners to work, requiring a work permit as well as a visa or a temporary residency permit. Given these complications, making contact with prospective employers within the country is a good way to expedite permits or arrange work-for-accommodation swaps. US students and young adults may also wish to make use of a service such as the Council on International Educational Exchange p. 41, which help applicants find work in their chosen country.

LONG-TERM WORK

If you're planning on spending a substantial amount of time (more than 2 or 3 months) working in Berlin, Prague, or Budapest, search for a job well in advance. International placement agencies are often the easiest way to find employment abroad, especially for those interested in teaching. Although they are often only available to college students, **internships** are a good way to ease into working abroad. Many students say the interning experience is well worth it, despite low pay (if you're lucky enough to get paid at all). Be wary of advertisements for companies claiming to be able get you a job abroad for a fee—the same listings are often available online or in newspapers. **Transitions Abroad** (www.transitionsabroad.com) offers an updated online listing of teaching and other work opportunities. Some reputable organizations that may be useful include:

CA Education Programs (CAEP), 112 E. Lincoln Ave., Fergus Falls, MN 56538, USA (☎+1-218-739-3241; www.caepinc.org). Coordinates educational experiences with agricultural organizations in over 40 countries, including Germany. Jobs range from farming to wine-making. Pay and/or college credit available.

Carl Duisberg Gesellschaft e.V. (CDG), Weyerstr. 79-83, 50676 Cologne, DEU (☎0221 209 80; www.cdg.de). Professional training for students and young people from Germany and abroad.

CDS International, 871 United Nations Plaza, New York, NY 10017, USA (☎+1-212-497-3500; www.cdsintl.org). Arranges 6- to 12-month paid internships in Germany for students and recent graduates of accredited US colleges and universities.

Central European University (CEU) Professional Internship Program, affiliated with Bard College: Institute for International Liberal Education, 30 Campus Road, P.O. Box 5000, Annandale-on-Hudson, New York 12504, USA (☎+1-845-758-7875; ceu.bard.edu/internship). Arranges 2- to 6-month unpaid internships in Budapest for students of accredited US colleges and universities.

International Association for the Exchange of Students for Technical Experience (IAESTES), 10400 Little Patuxent Pkwy., Ste. 250 Columbia, MD 21044, USA (☎+1-410-997-3069; www.iaesteunitedstates.org). 8- to 12-week internships in Germany for college students with 2 years of technical study. US$50 application fee.

International Cooperative Education, 15 Spiros Way, Menlo Park, CA 94025, USA (☎+1-650-323-4944; www.icemenlo.com). Finds summer jobs for students in Germany. Semester- and year-long jobs also available. Costs include a US$250 application fee and a US$700 fee for placement.

Multicultural Center Prague, Vodičkova 36 (Palác Lucerna), 116 02 Prague 1 (☎420 296 325 345; www.mkc.cz). Offers short-term and long-term internships to students. Interns can focus on multicultural education, cultural events, or the day-to-day operation of an NGO.

Organization for Security and Cooperation in Europe (OSCE), náměstí Pod Kastany 2, 160 00 Prague 6 (Fax: 420 233 085 484; www.osce.org). Offers 2- to 6-month internships to graduate students under the age of 30 in the OSCE Prague office.

Research Internships in Science and Engineering (RISE), Deutscher Akademischer Austausch Dienst (DAAD), Michaela Gottschling, Referat 315, Kennedyallee 50, D-53175 Bonn, DEU (☎0228 882 567; www.daad.de/rise). Pairs German PhD candidates with North American undergraduates. Stipend provided.

TEACHING ENGLISH

Though George Eliot infamously said, "correct English is the slang of prigs," we here at Let's Go encourage you to revel in your priggishness and teach English correctly. Teaching jobs abroad provide great opportunities to engage with a foreign community. Volunteer teachers often receive some sort of a daily stipend to help with living expenses. Due to the recent world financial crisis, getting teaching jobs abroad has become more difficult, both because of hiring cuts and because the local governments are making it harder to obtain necessary visas for long-term work. Don't let that deter you—there are still jobs out there. In almost all cases, you must have at least a bachelor's degree to be a full-fledged teacher, although college undergraduates can often get summer positions teaching or tutoring. Many schools require teachers to have a **Teaching English as a Foreign Language (TEFL)** certificate. You may still be able to find a teaching job without one, but certified teachers often find higher-paying jobs.

The German-, Czech-, or Hungarian-impaired don't have to give up their dreams of teaching, either. Private schools usually hire native English speakers for English-immersion classrooms where only English is spoken. (Teachers in public schools will more likely work in both English and the local language.) Placement agencies or university fellowship programs are the best resources for finding teaching jobs. The alternatives are to contact schools directly or try your luck once you arrive. In the latter case, the best time to look is several weeks before the start of the school year. The following organizations are helpful in placing and training teachers:

Central European Teaching Program, 3800 NE 72nd Ave., Portland, OR 97213, USA (☎+1-503-287-4977; www.cetp.info). Places English teachers in state schools in Hungary for one semester (US$1800) or a full school year (US$2500).

Czech Academic Information Agency, Dům Zahraničních Služeb, Senovážné náměstí 26, P.O. Box 8, 110 06 Prague 6 (☎420 224 229 698). Helps prospective English teachers find posts in state primary and secondary schools in small Czech towns.

International Schools Services (ISS), 15 Roszel Rd., P.O. Box 5910, Princeton, NJ 08543, USA (☎+1-609-452-0990; www.iss.edu). Hires teachers for more than 200 overseas schools, including ones in Berlin, Prague, and Budapest. Candidates should have teaching experience and a bachelor's degree. A 2-year commitment is the norm.

International Teacher Training Organization (ITTO), Madero No.469, Guadalajara, Jalisco 44100, MEX (☎+52 33 3658 3224 or toll-free from the US 1-866-514 7479; www.teflcertificatecourses.com/). ITTO offers a 4-week, 130-hour TEFL certificate course in Prague. Also has free Czech language lessons and guaranteed paid job placement in the Czech Republic. About US$1760.

Office of Overseas Schools, US Department of State, Room H328, SA-1, Washington, D.C. 20522, USA (☎+1-202-261-8200; www.state.gov/m/a/os). Keeps comprehensive lists of schools abroad and agencies that place American teachers.

Oxford Seminars, 244 5th Ave., Ste. J262, New York, NY 10001, USA (☎+1-212-213-8978; www.oxfordseminars.com). Offers TEFL programs in the USA and job placement in Germany and other European countries. TEFL certification course US$1095.

Teach Abroad, 7800 Point Meadows Dr., Ste. 218, Jacksonville, FL 32256, USA (☎+1-720-570-1702; www.teachabroad.com). A great resource for finding teaching positions in Berlin, Prague, or Budapest. Also has info on TEFL certification as well as study, internship, and volunteer opportunities.

TEFL Worldwide, Freyova 12/1., 190 00 Prague 9 (☎420 603 486 830; www.teflworldwideprague.com). TEFL Worldwide offers a 4-week internationally recognized TEFL certificate course in Prague (about US$1840, housing about an additional US$440).

TESall.com, (www.tesall.com). The original search engine for teaching jobs abroad maintains one of the most extensive, if hard-to-navigate, databases. Site also features other jobs in Central and Eastern Europe.

AU PAIR WORK

Au pairs are typically women (although men are increasingly entering the field) aged 18-24 who work as live-in nannies, caring for children and doing light housework in foreign countries in exchange for room, board, and a small spending allowance or stipend. One perk of the job is that it allows you to get to know the country you are in without large travel expenses. Drawbacks, however, can include mediocre pay and long hours. Also, you might get hand cramps from a hard day's work of finger-painting. Average salary (often thought of as pocket money) for au pairs in Germany, the Czech Republic, and Hungary is running about US$300 or so per month. Much of the au pair experience depends on the family with which you are placed. The agencies below are a good starting point for looking for employment:

AuPairConnect, Max Global, Inc., 8370 W. Cheyenne Ave. #76, Las Vegas, NV 89129, USA (www.aupairconnect.com). Finds work in a variety of Central and Eastern European countries.

Childcare International, Trafalgar House, Grenville Pl., London NW7 3SA, UK (☎+44 20 8906 3116; www.childint.co.uk).

Great Au Pair, 1329 HWY 395, Ste. 10-333, Gardnerville, NV 89410, USA (☎+1-775-215-5770; www.greataupair.com). An Au Pair & Nanny Agency that is basically the Craigslist of au pairs.

InterExchange, 161 6th Ave., New York, NY 10013, USA (☎+1-212-924-0446 or 800-AU-PAIRS/287-2477; www.interexchange.org).

SHORT-TERM WORK

Traveling for long periods of time can be hard on finances; many travelers try their hand at odd jobs for a few weeks at a time to help pay for another month or two of travel. Working in a hostel or restaurant or teaching English are the most common forms of employment among travelers to Central and Eastern Europe. Opportunities are more abundant in larger cities like Berlin, Prague, and Budapest, but there are also more prospective workers—especially in the current economy. Word-of-mouth is often the best resource when seeking a job; ask other backpackers and friendly hostel or restaurant owners for tips. Another popular option is to work several hours a day at a hostel in exchange for free or discounted room or board. Due to high turnover in the tourism industry, many places are eager for help, even if it is only temporary. *Let's Go* lists temporary jobs of this nature whenever possible; look in the **Practical Information** sections of each city.

FURTHER READING ON BEYOND TOURISM

Alternatives to the Peace Corps: A Guide of Global Volunteer Opportunities, edited by Paul Backhurst. Food First, 2005.

The Back Door Guide to Short-Term Job Adventures: Internships, Summer Jobs, Seasonal Work, Volunteer Vacations, and Transitions Abroad, by Michael Landes. Ten Speed Press, 2005.

Green Volunteers: The World Guide to Voluntary Work in Nature Conservation, by Fabio Ausenda. Universe, 2009.

How to Get a Job in Europe, by Cheryl Matherly and Robert Sanborn. Planning Communications, 2003.

How to Live Your Dream of Volunteering Overseas, by Joseph Collins, Stefano DeZerega, and Zahara Heckscher. Penguin Books, 2001.

International Job Finder: Where the Jobs Are Worldwide, by Daniel Lauber and Kraig Rice. Planning Communications, 2002.

Live and Work Abroad: A Guide for Modern Nomads, by Huw Francis and Michelyne Callan. Vacation Work Publications, 2001.

Volunteer Vacations: Short-Term Adventures That Will Benefit You and Others, by Doug Cutchins, Anne Geissinger, and Bill McMillon. Chicago Review Press, 2009.

Work Abroad: The Complete Guide to Finding a Job Overseas, edited by Clayton A. Hubbs. Transitions Abroad, 2002.

Work Your Way Around the World, by Susan Griffith. Vacation Work Publications, 2008.

BEYOND TOURISM

BERLIN

Berlin is bigger than Paris, up later than New York, wilder than Amsterdam, and more eclectic than London. Simultaneously cosmopolitan, dynamic, and in some regards oblivious, the city is in the midst of a profound transition from a reunited post-Cold War metropolis into the thriving center of an eastward-expanding European Union. Everything in this city of 3.4 million is changing, from the demographics of the diverse population to which *Bezirk* (neighborhood) is currently "in." The long, agonizing period of division and the unanticipated and abrupt reunification in 1989—which saw the Berlin Wall literally shattered at the hands of eager civilians—resulted in a turbulent decade filled with euphoria, disillusionment, wild despair, and even wilder optimism. In 1999, the unified federal government moved from Bonn to Berlin, throwing the new capital back into chaos as construction sites sprang up everywhere and droves of bureaucrats provided a sudden contrast to the wayward artists and nihilistic punks that had freely ruled the city streets. Amid lingering turmoil, ambitious plans for the city's renovation now speed toward completion. The glass and steel Potsdamer Platz now towers where the *Mauer* used to stand, and the new Hauptbahnhof, Europe's largest train station, connects Berlin to the rest of the continent without the blockades that once marred its path. But while Berlin surges ahead, memories of a long and complicated past remain etched into the city's geography, architecture, and the texture of its daily life.

Many Berliners remain strikingly ambivalent to the sweeping transformation taking place all around them. The problem of *Mauer im Kopf* (literally translated as "wall in the head") seems more prevalent here than anywhere else in the country, and feelings of division persist. *Wessis* (West Berliners) resent spending so much on taxes to prop up their less-affluent eastern neighbors. *Ossis* (East Berliners) disdain the West's corporate demeanor and air of superiority. Conflicted yet brilliant, the resulting city exudes a creative vibrancy that has established Berlin as an epicenter of global culture.

HIGHLIGHTS OF BERLIN

ABANDON MODESTY AND MODERATION while diving into Berlin's notorious **nightlife** (p. 114) in the districts of Mitte, Kreuzberg, Prenzlauer Berg, and Friedrichshain, or while experiencing the unparalleled **gay scene** in Schöneberg.

CHECK OUT CUTTING-EDGE ARCHITECTURE, among the best in Europe, on a walking tour that includes an **aquarium-cum-elevator** (p. 104).

ASCEND the sleek spiraling glass dome atop the **Reichstag** (p. 95) and wonder how many other countries have a **solar-powered parliament.**

ABSORB OBSCENE AMOUNTS OF ART by Old Masters and contemporary renegades alike in **Museumsinsel** (p. 93), **Kulturforum** (p. 106), and **Dahlem** (p. 109).

MINGLE WITH THE HIPSTERS in **Hackescher Markt** before relaxing with a foaming *Milchkaffee* at one of the many cafes in the **Hackesche Höfe**.

RELIVE THE COLD WAR at **Checkpoint Charlie** (p. 108) or at the longest surviving stretch of the Berlin Wall, now the canvas for the **East Side Gallery** (p. 98).

Unlike most major capitals, Berlin has no "downtown" in the traditional sense; instead, the city is composed of many *Bezirke*. These neighborhoods began as individual settlements on the Spree River, growing together over generations into a city with a surface area ten times the size of Paris.

Neighborhoods struggle to maintain their individuality in the face of increasing integration. Areas that no one would have dreamed of visiting five years ago are now nightlife hotspots, and districts where everyone wanted to live last week will be passé tomorrow. Berlin is the most tolerant Germany city, with a world-famous gay and lesbian scene and few hate crimes. The city's progressiveness extends even into its urban development scheme. But, as Berlin rushes into the future, this very dynamism could endanger the preservation of its rich history. In Mitte, controversy rages over plans to tear down the DDR-era Palast der Republik, while the longest remaining portion of the Berlin Wall is rapidly being defaced by tourist scribblings. Come watch Berlin change before your very eyes; as an old German song goes, *"Es gibt nur einmal, und kommt nicht wieder"* ("It will only happen once, and never again").

NEIGHBORHOODS OF BERLIN

The **River Spree** snakes west to east through Berlin, north of the narrower **Landwehrkanal** that flows into it. The vast **Tiergarten,** Berlin's beloved park, lies between the waterways at the city's center. If you see a radio tower, it's either the **Funkturm** (pointed and Eiffel-like) in the west or the **Fernsehturm** (with the globe) in the east at **Alexanderplatz.** Major streets include **Kurfürstendamm** (nicknamed the Ku'damm), lined with department stores and running into the **Bahnhof Zoo,** the regional transit hub of West Berlin. The eloquent ruins of the **Kaiser-Wilhelm Gedächtniskirche** are near Bahnhof Zoo, as is the **Europacenter,** one of Berlin's few real skyscrapers.

FACTS AND FIGURES

METRO AREA POPULATION: 3,416,255	**AVERAGE MALE LIFE EXPECTANCY:** 77
TOTAL AREA: 892 sq. km	**AVERAGE FEMALE LIFE EXPECTANCY:** 82
LARGEST BERZIRK: Treptow-Köpenick at 168 sq. km	**PERCENTAGE OF POPULATION AGED 18-25:** 9
OFFICIAL CURRENCY: the Euro (€)	**NUMBER OF TRAFFIC ACCIDENTS ANNUALLY:** 123,592
NUMBER OF PLAYGROUNDS: 1,824	
NUMBER OF DOGS: 108,509	**APPROXIMATE NUMBER OF JOBS IN BERLIN'S TOURIST INDUSTRY:** 170,000
TURKISH CITIZENS LIVING IN BERLIN: 117,624.	**NUMBER OF SWIMMING POOLS:** 101
NUMBER OF REGISTERED TAXIS: 6800	**NUMBER OF PUBLIC LIBRARIES:** 108
UNEMPLOYMENT RATE: 15.5%.	**STUDENTS IN BERLIN'S UNIVERSITY SYSTEM:** 141,010
NUMBER OF DENTISTS: 3,162	
NUMBER OF MUSEUMS: 170	**HIGHEST ELEVATION:** The Müggelberge and Teufelsberg hills at a staggering 115m.
TOTAL LENGTH OF SUBWAY, SUBURBAN RAIL, STREETCAR, AND BUS LINES: 2,368 km	

The grand, tree-lined **Straße des 17 Juni** runs east-west through the Tiergarten, ending at the triumphant **Brandenburger Tor** at the park's eastern border. From here it becomes **Unter den Linden,** flanked by the bulk of Berlin's imperial architecture (**Sights,** p. 88). Next to the Brandenburger Tor is the **Reichstag,** and several blocks south, **Potsdamer Platz** is shadowed by the glittering **Sony Center** and the Deutsche Bahn headquarters. Streets in Berlin are short and frequently change names. Street numbers often climb to the end of the street and wrap around to the other side, (not so) conveniently making the highest- and lowest-numbered buildings opposite one another. A map with an index is invaluable.

The former West, including **Charlottenburg** and **Schöneberg,** is still the commercial heart of Berlin. The former East holds the most happening neighborhoods: swanky **Mitte,** hipster-populated **Prenzlauer Berg,** and the newest scene, **Friedrichshain.** Counterculture-heavy **Kreuzberg** was part of West Berlin, but falls in the east geographically. Berlin is rightly called a collection of towns, not a homogeneous city: each *Bezirk* maintains an individual history and identity. Every year, for example, citizens of Kreuzberg and Friedrichshain battle with vegetables for possession of the **Oberbaumbrücke** on the border between them.

CHARLOTTENBURG

S3, S5, S7, S9, or S75 to Bahnhof Zoo, Charlottenburg, Pichelsburg, Savigny Platz, or Zoologischer Garten. U1, U2, U5, or U7 to Ernst-Reuter Platz, Konstanzer Str., Sophie-Charlotte Platz, or Uhlandstr. See also: Accommodations (p. 71), Food (p. 83), and Sights (p. 88).

Like any good hipster, Berlin does its best to steer clear of the European mainstream: it buys all of its clothes at flea markets, it drinks PBR on the weekends, and it eschews Camel Lights in favor of hand-rolled. Should you forget you're in an old-school European capital, Charlottenburg will quickly remind you. Originally a separate town founded around the grounds of Friedrich I's imperial palace, Charlottenburg became an affluent cultural center during the Weimar years, home to dozens of fashionable cabarets. Today the neighborhood maintains its bougie, old-world feel with upscale Beaux-Arts apartments that house a quiet, somewhat older crowd. Nightlife options are few and far between, but there is no shortage of yuppie couples walking silly little dogs in Charlottenburg's well manicured (and beautiful) **Tiergarten.** The area around the **Bahnof Zoo,** which includes Berlin's main shopping strip, the **Kurfürstendamm,** is slightly more lively than the rest of the neighborhood—but not by much. Ku'Damm, as the locals know it, is home to department stores, street performers, teenagers darting in and out of H&M, and enough hot-dog stands to give midtown Manhattan a run for its money. Charlottenburg is also home to Europe's largest department store, **KaDeWe (p. 122).** Five massive floors keep the neighbors outfitted in Prada and Chanel, while the gourmet floor up top keeps their pantries well-stocked with truffle oils, chichi mustards, and over 1300 varieties of smelly cheese.

SCHÖNEBERG AND WILMERSDORF

S1 to Julius-Leber-Brücke. U1, U2, U3, U4, U7, U9, or U15 to Bülowstr., Eisenacher Str., Fehrbelliner Platz, Guntzelstr., Nollendorfplatz, Rathaus Schöneberg, Wittenbergplatz, or Yorckstr. See also: Accommodations (p. 73), Food (p. 83), and Sights (p. 90).

South of the Ku'damm, Schöneberg and Wilmersdorf are middle-class residential districts noted for their world-class restaurants and shopping. The area around Nollendorfplatz, where even the military store is draped with rainbow flags, is the nexus of Berlin's gay and lesbian community, and the streets surrounding Hauptstr. are home to a sizable Turkish population. The birthplace of Marlene Dietrich and former stomping grounds of Christopher Isherwood, Schöneberg maintains a decidedly mellow mood.

MITTE

S1, S2, S3, S5, S7, S9, S25, or S75 to Alexanderplatz, Anhalter Bahnhof, Bellevue, Hackescher Markt, Oranienburger Str., or Unter den Linden. U2, U5, U6, or U8 to Französische Str., Oranienburger Tor, Potsdamer Platz, Rosa-Luxemburg-Platz, Rosenthaler Platz, Stadtmitte, Weinmeisterstr., or Zinnowitzer Str. See also: Accommodations (p. 74), Food (p. 84), and Sights (p. 90).

If you spend one day in Berlin, spend it in Mitte. It is in Mitte, once the heart of Berlin, that the contrast between East and West is most palpable and alive. Much of the Eastern segment languished in disrepair when the district was split down the middle by the wall, but the wave of revitalization that swept post-wall Berlin hit Mitte first. Today, monstrous relics of the DDR era, including the enormous **Fernsehturm** (TV tower) and colossal statues of Marx and Engels, compete for attention with spruced-up Imperial architecture. Tourists spend most of their time in Mitte, hitting major sights like the **Museumsinsel** (Museum Island), **Brandenburg Gate,** and the recently renovated **Reichstag. Unter din Linden,** Mitte's elegant, tree-lined boulevard, is also a must for any visit to Berlin. When you tire of museum-going, hop in line at the famous **Cafe Einstein** (p. 84) for an elegant, Viennese pastry pick-me-up. Though Mitte is still home to first-rate nightlife, the best clubs have closed—they were the illegal ones, as every good Berliner knows—as the city's nightlife culture swept farther East. Mitte may have received a final coat of polish, but you can still find devastated war wrecks squeezed in among grandiose Prussian palaces, glittering modern constructions, and swank galleries.

🞄 LET'S GO PICKS

BEST WAY TO CURE A HANGOVER: A smorgasbord buffet brunch at **Cafe Morgenland** (p. 87) in Kreuzberg.

BEST PLACE (OR MAYBE THE ONLY PLACE) TO SPOT CELEBRITIES AND POLITICIANS: Paris Bar (p. 83) in Charlottenburg.

BEST PLACE TO GET A HIP, NEW (USED) WARDROBE: Stop in at **Made in Berlin** (p. 123) in Mitte.

BEST PLACE TO SPOT NUDE SUNBATHERS: around the **Victory Column (p. 96)** in the Tiergarten.

BEST DRUNK MUNCHIES: The chicken shawarma at 🞄**Maroush** (p. 87) in Kreuzberg.

BEST PLACE TO SWIM IN A POOL THAT FLOATS IN THE SPREE: the **Badeschiff**.

BEST REINVENTED CURRYWURST: Friederichshain's 🞄**Frittiersalon** (p. 86)–a "frying salon" with an organic twist.

BEST PLACE TO BUY BOOKS YOU CAN ACTUALLY READ: St. George's Bookstore (p. 123).

BEST PLACE TO SIT ON KARL MARX'S LAP: Get up close and personal at the **Marx-Engels forum** (p. 94).

BEST PLACE TO WRITE YOUR EX-PAT NOVEL: In the midst of Schöneberg's cafe culture at 🞄**Cafe Bilderbuch** (p. 83).

BEST PLACE TO BUY DDR SOUVENIRS: the **secondhand market** on Su in Prenzlauer Berg's Mauerpark **(p. 122).**

BEST PLACE TO WEIN: the Weinerei (p. 117) in Prenzlauer Berg.

BEST PLACE TO DINE: For an authentic German feast, head to **Schwarzwaldstuben (p. 84)** in Mitte.

BEST U-BAHN: all of them, because you can drink beer on the subway and it never ever gets old.

BEST BATHROOMS: Check out the bathroom "art" at the **Schwarzes Cafe** (p. 83)–it's like peeing in a Prince video.

BEST POLAR BEAR AND WHERE TO FIND HIM: His name is **Knut** and he lives in the **Zoologischer Garten (p. 88)** in Charlottenburg.

PRENZLAUER BERG

S8, S41, or S42 to Prenzlauer Allee or Schönhauser Allee. U2 or U8 to Bernhauer Str., Eberswalder Str., Rosenthaler Platz, Senefelderplatz, or Voltastr. See also: Accommodations (p. 78), Food (p. 85), and Sights (p. 97).

Though largely overlooked during post-war reconstruction efforts, Prenzlberg (as locals call it) has been transformed in recent years from a heap of crumbling, graffiti-covered buildings into perhaps the trendiest of Berlin's

Bezirke. Attracted by low rents, students and artists stormed the neighborhood after reunification. Today, the streets are owned by well-dressed first graders and their young, effortlessly hip parents and studded with cool, costly second-hand clothing stores. In Prenzlauer Berg, everything used to be something else, including the expats dropping English phrases in neighborhood cafes. Scrumptious brunches unfold every Sunday in what were once butcher shops, a former power plant stages thoughtful furniture exhibitions, and students cavort in breweries-turned-nightclubs. Relics of Prenzlberg's past life are disappearing, but cafe-bar owners know shabby-chic when they see it: mismatched sofas and painted advertisements for cabbage remain the decorating standard. Though by now you've probably missed the boat, you can still find traces of Prenzlberg's graffitied past among the strollers and baby bjorns in **Mauerpark** (literally, Wall Park). Also check out **Kasthanianallee** and **Oderbergerstrasse,** where you can still find pockets of young and hip in the form of cheaper vintage stores and trendy bars. In general, Prenzlberg is the bar scene to Friedrischain's club culture—if you prefer drinking against a backdrop of studied cool to gyrating in the dark, this is the neighborhood for you.

FRIEDRICHSHAIN

S3, S5, S6, S7, S9, or S75 to Ostbahnhof or Warschauer Str. U5 or U15 to Frankfurter Tor, Magdalenenstr., Samariter Str., or Strausberger Platz. See also: Accommodations (p. 78), Food (p. 86), and Sights (p. 98).

As the avant-garde crowd follows low rents ever eastward and farther from the geographical center of the city, Friedrichshain is becoming a new temple of bohemian—make that punk-rock—living. While this *Bezirk* still retains much of its DDR atmosphere, from the pre-fab apartment houses and gray concrete to the massive remains of the Wall, some of its long-standing proponents complain that gentrification has found its way even here. The oppressive architecture of central axis **Frankfurter Allee** is overtaken by more traditional residential areas, while the main drag for the young populace is **Simon-Dach-Strasse** and **Boxhagenerplatz,** covered with sun-soaked outdoor seating and crowds of chic 20-somethings. Farther north, **Rigaerstrasse** is a stronghold of Berlin's legendary underground, home to squatter bars, makeshift clubs, and sidewalk punks. Friedrichshain is definitely the place to be for hardcore shows in someone's basement or radical, anarchist actions—just keep an eye out at night, as Friederichshain is still a little rough around the edges, and can be desolate in some spots.

KREUZBERG

U1, U2, U6, U7, or U15 to Gleisdreieck, Gneisenaustr., Görlitzer Bahnhof, Kochstr., Kottbusser Tor, Mehringdamm, Möckernbrücke, Platz der Luftbrücke, Prinzenstr., Schlesisches Tor., or Yorckstr. See also: Accommodations (p. 80), Food (p. 86), and Sights (p. 99).

If Prenzlberg is too bougie and Friederichshain too punk-rock, then Kreuzberg may be just right. Across the Spree and over the wall from Freidrichshain, Kreuzberg ladles out West Germany's dose of counter-culture. A center of Berlin's alternative scene, Kreuzberg's only certainty is unpredictability. In the 1960s and 70s, much of the area was occupied by *Hausbesetzer* (squatters) until a conservative city government forcibly evicted most of them in the early 80s. The ensuing riots threw the city into chaos; during President Reagan's 1985 visit to Berlin, authorities so feared protests from Kreuzberg that they cordoned off the entire district. This *Bezirk*'s anti-establishment reputation exists alongside an incredibly diverse demographic. Home to an especially large number of the city's immigrants, Kreuzberg is a neighborhood of sidewalk

food stands, fruit vendors, and cafes. Much of Kreuzberg's immigrant population is Turkish, which means Turkish bakeries, Turkish grocery stores, and
the famous **Türkische Markt** every Tuesday and Friday (p. 86). Its increasing
trendiness has attracted a wave of gentrification in the form of yuppies and
sober government workers, particularly in the western half; farther east, the
neighborhood remains as forward-looking as ever. Kreuzberg defiantly rejects
stereotypes, presenting instead a kaleidoscopic mix of people who keep the
dynamic scene alive with a tireless supply of partiers.

OUTER DISTRICTS AND DAYTRIPS

Berlin's outer districts, primarily residential neighborhoods surrounded by
greenery, provide a pleasant respite from the bustle of the metropolis. The
vast Treptow park is a relaxing locale for summer lounging, Berlin goes to the
beach at Wannsee, and Oranienburg contains the grim former Sachsenhausen
concentration camp. Dahlem's suburban streets are home to affluent professionals, the sprawling *Freie Universität*, and one of Berlin's federal museum
complexes. Spandau is one of the oldest parts of Berlin and in many ways
remains a stubbornly independent city, with a lively pedestrian zone, stately
archaic houses, and glitzy car dealerships. Neighboring Steglitz is remarkable
only for its trendy shopping district (U9 to Schloßstr.) and expansive botanical
garden. All of these districts are 20-50min. by train from the city.

LIFE AND TIMES

HISTORY

THE BEGINNING: LOTS OF WAR. Berlin, now Germany's most populous city,
was originally the site of small Slavic settlements in the marshlands along
the Havel and Spree Rivers during the early Middle Ages. Berlin takes its
name from the Slavonic word *birl* (swamp). The Saxon duke **Albrecht der Bär**
(Albert the Bear) came to power in Brandenburg during the 12th century and
removed the Slavs from the region, resettling with immigrants from the west.
By the 13th century, the trading posts Cölln and Berlin were founded, and in
1307 the two formally united. The electors of Brandenburg seized control
in 1411 and built a capital to match their dreams of glory. With the Edict of
Potsdam (1685), **Friedrich Wilhelm** bolstered the city's population by accepting
Huguenot and Jewish refugees from newly intolerant France, and in 1701
Berlin became the capital of the Kingdom of Prussia. Berlin flourished as an
intellectual hotspot thanks to thinkers like dramatist **Gotthold Ephraim Lessing,**
educators like the **Humboldt brothers,** and the ruler **Friedrich II**—whose penchant for martial pomp and circumstance turned the city into an assortment
of broad avenues and grandiose parade grounds. Conquered by **Napoleon** in
1806 and beset by revolution in 1848, the city fell into a decline until **Otto von
Bismarck** unified Germany in 1871. Though Berlin was made capital of the
fledgling empire, it never became the center of the new nation, and most
Germans felt little affection for the capital.

BETWEEN WARS: REBELLION AND POVERTY. WWI and the Allied blockade
reduced Berlin to poverty. A popular uprising led to Kaiser Wilhelm II's abdi-
cation and **Karl Liebknecht's** declaration of a socialist republic with Berlin as its
capital on November 9, 1918. Locally, the revolt, led by Liebknecht and **Rosa
Luxemburg,** turned into a full-fledged workers' revolution that controlled the
city for several days. The rival Social Democratic government led by **Philipp**

Scheidemann enlisted the aid of right-wing merce-naries, **the Freikorps,** to suppress the rebellion and murder Liebknecht and Luxemburg. As Berlin recovered from economic and political instability, it grew into one of the major cultural centers of Europe. Expressionist painting flourished, Bertolt Brecht (p. 97) revolutionized theater, and artists and writers from all over the world flocked to the city. The city's "Golden Twenties" ended abruptly with the 1929 economic collapse, when the city erupted with bloody riots and political chaos.

WAR AGAIN: A CITY DIVIDED. With economic woes came a rise in the popularity of the extremist Nazi party. When Hitler took power on January 30, 1933, traditionally left-wing "Red Berlin" was not one of his strongholds. Furious at the radical city, Hitler famously declared: "Berliners are not fit to be German!" He finally consolidated control over the city through economic improvements and totalitarian measures, marshalling support for the savage anti-Semitic pogrom of November 9, 1938, known as **Kristallnacht.** Only 7000 members of Berlin's once-thriving Jewish community of 160,000 survived the Holocaust. Allied bombing and the Battle of Berlin leveled one-fifth of the city, killing 80,000 citizens. The pre-war population of 4.3 million was reduced to a mere 2.8 million by 1945. With nearly all healthy men dead or gone, it was Berlin's **Trümmerfrauen** (rubble women) who literally picked up the pieces of the city.

The Allies divided post-war Germany into American, British, French, and Soviet sectors, controlled by a joint **Allied Command.** On June 16, 1948, the Soviets withdrew from the alliance and demanded full control over Berlin. Ten days later, they blockaded the land and water routes that led into the non-Soviet sectors. The Allies saved West Berlin from starvation through a massive airlift of supplies, called the **Luftbrücke (Berlin Airlift).** On May 12, 1949, the Soviets ceded control of West Berlin to the Allies.

THE DDR YEARS: CONCRETE AND CHECKPOINTS. On October 5, 1949, the Soviet-controlled German Democratic Republic was formally established with East Berlin as its capital. East Berliners, dissatisfied with their government, staged a **workers' uprising** on June 17, 1953. Soviet tanks overwhelmed the demonstrators, and when the dust settled, the only upshot of the day's events was the renaming of a major West Berlin thoroughfare to "Straße des 17. Juni" in a gesture of solidarity between *Ossis* and *Wessis.* Many fled the repressive state for West Berlin—200,000 in 1960 alone.

LOCAL LEGEND

I'M A JELLY DONUT

On June 26, 1963, President John F. Kennedy ended his speech to the citizens of Berlin with the words *"Ich bin ein Berliner"* in a declaration of international solidarity against the encroachments of the Soviet Union. After he spoke these words, the American media claimed that he should have said *"Ich bin Berliner,"* and that by adding the indefinite article *ein,* he actually spoke the words "I am a jelly donut." On June 27, 1963, newspapers from Tulsa to Tokyo were plastered with caricatures of talking pastries.

But the notion that Kennedy committed a major faux pas is more myth than reality. A "Berliner" is indeed a common name for a type of donut that originated in Berlin. And indeed, by adding *ein* to his statement, Kennedy's words could have been interpreted as a declaration of solidarity with fried dough. Nevertheless, nobody in Berlin would have misunderstood his words. For, though "Berliner" is a common term in the rest of Germany, Berliners themselves refer to the donut as a *Krapfen.* And though *ein* is often omitted when speaking of a particular individual, it is grammatically necessary when speaking figuratively, as Kennedy was doing.

Whatever the grammar police say, it's also possible that Kennedy was just taking the saying "You are what you eat" a bit too literally.

On the morning of August 13, 1961, the East German government responded to the exodus of its workforce with the overnight construction of the **Berlin Wall**, a 165km-long "anti-fascist protective barrier," separating families and friends, and in some places even running through people's homes. In the early 1970s, a second wall was erected parallel to the first; the space between them was filled with barbed wire, land mines, and glass shards and patrolled by armed East German guards. Known as the **Todesstreifen** (death strip), this wasteland claimed hundreds of lives. The Western Allies responded to West Berlin's isolation by pouring millions of dollars into the city's reconstruction, turning it into *das Schaufenster des Westens* (the shop-window of the West).

Even though West Berliners elected a mayor, the Allies retained ultimate authority over the city—never officially a part of the Federal Republic—until German reunification in 1990. One perk of this "special status" was West Berliners' exemption from military conscription. Thousands of German artists, punks, homosexuals, and left-wing activists moved to West Berlin to escape the draft, forming an unparalleled alternative scene. The West German government, determined to make a Cold War showcase of the city, directly subsidized Berlin's economy and cultural scene.

THE WALL COMES DOWN. On November 9, 1989—the 71st anniversary of the proclamation of the Weimar Republic, the 66th anniversary of Hitler's Beer Hall Putsch, and the 51st anniversary of Kristallnacht—a series of popular demonstrations erupted throughout East Germany. The public unrest rode on a decade of discontent and a year of rapid change in Eastern Europe, and it culminated in the opening of the Berlin Wall. Photos of Berliners embracing beneath the Brandenburg Gate (p. 90) that night provided some of the most memorable images of the century. Berlin was officially reunited (and freed from Allied control) along with the rest of Germany on October 3, 1990, a result that was met with widespread celebration. Since then, the euphoria has evaporated. Resignation to reconstruction has taken the place of the biting criticism and tasteless jokes that were standard just after reunification. After a decade of planning, the **Bundestag** (German Parliament) finally moved from Bonn to Berlin in 1999, restoring Berlin to its pre-war status as the locus of German political power.

THE ARTS

If Germany is the land of *Dichter und Denker*—poets and thinkers—then Berlin is Germany's capital of *Kunst*: the nation's center of artistic innovation and international influence. In Berlin, hipsters gather in low-rent lofts, artists hobnob in streamlined galleries, and experimental installations compete for space in concert halls. Berlin's gleaming new train station, the Hauptbahnhof, is one of Europe's most architecturally innovative transport hubs, providing a glimpse of the city's style that extends far beyond the station's glass walls. The presence of the arts comes through in Berlin's countless festivals, plays, boutiques and museums, as well as through the creative flair of Berliners themselves.

LITERATURE

While German literature has a long and illustrious history, with poets such as Wolfgang von Goethe lending their talents to poetry, novels, and German legends, Berlin gained international literary renown only with the rise of later political and modernist movements.

MODERN LOVE. Around the time of the 1848 revolutions, Romanticism gave way to Realist political literature. **Heinrich Heine** was the finest member of the

Junges Deutschland (Young Germany) movement and one of the first German Jews to achieve literary fame. **Hermann Hesse** incorporated Eastern spirituality into his writings (his 1922 novel *Siddhartha* became a paperback sensation in the 1960s), while **Thomas Mann** carried the Modernist novel to its zenith with *Der Zauberberg* (*The Magic Mountain;* 1924).

BURNING QUESTIONS. In the years preceding WWI, Germany produced a violent strain of Expressionist poetry that reflected simultaneous moves in visual art. In the aftermath of the war, Berlin saw a wealth of artistic creation, most famously **Erich Maria Remarque's** bleak portrayal of the Great War, *All Quiet on the Western Front* (1929) and **Bertolt Brecht's** explorations of man's grotesque absurdity. It was during the interwar period that cultural critic **Walter Benjamin** wrote his seminal *The Work of Art in the Age of its Technological Reproducibility* (1935) and began his *Arcades Project* (1927-1940), a sprawling account of Paris in the 19th century that went unfinished when Benjamin was forced to flee the Nazis in 1940. Under Hitler, artistic production all but stopped. The Nazi attitude toward literature can be summed up by Nazi propaganda chief Joseph Goebbels: "Whenever I hear the word 'culture,' I reach for my gun." The Third Reich burned more books than it published, destroying 20,000 in front of Berlin's Staatsbibliothek (p. 91) on May 10, 1933.

EXPRESSING THE INEXPRESSIBLE. The Holocaust left a traumatized literature in its wake. While philosopher **Theodor Adorno** pronounced that "writing poetry after Auschwitz is barbaric," poets have presented powerful challenges to this assertion with work like **Paul Celan's** *Todesfuge (Death Fugue)*, which detailed life in a concentration camp. Though survivors such as **Elie Wiesel** and **Edgar Hilsenrath** have attempted to chronicle the inhumanity of the Holocaust in poignant works, the genocide destroyed many more writers than it created.

LOOKING BACK IN ANGER. WWII left Germany's artistic consciousness in shambles. To nurse German literature back to health, several writers formed **Gruppe 47,** so named for the year of its founding. Renowned authors like **Günter Grass** and Celan delved into Germany's Nazi past, while others turned a critical eye to post-war West Germany. In East Germany, meanwhile, many expatriates, particularly those with Marxist leanings, returned to the East with high hopes; unfortunately for them, the Communist leadership had little interest in free artistic expression.

SUGGESTED READING

ALFRED DÖBLIN. *Berlin Alexanderplatz.* An early modernist masterpiece, influenced by Joyce, that uses multiple perspective and montage to tell the story of a petty criminal.

CHRISTOPHER ISHERWOOD. *The Berlin Stories.* Isherwood's two semi-autobiographical novels together form an exposé of Berlin just before the Nazis move in.

PETER SCHNEIDER. *The Wall-Jumper.* Schenider's impressions of a perversely divided Berlin, and one of the few novels to engage with the experience of the Berlin Wall.

IAN MCEWAN. *The Innocent.* A story of intrigue, (first-time) sex, and espionage in Cold War-era Berlin. Not le Carré, but not bad.

JOSEPH ROTH. *What I Saw: Reports from Berlin, 1920-1933.* Roth, a journalist with poetic flair, evokes the confused, teetering Berlin of the Weimar Republic, on the verge of destruction and upheaval of so many orders.

ANNA FUNDER. *Stasiland.* Funder, an Australian lawyer, traveled to Berlin after the Wall fell and catalogued stories of people who resisted the Stasi, the Kafkaesque police apparatus that haunted Berlin.

BERLIN

BOOKING IT. Günter Grass's receipt of the Nobel Prize for Literature in 1999 provided a newly reunited Germany with its first literary icon, though Grass's reputation was tarnished in 2006 when he revealed that he had served in the SS, the Nazi security force, during WWII. **W.G. Sebald's** novels push the boundaries between fiction and nonfiction, while works by German writers such as **Monika Maron, Peter Schneider,** and **Bernhard Schlink** have been translated into dozens of languages around the world. Most recently, the film adaptation of Schlink's *The Reader* garnered international accolades at the 2009 Academy Awards.

VISUAL ARTS

SAY IT LOUD. German art flourished in the 20th century with a cluster of Modernist movements. **Expressionism** echoed the Symbolist tendencies of Viennese Jugendstil and French Fauvism. In 1905, painter **Ernst Ludwig Kirchner** founded one of the earliest Expressionist groups, **Die Brücke** (The Bridge), in Dresden. Painters **Emil Nölde** and **Max Pechstein** soon joined the fold. Die Brücke was short-lived; **Wassily Kandinsky, Franz Marc, Gabriele Münter, Lyonel Feininger,** and several others followed up with a second Expressionist movement, **Der Blaue Reiter,** in 1911. Legend has it that the name (The Blue Rider) derives from Marc's love of horses and Kandinsky's love of the color blue, but they could have just been messing with us. Gone were the days of painstaking 19th-century Realism: jarring colors and feverish outlines now reigned supreme.

WEIMAR A-GO-GO. WWI left Germany's artists and intellectuals stunned. Painters like **Max Beckmann,** Kirchner, and particularly **Otto Dix** abandoned the childlike revery and nostalgia that characterized Expressionism's early years and began to take on the physical and emotional trauma of war in the trenches. For Berlin's **Dada** movement, easel painting was not a radical enough departure from pre-war artistic movements. Instead, **George Grosz, John Heartfield,** and **Raoul Hausmann** dismantled the burgeoning print industry by slicing and dicing magazines and newspapers to create politically subversive **photomontages.** In 1919, **Hannah Höch,** one of the movement's few female members, lampooned Berlin's political and intellectual scene with her fabulous *Cut With the Kitchen Knife Dada Through the Last Weimar Beer-Belly Cultural Epoch of Germany.*

Easel painting managed to survive the 1920s and 1930s in Germany—some artists just couldn't quit. In a movement known as **Neue Sachlichkeit** (New Objectivity), painters like Max Beckmann and **Christian Schad** eschewed scissors and newspaper, and attempted instead to address the contradictions of Weimar society with a paintbrush and a heady dose of verism. A parallel movement took place in the realm of photography: **August Sander,** for instance, created a portrait archive with over 40,000 images of German society during the 1920s and 1930s. Interwar Germany also saw the rise of a number of female photographers, including **Gisele Freund, Germaine Krull,** and **Lotte Jacobi.**

A LONG EXILE. Themes of **Blut und Boden** (Blood and Soil) dominated Nazi art, depicting the union of native Teutonic blood and German land in romanticized images of laborers and soldiers. Reactionary artists like **Arno Breker** created classicizing sculptures. In 1937, the Nazis' infamous **Entartete Kunst** (degenerate art) exhibit ridiculed art from the Weimar period by displaying it next to paintings by psychotics and mental patients.

EAST AND WEST. After the war, state-supported **Socialist Realism** dominated in East Germany, while West Germany turned to abstraction. Like their literary counterparts, the generation of artists that followed WWII struggled with the legacy of fascism and the Holocaust. Postwar painter and photographer **Gerhard Richter,** for instance, confronted his family's traumatic past in his *Atlas* project, a massive photo archive (in the vein of Sanders', a generation earlier) that lays images of liberated concentration camps family portraits and candids.

UNDER KUNSTRUCTION. Today, Germany exhibits a huge array of modern art, from multimedia installations to avant-garde painting and sculpture, and the state supports contemporary art through *Kunstfonds* (art funds). **Wolfgang Laib,** a minimalist who gathers his materials from nature, and **Günter Förg,** who creates geometric abstractions, are among Germany's most dynamic and prolific contemporary artists. Berlin's **Hamburger Bahnhof** (p. 107) and exhibits along the **Museumsinsel** (p. 93) are not to be missed.

ARCHITECTURE

STARTER HOMES. German churches and castles showcase stunning Romanesque, Gothic, and Baroque styles. By 1550, when Lutheran reforms had put a damper on the ornamentation of northern cathedrals, the **Counter-Reformation** spurred the extravagant new Baroque style. This opulence reached its extreme with **Rococo,** exemplified by **Schloß Sanssouci** in Potsdam (p. 126). The late 18th century resurgence of Greco-Roman influences found expression in the Neoclassical style; examples of it include the **Brandenburg Gate** and the buildings along **Unter den Linden** in Berlin (p. 90).

OUR HOUSE IS BAUHAUS. In 1919, **Walter Gropius** founded the **Bauhaus school** of Weimar, which sought to unite the principles of form and function in designs aimed at Germany's working class. The sterling silver teacups and chess sets didn't take off with the masses in quite the way that Gropius had hoped, but the school had a lasting impact: a sleek, proletarian-ready desk set can still be yours for a mere US$3,000.

STRICTURES AND STRUCTURES. Hitler disapproved of Walt's innovations, appointing **Albert Speer** as his minister of architecture and commissioning imposing buildings intended to last throughout his "thousand-year Reich." These included the **Olympic Stadium** in Berlin (p. 89), newly renovated for the 2006 World Cup. After the war, Soviet architecture cluttered East Germany, reaching its pinnacle with the 368m **Fernsehturm** (TV tower) in Berlin (p. 93). Berlin's **Karl-Marx-Allee** is rich in **Plattenbauten,** bleak pre-fab apartment buildings still scattered throughout eastern Germany.

ALL FALLS DOWN. Since the fall of the Berlin Wall, new construction has once again put Germany at the top of the world architecture scene. Berlin is home to high-profile projects such as **Sir Norman Foster's** glass cupola on the **Reichstag** (p. 95) and the reconstructed **Potsdamer Platz** (p. 92), anchored by the imposing steel and glass **Sony Center.** **Daniel Libeskind's** zigzagging, ruptured **Jewish Museum** (p. 108) opened in 2002, and American architect **Peter Eisenman's** stark **Holocaust memorial** (p. 95) was unveiled in 2005. Meanwhile, the 2006 completion of Berlin's central train station, the **Hauptbahnhof,** has raised Berlin's urban planning to towering heights.

PHILOSOPHY

A GERMAN DELICACY. German philosophy is like wurst: thick and difficult to digest, but ultimately satisfying. **Immanuel Kant,** the foremost thinker of the German Enlightenment, centered his philosophy around a rejection of traditional metaphysics and epistemology and enshrined reason as the discipline's highest value. Meanwhile, **Johann Gottlieb Fichte** spearheaded the German **Idealist movement,** which stressed the importance of "Spirit" *(Geist)* in interpreting experience. In 1810, Fichte was appointed rector and the first chair of philosophy at

BERLIN

the University of Berlin (now *Humboldt-Universität zu Berlin*). **G. W. F. Hegel** succeeded Fichte in his Berlin post in 1810. Continuing in the Idealist tradition, Hegel espoused the idea that history could be understood as a series of dialectical struggles that enabled growth and progress. Hegel's view of world history would, after some distortion, provide the theoretical foundations for **German nationalism.** Hegel's work underwent a radical reinterpretation at the hands of **Karl Marx,** who asserted that class conflict was the world's major force—and profoundly altered the course of 20th-century history.

Max Weber, who began his career at the University of Berlin in 1884, is famous for his exposition of the dehumanizing and bureaucratizing tendencies of modernity. These notions are epitomized in popular culture by the iron cage of rationality. His contemporary, **Martin Heidegger,** made his name with *Sein und Zeit (Being and Time)*. His notoriously dense text probes questions of morality, anxiety, and existential alienation in modern times The most celebrated post-war German philosopher, **Jürgen Habermas,** authored an innovative theory of communicative rationality and deliberative democracy. He also dabbled in politics, criticizing German reunification for attempting to integrate two nations that had grown to adopt two very different cultures.

MUSIC

Berlin's current music scene embraces age-old trends of German music: creativity and a penchant for music theory. From pop to pounding techno, the city's musicians strive to find new sounds, jar the ear, and make their beats heard.

FIRST NOTES. German theorists aided in the development of **Western musical notation** and **polyphony,** which started as the addition of new musical lines to the chant form. In the 17th century, German composers adopted Italy's elaborate forms: **cantatas, oratorios,** and **passions. J.S. Bach's** *St. Matthew Passion* has become one of the world's most famous musical narratives of the death of Christ. **Joseph Haydn** and **Wolfgang Amadeus Mozart** were crucial players in the Austro-German tradition of Classical and Romantic music, while **Ludwig van Beethoven** became a legend as a brilliant improviser and composer.

SWEET SOUNDS. Early 19th-century Romantic composers **Franz Schubert** and **Robert Schumann** expressed an ineffable longing in their *Lieder* (songs) and piano pieces. The **New German School** emphasized the production of music that doubled as narrative, and encouraged work such as **Richard Wagner's** massive operas, which drew their inspiration from medieval German epics. These nationalistic pieces were later appropriated by Hitler and the Nazis.

BROKEN CHORDS. The modern era saw a fragmentation of the grand dreams of the Romantics. **German Neoclassicists** embraced orderly Baroque forms as a reaction to the destructive passions of WWI, while emerging musical forms like jazz flourished under the unstable Weimar Republic. Schmaltzy **Schlagermusik** (pop music) and the esoteric avant-garde "art" music of the **Darmstadt school** both dominated the immediate post-war period.

LIKE A ROCK. Berlin's music scene today melds international sounds with forms that are uniquely German. Rock forefather **Udo Lindenberg** has been a musical and political legend since the 1980s; other notable rock acts such as **Die Ärzte, Wir sind Helden, Einstürzende Neubauten,** and **The Notwist** play regularly in Berlin. In the 1980s and 90s, the **Hamburger Schule** combined intelligent lyrics, punk, grunge, and pop in such indie groups as **Die Sterne, Kante, Tomte,** and **Blumfeld.** Berlin has been an inspiration to foreign musicians: **David Bowie** and **Iggy Pop** recorded their 1977 *Lust for Life* in Schöneberg, while **U2** recorded *Achtung*

Baby among the city's post-wall euphoria in 1991. The first track, "Zoo Station," is named after the Metro stop along—coincidentally—Berlin's U2 line.

BRINGING DOWN THE HOUSE. Meanwhile, younger and edgier sounds find expression through German hip-hop groups like **Die fantastischen Vier, Fünf Sterne Deluxe,** and **Fettes Brot.** Popular rappers are often connected to the international immigrant communities in neighborhoods like Kreuzberg, a center of hip-hop, breakdance, and rap in Berlin. They include **Sabrina Setlur, Xavier Naidoo,** and **Illmatic.** Berlin was a pioneer in techno music, and its beats continue to electrify the city's club scene.

FILM

Berlin's love of film blossoms at the **Berlinale,** the city's international film festival, held each year in early February. Film has consistently served to capture the 20th century's upheaval, destruction, introspection, and foreign outlook, and is today a dynamic component of Berlin's alternative scene.

NEW ART. The newborn medium exploded onto the German art scene in the Weimar era thanks to a number of brilliant directors. **Fritz Lang's** remarkable films include *M., Dr. Mabuse der Spieler,* and *Metropolis,* which give a dark portrait of the techno-fascist city of the future. Meanwhile, **Josef von Sternberg** extended the tradition into sound with his satiric *Der blaue Engel (The Blue Angel),* starring Berlin bombshell **Marlene Dietrich.**

PROPAGANDA DAZE. Heeding Hitler's prediction that "without motor-cars, sound films, and wireless, (there can be) no victory for National Socialism," propaganda minister **Joseph Goebbels** became a masterful manipulator of sights and sounds, while filmmaker **Leni Riefenstahl's** *Olympia* recorded the infamous **1936 Olympic Games** in Berlin.

POST-WAR PROWESS. Germany's film Renaissance began in 1962 with the **Oberhausen Manifesto,** a declaration by independent filmmakers demanding artistic freedom and the right to create new feature films. **Rainer Werner Fassbinder** told fatalistic stories of people defeated by society, including an epic production of **Alfred Döblin's** celebrated 1929 novel *Berlin Alexanderplatz.* Fassbinder's film *Die Ehe der Maria Braun (The Marriage of Maria Braun)* and **Volker Schlöndorff's** *Die Blechtrommel (The Tin Drum),* based on Günter Grass's novel, brought this new German wave to an international audience.

PLAYING DDR. East German film had to be created under the supervision of the state-run German Film Corporation (DEFA). **Slatan Dudow** produced the first of the DEFA's films, *Unser täglich Brot (Our Daily Bread),* a paean to the nationalization of industry. After a brief post-Stalinist thaw, few East German films departed from the standard format of socialist heroism or love stories, with the exception of feminist director **Egon Günther's** 1965 film *Lots Weib (Lot's Wife).* **Frank Beyer's** politically daring *Spur der Steine (Trace of Stones)* was a reflection on corruption and intrigue in a communal construction project.

LIFTING THE (IRON) CURTAIN. **Tom Tykwer** wowed international audiences in 1998 with his stylish, high-energy *Lola Rennt (Run Lola Run),* a film that is an icon of reunified, postmodern Germany, keeping apace with its throbbing techno and bodies in relentless motion. Wim Wenders's 1998 *Der Himmel über Berlin (Wings of Desire)* became a sensation with its story of a lovelorn angel roaming the city's streets, while **Wolfgang Becker's** 2003 hit *Goodbye, Lenin!* took a satirical look at family life in the Democratic Republic post- reunification. In 2007, **Florian Henckel von Donnersmarck's** *Das Leben der Anderen (The Lives*

BERLIN

of Others), a gripping tale of *Stasi* surveillance in Berlin, won the Academy Award for Best Foreign Film.

◼ INTERCITY TRANSPORTATION

Located on the plains of northeastern Germany, Berlin is rapidly becoming the hub of both domestic and international rail networks. Three hours southeast of Hamburg by train and seven hours north of Munich, Berlin has rail and air connections to most European capitals, including those in Eastern Europe. Nearly all European airlines have frequent service to one of Berlin's airports.

Flights: For information on Berlin's airports, call ☎0180 500 0186 or visit www.ber-lin-airport.de. Berlin is currently restructuring its airport system to send all travelers through the state-of-the-art **Capital Airport Berlin Brandenburg International (BBI)**, an expansion of the current **Flughafen Schönefeld Airport.** As part of this process, Tempelhof Airport was closed on Oct. 30, 2008, and in 2011, **Tegel Airport** will be closed in preparation for BBI's big debut. To get to Tegel, take express bus #X9 or #109 from Jakob-Kaiser-Platz on U7, bus #128 from Kurt-Schumacher-Platz on U6, or bus TXL from Beusselstr. on S42 and S41. Follow signs in the airport for ground transportation. To get to Flughafen Schönefeld, take S9 or S45 to Flughafen Berlin Schönefeld or the Schönefeld Express train, which runs every 30min. through most major S-Bahn stations, including Alexanderplatz, Friedrichstr. Hauptbahnhof, and Ostbahnhof.

Train Stations: Berlin's massive new **Hauptbahnhof,** which opened just in time for the World Cup in 2006, is now the city's major transit hub, with some international and national trains continuing on to **Ostbahnhof** in Friedrichshain. **Zoologischer Garten** (almost always called **Bahnhof Zoo**), formerly West Berlin's main station, connects to regional destinations and offers S-bahn service. Many trains also connect to **Schönefeld** airport. A number of S-Bahn lines make stops at **Oranienburg, Spandau,** and **Potsdam.** Trains in the Brandenburg regional transit system tend to stop at all major stations, as well as Friedrichstr. and Alexanderplatz.

Trains: Hourly to: **Cologne** (4¾hr., €122); **Frankfurt** (4½hr., €129); **Hamburg** (2hr., €81); **Leipzig** (1¼hr., €46). Every 2hr. to: **Dresden** (2½hr., €46); **Munich** (7-8hr., €130); **Rostock** (2¾hr., €49). International connections to: **Amsterdam, NTH** (6½hr.); **Brussels, BEL** (7hr.); **Budapest, HUN** (13hr.); **Copenhagen, DNK** (7hr.); **Kraków, POL** (10hr.); **Paris, FRA** (9hr.); **Prague, CZR** (5hr.); **Stockholm, SWE** (13½hr.); **Vienna, AUS** (9½hr.); **Warsaw, POL** (6hr.); **Zurich, CHE** (11hr.). Times and prices change frequently—check at the computers located in the train stations. Prices depend on when you book—save 25-50% by booking **3 weeks to 3 days in advance.**

Rail Information: Deutsche Bahn Information (☎0180 599 6633; www.bahn.de). Long lines snake out the door of the **Reisezentrum** (Travel Center) in the Hauptbahnhof (open daily 6am-10pm), Bahnhof Zoo, and Ostbahnhof.

Buses: ZOB, Masurenallee 4, the central bus station (☎030 301 0380), by the Funk-turm near Kaiserdamm. U2 to Kaiserdamm or S4, S45, or S46 to Messe Nord/ICC. Open M-F 6am-9pm, Sa-Su and holidays 6am-8pm. To **Paris, FRA** (15hr., €85), **Prague, CZR** (5hr.; €40), and **Budapest, HUN** (14½hr.; €76). **Gullivers,** at ZOB (☎030 31 10 21 10; www.gullivers.de) often has good deals on buses.

Mitfahrzentralen (Ride Share): Mitfahrzentrale, Theaterstr. 22, D-53111 Bonn (☎228 410 110; www.mitfahrzentrale.de). Rideshare in Germany is a popular, relatively afford-able way to get around. Mitfahrzentrale is one of the largest and most popular websites; it allows you to search for and map rides and calculate fares. Rates vary; prices listed are approximate. To: **Hamburg** (€16); **Hannover** (€16); **Frankfurt** (€30).

Hitchhiking: Let's Go does not recommend hitchhiking as a safe mode of transportation. Hitching is rare in Berlin and also illegal at rest stops or anywhere along the highway.

▆ LOCAL TRANSPORTATION

Berlin may be the second largest city in Europe, but with a train pass and a city map, it's yours. Maps cost €1 at any tourist office and include a **transit map** of S-Bahn and U-Bahn lines, enough to get you almost anywhere. Make sure to pick up a *Nachtnetz* (night bus map) if you plan to be out past midnight on weeknights, as most U-Bahn and several S-Bahn lines shut down until 4am.

Public Transportation: The **BVG** (Berliner Verkehrsbetriebe; www.bvg.de) is one of the most efficient transportation systems in the world. Disruptions in service are rare.

Orientation and Basic Fares: It is futile to try to see all of Berlin on foot. Fortunately, the extensive **Bus, Straßenbahn** (streetcar or tram), **U-Bahn** (subway), and **S-Bahn** (surface rail) systems will get you to your destination safely and relatively quickly. Berlin is divided into 3 transit zones. **Zone A** encompasses central Berlin. The rest of Berlin, including Tegel Airport, is in **Zone B.** Those looking to explore Berlin's great outdoors should visit **Zone C,** which covers the outlying areas. (Zones AB €2.10, BC €2.50, ABC €2.80. Children under 6 free with an adult, under 14 reduced fare.) Tickets are valid for 2hr. **Within the validation period, they may be used on any S-Bahn, U-Bahn, bus, or tram.**

Special Passes: Single tickets are seldom worth purchasing during a visit to Berlin. A day pass (AB €6.10, BC €6.30, ABC €6.50) is good from the time of validation until 3am the next day. The **WelcomeCard** (sold at tourist offices) is valid on all lines for 48hr. (€16.50 for AB, €21.50 for ABC), 72hr. (€18/24.50) or 5 days (€29.50/34.50) and includes discounts on select tours. The **CityTourCard** is good for 48hr. (€15.90 for AB, €17.90 for ABC), 72hr. (€20.90/22.90), or 5 days (€28.90/33.90) and offers discounts at over 50 attractions. The **7-Tages-Karte** (AB €26.20, BC €27, ABC €32.30) is good for 7 days of travel. A **VBB Umweltkarte** (AB €72, BC €73, ABC €88.50) is valid for 1 month. **Bikes** require a supplemental ticket (AB €1.50 per trip, BC €1.70, ABC €2), and are permitted on the U-Bahn, S-Bahn, and select trams.

Purchasing Tickets: Buy tickets, including monthly passes, from **Automaten** (machines), bus drivers, or ticket windows in the U- and S-Bahn stations. When using an *Automat,* make your selection before inserting money. Machines will not give more than €10 change. Also, many machines do not take bills—save coins or use a ticket window to buy more expensive day or week passes. Some machines accept credit cards. **Validate your ticket** by inserting it into the machines marked *hier entwerfen* **before boarding!**

LOCAL LEGEND

CONTROVERSY IN THE CROSSWALK

The most powerful person in Berlin is not Mayor Klaus. Nor is it the bouncer at Berghain. There is but one individual who reigns supreme, whom the entire German populace consciously or unconsciously obeys. With a simple wave of his arm, entire crowds march at his command. And with another wave, he can make them stop in their tracks, even in the middle of a busy street.

Who is this man? He is about 8 inches tall. He is sometimes red and sometimes green. He is the Ampel-Männchen, and he lives in a traffic light. Created by traffic psychologist Karl Peglau in 1961 during the days of the DDR, the cheerful design was meant to appeal to children, but it quickly developed followers of all ages.

When the city was reunified, plans were made to standardize the symbols. Distraught eastern Berliners, however, started a "Save the Ampel-Männchen" campaign; not only did the little man remain on traffic lights, but he cropped up on a whole host of paraphernalia. Even as the city moves beyond its past division, the Ampel-Männchen allows the East to preserve a small shard of its prior identity as it is increasingly folded into the West.

THERE ARE NO FREE RIDES. You may have noticed that getting on and off the U-Bahn, S-Bahn, tram, or bus doesn't involve that ticket that you just bought. Does Berlin public transportation work on the honor system? No way! Every so often, plainclothes officials will board your car and ask to see your ticket once the doors close. They accept no excuses for *Schwarzfahren* (riding without paying), and if you fail to produce a validated ticket you'll be slapped with a €40 fine, due on the spot if you can't provide identification.

Maps and Information: The BVG's numerous **Fahrscheine und Mehr** (tickets and more) stations have tons of maps. They can be found in most major transfer stations (e.g., Alexanderplatz). Liniennetz maps of the U-Bahn, S-Bahn, bus lines, and night bus lines are free. BVG information line: ☎030 194 49, open 24hr.; www.bvg.de.

Night Transport: U- and S-Bahn lines generally do not run M-F 1:30-4am. On F-Sa nights, S-Bahn and U-Bahn lines continue to run, though less frequently. An extensive system of just under 100 **night buses** runs every 20-30min. and tends to follow major transit lines; pick up the free Nachtliniennetz map at a Fahrscheine und Mehr office. The **letter "N"** precedes night bus numbers. Some trams also continue to run at night.

Ferries: Stern und Kreis Schifffahrt, Puschkinallee 15 (☎030 5363 6026; www.sternundkreis.de), in Treptower Park. Operates along the Spree Apr.-Oct. Ferries leave from locations daily 10am-4:20pm throughout the city, including Friedrichstr., Jannowitzbrucke, and the Nikolaiviertel. Fares (€7.50-16) depend on distance traveled. Pleasure cruises available. *Fahrscheine und Mehr* counters offer information. Advance sale at their office at the Treptow S-Bahn Station (M-F 9am-6pm, Sa 9am-2pm).

Taxis: (☎030 26 10 26, toll-free 0800 263 0000). Call 15min. in advance. Women can request female drivers. Trips within the city cost up to €21.

INSIDE SCOOP. If you feel like splurging on a cab but don't want pay the hefty metered rates, ask the driver for a *Kurzstrecke*—a special deal whereby, for only €3, you can travel 2km in any given direction. You probably won't get all the way to your doorstep, but you may get close. The *Kurzstrecke* applies only for cabs that you hail, not those you call.

Car Rental: Most companies have counters at the airports and around Bahnhof Zoo, Ostbahnhof, and Friedrichstr. stations. Offices are also in the Europa Center with entrances at Budapester Str. 39-41. Rates average around €65 for a small car. 19+. Try **Avis,** Budapesterstr. 41 (☎030 230 9370; open daily 24hr.) or **Hertz,** Budapesterstr. 39 (☎030 261 1053; open M-F 7am-7pm, Sa 8am-2pm, Su 9am-1:30pm).

Bike Rental: Fat Tire Bike Rental (☎030 24 04 79 91; www.berlinfahrradverleih.com) has 2 locations in Berlin: one in the East directly under the TV Tower in Alexanderplatz (U2 to Alexanderplatz), and one in the West at the Zoologischer Garten (Zoo Station). €12 per day, €7 for half day (up to 4hr.). Rates decrease with longer rental periods.Open daily Mar. 1-Apr. 9 and Oct. 1-Nov 30 (9:30am-6pm), Apr. 10-Sept. 30 (9:30am-8pm). **Velomondo,** Motzstr. 12 (☎030 21 75 30 46; www.velomondo.de), U1-U4 to Nollendorfplatz. €10 per day, €49 per week. Open M-F 10am-7pm, Sa 10am-2pm. Deutsche Bahn **Call-A-Bike** (☎0700 522 5522; www.callabike.de) are parked all over the city. €0.08 per min. (up to €9 per 24hr.) or €36 per week.

🔊 PRACTICAL INFORMATION

CITY CODE:	The city code for all of Berlin is ☎**030**.

TOURIST OFFICES

Now privately owned, tourist offices provide a narrower range of free services and information than they once did. They still sell a useful **city map** (€1) on which sights and transit stations are clearly marked, and book same-day **hotel rooms** for a €3 fee—room prices start around €30. The monthly *Berlin Programm* (€1.75) lists museums, sights, restaurants, and hotels, and opera, theater, and classical music performances. German speakers should get *Tip* (€2.70) or *Zitty* (€2.70) for full listings of film, theater, concerts, and clubs. *Siegessäule, Sergej*, and *Gay-Yellowpages* have gay and lesbian event and club listings. English-language movie and theater reviews are in the *Ex-Berliner* (€2), and www.berlin.de has quality information on all aspects of the city.

EurAide (☎1+781-828-2488; euraide@verizon.net), in the Hauptbahnhof, across from the McDonald's. Sells rail tickets, maps, phone cards, and walking tour tickets.

Tourist Info Centers, Berlin Tourismus Marketing GmbH, Am Karlsbad 11, 10785 (☎030 25 00 25; www.berlin-tourist-information.de) reserve rooms for a €3-6 fee, with friendly service in English. A list of campgrounds and pensions is available. Transit maps (free) and city maps (€1). There's an office located on the ground fl. of the **Hauptbahnhof.** The entrance is on Europlatz. Open daily 8am-10pm. Another is located near the **Brandenburger Tor,** S1, S2, or S25 or bus #100 to Unter den Linden, on your left as you face the pillars from the Unter den Linden side. Open daily 10am-6pm.

CITY TOURS

Unless otherwise noted, the tours listed below are conducted in English.

▨ **Terry Brewer's Best of Berlin** (☎0177 388 1537; www.brewersberlintours.com). Terry and his guides are legendary for vast knowledge and engaging personalities, making the 6hr.+ walk well worth it. Tours leave daily from in front of the Bandy Brooks shop on Friedrichstr. (S5, S7, S9, S75, or U6 to Friedrichstr.) at 10:30am. €12. Not exactly a family affair, the **Sinful Berlin** tour meets Th and Sa at 8pm, and includes entrance into Europe's largest erotic museum.

Insider Tour (☎030 692 3149; www.insidertour.com) offers a variety of fun, erudite tours that hit all the major sights. More importantly, the guides' enthusiasm for Berlin is contagious and their accents span the English-speaking world. The **Famous Insider Walk** picks up daily from Apr.1 to Oct. 31 at 10am and 2:30pm at the McDonald's outside the Zoo Station, 30min. later from the Coffeemamas at Hackescher Markt; from Nov. 1 to Mar. 30 10am from the Zoo Station and 10:30am at Hackescher Markt only. Tours last 4hr. €12, under 26 or with WelcomeCard or ISIC €10. **Bike tours** (4hr.) meet by the Coffee Mamas at Hackescher Markt. From June 1 to Sept. 15 at 10:30am and 3pm, from Apr. 1 to Nov. 15 10:30am only. €20/18. Offers tours of Nazi Berlin, Cold War Berlin, Potsdam, and a Berlin Pub Crawl as well as daytrip tours to Dresden.

Original Berlin Walks (☎030 301 9194; www.berlinwalks.de) offers a range of English-language walking tours, including "Infamous Third Reich Sites," "Jewish Life in Berlin," "Nest of Spies," and "Discover Potsdam." Their **Discover Berlin Walk** (4hr.; €12, under 26 €10, WelcomeCard and ISIC €9) is a great way to get acquainted with the city. Guides' knowledge complements their eager attitude. Tours meet Apr.-Oct. at 10am and 2:30pm at the taxi stand in front of Bahnhof Zoo and at 10:30am and 3pm at the Hackescher Markt Häagen-Dazs, Nov.-Mar. 10am and 10:30am only.

New Berlin (☎030 51 05 00 30; www.newberlintours.com) offers free tours (on a tips only basis, which means some pandering from the guides) of Berlin's biggest sights, and special tours (Sachsenhausen, Third Reich tour, pub crawl, etc.) for a fee. Backpackers with little cash are encouraged to take the tour, but occasionally dislike the cursory nature of the set-up. Tours leave every day from the Brandenburg Gate Starbucks (11am, 1, 4pm) and the Zoologischer Garten Dunkin' Donuts (10:30am, 12:30, and 3:30pm). A new **bike tour** (€15 with bike, €12 without) meets daily at 11am and 2pm in front of the Postfuhramt, on the corner of Oranienburgerstr. and Tucholskystr., S-Bahn to Oranienburger Straße.

Bus tours: Severin + Kühn's Stadtrundfahrt (☎030 880 4190; www.severin-kuehn-berlin.de). Tours start M-Th 10am and F-Su 10am and 2pm at Ku'damm 216 (in front of Hotel Kempinski). €19, ages 6-14 €9.50.

TRAVEL AGENCIES

STA: Books flights and hotels and sells ISIC cards. Branches at: **Dorotheenstr. 30** (☎030 20 16 50 63). S3, S5, S7, S9, S75, or U6 to Friedrichstr. Open M-F 10am-7pm, Sa 11am-3pm. **Gleimstraße 28.** S4, S8, S85, or U2 to Schönhauser Allee. Open M-F 10am-7pm, Sa 11am-4pm. **Hardenbergerstraße 9.** U2 to Ernst-Reuter-Platz. Open M-F 10am-7pm, Sa 11am-3pm. **Takustraße 47.** Open M-F 10am-7pm, Sa 10am-2pm.

EMBASSIES AND CONSULATES

Berlin's construction plans include a new complex to house foreign dignitaries. Though most have moved to their new homes, the locations of some embassies and consulates remain in a state of flux. For the latest information, call the **Auswärtiges Amt Dienststelle Berlin** (☎030 500 00; www.auswaertiges-amt.de) or visit their office on the Werderscher Markt (U2 to Hausvogteiplatz). See **Consular Services Abroad**, p. 8, for embassy and consulate contact information.

FINANCIAL SERVICES

Currency Exchange: The best rates are usually found at exchange offices with *Wechselstube* signs outside, at most major train stations, and in large squares. **ReiseBank,** at the Hauptbahnhof (☎030 20 45 37 61; M-Sa 8am-10pm), at **Bahnhof Zoo** (☎030 881 7117), and at **Ostbahnhof** (☎030 296 4393), is conveniently located, but has poor rates.

Bank and ATM: ATMs are labeled *Geldautomat*. **Berliner Sparkasse** and **Deutsche Bank** have branches everywhere. Their ATMs usually accept MC/V. **Citibank** has 23 branches in Berlin with **24hr. ATMs,** including Friedrichstr. 194-99 (U-Bahn to Stadtmitte).

American Express: Main Office, Bayreuther Str. 37-38 (☎030 21 47 62 92). U1 or U2 to Wittenbergplatz. Holds mail and offers banking services. No commission for cashing American Express Traveler's Cheques. Expect out-the-door lines F-Sa. Open M-F 9am-7pm, Sa 10am-2pm. **Branch,** Friedrichstr. 172 (☎030 201 7400). U6 to Französische Str. Same services and hours.

LOCAL SERVICES

Luggage Storage: In the **Hauptbahnhof**, in DB Gepack Center, 1st fl., East side. €4 per day. In **Bahnhof Zoo,** lockers €3-5 per day, depending on size. Max. 2hr. Open daily 6:15am-10:30pm. 24hr. lockers are also at **Ostbahnhof** and **Alexanderplatz.**

Bookstores:

Marga Schöller Bücherstube, Knesebeckstr. 33 (☎030 881 1112). S5, S7, S9, or S75 to Savignyplatz Off-beat and contemporary reading material in English. Open M-W 9:30am-7pm, Th-F 9:30am-8pm, Sa 9:30am-4pm.

Hugendubel is a massive chain-store. Branches at Tauentzienstr. 13 (☎030 48 44 84; www.hugendubel.de) by the Ku'damm; Karl-Marx-Str. 66; Alte Potsdamer Str. 7; Wilmersdorfer Str. 121. Open M-Sa 10am-8pm.

Dussmann, Friedrichstr. 90 (☎030 20 25 11 11). S1-S3, S5, S7, S9, S25, S75, or U6 to Friedrichstr. Another immense bookstore, with an English section on the 2nd fl. Open M-Sa 10am-10pm.

Libraries: Staatsbibliothek Preußischer Kulturbesitz, Potsdamer Str. 33 (☎030 26 60). A book for every Berliner; 3.5 million in all. Lots of English-language newspapers. Built for West Berlin in the 1960s, after the Iron Curtain cut off the original *Staabi* at Unter den Linden 8, next to the Humboldt-Universität (p. 91). Now you can choose between them. Both open M-F 9am-9pm, Sa 9am-5pm; Potsdamer Str. also Sa until 7pm. Day pass (€0.50) required for entry.

EMERGENCY AND COMMUNICATIONS

Police: Platz der Luftbrücke 6. U6 to Platz der Luftbrücke. **Emergency** ☎110. **Ambulance** and **Fire** ☎112. **Non-emergency advice hotline** ☎030 46 64 46 64.

 SAFETY PRECAUTION. Berlin is by far the most tolerant city in Germany, and, among major cities, Berlin has the fewest hate crimes per capita and very few neo-Nazi skinheads. However, minorities, gays, and lesbians should exercise caution in the outlying eastern suburbs at night. If you see skinheads wearing dark combat boots (especially with white laces), proceed with caution, but do not panic, and avoid drawing attention to yourself.

Crisis Lines: English spoken at most crisis lines.

American Hotline (☎0177 814 15 10). Crisis and referral service.

Poison Control (☎030 192 40).

Berliner Behindertenverband, Jägerstr. 63d (☎030 204 38 47; www.bbv-ev.de). Advice for the handicapped. Open W noon-5pm and by appointment.

Deutsche AIDS-Hilfe, Wilhelmstr. 138 (☎030 690 0870; www.aidshilfe.de).

Drug Crisis (☎030 192 37) 24hr.

Women's Resources: Frauenkrisentelefon (☎030 615 4243; www.frauenkrisentelefon.de). Women's crisis line. Open M and Th 10am-noon; Tu-W, F 7pm-9pm; Sa-Su 5pm-7pm.

Lesbenberatung, Kulmer Str. 20 (☎030 215 2000; www.lesbenberatung-berlin.de). Lesbian counseling.

Schwulenberatung, Mommsenstr. 45 (☎030 194 46; www.schwulenberatungberlin.de). Gay men's counseling.

Maneo (☎030 216 3336; www.maneo.de). Legal help for gay violence victims. Daily 5pm-7pm.

LARA, Fuggerstr. 19 (☎030 216 8888; www.lara-berlin.de) Sexual assault help. M-F 9am-6pm.

Pharmacies: Ubiquitous in Berlin. **Apotheke im Bahnhof Zoo** (☎030 31 50 33 61) located within Bahnhof Zoologischer Garten. Open M-F 7am-8pm, Sa 8am-8pm, Su 11am-6pm. Pharmacies list a rotating schedule of 24hr. service.

Medical Services: The American and British embassies list English-speaking doctors. **Emergency doctor** (☎030 31 00 31); **Emergency dentist** (☎030 89 00 43 33).

Internet Access: Free internet with admission to the **Staatsbibliothek** (see **Libraries**). Also try: **Netlounge,** Auguststr. 89 (☎030 24 34 25 97; www.netlounge-berlin.de). U-Bahn to Oranienburger Str. €2.50 per hr. Open daily noon-midnight. **Easy Internet** has several locations throughout Berlin: Karl-Marx-Str. 78, Ku'damm 224, Schloßstr. 102, Sony Center, and Rathausstr. 5. **Wi-Fi** can be found throughout Berlin, both free and charge-based services (see **Essentials,** p. 7).

Post Offices: Joachimstaler Str. 7 (☎030 88 70 86 11), down Joachimstaler Str. from Bahnhof Zoo and near Kantstr. Open M-Sa 9am-8pm. Branches: **Tegel Airport,** open

BERLIN

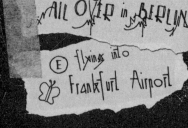
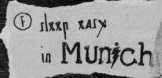

M-F 8am-6pm, Sa 8am-noon; **Ostbahnhof,** open M-F 8am-8pm, Sa-Su 10am-6pm. Most branches open M-F 9am-7pm, Sa 9am-1pm. **Postal Code:** 10706.

⛰ ACCOMMODATIONS

Same-day accommodations in Berlin aren't impossible to find, but you may need to wait until late in the day when establishments have vacancies due to cancellations. If you want to stay in the same place longer than a couple of days or on weekends, reservations are essential. Book a week ahead to get a room and a month ahead to have a selection. For a €3-6 fee, **tourist offices** will find you a room in a hostel, pension, or hotel. Be prepared to pay at least €30 for a single and €50 for a double. Some tourist offices also have the pamphlet *Hotels und Pensionen*, listing accommodations across the price spectrum.

For longer stays, **Mitwohnzentrale** (home share companies) find rooms in *Wohngemeinschäfte* ("WGs," shared apartments). Leases typically require a passport and payment up front for those without a German bank account. Rooms start at €250 per month. Private apartments run at least €350 per month. *Mitwohnzentralen* charge commission on the monthly rent; the longer the stay, the lower the percentage. **Home Company Mitwohnzentrale,** Bundesallee 39-40A, is the biggest. Commission is 25% for stays up to one month. (U7 to Berlinerstr."☎030 194 45; www.berlin.homecompany.de. Open M-Th 9am-6pm, F 9am-5pm, Sa 10am-1pm.) Located in Mitte, **City-Wohnen,** Linienstr. 111, has pictures of the rooms it rents. Commission starts at 25%. (S1 to Oranienburgerstr. ☎030 194 30; www.city-wohnen.de. Open M-F 10am-6pm, Sa 10am-3pm.) **Erste,** Sybelstr. 53, charges 29% commission, but adds a personal touch. (U7 to Adenauerplatz ☎030 324 3031; www.mitwohn.com. Open M-F 9am-7pm, Sa 10am-3pm.) **Fine+Mine,** Neue Schönhauser Str. 20, is in the Hackescher Markt. (☎235 51 20; www.fineandmine.de. Open M-F 9am-7pm, Sa 10am-6pm.)

Another long-term option is to live in a **Wohnheim** (residential hostel). **Studentenwerk** (www.studentenwerk-berlin.de) manages over 40 of these apartments, limited to students studying in Berlin. For long-term stays like internships, **Wohnheim Berlin Junge Politik** in Charlottenburg offers single rooms from €180 per month and apartments from €230 (www.wohnheim-berlin.de).

HOSTELS AND DORMITORIES

HI hostels in Berlin are state-owned and usually clean, reliable, and filled with German school groups. Some impose a curfew or require an access code for late entry. Most require a membership card and charge an extra €3 per night without one. Purchase an **HI membership card** at any HI hostel. For a more party-ready crew, crash at a **private hostel,** popular among international travelers. These epicenters for the hip are often located near train stations and nightlife areas and have a turnover rate of two days—you'll never be bored.

PENSIONS

Pensions are generally smaller and shabbier than hotels, but way cheaper. Most are also amenable to *Mehrbettzimmer,* where extra beds are moved into a large double or triple. Most affordable hotels are in western Berlin, though inexpensive options are beginning to appear in the east, notably around Mitte's **Oranienburger Strasse.** Find cheap rooms is Charlottenburg, especially around **Savignyplatz** and **Wilmersdorfer Strasse.**

BERLIN

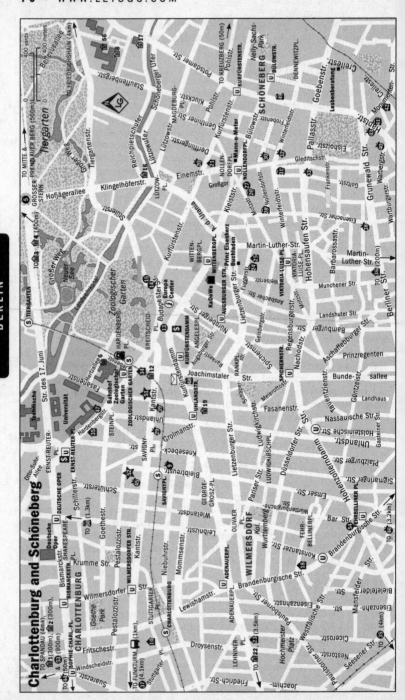

Charlottenburg and Schöneberg

Charlottenburg and Schöneberg

🏠 ACCOMMODATIONS

A&O Hostel, **34**
Art Hotel Connection, **25**
Berolina Backpacker, **10**
CVJM-Haus, **21**
Frauenhotel Artemisia, **18**
Jugendagästehaus am Zoo, **35**
JetPAK, **23**
Jugendhotel Berlincity, **42**
Meininger City Hostel, **36**

🍴 BARS & ★ NIGHTLIFE

Alt Berliner Biersalon, **48**
Begine, **49**
Connection, **24**
Hafen, **28**
Heile Welt, **26**
Neue Ufer, **41**
Quasimodo, **51**
Salz, **50**
Slumberland, **31**
Trane, **52**

🍴 FOOD & DRINK

Am Nil, **44**
Baharat Falafel, **32**
Bar Tolucci, **38**
Cafe Berio, **30**
Cafe Einstein, **20**
Cafe Bilderbuch, **43**
Die Feinbeckerei, **40**
Kuchi, **45**
Mensa TU, **47**
Paris Bar, **39**
Restaurant-Café Bleibtreu, **9**
Schwarzes Cafe, **29**
Seidles Gotenstraße, **46**
Vegetables and Fish, **33**

● SIGHTS

Aquarium, **15**
Elefantententor, **14**
Fehrbelliner Platz, **54**
Gay Memorial, **27**

Kaiser-Wilhelm-Gedächtiskirche, **13**
Olympia-Stadion, **37**
Schloss Charlottenburg, **53**
Siegessäule, **5**

🏛 MUSEUMS

Akademie der Künste, **3**
Bauhaus-Archiv, **16**
Bröhanmuseum, **1**
Brücke Museum, **22**
Erotik Museum, **12**
Gemäldegalerie, **8**
Käthe-Kollwitz Museum, **19**
Kunstgewerbemuseum, **7**
Kupferstichkabinett, **56**
Neue Nationalgalerie, **17**
Museum Berggruen, **2**
Museum Für Fotografie, **6**
Schloß Bellevue, **4**

CAMPING

Deutscher Camping-Club runs campgrounds in Wannsee, Spandau, and Köpenick. Reservations are recommended; write to Deutscher Camping-Club Berlin, Geisbergstr. 11, 10777 Berlin, or call in advance. (☎030 218 6071; www.dccberlin. de. Sites charge €5.60 per person, €2.50 per child, €4 per tent.) One convenient campground is **Kladow 1 ❶**, Krampnitzer Weg 111-117 (☎030 365 2797). Take U7 to Rathaus Spandau, then bus #135 (dir.: Alt-Kladow) to the end. Switch to bus #234 to Krampnitzer Weg/Selbitzerstr., then follow Krampnitzer Weg 500m. This far-off suburban locale rewards with a store, restaurant, and swimmable lake. (Open year-round. €5.60 per person. Cash only.)

CHARLOTTENBURG

Hotels and hostels tend to be quieter and slightly more upscale here than in other parts of the city. While central locations listed below may be in the center of Charlottenburg, Zoologischer Garten is a solid 20min. U-Bahn ride away from the tourist stretch along Unter den Linden.

▨ **Berolina Backpacker,** Stuttgarter Platz 17 (☎030 32 70 90 72; www.berolinaback-packer.de). S3, S5, S7, S9, or S75 to Charlottenburg. This quiet hostel with an ivy-laced facade keeps things elegant with print art in the bunk-free dorms and daisies on the breakfast table. Surrounding cafes and proximity to the S-Bahn make up for its distance from the rush of the city. Communal and private kitchens (communal €1 per day, private €9.50) available for use. Breakfast buffet €7; "backpackers' breakfast" (a roll with cheese and coffee) €3.50. Internet €0.50 per 15min. Reception 24hr. Check-out 11am. 5-bed dorms €10-13.50; singles €29.50-35.50; doubles €37-47; triples €39-64; quads €46-60. AmEx/MC/V. ❶

Frauenhotel Artemisia, Brandenburgische Str. 18 (☎030 873 89 05; www.frauenhotel-berlin.de). U7 to Konstanzer Str. Pricey but rare—an elegant hotel for women only, the 1st of its kind in Germany. Outdoor terrace provides a sweeping view of Berlin. Named after Italian painter Artemisia Gentileschi, the hotel hosts rotating art exhibitions. Phone and TV by request. Breakfast buffet €7. Free Wi-Fi. Reception 7am-9:30pm. Singles €49-54, with bath €64-79; doubles €78/78-108. Additional beds €20. Ages 3-8 €10 per night, under 3 one-time €10 fee. Discounts for longer stays. AmEx/MC/V. ❺

BERLIN

READY. SET.

LET'S GO

www.letsgo.com

THE STUDENT TRAVEL GUIDE

Jugendgästehaus am Zoo, Hardenbergstr. 9A (☎030 312 94 10; www.jgh-zoo.de). Take bus #245 to Steinplatz or walk from Bahnhof Zoo down Hardenbergstr. Tucked away in a quiet, late 19th-century building. 85 beds in simple rooms. Low prices and proximity to Zoo makes escapes to Mitte and Kreuzberg easy. Reception 24hr. Check-out 10am. Lockout 10am-2pm. 4- to 8-bed dorms €18, in the high season €21; singles €26/29; doubles €46/52. Surcharge for those over 27 €3. Cash only. ❸

A&O Hostel, Joachimstaler Str. 1-3 (☎030 809 47 53 00; www.aohostels.com), 30m from Bahnhof Zoo. Reliable dorms right on Zoo. Lobby, bar, and rooftop terrace stay packed at night. Private rooms include linens, bath, and breakfast. Breakfast buffet €6. Linens €3. Internet €5 per day. Bike rental €12 1st day, less each additional day. Reception 24hr. 8- to 10-bed dorms from €8; smaller dorms from €10.50; singles from €25; doubles from €30. Prices fluctuate with season and availability. Branches in Mitte and Friedrichshain. MC/V. ❶

SCHÖNEBERG AND WILMERSDORF

Jugendhotel Berlincity, Crellestr. 22 (☎030 7870 2130; www.jugendhotel-berlin.de). U7 to Kleistpark or Yorckstr. The high ceilings and enormous windows in this former factory provide guests with spacious, airy rooms. Funky light fixtures shaped like fried eggs illuminate the hallways, which are lined with dark hard wood. Request a room with a view of the TV tower. Breakfast and linens included. Wi-Fi €1 per 20min., €5 per day. Reception 24hr. Singles €38, with bath €52; doubles €60/79; triples €87/102; quads €112/126; quints €124/150; 6-person room €146/168. MC/V. ❺

JetPAK, Pücklerstr. 54, Dahlem (☎030 8325 011; www.jetpak.de). U3 to Fehrbelliner Platz or U9 to Güntzelstr., then bus #115 (dir.: Neuruppiner Str.) to Pücklerstr. Follow sign to Grunewald and turn left on Pücklerstr. Turn left again when the JetPAK sign directs you at the edge of the forest. Hidden in an old *Wehrmacht* military complex in the Grunewald forest, this casual hostel has a summer-camp feel that belies its history and makes up for the distance. Ping-pong table and basketball hoop outside. Common room with computers and foosball. Breakfast and linens included. Free internet. Dorms €14-18; singles €30; doubles €50. Additional €1 charge on F-Sa. Cash only. ❷

CVJM Jugendgastehaus, Einemstr. 10 (☎030 264 10 88; www.cvjm-jugendgaestehaus. de). U1, U2, U4, or U15 to Nollendorfplatz. An inexpensive, basic alternative to a dorm. Breakfast buffet included and packed lunch available (€3.20-€3.50). Linens €4, free for stays of over 3 days. Reception M-F 8am-5pm. Quiet hours 11pm-7am. Reserve well ahead. Singles €37; doubles €45; 4- to 6-bed rooms €23.50 per person. €3 per night surcharge for guests over 27. Cash only. ❺

Art-Hotel Connection, Fuggerstr. 33 (☎030 210 21 88 00; www.arthotel-connection. de). U1, U2, or U15 to Wittenbergplatz, off Martin-Luther-Str. Located above the club Connection (p. 116) on the 3rd fl. of an apartment building. The airbrushed imitation of Michaelangelo's *The Creation of Adam* on the ceiling is the first clue that this establishment is for men only. 17 rooms with phone, TV, and bath. "Playrooms" have slings and other sex toys. Singles €59; doubles €79-110; playrooms €103-130. Cheaper M-Th, in winter, with advanced booking, or for stays over 3 nights. AmEx/MC/V. ❺

Meininger City Hostel, Meininger Str. 10 (☎0800 634 64 64; www.meininger-hostels. de). U4, bus #146 or N46 to Rathaus Schöneberg. Walk toward the Rathaus tower on Freiherr-vom-Stein-Str., turn left on Martin-Luther-Str., then right on Meininger Str. Lively atmosphere and superb value in a hostel that has its own terrace, beer garden, and pool table. All-female dorms available. Breakfast €3.50. Linens included. Free Wi-Fi. Reception 24hr. Door locked at midnight; ring to enter. Book in advance. 5- to 6- bed dorms €18-26; 4- to 6- bed dorms €20-36; singles €49-69; doubles €66-98; triples €81-117. Branches at Hallesches Ufer, Tempelhofer Ufer, Senefelderplatz and a new one at the Hauptbahnhof (main train station) with same rates. MC/V. ❸

BERLIN

MITTE

For those who stay in Berlin only one night, it makes sense to find accommodations in sightseeing central. Those here longer or looking to party would do better in Kreuzberg or Friedrichshain.

🏨 **Mitte's Backpacker Hostel,** Chausseestr. 102 (☎030 28 39 09 65; www.backpacker.de). U6 to Zinnowitzer Str. The apex of hostel hipness, with a gregarious English-speaking staff and themed rooms, from "Aztec" to "skyline" (of Berlin, of course). The social common room is lined with antique theater sets. A pickup spot for Terry Brewer's Tours and Insider Tours bike tours (p. 65). Sheets €2.50. Laundry €7. Internet €3 per hr. Bike rental €10 per day. Reception 24hr. Dorms €14-19; singles €30-34; doubles €48-54; quads €80-84. AmEx/MC/V. ❷

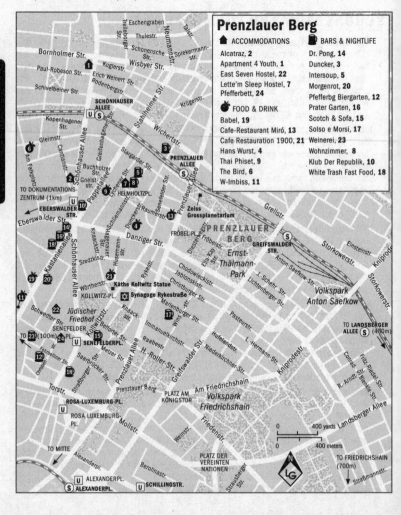

Prenzlauer Berg

🏠 **ACCOMMODATIONS**
Alcatraz, **2**
Apartment 4 Youth, **1**
East Seven Hostel, **22**
Lette'm Sleep Hostel, **7**
Pfefferbett, **24**

🍴 **FOOD & DRINK**
Babel, **19**
Cafe-Restaurant Miró, **13**
Cafe Restauration 1900, **21**
Hans Wurst, **4**
Thai Phiset, **9**
The Bird, **6**
W-Imbiss, **11**

🍸 **BARS & NIGHTLIFE**
Dr. Pong, **14**
Duncker, **3**
Intersoup, **5**
Morgenrot, **20**
Pfefferbg Biergarten, **12**
Prater Garten, **16**
Scotch & Sofa, **15**
Solso e Morsi, **17**
Weinerei, **23**
Wohnzimmer, **8**
Klub Der Republik, **10**
White Trash Fast Food, **18**

Berlin Mitte

ACCOMMODATIONS
BaxPax Downtown Hostel, 24
Circus, 4 & 17
CityStay Hostel, 34
Heart of Gold, 18
Helter Skelter, 23
Mitte's Backpacker Hostel, 2
Three Little Pigs, 73
Wombat's Hostel, 8

FOOD & DRINK
Beth Cafe, 10
Cafe Fleury, 27
Café Sankt Oberholz, 14
Dada Falafel, 9
Leo Bettini, 25
Maedchenitaliener, 21
Monsieur Vuong, 21
Schokogalerie, 28
Schwarzwaldstuben, 71
Sophien 11, 15
Tadshickishe Teestube, 68

BARS & NIGHTLIFE
Bang Bang Club, 31
Clärchen's Ballhouse, 65
Cookies, 42
Delicious Doughnuts, 12
Kaffee Burger, 37
Tacheles, 13
Tape, 77
Week-End, 29
CCCP, 3

ENTERTAINMENT
Berliner Ensemble, 49
Deutsche Staatsoper, 57
Deutsches Theater, 33
Die Distel, 51
English Theater Berlin, 50
Hebbel-Theater, 48
Komische Oper, 79
Konzerthaus, 62
Maxim-Gorki-Theater, 80
Philharmonie, 69
Volksbühne, 81

CHURCHES
Berliner Dom, 49
Deutscher Dom, 64
Französischer Dom, 61
Marienkirche, 38
St.-Hedwigs-Kathedrale, 58

MUSEUMS
Alte Nationalgalerie, 36
Altes Museum, 48
Anne Frank Zentrum, 32
Art Center Berlin, 22
Bodemuseum, 30
Deutsche Guggenheim Berlin, 55
Deutsches Hist. Museum, 46
Filmmuseum Berlin, 70
Gemäldegalerie, 67
Hamburger Bahnhof, 5
Hanfmuseum, 60
Haus am Checkpoint Charlie, 78
Kunst-Werke Berlin, 11
Martin-Gropius-Bau, 74
Neue Nationalgalerie, 72

Neuer Berliner Kunstverein, 7
Pergamonmuseum, 35
Musikinstrumenten Museum, 66
Schinkelmuseum, 59
Topographie des Terrors, 75

SIGHTS
Alte Bibliothek, 56
Alter-Jüdischer Friedhof, 26
Bertolt-Brecht-Haus, 1
Denkam Für Die Ermordeten Juden Europas, 82
Fernsehturm, 39
Franziskaner-Klosterkirche, 83
Französischer Dom, 84
Führerbunker, 63
Gay Memorial, 85
Hi-Flyer Balloon, 76
Humboldt-Universität, 44
Juediscke Knabenschule, 20
Lustgarten, 47
Köllnischen Park, 86
Marx-Engels-Forum, 52
Missing House, 89
Neue Wache, 45
Neue Synagoge, 19

Russian Embassy, 54
Siegessäule, 87
Sowjetisches Ehrenmal, 88
Staatsbibliothek zu Berlin, 43
The Kennedys Museum, 41

Circus, Weinbergersweg 1A (☎030 28 39 14 33; www.circus-berlin.de). U8 to Rosenthaler Platz. Designed with the English-speaking traveler in mind. Nightly happy hours and W karaoke. Breakfast €2-5 until 1pm. Free laundry. Wi-Fi in rooms; internet €0.05 per min. Wheelchair-accessible. Reception and bar 24hr. 4- to 8-bed dorms €19-23; singles €40, with bath €50; doubles €56/70; triples €75. A larger branch at Rosenthaler Platz on Rosenthaler Str. 1. MC/V. ❷

BaxPax Downtown Hostel/Hotel, Ziegelstr. 28 (☎030 251 52 02; www.baxpax-downtown.de). S1, S2, or S25 to Oranienburger Str. or U6 to Oranienbuger Tor. The sleeker sibling of the Kreuzberg branch has all the usual amenities plus a bar/lounge with fireplace and a rooftop bar with a huge kiddie pool. All-female dorm rooms available. Breakfast €5.50. Laundry facilities available. Internet €3 per hr. Dorms €13-17; singles €29-45; doubles €60-65; triples €70. MC/V. ❷

Three Little Pigs, Stresemannstr. 66 (☎030 32 66 29 55; www.three-little-pigs.de). S1, S2, or S25 to Anhalter Bahnhof or U2 to Potsdamer Platz Next door to a church and itself a former nunnery, this quiet hostel is minutes from the glitzy Potsdamer Platz. Free city tours. Breakfast €4.50. Linens €2.50. Laundry service €5. Internet €1 per 30min. Bike rental €12 per day. Reception 24hr. Dorms €13-16; singles €35, with bath €45; doubles €22-23/32; triples €20; quads €18. €1 discount in winter. AmEx/MC/V. ❷

Wombat's Hostel, Alte Schönhauser Str. 2 (☎030 84 71 08 20; www.wombatshostels.com). U2 to Rosa-Luxemburg-Platz. With an eye-poppingly bright interior and a space-age exterior, this year-old newcomer features a pool table, rooftop terrace with a view of the TV tower, a cheap breakfast buffet (€3.50), and free Wi-Fi. The chic womBar downstairs is open daily 6pm-2am. Happy hour 6-8pm. Free drink and city map with check-in. Kitchen access. Reception 24hr. 4- to 6-bed dorms €17-21, 2-bed €25-29; doubles €40. MC/V. ❷

CityStay Hostel, Rosenstr. 16 (☎030 23 62 40 31; www.citystay.de). S5, S7, S9, or S75 to Hackescher Markt or U2, U5, or U8 to Alexanderplatz. A social hostel with ample amenities—an all-night bar, courtyard barbecues, clean dorms, and private showers—smack in the middle of Berlin. Women-only dorms on request. Kitchen available. Breakfast €4. Free lockers. Linens €2.50. Laundry €5. Internet €3 per hr.; free Wi-Fi. Dorms €14-20; singles €40, with bath €55; doubles €50/64; quads €84. Cash only. ❷

Berlin Mitte

BERLIN

Volkspark Friedrichshain

TO PRENZLAUER BERG

Prenzlauer Allee

TO PRENZLAUER BERG

Friedenstr.

Am Friedrichshain-Königrode-Allee

Lichtenberger Str.

STRAUSBERGER PL.

Singerstr.

Andreasstr.

Mollstr.

Otto-Braun-Str.

Karl-Marx-Allee

STRAUSBERGER PL.

Neuen Blumenstr.

Singerstr.

Lichtenberger Str.

Spree

TO BADESCHIFF (2.3km)

Mollstr.

SCHILLINGSTR.

Schillingstr.

JANNOWITZBR.

Holzmarktstr.

Michaelkirchstr.

TO KREUZBERG

Alexanderstr.

Dircksenstr.

Brückenstr.

Köpenicker Str.

Heinrich-Heine-Str.

MICHAEL-KIRCHPL.

ROSA-LUXEMBURG-PL.

ROSA-LUXEMBURG-STR.

Torstr.

M-Beer-Str.

R.-Luxemburg-Str.

Alexander Pl.

ALEXANDERPL.

Gruner str.

Dircksenstr.

Klosterstr.

Stralauerstr.

Jannowitzbrücke

N.-HEINE-STR.

Sebastianstr.

Alte Jakobstr.

400 yards

400 meters

TO (200m)

Gormannstr.

Linienstr.

Alte Schönh. Str.

Almstädtstr.

Münz Str.

R.-Luxemburg-Str.

HACKESCHER MARKT

Rosenstr.

Rathausstr.

KLOSTERSTR.

MARK. MUS.

Spree

WEINMEISTERSTR.

Gipsstr.

Rosenthaler Str.

An der Spandauer Brücke

Dircksenstr.

Karl-Liebknecht-Str.

MARX ENGELS FORUM

NIKOLAIVIERTEL

Mühlendamm

Fischerinsel

SPITTELMARKT

ROSENTHALER PL.

Sophienstr.

Gr. Hamburger Str.

Krausnickstr.

Oranienburger Str.

Monbijou

Museumsinsel

Bodestr.

Lustgarten

SCHLOSSPL.

Breite Str.

Weder Markt

Gertraudenstr.

Leipziger Str.

Krausenstr.

Schützenstr.

Zimmerstr.

Linienstr.

Augustr.

Tucholskystr.

Oranienburger Str.

ORANIENBURGER STR.

Johannisstr.

Ziegelstr.

Am Weidendamm

Kupfergraben

Zeughaus

Museumsinsel

Oberwallstr.

HAUSVOGTEIPL.

HAUSVOGTEI-PL.

Niederwallstr.

Mohrenstr.

Markgrafenstr.

Former Berlin Wall

Rudi-Dutschke-Str.

ORANIENBURGER TOR

Chausseestr.

Dorotheen städtische Friedhof

VOR DEN NEUEN TOR

Torstr.

Hannoversche Str.

FRIEDRICHSTR.

Georgenstr.

Universitätsstr.

Charlottenstr.

BEBEL PL.

Französische Str.

GENDARMENMARKT

STADTMITTE

Kronenstr.

Friedrichstr.

Invaliden Park

Invalidenstr.

Friedrichstr.

Johannisstr.

Friedrichstr.

Albrechtstr.

Dorotheenstr.

Unter den Linden

Behrenstr.

FRANZ. STR.

Jäger- str.

Tauben- str.

Mohrenstr.

MOHRENSTR.

Mauerstr.

Friedrichstr.

Reinhardtstr.

Marienstr.

Schiffbauerdamm

UNTER DEN LINDEN

Glinkastr.

Mauerstr.

Wilhelmstr.

Leipzigerstr.

Niederkirchnerstr.

Luisenstr.

Schumannstr.

Reichstagufer

Dorotheenstr.

PARISER PL.

Brandenburger Tor

Former Berlin Wall

Ebertstr.

Voßstr.

POTSDAMER PL.

Stresemannstr.

Heidestr.

Humboldthafen

HAUPTBAHNHOF

Invalidenstr.

Willy-Brandt-Str.

Alt-Moabit

Spree

Paul-Löbe-Allee

PL. DER REPUBLIK

Kronprinzenufer

Scheidemannstr.

Bundesstr.

Reichstag

Dorotheenstr.

PARISER PL.

POTSDAMER PL.

Sony Center

KEMPERPL.

Kulturforum

Entlastungstr.

TO CHARLOTTENBURG (1900m)

Straße des 17. Juni

Tiergarten

Bellevueallee

Sigismundstr.

Potsdamer Str.

TO SCHÖNEBERG

Waldeckpark

Lindenstr.

Sebastianstr.

TO SCHONEBERG

Heart of Gold Hostel, Johannisstr. 11 (☎030 29 00 33 00; www.heartofgold-hostel. de). S1, S2, or S25 to Oranienburger Str. or U6 to Oranienburger Tor. Designed as a tribute to *The Hitchhiker's Guide to the Galaxy*, this kooky hostel is space-age clean. Breakfast €3. Laundry €3. Internet €1 per hr.; free Wi-Fi. Reception and bar 24hr. Check-out at noon. 8-bed dorms €15; 6-bed dorms €18; 3- to 4-bed dorms €22; doubles with bath €60. AmEx/MC/V. ❷

Helter Skelter, Kalkscheunestr. 4-5 (☎030 28 04 49 97; www.helterskelterhostel. com). S1, S2, or S25 to to Oranienburger Str. or U6 to Oranienburger Tor. Convenient access to Oranienburger Str.'s rather touristy nightlife and Mitte sights, with a casual atmosphere. Terry Brewer's Tours pick up guests daily at 10:15am. Breakfast buffet €3. Linens included. Internet €0.50 per 5min. Reception and bar 24hr. Reserve rooms at least 2-3 days in advance. 13-bed dorms €14, 5- to 7-bed €18; doubles €54; triples €66; quads €88. AmEx/MC/V. ❶

PRENZLAUER BERG

There are only a handful of hostels in Prenzlauer Berg, where students have been priced out by yuppies in the bed department, if not in the beer department (see **Nightlife, p. 114**).

▨ **East Seven Hostel,** Schwedter Str. 7 (☎030 93 62 22 40; www.eastseven.de). U2 to Senefelderplatz. No bunks in the well-lit, beautifully painted dorms. The grill area in the garden out back is friendly and social. Kitchen available. Linens €3. Towels €1. Laundry €4. Internet €0.50 per 20min; free Wi-Fi. Reception 7am-midnight. Dorms €13-17; singles in low-season €30, in high season €37; doubles €42/50; triples €52.50/63; quads €66/76. Cash only. ❷

▨ **Pfefferbett,** Christinenstraße 18-19 (☎030 93 93 58 58; www.pfefferbett.de). U2 to Senefelderplatz. Juxtaposing its original 19th-century brick walls with contemporary design, this hostel has a roof deck and some of the best deals in Berlin. Named after the nearby beer garden. Breakfast buffet €4. Linens €2.50. Free Wi-Fi. Reception and bar open 24hr. 6- to 8-bed dorms with shared bath from €12; 4- to 6-bed dorms with private bath from €17.50. Doubles with private bath, TV, and telephone €27. Cash only. ❶

Alcatraz, Schönhauser Allee 133A (☎030 48 49 68 15; www.alcatraz-backpacker.de). U2 to Eberswalder Str. Tucked away in a spray-painted courtyard. 80 beds in small but carefully decorated rooms. The "chill out room" is quite the hangout after dark. Kitchen facilities. Linens €2. Free internet and Wi-Fi. Bike rental €5. 8-bed dorms in summer €16, in winter €13; singles €40/30; doubles €50/42; triples €66/54; quads €72/60. 5% discount per night with ISIC Card. MC/V. ❷

Lette'm Sleep Hostel, Lettestr. 7 (☎030 44 73 36 23; www.backpackers.de). U2 to Eberswalder Str. If it weren't for the bright paint job, you could mistake the hostel for one of the cafes and bars lining Helmholtzplatz, one of the neighborhood's most lively areas. The big kitchen, complete with comfy red couches, is the social nexus of this 48-bed hostel. Linens €2. Free internet. Wheelchair-accessible. Reception 24hr. Apr.-Oct. 4- to 7-bed dorms €17-23, doubles with sheets €55, triples €68; Nov.-Mar. €11-20/40/60. AmEx/MC/V. ❷

Apartment4Youth, Schönhauser Allee 103 (☎030446 77 83; www.hotel4youth.de). S42 to Schönhauser Allee. Although pricey for a single, one of these airy apartments is a good deal for a group. A definite step-up from hostels. 24hr. reception and bar. Complimentary breakfast buffet. Free internet and Wi-Fi. Singles €43; doubles €66. AmEx/MC/V. ❺

FRIEDRICHSHAIN

If you want to stay near Friedrichshain's legendary nightlife, base yourself near **Warschauer Strasse,** which can be reached from the U15, S3, S5-7, S9, and S75.

BERLIN

Friedrichshain

ACCOMMODATIONS
All in Hostel, 6
Eastern Comfort Hostelboat, 18
Globetrotter Hostel Odyssee, 3
Sunflower Hostel, 12

FOOD & DRINK
Aunt Benny, 2
Der Fliegender Tisch, 7
Frittiersalon, 9
Lemongrass, 5

SIGHTS
East Side Gallery, 17
Gedenkstätte
Normannenstraße, 1

BARS & NIGHTLIFE
Astro-Bar, 8
Berghain/Panorama Bar, 4
Cassiopeia, 15
Dachkammer Bar, 10
Habermeyer, 14
Maria am Ostbahnhof, 13
Matrix, 16
Sanitorium 23, 11

LICHTENBERG

FRIEDRICHSHAIN

RUMMELSBURG

Stadtpark

Spree

East Side Gallery

OSTBAHNHOF

OSTKREUZ

FRANKFURTER ALLEE

FRANKFURTER TOR

WARSCHAUER STR.

SCHLESISCHES TOR

STRAUSBERGER PL.

WEBERWIESE

SAMARITERSTR.

TO VOLKSPARK
FRIEDRICHSHAIN (50m)

TO PRENZLAUER BERG

TO MITTE

0   200 yards
0   200 meters

Sunflower Hostel, Helsingforser Str. 17 (☎030 44 04 42 50; www.sunflower-hostel. de). This relaxed, eclectic hostel features a vine-hung bright orange lounge. Spotless dorms are a marked contrast to the studied chaos of the common areas. The staff knows the nightlife scene well. Breakfast buffet €3. Locks and linens €3 deposit each. Laundry €4.50. Internet €0.50 per 10min.; free Wi-Fi. Reception 24hr. 7- to 8-bed dorms €10-14.50; 5- to 6-bed dorms €12.50-16.50; singles €30-36.50; doubles €38-46.50; triples €51-61.50; quads €60-79.50. 7th night free. MC/V. ❶

Eastern Comfort Hostelboat, Mühlenstr. 73-77 (☎030 66 76 38 06; www.eastern-comfort.com). Enter through the first opening in the East Side Gallery (p. 98). Those willing to brave narrow corridors and cramped quarters will be rewarded with Berlin's most adventurous hostel: a docked boat. The truly bold can sleep outside on the deck in summer for the cheapest view of the river in town. Breakfast €4. Linens €5. Laundry €5 per load. Internet €2 per hr. Tent/open-air €12; dorms €16; 1st-class singles €64, 2nd-class €50; doubles €78/58; triples €69; quads €76. 2-night bookings only on weekends. The new sister ship, Western Comfort, is docked on the opposite side of the Spree and rents pricier rooms and no dorms. MC/V. ❶

Globetrotter Hostel Odyssee, Grünberger Str. 23 (☎030 29 00 00 81; www.globetrot-terhostel.de). Convenient base for nightlife "sightseeing." Rooms with psychedelic swirls of paint, an outdoor courtyard, and a pool table by the bar make this a backpacker favorite. Bar open until dawn. Breakfast €3. Sheets included with deposit. Internet €0.50 per 10min; free Wi-Fi. Reception 24hr. 8-bed dorms in summer €13, in winter €10; 6-bed dorms €15/12; doubles €45/39, with shower €52/46; triples €57/48; quads €68/56. 7th, 13th, and 14th nights free. MC/V. ❶

All In Hostel, Grünberger Str. 54 (☎030 288 7683; www.all-in-hostel.com). A sleek if institutional new hostel that, with 400 beds, anticipates the rising demand for Friedrichshain's booming nightlife scene. Breakfast and linens included. Internet €1 per 10min.; free Wi-F. Reception 24hr. 8-bed dorms €10-27; 4- to 6-bed dorms €18-35; singles with private bath €39-69; doubles €50-160. AmEx/MC/V. ❷

KREUZBERG

Bax Pax, Skalitzer Str. 104 (☎030 69 51 83 22; www.baxpax-kreuzberg.de). U1 or U15 to Görlitzer Bahnhof, right across the street. Run by the same friendly people as Mitte's Backpacker Hostel. Around the corner from Oranienstr., with a pool table, roomy common spaces, walls painted with film reels, and a bed inside an antique VW Bug (ask for room 3). Kitchen facilities and an outdoor terrace. Breakfast €4.50. Linens €2.50. Internet €2 per 30min. Bike rental 1st day for €12, 2nd €10, additional days €5. Reception 24hr. Big dorms in high season €16, in low season €15; 7- to 8-bed dorms €17/15; 5- to 6-bed rooms €18/17; singles €31/30; doubles €48/46, with bath €60/56; triples €63/60; quads €76/72. AmEx/MC/V. ❷

Hostel X Berger, Schlesische Str. 22 (☎030 69 53 18 63; www.hostelxberger.com). U1 or U15 to Schlesisches Tor, or night bus #N65 to Taborstr. This social hostel is a good launching pad for the one Kreuzberg area that might be more fun at night than Oranienstr. The colorful graffiti outside is more exciting than the basic, roomy dorms. Female-only dorms available. Sheets €2, towel €1. Free internet. Reception 24hr. Dorms €11-15; singles €28-32; doubles €36-40; triples €36-38; quads €60-64. Cash only. ❶

Berlin Boutique Hostel, Gneisenaustr. 109 (☎030 69 81 923). U6, U7, or night bus #N19 to Mehringdamm. The name refers to pleasant details like chiffon curtains, plants, and beautiful pillows in the otherwise standard dorms. On the quieter side of Kreuzberg. Continental breakfast and linens included. Free internet. 12- to 8-bed dorms €12-15; 4- to 5-bed dorms €14-16. AmEx/MC/V. ❷

Pension Kreuzberg, Großbeerenstr. 64 (☎030 251 1362; www.pension-kreuzberg. de). U6, U7, or night bus #N19 to Mehringdamm. Elegant, old-fashioned staircases, a

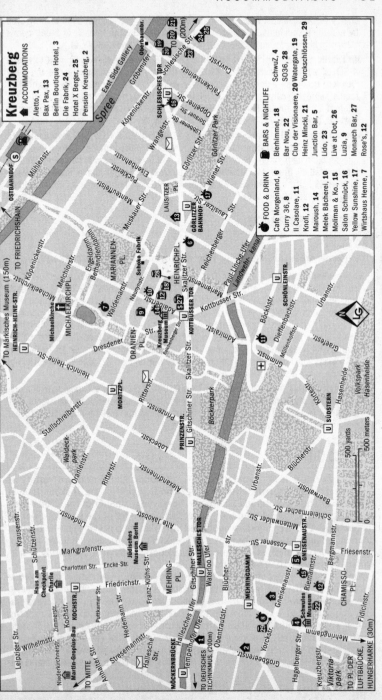

Kreuzberg

ACCOMMODATIONS

Aletto, **1**
Bax Pax, **13**
Berlin Boutique Hotel, **3**
Die Fabrik, **24**
Hotel X Berger, **25**
Pension Kreuzberg, **2**

BARS & NIGHTLIFE

Bierhimmel, **18**
Bar Nou, **22**
Club der Visionaere, **20**
Heinz Mincki, **21**
Junction Bar, **5**
Lido, **23**
Live at Dot, **26**
Luzia, **9**
Monarch Bar, **27**
Rose's, **12**
SchwuZ, **4**
SO36, **28**
Watergate, **19**
Yorckschlössen, **29**

FOOD & DRINK

Cafe Morgenland, **6**
Curry 36, **8**
Il Casolare, **11**
Knofi, **12**
Maroush, **14**
Melek Bäckerei, **10**
Moliman & Ko., **15**
Salon Schmück, **16**
Yellow Sunshine, **17**
Wirtshaus Henne, **7**

BERLIN

cheery yellow breakfast room, and antique iron stoves. The neighborhood is lively, even by Kreuzberg standards. Breakfast included. Reception 8am-9pm. 3- to 5-bed dorms €25, with bath €27; singles €42/60; doubles €58/69. AmEx/MC/V. ❸

Die Fabrik, Schlesische Str. 18 (☎030 611 7116; www.diefabrik.com), next to Hostel X Berger. U1 to Schlesische Tor. S1, S5, S7, S9 to Warschauerstr. Despite the party location, a slightly older, calmer clientele gathers at this former factory. Light-filled rooms, some with carpets, leather furniture, and oriental carpets. Breakfast €3.50-6.50. Internet €1 per 20min; free Wi-Fi. Reception 24hr. Dorms €18; singles €38; doubles €46-58; triples €60-78; quads €75-90. Cash only. ❷

Aletto Jugendhotels, Tempelhofer Ufer 8-9 (☎030 25 93 04 80; www.aletto.de). U1, U7, or U15 to Möckernbrücke. Spacious, well-outfitted rooms in an institutional-looking building right on the Landwehrkanal. Additional rooms with flatscreen TVs and foosball tables. Breakfast buffet included. Internet €0.50 per 15min. Reception 24hr. Singles €35-55; doubles €39-75; triples €51-90. Another location at Grunewaldstr. 33 in Schoneberg. MC/V. ❺

OUTER DISTRICTS

TEGEL

Two hostels are north of the city, near the beautiful Tegeler See lake.

Backpacker's Paradise, Ziekowstr. 161 (☎030 433 86 40; www.backpackersparadise. de). Take the U6 to Alt-Tegel, and then bus #222 or night bus #N22 (dir.: Alt-Lübars) to Titusweg. Alternatively, take the S25 to Tegel, take a right out of the station, and walk 20m to catch the #222. Nightly campfires, hot showers, and a free-spirited vibe in a little yard behind the Jugendgästehaus. Cheapest overnight stays in Berlin. Space is nearly always available, except when overrun by school groups. Breakfast buffet €2.50. Laundry €4. Free internet. Bike rental €4. Reception 24hr. Open May 15 to Sept. 1. €8.50 gets you a blanket and foam pad in a 20-person tent, €1 more buys a cot to put them on. Bring a sleeping bag. Cash only. ❶

Jugendgästehaus Tegel, Ziekowstr. 161 (☎030 433 30 46; www.jugendgaestehaus-tegel.de). A dignified red brick building with an institutional, boarding-school feel. Breakfast included. Linens €3. Free internet. Reception 7:30am-midnight. €20 per person. Under 27 only. Cash only. ❷

◪ FOOD

Food in Berlin is less German than it is cosmopolitan. Besides a variety of tasty local options, terrific ethnic food abounds thanks to the Turkish, Indian, Italian, and Thai populations. There are, however, a number of traditional German restaurants; in early summer, expect an onslaught of the popular *Spargel* (asparagus). Fall is pumpkin season, and pumpkin soup is everywhere. Berlin's dearest culinary tradition, however, is breakfast, a gloriously civilized institution often served in cafes well into the afternoon. Relax over a leisurely *Milch-kaffee*, a bowl of coffee foaming with milk.

Almost every street in Berlin has its own Turkish restaurant and *Imbiß* (snack bar). Most are open ridiculously late, some 24hr. The *döner kebap* (shaved roast lamb or chicken in a toasted flatbread and topped with vegetables and garlic sauce) has cornered the fast-food market, with falafel running a close second. Another budget option for travelers is to buy *belegte Brötchen*, or stuffed baguettes, at a local *Bäckerei* or *Konditorei* (€2.50-3.50). Quality Indian and Italian eateries are everywhere, and the city of course has its fair share of *Currywurst* and *Bratwurst*. **Aldi, Plus, Spar, Edeka,** and **Penny Markt** are the cheapest supermarket chains, followed by **Bolle, Reichelt,** and the ubiquitous **Kaisers.** Supermarkets are usually open M-F 9am-6pm and Sa 9am-4pm, though some are open as late as 8pm on weekdays. **Ullrich** at Bahnhof Zoo is open M-Sa 9am-10pm, Sa 11am-10pm. Bahnhof Zoo's open-air market fires up Saturday mornings on **Winterfeldtplatz,** and almost every neighborhood has its own market. For cheap veggies and huge wheels of *Fladenbrot* (pita bread), hit the kaleidoscopic **Turkish market** in Kreuzberg, along Maybachufer on the Landwehrkanal (U1 or U8 to Kottbusser Tor. Open Tu and F 10am-6pm.)

CHARLOTTENBURG

▧ **Schwarzes Cafe,** Kantstr. 148 (☎030 313 8038). S3, S5, S7, S9, or S75 to Savignyplatz. The most popular boho cafe in the area for a reason: absinthe all night in the dimly lit, frescoed space, followed by delicious breakfast when the sun comes up. Weekly specials served 11:30am-8pm (€7-10). Breakfast always available (€5-8.50). Open 24hr., (except Tu 3am-11am). Cash only. ❸

▧ **Am Nil,** Kaiserdamm 114 (☎30 321 44 06) U2 to Sophie-Charlotte Platz. Recline on the Oriental carpets and enjoy platters of spiced Egyptian food (€7-14). Belly dancer F and Sa 9pm. Open Tu-Su 3pm-1am. Cash only. ❸

Kuchi, Kochstr. 30 (☎030 31 50 78 15). S5, S7, S9 or S75 to Savignyplatz. A bit more pricey than the sushi *Imbisse,* but you can be sure you are eating real fish in this trendy little restaurant. Sushi rolls from €4. Hot Japanese entrees. Open M-Th noon-midnight, F-Su 12:30pm-1am. Cash only. ❷

Mensa TU, Hardenbergstr. 34 (☎030 939 39 7439). U2 to Ernst-Reuter Platz bus #245 to Steinplatz, a 10min. walk from Bahnhof Zoo. You'll find the cheapest hot meal around in this cafeteria. 3 entree choices as well as vegetarian options. Meals €2-4, students €2-3. Cafeteria downstairs has slightly higher prices. Open M-F 11am-2:30pm. Cafeteria open M-F 11am-3:30pm, coffee bar M-F 11am-6pm, and cake shop M-F 7:30am-2:30pm. Cash only. ❶

Paris Bar, Kantstrasse 152 (☎030 313 8052) U1 to Uhlandstr. One of the most popular restaurants of the former West Berlin is still a gathering point for hot artists, popular politicians, uber-celebs who enjoy the bistro food, and students who can only afford the desserts. Entrees €10-25. Open daily noon-2am. AmEx/MC/V. ❺

Restaurant-Cafe Bleibtreu, Bleibtreustr. 45 (☎030 881 4756; www.cafe-bleibtreu.de). S5, S7, S9, or S75 to Savignyplatz Audrey Hepburn and James Dean watch you eat in this time warp adorned with classic film posters and a London phone booth. Pasta and vegetarian plates €5-6. Meat and fish entrees €8-13. Breakfast buffet Sa-Su 9:30am-3:30pm; €6, children €3. Open M-F 9:30am-1am, Sa-Su 9:30am-2am. AmEx/MC/V. ❷

SCHÖNEBERG AND WILMERSDORF

To experience Schöneberg's relaxed cafe culture look no farther than the intersection of **Maaßenstraße** and **Winterfeldstraße.**

▧ **Cafe Bilderbuch,** Akazienstr. 28 (☎030 78 70 60 57; www.cafe-bilderbuch.de). U7 to Eisenacher Str. Fringed lamps, oak bookcases, and velvety couches give this cafe the feel of a Venetian library. The tasty brunch baskets, served around the clock, reach their pinnacle in a sumptuous Sunday buffet (€8). Dinner specials €5-8.50. Open M-Th 9am-1am, F-Sa 9am-2am, Su 10am-1am. Kitchen open 9am-11pm. Cash only. ❷

▧ **Seidls Gotenstraße 1** (030 78 09 79 97; www.seidls-berlin.de). S1 to Julius-Leber-Brücke. This airy, out-of-the-way restaurant with artwork and tablecloths is the best splurge in the area. Entrees €9-17. Open M-Sa noon-1am, Su 9-1am. Cash only. ❷

▧ **Baharat Falafel,** Winterfeldtstr. 37 (☎030 216 8301). U1-U4 to Nollendorfplatz. This isn't your average *Döner* stand—it's all about falafel fried to order and a place to sit

BERLIN

down. Get your choice of 3 or 5 chickpea balls in a fluffy pita with veggies and tahini mango, or chili sauce (€3/4). Plates €6-8, with hummus, tabouleh, and salad. Wash it down with fresh-squeezed *Gute Laune Saft* (good-mood juice; €1-2). Open M-Sa 11am-2am, Su noon-2am. MC/V. ❷

Cafe Berio, Maaßenstr. 7 (☎030 216 1946; www.cafe-berio.de). U1, U2, U4, or U15 to Nollendorfplatz. Always jam-packed with (mostly gay) locals, this 2-floor Viennese-style cafe tempts passersby off the street with its unbeatable breakfast menu (€3-11). The place to go before clubbing. Entrees €5-9. Happy hour mixed drinks 2-for-1 M-Th and Su 7pm-midnight and F-Sa 7-9pm. Open M-Th and Su 8am-midnight, F-Sa 8am-1am. Kitchen open daily 8am-11pm. Cash only. ❸

Cafe Einstein, Kurfurstenstr. 58 (☎030 261 5096; www.cafeeinstein.com). U1, U2, U3, or U4 to Nollendorf Platz. An obligatory stop (yes, for the other tourists, too). Berlin's premier Viennese coffee shop will make you drool for the apple strudel and home-roasted coffee. Elegant wood-panneled interior and outdoor garden. Entrees €15-19. Open daily 8am-1am. The bar **Lebensstern** is open 7pm-1am, all mixed drinks €9. AmEx/MC/V. ❹

Bar Tolucci, Eisenacher Str. 86 (☎030 214 1607; www.bar-tolucci.de). U7 to Eisenacher Str. This tastefully understated Tuscan restaurant pays homage to the Italian filmmaker Bertolluci by decorating the walls with images from his films. The small garden is a perfect place to enjoy a leisurely meal (entrees €6-9). Stone-oven pizza served 5pm-midnight (€4-8), just one option on the exhaustive menu. Open daily 10am-1am, garden 10am-midnight. MC/V. ❷

Vegetables & Fish, Goltzstr. 32 (☎030 215 7455). U1, U2, U4, or U15 to Nollendorfplatz. Order generous portions (€4-6) of the eponymous food groups or meat from a little counter in the back of this tasty Thai spot and enjoy them on the eye-catching outdoor tables covered in bright orange plaid. Go for the dishes with *Kokosmilch* (coconut milk). Open daily noon-midnight. Cash only. ❷

Die Feinbäckerei, Vorbergstr. 2 (☎030 81 49 42 40; www.feinbaeck.de). U7 to Kleistpark. Like Die Feinbäckerei's pub-like interior and low-key outdoor seeting, its Swabian cuisine is unassuming and traditional. Try the one of the many varieties of *Spätzle* (noodles; €6.90) and all-you-can-eat specials. Sa-Su brunch served noon-4pm. Open daily noon-1am. Cash only. ❷

MITTE

Steer clear of the enormous tourist-trap restaurants along Oranienburger Str. The best bet for a moderately priced sit-down meal is one of the small restaurants in the **Scheunenviertel** (p. 94).

☒ **Schwarzwaldstuben,** Tucholskystr. 48, (☎030 28 09 80 84). S-Bahn to Oranienburger Str. Fitted out like a rustic southern German restaurant with sofas between the tables and stuffed boar heads on the wall, this is the best place for a schnitzel and Rothaus beer, made in the only state brewery left in Germany. Reserve on weekends, or drop by during the day for a *Flammkuchen* (€4.50-8), a sort of German pizza, and to read by the light of the fringed lamps. Entrees €8-18. ❹

☒ **Tadshickische Teestube,** Am Festungsgraben 1, (☎030 204 1112). S3, 5, 7, 9, or 75 to Hackescher Markt. Dating back to the Soviet days, this Tajik teahouse is a hidden haven of oriental carpets, tea served in samovars (€2-6), and sour cream covered meat pierogi (€5). Take off your shoes before settling cross-legged onto the cushions around the low tables. Open M-F 5pm-midnight, Sa-Su 3pm-midnight. Cash only. ❷

☒ **Monsieur Vuong,** Alte Schönhauser Str. 46 (☎030 99 29 69 24; www.monsieurvuong.de). U8 to Weinmeisterstr. or U2 to Rosa Luxembourg Platz. Gallerists, artists, and, yes, tourists (the word is out) perch on the red cube seats in this trendy, extremely popular Vietnamese restaurant. Fresh fruit drinks €3.40. Entrees €6-9. Open daily noon-midnight. Cash only. ❷

Cafe Fleury, Weinbergsweg 20 (☎030 044 03 41 44). U8 to Rosenthaler Platz. One Berlin-dweller imported some blue and white wallpaper, photographs, and knicknacks from her native France and turned her hobby into a job, opening this gorgeous cafe. Unbeatable croque monsieur and fresh soups and snacks. Entrees €5-6. Open M-F 8am-10pm, Sa-Su 10am-10pm. Cash only. ❷

Dada Falafel, Linienstr. 132 (☎030 27 59 69 27). U6 to Oranienburger Tor. Located just off of Oranienburger Str. Lebanese *Imbiss*. Caters to executives during the day and clubgoers at night. Though seating in this cubbyhole is limited, take your meal next door to Dada's Galerie and eat while enjoying rotating art exhibitions and the occasional live music. Spicy falafel or beef shawarma sandwich (€3.50), platter (€4.50), vegetarian platter for 2 (€6.50). Open daily 10am-2am; F-Sa until 3am. Cash only. ❶

Beth Cafe, Tucholskystr. 40 (☎030 281 3135), just off Auguststr. S-Bahn to Oranienburger Str. A favorite of the local Jewish community, Beth Cafe sports an "I Love Kosher" bumper sticker in its window and offers a menu with Hebrew translations. The restaurant serves quality classics like bagels with lox and cream cheese (€2.50). Other dishes €3-8. Open M-Th and Sa-Su 11am-6:30pm. AmEx/MC/V. ❷

Maedchenitaliener, Alte Schönhauser Str. 12. (☎030 40 04 17 87) U8 to Weinmeisterstr. or U2 to Rosa Luxembourg Platz. It may not look like much, it may not even look like a restaurant given the lack of signage—but this is the best inexpensive Italian food in town. Settle in at your candlelit table and order ½-L of wine (€6-12) and one of the 3 dishes on the chalkboard menu. Pasta with fresh figs, fennel, and parmesan (€12), one of the few menu regulars, is always a good bet. Entrees €8-15. Open daily 5pm-late. Cash only. ❸

Leo Bettini, Mulackstr. 33 (☎030 60 50 74 49). U8 to Weinmeisterstr. The 2 owners make only dumplings, but what dumplings. Most are Knödel, a sort of German bread ball, studded with vegetables, fruit, and seasonings. Takeaway available. Entrees €3.50-7.90, side salad €2. Open M-Th 9:30am-6pm, F-Sa noon-8pm. Cash only. ❷

Sophien 11, Sophienstr. 11 (☎030 2832136). This unassuming pub is housed in one of the oldest homes in Berlin, but the star is the secluded garden courtyard with stunning flowers. Serves traditional German fare, but stays relaxed and inexpensive. Entrees €3-10. Open M-F 5pm-late, Sa-Su 3pm-late. Cash only. ❷

Cafe Sankt Oberholz, Rosenthaler Str. 72A (☎030 240 855 86; www.sanktoberholz. de). The Mac-users come for the free Wi-Fi and stay for the well-lit, airy space and generous bowls of spaghetti bolognese (€5.50). Wear a hoodie and nerd glasses to fit in. Coffee drinks €1.80-3. Open M-F 8am-midnight, Sa-Su 9am-midnight. Cash only. ❶

Schokogalerie, Große Hamburger Str. 35 (☎030 4005 5993). U8 to Weinmeisterstr. Berlin is chockablock with chocolate shops, but this is the only one, tucked in among fellow galleries in the Scheunenviertel, that deserves to call itself art. If you are on a student's budget, it may be better just to window shop. Open daily 11am-6pm.

PRENZLAUER BERG

Prenzlauer Berg is flooded with all manner of restaurants, particularly at the borders of **Helmholzplatz** and **Kollwitzplatz**. The little streets around **Kastanienallee** are also good places to explore. On most Sundays, when virtually every restaurant serves brunch, you'll be hard-pressed to find a free table outside unless you get an early start.

▨ **Hans Wurst,** Dunckerstr. 2A (☎030 41 71 78 22). U2 to Eberswalderstr., M10 to Husemannstr. This cafe/restaurant-on-a-mission serves only organic, vegan foods with no flavor enhancers. Readings, DJs, and acoustic concerts in the evenings. The menu changes daily, with seasonal offerings and fresh creations (€3.70-8). Free Wi-Fi. Brunch Sa-Su 11am-5pm. Open Tu-Th noon-midnight, F-Sa noon-late.❷

🔲 **Cafe-Restaurant Miró,** Raumerstr. 29 (☎030 44 73 30 13; www.miro-restaurant.de). U2 to Eberswalder Str. A Mediterranean cafe whose candelit, pillowed back room and fresh entrees (€8-11) capture the region's essence perfectly. Breakfast €4.50-8.25. Soups €3.20-3.70. Large appetizers and salads €4-9. Open daily 10am-late. Kitchen closes at midnight. ❸

The Bird, Am Falkplatz 5 (☎0305 105 3283). U8 to Voltastr. One of the few, if not the only, places to get an honest-to-goodness burger in Berlin, cooked by 2 gruff New York transplants in their exposed-brick restaurant. Everything is made from scratch daily, including the sauce for the aptly named "napalm wings" (€6). Burgers €9-12. Angry hour (buy 1 beer get 1 free) 6-8pm. Open M-Sa 6pm-late, Su noon-late. Cash only. ❸

W-Imbiss, Kastanienallee 49 (☎030 4849 2657). U8 to Rosenthaler Platz. Look for the upside-down McDonald's sign and crowded outdoor seating at this casual spot. Naan cooked fresh to order and covered with your choice of toppings to make a sort of Indian pizza. Entrees €2.50-6. Open daily in summer noon-midnight, in winter 12:30-11:30pm. Cash only. ❷

Babel, Kastanienalle 33 (☎030 44 03 13 18). U8 to Bernauer Str. Locals obsessed with Babel's falafel (€3-6) keep this neighborhood Middle Eastern joint busy at all hours. Grab your food to go, or lap up the large portions under the garlic dangling from the ceiling. Open daily 11am-2am. Cash only. ❷

Thai Phiset, Pappelallee 19 (☎030 44 04 49 29), on Raumerstr. U2 to Eberswalder Str. The cheapest lunch in Prenzlberg that still comes on a plate. Noodle dishes from €2.80. Chicken €3.20-4.50. Open daily 11:30am-11pm. Cash only. ❶

Cafe Restauration 1900, Husemannstr. 1 (☎030 442 2494; www.restauration1900. de), at Kollwitzplatz. U2 to Senefelderplatz. A fashionable set frequents this ideally located cafe. The salad for 2 (€23) challenges conventional notions of what "salad" should include. Brunch buffet Sa-Su 10am-4pm (€9.50). Open daily 10am-late. Kitchen closes at midnight. MC/V. ❸

FRIEDRICHSHAIN

Most come to Friedrichshain for the techtonic dancing, but that can make you hungry. The areas around **Simon-Dach-Strrasse** and before the bridge over the **Spree** are full of late-night options.

🔲 **Frittiersalon,** Boxhagener Straße 104 (☎030 25 93 39 06). U5 to Frankfurter Tor. Multicultural, all-organic "frying salon" serves french fries and organic burgers with all kinds of fusion twists, including a meatless currywurst. The cheery place has won prizes for Berlin's best currywurst and best hangover breakfast, among other honors. Everything €2.20-9. Open M 6pm-late, Tu-F noon-late, Sa-Su 1pm-late. Cash only. ❷

Der Fliegender Tisch, Mainzer Strasse 10 (☎030297 7648). U5 to Samariter Str. A cozy candelit spot serves inexpensive Italian food to its local devotees. The pizza is good but the pasta and risotto are better. Entrees €6-7. Open M-F and Su noon-midnight, Sa 5pm-midnight. Cash only. ❷

Lemongrass, Simon-Dach-Str. 2 (☎030 20 05 69 75). Laid-back decor and classic Thai specialties cooked within view make this a neighborhood favorite. Entrees €5.50-8. Open daily noon-midnight. Cash only. ❷

Aunt Benny, Oderstr. 7 (☎030 66 40 53 00). The love is in the details at this new cafe: check out the gorgeous lamps and little rock garden set into the wall. Everything from the lemon squares to the chickpea chili salad is made by hand. Free Wi-Fi. Everything under €10. Open M-F 8:30am-7:30pm, Sa-Su 10am-late. Cash only. ❷

KREUZBERG

Kreuzberg is packed with small restaurants, cafes, and no shortage of kebab stands. You'll find most eateries along Bergmannst. and Oranienstr., and cheaper places on the sidestreets off of them. But if you're looking for the best deal, the **Turkish market** along Maybachufer (Tu and F 11am-6:30pm) should not be missed. Rings of sesame bread, all kinds of spreads, cheeses, and cured olives make great sandwiches.

▦ Maroush, Adalbertstr. 93 (☎030 69 53 61 71). U1 or U15 to Kotbusser Tor. Tourists flock to Turkish Hasir, across the street, which claims to have invented the *Döner* kebab, but this Lebanese *Imbiss* is cozier and much cheaper. Favorite choices from the menu, handwritten in Arabic and German, are chicken shawarma wrap (€2.50) and a vegetarian platter with falafel and salads (€6). Open daily 11am-2am. Cash only. ❷

Wirtshaus Henne, Leuschnerdamm 25 (☎030 614 7730; www.henne-berlin.de). U1, or U15 to Kottbusser Tor. Though this slightly out-of-the-way German restaurant does serve other dishes (€2.50-6), virtually everyone orders the famous *Brathähnchen* (fried chicken), arguably the best in Berlin. It has a small beer garden, but the real charm is in its dark wood interior, with plaid tablecloths and antique lanterns. Always packed, so reserve in advance. Open Tu-Sa from 7pm, Su from 5pm. Cash only. ❷

Curry 36, Mehringdamm 36. U7 or U8 to Mehringdamm. A Berlin institution, currywurst is sliced sausage with ketchup and curry powder, served with fries and eaten with a miniature plastic fork. Connoisseurs say this stand is the best in the city. Non-connoisseurs say it is a convenient location for a post-clubbing or drinking snack, the only time they can stomach the stuff. "Red and white meal" (sausage with curry ketchup, mayonnaise, and fries; €2.40). Open M-F 9am-4am, Sa 10am-4am, Su 11am-3am. Cash only. ❶

Molinari & Ko., Riemannstr. 13 (☎030 691 3903). U7 to Gneisenaustr. Students come here in 2 waves each day, mornings to enjoy Italian coffee (€1.80-2.80) with their newspaper and evenings to share large Italian entrees with friends (€5-14). The interior has a rustic feel, with wooden school desks, checked tablecloths, and the obligatory dripping candles. Open M-F 8am-1am, Sa-Su 9am-1am. Cash only. ❸

Salon Schmück, Skalitzer Str. 80 (☎030 69 00 47 75). U1 to Schlesisches Tor. The coffee, cakes, and snacks are good, but the real draw is the soft armchairs and sofas and secondhand clothing store in the back of the cafe. The place morphs into a bar at night, with a DJ on W and living-room style concerts on Su in a range of genres. Food €2-8. Beer €2.20. Open M-F 9am-late, Sa-Su 10am-late. Cash only. ❷

Cafe Morgenland, Skalitzer Str. 35 (☎030611 3291). U1 or U15 to Görlitzer Bahnhof. Morgenland deserves its reputation as Kreuzberg's best brunch spot with its varied spread of seafood salads, rice dishes, and rich desserts alongside more traditional offerings like rolls, cheese, and sausage. Unfortunately, the secret is out, so make a reservation, avoid Sundays, arrive early—or, better, all three. All-you-can-eat brunch €9. Entrees €5-16. Open M-F 9am-1am, Sa-Su 10am-1am. Cash only. ❸

Yellow Sunshine, Wiener Str. 19 (☎030 69 59 87 20; www.yellow-sunshine.com). U1 or U15 to Görlitzter Bahnhof. This is the spot to meet dreadlocked German 20-somethings indulging in organic vegetarian and vegan "burgers" at tables overlooking the park. The burgers are a little tasteless, but the variety of sauces makes up for it and the fries are delicious. Burger with fries and salad €6.65. Open M-Th and Su noon-midnight. F-Sa noon-1am. AmEx/MC/V. ❷

Knofi, Bergmannstr. 98 and Bergmannstr. 11 (☎030 494 5807). U6 or U7 to Mehringdamm. You aren't seeing double. One Knofi (north side) sells nuts, spreads, pastas, fine olive oil, and more, while the Knofi on the other side of the street (south) is a Mediterranean cafe that doubles as a bakery. Outdoor seating and one of the few reasonably priced meals on Bergmannstr. are available at both. Entrees including filled crepes, meat dishes, and salad plates €2.50-10. Glass of wine €2.50. Open daily 9am-9pm. Cash only. ❷

Il Casolare, Grimmstr. 30 (☎030 69 50 66 10). U1 or U15 to Prinzenstr. The brusque waiters will yell at you for putting extra parmesan on your pizza, your bill will come...

FOOTBALL FANTASIES

Germans are renowned for their football fanaticism. They love the game of soccer and sometimes that love drives them to do ridiculous things. During the 2008 Euro Cup, Germany announced a victory celebration before the Finals were played. Suffice it to say that a 1-0 loss to Spain rained on that parade.

In 2006, when Germany hosted the World Cup, Berlin was changed into something called Fan Fest Berlin, an all-out soccer bonanza. Huge screens were put up throughout the city, stages were brought in, and people gathered in astronomic numbers. At 16 locations throughout the city, near these Fan Fest areas, there were also soccer balls chained to poles, trees, and street lights, with signs above them reading "Can you kick it?"

However, these balls weren't there just for a knock around. They were filled with concrete. Unfortunately, two people injured themselves when trying to give these balls a whack. When the men who had set up these 16 stations were found they protested that it was just art, that the cement-filled balls were "neither a source of danger nor a trap," and that the art meant "soccer is something for everyone." And that's true, soccer is something for everyone in Germany—well, except for the two casualties—they had to heal up before they got back out on the pitch.

eventually... and one of the pizzas is covered in horse meat (!). But any unpleasantness is more than made up for by the excellent thin-crust pizzas and wonderful views of the canal from the outside seating in summer. Feel free to grab a marker and leave your own graffiti on the yellow walls, alongside that of punk rockers and teenage couples. Pizzas €4.50-8. Entrees €8-14. Open M-Sa 9am-6pm. Cash only. ❷

Melek Bäckerei, Oranienstr. 28 (☎030 61 20 19 58). U1, U8, or U15 to Kottbusser Tor. Turkish pastries and breads are available for pocket change at this popular sweets shop. *Baklava cevizli* €0.75. Open 24hr. Cash only. ❶

◉ SIGHTS

Most of central Berlin's major sights are along the route of **bus #100**, which travels from Bahnhof Zoo to Alexanderplatz, passing the Siegessäule, Brandenburg Gate, Unter den Linden, and the Berliner Dom, among others. Tickets for individual bus rides quickly add up—buy a day pass to save money (see **Local Transportation,** p. 63). There are only a few places to see **remnants of the Berlin Wall:** a narrow band stands in Potsdamer Platz; the touristed **Haus Am Checkpoint Charlie** guards another piece p. 108; the sobering **Documentation Center** in Prenzlauer Berg has preserved an entire city block p. 97; and a much-embellished section of the wall in Friedrichshain has become the **East Side Gallery** p. 98. A line of double bricks in the pavement (usually unmarked) traces the former location of the wall; if you're interested, you can hoof the whole thing.

CHARLOTTENBURG

During the city's division, West Berlin centered around Bahnhof Zoo, the station that inspired U2's "Zoo TV" tour. The area around the station is dominated by department stores and peep shows intermingled with souvenir shops and more G-rated attractions.

ZOOLOGISCHER GARTEN. Germany's oldest zoo houses around 14,000 animals of 1500 species, most in open-air habitats. The southern entrance is the famous **Elefantentor** (across from Europa-Center), a decorated elephant pagoda standing at Budapester Str. 34. You had better visit the world-famous polar bear █**Knut;** otherwise he might go berserk. Originally deemed the cutest polar bear alive, Knut has been diagnosed by animal specialists as a psychopath who is addicted to human attention. (☎030 25 40 10; www.zoo-berlin.de. Park open daily 9am-7:30pm, animal *houses open 9am-6pm; entrance closes at 6:30pm. €12, students €9, children €6. Combination ticket to zoo and aquarium €18/14/9.)*

AQUARIUM. Within the walls of the zoo, but independently accessible, is an aquarium, with three floors of fish, reptiles, amphibians, and insects. Highlights include the psychedelic jellyfish, freaky eels, and carp petting zoo. *(Budapester Str. 32. ☎030 25 40 10; www.aquarium-berlin.de. Open daily 9am-6pm. €12, students €9, children €6. See above for Aquarium-Zoo combo tickets.)*

KAISER-WILHELM-GEDÄCHTNISKIRCH (MEMORIAL CHURCH). Berliners nicknamed the older part of the complex **Hohler Zahn** (hollow tooth) for its jagged steeple, left bombed out after WWII as a testament to warfare. Finished in 1895 in a neo-Romanesque/Byzantine style, the church has a striking interior lined with cracked, colorful mosaics. Inside is a small exhibit showing what the church used to look like, as well as horrific photos of the city in the wake of WWII. The other part of the complex is the **New Church,** a separate nave and tower with a blue stained glass-interior, consecrated in 1992. Together they are nicknamed the "lipstick and case." *(☎030 218 5023. Exhibit open M-Sa 10am-4pm. Church open daily 9am-7pm.)*

SCHLOSS CHARLOTTENBURG (CHARLOTTENBURG PALACE). The broad Baroque palace, which was commissioned by Friedrich I in the 17th century for his second wife, Sophie-Charlotte, stands impassively at the end of a beautiful, tree-lined esplanade in northern Charlottenburg. The *Schloß*'s extensive grounds include the **Altes Schloß,** underneath the iconic dome topped with a statue of Fortuna; the **Große Orangerie,** which contains rooms filled with historic furnishings (much of it reconstructed as a result of war damage) and gratuitous gilding; the **Neuer Flügel,** which includes the marble receiving rooms and the more sober royal chambers; the **Neuer Pavillon,** a museum dedicated to Prussian architect Karl Friedrich Schinkel; the **Belvedere,** a small building housing the royal family's porcelain collection; and the **Mausoleum,** the final resting place for most of the family. Stroll the **Schloßgarten** behind the main buildings, an Elysium of small lakes, footbridges, fountains, and meticulously manicured trees. *(Spandauer Damm 10-22. Take bus #M45 from Bahnhof Zoo to Luisenplatz/Schloß Charlottenburg or U2 to Sophie-Charlotte Platz. ☎030 320 9275. Altes Schloß open Tu-Su Apr.-Oct. 10am-6pm, Nov.-Mar. 10am-5pm. Neuer Flügel open M and W-Su Apr.-Oct. 10am-6pm, Nov.-Mar. 10am-5pm. Belvedere and Mausoleum open daily Apr.-Oct. 10am-6pm, Nov.-Mar. noon-5pm. Altes Schloß €10, students €7; Neuer Flügel €6/5; Belvedere €2/1.50; Mausoleum €2/1.50. Audio tours, available in English, are included.)*

OLYMPIA-STADION. This massive Nazi-built stadium comes in a close second after Tempelhof Airport in the list of monumental Third Reich buildings in Berlin. It was erected for the infamous 1936 Olympic Games, in which African-American Jesse Owens won four gold medals. Hitler refused to congratulate Owens, a legendary runner who now has a Berlin street (Jesse-Owens-Allee) named after him. Film buffs will recognize the complex from Leni Riefenstahl's terrifying film *Olympia* (1938) while others will recognize it as the sight of the 2006 World Cup final. The **Glockenturm** (bell tower) provides a great lookout point and houses an exhibit on the history of German athletics. *(S5, S7, or U2 to Olympia-Stadion. For Glockenturm, S5 or S7 to Pichelsburg. ☎030 25 00 23 22; www.olympiastadion-berlin.de. Open daily Mar. 20-May 9am-7pm, Jun.-Sept. 15 9am-8pm, Sept. 16-Oct. 31 9am-7pm, Nov.-Mar. 19 9am-4pm. €4, students €3. Tour with guide €8, students €7; children under 6 free. Audio tour €2.50.)*

SCHÖNEBERG AND WILMERSDORF

Schöneberg sights are a mix of gorgeous park and whatever cultural bits and pieces ended up in this largely residential neighborhood.

GRUNEWALD. In summer, this 3 sq. km birch forest, the dog-walking turf of many a Berliner, provides an ideal retreat from the heat and chaos of the city. About 1km into the woods, the **Jagdschloß,** a restored royal hunting lodge, houses paintings by German artists like Graff and Cranach. The one-room hunting museum is worth skipping. Instead, walk around the grounds, or take a hike north in the forest to **Teufelsberg** ("devil's mountain"), the highest point in Berlin, made of overgrown rubble from WWII piled over a Nazi military school. *(Am Grunewaldsee 29. U3 or U7 to Fehrbelliner Platz, or S45 or S46 to Hohenzollerndamm, then bus #115 (dir.: Neuruppiner Str. or Spanische Alle/Potsdamer) to Pücklerstr. Turn left on Pücklerstr. following the signs and continue straight into the forest to reach the lodge. ☎ 030 813 3597; www. spsg.de. Open Tu-Su 10am-6pm. €4, students €3; with tour €5/4.)*

BRÜCKE MUSEUM. This museum features four rooms of bright, fierce paintings from Die Brücke (The Bridge), a short-lived component of German Expressionism. *(Bussardsteig 9. U3 or U7 to Fehrbelliner Platz then bus #115 (dir.: Neuruppiner Str. or Spanische Allee/Potsdamer) to Pücklerstr. ☎ 030 831 2029; www.bruecke-museum.de. Open M and W-Su 11am-5pm. €4, students €2.)*

GAY MEMORIAL. Just outside the Nollendorfplatz U-Bahn station, heading in the Motzstr. direction, stands an unassuming and unmarked memorial to gay victims of the Holocaust.

FEHRBELLINER PLATZ. This square was erected by the Nazis as a vision of the Fascist architectural future. The austerely regular, prison-like blocks were model apartment houses, since enlivened by the strangest-looking U-Bahn station in Berlin. More optimistically, a park extends from the square where flea markets are held on weekends and children play soccer. *(U3 or U7 to Fehrbelliner Platz.)*

MITTE

The sights of Mitte alone could keep a tourist busy for weeks. The most efficient approach is to start at the Brandenburg Gate and either walk due east on Unter den Linden or take the #100 bus to do a drive-by of Imperial Berlin.

UNTER DEN LINDEN

This famous street was named "under the linden trees" for the 18th-century specimens that still line what was the spine of Imperial Berlin and what has become the nerve center of tourist Berlin. During the DDR days, it was known as the "idiot's mile," because it was often all that visitors saw, giving them little idea of what the eastern part of the city was really like. Originating in Pariser Platz, dominated by Brandenburger Tor, the street runs east through Bebelplatz and the Lustgarten, passing most of what remains of the city's still-impressive imperial architecture. *(S1, S2, or S25 to Unter den Linden. Bus #100 runs the length of the street every 4-6min.)*

▓BRANDENBURGER TOR (BRANDENBURG GATE). Don't deny yourself the obligatory photo op. Berlin's only remaining city gate and and most recognizable symbol was built by Friedrich Wilhelm II in the 18th century as a symbol of victory, although in recent years this has been rephrased as "The Victory of Peace" in a fit of political correctness. During the Cold War, when it sat along the wall and served as a barricaded gateway, it became the symbol of a divided Berlin. Today, it is the most powerful emblem of reunited Germany—in 1987,

Reagan chose this spot to make his "Tear down this wall" speech. The **Room of Silence** in the northern end of the gate provides a non-denominational place for meditation and reflection. *(Open daily 11am-6pm.)*

PARISER PLATZ. Why is Berlin's most historic square named after its nemesis city? The 1814 Prussian overthrow of Napoleon was apparently reason enough. Arguably the most spectacular post WWII renovation in the square is the **Hotel Adlon,** once the premier address for visiting dignitaries and, more recently, the site of the infamous Michael Jackson baby-dangling incident. *(The square is in front of the Brandenburger Tor.)*

THE KENNEDYS. His "Ich bin ein Berliner" speech reserved JFK a special place in Berliners' hearts and their most important square, now home to one of the world's most extensive compilations of the family's photographs, official documents, private letters, and memorabilia. *(Pariser Platz 4A. Take S-Bahn to Unter den Linden. ☎ 030 20 65 35 70; www.thekennedys.de. Open daily 10am-6pm. €7, students €3.50.)*

RUSSIAN EMBASSY. Rebuilding the edifices of the rich and famous wasn't a major priority in the workers' state of the DDR. The exception was Berlin's largest embassy, which covers almost an entire city block. The quiet removal of the enormous Lenin bust at the end of the Cold War completed its transformation into just another embassy. *(Unter den Linden 65.)*

STAATSBIBLIOTHEK ZU BERLIN (BERLIN STATE LIBRARY). The stately library features an ivy-covered courtyard filled with lounging intellectuals. It was founded in 1661, making it one of the oldest buildings in all of Berlin. Inside are over 10 million books, along with an endless list of cultural assets. *(Unter den Linden 8. ☎ 030 26 60. Open M-F 9am-9pm, Sa 9am-5pm. Free internet with admission. €0.50.)*

HUMBOLDT-UNIVERSITÄT (HUMBOLDT UNIVERSITY). Just beyond the Staatsbibliothek lies the H-shaped main building of Humboldt University, whose hallowed halls have been paced by the likes of Hegel, Einstein, Bismarck, the Brothers Grimm, and Karl Marx. In the wake of post-1989 academic warfare, in which many departments were purged of Marxist leanings, international scholars have descended upon the university to take part in its dynamic renewal. Budding socialists can peruse the works of Marx and Lenin at the book vendors outside under the statue of a triumphant **Frederick the Great.** *(Unter den Linden 6.)*

▨NEUE WACHE. The combination of Prussian Neoclassicism and a copy of an Expressionist statue by Käthe Kollwitz, *Mutter mit totem Sohn* (*Mother with Dead Son*), makes for an oddly moving memorial to "the victims of war and tyranny." The "New Guardhouse" was designed by architect Karl Friedrich Schinkel, turned into a memorial to victims of "fascism and militarism," and closed after reunification. Today, the remains of an unknown soldier and an unknown concentration camp victim are buried inside with earth from the camps at Buchenwald and Mauthausen and from the battlefields of Stalingrad, El Alamein, and Normandy. *(Unter den Linden 4. Open daily 10am-6pm.)*

BEBELPLATZ. On May 10, 1933, Nazi students ransacked the nearby state library and burned nearly 20,000 books here by "subversive" authors such as Heinrich Heine, Albert Einstein, and Sigmund Freud. A plaque in the center of the square is engraved with Heine's eerie 1820 German epigram: "Wherever they burn books, eventually they will burn people too." A glass square in the center of the Platz provides a view into an underground memorial: a white room lined with empty bookshelves. On the west side of the square, the building with the curved facade is the **Alte Bibliothek.** Once the royal library, it is now home to Humboldt's law faculty. On the other side of the square is the

Deutsche Staatsoper, one of Berlin's three opera houses, fully rebuilt after the war from original sketches by Knobelsdorff, the architect who designed Schloß Sanssouci in Potsdam (p. 126). The distinctive blue-green dome at the end of the square belongs to the 1773 **Sankt-Hedwigs-Kathedrale**, Berlin's first Catholic church built after the Reformation. Organ concerts draw visitors on Wednesday at 3pm. *(Cathedral open M-Sa 10am-5pm, Su 1-5pm. Free.)*

POTSDAMER PLATZ

POTSDAMER PLATZ. Both Berlin's shiniest commercial center and the site of its most high-profile architectural failures, Potsdamer Platz is amazing for the sheer speed of its construction. Built under Friedrich Wilhelm I (in imitation of Parisian boulevards) as a launch pad for troops, the area became the commercial and transportation hub of pre-war Berlin, regulated by Europe's first traffic lights (the massive clock is set into a replica of what they looked like). But the square was flattened by bombers in WWII and caught in the death strip between East and West during the Cold War. In the decade that followed reunification, a number of commercial buildings sprouted up, the most recognizable being an off-kilter glass recreation of Mt. Fuji. *(U2, or S1, S2, or S25 to Potsdamer Platz.)*

FÜHRERBUNKER. Near Potsdamer Platz, unmarked and inconspicuous, is the site of the bunker where Hitler married Eva Braun and then shot himself. During WWII, it held 32 rooms, including private apartments, and was connected to Hitler's chancellery building (since destroyed). Plans to restore the bunker were shelved for fear that the site would become a pilgrimage spot for neo-Nazis; all that remains is a dirt expanse and the occasional tourist. *(Under the parking lot at the corner of In den Ministergärten and Gertrud-Kolmar-Str.)*

GENDARMENMARKT

Several blocks south of Unter den Linden, Berlin's most typically Old Europe square became the French quarter in the 18th century after the arrival of an influx of Huguenots fleeing persecution by Louis XIV. During the last week of June and the first week of July, the square becomes an outdoor stage for open-air classical concerts. *(U6 to Französische Str. or U2 or U6 to Stadtmitte.)*

DEUTSCHER DOM. Though destroyed during WWII, the cathedral was rebuilt to its Renaissance glory in the 1970s. Once again gracing the southern end of the square, the Dom is not currently used as a church but instead houses **Wege Irrwege Umwege** ("Milestones, Setbacks, Sidetracks"), a humble exhibit tracing German political history from despotism to democracy. *(Gendarmenmarkt 1. ☎ 030 22 73 04 31. Open Tu-Su and holidays 10am-6pm. Free.)*

FRANZÖSISCHER DOM. Built in the early 18th century by French Huguenots, the Dom now holds a restaurant and small museum on the Huguenot diaspora. The tower commands a sweeping view of the city. *(Gendarmenmarkt 5. ☎ 030 229 17 60; www.franzoesischer-dom.de. Open Tu-Su noon-5pm. Tower open daily 9am-7pm. Museum €2, students €1. Tower €2/1.50.)*

▨ FASSBENDER & RAUCH CHOCOLATIERS. This fancy chocolate store provides the perfect opportunity to review or preview your Berlin sightseeing with enormous models of the **Kaiser Wilhelm Memorial Church (p. 89)**, **Reichstag (p. 95)**, and the **Brandenburg Gate (p. 90)**, all rendered in chocolate and wafers. *(Charlottenstr. 60. ☎ 030 20 45 84 40. Open M-Sa 10am-8pm, Su 11am-8pm.)*

MUSEUMSINSEL (MUSEUM ISLAND)

There are more than a handful of reasons to set aside a good chunk of time for Museum Island, the entirety of which is a **UNESCO World Heritage Sight.** After crossing the Schloßbrücke over the Spree, Unter den Linden becomes Karl-Liebknecht-Str. and cuts through the Museumsinsel, which is home to five major museums and the **Berliner Dom.** *(Take S3, S5, S7, S9, or S75 to Hackescher Markt and walk toward the Dom. Alternatively, pick up bus #100 along Unter den Linden and get off at Lustgarten. For information on the Altes Museum, Pergamon, Bodemuseum, and Alte Nationalgalerie, see Museums, p. 102.)*

■**BERLINER DOM.** One of Berlin's most recognizable landmarks, this elegantly bulky, multiple-domed cathedral proves that Protestants can design buildings as dramatically as Catholics. Built during the reign of Kaiser Wilhelm II in a faux-Renaissance style, the cathedral suffered severe damage in a 1944 air raid and took 20 years to fully reconstruct. Look for the Protestant icons (Calvin, Zwingli, and Luther) that adorn the decadent interior, or soak up the glorious view of Berlin from the top of the cupola. *(☎ 030 20 26 91 19; www.berlinerdom.de. Open M-Sa 9am-8pm, Su noon-8pm, closed during services 6:30-7:30pm. Free organ recitals W-F 3pm. Frequent concerts in summer; buy tickets in the church or call ahead. Combined admission to Dom, crypt, tower, and galleries €5, students €3. Audio tour €3.)*

LUSTGARTEN. The "pleasure garden," is bounded by the Karl Friedrich Schinkel-designed Altes Museum to the north and the Berliner Dom to the east. The massive granite bowl in front of the museum was meant to adorn the main hall but didn't fit through the door.

SCHLOSSPLATZ. Known as Marx-Engels-Platz during the days of the DDR, the "palace square" is at the heart of Berlin's biggest architectural and urban-planning controversy. The Berliner Schloß, the Hohenzollern Imperial palace, used to stand here, but was torn down in 1950 by the East German authorities to overwhelming (mostly West Berliner) protest. The Schloß was replaced by the concrete Palast der Republik, where the East German parliament met. After reunification, the Palast was knocked down to make way for a replica of, you guessed it, the Schloß, to enormous (mostly East Berliner) protest. *(Across the street from the Lustgarten.)*

ALEXANDERPLATZ AND NIKOLAIVIERTEL

Formerly the heart of Weimar Berlin, **Alexanderplatz** became the center of East Berlin, an urban wasteland of fountains, pre-fab concrete apartment buildings, and—more recently—chain stores and malls. **Karl-Liebknecht-Strrasse,** which divides the Museuminsel, leads into the monolithic Alexanderplatz, a former cattle market. Behind the Marx-Engels-Forum, the preserved cobblestone streets of **Nikolaiviertel** (Nicholas' Quarter) stretch toward Mühlendamm. *(Take U2, U5, or U8, or S3, S5, S7, S9, or S75 to Alexanderplatz.)*

■**FERNSEHTURM** (TV TOWER). The tremendous and bizarre tower, the tallest structure in Berlin (368m, was originally intended to prove East Germany's technological capabilities, though Swedish engineers were ultimately brought in when construction faltered. As a result, the tower has acquired some colorful, politically infused nicknames, among them "Walter Ulbricht's Last Erection." Look at the windows when the sun is out to see the cross-shaped glint pattern known as the *Papsts Rache* (Pope's Revenge), so named because it defied the Communist government's attempt to rid the city of religious symbols. An elevator whisks tourists up to the magnificent view from the spherical node (203m) and a slowly rotating cafe one floor up serves international meals

94 • WWW.LETSGO.COM

for €8-16. (☎030 242 3333; www.berlinerfernsehturm.de. Open daily Mar.-Oct. 9am-midnight, Nov.-Feb. 10am-midnight. €10, under 16 €4.50.)

MARIENKIRCHE. The non-bombed and non-reconstructed church (Berlin's second oldest) is Gothic, the altar and pulpit Rococo, and the tower Neo-Romantic, thanks to centuries of additions to the original structure. Knowledgeable guides explain the artifacts as well as the painting collection, which features works from the Dürer and Cranach schools. *(☎030 242 4467. Open daily in summer 10am-9pm, in winter 10am-6pm.)*

ROTES RATHAUS (RED TOWN HALL). The name of the high-Italian Renaissance-style city hall refers to its gorgeous brick facade, not its politics—although it was the city hall of Communist East Berlin. Since 1991 it has served as the city hall for the reunified Berlin. *(Closed to the public.)*

MARX-ENGELS FORUM. Across the river from Museumsinsel on the south side of Karl-Liebknecht-Str. is this rectangular park with a memorial of imprinted steel tablets dedicated to the worldwide workers' struggle against fascism and imperialism. Somber statues of Marx and Engels preside over the oft-graffitied tablets. Tourists jump into Marx's lap for a popular photo-op—we won't judge you if you join in.

SCHEUNENVIERTEL AND ORANIENBURGER STRASSE

Northwest of Alexanderplatz, near Oranienburger Str. and Große Hamburger Str., is the **Scheunenviertel** (Barn Quarter), once the center of Berlin's Orthodox Jewish community. Prior to WWII, wealthier and more assimilated Jews tended to live in Western Berlin, while Orthodox Jews from Eastern Europe settled in the Scheunenviertel (originally a derogatory term coined by Nazis). Full of cobblestone streets, Judaica-oriented bookstores and art galleries, this is one of the most pleasant strolls in all of Berlin. *(S1, S2, or S25 to Oranienburger Str. or U6 to Oranienburger Tor.)*

NEUE SYNAGOGUE. This huge building, modeled after the Alhambra, was designed by Berlin architect Eduard Knoblauch in the 1850s. The synagogue, which seated 3200, was used for worship until 1940, when the Nazis occupied it and used it for storage. Amazingly, the building survived *Kristallnacht*—the SS torched it, but a local police chief bluffed his way past SS officers to order the fire extinguished. The synagogue was later destroyed by bombing, but its restoration, largely financed by international Jewish organizations, began in 1988 and was completed in 1995. Too big for Berlin's remaining Jewish community, the striking building is no longer used for services and instead houses an exhibit chronicling its history as well as that of the Jewish community that once thrived in the surrounding neighborhood. *(Oranienburger Str. 29. ☎030 88 02 83 00; www.cjudaicum.de. Open Apr.-Sept. M and Su 10am-5pm, Tu-Th 10am-6pm, F 10am-5pm; Mar. and Oct. M and Su 10am-2pm, Tu-Th 10am-8pm, F 10am-6pm; Nov.-Feb. M and Su 10am-2pm, Tu-F 10am-6pm. Last entry 30min. before closing. Permanent exhibition "Open Ye the Gates" €3, students €2. Dome €1.50/1. Temporary exhibition €3/2.)*

ALTER JÜDISCHER FRIEDHOF (OLD JEWISH CEMETERY). Obliterated by the Nazis, the cemetery now contains only the restored gravestone of Enlightenment philosopher and scholar Moses Mendelssohn; the rest is a quiet park. In front, a prominent plaque marks the site of the **Jüdisches Altersheim** (Jewish Old-age Home), which served as a holding place for Jews before their deportation to concentration camps. *(At the end of Große Hamburger Str., near Oranienburger Str.)*

JUEDISCHE KNABENSCHULE (JEWISH BOYS' SCHOOL). Next to the cemetery on Große Hamburger Str. stands Berlin's oldest Jewish school, where Moses

Mendelssohn once taught. Today, it's a co-ed, non-denominational school. The plaque adorning the building memorializes Mendelssohn, "the German Socrates," who translated the Hebrew Bible into German and supported Jewish rights and education in Germany.

THE MISSING HOUSE. Across the street from the Jewish Boys' school is a 1990 art installation by Christian Boltanski in the space where a house was bombed during WWII. Boltanski researched the apartment's earlier inhabitants—Jews and non-Jews alike—and put plaques on the walls of the surrounding buildings at the approximate height of their apartment floors with their names, dates of birth and death, and professions. *(Große Hamburger Strasse.)*

TIERGARTEN

Stretching from Bahnhof Zoo in the west to the Brandenburg Gate in the east, this vast landscaped park was formerly used by Prussian monarchs as a hunting and parade ground. Today, it is frequented by strolling families, elderly couples. **Straße des 17. Juni** bisects the park from west to east, connecting Ernst-Reuter-Platz to the Brandenburg Gate. The street is the site of many demonstrations and parades, including Barack Obama's 2008 speech, which attracted over 200,000 viewers.

THE REICHSTAG. The current home of Germany's governing body, the **Bundestag,** the Reichstag has seen some critical historical moments in its day. Philipp Scheidemann proclaimed *"Es lebe die Deutsche Republik"* ("Long live the German Republic") here in 1918. In 1933 Adolf Hitler used a fire at the Reichstag as an excuse to declare a state of emergency and seize power. In 1997, a glass dome was added to the top, built around the upside-down solar cone that powers the building. A walkway spirals up the inside of the dome, providing visitors with information about the building, panoramic views of the city, and a view of the parliament meeting inside—a powerful symbol of government transparency. Braving the line is worth it. *(☎030 22 73 21 52; www.bundestag.de. Open daily 8am-midnight. Last entry 10pm. Free.)*

DENKMAL FÜR DIE ERMORDETEN JUDEN EUROPAS (MEMORIAL FOR THE MURDERED JEWS OF EUROPE). Just looking at the block of concrete stelae—large rectangular columns of concrete varying in height—it is hard to know what this prominent memorial, opened in the spring of 2005 and designed by architect Peter Eisenman, represents. Most agree, however, that it is quite moving. An underground information center tells the stories of specific families murdered during the Holocaust. *(Cora-Berliner-Str. 1, at the corner of Behrenstr. and Ebertstr. near the Brandenburg Gate. ☎030 26 39 43 36; www.stiftung-denkmal.de. Open daily 10am-8pm. Last entry Apr.-Sept. 7:15pm, Oct.-Mar. 6:15pm. Free audio tour. Guided public tours Sa-Su 11am and 2pm in German and Su 4pm in English. Admission €3, students €2.50.)*

AROUND THE REICHSTAG. Also known as the *Kohllosseum* for its size and first resident (Helmut Kohl), the huge white and blue **Chancellory** was reportedly a source of embarrassment to former Chancellor Gerhard Schröder, who wished to keep a low profile. Tourists aren't permitted inside. The **Palais am Pariser Platz,** directly north of the Brandenburg Gate, was once the site of a castle; enter the courtyard to find Stephen Balkenhol's startling 1998 statue *Großer Mann mit kleinem Mann* (Big Man with Little Man).

WEISSE KREUZE (WHITE CROSS) **MEMORIAL.** White crosses along the bank of the Spree behind the Reichstag commemorate those who were killed trying to cross over to West Berlin. Ten meters down the waterfront are ten glass panels inscribed with the German Bill of Human Rights. Some Berliners refer to the memorial as "the washing machine," and it's not hard to see why.

IN RECENT NEWS

KISSED GOODBYE

Communists Leonid Brezhnev and Erich Honecker will no longer lock lips along the banks of the Spree River. In their restoration of the East Side Gallery, Berlin officials gave "The Kiss,"—the most famous of its murals—the kiss of death.

Since its creation in 1989, "The Kiss" has become a stop on the Berlin tourist circuit. The image graces souvenir coffee mugs, t-shirts and postcards. But while the image remains iconic, the mural itself was aging noticeably. Plagued by constant pollution and traffic, the cheap paint began to flake off. The image, say Berlin officials, was beyond rescue. And so, in preparation for the large-scale refurbishment celebrating the East Side Gallery's 20-year anniversary, they just destroyed it.

Taking down the image was a stealth operation. Officials warned no one, not even the artist. In fact, it was only when he received a €3000 check in the mail that Russian-born Dmitri Vrubel learned that that his art stood no more. Enclosed with the check was an invitation to recreate the picture with new, longer-lasting paint.

But Vrubel refuses to let politicians dictate his creative endeavors. "I simply cannot paint a new picture like making a sandwich," said Vrubel.

SIEGESSÄULE (VICTORY COLUMN). In the heart of the Tiergarten, this slender 70m monument commemorates Prussia's victory over France in 1870. The statue at the top—Victoria, the goddess of victory—is made of melted-down French cannons. In a less-than-subtle affront to the French, the Nazis moved the monument here in 1938 from its former spot in front of the Reichstag in order to increase its visibility. Climb the monument's 285 steps for a panorama of the city. *(Großer Stern. Take bus #100 or 187 to Großer Stern or S5, S7, or S9 to Tiergarten. Accessible via the stairs at the west corner around the traffic circle. ☎ 030 391 2961. Open Apr.-Nov. M-F 9:30am-6:30pm, Sa-Su 9:30am-7pm; Dec.-Mar. M-F 10am-5pm, Sa-Su 10am-5:30pm. €2.20, students €1.50.)*

SOWJETISCHES EHRENMAL (SOVIET CENOTAPH). At the eastern end of the Tiergarten, a Soviet memorial rises (yes, in western Berlin) above a pair of red star-emblazoned tanks, the first two to enter Berlin in 1945. The position of the soldier's hand is an inverted Nazi salute. *(Bus #100 to Platz der Republik.)*

GAY MEMORIAL. Berlin's mayor unveiled a memorial to homosexuals persecuted by the Nazis on the eastern end of the Tiergarten in 2008. Peer into the 4m concrete block to see a video of two men kissing on continuous loop. *(Bus #100 to Platz der Republik.)*

WALKING ON HISTORY. It is possible to literally trip over Berlin's most pervasive memorial. Small plaques are set into the sidewalk outside apartment buildings from which Jews were deported and murdered during WWII with their names. German artist Gunther Demnig started installing the "stumbling blocks" in 1993.

FISCHERINSEL

The other half of the island that holds Museum Island, "Fisher Island" was the first part of Berlin to be settled, back when the city was called Cölln. It is well off the tourist track but worth a stop if only visit the two special Berliners living in the Köllnischen Park. *(U2 to Klosterstr.)*

KÖLLNISCHEN PARK. The most memorable part of this rambling park is the "bear pit," surrounded by a moat and containing Schnute and Maxi, two live brown bears. Living versions of the city mascot have called the park home for centuries, and were among the casualties during bombings in WWII. The only other attraction is an unremarkable statue of artist Heinrich Zille. *(Open dawn to dusk.)*

FRANZISKANER-KLOSTERKIRCHE (FRANCISCAN CLOISTERS). What used to be a working monastery beginning in the 14th century is now a stunning shell of a building, bombed during WWII. An experimental theater groups stages performances here in the summer. *(Open from dawn to dusk)*

OTHER SIGHTS IN MITTE

◪**DIE HACKESCHE HÖFE.** Built in the early 1900s, this gorgeous series of Art Deco courtyards house a combination of theaters, art galleries, bars and offices. Berlin's best art house cinema is just to the right as you enter. *(Rosenthaler Str. 40/41. www.hackesche-hoefe.com.)*

BERTOLT-BRECHT-HAUS. If any one man personifies the maelstrom of Berlin's political and aesthetic contradictions, it is the playwright Bertolt Brecht, who lived and worked in this house from 1953 to 1956. "There is a reason to prefer Berlin to other cities," the playwright once said, "because it is constantly changing. What is bad today can be improved tomorrow." The **Literaturforum im Brecht-Haus** on the second floor sponsors exhibits and lectures. *(Chausseestr. 125. U6 to Oranienburger Tor or Zinnowitzer Str. ☎ 030 28 22 003. Tours in German—required for entrance—every 30min. Tu, W, F 10-11:30am; Th 10-11:30am and 5-6:30pm; Sa 9:30am-1:30pm; Su 11am-6pm. Max. 8 people. €5, students €2.50.)*

DOROTHEENSTÄDTISCHER FRIEDHOF (DOROTHEEN MUNICIPAL CEMETERY). Attached to Brecht's house is the cemetery where he and his wife, Helene Weigel, are buried in simple graves. Other famous personages interred in the cemetery include Karl Friedrich Schinkel, Heinrich Mann, and Georg Hegel and Johann Fichte, who lie side-by-side in the middle of the yard. A map near the entrance points out locations of notable graves. *(Open daily 8am-dusk.)*

SCHLOSS BELLEVUE. Finished in 1786, this palace was the first in Berlin to be built in the Neoclassical style. The sprawling property near the Tiergarten once housed the Crown Prince of Germany and official guests of the Nazi party, and is now the official residence of the federal President. *(Closed to the public. Spreeweg 1. S5, S7, S9, or S75 to Bellevue or bus #100 to Schloß Bellevue. ☎ 030 20 00 00.)*

HI-FLYER BALLOON. Tethered to the ground near Potsdamer Platz, this hot-air balloon rises 150m into the air every 15min. for a bird's-eye view of the surrounding area. *(At the corner of Wilhelmstr. and Niederkirchnerstr. ☎ 030 226 67 88 11; www.air-service-berlin.de. Open in summer M-Th and Su 10am-10pm, F-Sa 10am-12:30am; in winter M-Th and Su 11am-6pm, F-Sa 11am-7pm. €19, students €13.)*

PRENZLAUER BERG

BERLINER MAUER DOKUMENTATIONZENTRUM (BERLIN WALL DOCUMENTATION CENTER). A museum, a chapel, and an entire city block of the preserved Berlin Wall—two concrete barriers separated by the open *Todesstreife* (death strip)—come together in a memorial to "victims of the Communist tyranny." The museum has assembled a comprehensive collection of all things Wall. Exhibits include photos, film clips, and sound bites. The collection here is both cheaper and more informative than the private museum at Checkpoint Charlie, which covers similar material. *(Bernauer Str. 111; www.berliner-mauer-dokumentationszentrum. de. ☎ 030 464 1030. U8 to Bernauer Str., switch to S1 or S2 to Nordbahnhof. Open Tu-Su Apr.-Oct. 10am-6pm, Nov.-Mar. 10am-5pm. Free.)*

BERLIN

JÜDISCHER FRIEDHOF (JEWISH CEMETERY). Prenzlauer Berg was one of the major centers of Jewish Berlin during the 19th and early 20th centuries. The ivy-covered Jewish cemetery on Schönhauser Allee contains the graves of composer Giacomo Meyerbeer and painter Max Liebermann. *(Enter by the Lapi-darium. Open M-Th 8am-4pm, F 8am-1pm. Men must cover their heads.)* Nearby, **Synagoge Rykestraße,** Rykestr. 53, is one of Berlin's loveliest synagogues. It was spared on *Kristallnacht* thanks to its inconspicuous location. Unfortunately, visitors are not allowed in, as the synagogue still operates as a school.

KOLLWITZPLATZ. This little triangle of greenery is one big playground, with toddlers climbing even on the statue of Käthe Kollwitz, the renowned painter. Non-parents are drawn by the upscale ▓market on Saturdays where vendors sell everything from boar meat sausage to handmade ravioli. *(U2 to Senefelderplatz.)*

ZEISS-GROSSPLANETARIUM. In 1987 this planetarium opened as the most modern facility of its kind in the DDR. Compared to its peers in the West, it seems about as technologically advanced as a Trabi (the East German car and butt of many jokes) but it can still show you the stars. Call or check the website for showtimes and special events. *(Prenzlauer Allee 80. S8, S41, S42, or tram M2 to Prenzlauer Allee; the planetarium is across the bridge. ☎ 030 421 8450; www.astw.de. Open Tu and Th 9am-noon, W 9am-noon and 1:30-3pm, F 7-9pm, Sa 2:30-9pm, Su 1:30-5pm. €5, students €4.)*

FRIEDRICHSHAIN

▓**EAST SIDE GALLERY.** The longest remaining portion of the Berlin Wall, this 1.3km stretch of cement slabs also serves as the world's largest open-air art gallery. The murals are not remnants of Cold War graffiti, but rather the organized efforts of an international group of artists who gathered here in 1989 to celebrate the end of the city's division. The stretch of street remains unsupervised and, on the Warschauer Str. side, open at all hours. *(Along Mühlenstr. Take U1 or U15 or S3, S5-S7, S9, or S75 to Warschauer Str. or S5, S7, S9, or S75 to Ostbahnhof and walk back toward the river. www.eastsidegallery.com.)*

STASI MUSEUM. The Lichtenberg suburb harbors perhaps the most hated and feared building of the DDR regime: the headquarters of the East German secret police, the *Staatssicherheit* or Stasi. During the Cold War, the Stasi kept dossiers on some six million of East Germany's own citizens, an amazing feat and a testament to the huge number of civilian informers in a country of only 16 million people. On January 15, 1990, a crowd of 100,000 Berliners stormed and vandalized the building to celebrate the demise of the police state. Since a 1991 law returned the records to the people, the "Horror Files" have rocked Germany, exposing millions of informants—and wrecking careers, marriages, and friendships—at every level of German society. Officially known today as the **Forschungs und Gedenkstätte Normannenstraße,** the building maintains its oppressive Orwellian gloom and much of its worn 1970s aesthetic. The exhibit displays the extensive offices of Erich Mielke, the loathed Minister for State Security from 1957 to 1989, a large collection of tiny microphones and hidden cameras used for surveillance by the Stasi, and a replica of a Stasi prison cell. *(Ruschestr. 103, Haus 1. U5 to Magdalenenstr. ☎ 030 553 6854; www.stasimuseum.de. Exhibits in German. English info booklet €3. Open M-F 11am-6pm, Sa-Su 2-6pm. €4, students €3.)*

CONFRONTING THE PAST. Files housed in the Stasi Museum are now officially open to the public, but privacy rules dictate that you can only look up the name of informants if they were informing on you. A beautiful German film addressing this topic is Florian Henckel von Donnersmarck's ▓**Das Leben der Anderen** (The Lives of Others).

KARL-MARX-ALLEE. Formerly known as Stalinallee, this was the main drag of the East German Potempkin Village, where party members staged elaborate military parades. Built in the early 1950s and widened in the 1960s, it is flanked by hideous gray pre-fab buildings that give way to the wedding-cake style "people's palaces" at Strausberger Platz. (U5 to Strausberger Platz.)

KREUZBERG

Kreuzberg sights are mostly devoted to the area's hybrid history as a hub for both punks and immigrants.

SOUTHERN KREUZBERG. The cobblestone streets and pre-war ornamented apartment blocks just east of Mehringdamm form the most gentrified area of Kreuzberg—witness the outdoor organic food market on Saturdays in Chamissoplatz. The spine of of the area is **Bergmannstraße,** a stretch of cafes, secondhand clothing and record stores, and bookshops. West of Mehringdamm, forested Viktoria Park is the highest natural point in Berlin at 66m. A huge neo-Gothic memorial commemorating the Napoleonic Wars provides a great view of Berlin. Vineyards first planted by the Knights Templar and a number of small restaurants and beer gardens—including philosopher Georg Friedrich Hegel's favorite watering hole—are tucked away in the park near the artificial waterfall. Farther south down Mehringdamm is **Tempelhof Airport,** built by Nazi architect Albrecht Speer but most famous as the site of the Berlin Airlift, 1948-1949, one of the most dramatic crises of the Cold War. The German government closed the airport in 2008, but still visible in a flower-ringed field is a monument known as the **Hungerharke** (hunger rake) representing the three air corridors and dedicated to the 78 pilots who lost their lives in the 328 days of the airlift. (U6 to Platz der Luftbrücke or U6 or U7 to Mehringdamm.)

EASTERN KREUZBERG. The **Landwehrkanal,** a channel bisecting Kreuzberg, is a lovely place to take a stroll, with moored boats doubling as on-the-water cafes. Its history is less pleasant: it is where the conservative, nationalist Freikorps threw the body of left-wing activist and Communist revolutionary Rosa Luxemburg after murdering her in 1919. The Berlin Wall once ran near **Schlesisches Tor,** a nightlife hotspot with a huge Turkish and Balkan influence and featuring arguably the best street art and graffiti in the city—especially around Wrangelstraße. The **Oberbaumbrücke,** an iconic double-decker brick bridge, spans the Spree River. Once a border crossing into East Berlin, it now connects Kreuzberg to Friedrichshain. Residents of the rival neighborhoods duke it out in a "water fight" on the bridge each July 27, with up to a thousand people throwing water and rotten vegetables at one another. (U1 or U15 to Schlesisches Tor.)

ORANIENSTRASSE. This strip's colorful mix of cafes, bars, and stores is home to the city's punk and radical elements. May Day parades, which start on Oranienplatz, were the scene of violent riots in the 1980s, although May 1 has since become a family holiday complete with a big block party. The street's **Heinrichplatz** boasts, in addition to great cafes, a women-only Turkish-style bath, **Schoko Fabrik,** which doubles as a community center (www.schokofabrik.de;

open M 3-11pm, Tu-Su noon-11pm). Squatters still occupy the **Bethanien Kunst-haus** in Marienplatz (www.bethanien.de), which hosts frequent exhibitions and an open-air cinema in summer. *(U1 or U15 to Kottbusser Tor or Görlitzer Bahnhof.)*

GÖRLITZER PARK. Built on the ruins of an old train station, Görlitzer Park is a bizarre landscape of graffitied ruins, freestanding sculpture, and—in summer—neighborhood hipsters playing frisbee and families grilling on portable barbecues. In the center, you'll find a basin, marked by a large iron sculpture; to the northeast is a small playground and petting zoo. What remains of the old station building is now a Heidi-in-the-Alps-themed cafe, **Das Edelweiß,** complete with beach chairs and outdoor screenings of soccer games in summer. *(Cafe open 11am-late.)*

OUTER DISTRICTS

WANNSEE

Most Berliners think of the town of Wannsee, on a lake of the same name, as the beach. Wannsee has one of Europe's longest inland stretches of beach along the **Havel-Uferpromenade,** and the roads behind the beaches are crowded with vacation villas. To reach the locally beloved baths, **Strandbad Wannsee,** take S1 or S7 to Nikolassee, cross the bridge in front of the main exit, continue through the park, and follow the signs down the road. Getting to the beach along the Uferpromenade is more complicated: walk along Am Großen Wannsee to Haveleck. Alternatively, take bus #218 from the Wannsee station to Pfaueninsel, backtrack to Pfaueninsel-Chaussee, and ride it to Uferprom-enade, which will appear on your right. On summer weekends, a special bus shuttles bathers from the train station. The beach fills up absurdly early with German families on weekends; be prepared to battle the crowds for choice spots. *(Wannseebad 5. Open from May to mid-July M-F 10am-7pm and Sa-Su 8am-8pm, from mid-July to Aug. M-F 9am-8pm and Sa-Su 8am-9pm, Sept.-Apr. M-Su 10am-7pm. €4, students €2.50; after 5:30pm €2/2.)*

▦PFAUENINSEL (PEACOCK ISLAND). The banks of Pfaueninsel (the second largest island in Berlin) served as the perfect setting for Friedrich Wilhelm II's "ruined" castle, where he and his mistress could romp for hours. Far more impressive than this underwhelming fortification, however, are the perfectly manicured orchards and trails that open up to lake vistas. A flock of the island's namesake fowl roams about the gardens. *(Take bus #218 from the Wannsee S-Bahn station to Pfaueninsel and wait for the ferry. Ferry runs daily May-Aug. 8am-9pm, Mar.-Apr. and Sept.-Oct. 9am-6pm, Nov.-Feb. 10am-4pm. Ferry €2, students €1. Castle open Apr.-Oct. Tu-Su 10am-5pm. Ticket office closed 1-1:30pm. Castle by tour only, every 30min. Last tour 4:30pm. €3, students €2.50.)*

HAUS DER WANNSEE-KONFERENZ. This area attained international notoriety after the the the **Wannsee Conference** on January 20, 1942. Leading officials of the SS completed the details for the implementation of the "Final Solution"—the deportation and murder of Europe's Jewish population—in the **Wannsee Villa,** formerly a Gestapo intelligence center. In January 1992, the 50th anniversary of the Nazi death-pact, the villa reopened as a museum with permanent Holocaust exhibits (mostly in German) and a documentary film series. *(Am Großen Wannsee 56-58. Take bus #114 from the S-Bahn station to Haus der Wannsee-Konferenz. ☎030 805 0010; www.ghwk.de. Exhibition and garden open daily 10am-6pm. Last entry 5:45pm. Library open M-F 10am-6pm. Free. Free guided tours in German and English.)*

MAX LIEBERMANN VILLA. The former summer home of Jewish painter Max Liebermann displays the artist's pastels, etchings, and paintings along with special exhibitions in his lovely villa, into which the artist retreated after persecution by the Nazis. The garden out back was reconstructed according to designs by Liebermann himself. *(Colomierstr. 3, at the corner of Am Großen Wannsee. S1 to Wannsee.* ☎ *030 80 58 59 00. Open Apr.-Sept. M, W, and F-Su 10am-6pm, Th 10am-8pm; Oct.-Mar. M and W-Su 11am-5pm. €6, students €4.)*

GLIENICKER BRÜCKE. At the southwestern corner of the district, this unspectacular bridge with spectacular history crosses the Havel River into Potsdam and the former DDR. Closed to traffic during the Cold War, it was the spot where East and West once exchanged captured spies. The most famous incident involved the trade of American U-2 pilot Gary Powers, shot down over Russia, and Yale student Frederic Pryor for Soviet spy Vilyam Genrikovich Abel. *(Bus #316 from the S-Bahn station Wannsee to Glienicker Brücke-Potsdam.)*

TREPTOW

SOWJETISCHES EHRENMAL. The Soviet War Memorial, a promenade built with marble taken from Hitler's Chancellery, is moving if only for its awesome scale. The Soviets dedicated the site in 1948 to honor the millions of Red Army soldiers who fell in what Russians call the "Great Patriotic War." The colossal bronze figure at the head of the promenade symbolically crushes Nazism underfoot (yes, that's a swastika—it's legal because it's partially obscured). The memorial doubles as a massive graveyard, with the bodies of 5000 unidentified Soviet soldiers buried underfoot. *(S4, S6, S8, S9, or S85 to Treptower Park. Turn left on Puschkinallee and follow the signs; it's about 900m down.)*

ORANIENBURG AND SACHSENHAUSEN

KZ SACHSENHAUSEN. The small town of Oranienburg, just north of Berlin, was home to the Nazi concentration camp Sachsenhausen, where more than 100,000 Jews, Communists, intellectuals, gypsies, and homosexuals were killed between 1936 and 1945. The **Gedenkstätte Sachsenhausen,** a memorial preserving the remains of the camp and recalling those imprisoned in it, was opened by the DDR in 1961. The blunt gray buildings, barbed-wire fencing, and vast, bleak spaces express the camp's brutality and despair. Some buildings have been preserved in their original forms. Sets of cramped barracks remain, along with the cell block where particularly "dangerous" prisoners were kept in solitary confinement and tortured daily, and the pathology department where Nazis performed medical experiments on inmates both dead and alive. Only the foundations of **Station Z,** where prisoners were methodically exterminated, remain. A stone monolith commemorating the camp's victims stands sentinel over the wind-swept grounds and several small museums. Barracks 38 and 39, the special "Jewish-only" barracks torched by neo-Nazis in 1992 and since reconstructed, feature displays on daily life in the camp. The prison contains a **museum** housed in five original cells of the one remaining wing of the cell block. The museum buildings and industrial yard contain broader exhibits on the history of Sachsenhausen, both as a concentration camp and a memorial site. DDR-era political slant is still apparent in the main museum building, which features Socialist Realist stained-glass windows memorializing "German Anti-Fascist Martyrs." *(Str. der Nationen 22. S1 (dir.: Oranienburg) to the end (40min.). Then either use the infrequent bus service on lines #804 and 821 to Gedenkstätte or take a 20min. walk from the station. Follow the signs from Stralsundstr., turn right on Bernauer Str., left on Str. der Einheit, and right on Str. der Nationen.* ☎ *03301 20 00; www.gedenkstaette-sachsenhausen.de. Open daily Mar. 15-Oct. 14 8:30am-6pm; Oct. 15-Mar. 14 8:30am-4:30pm. Last entry 30min. before closing. Archive and library open Tu-F 9am-4:30pm. Open air exhibition "Murder and Mass Murder in*

Sachsenhausen Concentration Camp" and site of commemoration "Station Z" open daily. Exhibition "System of Terror" in the T-Building open M-F 8am-6pm, Sa-Su noon-4pm. Free. Audio tour €3.)

SCHLOSS ORANIENBURG. Friedrich Wilhelm I converted his hunting lodge into a Dutch-influenced orange and white palace, which later served as a barracks for the East German army. Today, the **Schloßmuseum** showcases room after room of art from the Dutch masters and a beautiful gold *étagère* holding intricately painted china. The corresponding **Kreismuseum** features exhibits on local history. *(☎ 03301 53 74 37; www.spsg.de. Schloßmuseum accessible by guided tour only. Open Apr.-Oct. Sa-Su 10am-5pm and Tu-F 10am-5pm, Nov.-May Sa-Su 10am-4pm. Kreismuseum open Apr.-Oct. Tu-Su 10am-6pm, Nov.-Mar. Sa-Su 10am-5pm; last entry 30min. before closing.)*

SPANDAU

ZITADELLE. Rising starkly from the water, this Renaissance citadel is accessible only by a single stone bridge and was considered impregnable in the 16th and 17th centuries. During WWII, the Nazis used the fort as a chemical weapons lab, and in 1945 the Allies employed it as a prison to hold war criminals before the Nuremberg Trials. Nowadays, the citadel is an overgrown, weedy ghost of its former self, filled with old field-cannons, statues, and a **medieval history museum,** and a variety of art galleries. The thickly fortified **Juliusturm** (Julius Tower), dating from 1200, is the unofficial symbol of Spandau. *(Am Juliusturm. Take U7 to Zitadelle and follow the signs. ☎ 030 354 9440. Open daily 10am-5pm. Last entry 30min. before closing. Guided tours May-Oct. Sa-Su at noon, 2, and 4pm; Mar.-Apr. and Nov. at noon and 2pm. Museum and tower €4.50, students €2.50. Audio tour €2.)*

STEGLITZ

BOTANISCHER GARTEN. The Botanischer Garten is one of the most comprehensive botanical gardens in the world, featuring everything from orderly English gardens and Japanese *koi* ponds to vast greenhouses, which stay lush even in winter. *(Königin-Luise-Str. 6-8. S1 to Botanischer Garten. Follow the signs from the S-Bahn station; entrance on Unter den Eichen. ☎ 030 83 85 01 00; www.bgbm.org. Open daily May-July 9am-9pm, Aug. and Apr. 9am-8pm, Oct. and Mar. 9am-6pm, Nov.-Jan. 9am-4pm, Feb. 9am-5pm. Last entry 30min. before closing. €5, students €2.50; 2hr. before closing €2/1. Museum open daily 10am-6pm. Library open M-F 9am-6pm.)*

🏛 MUSEUMS

Berlin is one of the world's great museum cities, with collections of art and artifacts encompassing all subjects and eras. The **Staatliche Museen zu Berlin** (**Stiftung Preußischer Kulturbesitz** or **SPK,** or simply **SMB**) runs over 20 museums in four major regions—**Museumsinsel** (an island of historic museums in the middle of the Spree), **Kulturforum, Charlottenburg,** and **Dahlem**—as well as elsewhere in Mitte and around the Tiergarten. Prices are generally standardized: €8, students €4 for Hamburger Bahnhof, Charlottenburg, the KulturForum, and Museumsinsel houses. Dahlem museums are €6, students 3. Tickets are valid for all SMB-PK museums in a given complex on the day of purchase. The **Drei-Tage-Karte** (€19, students €9.50) is valid for three consecutive days. Buy either card at any SMB-PK museum. Admission is free the first Sunday of every month. Non-SMB-PK-affiliated museums tend to be smaller and more specialized, dealing with everything from Käthe Kollwitz to the cultural history of marijuana. *Berlin Programm* (€1.75) lists museums and galleries. Most state museums close on Mondays and are free Thursday nights 6-10pm. Twice every year, all state museums stay open all night on the **Long Night of the Museums.** Check online for more information (www.smb.museum).

CHARLOTTENBURG

Charlottenburg's museums range from high culture to smut and house one of the strongest collections of Picasso outside of Barcelona.

▓**MUSEUM BERGGRUEN.** This intimate three-floor museum exhibits some wonderful Picassos alongside works that influenced the artist, including African masks and late French Impressionist paintings by Matisse. The top floor showcases paintings by Bauhaus teacher Paul Klee and Alberto Giacometti's surreally elongated sculptures. *(Schloßstr. 1. Near the Schloß Charlottenburg. Take bus #M45 from Bahnhof Zoo to Luisenplatz/Schloß Charlottenburg or U2 to Sophie-Charlotte-Platz.* ☎ *030 3269 580. Open Tu-Su 10am-6pm. €6, students €3, children free. Audio guide free.)*

▓**KÄTHE-KOLLWITZ-MUSEUM.** Through both World Wars, Käthe Kollwitz, a member of the Berlin *Sezession* (Secession) movement and one of Germany's most prominent 20th-century artists, protested war and the condition of the working class through her haunting depictions of death, poverty, and suffering. The artist's biographical details—her son died in World War II and she withdrew into so-called inner migration during the DDR—provide context for her depictions of death, pregnancy, and starvation and for her somber self-portraits shown in what used to be a private home. *(Fasanenstr. 24. U1 to Uhlandstr.* ☎ *030 882 5210; www.kaethe-kollwitz.de. Open daily 11am-6pm. €5, students €2.50. Audio guide €3.)*

BRÖHANMUSEUM. This sleek building is full of Jugendstil (a.k.a Art Nouveau) and Art Deco paintings, houseware, and furniture. The ground floor consists of several ensembles of furniture, complete with accompanying paintings from the same time period (1889-1939). The first floor is a small gallery dedicated to the Modernist Berlin *Sezession* painters and the top floor houses special exhibitions. *(Schloßstr. 1A, next to the Berggruen, across from the Schloß.* ☎ *030 32 69 06 00; www.broehan-museum.de. Open Tu-Su 10am-6pm. €5, students €4.)*

MUSEUM FÜR FOTOGRAFIE. The former Landwehr-Casino building became a museum in June 2004, devoted principally to displaying the work of Helmut Newton in ever-changing guises. In the former brick ballroom on the third floor, rotating exhibits join the alternating collection of Newton's quasi-pornographic photos. *(Jebensstr. 2, directly behind the Zoo station.* ☎ *030 2662188. Open Tu-Su 10am-6pm, Th 10am-10pm. €6, students €3. SMB Museum cards accepted.)*

BEATE UHSE EROTIK MUSEUM. The world's largest sex museum contains over 5000 sex artifacts from around the world. Attracting a quarter of a million visitors per year, it is Berlin's fifth-most popular tourist attraction. Visitors come to see erotica ranging from naughty carvings on a 17th-century Italian deer-hunting knife to a 1955 calendar featuring Marilyn Monroe in the nude. A small exhibit describes the life of Beate Uhse, a pilot-turned-entrepreneur who pioneered Europe's first and largest sex shop chain. *(Joachimstalerstr. 4.* ☎ *030 886 0666; www.erotikmuseum.de. Museum open daily 9am-midnight. €6, students €5. Gift store open M-Sa 9am-9pm, Su 1-10pm.)*

MITTE

MUSEUMSINSEL (MUSEUM ISLAND)

The Museumsinsel holds five separate museums on an area cordoned off from the rest of Mitte by two arms of the Spree. The museums were built in the 19th- and 20th centuries, suffered bombing during World War II and isolation and neglect afterwards, but have all been recently and extensively renovated. *(S3, S5, S7, S9, or S75 to Hackescher Markt or bus #100 to Lustgarten.* ☎ *030 266 3666. All national museums, unless otherwise noted, open Tu-W and F-Su 10am-6pm, Th 10am-10pm. Free audio*

BERLIN

START: Radisson Hotel on Karl-Liebnecht-Str.

FINISH: Sony Center on Potsdamer Pl.

DURATION: 1½-3hr.

WHEN TO GO: Late afternoon.

If there is anything that single-handedly embodies the strange spirit of Berlin's weighty histo and its forward-thinking hyper-modernity, it's the city's architecture. Although remnants of i imperial past still line Unter den Linden, a stroll through the heart of the city shows that Berlin reputation for edginess and artistry is well deserved. The construction cranes punctuating th skyline mean that while the buildings listed here may represent some of the greatest feats contemporary architecture, they are in fact only the beginning of Berlin's steamroll toward a ne kind of cosmopolitan future.

1. AQUADOM. In the lobby of the Radisson Hotel, built in a square formation around a centr courtyard, towers a massive elevator shaft. And not just any elevator shaft: it's a roughly five-sto cylindrical aquarium on a concrete foundation, with thousands of colorful fish swirling about sparkling blue water. While you have to pay entrance to the neighboring aquarium to ride up th "AquaDom," simply ask the concierge's permission to enter the building and get a glimpse.

2. LUSTGARTEN. This is a typical Berlin contrast between the formidably old and jarringly ne You'll find yourself surrounded on one side by the **Altes Museum** (p. 106), designed by imperi architect Karl Friedrich Schinkel, and the towering **Berliner Dom** (p. 93). On the other, Schlo platz holds the modern **Staatsrat**, a federal government building, which incorporates a fragme of the old facade. Decide for yourself why the park is called Lustgarten (Pleasure Garden).

3. DEUTSCHES HISTORY MUSEUM. One of the newest additions to Berlin's trove of cu tural treasures, I.M. Pei's 2004 masterpiece stands hidden behind the **Zeughaus** on Unt den Linden and houses the temporary exhibits of the German History Museum. The buildin however, tends to outdo its contents. A conical glass structure with a spiraling staircase lin the different floors. The new marble supports blend into the more traditional segments of th old building, framing the glass entrance hall. The interior, largely visible from outside, contai crisscrossed, multi-tiered walkways leading to different floors of the museum. In back, imposin marble is interrupted by a triangular balcony with a window overlooking a single tree, while th front contains an indentation resembling a half-column, perhaps a contemporary reference t the imperial structures along neighboring Unter den Linden.

4. INTERNATIONALES HANDELSZENTRUM, FRIEDRICHSTRAβE, AND SCHIFFBAU ERDAMM. From the museum, continue away from Under den Linden and turn left on Dor theenstr. As you follow this to Friedrichstr., you'll pass the **Internationales Handelszentru** (Trade Center), built in 1978 and a very prominent feature of the Berlin skyline. Heading righ on Friedrichstr., take in the wavy glass-plated facade at **#148** before crossing the Spree an heading left on Schiffbauerdamm, which is lined with a mish-mash of modern buildings.

5. GOVERNMENT COMPLEX. Schiffbauerdamm will lead you to some of Berlin's mo unusual architectural marvels. Opposite the glass-domed **Reichstag** (p. 95) spans a stretc of government buildings dating from 1997-2003: they begin with the **Marie-Elisabeth Lüde Building**, designed by Stephan Braunfels and home to the Bundestag's library; cross over th river to Braunfels' **Paul Löbe Building**, which holds the Bundestag's many committees; an continue to the **Federal Chancellery**, the hyper-modern structure imagined by Axel Schulte and Charlotte Frank and best known for the huge circular windows on its sides. The contra between fluid shapes and sharp angles in these buildings mark a departure from conventional stiff, bureaucratic architecture. The walkway over the Spree, an area once located in the dea strip, symbolizes a newly reunified Germany. To the northwest, you can spot the shimmerin Hauptbahnhof, the largest train station in Europe.

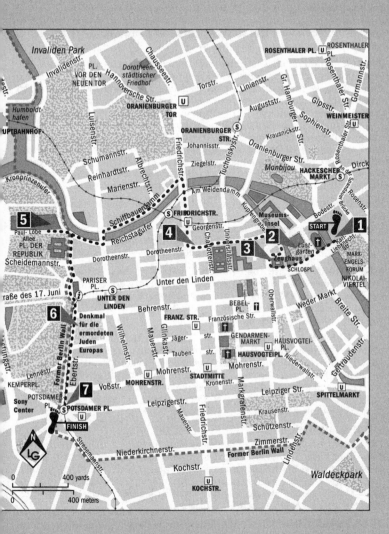

DENKMAL FÜR DIE ERMORDETEN JUDEN EUROPAS (MEMORIAL FOR THE MURDERED JEWS OF EUROPE). Cutting across the top of the Tiergarten, you'll reach this new memorial, opened in 2005. Designed by Peter Eisenman, it spans 19,000 sq. m and allows you to walk unsteadily on wavy ground between slabs of concrete. Their varying heights, coupled with the uneven walkways, will leave you feeling (appropriately) unsettled.

POTSDAMER PLATZ. Welcome to the glittering hub of modern Berlin, surrounded by an array of towering contemporary buildings, with more on the way. None is more striking than the **Deutsche Bahn Tower,** which commands attention with its curved glass front, jutting upward at an abrupt angle. Next door, the triangular Sony Center lures in spectators with its courtyard arena, which is covered in a strangely asymmetrical structure resembling a circus tent.

tours in English. Admission to each €8, students €4. All sell a 3-day card good for admission to every museum; €14, students €7.)

◼PERGAMONMUSEUM. One of the world's great ancient history museums, the Pergamon dates from the days when Heinrich Schliemann and other zealous 19th-century German archaeologists dismantled the remnants of collapsed empires the world over and sent them home for reassembly. Named for Pergamon, the city in present-day Turkey from which the enormous **Altar of Zeus** (180 BC) was taken, the museum features gargantuan pieces of ancient Mediterranean and Near Eastern civilizations from as far back as the 10th century BC. The colossal blue **Ishtar Gate** of Babylon (575 BC) and the **Roman Market Gate** of Miletus are just two more massive pieces in a collection that also includes Greek, Assyrian, and Far Eastern art. *(Bodestr. 1-3. ☎030 2090 5577. Open M-Su 10am-6pm, Th 10am-10pm. Last entry 30min. before closing. €8, students €4.)*

BODE-MUSEUM. The island's most attractive museum, which looks like it rises straight up from the water, reopened in 2006 after six years of renovations. It houses a hodgepodge of classical sculpture, Byzantine art, and oil painting. Its numismatic collection (coins and monies) is one of the largest in the world. *(Monbijoubrücke. ☎030 266 3666. Open Tu-W and F-Su 10am-6pm. Th 10am-10pm. €8, students €4.)*

ALTE NATIONALGALERIE (OLD NATIONAL GALLERY). After extensive renovations, this museum is open to lovers of 19th-century art, showcasing everything from German Realism to French Impressionism. Camille Pisarro leads the all-star cast of featured artists. *(Am Lustgarten. ☎030 2090 5577. Open Tu-W and F-Su 10am-6pm. Th 10am-10pm. €8, students €4.)*

ALTES MUSEUM. At the far end of the Lustgarten, the museum in the stately columned building designed by Karl Friedrich Schinkel is surprisingly untouristed. The lower level contains a permanent collection of ancient Greco-Roman (especially Etruscan) decorative art. The highlight of the upstairs Egyptian collection, and probably the whole museum, is the amazingly realistic bust of Nefertiti. *(AmLustgarten. ☎030 266 3660. Open M-W and F-Su 10am-6pm. Th 10am-10pm. €8, students €4. Free audio tour.)*

KULTURFORUM

The Kulturforum is a cluster of museums, concert halls, and libraries right off Potsdamer Platz. Two of its most recognizable buildings are the twin **Philharmonie** and the **Neue Staatsbibliothek** (new state library), both a warm honey color. *(S1, S2, S25 or U2 to Potsdamer Platz and walk down Potsdamer Str.; the museums will be on your right on Matthäikirchplatz. www.kulturforum-berlin.com. Full day ticket to the entire Kulturforum €8, students €4. Opening times vary; all free Th 6-10pm.)*

◼GEMÄLDEGALERIE (PICTURE GALLERY). This is the place to come in Berlin, and arguably in Germany, for painting. The city's most famous museum houses a collection of 2700 13th- to 18th-century masterpieces by Dutch, Flemish, German, and Italian masters, including works by Botticelli, Bruegel, Dürer, Gainsborough, Raphael, Rembrandt, Rubens, Titian, Velazquez, and many, many others. *(Matthäikirchplatz 4-6. ☎030 266 2951. Open Tu-W and F-Su 10am-6pm, Th 10am-10pm.)*

NEUE NATIONALGALERIE (NEW NATIONAL GALLERY). This sleek building, designed by **Mies van der Rohe** at the height of 1960s Minimalism, contains often wacky temporary exhibits in the glass entrance hall and gallery downstairs. The real draw is its formidable permanent collection of 20th-century art, including works by Warhol, Munch, Kirchner, and Beckmann. *(Potsdamer Str. 50. ☎030 266 2651. Open Tu-W and F 10am-6pm, Th 10am-10pm, Sa-Su 11am-6pm.€8, students €4.)*

KUPFERSTICHKABINETT (MUSEUM OF PRINTS AND DRAWINGS). Sketches by everyone from Botticelli to Picasso to Warhol show that sometimes it is more thrilling to see genius' works-in-progress than it is to see the "finished" product. *(Matthäikirchplatz 8. ☎ 030 266 2002. Open Tu-F 10am-6pm, Sa-Su 11am-6pm.)*

MUSIKINSTRUMENTEN-MUSEUM (MUSICAL INSTRUMENT MUSEUM). Benjamin Franklin's design for a glass harmonica, J.S. Bach's *cembalo*, and a few of King Friedrich II's old flutes are just some of the instruments on display here. It is worth taking the tour to hear the "Mighty Wurlitzer," a monstrous organ, played live. *(Tiergartenstr. 1. ☎ 030 25 48 11 78. Open Tu-F 9am-5pm, Th 9am-8pm, Sa-Su 10am-5pm. Tours Th 6pm and Sa 11am, €2.)*

OTHER MUSEUMS IN MITTE AND TIERGARTEN

▓**HAMBURGER BAHNHOF: MUSEUM FÜR GEGENWART** (MUSEUM FOR THE PRESENT). With a colossal 10,000 sq. m of exhibition space, this converted train station houses Berlin's foremost collection of contemporary art. The museum features several whimsical works by Warhol as well as pieces by Twombly and Kiefer and some more puzzling exhibits in its vast white spaces. *(Invalidenstr. 50-51. S3, S5, S7, S9, or S75 to Hauptbahnhof or U6 to Zinnowitzer Str. ☎ 030 3978 3411; www.hamburgerbahnhof.de. Open Tu-F 10am-6pm, Sa 11am-8pm, Su 11am-6pm. €8, students €4; Th 2-6pm free.)*

ANNE FRANK ZENTRUM (ANNE FRANK CENTER). If you can't get to Amsterdam to see the Anne Frank House, the permanent exhibit "Anne Frank—A Story for Today" provides the basics and a timeline of her short life. Tucked into a courtyard, the center's mission is to fight discrimination and anti-Semitism through workshops and exhibitions. *(Rosenthaler Str. 39. ☎ 030 28886 5610; www.annefrank.de. Open May-Sept. Tu-Su 10am-8pm; Oct.-Apr. 10am-6pm. €4, students €2.50.)*

SCHINKELMUSEUM. In Berlin, if it's made of stone, Karl Friedrich Schinkel probably designed it, and the lovely Friedrichwerdersche Kirche is no exception. The museum's renovated interior houses 19th-century French and German sculpture and an exhibit on the Prussian architect's life and work. *(Werderscher Markt, on the corner of Oberwallstr., south of Unter den Linden. U2 to Hausvogteiplatz. ☎ 030 208 1323. Open daily 10am-6pm. Free.)*

INDEPENDENT MUSEUMS

▓**DEUTSCHE HISTORISCHES MUSEUM** (GERMAN HISTORY MUSEUM). The oldest building on Unter den Linden, a baroque former military arsenal dating to 1730, the museum now houses a thorough exploration of German history, from Neanderthals to the Nazis to the fall of the Wall. Temporary exhibitions focus on the last 50 years, with plenty of depictions of smiling workers from the DDR era. Behind the main building stands its modern counterpart, a new wing designed by I. M. Pei that further bolsters Berlin's reputation for cutting-edge architecture. *(Unter den Linden 2. S3, 5, 7, 9, or 75 to Hackescher Markt. ☎ 030 2030 4444; www.dhm.de. Open daily 10am-6pm. €5, 18 and under free. Audio tour €3.)*

▓**KUNST-WERKE BERLIN** (INSTITUTE OF CONTEMPORARY ART). MoMA curator Klaus Biesnbach transformed this former margarine factory into a non-profit "art laboratory," with constantly changing exhibitions, an open library of art magazines and journals, and a number of artists' *ateliers*. It is perhaps best known as the home of the **Berlin Biennale**, a contemporary art fair, when the normally tranquil garden cafe is overrun. *(Auguststr. 69. U6 to Oranienburger Tor. ☎ 030 243 4590; www.kw-berlin.de. Open Tu-W and F-Su noon-7pm, Th noon-9pm. Check the website for current shows. €6, students €4. Garden and cafe open daily 9am-8pm. Free.)*

BERLIN

DEUTSCHE KINEMATHEK. The museum chronicles the development of German film with a special focus on older works like Fritz Lang's *Metropolis* (1927), but for non-film buffs, the best part is the futuristic mirrored entrance. There is a mix of old film (whole rooms are devoted to such icons as Marlene Dietrich) and new, with a permanent display on television that was unveiled in 2006. Captions are in English. *(Potsdamer Str. 2; 3rd and 4th fl. of the Sony Center. S1, S2, S25 or U2 to Potsdamer Platz. ☎ 030 300 9030; www.filmmuseum-berlin.de. Tickets sold on ground fl. Open Tu-W and F-Su 10am-6pm, Th 10am-8pm. €6, students €4.50, children €2.)*

DEUTSCHE GUGGENHEIM BERLIN. Together, the Guggenheim Foundation and Deutsche Bank scrounged together enough money to commission and feature three to four exhibitions of contemporary art per year in this non-descript exhibition space. *(Unter den Linden 13-15. ☎ 030 202 0930; www.deutsche-guggenheim.de. Open M-W and F-Su 10am-8pm, Th 10am-10pm. Free guided tours daily 6pm. €4, students €3; M free.)*

BAUHAUS-ARCHIV MUSEUM FÜR GESTALTUNG (BAUHAUS ARCHIVE MUSEUM FOR DESIGN). A must-visit for design fans, this building was conceived by Bauhaus founder **Walter Gropius** and houses rotating exhibits of paintings, sculptures, and of course, the famous furniture. *(Klingelhöferstr. 14. Bus #100, 187, 200, or 341 to Nordische Botschaften/Adenauer-Stiftung or U1, U2, U3, or U4 to Nollendorfplatz. ☎ 030 254 0020; www.bauhaus.de. Open M and W-Su 10am-5pm. M-Tu and Sa-Su €7, students €4; W-F €6/3. Audio tour free.)*

HANFMUSEUM (HEMP MUSEUM). Catering to the curious and the devoted, this museum details the medical and textile uses of hemp, as well as the debate over its legality. *(Mühlendamm 5. U2 to Klosterstr. ☎ 030 242 4827; www.hanfmuseum.de. Open Tu-F 10am-8pm, Sa-Su noon-8pm. €3.)*

KREUZBERG

Museums in Kreuzberg are a grab-bag. This area has one must-see (the Jewish Museum). You can see the rest if it's raining out or you're feeling especially ambitious.

▓JÜDISCHES MUSEM (JEWISH MUSEUM). Architect Daniel Libeskind's design for the zinc-plated Jewish Museum is fascinating even as an architectural experience. No two walls are parallel, creating a sensation of perpetual discomfort. Underground, three symbolic hallways—the **Axis of the Holocaust,** the **Axis of Exile,** and the **Axis of Continuity**—are intended to represent the trials of death, escape, and survival. The labyrinthine "Garden of Exile" replicates the dizzying effects of dislocation and the eerie "Holocaust Tower," a giant, asymmetrical concrete room nearly devoid of light and sound, encourages reflection. Exhibits feature works by contemporary artists, memorials to victims of the Holocaust, and a history of Jews in Germany. Enter at the top of the stairs from the Axis of Continuity. *(Lindenstr. 9-14. U6 to Kochstr., or U1, U6, or U15 to Prinzenstr. ☎ 030 25 99 33 00. Open M 10am-10pm, Tu-Su 10am-8pm. Last entry 1hr. before closing. €5, students €2.50. Special exhibits €4. Audio tour €2.)*

MARTIN-GROPIUS-BAU. After standing for years in the shadow of the Wall, Martin-Gropius-Bau has returned to its rightful place as the city's most beautiful and important exhibition space. Bauhaus founder Walter Gropius' great-uncle designed the building, which houses temporary exhibits of photography, painting, and decorative art. *(Niederkirchnerstr. 7. U6 to Kochstr. ☎ 030 254 860; www.gropiusbau.de. Open M and W-Su 10am-8pm. Price varies by exhibition. Free tours of the space once per month; check the website.)*

HAUS AM CHECKPOINT CHARLIE. Checkpoint Charlie, the border crossing between former East and West Berlin has become one of Berlin's most popular attractions, with tour buses, stands selling DDR memorabilia, actors clad as soldiers, and a table where you can get your passport "stamped." Perhaps the biggest rip-off (those actors only charge €1 per photo) in the area is the **Haus am Checkpoint Charlie,** a two-bedroom apartment turned private museum. The exhibits detail how women curled up in loudspeakers, students dug tunnels with their fingers, and others found ingenious ways of getting into the West. Much of the same information can be gleaned for free by reading the placards along **Kochstraße,** where the wall used to run. *(Friedrichstr. 43-45. U6 to Kochstr. ☎ 030 253 7250; www.mauer-museum.de. Museum open daily 9am-10pm. German-language films with English subtitles every 2hr. from 9:30am. €12.50, students €9.50. Audio tour €3.)*

DEUTSCHES TECHNIKMUSEUM. The airplane on the roof is a C-47, one of the original fleet of "raisin bombers" that kept West Berlin fed during the airlift. Inside, a colossal museum features aged trains, a history of film technology, and full-size model ships through which you're free to wander. Across the parking lot, another building features a collection of classic cars, music-makers, a plethora of science experiments involving optical illusions, and—best of all—a revolving playhouse. The new aeronautical wing documents the history of flight; its displays range from life-size planes to a whole room full of engines. Some exhibits are in English. *(Trebbiner Str. 9. U1, U2, or U15 to Gleisdreieck, or U1, U7, or U15 to Möckernbrücke. ☎ 030 902 540; www.stdb.de. Open Tu-F 9am-6pm, Sa-Su 10am-6pm. Last entry 30min. before closing. €4.50, students €2.50. Audio guides €2. Some special exhibits cost extra. 1st Su of the month free.)*

TOPOGRAPHIE DES TERRORS (TOPOGRAPHY OF TERROR). This "temporary outdoor museum" on an eerie, open field marks the location of the former SS Gestapo headquarters with terrifying exhibits on the history of the Gestapo. A permanent exhibition is slated to open in 2010. *(Niederkirchnerstr. 8. U6 to Kochstr. ☎ 030 2545 0950. Exhibits in German; English audio guides. Open May-Sept. 10am-8pm; Oct.-Apr. 10am-dusk. Audio guides free.)*

SCHWULES MUSEUM (GAY MUSEUM). Tucked into a courtyard off Mehringdamm, the only federally funded museum focused on gay culture in the world recounts the history of homosexuals in Germany from 1800 to 1970, with a focus on persecution under the Nazis. A lending library contains thousands of periodicals, books, and films. *(Mehringdamm 61. ☎ 030 6959 9050. Open Tu-F 2-6pm, Sa 2-7pm. €5, students €3.)*

OUTER DISTRICTS

MUSEEN DAHLEM. The Museen Dahlem consists of three museums housed within Dahlem's *Freie Universität.* The **Ethnologisches Museum** (Ethnology Museum) dominates the main building, a white Bauhaus complex. The exhibits are stunning, ranging from massive pieces of ancient Central American stonework to African elephant tusk statuettes. Most surprising are the enormous, authentic boats from the South Pacific and the model huts that you can actually enter. Under the same roof, the recently inaugurated **Museum für Asiatiche Kunst** (Museum for Asian Art) combines Dahlem's collection of Indian art, featuring ornate gilded shrines and brightly painted murals, with East Asian holdings, including dynastic furniture and tapestries. The **Museum Europäischer Kulturen** (Museum of European Culture) is around the corner, fronted by an imposing columned facade. *(Arnimallee 27. U3 to Dahlem-Dorf; follow the "Museen" signs to get to the main building. ☎ 030 830 1438. Open Tu-F 10am-6pm, Sa-Su 11am-6pm. 1 ticket grants entry to all 3 museums. €6, students €3. Th free from 2pm.)*

TOP 10 TASKS FOR THE MOVIE BUFF IN BERLIN

Run across the **Oberbaumbrücke,** where *Run Lola Run* (1998) shot some of its most beautiful footage. Meander along the scenic routes Lola takes to collect the money that will save her boyfriend. (Or, if you're truly hardcore, take the *Lola Rennt* running tour.)

Come to the *Cabaret* (1972) and look for Sally Bowles at the **KitKatClub.** Although the present fetish incarnation is a far cry from the interwar nightclub of the film, your chances of seeing someone dressed as the Emcee are fairly good. Not for the faint of heart, though: patrons are allowed to have sex on the dance floor.

Take a bunch of pictures in the **Alexanderplatz.** When you get home, Photoshop out all the Westernized billboards in homage to Alex in *Good-Bye, Lenin* (2003) and his desperate attempt to protect his sickly mother from the reality of the fall of the Berlin Wall.

Since you're already in "der Alex," arrange a meeting with someone mysterious at the **World Clock.** You probably know who you are, but why not take in the city à la Jason Bourne in *The Bourne Supremacy* (2004).

Have a drink at **Cafe Adler** and take a look at **Checkpoint Charlie.** Then imagine the diggers of *Der Tunnel* (2001) burrowing beneath you to save their families

DOMÄNE DAHLEM. Everything you ever wanted to know and more about the process of producing food, from the farm to the shopping bag. Check out the live demonstrations on pulling honey from the hive. (*Königin-Luise-Str. 49. U3 to Dahlem-Dorf. From the station, cross the street and head left on Königin-Luise-Str. ☎ 030 666 3000; www.domaene-dahlem.de. Open M and W-Su 10am-6pm. €3, students €1.50.*)

🏛 GALLERIES

Berlin has an extremely well-funded art scene, with many first-rate galleries. The work is as diverse as Berlin's cultural landscape and includes everything from early Christian antiques in Charlottenburg to conceptual installations in Mitte. A few good pamphlets, all with maps and available just about anywhere in the city, are: *ARTery Berlin* (€2.50), with complete show listings in English and German; *Berliner Kunst Kalender* (€2); and *Berliner Galerien* (free). The normal city guide, *Zitty*, also lists the major openings.

The center of Berlin's gallery world is Mitte, which has more contemporary work than classics; the *Berlin Mitte* pamphlet provides listings and a map. Five times a year, Mitte offers a *Galerienrundgang* tour of the galleries (dates are listed in the pamphlets). On nearby **Sophienstaße, Gipsstraße, Auguststraße,** and **Linienstraße,** galleries pack the streets and *Hinterhöfe* (courtyards hidden behind building facades). Charlottenburg also has a large selection of galleries, many of which are more upscale. Kreuzberg hosts a handful of galleries, many with a political focus, and there's a new, small scene in Prenzlauer Berg off **Danziger Straße.** Be sure to pick up some 🍷**free wine** at many of the openings.

The galleries below are some of the more prominent ones; all are located in Mitte.

AKADEMIE DER KUNST. This 300-year-old institution has been the core of Berlin's art community for years, with students and artists working in every medium from film to painting to music and more. The Akademie sponsors a variety of prizes and hosts exhibitions in its Hanseatenweg location. A futuristic branch, at Pariser Platz 4, houses the Akademie archives and five additional exhibition halls. (*Hanseatenweg 10. S3, S5, S7, S9, or S75 to Bellevue, or U9 to Hansaplatz. ☎ 030 390 760; www.adk.de. Open Tu-Su 11am-8pm. Exhibitions range from free to €12, students €10. Last Su of the month free.*)

NEUER BERLINER KUNSTVEREIN. Besides hosting a gallery space, Berlin's most democratic art organization sponsors the weekly "Treffpunkt NBK," a series of lectures, discussions with artists, performances, and more. It also lends reproductions of masterpieces to Berlin residents for €0.50 per month through the **Artothek** and has thousands of videos available to the public via the **Video-Forum.** *(Chausseestr. 128-129. ☎030 280 7020; www.nbk.org. Artothek ☎0881 927 0400. Gallery open Tu-F noon-6pm, Sa-Su 2-6pm. Video-Forum www.nbk.org. Open Tu and Th 2-6pm, W and F noon-5pm.)*

ART CENTER BERLIN. The impressive waterfall wall marks the complex for the Art Center Berlin, a forum for contemporary art. The multi-level glass-heavy space showcases international galleries and collections in a central exhibition location. Recent exhibitions have included master sculptors of Zimbabwe, aboriginal painting from Australia, and conceptual art from Korea. *(Friedrichstr. 134. ☎030 27 87 90 27; www.art-center-berlin.de. Open daily 11am-9pm. Guided tours by request. €5, students €3.50.)*

🎭 ENTERTAINMENT

Berlin's vibrant cultural scene is bustling with exhibitions, concerts, plays, and dance performances. The city generously subsidizes its artists despite recent cutbacks, and tickets are usually reasonable, especially with student discounts. Reservations can be made through the box office. Most theaters and concert halls offer up to 50% discounts for students who buy at the *Abendkasse* (evening box office), which generally opens 1hr. before shows. Other ticket outlets charge 15-18% commissions and do not offer student discounts. There is also a ticket counter on the sixth floor of the **KaDeWe.** (See p. 122. ☎030 217 7754; www.showtimetickets. de. Open M-F 10am-8pm, Sa 10am-4pm.) Theaters generally accept credit cards, but many ticket outlets do not. Most theaters and operas close from mid-July to late August.

Hekticket, Hardenbergplatz (☎030 230 9930; www. hekticket.de), near the Cineplex. 2nd branch at Alexanderplatz, Karl-Liebknecht-Str. 12.Last-minute tickets up to 50% off. Open M-Sa 10am-8pm, Su 2-6pm; closed July to mid-Aug.

Berlin Ticket (☎030 2309 9333; www.berlin-ticket.de). Tickets for everything from sporting events and club parties to classical music concerts. *Klassik Kard* (€20) allows under 25 patrons to buy last minute €10 tickets for the opera or ballet.

stranded in East Berlin or James Bond sneaking through in search of *Octopussy* (1983).

Boogie-woogie all night at the **Rock'n'Roll Club Spreeathen** and try to pick up one of the *Swing Kids* (1993).

Pop by the **Gendarmen Market.** Get a snack and have a flashback to the *V for Vendetta* (2005) Norsefire rally.

Stroll around the **Charlottenburg Palace** and pretend you're in Paris, like Jackie Chan in *Around the World in 80 Days* (2004). Marvel at the idea that someone who can't even tell Paris from Berlin would try to travel around the world via hot air balloon.

Walk through the **Brandenburg Gate,** like the actors in Billy Wilder's *One, Two, Three* (1961). Ponder the fact that the gate closed during the filming, and nobody made that trip again until the Wall fell. Ponder further whether the closing was due to the Communism=bad, Coca-Cola=awesome plot of the movie.

Find a smoky jazz club, order something made with blue gin, and dream of another Lola—Marlene Dietrich as the sexy cabaret singer who causes the downfall of a university professor in *The Blue Angel* (1930).

CONCERTS, DANCE, AND OPERA

Berlin reaches its musical zenith in September during the fabulous **Berliner Festwochen,** which draws the world's best orchestras and soloists. The **Berliner Jazzstage** in November, featuring top jazz musicians, also brings in the crowds. For tickets (which sell out months in advance) and more information for both festivals, call or write to **Berliner Festspiele** (☎030 25 48 90; www.berlinerfestspiele.de). In mid-July, the **Bachtage** feature an intense week of classical music, while every Saturday night in August the **Sommer Festspiele** turns the Ku'damm into a concert hall with genres from punk to folk competing for attention.

The monthly pamphlets *Konzerte und Theater* in Berlin und Brandenburg (free) and *Berlin Programm* (€1.75) list concerts, as do the biweekly *Zitty* and *Tip.* Tickets for the Philharmonie and the Oper are nearly impossible to get without writing months in advance, except by standing outside before performances with a small sign saying *"Suche Karte"* (seeking ticket)—people often try to unload tickets at the last moment, usually at outrageous prices.

▨ **Berliner Philharmonisches Orchester,** Herbert-von-Karajan-Str. 1 (☎030 25 48 89 99; www.berlin-philharmonic.com). S1, S2, or S25 or U2 to Potsdamer Platz and walk up Potsdamer Str. It may look bizarre, but this yellow building, designed by Scharoun in 1963, is acoustically perfect: every audience member hears the music exactly as it is meant to sound. The Berliner Philharmoniker, led by the eminent Sir Simon Rattle, is one of the world's finest orchestras. It's tough to get a seat; check 1hr. before concert time or write at least 8 weeks in advance. Closed from late June to early Sept. Box office open M-F 3-6pm, Sa-Su 11am-2pm. Tickets from €7 for standing room, from €13 for seats.

Konzerthaus (Schauspielhaus am Gendarmenmarkt), Gendarmenmarkt 2 (☎030 203 092 101; www.konzerthaus.de). U2 or U6 to Stadtmitte. The opulent home of Berlin's symphony orchestra. Last-minute tickets are somewhat easier to come by. No performances from mid-July to Aug. Box office open M-Sa noon-7pm, Su noon-4pm. Open in July M-Sa noon-6pm.

Deutsche Staatsoper, Unter den Linden 7 (☎030 2035 4555; www.staatsoper-berlin. de). U6 to Französische Str. or bus #100, 157, or 348 to Deutsche Staatsoper. Eastern Berlin's leading opera company. Box office open M-F 11am-7pm, Sa-Su 2-7pm, and 1hr. before performances. Closed from mid-July to Aug. Tickets €5-160; students €12, if purchased 30min. before shows and ½-price on cheaper seats for certain performances.

Deutsche Oper Berlin, Bismarckstr. 35 (tickets ☎030 34 38 43 43; www.deutscheoperberlin.de). U2 to Deutsche Oper. Berlin's best and youngest opera. Box office open M-Sa 11am until 1hr. before performance (11am-7pm on days without performances), Su 10am-2pm. Evening tickets available 1hr. before performances. Closed July-Aug. Tickets €12-118. 25% student discounts.

Komische Oper, Unter den Linden 41 (☎030 4799 7400; www.komische-oper-berlin. de). U6 to Französische Str., or S1, S2, S25 to Unter den Linden. Started by zany director Walter Felsenstein and now under the direction of Andreas Homoki, the 112-year-old opera is known for fresh takes on the classics. Box office open M-Sa 11am-7pm, Su 1-4pm. Tickets €8-93. 25% student discounts available 1hr. before curtain.

THEATER

Theater listings, found on the yellow and blue posters in most U-Bahn stations, are available in the monthly pamphlets *Kultur!news* and *Berlin Programm,* as well as in *030, Zitty,* and *Tip.* In addition to the world's best German-language theater, Berlin also has a lively English-language scene; look for listings in *Zitty* or *Tip* that say *"in englischer Sprache"* (in English). A number of privately run companies called **Off-Theaters** also occasionally feature English-language plays.

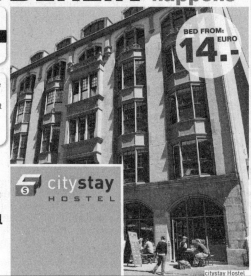
As with concert halls, virtually all theaters are closed in July and August (closings are indicated by the words *Theaterferien* or *Sommerpause*).

Deutsches Theater, Schumannstr. 13A (☎030 2844 1225; www.deutschestheater. de). U6, S1, S2, S5, S7, S9, S25, or S75 to Friedrichstr. Even western Berlin admits it: this is the best theater in Germany. The **Kammerspiele** stages smaller, provocative productions. Box office open July M-F 1-7pm; Aug.-June M-Sa 11am-6:30pm, Su 3pm-6:30pm. Tickets for Deutsches Theater €5-43, for Kammerspiel €14-30; students €6-10.

Berliner Ensemble, Bertolt-Brecht-Platz 1 (☎030 28 40 81 55; www.berliner-ensemble. de). U6 or S1, S2, S5, S7, S9, S25, or S75 to Friedrichstr. The theater, established by Brecht, is enjoying a renaissance under the leadership of Claus Peymann. Hip repertoire with Heiner Müller, young American playwrights, and Brecht. Box office open M-F 8am-6pm, Sa-Su 11am-6pm, and 1hr. before shows. Tickets €2-30, students €7.

Volksbühne, Am Rosa-Luxemburg-Platz (☎030 24 06 55; www.volksbuehne-berlin.de). U2 to Rosa-Luxemburg-Platz. High on shock value, low on name recognition. Box office open daily noon-6pm. Tickets €10-30, students €6-15. The Volksbühne also features 2 nightclubs for the proletariat: the Roter Salon and Grüner Salon. Ask permission to eat downstairs with the actors in the cantina.

English Theater Berlin, Fidicinstr. 40 (☎030 691 1211; www.etberlin.de). U6 to Platz der Luftbrücke. This smaller, less well-funded stage produces new, experimental works and old favorites by the likes of Samuel Beckett and Tennessee Williams. Box office opens 1hr. prior to showtime. Most shows at 8pm. Tickets €8-15.

Hebbel-Theater, Stresemannstr. 29 (☎030 2590 0427; www.hebbel-theater.de). U1, U6, or U15 to Hallesches Tor. The most avant of Berlin's avant-garde theaters attracts innovative talent from all over the world. Order tickets from the box office (open daily noon-7pm) on Stresemannstr., by phone daily 4-7pm, or show up 1hr. before shows. Tickets €11-18, students €7.

Maxim-Gorki-Theater, Am Festungsgraben 2 (☎030 2022 1115; www.gorki.de). U6, S1, S2, S5, S7, S9, S25, or S75 to Friedrichstr., or bus #100, 157, or 348 to Deutsche Staatsoper. Contemporary theater with a wide repertoire. Box office open M-Sa noon-6:30pm, Su 4-6:30pm, and 1hr. before shows. Tickets €10-30, students €9.

Die Distel, Friedrichstr. 101 (☎030 204 4704; www.distel-berlin.de). U6, S1, S2, S5, S7, S9, S25, or S75 to Friedrichstr. During the DDR days, this cabaret was renowned for political satire. As popular as ever, the shows feature lots of snappy dialogue and German slang, making it hard for non-native speakers to follow. Box office open M-F noon-6pm and 2hr. before performances. Tickets €13-27; students 25% off 2hr. before M-Th and Su performances (excluding premieres).

FILM

On any night in Berlin you can choose from over 150 different films. **O.F.** or **O.V.** next to a movie listing means original version (i.e., not dubbed in German); **O.m.U.** means original version with German subtitles; **O.m.e. U.** means original with English subtitles. Check *Tip, Zitty,* or *030* for theater schedules. Monday through Wednesday are Kinotage at most theaters, with reduced prices and further discounts for those with a student ID. The city also hosts the international **Berlinale film festival** (early February).

Arsenal, (☎030 26 95 51 00; www.fdk-berlin.de), in the Filmhaus at Potsdamer Platz. U2, S1, S2, or S25 to Potsdamer Platz. Run by the founders of the Berlinale, Arsenal showcases indie films and some classics (€6.50). Frequent appearances by guest directors make the theater a popular meeting place for Berlin's filmmakers.

Filmkunsthaus Babylon, Rosa-Luxemburg-Str. 30 (☎030 242 59 69; www.babylon-berlin.de). U2 to Rosa-Luxemburg-Platz. Shows classics like *Goodfellas* in the main theater and art films from around the world in the intellectual **Studiokino** (entrance on Hirtenstr.). Most English-language films not dubbed in German. Main theater M-W €5.50, Th-Su €6.50.

Odeon, Hauptstr. 116 (☎030 7870 4019; www.yorck.de). U4 to Innsbrucker Platz. One of the 1st English-language theaters in Berlin, Odeon shows mainstream American and British flicks, sometimes dubbed in German and sometimes with subtitles. €7.50, students €7; M €5, Tu-W €6.

CineStar, in the Sony Center, Potsdamer Platz 4 (☎030 2606 6260; www.cinestar.de). S1, S2, or U2 to Potsdamer Platz. English-language blockbusters in a huge theater with stadium seating so steep you'll fear for your life. Last showing around 11pm, M no late show. M and W €6.50, Tu €4.50, F-Sa €7.50; students M and W-Th €5.50, F-Su €6.

Freiluftkino: Berlin buzzes with outdoor movies in the summer. Check out the ones below.

Freiluftkino Hasenheide (☎030 283 4603; www.freiluftkino-hasenheide.de), at the Sputnik in Hasenheide park. U7 or U8 to Hermannplatz. Screens silent films and last year's blockbusters. €6.

Freiluftkino Kreuzberg, Mariannenplatz 2 (☎030 2936 1628; www.freiluftkino-kreuzberg.de). U1 or U8 to Kottbusser Tor. Screens foreign films. €6.

Freiluftkino Friedrichshain (☎030 2936 1629; www.freiluftkino-berlin.de), in Volkspark Friedrichshain. U5 to Straußberger Platz. Shows modern Hollywood and German films. €6.

◪ NIGHTLIFE

Berlin's nightlife is world-renowned absolute madness—a teeming cauldron of debauchery that bubbles around the clock. Bars typically open at 6pm and get crowded around 10pm, just as the clubs open their doors. Bar scenes wind down anywhere between midnight and 6am; meanwhile, around 1am, dance floors fill up and the lights flash at clubs that keep pumping beats until dawn, when a variety of after-parties keep up the perpetual motion. In summer months it's only dark from 10:30pm to 4am, so it's easy to be unintentionally included in the early morning crowd, watching the sun rise on Berlin's landmarks and waiting for the cafes to open. From 1-4am on weekdays, 70 night buses operate throughout the city, and on Friday and Saturday nights the U- and S-Bahn run on a limited schedule throughout the night. The best sources of information about bands and dance venues are the bi-weekly magazines *Tip* (€2.70) and the superior *Zitty* (€2.70), available at all newsstands, or the free *030*, distributed in hostels, cafes, shops, and bars.

CHARLOTTENBURG

Charlottenburg's quiet cafes and music venues cater to the 30-something set. It's a nice place for a mellow evening or to hear the city's best jazz, but the real parties are eastward. **The Ku'damm** is best avoided at night, unless you enjoy fraternizing with drunk businessmen.

▓ **Trane,** Bleibtreustr. 1 (☎030 313 2550; www.a-trane.de). S3, S5, S7, S9, or S75 to Savignyplatz. Cozy tables litter the floor of this comfortably sized club for serious jazz fans. Classic black and white photographs adorn walls, and a small chalkboard next to the stage lists the night's performers. Herbie Hancock, Wynton Marsalis—all the classics have played here. Late-night jam with no cover Sa from 12:30am. Cover €7-15, students €5-13. Open M-Th and Su 9pm-2am, F-Sa 9pm-late. Reserve a table online in advance. Cash only.

Salz, Salzufer 20 (☎01702 833504; www.salz-club.de). U2 to Ernst-Reuter-Platz. Exposed brick walls keep the disco-ball-lit dance floor looking classy at this salt warehouse turned techno club. The two real prizes: a gorgeous patio with tiki lamps and never, ever a cover. Check the website for music schedule. Open F-Sa 8pm-late.

Quasimodo, Kantstr. 12A (☎030 312 8086; www.quasimodo.de). U2, S5, S7, S9, or S75 to Zoologischer Garten. Beneath a huge cafe, this grownup, spacious venue showcases soul, R&B, and jazz. Drinks €2.50-4.50. Cover for concerts €8-30. Tickets available F from 4:30pm or Sa-Su from 11am at the cafe upstairs or from KonzertKasse ticket service (☎030 61 10 13 13); cheaper if reserved in advance. Check website for schedule. Open daily 9pm-late. Cash only.

SCHÖNEBERG AND WILMERSDORF

▓ **Slumberland,** Goltzstr. 24 (☎030 216 5349). U1-U4 to Nollendorfplatz. Palm trees, rotating art from Africa and, yes, a real sand floor that transports you to the Bahamas in what is otherwise a standard looking pub. Listen to reggae while sipping a mixed drink (€5). The secret to the frappés (€2.30)? Coffee crystals. Most drinks €2-5. Open M-Th and Su 6pm-2am, F 6pm-4am, Sa 11am-4am. Cash only.

Alt Berliner Biersalon, Ku'damm 225 (☎030 88 43 990). Go for a taste of the former West Berlin opulence at this spacious pub-like bar. For all the gorgeous wooden paneling the atmosphere is far from stuffy: locals gather to watch German league (Bundesliga) soccer games here on Sa. (Hint: root for Hertha and you will make friends.) Beer €3-4.50. Open 24hr.

GAY AND LESBIAN

Schöneberg is Berlin's unofficial "gay district" and teems with GLBT nightlife.

Hafen, Motzstr. 19 (☎030 211 4118; www.hafen-berlin.de). U1-U4 to Nollendorfplatz. Nearly 20 years old, this bar has become a landmark for Berlin's gay community. The sign outside specifically invites in "drop dead gorgeous looking tourists," but there are plenty of locals here, too. The mostly male crowd jams the surrounding sidewalk in summer. Weekly pub quiz M 8pm (1st M of the month in English). New DJs W. Open daily 8am-4am. Cash only.

Connection, Fuggerstr. 33 (☎030 218 1432; www.connection-berlin.de). U1 or U2 to Wittenbergplatz. The name says it all. Find your soulmate (or one-night stand) in the disco, then go next door to the labyrinthine **Connection Garage** to get acquainted. First F of the month mixed; otherwise, men only. Cover €7, includes 1st drink. Club open F-Sa 11pm-late; Garage open M-Sa 10am-1am, Su and holidays 2pm-1am. AmEx/MC/V.

Begine, Potsdamer Str. 139 (☎030 215 1414; www.begine.de). U2 to Bülowstr. In a neighborhood dominated by sceney gay clubs, this is a welcome retreat for women. Named after a now-defunct lesbian squat, Berlin's biggest lesbian community center has a popular, low-key cafe/bar with live music and readings at night. No cover. Open M-F 6pm-late, Sa-Su 9:30pm-late.

Heile Welt, Motzstr. 5 (☎030 2191 7507). U1-U4 to Nollendorfplatz. Despite the addition of 2 enormous, quiet inner sitting rooms, the 20-something clientele still pack the bar and spill into the street. Aside from a fur-covered wall and single tiara hanging above the bar, both the decor and mood are reserved. Mostly male crowd during "prime time;" more women in the early evening, on weekdays, and in the early morning. Open daily 6pm-4am, sometimes later. Cash only.

Neue Ufer, Hauptstr. 157 (☎030 7895 7900). U7 to Kleistpark. Formerly Anderes Ufer (The Other Shore), this long-running cafe has become "the new shore," abandoning the rainbow ship that once decorated the interior. A photo of David Bowie commemorates the many hours he spent drinking here. The beer (€2.80-3.80) and coffee (€2.20-2.80) flow and the mood is still mellow. Open daily 11am-2am. Cash only.

MITTE

The Mitte nightlife scene centers on **Hackescher Markt** and **Oranienburger Straße** (also, incidentally, the city's most conspicuous prostitution drag). The pricey, packed strip offers a mixture of both world-renowned and touristy bars and clubs. If you'd prefer to get off the beaten track, head to the outskirts of Mitte or its eastern neighborhoods.

Week-End, Alexanderplatz 5 (☎030 24 63 16 76; www.week-end-berlin.de), on the 12th and 15th fl. of the building with the "Sharp" sign overlooking the city. A staple of the Berlin club scene, where minimal techno fuels the floor until the sun rises over the block-housing of East Berlin. Wheelchair-accessible. Cover €8-12. Open F-Su 11pm-late. Cash only.

Tape, Heidestr. 14 (☎030 848 4873; www.tapeberlin.de), near a few art galleries along a strip close to the Hauptbahnhof. This converted warehouse is worth the trip. The walls, the entrance, and ravers' hands are all stamped with images of cassette tapes, the club's symbol. An artsy crowd dances in the enormous main room and hangs out on couches in the silver lounge. Cover varies. Open F-Sa 11pm-late.

Clärchen's Ballhouse, Auguststr. 24 (☎030 282 92 95; www.ballhaus.de). This odd-looking building was a ballroom before WWI, and now it is again. Older couples gather to tango and swing, while younger groups attempt to join in or enjoy beer in the flower-filled courtyard. Free introductory "swing tease" lesson W. Classical concerts and cha-cha brunch W. Open daily noon-late.

Bang Bang Club, Neue Promenade 10 (☎030 60 40 53 10; www.bangbang-club.de). Twiggy look-alikes run around a dance floor while guys in fedoras nod and smile. Grab your best tight jeans and ankle boots for "Death by Britpop" on F. Opening days and times vary. Check website or show up after midnight.

CCCP Klub, Torstr. 136 (☎0179 69 29 13). The only marker is the red star above the rusty iron door. Inside, this bar looks like your crazy aunt's closet—in a good way. There's a skeleton on one wall and a bearskin rug on another. Listen for the old Russian pop music or seek out indie and electro. Open Tu-Sa 11pm-late. Cash only.

Kaffee Burger, Torstr. 60 (☎030 28 04 64 95; www.kaffeeburger.de). U2 to Rosa-Lux-emburg-Platz. Iconic retro DDR-style bar draws huge crowds for twice monthly "Russian disco" night. Connected to the more laid-back **Burger Bar** (Torstr. 58) through a cloak-room guarded by a life-size statue of a Russian soldier. Live bands Th 10pm. Cover M-Th €1, F-Sa €5-6. Open M-Sa 10pm-late, Su 7pm-late. Cash only.

Cookies, Friedrichstr. at Unter den Linden (☎030 27 49 29 40; www.cookies-berlin.de). U6 to Französiche Str. Once a mobile weekly dance party among a group of friends, the party is now open to the public, as is the hip restaurant, **Cookies Cream.** Go dancing Tu and Th 11pm-6am. Restaurant open Tu-Sa from 8pm. The affiliated **Crush** party happens Sa at Behrenstr. 55. Open midnight-late. Cash only.

Tacheles, Oranienburger Str. 54-56 (☎030 282 6185; www.tacheles.de). U6 to Oranien-burger Tor or S1, S2, or S25 to Oranienburger Str. or night buses N6 or N84. Housed in a bombed-out former department store and the adjacent courtyard, this edgy complex boasts a motif of graffiti and scrap metal artwork. A playground for artists, punks, and curious tourists, the labyrinth leads into several art galleries, movie theaters, and bal-cony bars. Opening times for the theater and galleries vary, as do party dates—check the website. For theater tickets, call ☎030 28 09 68 35.

Delicious Doughnuts, Rosenthaler Str. 9 (☎030 28 09 92 74; www.delicious-dough-nuts.de). U8 to Rosenthaler Platz. This backpacker hangout's curved design draws you into one of the loungeable booths. Other facilities include pinball and a pocket-sized dance floor. Shades keep early-morning stragglers protected from the sun. Cover M-Th and Su €3, F-Sa €5. Open daily 10pm-late. Cash only.

 TROPICAL BERLIN. Berliners like to do everything outside in sum-mer: grill meat in the parks, attend outdoor cinemas (www.freiluft-kino.de), and play on tropical beaches—manmade tropical beaches, that is, with sand and deck chairs laid out to make temporary bars. One of the most popular is along **Monbjou Park** (S-Bahn Hackescher Markt) but they're everywhere along the Spree.

PRENZLAUER BERG

Prenzlauer Berg is the place to go for a slightly more relaxed, less techno oriented scene than the elsewhere in Berlin. Trendy bars and late-night cafes cluster around **Kastanienallee** (U2 to Eberswalder Str.) while the areas around **Helmholtzplatz** (S-Bahn to Prenzlauer Allee) are your best bet for the neighbor-hood's trademark shabby chic.

▓ **The Weinerei,** Veteranenstr. 14 (☎030 440 6983). The unmarked wine bar has gone from local secret to local legend, based on comfortable elegance and a strange pricing system. Pay €1 for a glass, sample all of the wines, sample again, and again, and before leaving pay however much you think you owe. Open daily 10am-very late. Cash only.

▓ **Klub Der Republik (KDR Bar),** Pappelallee 81. U2 to Eberswalder Str., M10, N2, N42. Turn into what looks like a deserted parking lot and climb the stairs of a dance studio to find a preserved DDR ballroom turned favorite post-wall watering hole. Cheap drinks for the neighborhood (€2-4). Open daily in summer from 9pm, in winter from 8pm. Cash only.

BERLIN

Wohnzimmer, Lettestr. 6 (☎030 445 5458). U2 to Eberswalder Str. The name means living room, and they aren't kidding. With wood-beam floors, the bar resembles an old-fashioned kitchen, and glassware cabinets line the walls. You'll feel right at home as you settle into a velvet armchair with a matching mixed drink. Damn good mojito €5. Open daily 9am-4am. Cash only.

Solsi e Morsi, Marienburger Str. 10. Owner Johnny Petrongolo flits around his always packed familial wine bar opening bottles and bestowing plates of free *parma* ham, cheese, and olives. The young clientele love their Galouises: Solsi e Morsi is not for the faint of lung. Open daily 6pm-late.

Dr. Pong, Eberswalder Str. 21. U2 to Eberswalder Str. The centerpiece at this minimalist bar is a ping-pong table, ringed with intense hipsters gripping their paddles. Beginners and the severely intoxicated are both equally welcome. Drinks €2-5.50. Open M-Sa 8pm-late, Su from 2pm. Cash only.

Prater Garten, Kastanienallee 7-9 (☎030 448 5688; www.pratergarten.de). U2 to Eberswalder Str. Giant chestnut trees hung with lanterns overhang sprawling picnic tables and umbrellas at what is arguably Berlin's most pleasant beer garden. Outdoor theater and TV. Bratwurst €2.50. Beer €2.50-3.50. Open in good weather Apr.-Sept. daily from noon until late. Cash only.

White Trash Fast Food, Schönhauser Alle 6-7 (☎030 50 34 86 67; www.whitetrashfastfood.com). Guarded by 2 gilded lions out front, 4 levels of kitsch and irony provide endless eye-candy inside. Fish tanks, rabbit skins, and movie memorabilia abound. Drinks come with honest, English explanations. Try a "Zombie" (€8): "blast your head into 1000 pieces!" There's also a pinball machine. Open daily 6pm-late. Cash only.

Intersoup, Schliemannstr. 31 (☎030 23 27 30 45; www.intersoup.de). U2 to Eberswalder Str. Named after DDR-era general stores (Intershop), this shabby bar eschews fancy designer drinks and popular music in favor of worn 70s furniture, soup specials (€4.50-5), and retro floral wallpaper. Downstairs, the small club **undersoup** keeps things wild with live music (most W and Sa nights), karaoke, occasional films, and a puppet theater (M and Tu). DJs most nights. Club cover €5 and under. Free Wi-Fi. Open M-Sa 6pm-3am, Su 5pm-2am. Cash only.

Pfefferberg Biergarten, Fehrbelliner Str. 92 (☎030 4438 3485). U2 to Senefelderplatz. Berlin's oldest beer garden, on a courtyard elevated from the noise of Schönhauser Allee. Live music some nights, but a slightly more staid, family atmosphere than that of the Prater. Beer €2-4. Sausage €1.50. Cash only.

Morgenrot, Kastanienallee 85 (☎030 44 31 78 44; www.cafe-morgenrot.de). U2 to Eberswalder Str. Candy-print wallpaper and abrupt art lure hipsters off the Kastanienallee strip. By day, it's a vegan hangout with a great brunch—by night, there are frosty vodka shots (€2). Open Tu-Th 10am-1am, F 10am-3am, Sa 11am-3am, Su 11am-1am. Cash only.

Duncker, Dunckerstr. 64 (☎030 445 9509; www.dunckerclub.de). S8, S41, or S85 to Prenzlauer Allee. This intense club draws crowds with its insider vibe. Grill in back. Ring the bell for entry. M and Su goth, Tu hippie, Th live bands. Cover €1.50-4, Th often free. Open M-Tu and Th-Su 8pm-late. Heats up around 1am. On F and Sa, all drinks €2 max. Cash only.

Scotch & Sofa, Kollwitzstr. 18 (☎030 44 04 23 71). U2 to Senefelderplatz. Exactly what the name promises, (and a very comfortable sofa at that). Hangout of intellectual types who spill over from the nearby bookstores to enjoy the good music, which often includes some soul. Smoking downstairs, banned upstairs. Open daily 2pm-very late. Cash only.

FRIEDRICHSHAIN

When people think of Berlin techno clubs, they're thinking of Friedrichshain. There are more legendary converted factory or warehouse clubs in this neighborhood than you can shake a stick at. The more low-key bars cluster around **Simon-Dach-Strrasse.** Raging dance venues are scattered between the car dealerships and empty lots on **Mühlenstrasse.**

◪ **Berghain/Panorama Bar,** Am Wriezener Bahnhof (☎030 29 00 05 97; www.berghain. de). S3, S5, S7, S9, or S75 to Ostbahnhof. Heading up Str. der Pariser Kommune, take the 3rd right into what looks like a parking lot. The granddaddy of Berlin's "it" clubs deserves its reputation as a must-visit. Beneath the towering ceilings of this former power plant, spaced-out techno-fiends pulse to the reverberating music. Cover generally €12. Open F-Sa and occasionally W from midnight. Cash only.

◪ **Maria am Ostbahnhof,** Am der Schillingbrücke (☎030 21 23 81 90; www.clubmaria. de). S-Bahn to Ostbahnhof. From Stralauer Platz exit, take Str. der Pariser Kommune to Stralauer Platz, follow it right along the wall, turn left at the bridge, and look for the red lights by the water. Tucked away by the river in an old factory, this club embodies the industrial legacy of Friedrichshain's scene. Sizable—and usually full—dance floor. Mostly electronic music, occasional punk, and reggae. Beer €2.50-3.50. Cover €10-12. Open F-Sa 11pm-late, weekdays for concerts and events only. Cash only.

Sanitorium 23, Frankfurter Allee 23 (☎030 42 02 11 93; www.sanatorium23.de). Large windows look into a sterile yet hip interior of this sleek break from converted warehouses. Hang your coat on the overturned gurney and try the "Moscow Mule" (€5). Open daily 2pm-late. Chic rooms available above. Singles €40; doubles €55. Cash only.

Häbermeyer, Gärtnerstr. 6 (☎030 29 77 18 87). U5 to Samariterstr. Retro stylings and soft red lighting from funky lamps complement the New Wave DJ sessions. Foosball table in back lends a competitive edge to the otherwise relaxed atmosphere. Mixed drinks €5.90-7.40. Open daily 7pm-late. Cash only.

Dachkammer Bar (DK), Simon-Dach-Str. 39 (☎030 296 1673). U5 to Frankfurter Tor. Draped vines give this bar a rustic feel, along with plenty of brick, wood, and comfy nooks adorned with vintage furniture. Quieter than its neighbors, DK is the place for conversation along with mixed drinks (€5-8), snacks (from €3.50), and a huge variety of beer on tap. Breakfast buffet 1am-3pm (€6.50). Open daily noon-late. Cash only.

Matrix, Warschauer Platz 18 (☎030 29 36 99 90). S3, S5, S7, S9, S75, or U1 to Warschauer Str. No, you aren't imagining the pounding bass coming from under the station—4 dance floors and multiple bars extend under the tracks. The stylish can opt for a mixed drink (€4.50-7.50) in the VIP lounge. No sneakers. Cover €3-6. 18+ (bring ID). Open daily 10pm-late. Cash only.

Astro-Bar, Simon-Dach-Str. 40 (www.astro-bar.de). U5 to Frankfurter Tor. Gritty retro-galactic bar with plastic robots in action poses proves yet again that Berlin is anything but normal. DJs play everything from R&B to electronica. Mixed drinks €3-5.50. Open daily from 6pm. Cash only.

Cassiopeia, Revaler Str. 99 (☎030 29 36 29 66). U- or S-Bahn to Warschauer Str. A sprawling nightlife oasis in an abandoned train repairs factory, this club/beer garden/restaurant/theater has outdoor couches that provide relief from the packed dance floor. Beer €2-3. Movies €5-6. Cover €3-10. Open F-Sa from 11pm; check website for weekdays. Cash only.

KREUZBERG

Although clubs are emerging throughout the rest of eastern Berlin (especially Friedrichshain), Kreuzberg is still a nightlife stronghold, full of options for virtually every demographic. Although there is no shortage of bars, **Oranienstraße** has the densest and coolest stretches of nightlife offerings. A unique row of bars along the water on **Schlesisches Straße** allow travelers to watch the sun set and then sip drinks until it rises again.

◪ **Club der Visionaere,** Am Flutgraben 1 (☎030 69 51 89 42; www.clubdervisionaererecords.com). U1 or U15 to Schlesisches Tor or night bus #N65 to Heckmannufer. Lounging around on their torch-lit raft in the canal in summer is the single most pleasant bar

BERLIN

experience in Berlin. Legend has it that bargoers occasionally fall into the water, but more common activities include dancing to house music or downing a pizza (€5-8) along with your drink. Beer €3. Open M-F 2pm-late, Sa-Su noon-late. Cash only.

Monarch Bar, Skalitzer Str. 134. U1 or U15 to Kotbusser Tor. Don't be put off by the urine smell in the staircase that leads up to this small, unmarked bar above Kaiser's supermarket. Some of the cheapest beer (€1 and up) around, a panoramic view of the raised S-Bahn thundering by, and a nightly DJ spinning electronica. Open 10pm-late. Cover €1.

Watergate, Falckensteinstr. 49 (☎030 61 28 03 96; www.water-gate.de). U1 or U15 to Schlesisches Tor. Depending on who is spinning, this can be the best party in the city on any given night. 2 constants: the polka-dot light show on the ceiling and the unbeatable view of the Spree from the "Water Floor" lounge and terrace. Crowds pick up at 2am. Cover W €6, F-Sa €10. Open W and F 11pm-late and Sa midnight-late. Cash only.

Live At Dot, Falckensteinstr. (☎030 76 76 62 67; www.liveatdot.com) U1 or U15 to Schlesisches Tor. This new 2-story bar and alternative live music venue is slicker than most places in the neighborhood. Skip the downstairs restaurant and head straight for the concert above, where the acoustics are so good there are often live recordings taking place. Cover €5-10. Hours vary, open most nights; check the website for a schedule. Cash only.

Luzia, Oranienstr. 34 (☎030 81 79 99 58; www.luzia.tc). U1 or U15 to Kotbusser Tor. Movie theater chairs, dark gold walls, and lofts accessible by ladders make Luzia the darling of a young, international crowd. That guy ordering a Krusovice on tap (€3) next to you at the bar is probably a freelance video artist. No cover. Open daily 9pm-late

Lido, Cuvrystr. 7 (☎030 81 79 99 58; www.lido-berlin.de). U1 or U15 to Schlesisches Tor. Despite its unassuming exterior plastered with peeling posters, this former cinema provides Kreuzberg and greater Berlin with parties (cover €3-6) and concerts (€12-15) that feature internationally popular indie and rock groups.

Bar Nou, Bergmannstr. 104 (☎030 74 07 30 50). U7 to Gneisenaustr., or night bus #N4 or N19 to Zossener Str. Bartenders joke about a 1 guest, 1 drink rule, but should think about enforcing it for real—these are some strong, strong drinks. Between the booze, the sexy red lighting, and communal sofa seating, more pickups happen here than at most German bars. Mixed drinks €7.50-9.50. Open daily 8pm-4am.

Yorckschlösschen, Yorckstr.15 (☎030 215 80 70; www.yorckschloesschen.de). U7 or S1 to Yorckstr. Local radicals mix with international students in the "small castle," which opened as a corner pub at the turn of the century. These days, it is Berlin's most relaxed jazz club. Live jazz, blues, and funk W and Sa (9pm-midnight) and Su (2-6pm). Cover €4. Open M-F 5pm-3am, Su 10am-3am.

Junction Bar, Gneisenaustr. 18 (☎030 694 6602; www.junction-bar.de). U7 to Gneisenaustr., or night bus #N4 or N19 to Zossener Str. Small but energetic venue for classic and pop rock, with nightly shows on an intimate subterranean stage. Can be packed or oddly empty depending on the night. Take a break at **Junction Cafe** upstairs (open 11am-2am). Live rock, soul, funk, jazz, or blues M-Th and Su from 9pm, F-Sa from 10pm. DJs start M-Th and Su 11:30pm, F-Sa 12:30am. Cover €5-8 for live music. Cover for DJs M-Th and Su €3, women free; F-Sa €4. Open daily 8pm-5am. Cash only.

Heinz Minki, Vor dem Schlesischen Tor 3 (☎030 69 53 37 66; www.heinzminki.de). U1 or U15 to Schlesisches Tor or night bus #N65 to Heckmannufer. A beer garden that (shockingly) is actually a garden. Plush drapery lines the small interior, but the real fun is outside. Patrons pound beers (½L €3.10) at long tables under hanging colored lights and surrounded by greenery. Gourmet pizza €2.60-2.90. Grilled bratwurst €2. Foosball tournament last Su of every month. Open daily noon-late; check website for winter hours. Cash only.

BERLIN

Potsdam

FOOD & DRINK
Kashmir Haus, **1**
Siam, **3**
Café Heider, **2**

ACCOMMODATIONS
Jugendherberge Potsdam (HI), **5**
Campingplatz Sanssouci-Gaisberg, **4**

400 yards
400 meters

TO SCHLOSS CECILIENHOF (800m)

Neuer Garten

Heiliger See

Marmorpalais

Am Neuen Garten

TO SCHLOßPARK GLIENICKE, GLIENICKER BRÜCKE (1km)

TO KAPELLE ALEXANDER NEWSKI (300m)

Puschkinallee

Russische Kolonie

Am Schragen

Hebbelstr.

Kurfürstenstr.

HOLLÄNDISCHES VIERTEL

Französische Kirche

Französische Str.

BASSIN-PLATZ

Am Kanal

Am Bassin

Kirche St. Peter und Paul

Altes Rathaus

Babelsberger Str.

Cityrad

Potsdam Hauptbahnhof

Neue Fahrt

Lange Brücke

Obelisk

Nikolaikirche

Filmmuseum

Schloß

AM NEUEN MARKT

PLATZ DER EINHEIT

Am Alten Markt

Dortustr.

Yorckstr.

Breite Str.

Lindenstr.

Charlottenstr.

Brandenburger Str.

Jägerstr.

Gutenbergstr.

Friedrich-Ebert-Str.

Nauener Tor

Jägerallee

Hegelallee

Jäger-tor

Obeliskportal

Triumphtor

Bildergalerie

Neptun-grotte

Gregor-Mendel-Str.

Voltaireweg

Bornstedter Str.

Zur Historische Mühle

Schloß Sanssouci

Neue Kammern

Große Fontäne

Marlygarten

Alte nach Sanssouci

Brandenburger Tor

Friedenskirche

Schopenhauerstr.

LUISEN-PLATZ

Dampfmaschinen-haus

Neustädter Havelbucht

Am Neuen Markt

Lindenstr.

Feuerbachstr.

Lennéstr.

Am Grünen

Zeppelinstr.

BRANDENBURGER VORSTADT

Maschinen-teich

Schafgraben

Ökonomieweg

Chinesisches Teehaus

Sizilianischer Garten

Nordischer Garten

An der Orangerie

Maulbeerallee

Hauptallee

Rosengarten

Orangerie

Botanischer Garten

Drachenhaus

Bornstedter See

Ribbeckstr.

Eichenallee

Amundsenstr.

Ruinenbergstr.

Pappelallee

Park Sanssouci

Antikentempel

Freundschafts-tempel

Fasanerie

Hippodrom

Schloß Charlottenhof

Römische Bäder

Lindstedter Weg

Am Neuen Palais

Neues Palais

Bahnhof Park Sanssouci

Lindenavenue

Geschwister-Scholl-Str.

TO WISSENSCHAFTSPARK "ALBERT EINSTEIN" (1km)

(2km)

GAY AND LESBIAN

GLBT-friendly nightlife in Keuzberg is clustered around **Oranienstraße** between Lausitzer Platz and Oranienplatz and **Mehringdamm** north of the Platz der Luftbrücke.

■ **Rose's,** Oranienstr. 187 (☎615 65 70). U1 to Görlitzer Bahnhof. Marked only by "Bar" over the door. It's Liberace meets Cupid meets Satan. A friendly, gay and lesbian clientele packs this intense and claustrophobic party spot all night. The voluptuous dark-red interior is accessorized madness, boasting hearts, glowing lips, furry ceilings, feathers, and glitter. The small menu covers the basics with whiskey (€5) and schnapps (€2). Open M-Th and Su 11pm-6am, F-Sa 11pm-8am. Cash only.

SchwuZ, Mehringdamm 61 (☎030 629 0880; www.schwuz.de). U6 or U7 to Mehringdamm. Enter through Melitta Sundström, a popular gay and lesbian cafe. The city's longest-running gay bar features 2 dance floors and a loungy underground area lined with pipes and its own DJ and disco lights. Music varies from alternative to house depending on the night, and the crowd varies from young to very young. Lesbian night every 2nd F of the month. Cover F €5 before midnight, €6 after; Sa €6/7. Open F-Sa 11pm-late. Cash only.

SO36, Oranienstr. 190 (☎030 61 40 13 06; www.so36.de). U1 to Görlitzer Bahnhof. One of Kreuzberg's oldest, grungiest, and best punk venues, named after the neighborhood's postal code, doubles as a gay nightclub. "Gayhane," Berlin's only Turkish gay night, is especially popular. Cover €3-10. Open 10pm-late. Cash only.

Bierhimmel, Oranienstr. 183 (☎030 61 53 122). U1 to Görlitzer Bahnhof. Translating to "beer heaven," this place is also a heaven of good coffee and homemade cake during the day and a heaven of handsome men in the very dark back lounge at night. Mixed crowd uses it as a stop on the way to SO36. Open 11am-3am. Cash only.

🗋 SHOPPING

When West Berlin was a lonely outpost amid the consumer wilderness of the Eastern Bloc, West Berliners had no choice but to buy locally. As a result, the city has a mind-boggling array of things for sale.

FLEA MARKETS

Some of Berlin's most popular shopping is at its many flea markets. The **market** on Str. des 17. Juni has the best selection in the area, but the prices are higher than those at other markets. (S5, S7, S9, or S75 to Tiergarten. Open Sa-Su 10am-5pm.) Sundays in Prenzlauer Berg's **Mauerpark** see a secondhand market take over the park, selling everything from food to furniture to bicycles (many stolen). Other markets are around **Ostbahnhof** in **Friedrichshain** (near Erich-Steinfurth-Str.; S3, S5, S7, S9, or S75 to Ostbahnhof; info ☎030 2900 2010; open Sa, Su 10am-5pm), on **Am Kupfergraben** by the Museuminsel (S-Bahn or U6 to Friedrichstr.; open Sa 11am-5pm, Su 10am-4pm; info: ☎0172 301 8873) and on **John-F.-Kennedy-Platz** (U4 to Rathaus Schöneberg; open F-Su 8am-4pm).

CLOTHING AND ACCESSORIES

■ **KaDeWe,** Tauentzienstr. 21-24 (☎030 212 10). U2 or U5 to Wittenbergplatz. Berlin's high temple of consumerism is the 7-story Kaufhaus des Westens (Shopping Mall of the West) the largest department store on the continent. Everything from designer clothing to a food shop with an American section full of marshmallows. Open M-Th 10am-8pm, F 10am-9pm, Sa 9:30am-8pm. AmEx/MC/V.

Revanche de la Femme, Uhlandstr. 50 (☎03088912672) U to Uhlandstr. It stands to reason that the sexiest lingerie is available near the former Cabaret hotspots in the

West. Get lucky, hit a sale, and pick up some gorgeous corsets for cheap. Open M-F 11am-7pm, Sa 11am-3pm. MC/V.

Kwikshop, Kastanienallee 44 (☎030 4199 7150). So gimmicky but so cute, this Prenzlauer Berg fixture has a drive-by-style pickup window for picking up a sweater or socks on the fly. Good for gifts under €5. Open M-Sa 11am-7pm. Cash only.

SECONDHAND SHOPS

Zweite Hand (€2) appears Tuesday, Thursday, and Saturday with listings for everything under the sun: plane tickets, silk dresses, cats, and terrific deals on bikes. Boutiques on **Kastanianallee** and **Oranienburger Straße** sell chic secondhand clothes for first-hand prices. Kreuzberg's strip for used clothing and cheap antiques is **Bergmannstraße.**

Lunette's Brillenagentur, Marienburger Str. 11 (☎030 3408 2789). Ringbahn to Prenzlauer Allee. A quirky store that sells only vintage sunglasses, mostly pre-1950s. The staff will help with frame/face-shape issues. Open M-F 11am-8pm, Sa noon-6pm.

Made in Berlin, Neue Schönhauser Str. 19. (☎030 899 50). The source for all of your leather jacket needs, hipster. Open M-Sa noon-8pm.

Garage, Ahornstr. 3 (☎030 211 2760), in Nollendorfplatz. Heaps of quirky and vintage used clothing for sale by the kilo. Open M-F 11am-7pm, Sa 11am-6pm.

Hands Up! Schlesische Str. 19. In case you simply must have a new old vest to wear dancing. Open M-Sa noon-8pm.

Trash-Schick, Wülischstr. 31 (☎030 2757 4437) in Frierichshain. More vintage wear. Open daily noon-8pm.

MUSIC AND BOOKS

If you're looking for used CDs or LPs, snoop around the streets near **Schlesische Straße** and **Bergmannstraße.** (U1 or U15 to Schlesisches Tor.)

🖼 **St. George's Bookstore,** Wörtherstr. 27 (☎030 8179 8333). U2 to Senefelderplatz. The largest collection of secondhand books in Berlin, with an especially good selection of fiction and German history. The wonderful English-speaking staff will order new books for you. Tu movie night (€3, includes movie and a glass of wine or beer). Various readings and concerts. Open M-Sa 11am-8pm, Sa 11am-7pm. Cash only.

Rock Steady Records, Motzstr. 9 (☎030 217 27 20) U1, U2, U3, or U4 to Nollendorf Platz. Berlin is full of record junkies and they all know to come here. 10,000 plus LPs in an effort to "save the vinyl." Open M-F 11am-7pm, Sa 10am-4pm. Cash only.

SpaceHall, Zossener Str. 33 (☎030 694 7664). U7 to Gneisenaustr. This is a serious shop for those who are serious about their techno. There are some serious techno T-shirts for sale, too. Open M-F 11am-8pm, Sa 11am-7pm. Cash only.

Saturn, Alexanderplatz 8. (☎030 247 516). U2, U5, U8, S3, S5, S7, S9, or S75 to Alexanderplatz. Berlin's enormous electronics store has a respectable CD collection in its basement. Open M-F 9:30am-8pm, Sa 9am-8pm.

Cover, Turmstr. 52 (☎030 395 8762). U9 to Turmstr. Pop music rules the day here. A variety of used CDs and records. Open M-F 10am-8pm, Sa 10am-4pm.

Freak Out, Prenzlauer Allee 49 (☎030 442 7615). U2 to Eberswald Str. Somewhat outside-the-mainstream music, ranging from electronica to reggae. The back room contains used CDs and LPs, most around €5. Open M-F 11am-7:30pm, Sa 11am-4pm.

Hard Wax, Paul-Lincke-Ufer 44A (☎030 6113 0111; www.hardwax.com). U8 to Kottbusser Tor. An absolutely mind-boggling vinyl collection. Open M-Sa noon-8pm.

⬛ EXCURSIONS FROM BERLIN

Completely surrounding Berlin, the Land of Brandenburg is a perfect escape from the sprawling urban behemoth resting at its center. The infamous Hohenzollern family emerged from the province's forests to become the rulers of Prussia, leaving their mark on the region in the shape of more than 30 stunning palaces. The castles attract their share of visitors to Brandenburg, especially the sprawling Sanssouci, only a 30min. train trip from the nation's capital making this Prussian take on Versailles a favorite jaunt for native Berliners.

POTSDAM
☎0331

Visitors disappointed by Berlin's distinctly unroyal demeanor can get their Kaiserly fix by taking the S-Bahn to Potsdam (pop. 146,000), the glittering city of Friedrich II (the Great). While his father, Friedrich Wilhelm I (the "Soldier King"), wanted to turn Potsdam into a huge garrison of the tall, tall men he had kidnapped to serve as his toy soldiers, the more aesthetically-minded Friedrich II beautified the city. His additions include Schloß Sanssouci and the surrounding park, and the nearby Neues Garten with its Marmorpalais. Potsdam was Germany's "Little Hollywood" in the 1920s and 30s, when the suburb of Babelsberg played a critical role in the early film industry. A 20min. air raid in April 1945 brought Potsdam's cinematic glory days to an end. As the site of the 1945 Potsdam Conference, in which the Allies divvied up the country, Potsdam's name became synonymous with German defeat. After hosting Communist Party fat cats for 45 years, the 1000-year-old city gained independence from Berlin in 1991, recovering its eminent status as capital of the Land. Much of the residential city has been renovated to create long boulevards adorned with gateways and historic buildings. Today, the city moves at a leisurely pace, its palaces and avenues swelling with curious visitors.

▌ TRANSPORTATION

Trains: S7 runs to Potsdam's Hauptbahnhof, as does the RE1 from Berlin's Friedrichstr., Alexanderplatz, and other major stations (40min. or 25min., €2.80). Trains every hr. to: **Dessau** (2hr., €32); **Leipzig** (1¾hr., €44); **Magdeburg** (1¼hr., €19.20).

Public Transportation: Potsdam is in Zone C of Berlin's BVG transit network. It is also divided into its own subdivisions of A, B, and C; special Potsdam-only tickets can be purchased on any bus or tram (€1.20, valid 1hr.; all-day €3.70-5.50). The **Berlin Welcome Card** (€18-24.50) is also valid in Potsdam.

Bike Rental and Tours: Potsdam is best seen by bike, and bike rental places often map out the best way to see all the sights. ⬛**Potsdam Per Pedales** (☎0331 748 0057; www.pedales.de) rents them out from their main location at Rudolf-Breitscheid-Str. 201, in the Griebnitzsee S-Bahn station or on the S-Bahn platform at Potsdam Hauptbahnhof. From the former, pay to take your bike on the S-Bahn (special bike pass €1.20-1.80 at any BVG ticket office). Bike tours in English (reserve ahead) and German (€10.50, students €8.50; €6 audio guide.) **Canoe** and **kayak** rental €28-30 per day. Griebnitzsee Station open Good Friday-Oct. daily 9am-6:30pm; Potsdam Hauptbahnhof open May-Sept. daily 9am-7pm. **Cityrad** rents **bikes** right across from the Babelsbergerstr. exit of the Hauptbahnhof. (☎0177 825 4746; www.cityrad-rebhan.de. €11 per day. Open Apr. 1-Oct. 31 M-F 9am-7pm, Sa-Su 9am-8pm).

🔁 PRACTICAL INFORMATION

Tourist Office: Brandenburger Str. 3 (☎0331 27 55 80; www.potsdamtourismus.de) by Brandenburg Gate. Buy city maps and book a room (from €15). Open Apr.-Oct. M-F 9:30am-6pm Sa-Su 9:30am-4pm; Nov.-Mar. M-F 10am-6pm, Sa-Su 9:30am-2pm.

Tours: The tourist office runs 2hr. tours of the city; inquire at the office (€8, departs May-Sept. daily 3pm). Original Berlin Walks has 5-6hr. walking tours that leave from the taxi stand outside Berlin's Bahnhof Zoo Apr.-Oct., Th and Su 9:50am. €15, under age 26 €11.50. Double-decker buses from **Potsdam City Tours** leave daily on the hour from Hauptbahnhof 10:45am-3:45pm. €14, students €11.

Post Office: Platz der Einheit. Open M-F 9am-6:30pm, Sa 9am-1pm. **Postal Code:** 14476.

🏠 📷 ACCOMMODATIONS AND CAMPING

Budget options are limited in Potsdam. The tourist office finds private rooms and has a list of campgrounds in the area. Consider staying in Wannsee (p. 100), 10min. away by S-Bahn, or at one of the many hostels in central Berlin.

Jugendherberge Potsdam (HI), Schulstr. 9 (☎030 264 9520; www.jh-potsdam.de), located in Babelsberg just one S-Bahn stop from the Potsdam Hauptbahnhof. Head left out of the S-Bahn station and take the 1st left. Breakfast and sheets included. Internet €0.50 for 10min. Dorms €15, over 27 €18; singles €31.50/34.50; doubles €26.50/29.50. Nov.-Feb. all rooms €15 per person. Cash only. ❷

Campingplatz Sanssouci-Gaisberg, An der Pirschheide 41 (☎0331 951 0988; www.campingpark-sanssouci-potsdam.com) on the scenic banks of the Templiner See. Take S7 to Potsdam Hauptbahnof, then tram #91 to Bahnhof Pirschheide. Call 8:45am-9pm for free shuttle to campsite. Phone reception 8am-1pm and 3-8pm. €10.50 per person. Internet available for €2 per day. Laundry €4. ❶

🍴 FOOD

Bright, renovated **Brandenburger Str.,** the local pedestrian zone, encompasses many of the city's restaurants, fast-food stands, and markets. The dozens of cafes near Brandenburger Tor are lovely but pricey, as are the cafes and restaurants along parts of Friedrich-Ebert-Str. and the **Holländisches Viertel.** Head to the **flea market** on Bassinplatz for fresh produce. (Open M-F 9am-6pm.) In the Hauptbahnhof is a massive **Kaufland** grocery store. (Open daily 6am-8pm.)

Siam, Friedrich-Ebert-Str. 13 (☎0311 200 9292). Prepares tasty Thai food (€5-8) right before your eyes in a bamboo-laden interior. Open daily 11:30am-11pm. Cash only. ❷

Kashmir Haus, Jägerstr. 1 (☎0331 870 9580). Offers Indian food in a trapestry-draped setting removed from the tourist bustle. The weekday lunch special (€4.50-6.50, 11am-4pm) includes vegetarian options and is an unbeatable deal. Open M-F 11am-11pm, Sa-Su 11am-midnight. Cash only. ❸

Cafe Heider, Friedrich-Ebert-Str. 29 (☎0331 270 5596). Heider is a beautiful outdoor cafe, located right on the border of the Hollandisches Viertel. Entrees €8-12. Open M-F from 8am, Sa from 9am, Su from 10am. ❸

📷 SIGHTS

A **Premium Day Ticket** (€15, students €10) is a good investment for anyone interested in serious sightseeing. It is valid and available at all castles in Potsdam, including Sanssouci, which requires separate admission.

PARK AND SCHLOSS SANSSOUCI

◪**PARK SANSSOUCI.** Schloß Sanssouci's 600-acre "backyard," a testament to the size of Friedrich II's treasury and the diversity of his aesthetic tastes, has two distinct areas to explore. Half of the park is done in the Baroque style, with straight paths intersecting at topiaries and statues of nude nymphs arranged in geometrically pleasing patterns. The other half is in the rambling, rolling style of English landscape gardens. The sheer magnitude of the park—encompassing wheat fields, rose trellises, and lush, immaculate gardens—makes it a compelling place to spend an afternoon. For information on the park's many attractions, from Rococo sculptures to beautiful fountains, head to the visitors center next to the windmill, behind the *Schloß*. (☎0331 969 4200. Open daily Mar.-Oct. 8am-10pm; Nov.-Feb. 9am-8pm.)

SCHLOSS SANSSOUCI. The park's main attraction, the very-Versailles *Schloß*, sits atop a landscaped hill. Designed by Georg Wenzeslaus von Knobelsdorff in 1747, the yellow palace is small and airy, adorned with rich depictions of Dionysus and other Greek gods. Inside Sanssouci (French for "without worry"), the style is cloud-like French Rococo—all pinks and greens with gaudy gold trim. Friedrich, an unrepentant Francophile until his death, built the exotic **Voltairezimmer** (Voltaire Room), decorated with carved reliefs of parrots and tropical fruit, in honor of Voltaire, though the writer never stayed here. The library reveals another of Friedrich's eccentricities: whenever he wanted to read a book, he had a copy printed for each of his palaces—*en français*, of course. Also on display in the palace is Andy Warhol's modern interpretation of the king's portrait. (Bus #695 or X15 to Schloß Sanssouci. ☎0331 969 42 00. Open Tu-Su Apr.-Oct. 10am-6pm, last entry 5:30pm; Nov.-Mar. 10am-5pm, last entry 4:30. Price of admission for Schloß Sanssouci and Buldergalerie together: €12, students €8. Audio guide included.)

NEUES PALAIS. At the opposite end of the park, the New Palace is the largest and latest of the park's four castles. Commissioned by Friedrich the Great to emphasize Prussia's power after the Seven Years' War, this 200-room ornate pink *Schloß* features royal apartments, festival halls, and the impressive Grottensaal, whose shimmering walls are literally coated with seashells. (☎0331 96 94 361. Open Apr.-Oct. M and W-Su 10am-6pm, last entry 5:30pm; Nov.-Mar. and 10am-5pm, last entry 4:30.. €5, students €4. Tours €1 extra in summer.)

OTHER BUILDINGS IN THE PARK. Next to the Schloß Sanssouci, the **Bildergalerie's** collection of Caravaggio, van Dyck, and Reubens crowd a long hall of massive and elaborate canvases. (☎0331 969 4181. Open Apr. 1-Oct. 31. Tu-Su 10am-5:30pm. €3, students €2.50. Audio Guide €1.) The **Neue Kammern** (New Chambers) are former the *Schloß*'s guesthouse and recital hall. The ball and festival rooms are symbolically decorated with Baroque circumstance. The wall gildings depict Ovid's *Metamorphosis*, while a painting of Venus looks down onto the carefully painted ceiling in order to emphasize the importance of beauty. (Open Apr 1-Apr 30 Sa-Su 10am-6pm; May 1-Oct 31 Tu-Su 10am-6pm. Last entry 5:30pm. €4, students €3. Audioguide included. Tour €1.) The stunning **Sizilianer Garten** (Sicilian Garden) is next door. Overlooking the park from the north, the pseudo-Italian **Orangerie** is famous for its 67 dubious Raphael imitations that replace originals swiped by Napoleon. (Open from mid-May to mid-Oct. Tu-Su 10am-12:30pm and 1-5pm. Mandatory tours €3, students €2.50. Tower only €2.) Romantic **Schloß Charlottenhof**, whose park surroundings were a Christmas gift from Friedrich Wilhelm III to his son Friedrich Wilhelm IV, melts into landscaped gardens and grape arbors to the south. (Open May-Oct. Tu-Su 10am-6pm. €4, students €3.) Nearby are the **Römische Bäder** (Roman baths), alongside a reedy pond with a miniature bridge. Meant to provide a contrast to the Italian villas, the gold-plated **Chinesisches Teehaus** stands complete with a parasol-wielding rooftop Buddha and 18th-century *chinois* porcelain inside. *(Open May-Oct. Tu-Su 10am-6pm. €3, students €2.50)* The almost industrial-looking **Friedenskirche** at the east entrance of the park contains the graves of Friedrich Wilhelm IV and his wife Elizabeth below glittering mosaics.

OTHER SIGHTS

NEUER GARTEN. Running alongside the Heiliger See, Potsdam's second park contains several royal residences. **Schloß Cecilienhof,** built in the image of an English Tudor manor, houses exhibits on the **Potsdam Treaty,** signed at the palace in 1945. Visitors can see numerous Potsdam Conference items, including the table at which the Big Three bargained over Europe's fate, and can stand in the very room Stalin used as his study. *(☎0331 969 4244. Open Tu-Su Apr.-Oct. 10am-6pm; Nov.-Mar. 10am-5pm. €5, students €4. Tours in summer €1 extra.)* The garden also contains the centerpiece of the park, the **Marmorpalais** (Marble Palace). One of the quirkier buildings is a replica of an Egyptian pyramid formerly used for food storage. *(Take bus #692 to Schloß Cecilienhof. Marmorpalais open Apr.-Oct. Tu-Su 10am-6pm; Nov.-Mar. Sa-Su 10am-5pm. €4, students €3. Tour extra €1 in summer.)* At the far end of the park, beachgoers bare all by the lake. Another palace-park, **Schloßpark Glienicke** contains a casino and **Schloß Glienicke,** built by Karl Friedrich Schinkel in 1828 for Prince Karl of Prussia. The nearby **Mauerweg** (Wall Path) follows the 160km route along which the Wall separated West Berlin from the surrounding DDR territory. *(Take tram #93 to Glienicker Brücke and continue along Berliner Str. to the bridge; the castle is just on the other side to the left. Open from mid-May to mid-Oct. Sa-Su 10am-5pm).* A walk back on Berliner Str. leads to the **Glienicker Brücke** (a.k.a. "The James Bond Bridge"), swallowed up by the death strip between the DDR and West Berlin. Closed to traffic until 1989, it was instead used for the exchange of spies and known ironically as the "Bridge of Unity."

RUSSISCHE KOLONIE. In the beginning of the 19th century, General Yorck brought 500 Russian soldiers to Prussia. Friedrich Wilhelm III, a great fan of Russian culture and handsome soldiers, discovered that many of them had singing talent. Unfortunately, only 12 of the original group were left by the 1820s. To mitigate the depressing atmosphere, Friedrich III built each soldier a small, shingled wooden house trimmed with ornate carvings. The nearby pink, onion-domed Kapelle Alexander Newski, designed by Schinkel, was also intended as compensation. *(Tram #90, 92, or 95 to Puschkinalle; follow the street north.)*

FILMMUSEUM. Housed in an old orangerie that once held Friedrich's stables, this museum documents Potsdam's days as a film mecca, with artifacts like Marlene Dietrich's costumes, as well as a silent film archive and a small **movie theater.** *(On the corner of Breite Str. and Schloßstr. ☎0331 271 8112; www.filmmuseum-potsdam.de. Open daily 10am-6pm. €3.50, students €2.50. Movies from M-W 6 and 8pm, Th-Su 6pm, 8pm, and 10pm. Theater open daily noon-1am. €5, students €4. €3 on M.)*

HOLLÄNDISCHES VIERTEL. Friedrich's attempt to import Dutch craftsmen to beautify the city produced the Dutch Quarter, which lies in the center of the town around Friedrich-Ebert-Str. Though it fell into disrepair during the mid-20th century, the neighborhood was revitalized when entrepreneurs converted the beautiful old buildings into a row of shops and restaurants in 1990.

NIKOLAIKIRCHE. Toward the waterfront, the impressive dome of the Nikolaikirche rises above its neighbors. With closer inspection, the dome and the granite cube upon which it sits don't seem to match. While the cap is light and spacious, the interior was renovated à la DDR with glass and sound-tiles that somehow dampen the aesthetic impact. An obelisk decorated with sphinxes and ram skulls, dedicated to Schinkel, stands in front. (Am Alten Markt. ☎ 0331 270 8602; www.nikolaipotsdam.de. Open daily 10am-7pm, in winter 10am-5pm.)

FILMPARK BABELSBERG. Back in the Golden Age of European cinema, the UFA-Fabrik in Babelsberg was *the* German studio, giving Marlene Dietrich, Hans Albers, and Leni Riefenstahl their first big breaks. Fritz Lang also made *Metropolis* here. That said, this amusement park has little to do with film, and little beyond the lunch-counter wurst is particularly German. Still, the park is fun and very family-conscious, with rides and huge walk-through exhibits geared toward children. (August-Bebel-Str. 26-53. Take S7 to Babelsberg, then bus #690 to Filmpark or take bus #601 or 690 to the same stop from Potsdam Hauptbahnhof. ☎ 0331 721 2750; www.filmpark.de. Open daily Mar 18-Nov 2 10am-6pm. Closed M and F in Jun. and Sept. €19, students €15.50. Tickets purchased 2½hr. before close discounted €12, students €10.50.)

BRANDENBURG AN DER HAVEL ☎ 03381

When Albert the Bear chose Brandenburg (pop. 74,000) "on the Havel" for the site of his cathedral in 1165, the small, unpretentious town had to deal with sudden prominence, reluctantly assuming a central political role in the region. In the end, Brandenburg's slow pace triumphed over the commercial demands imposed by its key river-side location. These days, the town has reclaimed its more peaceful past, cultivating an atmosphere lightyears away from its urbane neighbor as residents spend their time fishing by the Havel or strolling the Altstadt's cobblestone streets. The province's namesake moves at a leisurely gait and invites you to do the same along its scenic waterways.

🖅🔳 TRANSPORTATION AND PRACTICAL INFORMATION. Brandenburg is on the Magdeburg-Berlin regional express line, the RE1, with frequent **trains** to Berlin (45min., €7.60) and Magdeburg (45min, €18.40). Visitors from Berlin should consider buying a day ticket valid on all Berlin and Brandenburg public transportation (€19). The **tourist office,** Steinstr. 66/67, is at the tram stop Neustädtischer Markt. From the station, cross Am Hauptbahnhof, walk along Große Gartenstr., and follow it right onto Jakobstr., which becomes Steinstr. The staff books rooms for free, distributes English maps and brochures, and leads **walking tours** (1hr., May-Sept. Sa-Su at 11am, €3) and **boat tours,** which leave several times per day from near the Jahrtausendbrücke at the end of Hauptstr. (☎ 03381 20 87 69; www.stadt-brandenburg.de. Boat tours €5-6. Open M-F 9am-7pm, May 1-Sept. 30 Sa-Su 10am-3pm; Oct. 1-Apr. 30 Sa 10am-2pm.) The **Steinstr.** and **Neustädtischer Markt** areas are the town's main thoroughfares, while **Hauptstr.** offers more commercial shopping and chain stores.

🛏🍴 ACCOMMODATIONS AND FOOD. There aren't any youth hostels in Brandenburg, but private rooms are abundant and cheap—ask at the tourist office for a brochure or look for *Zimmer frei* signs. Hidden behind a cafe directly on Steinstr. is the **Pension Blaudruck ❷,** Steinstr. 21, with six small, charming rooms adorned with paintings and stray ivy creeping in from the windows. The proprietors dress in the same homemade blue fabric that adorns the rooms. Enter through the passage into the courtyard at #21. (☎ 03381 22 57 34; www.blaudruck-design.de. Breakfast €3.85. Reserve ahead. Singles €21; doubles €42. Cash only.) By a quiet canal between the Altstadt and the train station, **Pension**

"Haus am Jungfernsteig" ❸, Kirchhofstr. 9 Jungfernsteig 6a, run by two kindly violinists, has spacious rooms with TV, skylights, and shared bathrooms. (☎03381 20 15 11; www.pension-haus-am-jungfernsteig.de.) Wi-Fi available Breakfast included. Singles €28-32; doubles €49-52; triples €65-72. AmEx/MC/V.)

The main cafe and *Imbiß* scenes are on Steinstr. and perpendicular to Hauptstr., which also features an open-air **farmer's market** behind the Katharinenkirche. Along Mühlendamm, dockside cafes and snack stands let you sample the region's freshly-caught fish. (Open M-F 7am-5pm, Sa 7am-noon.) **Nummer 31** ❷, Steinstr. 31, offers tasty gourmet pizzas in a traditional German setting for €3-6. (☎03381 22 44 73; www.nummer31.de. Open M-Sa from 11am, Su from 5pm. Cash only.) The **Kartoffelkäfer** ❷, Steinstr. 56, serves delicious meals that take advantage of every possible variation of the potato. The outdoor cafe is a short walk from Neustädtischerer Markt. (☎03381 22 41 18; www.derkartoffelkaefer.de. Entrees €5-9. Open daily 11am-midnight. Cash only.) **Bismarck Terrassen** ❸, Bergstr. 20, is located at on the corner of Bergstr. and Am Marienburg, right at the base of the hill on which the Friedenswarte tower sits. Try authentic, traditional German fare (€6-10) in a room devoted to Otto von Bismarck. (☎03381 30 09 39. Open daily. Cash only.)

⧉ SIGHTS. Brandenburg's sights can be found along Steinstr. and its extension. Begin your tour of the Neustadt at the end of Steinstr. with the 14th-century **Steintorturm** (Stone Gate Tower), which holds a maritime history museum with displays on each level of the tower. Brave the steep, narrow spiral staircase for a view of the Havel and pedestrian Brandenburg. And you can ring a big bell. (☎03381 20 02 65. Tower open Tu-F 9am-5pm and Sa-Su 10am-5pm. €3, students €1, families €5, children under 6 free.) Work your way up the street to the cluttered rooms of DDR paraphenalia at the **Nostalgie-Museum,** Steinstr. 52. (☎03381 22 52 39; ww.n-ost-algie.de. Open Tu-Su 10am-noon and 1-4pm. €1.50.) The 14th-century **St. Katharinenkirche,** on the corner of Neustädter Markt, is a beautiful example of North-German *Backstein* (glazed brick) Gothic, now pockmarked by war damage. (Open M-Sa 10am-4pm, Su 1-4pm.) Walking through Molkenmarkt, across the river and along St. Petri will bring you to the famed **Dom St. Peter und Paul,** Burghof 11, a cathedral currently housing a rotating exhibition. Artwork is placed in the aisles with surprising abandon. The church is also adorned with its own art; architect Friedrich Schinkel couldn't resist adding a few touches like the "Schinkel-Rosette" and the window over the entrance. The **Dommuseum** inside displays an array of old clothing, local-history treasures, and medieval books. (☎03381 211 2221. Open M-Tu and Th-Sa 10am-5pm, W 10am-noon, Su 11:30am-5pm. Last entry for museum 4:30pm. €3, students €2.) Across the street, the **Petrikapelle** has gone from church to contemporary art gallery. (☎03381 20 03 25. Open M-Tu and Th-F 10am-4pm, W 10am-noon, Sa 10am-5pm, Su 11am-5pm.)

For those with time to spare, Brandenburg's **Altstadt,** across the Havel, has even more centuries-old buildings (including towers from the 12th-century walls), fewer glossy storefronts, and a more reserved feel. From St. Katharinenkirche, head down Hauptstr. across the river. For 500 years, a 6m statue of the epic hero Roland has stood here in front of the Rathaus. Farther afield, the modern and comically phallic **Friedenswarte tower,** on the Marienberg, directly uphill from Am Marienberg, provides a great view of the contrasting antiquity surrounding it. (Open Apr.-Oct. Tu-Su 10am-5pm. €2, students €1.)

SPREEWALD (SPREE FOREST)

The Spree River splits apart 100km southeast of Berlin and branches out over the countryside in an intricate maze of streams, canals, meadows, and primeval forests stretching over 1000 sq. km. The Spree Forest's tiny villages were first settled in the Middle Ages, and the folklore is an especially rich tradition. The **Sorbs,** Germany's native Slavic minority, originally settled the region and continue to influence its cultural identity.

Webbed by shaded canals, this popular vacation destination for Berliners is known as the "Venice of the North." Farmers row to their fields, and children paddle home from school. The fields and forests teem with owls, otter, and foxes, so that even a fleeting walk through the woods becomes strikingly idyllic. Now recognized as a biosphere nature reserve by the UN, some sections of the forest are off-limits to the public and others close during mating and breeding seasons. Tourist season bears its own fruit—campgrounds abound, bike paths proliferate, and excellent hiking trails weave through the trees. Bearing in mind the fragile state of the ecosystem, visit local tourist offices for advice on how to be environmentally responsible in protected areas.

Lübben and Lübbenau, two tiny towns that open into labyrinths of canals, are popular destinations within daytrip-range of Berlin, while nearby Cottbus is the area's largest transportation hub. The forest is divided into two sections. The Unterspreewald is a mountain biker's dream, while the Oberspreewald, surrounding Lübben and Lübbenau, is best explored by boat.

LÜBBENAU   ☎03542

Tiny Lübbenau (pop. 7000) is the most famous of the Spreewald towns and deservedly so—its interwoven canals and roads seem worlds away from the modern cities around it. For tourists, the village serves as a springboard for trips into the kingdom of the *Irrlichter* (will o' the wisp). The landscape here is dense with waterways, and has more gondolas than houses. Buried in the forest, the neighboring village Lehde has tiny houses with straw roofs and a museum that recreates life as it once was for the Spreewald Sorbs.

TRANSPORTATION AND PRACTICAL INFORMATION. Trains go to: Berlin (1hr., 2 per hr., €10.40); Cottbus (25min., every hr., €5.10); Lübben (10min., 2 per hr., €2.00). For a **taxi** call ☎03542 31 53. **Kowalsky's,** near the station at Poststr. 6, rents **bikes.** (☎03542 28 35. €7 per day. Open M-F 9am-12:30pm and 2-6pm, Sa 9am-noon, Su call in advance.) Rent a **kayak** at the campsite (below) or at **Franke,** Dammstr. 72., down the walkway over the bridge. From the station, turn right down Bahnhofstr. and left at Dammstr. (☎03542 27 22. Paddleboats €3-8per hr. Open Apr.-Oct. daily 8am-7pm.) **Hannemann,** Am Wasser 1, rents **boats** at the other port. Follow Spreestr. to the end, cross the bridge, and continue to the next bridge. (☎03542 36 47. 1-seaters €3-4 per hr. Call ahead to reserve a boat. Open daily Apr.-Oct. 8am-7pm.) The **tourist office,** Ehm-Welk-Str. 15, at the end of Poststr., has maps and finds rooms for a €3 fee. (☎03542 36 68; www. spreewald-online.de. Open Nov.-Mar. M-F 10am-4pm; Apr.-Oct. M-F 9am-7pm; Sa 9am-4pm; May-June Su 11am-3pm, Jul.-Sept 11am-4pm.) The **post office** is at Kirchplatz 6. (Open M-F 9am-6pm, Sa 9am-noon.) **Postal Code:** 03222.

ACCOMMODATIONS AND FOOD. Though the closest hostel is in Lübben, 10min. away by train (p. 132), finding a room isn't a problem in friendly Lübbenau. Check for *Zimmer frei* signs, particularly common along **Poststr.,** or ask for the *Gastgeberverzeichnis* brochure at the tourist office. **Pension Am Alten Bauernhafen ❸,** Stottoff 5 (☎03542 29 30; www.am-alten-bauern-hafen.de), between the train station and the center of town. From Poststr., take a left onto Ehm-Welk-Str., which becomes Karl-Marx-Str. Take a left on Stottoff. (Single €30-35; doubles €42-49; triples €65; quads €50-80. Bikes €7 per day; paddleboats €17 per day or €3.50 per person per hr. On the road to Lehde and surrounded by water, **Campingplatz "Am Schloßpark" ❶** has 125 tent plots with cooking and bathing facilities on-site, as well as a convenience store. (☎03542 35 33; www.spreewaldcamping.de. Bikes €8 per day; paddleboats €15 per day. Reception 7:30am-12:30pm and 2-10pm. €6 per person, €6 per child, 5-6 per tent. 2- to 4-person bungalows €20-50. Cash only.)

For cheap food—and pickles, beets, and beans by the barrel—check out the *Imbiße* (snack bars) and stands along the **Großer Hafen.** Cheerful yellow **Cafe Fontane ❸** dishes out delicious local cuisine just behind the church at Ehm-Wehk-Str. 42; try a salad with baguette (€9-10) or one of the homemade cakes. (Open daily from 11:30am. Cash only.) **Spreewald Idyll ❸,** Spreestr. 13, serves regional specialties like *Grützwurst* with potatoes (€7), fish dishes (€7-14), and salads (€2.60-6.60) within spitting distance of the Kleiner Hafen on an outdoor patio. (☎03542 22 51. Open M-Sa 10am-10pm, Su 10am-8:30pm. Cash only.)

▣▨ **SIGHTS AND HIKING.** The Altstadt is a 10min. walk from the station. Go straight on Poststr. until you reach the marketplace and the Baroque **Nikolai-kirche.** (Kirchplatz 3. ☎03542 27 78; www.kirche-luebbenau.de. Open May-Oct. M-Sa 2-4pm.) The requisite **Schloß** is now a handsome, pricy hotel and restaurant with lush grounds open to the public. Across the marketplace in the gatehouse (a prison until 1985) is the ▨**Spreewaldmuseum,** Topfmarkt 12, which gives a historical overview of the Spreewald and its customs. (☎03542 24 72; www.spreewald-web.de. Open from Apr. to mid-Oct. Tu-Su 10am-6pm. €3, students €2.) The **Haus für Mensch und Natur** (House for Man and Nature), Schulstr. 9, has a free exhibit on the local ecosystem. (Open Apr.-Oct. Tu-Su 10am-5pm.)

Gondola tours of the forest depart from the **Großer Hafen** and the **Kleiner Hafen** (larger and smaller ports, respectively). The Großer Hafen, along Dammstr. behind the church, offers a wider variety of tours, including 2-3hr. trips to Lehde. The boats take on customers starting at 9-10am and depart when full (about 20 passengers) throughout the day. **Genossenschaft der Kahnfährleute,** Dammstr. 77a, is the biggest company. (☎03542 22 25; www.grosser-hafen.de. Open Mar.-Oct. daily 9:30am-6pm. 2hr. round-trips to Lehde €8.50, children €4.25; 3hr. €10/5; 5hr. tour of the forest €13/6.50.) From the Kleiner Hafen, less-touristed but nearly identical wilderness trips are run by the **Kahnfährmannsverein der Spreewaldfreunde,** Spreestr. 10a. (☎03542 40 37 10. Open Apr.-Oct. daily 9am-6pm. Tours 2-10hr.; 4-5hr. tours recommended. €8-20, children €4-10.)

It's only a hop and a paddle from Lübbenau to the haystacks and thatched-roof houses of **Lehde,** a UNESCO-protected landmark that is accessible by foot (15min.), bike, or boat. Follow the signs from the Altstadt or Großer Hafen, or take a boat from the harbor. The **Freilandmuseum** (Open-Air Museum), a recreated 19th-century village, portrays a time when entire Spreewalder families slept in the same room and newlyweds literally went for a "romp in the hay." Follow the signs to Lehde; it's just behind the aquarium and over the bridge. (☎03542 24 72. Open daily Apr.-Sept. 10am-6pm, Oct. 10am-5pm. Last entry 5:30pm. €3, students and seniors €2, children €1.) Just before the bridge to the museum lies the **Fröhlichen Hecht ❷,** Dorfstr. 1, a large cafe, restaurant, and Biergarten with a patio right on a river. Enjoy a *Kartoffel mit Quark* (potatoes with curd cheese) in a special Spreewald sauce (€6.50) as gondolas drift. (☎03542 27 82; www.zumhecht.com. Open daily 11am-7pm.)

LÜBBEN ☎03546

With canals and trails fanning out from all ends, little Lübben (pop. 15,000) fills with German tourists milling around the colorful Altstadt and gliding by in kayaks, canoes, and gondolas. Lübben offers easy access to wooded bike paths and hiking trails, as well as a ceaseless supply of juicy *Gurken* (pickles, the region's specialty) and fresh fish that make for a woodland picnic.

▣▨ **TRANSPORTATION AND PRACTICAL INFORMATION.** Trains go to: Berlin Ostbahnhof and other major stations (1hr., 2 per hr., €9); Cottbus (45min., every hr., €6.30); Lübbenau (10min., 2 per hr., €2). For a **taxi** call ☎403546 812 or 30 39. Rent **bikes** at the tourist office (€6 per day, €25 per week). The **tourist office** is at Ernst-von-Houwald-Damm 15. From the station, head right on Bahnhofstr., make a left on Logenstr., which becomes Lindenstr., and cross the two bridges; the office will be to the right, on the *Schloßinsel.* The staff finds private rooms (€15-40) for a €3 fee. After hours, they post a list of private rooms outside the entrance. (☎03546 30 90 or 24 33. Open Apr.-Oct. daily 10am-6pm;

Nov.-Mar. M-F 10am-4pm.) The **post office**, Poststr. 4, has a 24hr. ATM. (Open M-F 9am-6pm, Sa 9am-noon.) **Postal Code:** 15907.

⌐⌐ ACCOMMODATIONS AND FOOD. The **Jugendherberge Lübben (HI) ❶**, Zum Wendenfürsten 8, is in a field at the edge of town. Follow Bahnhofstr. to its end, turn left on Luckauer Str. and then right on Burglehnstr. before the big crossing. Go right again on Puschkinstr., which becomes Cottbuser Str., then left on Dorfaue and follow signs from there. Though remote, the hostel is dreamily flanked by a river and a stretch of hayfields and offers easy access to wilderness paths. Playground, ping-pong, and canoes available. (☎03546 30 46; www.jh-luebben.de. Breakfast and Sheets included. Reception 9am-7pm. Dorms €14.50. Campsites €10. Cash only.) For convenience, **Pension am Markt ❸**, Hauptstr. 5, can't be beat. Each large room has a kitchen and fold-out couches. (☎03546 32 72; pension-am-markt@gmx.net. Breakfast included. Doubles €54-60; 2-4 person apartments €65-95. To get to **Spreewald-Camping Lübben ❶**, follow the directions to the Jugendherberge until Puschkinstr., and then turn left at the sign, where Puschkinstr. becomes Cottbusserstr, aross the street from the sign for Burglehnstr. (☎03546 70 53; www.spreewald-camping-luebben.de. Boat rental €3.50 per hr., €20 per day; for campers €2.70/16. Reception 8am-noon and 3pm-9pm. Open from mid-Mar. to Oct. €6.50per person, €3.50-4.50 per tent.)

Don't even think about leaving Lübben without sampling the Spreewald's pickled delicacies, famous throughout Germany. **Gurken Paule ❶**, at the entrance to the tourist office plaza on the *Schloßinsel*, is an outdoor stand offering the freshest of the Spreewald's unique pickle assortment: *Salzdillgurken* (dill), *Senfgurken* (mustard), and *Gewürzgurken* (spicy). They're sold by weight, averaging €0.50 per pickle and €2.50 per jar. (Open daily 9am-6pm.) Varied local cuisine and music ranging from *Schlager* to country can be found at **Bubak ❸**, Ernst-von-Houwald-Damm 9, named after the Sorbian bogeyman who carries naughty children off into the forest. Sample the *Gurken-Kartoffelsuppe* (pickle-potato soup; €3) with local entrees (€5.50-15). (☎03546 18 61 44; www.bubak.de. Open M-F 11:30am-3pm and 5:30-10:30pm, Sa-Su 11:30am-10:30pm.)

⌐⌐ SIGHTS AND OUTDOOR ACTIVITIES. The Altstadt's architectural pride is the newly restored **Paul-Gerhardt-Kirche**, named for the most famous German hymn writer since Martin Luther. (☎03546 31 42. Open May-Aug. W 10am-noon and 3-5pm.) Gerhardt is buried inside (no one knows quite where) and immortalized outside in stone. **Der Hain**, Lübben's forested park, lies at the end of Breite Str., a continuation of Haupstr. To the south, the **Schloßinsel**, an island whose park is more impressive than its namesake palace, houses the tourist office, docks, and pricey cafes. The **Schloß** contains an exhibit on Lübben's history and culture. (Ernst-von-Houwald-Damm 14. ☎03546 18 74 78; www.schloss-luebben.de. Open Apr.-Oct Tu-Su 10am-5pm; Nov-Mar W-F 10am-4pm, Sa-Su 1pm-4pm. €4, students €2.) Most of Lübben's attractions are in the forests surrounding the town. The **Fährmannsverein "Lustige Gurken" Lübben/Spreewald**, Ernst-von-Houwald-Damm 15 on the Schloßinsel, offers boat trips exploring the Spreewald. (☎03546 71 22; www.lustige-gurken.de. Open daily 9am-4pm. 1½-7hr., €8-18.) The **Fährmannsverein "Flottes Rudel,"** at the end of the parking lot across Lindenstr. from Am Spreeufer, offers boat and barge trips with picnics starting daily at 10am. (Eisenbahnstr. 9. ☎03546 82 69; www.flottes-rudel.de. 1½-8hr. tours €8-22.) Rent kayaks or canoes at **Bootsverleih Gebauer**, Lindenstr. 18. From Luckauer Str., turn right on Lindenstr. before the tourist office. (☎03546 71 94; www.spreewald-bootsverleih.de. ID required. Open daily Apr.-Oct. 9am-7pm. M-F 1-person kayaks €8 for first 2hr., €2.50 per additional hr., €16 per day. Sa-Su €9 for first 2hr., €3 per additional hr., €19 per day.)

BERLIN

PRAGUE

Prague traces its mythical origins back to one Libuše, professional prophetess and wife of an equally mythical husband. Legend has it that Libuše had a vision while taking a bath at Vyšehrad in which she saw a marvelous city growing from the seven hills to the north of castle. Sure enough, a city did grow outward from Vyšehrad and, in time, the town of Prague began to take shape. In the 14th century, King of Bohemia and Holy Roman Emperor Charles IV refashioned the town into a city of soaring cathedrals and lavish palaces. Throughout its 1100 year history, Prague has been the center of many cultural, political, and religious movements, even if they were not always appreciated in their time. In the early 15th century, Jan Hus was burned at the stake for sharing some thoughts on papal indulgences and the Crusades. Outrage over Hus's death led to the tumultuous Hussite Wars, the rise (and fall) of Prague's other favorite Jan, surname Žižkam, as well as the first of Prague's defenestrations. In the early 20th century, the city played a central role in the development of Franz Kafka, even if the author spent most of his adult life writing in German and trying to escape the city.

HIGHLIGHTS OF PRAGUE

GAZE hundreds of miles in every direction from **Prague Castle** (p. 185), one of the largest in the world and the seat of the Czech government for 1000 years.

RELIVE the legend at the **Franz Kafka Museum (p. 190)**.

OGLE with the crowds at the Staré Město's impressive **astronomical clock** (p. 180).

A maze of shady alleys lends Prague a dark, ethereal atmosphere, which continues to captivate writers, artists, and tourists alike. Nearly every landmark in Prague's Old Town has a rich history. Since the fall of Communism, that sense of magic has become one of the city's largest industries. In the summer, travelers from all over the world flood the city, while many of the locals literally take to the hills. During these months, the tourist-to-townie ratio soars to nine-to-one. If you find yourself stuck in an Old Town weekend crowd, surrounded by thousands of people speaking every language but Czech, you may wonder why on earth anyone comes here to begin with. Though the number of westerners living in Prague has decreased since the Czech Republic joined the EU, western influence has increased dramatically. Take the metro or tram just a few stops away from Old Town or Wenceslas Square, however, and there's still plenty to enchant. The cafes and bars away from the city center are the best places to get to know the Prague that locals actually inhabit.

NEIGHBORHOODS OF PRAGUE

Shouldering the river **Vltava,** greater Prague is a mess of suburbs and maze-like streets. The river runs south to north through central Prague, separating **Staré Město** (Old Town) and **Nové Město** (New Town) from **Malá Strana** (Lesser Side) and **Hradčany.** On the right bank, **Staroměstské náměstí** (Old Town Square) is Prague's focal point. Most of the city's historical landmarks are concentrated in the few blocks around the square. From the square, the elegant **Pařížská ulice** (Paris

Street) leads north into Josefov, the old Jewish quarter. West of Staroměstské náměstí, **Karlův Most** (Charles Bridge) spans the Vltava, connecting Staré Město with **Malostranské náměstí** (Lesser Town Square). **Pražský Hrad** (Prague Castle) overlooks Malostranské náměstí from Hradčany hill. The train station and bus station lie northeast of Václavské náměstí. To reach Staroměstské náměstí, take Metro A to Staroměstská and follow Kaprova away from the river.

South of Staré Město, Nové Město houses **Václavské náměstí** (Wenceslas Square), the city's commercial core, as well as a lot of places that you might actually want to visit. Nové Město is bordered on the south by mighty **Vyšehrad.** To the east, Vinohrady is a largely residential area with some expensive restaurants. To the north of Vinohrady, you can always spot the blue collar neighborhood turned watering hole **Žižkov** by Vitkov Hill or the TV tower. Across the river from Žižkov, **Holešovice** is a former industrial area in the middle of a cultural (or at least clubbing) Renaissance. It is also home to the Prague's other major train and bus station. Nearby **Letná Park** offers fantastic views of the more happening side of the Vltava. Last and probably least, **Dejvice** is a nice neighborhood to live in, but offers relatively little for travelers to appreciate.

FACTS AND FIGURES

PRAGUE FOUNDED: AD eighth century

POPULATION: 1,200,000

AS A PERCENTAGE OF THE CZECH REPUBLIC'S POPULATION: 12

TOTAL AREA: 496 sq. km

AVERAGE ELEVATION: 235m

OFFICIAL CURRENCY: the Crown (Kč)

NUMBER OF DISTRICTS: a whopping 57

NUMBER OF HILLS: nine (Letná, Vítkov, Opyš, Větrov, Skalka, Emauzy, Vyšehrad, Karlov, and Petřín)

ANNUAL RAINFALL: 21 in.

NUMBER OF PASSENGERS WHO PASS THROUGH PRAGUE'S RUZYNĚ AIRPORT EACH YEAR: 11,000,000

NUMBER OF ISLANDS IN THE VLTAVA RIVER: 9

NUMBER OF TOWERS: roughly 500

NUMBER OF CITIES IN THE US NAMED AFTER PRAGUE: four (in Minnesota, Nebraska, Oklahoma, and Texas)

NUMBER OF METRO CARS, TRAINS, AND BUSES: almost 2000

NUMBER OF TOWERS WITH BABY INFESTATIONS: 1 (p. 188)

PRAGUE

NOVÉ MĚSTO (NEW TOWN)

While "new" may not feel like the right adjective for a town more than 650 years old, Nové Město (New Town) is an interesting mix of modernity and history. On the Prague metro, New Town is marked by the once reviled, now iconic Dancing House, set against a backdrop of 500-year-old Baroque buildings, painted in pastel colors as though the tenants were making up for the monochromatic years under Communism.

Those who demonstrated against the Communist regime in 1989 probably did not envision the massive influx of western (predominantly American) influence and capital that would transform **Wenceslas Square.** While the historic buildings are the same, their tenants have become high-end western retailers and American fast-food chains. The square and its surrounding streets have become 21st-century Prague's commercial center.

Despite the intensely commercialized areas around Wenceslas, New Town still has many cool, authentic, and reasonably priced areas to explore. The area between the river and **Jungmannova** (bordered on the north by Národní and on the south by Resslova) has some of the best cafes, coffeehouses, and bookstores in the city, while the area south of Charles Square has more than its share of beautiful churches and quiet spots ideal for an afternoon of picnics or relaxation. Nové Město is also one of the best neighborhood for budget accommodations.

☑ LET'S GO PICKS

BEST PALACE THAT ISN'T REALLY A PALACE: ☑**Veletržní Palace (p. 190).** This museum's modern art collection is more a treasure than any chest of jewels.

BEST DRESSED WAITERS: Café Savoy (p. 170), where the servers wear striped vests and black bow ties.

BEST TOWER: New Town Hall (p. 177). Scale the heights for a most incredible view of the city below.

BEST FORMER SOVIET MONU-MENT: Stalin Memorial, now the Letná Park **metronome (p. 189).**

MOST ALIENATING MUSEUM: The Kafka Museum (p. 190).

MOST OFFENSIVE CLOCK: the **astro-nomical clock** (p. 180), pre-WWII.

MOST USELESS FORTIFICATION: the **Hunger Wall** on Petřín Hill (p. 144).

BEST HANGOVER CURE: a "Small Clear Head" from ☑**Lekha Hlava (p. 165).**

BEST PLACE TO BUY BOOKS YOU CAN ACTUALLY READ: ☑**The Globe Book-store and Cafe (p. 164).**

MOST UNNECESSARY UMLAUT: the "Žižkov Liberatör" at ☑**Blind Eye** (p. 201).

BEST ONE-EYED WAR HERO: Jan Žižka. Czech out his statue on Vítkov Hill (p. 188).

MOST NARCISSISTIC FRESCO: in the Main Hall of **Wallenstein Palace (p. 185).**

BEST RESTAURANT IN A BRICK CEL-LAR WITH A VAULTED CEILING: Koz-icka (p. 166); we give it bonus points for the dozens of metal goats.

BEST GOULASH: La Bastille (p. 169).

STARÉ MĚSTO (OLD TOWN)

The fortifications around Prague's Old Town were originally built to keep foreigners out, but now they only seem to draw them in. Like many histori-cal areas, Staré Město has turned its history into a commodity, sometimes at the expense of the history itself. Many of the statues that decorate the area's 500-year-old towers are modern replicas, with the originals stashed safely away from the forces of erosion and international tourism. It's hard to appre-ciate much of the area's charm in the daytime, as you will most likely be sur-rounded by thousands of other visitors and the tourist industry that accom-modates them. Avoiding the pitfalls of the area's many restaurants (they all charge extra for bread, outdoor seating, etc.) and clubs may be just as diffi-cult as navigating the 1000-year-old jumble of narrow streets and alleys. Don't let the tourist crowds deter you from such gems as the ☑**Mucha Museum (p. 190)** or the **Museum of Czech Cubism** (p. 190). Though the structures themselves will be closed, **Charles Bridge** (p. 179) and the **Church of Our Lady Before Týn (p. 180)** are particularly beautiful in the quiet of the night. If you need to escape the quiet, the ancient labyrinth comes alive after dark when the city's youth enlivens its many bars and jazz clubs.

JOSEFOV

Josefov, Prague's historic Jewish neighborhood and Central Europe's oldest Jewish settlement, lies north of **Staroměstské náměstí** along **Maiselova.** As a reac-tion to the Pope's 1179 decree that all Christians avoid contact with Jews,

Prague's citizens built a 4m wall around the area. The gates were opened in 1784, but the walls didn't come down until 1848, when the city's Jews were granted limited civil rights. The closed neighborhood bred many fantastical stories, often concerning the famed **Rabbi Loew ben Bezalel** (1512-1609) and his legendary **Golem,** a mud creature that supposedly came to life to protect Prague's Jews. The Golem is something of a mascot for the Jewish quarter, and books about the creature as well as tiny effigies can be purchased at most gift shops in the area. When the Nazis came to power, most of Josefov's Jews were deported to Terezín (p. 205) and the death camps. Hitler's decision to create a "museum of an extinct race" spared Josefov's cemetery and synagogues from destruction. These days, four of Josefov's five synagogues have in fact become museums (p. 182), and the entire area feels more like something preserved for posterity than a place where people live.

MALÁ STRANA

Easily the most Baroque of Prague's neighborhoods, Malá Strana (the Little Quarter or the Lesser Quarter, depending on your translation) also has some of the richest (read: most disastrous) history. Destroyed by fires in 1541 and rebuilt just in time to be sacked by the Swedes in 1648 at the end of the Thirty Years' War, Malá Strana has weathered its share of strife. These days, the area has a divided feel. The northern portion, around the Charles Bridge, has almost as many needlessly infuriating cobblestone alleys as Old Town, with the tourists to boot. At the same time, the area is also home to the foreign embassies, which gives many of its cafes and restaurants an international twist. While you may feel obligated to visit a few of the sights during the day, you should spend your evenings at the southernmost end of town. Probably one of the best neighborhoods of Prague, **Újezd** contains more than its share of excellent restaurants, bars, and coffeehouses, and remains (relatively) undiscovered by the teeming masses. Malá Strana lacks the homogeneity of many of Prague's other neighborhoods and it rewards the patient traveler.

 CZECH THE ADDRESS. Prague doesn't have street signs. Most streets are marked only with a red plaque on the side of a building—if they're marked at all. Building numbers appear on small, rectangular blue plaques, though with similar unpredictability.

THE INSIDER'S CITY
BEST OF PRAGUE

Prague may be a bit more manageable (at least size-wise) than Berlin, but trying to see it all in a matter of days can be overwhelming. In this list we've tried to take the pressure off by paring it down to the best in sights, museums, food, and nightlife.

Cafe Louvre, p. 165. If it was good enough for Kafka, then by God it's good enough for the rest of us. Oh, did we mention that Einstein was also a fan?

Letná Park, p. 189. The enormous eyesore that was the Joseph Stalin statue may be have been demolished long ago, but Letná is still a great place for a beer and a picnic.

☑Astronomical Clock, p. 180. Even if you have to share the moment with a thousand other picture-snapping tourists, it's probably the coolest clock you're going to see for a while.

Dancing House, p. 177. This once-reviled piece of postmodern architecture has finally come into its own. Czech out the controversial building for yourself.

☑Cross Club, p. 203. Finally, we no longer have to choose between tiki- and techno-themed clubs: Cross Club combines the two and sets them to the soundtrack of world-class DJs and live acts.

☑Veletržní Palace, p. 190. Prague's most underrated museum is well worth the metro ride. The excellent collection focuses on the push and pull between Czech and international Modernist movements.

☑Bar Bar, p. 169. They've done it. They've made a Bar Bar.

(We didn't think it was possible, either.) Keep an open mind and bring an appetite to this inventive little restaurant in Malá Strana.

Blind Eye, p. 201 The down-and-dirtiest bar in down-and-dirty Žižkov. Adios motherf***er!

Jan Žižka Statue, p. 188. The original one-eyed badass can't be contained by a puny chain-link fence.

Museum of Czech Cubism, p. 190. Admire the pretty pictures but do not try to sit on the furniture.

Mucha Museum, p. 190. This museum, devoted to Czech master and Art Nouveau pioneer Alfons Mucha, will make you wonder why Sarah Bernhardt isn't every graphic design student's pin-up of choice.

Saint Vitus Cathedral, p. 186. The 600-year work-in-progress almost lives up to your expectations after the half hour wait to get in.

Kafka Museum, p. 190. Prague's most awesomely alienating museum will make you look at filing cabinets in a whole new way.

Vyšehrad, p. 188. Prague's other castle offers a peaceful escape from the throngs.

HRADČANY

You might feel bad if you go to Prague without visiting the famed Castle District (Hradčany). Originally a separate district, it was joined with Staré Město, Nové Město, and Malá Strana in 1784 to form the modern entity of Prague. Now less a district and more an enormous tourist attraction, you're unlikely to find much authentic Czech charm, though you will find lots of old buildings, some cooler than others.

ŽIŽKOV

While Vinohrady has traditionally played home to Prague's upper crust, nearby Žižkov remains true to its working class roots, at least in spirit. Named for the Hussite general **Jan Žižka**, the area likes to cultivate a tough, blue collar image that is perhaps less accurate now than in years past. Nevertheless, its denizens proudly announce the commonly held belief that Žižkov has the highest number of pubs per capita of any city district in Europe. While this statement technically remains unproven, the area's many excellent bars and clubs make it one of the liveliest places to be after dark.

VINOHRADY

Vinohrady takes its name from the vineyards that covered the area in the 14th century. While the vineyards may be (mostly) gone, the tinge of refinement and bourgeois sensibility remains. The area around **Bruselská** and **Londýnská** has some of the most highly regarded (and highly priced) restaurants and wine bars in Prague. Additionally, Vinohrady houses a large segment of Prague's expatriate population, so don't be surprised if someone stops you on the street to ask for directions in English.

HOLEŠOVICE

Far away from the maddening crowds, Holešovice lacks the historical sights of Old and New Towns. Still, **Letná Park** (p. 189) provides residents and tourists with a fabulous green space, and **Veletržní Palace** (p. 190) is certainly one of the city's most underrated attractions. Once heavily industrialized, the area is still home to Prague's second largest train station and a number of warehouses and factories, which are often being reappropriated for surprising ends: many have turned into popular dance clubs. You'll also notice that the farther from the city center you get, the more extravagant the hostels (if that's even the right word for them) tend to become.

DEJVICE

Nearby Dejvice has historically been a high-end suburb, and remains a more desirable place to live than to visit; the large, Soviet-era roundabout is the closest thing to a sight the area has to offer. To its credit, Dejvice does have a wide variety of international cuisine for those who don't mind shelling out a little more than they're used to.

LIFE AND TIMES

HISTORY

AND SO IT BEGINS. The details are murky on the legend of Prague's founding. Some say that the city was born after the tribal leader Čech ascended Říp Mountain near its present-day site. Others claim that Čech's granddaughter decreed it, proclaiming that a city would spring up where all that existed was the threshold *(práh)* of a house. The historical record begins with the AD first-century arrival of the Celtic **Boii.** By the AD sixth century, **Slavs** had settled in the region, and by the 10th century, the Czechs were united under the **Přemyslid Dynasty. Wenceslas** (Václav), legendary patron saint, king of Bohemia, and protagonist of the Christmas carol, was one of the dynasty's earliest rulers. Under Přemyslid rule, the fortress at Prague soon developed into a thriving town. After Bohemia's entrance into the Holy Roman Empire in 1114, Prague saw a spate of church-building and increased commerce with the west.

IMPERIAL PRAGUE. Bohemia ascended to the status of hereditary kingdom with the ascension of **Ottokar I,** a German-allied Přemyslid prince. His reign saw an influx of German immigrants and the rise of Prague as a city to be reckoned with. In the following years, three towns around the castle of Prague merged with the modern city. While the old dynasty died out in 1306, the succeeding **House of Luxembourg** presided over continued progress. In the years of **Karel IV,** Prague became an archbishopric and **Charles University,** the oldest in Central Europe and one of the oldest in European civilization, was founded. The king promoted cathedral-building in the elaborate Bohemian school, and local artists, bankrolled by German and Italian merchants and bankers, became famous.

HUSSITE FIT. Karel's eldest legitimate son, **Václav,** saw much darker times. His father's extensive realms split up amongst the heirs, Václav's only dominion was Bohemia itself. A **1389 pogrom** of Prague's Jews marred the city. It was soon followed by the chaos of the Hussite controversy. The proto-Protestant preacher, **Jan Hus,** a teacher at the University in Prague, ignited a division in Czech society with his condemnations of the corruption of Rome and the Pope and his tirades against foreigners. While the King protected and encouraged Hus for some years, Hus was eventually burned at the stake to make peace with the Church. Hus became a martyr almost immediately, and **the Hussites,** a political-religious alliance of reformist nobility, arose. War began in 1419 when radical Hussites threw members of the city council from a window of the Council House in what became the **First Defenestration** of Prague. King Václav died soon after, and decades of civil war began. The passing of Bohemia to Hapsburg rule saw a few years of glory under **Rudolf II,** who moved the imperial capital to

Prague and kept a court of astronomers, scientists, alchemists, and magicians. The ultra-Catholic Hapsburg rule had some predictable consequences, and in the **Second Defenestration** of Prague, religious tensions set off the **Thirty Years' War** (1618-48), which engulfed all of Europe. (This time the victims survived; a pile of manure cushioned the blow.) The Protestants' eventual defeat was sealed after an early, harsh blow in the **Battle of White Mountain** in November 1620. Prague would suffer most at the hands of the Protestant Saxons and Swedes, who brutally sacked the city shortly thereafter.

BAROQUE AROUND THE CLOCK. By the early 1700s, Prague was turning around, in large part due to reconstruction after several earthquakes and heavy Jewish immigration. Peace was disrupted by the **Seven Years' War,** which saw attacks by Frederick the Great of Prussia to the north, but these were the last violent invasions the city would see until the cataclysms of the 20th century. After the peace, nobility from around the Hapsburg Empire came, building palaces and churches in the Baroque fashion. Prague, made into a city of toleration for ethnic and religious minorities by Joseph II's 1781 decree, became a power-house of the Industrial Revolution, drawing on the iron and coal of Bohemia to create new wealth. A railway to Vienna was built in 1845, but it was Prague's prosperity and intellectual culture as well as the migration of rural Czech to the cosmopolitan city that made it a center for newly stirring nationalism.

CZECHMATE. Nationalist sentiment took off after the **Congress of Vienna,** with the efforts of writers and public figures known as the "patriots." These patriots, luminaries such as **Josef Jungmann** and **Pavel Šafárik** among them, led efforts to revive the use of Czech, which had long since been replaced by German among the educated and urban classes. Grammar disputes gave way to guerrilla warfare as Prague saw participation in the great European upheavals of 1848; the revolt was followed by a swift imperial backlash. Over the following decades, Czech tension with Vienna grew, though Bohemia never achieved the autonomy from Austria that Hungary had. Nonetheless, the 19th century was one of peace for Prague: the city expanded and Czech national pride took on other forms, with the creation of the National Theater and National Museum and the rise of Bohemian music and academies.

METAMORPHOSIS. The sudden storm of WWI offered an opportunity for nationalists to seize power, and the Czechs and Slovaks made a joint go at independence. In the post-war confusion, **Edvard Beneš** and **Tomáš G. Masaryk** convinced the victorious Allies to legitimize a new state that united the old lands of Bohemia, Moravia, and Slovakia into a new state, Czechoslovakia. This **First Republic,** headquartered in Prague, remained mostly free from the economic collapse and ethnic strife that went on elsewhere in Central Europe. Prague became a city of astonishing size and ethnic diversity, home to Czechs, Germans, and Jews alike. The city and the nascent country did not last long, though: Hitler had his eye on the **the Sudetenland,** a region of the republic inhabited mostly by ethnic Germans. The western Allies, seeking a way out of conflict, appeased the Fuehrer with the 1938 **Munich Agreement,** which handed the Sudetenland to Germany. It turned out that was just the appetizer, and the entire nation of Czechoslovakia soon came into Hitler's fold. Prague was transformed as the Holocaust decimated the ancient Jewish community and imposed years of poverty and oppression. In a tragic farce, Allied soldiers stood by as Nazis put down a desperate uprising in May 1945, leaving the Soviets to clean up the mess. Soviet liberation placed the territory under firm Russian control.

UN-CRUSHED VELVET. Following the end of Nazi rule and the flight of most remaining ethnic Germans, the Communists won the 1946 elections, and seized permanent power in 1948. Over the next few years, Party leaders in Prague carried out a series of horrifying **Show Trials,** during which government officials were tortured and made to recite false confessions broadcasted throughout the nation. Convicted "traitors" (many of them Jewish) were either executed or given a life sentence. Though memories of the trials continued to haunt the Czech Republic throughout the Soviet era, full details of this dark period only came into the light after the Revolution of 1989.

The country's policies were handed over through the **Warsaw Pact** and Prague became a city of Communist block apartments and slowly decaying monuments. By the mid-1960s, the de-Stalinization currents already dominant in Russia reached Czechoslovakia, leading to a slightly freer arena of debate and reversals of convictions and purges. In 1968, Communist Party Secretary **Alexander Dubček** sought to open up the centrally controlled economy and political system in a period of liberalization known as **the Prague Spring,** an attempt to build "socialism with a human face." The Spring was met with the grim face of Soviet disapproval, and Warsaw Pact forces rolled into Prague, killing the few resisters and forcing out the reformists.

Gustáv Husák became Party Secretary in 1969, ushering in 20 years of repression: he denounced the Prague Spring, consolidated power, and bestowed the title of President upon himself in 1975. Czech intellectuals protested his human rights violations with the nonviolent **Charter 77 movement** and an explosion of dissident thought and activity, but they were helpless in the face of renewed authoritarianism.

The whole Communist edifice began to shake in the late 1980s, when cracks in the Berlin Wall and the fall of Hungary and Poland opened the way for Czechoslovakia's **Velvet Revolution,** named for the nearly bloodless transition to a multi-party state system (or, as rock fans claim, for the Velvet Underground). The Communist regime's violent suppression of a peaceful student demonstration led to mass civil resistance and a nation-wide strike on November 27. Within days the Communists resigned, and **Václav Havel,** a long-imprisoned playwright and the leader of both the Charter 77 and the Velvet Revolution, became president in December 1989. Slovak cries for independence grew stronger and, after some debate, the Czech and Slovak Republics parted ways on January 1, 1993.

TODAY. The Czech Republic has enjoyed a post-Communist status as one of the most stable countries in Eastern Europe. Playwright and former dissident Václav Havel, re-elected to the presidency in 1998 by the margin of a single vote in Parliament, remained the country's official head of state until the 2003 presidential election. Havel was succeeded by **Václav Klaus,** co-founder of the powerful **Civic Democratic Party (ODS)** and former Prime Minister. Klaus continues to enjoy a soaring popularity rating. In 2004, the Social Democrat **Stanislav Gross** succeeded **Vladimír Špidla** as prime minister, becoming the youngest Prime Minister in Europe at the age of 34. Allegations of misconduct led to his resignation less than a year later and **Jiří Paroubek** soon replaced him as the leader of the troubled party. This challenge proved daunting and Paroubek resigned in August of 2006 after an inconclusive lower-house election. His replacement, **Mirek Topolánek,** organized a center-right coalition that gained the confidence of the Chamber of Deputies in 2007, but came under scrutiny for financial irregularities, and was followed by a caretaker Prime Minister with no party affiliations, **Jan Fischer.**

The Czech Republic joined NATO in March 1999 and was admitted to the EU in May 2004. Klaus, who refers to himself as a Eurorealist, has often criticized the EU's centralization and bureaucracy, but the Republic has eagerly taken

PRAGUE

part in the open movement and trade within the European Union, a significant factor in the rapid growth of the Czech economy and standard of living since the end of Communism; in some respects Czech capitalism has surpassed that of its western neighbors. In January 2009, the Czech Republic even joined the rotation of EU leadership, and took its place as presiding country of the European Council for a six-month term. While Prague may have gained even more of a European character due to the influx of tourists from Western Europe, the euro will be a visitor long in coming, as plans for its adoption have stalled.

PEOPLE AND CULTURE

LANGUAGE

Czech is a West Slavic language, mutually intelligible with Slovak and closely related to Polish. Often baffling for its vowel-free words, travelers will find that English is understood by a majority of the population and especially by young people. Knowledge of German can be useful, especially in South Bohemia. In eastern regions, you're more likely to encounter Polish. Russian was taught to all schoolchildren under Communism, but use your *"privet"* carefully, as the language has fallen out of favor. If you care to brave the Bohemian language, a phrasebook and glossary can be found in the **Appendix** on p. 275.

DEMOGRAPHICS

The Czech Republic is comprised of 94% Czechs and 2% Slovaks, having lost most of its ethnic minorities to the migrations and tumult of the 20th century. Some significant remaining minorities include Germans, Ukrainians, and Roma. A new Vietnamese community has also recently sprouted up. Recent immigrants, which also include Greeks, Turks, and Yugoslavs, are most commonly found in multiethnic Prague.

 A CENTRAL CONCERN. When your new found Czech friends ask how you're enjoying your time in the Czech Republic, never respond by saying that you love Eastern Europe. Czechs consider themselves Central European, and often take offense at being lumped together with those other Slavs.

CUSTOMS AND ETIQUETTE

Firmly held customs govern wining and dining. When served beer, wait until all raise the common *"na zdraví"* (to your health) toast before drinking, and always look into the eyes of the person with whom you are toasting. Similarly, before biting into a saucy *knedlík*, wish everyone *"dobrou chut"* (to your health), especially at lunch, the main meal of the day. As a rule, foreigners should tip at servers and taxis at a rate of around 10%.

THE ARTS

LITERATURE

Czech writers have long held a privileged position, but this has been especially true in the Modern period. From the first Czechoslovak president, T.G. Masaryk, to the recently retired Václav Havel, the literary figures who have spoken most powerfully have often also assumed political prominence. Czech literature was slower in blossoming than other European literatures, but by the 19th century, Prague was host to a truly modern literature that took strength from and transcended national pride. In 1836, **Karel Hynek Mácha** penned his celebrated epic *May (Máj)*. Initially scorned as romantic and personal, it was eventually celebrated as a powerful, moving piece. The 1858 founding of the literary journal *Máj*, named after Mácha's poem, marked the beginning of an era known as the **National Revival.** One of its brightest stars, **Bozena Nwmcová,** introduced the novel to modern Czech literature with *Granny (Babička,* 1855). **Jaroslav Hašek's** satire, *The Good Soldier Švejk (Osudy dobrého vojáka Švejka za svetové války,* 1920-23), while never finished, was quickly enshrined as the classic commentary on the absurdities of the Hapsburg order. As a new Czechoslovak nation arose from that order, poet **Viktor Dyk** became an important figure in the Czech political arena.

While Kafka's work was in German, it was his experiences as a German-speaking Jew in his native Prague that were indispensable to the magical, complex, obscure character of his writing. After Kafka, **Jaroslav Seifert** and **Vítwzslav Nezval** produced image-rich works of poetry, and Czech writers such as **Karel Čapek** moved to the vanguard of science fiction, originating the very word "robot."

Socialist Realism was all that the Communist leadership could handle after it took power in 1948, but this didn't mean the death of Czech literature. The many contradictions of life under Soviet rule provided ample inspiration for an entire generation of writers, many of whom either fled to publish in exile or went underground and published in **samizdat** (literally "self-published). *Samizdat* editions were disseminated through the intellectual community via typewriter: often in the span of just a few short days, one was expected to read the work they were handed and to type complete copies of it on carbon paper that were then distributed to friends and colleagues. As long as readers and writers steered clear of photocopiers and took precautions such as signing original works in order to claim it as a "manuscript," they couldn't technically be prosecuted for participating in the underground network. One of these *samizdat* writers, Seifert, became the first Czech writer to receive a Nobel Prize in 1984.

The Czech literary tradition, re-emerged after the occlusion of Communism, remains strong today. The country's best-known contemporary writer is Milan Kundera, whose philosophical novel *The Unbearable Lightness of Being* met with international acclaim and quickly became a classic of postmodernism.

BOHEMIAN RHAPSODY

The 19th-century National Revival brought out the best in Czech music. The nation's most celebrated composers, **Antonín Dvořák, Leoš Janáček,** and **Bedřich Smetana,** are renowned for transforming Czech folk tunes into symphonies and operas. Dvořák's Symphony No. 9, *From the New World,* which combines Czech folk tradition with melodies gathered during the composer's trip to America, is probably the most famous Czech masterpiece, though his other symphonies and chamber music compositions were widely regarded by his contemporaries. Among Czechs, however, Smetana's symphonic poem *My Country (Má vlast)* remains most popular.

Jazz and bluegrass music have seen a recent spike in popularity, with bluegrass coming to life after a 1972 European festival was held just outside Prague and local band **Poutníci** took up the mantle. The rock scene was an incredibly influential factor in Czech dissident culture; it was the arrest of the seminal band **The Plastic People of the Universe** that prompted Charter 77. Their quirky example has been followed by the currents of New Wave and metal. **Support Lesbiens** is a popular band with New Age and rock features. American pop music has always been very popular here, but the lyrics are usually sung over in Czech.

START: Kafka Statue, corner Dušní and Žatecká.

FINISH: New Jewish Cemetery, Žižkov.

DURATION: 2½-4hr.

WHEN TO GO: Early afternoon.

CAVORTING WITH KAFKA

Though Prague is only mentioned by name a few times in any of Kafka's works, the city left indelible mark on the writer's psyche. A German-Jew, Kafka was doubly marginalized durin time when anti-foreign and anti-Semitic feelings were strong. Though he tried to leave Pra for Vienna and Berlin several times in his life, he always found himself drawn back to the cit his birth. The Prague of today is vastly different from Kafka's city, but many of his old haunts still worth a visit. We can only imagine how he would feel knowing that the city he felt so dist from has now made him one of its prime tourist attractions.

1. KAFKA STATUE. Between the Spanish Synagogue and a nearby catholic church stands only statue in Prague dedicated to its most alienated son. Jaroslav Rona's statue of Kafka quickly become one of the city's favorites. The writer appears seated on the shoulders of enormous set of clothes, his finger pointed forward as if to say, "That way!" or perhaps, "I th that guy owes me money" (p. 183).

2. FRANZ KAFKA'S BIRTHPLACE. The downer-to-be was born on July 3, 1883, in an tenement building on the corner of Kaprova and Maiselova streets. Though the tenement long since come down, there is a small marker on the side of the building marking the site.

3. DŮM U MINUTY. Kafka spent part of his childhood in the House on the Minute (Dům Minuty) across from the famed Astronomical Clock (p. 180), which at that time still spor an anti-Semitic statue, complete with beard and horns, for its depiction of Greed. While yo waiting with your thousand closest friends for the clock to strike, take a minute to admire building's two-tone frescos, which depict various biblical and classical scenes.

4. NATIONAL GALLERY AT GOLTZ-KINSKY PALACE. Kafka attended an elite second school on the second floor of the Goltz-Kinsky Palace. Every morning, he would make the w from the House on the Minute to the school, accompanied by his family's hostile cook. T seemingly inconsequential pattern seems to have had a profound effect on young Kafka, as mentions the routine more than once in his letters and journals.

5. FRANZ KAFKA MUSEUM. Across the river, the Franz Kafka museum attempts to tell K ka's story, largely through his relationship to Prague. The museum contains many of the write journals and letters as well as first editions of most of his works. The various audio-visual inst lations attempt to place you inside his mindset. If the haunting soundtrack and endless corrid of filing cabinets don't make you feel appropriately isolated and insignificant, then you might too cheery for this walking tour (p. 190).

6. PETŘÍN HILL. Petřín Hill was one of Kafka's favorite places to go as a teenager. It is a one of the only places ever mentioned explicitly by name in Kafka's works. His story, "Desc tion of a Struggle" warns against scaling its slopes during winter, though the view from the during a summer evening is still excellent. Rest up here for a while, and then prepare for long haul to Žižkov (p. 183).

7. CAFÉ LOUVRE. After the walk (or funicular ride) from Petřín, have a cup of coffee in elegant café. Kafka and his friends used to gather here every fortnight to debate current eve and philosophy. These are still perfectly acceptable topics of conversation, although nowad it's also a great place to reread "The Metamorphosis" (p. 165).

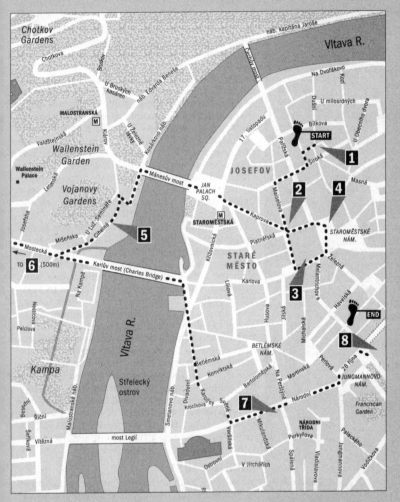

7.

GRAND HOTEL EUROPA. From Národní, make your way to the base of Wenceslas Square and start walking toward the National Museum. Though Wenceslas Square has undergone many changes over the past century, the Grand Hotel Europa, with much of its original Art Nouveau decor preserved inside and out, remains one of its most identifiable landmarks. On the second floor cafe, Kafka gave a reading of his recently completed story, "The Judgment," to an appreciative audience that didn't seem to mind having a damper put over their meal.

8. KAFKA'S GRAVE. Kafka died in 1924 at the age of 40. Though Kafka's relationship with his Jewish heritage was very complex, he received a traditional Jewish burial. His grave, along with those of his parents, can be found in the New Jewish Cemetery in Žižkov. From the main entrance, walk to the right of the ceremonial hall, and you will find signs pointing to the author's grave (sector 21, row 14, plot 33).

GOING ENTROPIC OVER ENTROPA

On January 12, 2009, the Czech Republic unveiled a massive art installation intended to celebrate its temporary presidency of the Council for the European Union (EU). *Entropa*, the brainchild of renowned Czech artist David Černý (see **Chumming with Černý**, p. 194), was commissioned to be the joint work of 27 artists, one from each of the EU countries. The piece was meant to include a representation of each country to show the EU's diversity and unity, but Černý's vision wasn't exactly what the good councilpeople had bargained for.

The portrayals of many of the countries were controversial, to say the least. Romania was represented as a Dracula theme park, France by a map embellished with *"GRÈVE!"* ("strike"), and Luxembourg by a lump of gold on sale for the highest bidder. Perhaps the icing on the cake was the depiction of Bulgaria as a Turkish toilet, which was subsequently covered in cloth at the outraged nation's request.

David Černý had no collaborators to speak of, either. He had created fake names and emails for the other 26 artists. He was initally accused of fraud, but all charges have been dropped.

After three tumultuous months, Černý requested that "Entropa" be taken down from its spot inside the European Council building in Brussels.

VISUAL ARTS

Czech artistry blossomed under Karel IV, who made Prague a center for painters such as **Master Theodoricus.** Under the kingship of the later Emperor Rudolph II, artists from across Europe again flocked to the Mother of Cities. Czech art became truly national in the 19th century, as painters such as **František Ženíšek** put their art into the service of the National Revival—his paintings can be seen today in the National Theater (see **Museums, p. 190**).

Modern art begins with one word: **Cubism.** One of the earliest names of Czech Cubism is **Emil Filla,** who incorporated the trauma of the world wars and the Buchenwald concentration camp into his art. The movement also includes **Josef Čapek,** brother of futurist writer Karl Čapek and a cartoonist best known for his satirical depiction of Hitler's ascent to power, and **Otto Gutfreund,** creator of the first Cubist sculpture, *Anxiety.* Surrealism, quite at home in Prague, the most surreal of cities, also reshaped Czech art, with the anti-war work of Prague native **Marie Čerminová Toyen.** Toyen later immigrated to Paris in the 1920s to work with André Breton, joining **Josef Šíma,** a noted and innovative painter.

One of the most important Czech artists of the 20th century, **Alfons Mucha** also worked in Paris and helped develop Art Nouveau. The capital hosts the annual **Art Prague** each May, a modern art exhibition that expands each year as interest increases. The prankster spirit of Czech art has been kept alive in modern times by **David Černý p. 195**, an artist reknowned for painting a Soviet war memorial pink and submitting the art for the Czech Republic's EU presidency; a wall of disparaging stereotypes of each European member state.

ARCHITECTURE

While few Czech architects have become household names, the country has a long and proud architectural tradition. During the 1300s, such monuments such as the St. Vitus Cathedral and the Charles Bridge were constructed. Picturesque neighborhoods such as **Český Krumlov** and **Kutná Hora (p. 205)** have been declared protected cultural monuments by UNESCO for their medieval buildings and winding streets. The first modern currents in Czech architecture were dominated by German and Italian architects, with the latter arriving in the Renaissance and establishing a small colony in the Malá Strana quarter of Prague, creating very unique takes on Baroque design. This style became truly Czech with the works of the Swiss-Czech architect **Jan Blažej Santini-Aichel.** As Bohemia entered modernity, native Cubist architects began to transform Prague through structures such as the **House of the Black Madonna** designed by **Josef Gočár.** Other famed architects of the day included **Pavel Janák,** one of the fathers of **Rondocubism,** an attempt to combine the modernity of Cubism and the humanity of folk styles and decoration. Czech architecture has taken to the world stage through such contemporary names as **Jan Kaplický.**

THEATER

The stage has always been important to Czech art, with writers such as the towering Václav Havel crossing from poetry or prose to playwriting and back. Czech-language theater was one of the key components of the National Revival under such actor-playwrights as **Prokop Šedivý.** These efforts culminated in the National Theater, one of the oldest institutions of Czech culture. Dvořák wrote 13 operas, of which the most globally acclaimed is *Rusalka.* Smetana's *The Bartered Bride* is another very well-known opera. The 20th century saw the immense output of **Leoš Janáček,** who integrated Czech language into the structure of his operas and dramas, of which *Jenufa* is perhaps most famous. His other works, including *Taras Bulba,* an adaptation of the Russian novel, are also classics of his time. Modern drama has been equally significant, and saw its beginnings in the German-language work of Prague writers such as **Paul Kornfeld,** later followed by the works of **Karel Čapek.** Former president Havel is the most renowned 20th-century Czech playwright. His plays, *The Garden Party* perhaps best-known among them, and his manifestos helped give voice to the dissident spirit of the 1970s.

FILM

Film quickly became a Czech forte, with the greatest achievements of the field coming with the **New Wave** filmmakers of the 1960s. These directors, who include **Miloš Forman, Ivan Passer,** and **Jiří Menzel,** were interested in experiment, realism, and humanistic observation. In 1965, *The Shop on Main Street,* directed by **Jan Kádár,** won the Academy Award for Best Foreign Film. Two years later Menzel's *Closely Watched Trains (Ostre sledované vlaky)* won the same award. **Barrandov Studios,** the Prague-located hub of Czech filmmaking, became known as the "Hollywood of the East." The fresh courage of these directors worried the Communist regime, and during Normalization, creativity was either stifled or forced abroad. Forman immigrated to the US in 1968 and conquered the film scene with the acclaimed *One Flew Over the Cuckoo's Nest* (1975). His 1984 film *Amadeus* won eight Oscars. In recent years, native cinema has become increasingly popular in the Czech Republic, and Karlovy Vary (p. 206) hosts a major film festival. In 1997, **Jan Svěrák's** *Kolya* won the Oscar for Best Foreign Language Film.

⌗ INTERCITY TRANSPORTATION

Flights: Ruzyně Airport (PRG; ☎220 111 111), 20km northwest of the city. Take bus #119 to ⓜA: Dejvická (12Kč, luggage 6Kč per bag); buy tickets from kiosks or machines. Airport **buses** run by Cedaz (☎220 114 296; 20-45 min., 2 per hr.) collect travelers from náměstí Republiky (120Kč); try to settle on a price before departing.

Trains: (☎221 111 122, international 224 615 249; www.vlak.cz). Prague has 4 main terminals. **Hlavní nádraží,** ⓜC: Hlavní nádraží (☎224 615 786) and **Nádraží Holešovice,** ⓜC: Nádraží Holešovice (☎224 624 632) are the largest and cover most international service. Domestic trains leave from **Masarykovo nádraží,** ⓜB: náměstí Republiky (☎840

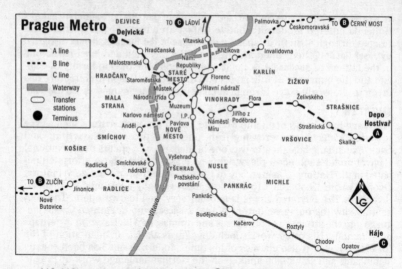

Prague Metro

- – – A line
- ···· B line
- — C line
- ▨ Waterway
- ◯ Transfer stations
- ● Terminus

DEJVICE
Dejvická Ⓐ
TO Ⓒ LÁDVÍ
Palmovka
Českomoravská
TO Ⓑ ČERNÝ MOST
Vltavská
Hradčanská
Křižíkova
Invalidovna
Malostranská
Nám.-Republiky
HRADČANY
Staroměstská
STARÉ MĚSTO
Florenc
KARLÍN
ŽIŽKOV
Můstek
Hlavní nádraží
Želivského
MALA STRANA
Národní třída
VINOHRADY
Flora
STRAŠNICE
Muzeum
Karlovo náměstí
I.P. Pavlova
Náměstí Míru
Jiřího z Poděbrad
Depo Hostivař
Anděl
NOVÉ MĚSTO
Strašnická
Skalka
SMÍCHOV
VRŠOVICE Ⓐ
KOŠIRE
Vyšehrad
Radlická
Smíchovské nádraží
VYŠEHRAD
Pražského povstání
NUSLE
MICHLE
TO Ⓑ ZLIČÍN
Jinonice
RADLICE
PANKRÁC
Nové Butovice
Pankrác
Budějovická
Kačerov
Roztyly
Háje Ⓒ
Chodov
Opatov

Vltava

112 113) and from **Smíchovské nádraží,** ⓂB: Smíchovské nádraží (☎972 226 150). International trains run to: **Berlin** (5hr., 6 per day, 1400Kč); **Bratislava, SLK** (5hr., 6 per day, 650Kč); **Budapest** (7-9hr., 5 per day, 1450Kč); **Kraków, POL** (7-8hr., 3 per day, 950Kč); **Moscow** (31hr., 1 per day, 3000Kč); **Munich, DEU** (7hr., 3 per day, 1400Kč); **Vienna, AUT** (4-5hr., 7 per day, 1000Kč); **Warsaw, POL** (9hr., 2 per day, 1300Kč).

Buses: (☎900 144 444; www.vlak-bus.cz.) State-run **ČSAD** (☎257 319 016) has several terminals. The biggest is **Florenc,** Křižíkova 4 (☎900 149 044; ⓂB or C: Florenc). Info office open daily 6am-9pm. To: **Berlin** (7hr., 2 per day, 900Kč); **Budapest** (8hr., 3 per day, 1600Kč); **Paris, FRA** (15hr., 2 per day, 2200Kč); **Sofia, BGR** (24hr., 2 per day, 1600Kč); **Vienna, AUT** (5hr., 1 per day, 600Kč). 10% ISIC discount. **Tourbus** office (☎224 218 680; www.eurolines.cz), at the terminal, sells Eurolines and airport shuttle tickets. Open M-F 7am-7pm, Sa 8am-7pm, Su 9am-7pm.

⊫ LOCAL TRANSPORTATION

Public Transportation: Buy interchangeable tickets for the bus, Metro, and tram at newsstands, *tabák* kiosks, machines in stations, or the DP (*Dopravní podnik;* transport authority) kiosks. Validate tickets in machines above escalators to avoid fines issued by plainclothes inspectors who roam transport lines. 3 **metro** lines run daily 5am-midnight: A is green on maps, B yellow, C red. **Night trams** #51-58 and **buses** #502-514 and 601 run after the last metro and cover the same areas as day trams and buses (2 per hr. 12:30am-4:30am); look for dark blue signs with white letters at bus stops. 18Kč tickets are good for a 20min. ride or 5 stops. 26Kč tickets are valid for 1hr., with transfers, for all travel in the same direction. Large bags and baby carriages 6Kč. DP offices (☎296 191 817; www.dpp.cz; open daily 7am-9pm), in the Muzeum stop on ⓂA and C lines, sell **multi-day passes** (1-day 100Kč, 3-day 330Kč, 5-day 500Kč).

Taxis: **City Taxi** (☎257 257 257) and **AAA** (☎140 14). 40Kč base, 25Kč per km, 5Kč per min. waiting. Hail a cab anywhere, but call ahead to avoid getting ripped off.

PRAGUE

GOING THE DISTANCE. To avoid being scammed by taxis, always ask in advance for a receipt (*Prosím, dejte mi paragon;* "please, give me a receipt") with distance traveled and price paid.

Car Rental: Europcar, Elišky Krásnohorské 9 (☎224 811 290; www.europcar.cz). Cars from 830Kč per day. Anyone planning on renting a car must have a European driver's license. Open daily 8am-8pm. AmEx/D/MC/V.

Bike Rental: City Bike, Královdorská 5 (☎776 180 284), rents bikes for 2, 3, or 4hr., or all day. All bikes come with a helmet, lock, map, and drink. First 2hr. 300Kč, each additional hr 50Kč up to maximum 500Kč. Open daily 9am-7pm. Cash only.

⚡ PRACTICAL INFORMATION

TOURIST AND FINANCIAL SERVICES

Tourist Offices: Green "i"s mark tourist offices. **Pražská Informační Služba** (**PIS**; Prague Information Service; ☎420 12 444; www.pis.cz) is in the **Staroměstské Radnice** (Old Town Hall). Open Apr.-Oct. daily 9am-7pm; Nov.-Mar. daily 9am-6pm. **Branches** at Na příkopě 20 and Hlavní nádraží. Open in summer M-F 9am-7pm, Sa-Su 9am-5pm; in winter M-F 9am-6pm, Sa 9am-3pm. Branch in the tower by the Malá Strana side of the Charles Bridge. Open Apr.-Oct. daily 10am-6pm.

Budget Travel: CKM, Mánesova 77 (☎222 721 595; www.ckm-praha.cz). ⓂA: Jiřího z Poděbrad. Sells budget airline tickets to those under 26. Also books accommodations in Prague from 350Kč. Open M-Th 10am-6pm, F 10am-4pm. **GTS,** Ve smečkách 27 (☎222 119 700; www.gtsint.cz). ⓂA or C: Muzeum. Offers student discounts on airline tickets (225-2500Kč in Europe). Open M-F 8am-10pm, Sa 10am-5pm.

Embassies and Consulates: See **Consular Services Abroad,** (p. 8).

Currency Exchange: Exchange counters are everywhere but rates vary wildly. Train stations have high rates. Never change money on the street. **Chequepoints** are plentiful and open late, but they often charge large commissions. **Komerční banka,** Na příkopě 33 (☎222 432 111), buys notes and checks at a 2% commission. Open M and W 8:30am-5pm, Tu and Th 8:30am-5pm, F 8:30am-5:30pm. There's a 24hr. **Citibank** at Rytířska 24.

American Express/Interchange: Václavské náměstí 56 (☎222 800 224). ⓂA or C: Muzeum. AmEx **ATM** outside. Western Union services available. MC and V **cash advances** (3% commission). Open daily 9am-7pm.

NO EASY RIDING. You might be tempted to try out one of the many bike tours offered throughout the city, but you may want to think twice: Prague's narrow streets weren't made to accommodate bikes (and drivers rarely bother), and the cobblestones may rattle your teeth out. If you really want to go on a tour, consider one of the many walking tours.

LOCAL SERVICES

Luggage Storage: Lockers in train and bus stations take 2 5Kč coins. For storage over 24hr., use the luggage offices to the left in the basement of Hlavní nádraží. 25Kč per day, bags over 15kg 40Kč. Fine for forgotten lock code 30Kč. Open daily 6-11am, 11:30am-5:30pm, and 6pm-5:30am.

English-Language Bookstore: ◪The Globe Bookstore, Ptrossova 6 (☎224 934 203; www.globebookstore.cz). ⓜB: Národní třída. Exit metro left on Spálená, take the 1st right on Ostrovní, and then the 3rd left on Pštrossova. Wide variety of new and used books and periodicals. Cafe upstairs with an expansive menu of teas, coffees, and mixed drinks. Internet 1Kč per min. Open daily 9:30am-1am.

EMERGENCY AND COMMUNICATIONS

Medical Services: Na Homolce (Hospital for Foreigners), Roentgenova 2 (☎257 271 111, after hours 257 272 146; www.homolka.cz). Bus #167. Open 24hr. **Canadian Medical Center,** Velesavínská 1 (☎235 360 133, after hours 724 300 301; www.cmc. praha.cz). Open M, W, and F 8am-6pm, Tu and Th 8am-8pm.

24hr. Pharmacy: U Lékárna Anděla, Štefánikova 6 (☎257 320 918, at night 257 324 686). ⓜB: Anděl. After hours, press the button marked "Pohotovost" to the left of the main door for service.

Telephones: Phone cards sold at kiosks, post offices, and some exchange establishments for 200Kč and 300Kč. Coins also accepted (local calls from 5Kč per min.).

Internet: The post office (see below), almost any cafe, and many restaurants will have Wi-Fi. ◪**Bohemia Bagel,** Masná 2 (☎224 812 560; www.bohemiabagel.cz), ⓜA: Staroměstská. 2Kč per min. Open M-F 7am-midnight, Sa-Su 8am-midnight.

Post Office: Jindřišská 14 (☎221 131 445). ⓜA or B: Můstek. Internet 1Kč per min. Open daily 2am-midnight. Windows open until 7:30pm. **Postal Code:** 11000.

⌂ ⛺ ACCOMMODATIONS AND CAMPING

Hotel prices are through the roof in Prague, especially anywhere near the city center. Reservations are a must; if you plan to visit in the summer, consider calling several months in advance. The situation at hostels is not much better. Rates are nothing like they were even two or three years ago. Hostels in the city center and some of the nicer ones on the outskirts often fill up during the summer, so don't show up with a rucksack and bags under your eyes at one in the morning and expect to find a room. Increasingly, travelers are turning to short term sublets. Websites like the **Craigslist** (prague.craigslist.com) and **Expats. cz** (www.expats.cz) often have ads posted from potential renters. As with anything you find on the internet, do your research, don't wire anybody any money, and never give out your driver's license, passport, or credit card numbers.

If you tote a backpack in **Hlavní nádraží** or **Holešovice** stations, you will likely be approached by hostel runners offering cheap beds. Many of these are university dorms vacated from June to August, and they often provide free transportation. These living situations might be less than ideal, however, as the summer staff at the dorms rarely speaks English and won't be able to help you if you can't find the dorm. More personal, better-appointed options can be had at similar prices. Staff at hostels almost always speak English and can be invaluable resources for information about the city. Budget hotels are scarce, and generally the better hostel options offer more bang for your buck.

Staré Město has hostels closest to the action, but that proximity means you're more likely to get something overpriced or unfurnished. Additionally, sound tends to travel right through the walls of the older buildings around the square, so roaming stag parties or pub crawls could make your evening less than restful. **Nové Město**provides a good balance between quality, price, and proximity. Unless you're looking for a swimming pool, this area is probably your best bet. Generally

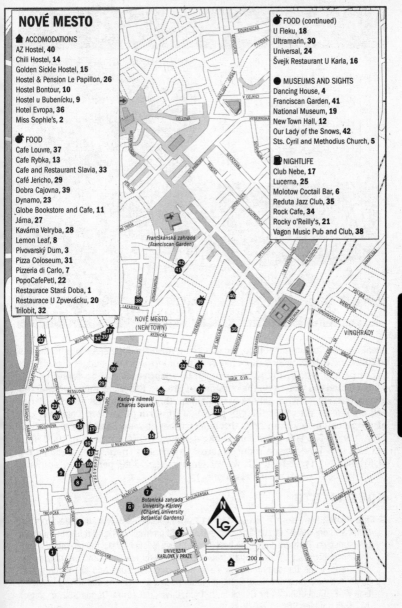

NOVÉ MESTO

ACCOMMODATIONS
AZ Hostel, **40**
Chili Hostel, **14**
Golden Sickle Hostel, **15**
Hostel & Pension Le Papillon, **26**
Hostel Bontour, **10**
Hostel u Bubenícku, **9**
Hotel Evropa, **36**
Miss Sophie's, **2**

FOOD
Cafe Louvre, **37**
Cafe Rybka, **13**
Cafe and Restaurant Slavia, **33**
Café Jericho, **29**
Dobra Cajovna, **39**
Dynamo, **23**
Globe Bookstore and Cafe, **11**
Jáma, **27**
Kavárna Velryba, **28**
Lemon Leaf, **8**
Pivovarský Dum, **3**
Pizza Coloseum, **31**
Pizzeria di Carlo, **7**
PopoCafePetl, **22**
Restaurace Stará Doba, **1**
Restaurace U Zpvevácku, **20**
Trilobit, **32**

FOOD (continued)
U Fleku, **18**
Ultramarin, **30**
Universal, **24**
Švejk Restaurant U Karla, **16**

MUSEUMS AND SIGHTS
Dancing House, **4**
Franciscan Garden, **41**
National Museum, **19**
New Town Hall, **12**
Our Lady of the Snows, **42**
Sts. Cyril and Methodius Church, **5**

NIGHTLIFE
Club Nebe, **17**
Lucerna, **25**
Molotow Coctail Bar, **6**
Reduta Jazz Club, **35**
Rock Cafe, **34**
Rocky o'Reilly's, **21**
Vagon Music Pub and Club, **38**

Frantškánská zahrada
(Franciscan Garden)

NOVÉ MESTO
(NEW TOWN)

VINOHRADY

Karlovo náměstí
(Charles Square)

Botanická zahrada
University Karlovy
(Charles University
Botanical Gardens)

UNIVERZITA
KARLOVA V PRAZE

0   200 yds
0   200 m

PRAGUE

speaking, the farther out you go, the nicer your hostel becomes. Accommodations in **Žižkov** and **Holešovice** look more like resorts for hipsters than budget digs.

For people who really want to rough it, **campgrounds** can be found on the Vltava Islands as well as on the outskirts of Prague. **Bungalows** must be reserved ahead, but tent sites are generally available without prior notice. Tourist offices sell a guide to sites near the city (20Kč). Just north of town in **Troja,** you can also rent campsites from April through October at **Camp Sokol Troja ❶,** Trojská 171A. (☎233 542 908; www.camp-sokol-troja.cz. 120Kč per person; 100-170Kč per tent site. Low-season reduced rates. Cash only.) There's also **Camp Herzog ❶,** Trojská 161. (☎283 850 472; www.campherzog.cz. 80Kč per person, students 55Kč; 60-150Kč per tent site. Cash only.)

NOVÉ MĚSTO

Chili Hostel, Pštrossova 7 (☎603 119 113; www.chili.dj). Ⓜ B: Národní třída. From the metro station, walk south on Spálená, make a right on Myslíkova, and then another right on Pštrossova. Perhaps one of the best located Nové Město hostels, though there's nothing especially spicy about it, apart from the orange and red walls and the racy anime posters that line the common area walls. The rooms, spacious and simply furnished, come in a wide range of sizes. Common room open 24 hr. Linens and towels included. Free Wi-Fi. Reception 24 hr. Check-in 2:30am. Check-out 11am. Dorms 322Kč; singles 1475Kč; doubles 966Kč. MC/V. ❶

Golden Sickle Hostel, Vodičkova 10 (☎222 230 773; www.goldensickle.com). Ⓜ B: Karlovo náměstí. From the metro station, cross the park and then turn left on Vodičkova; there will be small signs on the wall directing you to the hostel. In a 16th-century build-

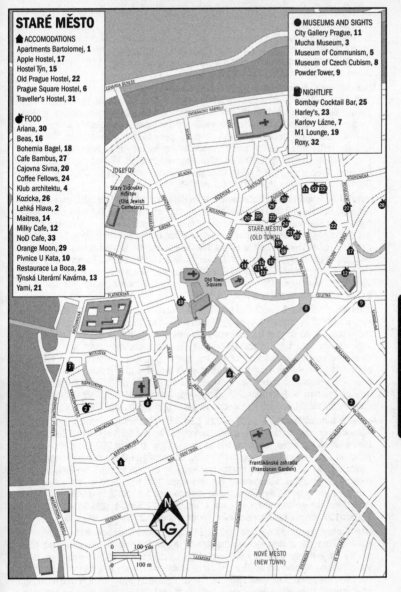

STARÉ MĚSTO

ACCOMODATIONS
Apartments Bartolomej, **1**
Apple Hostel, **17**
Hostel Týn, **15**
Old Prague Hostel, **22**
Prague Square Hostel, **6**
Traveller's Hostel, **31**

FOOD
Ariana, **30**
Beas, **16**
Bohemia Bagel, **18**
Cafe Bambus, **27**
Cajovna Sivna, **20**
Coffee Fellows, **24**
Klub architektu, **4**
Kozicka, **26**
Lehká Hlava, **2**
Maitrea, **14**
Milky Cafe, **12**
NoD Cafe, **33**
Orange Moon, **29**
Pivnice U Kata, **10**
Restaurace La Boca, **28**
Týnská Literární Kavárna, **13**
Yami, **21**

MUSEUMS AND SIGHTS
City Gallery Prague, **11**
Mucha Museum, **3**
Museum of Communism, **5**
Museum of Czech Cubism, **8**
Powder Tower, **9**

NIGHTLIFE
Bombay Cocktail Bar, **25**
Harley's, **23**
Karlovy Lázne, **7**
M1 Lounge, **19**
Roxy, **32**

JOSEFOV

Starý Zidovský
Hřbitov
(Old Jewish
Cemetery)

STARÉ MĚSTO
(OLD TOWN)

Old Town
Square

Frantskánská zahrada
(Franciscan Garden)

0   100 yds
0   100 m

N

LG

NOVÉ MĚSTO
(NEW TOWN)

PRAGUE

ing within view of New Town Hall. Clean, comfortable rooms overlooking a courtyard. Each dorm has its own bath and full kitchen. Hot breakfast can be arranged in advance for 100Kč. Towels and linens included. Free Wi-Fi and internet. Pickups from the airport 590Kč for groups of 1-4. Discounts at many nearby restaurants. Reception 9am-9pm, though arrangements can be made for late arrivals. Check-out 11am. Dorms 420Kč; 2-bed apartments 1680. Cash only. ❶

Miss Sophie's, Melounová 3 (☎296 303 530; www.missophies.com). Ⓜ C: IP Pavlova. Take 1st left from subway platform, then follow Katerinská to 1st right onto Melounová. This hostel is a little less centrally located than other places in Nové Město, but it makes up for its location with style to spare. Foregoes the worn-in, cozy feel of most small hostels for sleek, ultra modern bedroom furnishings. The dimly lit brick cellar would be the perfect place to smoke expensive cigarettes and chat suavely about deconstructivism, if smoking weren't banned. Kitchen available. Linens included. Free internet and Wi-Fi. Reception 24hr. Check-in 2pm. Check-out 11am. Dorms 590Kč; singles from 2100Kč. AmEx/MC/V.❷

Hostel U Melounu (by the Watermelons), Ke Karlovu 7 (☎224 918 322; www.hostelu-melounu.cz). Ⓜ C: I.P. Pavlova. From the metro station, walk down Legerova and make a right on Ke Karlovu. Follow it around the corner; the hostel will be on your right. A little out of the way, but with comfortable, medium-sized dorms and an inviting, TV-equipped common room. The real selling points are the cottage-like private rooms opening out onto a garden. Breakfast included. Lockers with a 100Kč deposit. Towels with a 50Kč deposit. Laundry available. Free Wi-Fi. Parking 150Kč per day. Reception 24hr. Check-in 2pm. Check-out 10am. Dorms 400Kč; private rooms in shared garden-side apartment 850Kč, with personal bath 990Kč. MC/V. ❶

AZ Hostel, Jindřišská 5 (☎224 241 664; www.hostel-az.cz). Ⓜ A or B: Můstek. From the metro, walk up the square toward the National Museum, then make a left on Jindřišská; the hostel will be on your left. This relatively new hostel offers simple yet flexible lodgings with no bunk beds, a self-service kitchen, and a common room with a TV/DVD player and comfy couches. And for a place located just off Wencelas Sq., the rates are surprisingly reasonable. Laundry included. Wi-Fi available on 1st floor and in common area, less reliable on higher floors. Wheelchair-accessible via lift, though the showers may be too narrow. Reception 24hr. Check-out 11am. Dorms 320Kč; singles 950Kč; doubles 500Kč. 10% discount for stays longer than 6 nights. MC/V. ❷

Hostel u Bubeníčků, Myslíkova 8 (☎222 539 539; ububenicku.hotel.cz). Ⓜ B: Karlovo náměstí. From the metro, take Resslova toward the river and then right on Na Zderaze and then a left on Myslíkova, the hostel will be on your right. In a UNESCO-protected building, attached to a restaurant of the same name. Combines great location with reasonable prices, and live jazz out on the terrace makes up for the lack of more conventional common areas. Apartments come with TVs and larger-than-normal beds. Hot breakfast of pancakes and eggs 100Kč. Linens included. Reception 1-11pm in the restaurant, though later times can be arranged. Check-out 11am. Dorms 200Kč; singles 1800Kč; doubles 960Kč. 10% discount at the restaurant. Children under 12 stay free. MC/V. ❶

Hotel Evropa, Václavské náměstí (☎224 215 387; www.lou-evropahotel.cz). Ⓜ A or B: Můstek. From the metro, walk up the square toward the National Museum; the hotel will be on your left. Built near the turn of the century in the Art Nouveau style, Hotel Evropa is one of the most opulent and recognizable buildings along Wencelas Sq. While the beds themselves are small, even by Prague standards, each room is well furnished. Student-rate floor with slightly more modest though significantly cheaper amenities. Book ahead using the website listed, as student rates aren't available at the reception desk. Free Wi-Fi. Check-in 1pm. Check-out 10am. Student rate singles 600Kč; doubles 900Kč. 10% discount for cash payment. AmEx/D/MC/V. ❷

Hostel Bontour, Myslíkova 22 (☎224 922 097; www.bontourhostel.cz). Ⓜ B: Karlovo náměstí. From the metro, take Karlovo náměstí north and then turn left on Odborů;

the hostel is on the corner. Cheap rooms with few amenities close to the metro stop. Shared bathrooms. Linens included. Laundry available. Free Wi-Fi. Reception 10am-8pm. Check-in 2pm. Check-out 11am. Dorms 380; singles 1050Kč; doubles 1200. Dorms only available to those under 30. MC/V. ❶

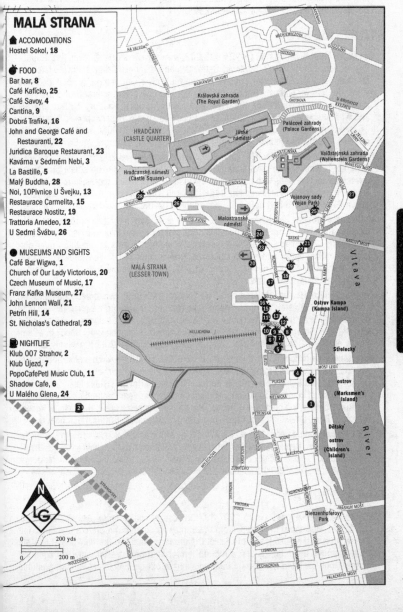

MALÁ STRANA

🏠 ACCOMODATIONS
Hostel Sokol, **18**

🍴 FOOD
Bar bar, **8**
Café Kafíčko, **25**
Café Savoy, **4**
Cantina, **9**
Dobrá Trafika, **16**
John and George Café and
Restauranti, **22**
Juridica Baroque Restaurant, **23**
Kavárna v Sedmém Nebi, **3**
La Bastille, **5**
Malý Buddha, **28**
Noi, 10Pivnice U Švejku, **13**
Restaurace Carmelita, **15**
Restaurace Nostitz, **19**
Trattoria Amedeo, **12**
U Sedmi Švábu, **26**

⬤ MUSEUMS AND SIGHTS
Café Bar Wigwa, **1**
Church of Our Lady Victorious, **20**
Czech Museum of Music, **17**
Franz Kafka Museum, **27**
John Lennon Wall, **21**
Petřín Hill, **14**
St. Nicholas's Cathedral, **29**

⬤ NIGHTLIFE
Klub 007 Strahov, **2**
Klub Újezd, **7**
PopoCafePetl Music Club, **11**
Shadow Cafe, **6**
U Malého Glena, **24**

PRAGUE

Hostel & Pension Le Papillon, Jungmannova 5 (☎606 854 123; www.papillon-hostel. cz). ⓂB: Národní třída. From the metro, take Charátova and then turn right on Jungmannova; the hostel is on the left through the big iron gate. In the middle of Nové Město commercial district and only a short walk from Karlovo náměstí, Papillon's location is definitely its major selling point. The dorms aren't the nicest around, however, and the only single looks as if it had been designed by an eight year old girl, not that there's anything wrong with that. Parking available in garage. Check-in 3pm. Check-out 10am. Dorms 318Kč; singles 800Kč. Cash only. ❶

STARÉ MĚSTO

Travellers' Hostel, Dlouhá 33 (☎224 826 662; www.travellers.cz). ⓂB: Náměstí. Republiky. Branches at Husova 3, Střelecký Ostrov 36, and U Lanové Dráhy 3. Private kitchens for each dorm and set of single rooms means you'll always have a pretty good idea who stole your leftover goulash. Bar on the 3rd floor is a convenient alternative to the standard pub crawl (beer 25Kč). Breakfast and linens included. Laundry 150Kč. Internet and Wi-Fi. Reception 24hr. Check-in 1pm. Check-out 10am. Reserve ahead in summer. 16-bed dorms 350Kč, 6-bed 480Kč, 4-bed 500Kč; singles 1190Kč, with bath 1390Kč; doubles 1380Kč per person, with bath 1600Kč. 40Kč ISIC discount. AmEx/MC/V. ❶

Hostel Týn, Týnská 19 (☎224 828 519; www.hostel-tyn.web2001.cz). ⓂB: Náměstí Republiky. Follow Týnská away from Old Town Sq. The dorms may be small, but they're never bunked. Soft beds with big pillows. Clean facilities. Kitchen access. In-room lockers. Free internet and Wi-Fi. Reception 24hr. Check-in 1pm. Check-out 10am. Quiet hours 10pm-6am. 4- and 5-bed dorms 420Kč; doubles 1240Kč. 200Kč deposit. Cash only. ❶

Old Prague Hostel, Benediktská 2 (☎224 829 058; www.oldpraguehostel.com). ⓂB: Náměstí Republiky. From the metro, walk north toward Revolučni and then turn left onto Beneditská. 2 common rooms and plenty of amenities. Tickets in reception offer discounts for bike rentals and area restaurants. Free internet and Wi-Fi. Wheelchair-accessible. Reception 24hr. Check-in 10am. Check-out 2pm. Dorms from 450Kč; singles 1200Kč; doubles 720Kč. Cash only. ❷

Prague Square Hostel, Melantrichova 10 (☎224 240 859; www.praguesquarehostel. com). ⓂA or B: Můstek. From the metro, take Na můstku away from Wenceslas Sq. until it becomes Melantrichova; the hostel will be on your right. Right between Wenceslas Sq. and Old Town Sq. Breakfast included. Wi-Fi. Key deposit. Reception 24hr. Check-in 10am. Check-out 2pm. Dorms from 420Kč; singles 1200Kč; doubles 720Kč. Cash only. ❶

Apartments Bartoloměj, Bartolomějská 3 (☎608 712 854; www.pension-apartment. cz). ⓂB: Národní třída. From the metro, take Národní toward the river and then turn right on Karoliny Světlé and veer right on Bartolomějská. Apartment-style suites for students who are tired of common bathrooms and kitchens. Large, clean bathrooms and pleasant furniture come at the cost of no internet, though several cafes are in the vicinity. Reception 9am-8pm. Check-in 3pm. Check-out 10am. Singles from 800Kč. Cash only. ❹

Apple Hostel, Královorská 16 (☎777 277 534). ⓂB: Náměstí Republiky. From the metro, walk north toward Revolučni and then turn left onto Královdvorská. Clean, no-frills rooms. Breakfast included. Internet 1Kč per min. Reception 24hr. Check-in 2pm. Check-out 10am. Dorms from 380Kč; singles 1190Kč, with bath 1290Kč; doubles 690Kč per person. Cash only. ❶

MALÁ STRANA

Hostel Sokol, Nosticova 2 (☎257 007 397; www.sokol-cos.cz/index_en.htm). Trams 12, 20, 22, 91, Hellichova tram stop. From the tram, walk south down Újezd and make a left on Hellichova; the hostel is in the Sokol Organization complex. The only hostel in Malá Strana proper. Basic dorms and a rooftop terrace that provides the only real common space. Good for people who want beds to sleep in but nothing fancy. Parking available

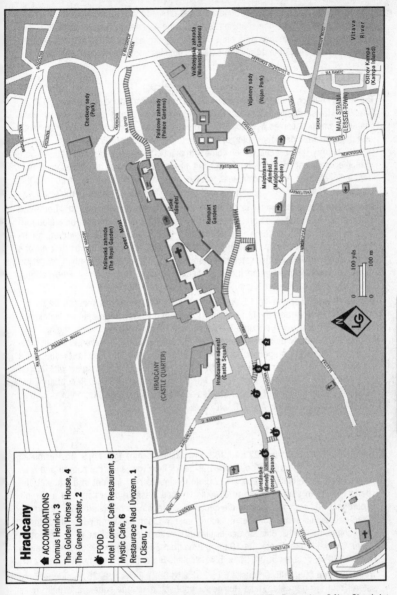

Hradčany

🛏 **ACCOMODATIONS**
Domus Henrici, **3**
The Golden Horse House, **4**
The Green Lobster, **2**

🍴 **FOOD**
Hotel Loreta Cafe Restaurant, **5**
Mystic Cafe, **6**
Restaurace Nad Úvozem, **1**
U Císaru, **7**

PRAGUE

100Kč per night. Linens and lockers included. Free Wi-Fi. Reception 24hr. Check-in 11am. Check-out 10am. Dorms 350Kč; doubles 900Kč. Cash only. ➊

Hostel 5, Plzeňská 23 (☎776 337 852; www.hostel5.com). Trams 4, 7, 9, 10, Bertramka tram stop. From the tram, walk east on Plzeňská; the hostel will be on your right. A ways south of Malá Strana in Smíchov, this place should be your absolute last resort. If the broken windows in the surrounding buildings don't dissuade you, be prepared for minimum accommodations, less-than-sparkling facilities, and a generally inattentive staff. Linens included. Wi-Fi in reception area only. Free parking. Reception 9am-noon and 1-10pm. Check-in 1pm. Check-out 1am. Dorms 360Kč; doubles from 420Kč. Cash only. ❶

HRADČANY

The Green Lobster, Nerudova 43 (☎257 532 158; www.garzottohotels.cz). Trams 12, 20, 22, 91, Malostranské náměstí tram stop. From the tram, head west on Malostranské náměstí, which becomes Nerudova; the hotel will be on your left. Best for a romantic evening or a truly decadent splurge, this hotel near the base of Prague Castle offers 3 levels of luxury. The best suites even come with bidets, if you're into that sort of thing. Soft, canopied beds and mercifully late check-out let you sleep off most bad decisions. Breakfast included. Free Wi-Fi in cafe, less reliable in the rooms. Pickup from airport 650Kč. Reception 24hr. Check-in 2pm. Check-out noon. Rooms 1850-3150Kč. AmEx/MC/V. ❺

The Golden Horse House, Úvoz 8 (☎603 841 790; www.goldenhorse.cz). Trams 12, 20, 22, 91, Malostranské náměstí tram stop. From the tram, head west on Malostranské náměstí, which becomes Nerudova, and then eventually Úvoz. Modern apartments in an old building. The couch and bed linens won't match, not that anyone really cares. Private baths, satellite TV, and a fully stocked kitchen might make you want to spend your vacation indoors. Highspeed internet and Wi-Fi. Free parking. Check-in 2pm. Check-out 10am. Apartments from 1420Kč. MC/V. ❺

Domus Henrici, Loretánská 11 (☎220 511 369; www.domus-henrici.cz). Trams 12, 20, 22, 91, Malostranské náměstí tram stop. From the tram, head west on Malostranské náměstí, which will become Nerudova, and then eventually Úvoz. Offers 8 minimally but tastefully decorated suites. The real selling point, however, is the terrace. The best rooms get a spectacular view of Petřín Hill, while the less fancy digs get a decent view of another building's roof. Suites and deluxe rooms come with added amenities like bathrobes. Free Wi-Fi. Pickup from airport 480Kč. Reception 24hr. Check-in 2pm. Check-out 10am. Singles 2220Kč; double 2450Kč, deluxe doubles 3030Kč; suites 2930Kč. AmEx/D/MC/V. ❺

ŽIŽKOV

Hostel Elf, Husitská 11 (☎222 540 963; www.hostelelf.com). Trams 5, 9, 26, Husinecká Tram stop. From the tram stop, follow Husinecká until you reach the square and then make a left at Orebitská, which will run into Husinecká right in front of the hostel. The perfect place to stay for those who wouldn't mind crashing on a couch in a friend's apartment. The common room is the center of hostel life, with 7 enormous, thoroughly lived-in couches and a communal kitchen nearby. Clean and simply furnished dorms with shared hall baths. Bike storage available. Breakfast included. Free Wi-Fi. Reception 24hr. Check-in 2pm. Check-out 10am. Dorms from 340Kč; singles 980Kč, with private bath 1230Kč; doubles 580/730Kč. 5% discounts in dorms for students. Cash only. ❶

Hotel Winston Churchill, Orebitská 6 (☎257 316 662). Trams 5, 9, 26, Husinecká Tram stop. From the tram stop, take Husinecká until you reach the square and then make a left at Orebitská. Surprisingly spacious rooms at the base of Vitkov hill. Computers available on request for 150Kč per day. Breakfast included. Pickup from the airport 700Kč. Parking 450Kč per day. Reception 24hr.; after 8pm, reception across the street. Check-in 2pm. Check-out 11am. Room prices vary; expect a standard double to run up to 2000Kč per night during the summer. AmEx/D/MC/V. ❻

VINOHRADY

Czech Inn, Francouzská 76 (☎267 267 600; www.czech-inn.com). ⓜA: Náměstí Míru. From the metro, follow Francouzská for about 2/3 km; the hostel will be on your right. As sleek and sexy as a hotel can be. From the black porcelain sinks to the large, drunk-friendly numbers painted on the doors, this place has your comfort and sense of style close to its heart. Standard dorms but with taller, more imposing bed-frames; smaller rooms come equipped with chandeliers and leather chairs. Breakfast 140Kč. Towels 100Kč. Free internet and Wi-Fi. Wheelchair-accessible. Reception 24hr. Check-in 2pm. Check-out 11am. Dorms from 472Kč; single suites 1694Kč; double suites 2057Kč. AmEx/MC/V. ❷

Hostel Advantage, Sokolská 11 (☎224 914 062; www.advantagehostel.cz). ⓜC: I.P. Pavlova. From the metro, follow Ječná toward the river and then make a left on Sokolská; the hostel will be on your right. Friendly and inviting. All the amenities you could want and no bunks. Breakfast (7:30-9:30am) included. Free Wi-Fi in rooms, computers available in common area. Reception 24hr. Check-in 10am. Check-out 2pm. Quiet hours 10pm-7am. Dorms 350Kč; doubles from 750Kč per person. 10% Hostelling International discount. AmEx/MC/V. ❶

HOLEŠOVICE

▓ Sir Toby's, Dělnická 24 (☎246 032 610; www.sirtobys.com). ⓜC: Nádraží Holešovice. From the metro, take the tram to Dělnická, walk to the corner of Dělnická, and turn left. Cultivates a welcoming, social atmosphere through thrice weekly film nights and a social cellar pub (beer 30Kč) furnished with antique bazaar decor. That's not to mention the lovely barbeque-ready terrace garden or the spacious and well-equipped guest kitchen. When you do need to turn in for the evening, you'll return to big, inviting rooms, some of which have been decorated with paintings from former guests. Buffet breakfast 100Kč. Laundry service 150Kč, self-service 100Kč. Free Wi-Fi. Wheelchairs can be accommodated with advanced notice. Reception 24hr. Check-in 3pm. Check-out 11am. Dorms 380-530Kč; singles 1400Kč; doubles 1950Kč. AmEx/MC/V. ❷

Plus Prague, Přívozní 1 (☎220 510 046; www.plusprague.com). ⓜC: Nádraží Holešovice. From the metro, take Verbenského east and then turn left on Přívozní. One of the most far-out hostels you're likely to find in Prague, but also one of the most resort-like. The massive complex can house up to 540 people, while the on-site restaurant, cafe, sauna, and swimming pool keep them entertained when they don't feel like making the trek to the city center. The pastel-colored dorms are nice enough, with desks and lamps, though the close-quarters of the bunks remind you that you are still, despite appearances, staying in a hostel. Breakfast 75Kč. Free Wi-Fi in lobby, computers 20Kč per 15min. Reception 24hr. Check-in 3pm. Check-out 10am. Dorms from 250Kč; triples 1290Kč. AmEx/MC/V. ❶

A&O Hostel, U Vystaviste 1 (☎220 870 252; www.aohostels.com). ⓜC: Vltavská. From the metro, take Bubenská north and then make a right on U Výstaviště. Small rooms where TVs and baths are standard but desks and chairs are not. A bar downstairs with occasional live music almost makes up for all the additional charges (1st beer free, after that 20Kč). Continental breakfast 60Kč, with Belgian waffle 70Kč. Locker deposit 300Kč. Linens 80Kč. Towels 30Kč. Wheelchairs can be accommodated on the 1st fl. with advanced notice. Reception 24hr. Check-in 2pm. Check-out 10am. Dorms from 360Kč; doubles 1080Kč. AmEx/MC/V, with a 70Kč surcharge. ❶

Hotel Extol Inn, Přístavní 2 (☎220 876 541; www.extolinn.cz). ⓜC: Nádraží Holešovice. From the metro, take the tram to Dělnická, walk north on Komunardů and then turn left onto Přístavní. Maybe it's the tile interior, or maybe it's the whirlpool, sauna, and fitness room, but this place feels less like a hostel and more like a celebrity rehab clinic. The

PAIRING FOOD WITH BEER: A CZECH TRADITION

As the French have a plethora of cheeses to complement their wines, the Czechs have developed dishes to accent their excellent beer. Billed *Proti velké Žízeni*, meaning "against great thirst and hunger," these dishes are a match made in Heaven to the adventurous beer lover. Try the *naakladanee hermeleen*, a pickled cheese, soft on the inside and covered with a thin white film. In the mood for meatier fair? The *Utopenci*, a sausage pickled in vinegar, oil, onion, red pepper, and spices are consistently delicious. For a different take on the sausage milieu, check out the region's massive selections of *Klobásy*, grilled sausages with horseradish and mustard, served on *chleb*, a hearty brown bread. Feeling homesick? Try the *párek v rohliku*, a mustard-topped twist on the classic American hot dog. These meaty morsels are sure to satiate even the most voracious of hunger twinges before, during, or after an evening of prodigious consumption. The morning after, take solace in the fact that Czech beer is often rich in B vitamins! For a true treat, cultivate your cravings at one of Prague's many beer gardens. Most offer only a single brand of beer, but the full array of aforementioned munchies is usually on the menu.

rooms themselves come in 1-, 2-, and 3-star varieties. The 2 stars have private baths and tables, while the 3 stars have TVs, minibars, and free access to the fitness facilities. Free Wi-Fi in lobby and 3-star rooms. Fitness room 70Kč. Sauna 100Kč. Wheelchair-accessible. Reception 24hr. Check-in 2pm. Check-out 10:30am. 1-star singles 820Kč, 2-star 1050Kč, 3-star 1500Kč; doubles 1400/1800/2350Kč. HI discount. AmEx/D/MC/V. ❹

🍴 FOOD

Eating out in Prague can be disorienting for people used to American service (or even Western European service). Do not expect a server to greet you at the door; you will be expected to seat yourself. When your server does find you, do not expect him or her to be cheery or talkative. While you might call this cold, negligent, or downright rude, the Czechs call this professionalism. Additionally, don't expect anything you order to come quickly. Dining out is supposed to be a relaxing social occasion where people talk and catch up; no good server would ever rush you by bringing your order too soon. During dinner hours, expect to wait at least 20-30 min. for food. While you're waiting, your server may leave a basket of bread and butter on your table. You will be charged for every piece of bread that you touch, and maybe for the butter, as well. Be sure to check the bill when it comes; even good restaurants may sometimes include a charge for *chleb* (bread) whether or not you actually had any, though calling this to the server's attention usually gets it removed without any trouble. At nicer restaurants, most people have coffee after dinner. When you're ready to pay, don't flag down your server, but stop them with a polite *"prosím"* the next time they pass. Perhaps because the service is often less than cheery, Prague servers do not expect large tips. For the most part, rounding up to the next 10Kč is usually sufficient, though for good service or larger orders a tip of about 10% may be in order.

Traditional Czech food is best described as hearty. Many restaurants will even have a special Czech section, often labeled "Old Czech Cuisine" to make it sound more authentic. Expect lots of beef and sausage. Pork knuckle and neck are usually specialties. Chicken is almost always available, though roast duck is traditionally a superior dish. Schnitzel—here called *řízek*—is also a staple.

Vegetarians will become well acquainted with potatoes and pickles. Dumplings of various sorts accompany most entrees. The most (in)famous item on Czech menus, though, remains the goulash: sometimes it's a stew, sometimes it's chunks of beef served in a puddle of paprika-laden sauce.

When all things roasted and boiled begin to lose their appeal, Prague has a few international restaurants. Italian restaurants are by far the most numerous (and usually most tasty) options available. Perhaps because of its strong dumpling-making tradition, Prague makes some of the best gnocchi to be had outside of Italy. There are also an inordinate number of good Thai places scattered pretty evenly throughout the city. Overpriced and bland sushi can be found anywhere there are tourists. Dozens of identical-looking Chinese restaurants can be found throughout the city, but they almost all offer the same low-quality, buffet-style food and most locals caution against them. Most restaurants will have at least a few vegetarian options, and exclusively vegetarian restaurants, ranging from Indian-style curry places to New Age organic buffets, are cropping up in many neighborhoods.

As a general rule, the closer you are to a tourist center, the more you will pay. The most overpriced restaurants in the city can be found around Old Town Square and across the river in Malá Strana near the Charles Bridge. The farther you get from these places, the more prices will start to resemble something reasonable. A decent meal with a drink should cost somewhere in the neighborhood of 150-200Kč, or about $7-10. Some of the city's most reasonably priced restaurants can be found in Nové Město in the area west of Spálená and in Malá Strana around Újezd. Farther out, Holešovice also has its share of budget-friendly and delicious restaurants. Nearby Dejivce, though lacking in most every other regard, has a surprising variety of international restaurants. Travelers tired of standard road grub may find it worthwhile to shave, put on something nice, and head over to Vinohrady. The restaurants here are some of, if not the most, expensive in the city, though unlike places in the tourist area, these prices are (usually) justified. If you keep your eye open, you can eat at a Michelin-rated restaurant for about half of what you could expect to pay in the States.

Those who are on a serious budget or those who might be nervous about scurvy may want to load up on basics at grocery stores. The city's major chains are **Albert, Billa,** and **Tesco.** You'll be able to find anything you'd expect to find at an American supermarket, including canned goods, fresh produce, and toiletries. Albert and Billa have locations within a stone's throw of one another at Karlovo náměstí (Albert open M-Sa 7am-9pm, Su 8am-9pm; Billa open M-Sa 7am-9pm, Su 8am-8pm). There's also a Tesco at Národní třída 26. (Open M-F 7am-10pm, Sa 8am-9pm, Su 9am-8pm.) Look for the daily **market** in Staré Město where you can grab better deals. Streetside **vendors** can be found all around Nové Město and the lower part of Malá Strana at similar prices. The various **bakeries** and Potraviny throughout the city usually sell pre-made sandwiches for 20-90Kč. They vary wildly in terms of size and quality, but will work in a pinch. After a night out, you may be tempted to grab a *párek v rohlíku* (hot dog) or a *smažený sýr* (fried cheese sandwich) from a **Václavské náměstí** vendor, but don't expect to feel so good about your choice the next morning.

NOVÉ MĚSTO

▨ **Dynamo,** Pštrossova 29 (☎224 932 020; www.restauracedynamo.com). Ⓜ️B: Národní
   třída. From the metro stop, walk down Ostrovní toward the river and then turn left on
   Pštrossova; Dynamo is on the right. A great place to take a break while exploring the

shops and bookstores in the area. Serves a mix of English-speakers and cool-looking locals in an award-winning restaurant. Full menu of duck, pork, and vegetarian options (135-180Kč); the real jewel is the tomato, mozzarella, and basil bruschetta (75Kč). Free Wi-Fi. Open daily 11:30am-midnight. AmEx/DC/MC/V. ❷

Restaurace Stará Doba, Gorazdoba 22 (☎224 922 511; www.staradoba.cz). ⓂB: Karlovo náměstí. From Karlovo náměstí, turn left on Resslova and then left again on Gorazdoba, the street directly behind the Dancing House. Melted candles line the entry and an honest-to-God beaver pelt awaits you at the bottom of the spiral stairs. Unabashedly kitschy in the best way with delicious food. Make sure you ask for the English menu so you can appreciate gems like the "Highlander's well-earned meal" (stuffed chicken breast with spinach and basil sauce; 150Kč) and the suspiciously named "Yeomanly blow-out" (stuffed steak with pepper sauce; 240Kč). Open M-F 11am-11pm, Sa 5:30-11pm. Cash only. ❸

Pizzeria di Carlo, Karlovo náměstí 30 (☎222 231 374; www.dicarlo.cz). ⓂB: Karlovo náměstí. From the metro station, walk to the other side of the park and turn left on Karlovo náměstí. Head through the arcade and down the stairs. A local favorite with a relaxed atmosphere and reasonably priced pizza and pasta. The tasteful decor, complete with black-and-white portraits of nondescript relatives, will make you feel like you're back in old country. Their 30 varieties of pizza (99-155Kč) and numerous pasta entrees include some unusual offerings like the tasty Riccardo III (smoked cheese, turkey, salami, and barbecue sauce; 135Kč). Outdoor seating available. Entrees 135-195Kč. Open M-F 11am-10:30pm, Sa-Su 11:30am-10:30pm. AmEx/D/MC/V. ❷

Jáma (The Hollow), V Jámě 7 (☎224 222 383; www.jamapub.cz). ⓂA or B: Muzeum. From the metro station, walk down Václavsté Naměstí and then turn left on Štěpanská and then a right on V jámě; Jáma will be on your right. An expat favorite, Jáma is an American-style grill that serves perhaps the only cheddar cheeseburger (175Kč) in Prague. Between the selection of burgers and the walls covered with posters of everything you could possibly miss (or not) about American culture—from Elvis, Fleetwood Mac and Muhammed Ali to Yoda and trashy Corona advertisements —you might think you were back in the USA, except that they charge you for condiments. Appetizers 65-185Kč. Soup 50Kč. Entrees 165-365Kč. Weekend brunch served until 5pm (149-199Kč). Open daily 11am-1am. MC/V. ❸

Lemon Leaf, Myslíkova 14 (☎224 919 056; www.lemon.cz). ⓂB: Karlovo náměstí. From Karlovo, take Resslova toward the river and then make a right on Na Zderaze. Though the address says Myslíkova, the entrance is on Na Zderaze. With bamboo placemats and a large, open dining room lit by large windows, Lemon Leaf is a welcome change from Prague's many basement establishments. The rotating lunch menu keeps things interesting, though many opt for lunch buffet on weekends (239Kč). Pad thai 166Kč. Free Wi-Fi. Open M-Th 11am-11pm, Sa 12:30pm-12:30am, Su 12:30-11pm. AmEx/DC/MC/V. ❸

Švejk Restaurant U Karla, Křemencova 7 (☎222 515 889; www.svejk-restaurant.cz). ⓂB: Karlovo náměstí. From the metro station, walk north on Karlovo náměstí, take a left at Myslíkova and then a right on Křemencova; the restaurant will be on your left. Just a few doors down from U Fleků but without the glut of tourists. Authentic Czech pub fare at reasonable prices, if you don't mind the portraits of the good soldier and his comrades which adorn the windows, chairs, and plates. Goulash (49Kč) comes in a delicious bread bowl. Free Wi-Fi. Appetizers 50-85Kč. Entrees 100-265Kč. Open daily 11am-11pm. AmEx/D/MC/V. ❸

Universal, V jirchářích 6 (☎224 934 416. www.universalrestaurant.cz). ⓂB: Národní třída. One of Nové Město's most celebrated restaurants—a fusion of Asian, French, and Mediterranean cuisines in an open dining area adorned with vintage advertisements and American movie posters. Highlights include tagliatelle with salmon (165 kč) and Chinese fondue (2 person min., 219 kč per person). Finish things off right with some Twelve Minutes chocolate mellow cake (65 kč). Huge salads 131-195Kč.

Entrees 165-329Kč. Su brunch buffet 235-265Kč. Open M-Sa 11:30am-midnight, Su 11am-midnight. AmEx/MC/V, 500Kč minimum. ❸

Kavárna Velryba, Opatovická 24 (☎ 224 931 444). ⓂB: Národní třída. From the metro station, walk down Ostrovní and then make a left on Opatovická; Velryba is on the left. A low-key Czech-Italian restaurant that has managed to resist tourist infiltration. Something of a haven for local artists—renowned Czech director Jan Svěrak even celebrated his Oscar win here. The enticing Captain Ahab (pork with balkan cheese; 122Kč) continues the nautical theme even as a more terrestrial dish. Entrees 88-155Kč. Open daily 11am-midnight. Cash only. ❷

Ultramarin, Ostrovní 32 (☎224 932 249; www.ultramarin.cz). ⓂB: Národní třída. Czech yuppies dig a mix of American and Thai dishes in a super stylish and sleek setting, though it's unclear if the "Elvis King Burger" (cheese, Irish bacon, onion jam, and mushrooms; 220Kč) is an ironic gesture or not. The Gurmán (dried fig salami and honey walnuts with blue cheese, brie, and goat cheese; 220Kč) is also appetizing. On Sa nights live jazz and the dual bars keep everyone well-liquored and groovy. Salads 100-198Kč. Entrees 188-290Kč. Open daily 10am-11pm. AmEx/D/MC/V. ❸

Trilobit, Palackého 15 (☎224 946 065; www.restauracetrilobit.cz). ⓂA or B: Můstek. From the metro, walk up Václavsté náměstí toward the National Museum, then turn left on Vodičkova and take the 1st right onto Palackého; Trilobit will be on your right. The trilobites and other Cambrian creatures on the stone basement walls give Trilobit the feel of an upscale fossil bed. The menu features many typical Czech entrees, including roast duck with cherry sauce (179Kč), as well as a few items under the colorful heading "Good things on a skewer" (169-259Kč). Reasonably classy, yet far enough away from Wenceslaus Sq. to be largely tourist-free. Appetizers 75-99Kč. Pasta 129-149Kč. Entrees 159-339Kč. Open M-Sa 11am-midnight, Su noon-11pm. AmEx/D/MC/V. ❸

Pizza Coloseum, Vodičkova 32 (☎224 214 914; www.pizzacoloseum.cz). ⓂA or B: Můstek. From the metro, walk up Václavsté náměstí toward the National Museum, then turn left on Vodičkova. Take a left in the arcade and the restaurant is down the stairs on your right. Fancier than most of Prague's Italian places, in a dimly lit, cellar-like atmosphere. The replica statues of Venus de Milo and others might make you think you're in the basement of a Roman antiquities pillager. If the standard pizza offerings (125-196Kč) don't do it for you, check out the butterfish and salmon (300Kč) or the *gnocchi d'agnello arrosto* (259Kč). Pasta 111-199Kč. Entrees 189-389Kč. Open M-Sa 11:30am-11:30pm, Su noon-11:30pm. AmEx/D/MC/V. ❸

Pivovarský Dům, Ječná 15 (☎296 216 666; www.gastroinfo.cz/pivodum). ⓂB: Karlovo náměstí. From the metro station, take Ječná east away from the river; the restaurant is on your right at the corner of Ječná and Štěpánská. The enormous brass vats in the middle of the dining area aren't just for show—the restaurant is also a working microbrewery that serves unfiltered, unpasteurized, and unconventional beer in addition to traditional Czech food. Regular house brews on tap include nettle, sour cherry, or banana beer (35Kč). If you're feeling ambitious, try "the giraffe," a towering, 4L beer with its own tap (245Kč). *Wiener schnitzel* 135Kč. Open daily 11am-11:30pm. Reservations recommended. AmEx/D/MC/V. ❸

Restaurace U Zpvěváčků, Na Struze 7 (☎777 145 742 or 608 774 573; www.restauraceuzpevacku.com). ⓂB: Národní třída. From Národní třída, walk down Ostrovní and then turn left onto Pštrossova; at the 1st intersection turn right. If the inside of this Czech-Italian establishment is a little too intimate for your taste, you can move to one of the sidewalk tables. The menu is heavy on pasta (105-138Kč) and includes an attractive array of salads (small 47-65Kč, large 98-145Kč) for those jonesing for some vegetables. Open M-F 8am-2am, Sa-Su 11am-2am. It might be worth calling ahead, as the place can be packed at lunch and dinner time. AmEx/D/MC/V. ❷

U Fleků, Křemencova 11 (☎224 934 805; www.ufleku.cz). ⓜB: Karlovo náměstí. From the metro station, walk north on Karlovo náměstí, take a left at Myslíkova and then a right on Křemencova; the restaurant is on your left. Perhaps the oldest and most (in)famous beer hall in Prague (its sign claims 1499 as its opening); now one of the most tourist-ridden. The sprawling interior houses a restaurant, bar, microbrewery, and beer museum (admission 50Kč). The menu consists mostly of "traditional" Czech fare, though you'll rarely see a Czech eating here. Expect to be serenaded by accordion and tuba at all hours of the day. Salads 59-149Kč. Entrees 189-369Kč. Cabaret shows nightly 8-9:45pm, 100Kč per person. Wheelchair-accessible. Open M-W and Su 10am-11pm, Th-Sa 10am-midnight. Reserve ahead for evenings and weekends, when massive groups of American, British, German, and Italian tourists descend. AmEx/D/MC/V. ❸

CAFES

🗺 **Globe Bookstore and Cafe,** Pštrossova 6 (☎224 934 203; www.globebookstore.cz). ⓜB: Karlovo náměstí. From the metro, take Resslova toward the river and then turn right on Na Zderaze, which becomes Pštrossova; the cafe is on your right. Owner of the largest collection of English-language books in Central Europe, the Globe is a favorite place for Anglophone expats to congregate. Even the poet Robert Creeley was known to stop by. In the evening, the Globe hosts a variety of events, including free classic movie screenings (Su 11pm) and trivia nights. Live music most weekends. Printing available and Wi-Fi 1Kč per min. Coffee and tea 50Kč. Espresso drinks 60-95Kč. Open daily 9:30am-1am. Kitchen open 9:30am-midnight. AmEx/MC/V. ❶

PopoCafePetl Bar Cafe/Bar, Italská 18 (☎777 944 672; www.popocafepetl.cz). ⓜA: Národní Muzeum, ⓜB: Náměstí Míru. From the National Museum, follow Vinohradská; the cafe will be on your right. A low-key cafe and bar where Prague's spiky-haired youth can enjoy reasonably priced bagels and 21 varieties of personal pizza (75Kč) in a setting best described as rusty-basement-chic. The low lighting and techno soundtrack make kids feel cool. Desserts include an array of chocolatey drinks (45Kč). Open M-F 1pm-2am, Sa-Su 4pm-2am. MC/V. ❶

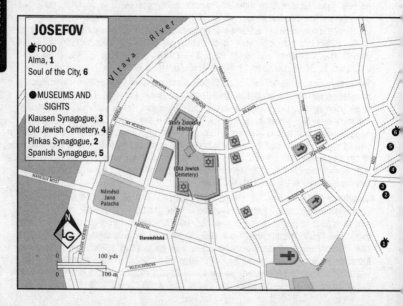

JOSEFOV

🍴FOOD
Alma, **1**
Soul of the City, **6**

● MUSEUMS AND
SIGHTS
Klausen Synagogue, **3**
Old Jewish Cemetery, **4**
Pinkas Synagogue, **2**
Spanish Synagogue, **5**

PRAGUE

Cafe Rybka, Opatovická 7 (☎224 932 260). ⓂB: Národní třída. From the metro, walk south on Spálená, then make a left onto Opatovická; the cafe is on the corner. A small, smoky bookstore and cafe that draws in the local intellectual and artistic crowd with cheap but tasty coffee (25-45Kč) and tea (22Kč). Alongside old typewriters are the musty shelves containing Czech translations of Camus and Leonard Cohen. Those looking for a little more inspiration might spring for the absinth (88Kč). Breakfast baguettes (40-45Kč) give unemployed artists a reason to wake up at a reasonable hour. Open daily 9:30am-10pm. Cash only. ❶

Cafe Louvre, Národní 22 (☎224 930 949; www.cafelouvre.cz). ⓂB: Národní třída. From the metro, walk north on Spálená and then turn left on Národní. Located in an old hotel, this ornate cafe has been serving thinkers like Einstein, Kafka, and Czech writer Karel Čapek (as well as mere mortals) for more than 100 years. Grab one of the tables next to the enormous windows for a beautiful street view while you enjoy your delicious (though pricey) meal, or take a break in the large billiard hall. Specialties include duck breast in cranberry sauce (229Kč) and roast rabbit filets (239Kč). Cold meals 69-80Kč. Tea 39Kč. Coffee 52Kč. Open daily 8am-11:30pm. AmEx/D/MC/V. ❸

Cafe and Restaurant Slavia, Smetanovo Nábřeží (☎224 218 493; www.cafeslavia. cz). ⓂB: Národní třída. From the metro, walk north on Spálená and then turn left on Národní; the restaurant is at the very end of the street, across from the National Theater, on your right. A combination of cafe and fancy diner that serves traditional Czech dishes like Old Prague Beef Goulash (149Kč) in addition to more standard diner fare. In the evenings, join the well-dressed locals for a pre-opera milkshake served in a wine glass (59Kč). Pasta 149Kč. Coffee 39-55Kč. Tea 39Kč. Free Wi-Fi. Open daily 8am-11pm. AmEx/D/MC/V. ❷

Dobra Cajorvna, Václavské Náměstí 14 (☎224 231 480; www.tea.cz/cajovna). ⓂA or B: Můstek. From the metro, walk up Václavsté náměstí toward the National Museum; the teahouse will be through the arcade on your right. Sip gourmet (read: expensive) teas (78-148Kč) from all over the world, in this strikingly Zen atmosphere. If your feet aren't too rank from days of traveling, take off your shoes and enjoy your tea in the lotus position in one of the cushioned alcoves with your new patchouli-scented friends. Wheelchair-accessible. Open M-F 10am-9:30pm, Sa-Su 2-9:30pm. Cash only. ❷

Café Jericho, Opatovická 26 (☎224 934 110). ⓂB: Národní třída. From the metro station, walk down Ostrovní and then make a left on Opatovická; Jericho is on the left, next to Velryba. Just like your favorite hole-in-the-wall coffeeshop back home, except it serves hard liquor and everyone speaks Czech. Students and other young people write sensitive things in their notebooks while enjoying reasonably priced panini (50-55Kč). Coffee 45Kč. Tea 28Kč. Beer 27Kč. Wheelchair-accessible. Open M-F 10am-10pm, Sa-Su noon-10pm. Cash only. ❶

STARÉ MĚSTO AND JOSEFOV

▨ **Klub architektů,** Betlémské náměstí. 169/5A (☎224 401 214). ⓂB: Národní třída. From the metro, take Spálená north and then make a left on Betlémské náměstí; the restaurant is through the courtyard on your right and in the basement. Finding this 12th-century cellar the first time feels like a true accomplishment. Rub elbows with the locals and stylish internationals in this intimate cavern of vaulted brick ceilings and low-hanging black lamps. Wide selection of dishes, some more wild than others, such as the chicken in cream sauce with peaches (160Kč). True gourmands will spring for the epicurean-only section, which includes ostrich filets (320Kč) among other adventurous options. Salads 70-150Kč. Veggie dishes 70-150Kč. Meat entrees 160-320Kč. Open daily 11:30am-midnight. AmEx/MC/V. ❸

▨ **Lehká Hlava,** Boršov 2 (☎222 220 665; www.lehkahlava.cz). ⓂA: Staroměstská. From the metro, take Křižovnická south, then veer left on Karoliny Světlé and turn left on

Boršov. Every nook and cranny of this tiny vegetarian and vegan restaurant has been turned into a seating area, complemented by colorful tapestries on the walls. If you can, try to score the table for two on the second level, where you'll be surrounded by plants and natural light pouring in from above. The "Small Clear Head" (eggplant, tabouli, and feta salad; 140Kč) will ease most hangovers. Su brunch (10:30am-3pm) comes in tiny (90Kč), standard (145Kč), and ideal (270Kč) portions. Entrees 95-210Kč. Open M-F 11:30am-11:30pm; Sa and Su noon-11:30pm. MC/V. ❷

Kozička, Kozí 1 (☎224 818 308; www.kozicka.cz). ⓂB: Náměstí Republiky. From the metro, walk north on Revoluční and then make a left on Dlouhá; follow it down to the sq. and then make a hard right onto Kozí. A relaxed Old Town cellar. Enjoy your meal while pretending not to notice the dozens of metal goats hanging menacingly from the walls and ceiling. For a mere 750Kč you can take a small version of the critters home as a memorable trinket. The chicken entrees, especially "Lilla" (chicken with tomato and mozzarella; 160Kč), are delicious. Entrees 120-350Kč. Open M-F noon-4am, Sa 6pm-4am, Su 6pm-3am. AmEx/MC/V. ❷

Beas, Týnská 19 (☎608 035 727; www.beas-dhaba.cz). ⓂB: Náměstí Republiky. Follow Týn-ská away from Old Town Square; the restaurant is located in the same courtyard as Hostel Týn (p.156). Reasonably priced meals of rice, curry, paneer, and lentils in varying combinations. Lacks the overbearing nature or exorbitant prices of some health food stores. Plates 88-133Kč. Fresh juices 36Kč. Open M-Sa 11am-8pm, Su noon-6pm. Cash only. ❷

Alma, Žatecká 10 (☎224 815 440; www.almarestaurace.cz). ⓂA: Staroměstská. From the metro, take Široká and then turn right on Žatecká; the restaurant will be on your left. Reasonably-priced Czech food with odd Italian or Mexican dish. Framed movie posters and paintings on the walls. Hungarian stuffed tenderloin 149Kč. Gnocchi with chicken, tomato, and onion 125Kč. Appetizers 65-115Kč. Pasta 95-135Kč. Entrees 115-259Kč. Open daily 11am-11pm. Cash only. ❷

Yami Restaurant, Masná 3 (☎222 312 756) ⓂB: Náměstí Republiky. From the metro, walk north on Revoluční and then make a left on Dlouhá; follow it down to the sq. and then make a hard left onto Masná. Japanese and Korean dishes in a sleek, relaxed dining room. A crowd devours Yami's fusion rolls (215-318Kč per 8 pieces), including the festive Mardi Gras roll (272Kč) and the deep-fried Seoul-to-Soul roll (268Kč). Sushi 60-90Kč. Entrees 238-332Kč. Open daily noon-11pm. AmEx/D/MC/V. ❸

Pivnice U Kata (The Executioner's Alehouse), U radnice 6 (☎224 236 363). ⓂA: Staroměstská. From the metro, take Kaprova east and then turn right at U radnice. A traditional Czech pub founded in the 17th century when the local executioner and his friends needed a place to go after a hard day's work. The walls are adorned with wicked-looking axes that not-so-subtly encourage you to behave as you tip back your Pilsner (35Kč). Smoked salted herring 50Kč. Devil's sausages 45Kč. Entrees 125-160Kč. Open M-Sa noon-12:30am, Su noon-11pm. Cash only. ❷

 CASH, CZECH, OR CREDIT? In the Czech Republic, everyone pays cash; very few establishments will accept credit cards. Your best bet is to take advantage of ATMs whenever you can. They will give you a much better rate than the ubiquitous currency exchanges, even if they're much less common.

Siam Thai Orchid, Na poříčí 21 (☎222 319 410; www.siamorchid.cz). ⓂB: Náměstí Republiky. From the metro stop, take Na poříčí past the Palladium and up another block; the restaurant is on the left, through the arcade and up the stairs. A real Thai place run by real Thai people. Diners enjoy traditional dishes while surrounded by hanging plants and bamboo. Phad Thai Kai (180Kč) comes served in delicious piles. Rice dishes 135-185Kč. Entrees 175-200Kč. Open daily 10am-10pm. AmEx/D/MC/V. ❷

Ariana, Rámová 6 (☎222 323 438; kabulrest.sweb.cz). ⓜB: Náměstí Republiky. From the metro, walk north on Revoluční and then make a left on Dlouhá; follow the street down to the square and then make a right onto Rámová. Upscale Afghan restaurant with a romantic atmosphere and enough tapestries and tassels to open an oriental rug store if the restaurant venture fails. English-speaking tourists who would like to think they're getting away from other English-speaking tourists opt for the *qorma chalaou* (meat and vegetables with white rice and mild curry; 179Kč) or one of the many kebabs (129-189Kč). Open daily 11am-11pm. Cash only. ❷

Hybernia Restaurant & Café, Hybernská 7 (☎224 226 004; www.hybernia.cz). ⓜB: Náměstí Republiky. From the metro, take Náměstí Republiky south and then make a right onto Hybernská; the restaurant will be on your left. A high-end cafe frequented by area professionals. The downstairs area features small tables and a curved stone ceiling. The *salmon tagliata* (145Kč) is a house specialty, though the real innovations are served Su, when you can customize your own schnitzel (200Kč) from a ½-dozen meats, fillings, and wrappings. Salads 132-146Kč. Entrees 145-336Kč. Open M-F 8am-11:30pm, Sa-Su 10:30am-11:30pm. AmEx/D/MC/V. ❸

Pizzeria Al Capone, Na poříčí 36 (☎224 819 007; alcapone.webnode.cz). ⓜB: Náměstí Republiky. From the metro, take Na poříčí past the Palladium and up another block; the restaurant is on your right. A reasonably priced Italian pizzeria and restaurant with a large salad selection (123-140Kč). The stone floors and ceiling in the basement evoke a 20s speakeasy. Pizzas 100-150Kč. Pasta 129-148Kč. Open M-F 11am-11pm, Sa-Su 11:30am-11pm. MC/V. ❷

Restaurace La Boca, Truhlářská 10 (☎222 312 073; www.laboca.cz). ⓜB: Náměstí Republiky. From the metro, take Truhlářská north; the restaurant is on the right. Between the slat wood overhang and the tapas selection (45-89Kč), you'll feel like you're in a Spanish courtyard where everyone happens to speak Czech. Highlights include grilled plum wrapped in bacon (56Kč) and octopus marinated in lime (78Kč). After a day of climbing the stairs to the tops of countless towers, the comfy pleather seats provide a welcome respite. Pasta 135-178Kč. Entrees 198-389Kč. Open M-F 10am-11pm, Sa-Su 11am-11pm. Reservations recommended. AmEx/D/MC/V. ❸

Orange Moon, Rámová 5 (☎222 325 119; www.orangemoon.cz). ⓜB: Náměstí Republiky. From the metro, walk north on Revoluční, make a left on Dlouhá and then a right on Rámová. A mix of Indian, Thai, and Burmese cuisine in a comfortable setting decorated with effigies of generic south Asian deities. Dishes include chicken in every possible combination of rice and sauce, as well as an assortment of vegetarian dishes (120-175Kč). Stand-bys like vindaloo (210Kč) and pad thai (190Kč) keep the menu tourist-friendly. Appetizers 60-165Kč. Entrees 175-365Kč. Open daily 11:30am-11:30pm. MC/V. ❷

Cafe Bambus, Benediktská 12 (☎224 828 110; www.cafebambus.com). ⓜB: Náměstí Republiky. From the metro, walk north on Revoluční and then make a left on Benediktská. Serves a culinary hodgepodge of Thai and Indian dishes (80-150Kč). The real specialties, however, are the Czech *palančinky* (crepes; 50-95Kč), which range from the basic Nutella crepe to the decadent macadamia, vanilla ice cream, and chocolate sauce variety. Pasta 95-155K. Beer from 48Kč. Open M-F 9am-2am, Sa 11am-2am, Su 11am-midnight. AmEx/D/MC/V. ❷

Soul of the City, Dušní 9 (☎222 315 852; www.soulofthecity.eu). ⓜA: Staroměstská. From the metro, take Široká and then turn left on Dušní at the Franz Kafka statue. Entrees are too expensive to bother with (225-420Kč), but many of the pasta dishes and skewers, particularly the Gala skewer (vegetables, pork, chicken, bacon, and cheese; 190Kč) will do just fine. Soups 20-35Kč. Pasta 165-200Kč. Open M-W 11am-midnight, Th-F 11am-1am, Sa 11:30am-1am, Su 11:30am-midnight. AmEx/D/MC/V. ❹

Restaurace Haštalský dědek, Haštalská 20 (☎224 827 196; www.hastalskydedek. cz). ⓜB: Náměstí Republiky. From the metro, walk north on Revoluční, make a left on

Dlouhá, then a right on Rybná, and finally a right on Haštalská. A standard Czech pub that prides itself on having the cheapest beer around (16Kč). Finding a seat on even a reasonably busy day can be a challenge, as half of the tables in the restaurant are reserved for various groups of older locals who've made the place something of a second home. Menu highlights include Old Man's sausage (169Kč) and the Burning Devil skewer (159Kč). Appetizers 45-59Kč. Pasta 129-139Kč. Entrees 109-129Kč. Open M-F 9am-11pm, Sa-Su 11am-11pm. AmEx/D/MC/V. ❷

Maitrea, Týnská ulička 6 (☎221 711 631; www.restaurace-maitrea.cz). Ⓜ️B: Náměstí Republiky. Vegetarian grub served beside walls covered in Sanskrit. Small, simple menu includes hummus made with pumpkin oil (60Kč) and the small-ish Mexican burrito (140Kč). Salads 60Kč. Entrees 105Kč. Wheelchair-accessible. Open daily 11am-9pm. Cash only. ❶

CAFES

NoD Cafe and Art Gallery, Dlouhá 33 (☎736 152 015; www.roxy.cz). Ⓜ️B: Náměstí Republiky. From the metro, walk north on Revoluční and then make a left on Dlouhá. This self-described "experimental venue" has quickly become a student favorite. A flexible performance area houses street art and doubles as a space for nonverbal theater performances. At least once a week, house or techno DJs get the students off their intellectual high horse and onto their feet. Tea 30Kč. Coffee 35Kč. Mixed drinks 80-90Kč. Open daily 10am-2am. Cash only. ❶

Bohemia Bagel, Masná 2 (☎224 812 569; www.bohemiabagel.cz). Ⓜ️B: Náměstí Republiky. From the metro, walk north on Revoluční and then make a left on Dlouhá; follow it down to the square and make a hard left onto Masná. Founded by expats, Bohemia Bagel is now a favorite of English-speaking tourists who consider themselves too hip for Starbucks. 11 varieties of bagel (11Kč, with cream cheese 65Kč), including chocolate chip and parmesan-oregano. The monstrous "I Don't Wanna Go Anywhere After This Breakfast" dish will cure any longing you have for eggs, bacon, sausage, or biscuits (169Kč). Other traditional meals include a good old fashioned Sloppy Joe (155Kč) and a BBQ bacon cheeseburger (155Kč). Wheelchair-accessible. Open daily 8am-11pm. Cash only. ❷

Čajovna Sivna, Masná 8 (☎222 315 983). Ⓜ️B: Náměstí Republiky. From the metro, walk north on Revoluční and then make a left on Dlouhá, follow it down to the square, and then make a hard left onto Masná. Small teahouse where local hippies hit up the hookah (100Kč for tobacco and coal) when they're not drinking tea (44Kč) or lounging on wooden benches. An assortment of tasty Middle Eastern appetizers include traditional hummus (50Kč) and rice-filled vine leaves (50Kč). Paintings of the Middle East and various wall hangings grace your surroundings. Coffee 44Kč. Open M-F noon-11:30pm, Sa 2-11:30pm, Su 2-10pm. Cash only. ❶

Coffee Fellows, Dlouhá 20 (☎222 310 200; www.coffee-fellows.cz). Ⓜ️B: Náměstí Republiky. From the metro, walk north on Revoluční and then make a left on Dlouhá. A modern, streamlined coffee shop decorated in varying shades of brown. Cube-shaped chairs provide interesting—if not entirely comfortable—seating while you're enjoying one of the few bagels to be found in this city (65-75Kč). American lemonade 45Kč. Espresso from 40Kč. Milkshakes from 62Kč. Free Wi-Fi. Wheelchair-accessible. Open daily 8am-9pm. Cash only. ❶

Týnská Literární Kavárna, Týnská 6 (☎224 827 807; www.knihytynska.cz). Ⓜ️B: Náměstí Republiky. From Old Town Square, take Týnská east; the cafe is around the corner. Attached to a small bookstore, this cafe serves local bookworms coffee (26Kč) and tea (28Kč) in homemade clay mugs. Espresso drinks from 40Kč. Open daily 10am-8pm. Cash only. ❶

Milky Cafe, Králodvorská 11 (☎222 310 248). Ⓜ️B: Náměstí Republiky. From the metro, take U Obecniho domu west and then turn right onto Králodvorská. Supplements the typical coffee and espresso options with a wide assortment of smoothies and desserts.

Specials include the Grasshopper (kiwi, apple juice, and banana; 75Kč) and the Black Banana (orange juice, black currant, and banana; 75Kč). Espresso drinks 43-63Kč. Desserts 69Kč. Wheelchair-accessible. Open M-S 8:30am-9:30pm. Cash only. ❶

MALÁ STRANA

Bar bar, Všehrdova 17 (☎257 313 246; www.bar-bar. cz). Ⓜ️A: Malostranská. From the metro, take the tram to Újezd, walk north on Újezd, and then turn right on Všehrdova. It's impossible to categorize this restaurant and bar with a zeal for combining things you would never imagine together. Unexpected hits include cheese-and-spinach-stuffed pancake topped with fried egg and bacon (129Kč) and Norwegian salmon with pesto and sun-dried tomato (159Kč). The decor is a similarly strange mix of abstract art and sculptures inside television sets. We don't know; we just go for the food. Savory pancakes 115-129Kč. Sweet pancakes 74-79Kč. Pasta 115-154Kč. Entrees 125-275Kč. Beer from 20Kč. Open M-Th and Su noon-midnight, F-Sa noon-2am. MC/V. ❷

Restaurace Carmelita, Újezd 31 (☎257 312 564; www.restauracecarmelita.cz). Ⓜ️A: Malostranská. From the metro, take the tram to Újezd. Reasonably priced (if you avoid the entrees) Italian food served in a classy, but not stuffy atmosphere that locals and visitors alike can enjoy. Greater variety than most Italian places in the area, and the indecisive will appreciate the *quattro stagioni* pizza, which contains 4 of their specialty pizzas in 1 easily divided dish (145Kč). The *gnocchi al forno* (baked gnocchi with chicken, bacon, mushrooms, cream sauce; 169Kč) is as filling as it is delicious. Appetizers 85-159Kč. Salads 98-169Kč. Pasta 109-169Kč. Entrees 175-349Kč. Wheelchair-accessible. Open M-Sa 11am-midnight. Cash only. ❸

La Bastille, Újezd 26 (☎257 312 830; www.labastille. cz). Ⓜ️A: Malostranská. From the metro, take the tram to Újezd. Both locals and visitors enjoy generous portions of tasty variations on conventional dishes surrounded by crossed swords, chains, and the requisite guillotine. The chicken spaghetti with mushrooms and curry sauce (140Kč) is delicious, and the piquant beef goulash with dumplings (135Kč) is some of the tastiest (if not the most traditional) in town. Salads 70-155Kč. Pasta 129-145Kč. Entrees 148-345Kč. Wheelchair-accessible. Open daily 11am-midnight. Cash only. ❸

Café Bar Wigwam, Zborovská 54 (☎257 311 707; www.cafebarwigwam.cz). Trams 6, 9, 12, 20, 22, 91, Újezd tram stop. From the tram, take Vítězná toward the river, then turn right on Zborovská. Tasty, reasonably priced restaurant with something of an identity

THE BIG SPLURGE

ROLLING ON THE RIVER

Tourists flock to the Charles Bridge to take in the sights of the Vltava River, but why not enjoy the view from on the river? The **Prague Dinner River Cruise** operates year-round, and takes passengers along a slow, scenic route with prime views of the Charles Bridge, Prague Castle, Malá Strana, and Vyšehrad Fortress, amongst others. Aside from the trip itself, this is an excursion that will feed and entertain you as well. Passengers nosh on an extensive buffet of classic Czech dishes whilst enjoying the repertoire of the live jazz band on deck. The cruise is an ideal location for a great date, and even better for a bad one, since your gentleman or lady friend can't desert you halfway through.

Travelers on a budget tend to avoid this sort of excursion as prices are usually quite high, but the river cruise comes at a surprisingly reasonable rate that includes the cruise, dinner buffet, and entertainment—a bargain when you consider the price of a meal in Old Town Square. Cocktail attire is appropriate, so leave your grungy backpacking clothes at home and spruce it up a bit for this worthwhile night on the town.

Cruises depart nightly at 7pm for 3hrs. Boarding point is the river embankment by the city center, near the Charles Bridge. Reservations can be made at the Prague Tourist Office in Old Town Square, online at www.pragueexperience. com. Cost is 790Kč per person.

crisis. The glowing blue bar and simple, modern tables and chairs seem at odds with the rest of the decor, which is a mix of Mezoamerican and Aboriginal influences. Tasty Thai-meets-Tex-Mex menu and creative salads, like the Tee Pee (greens, chicken, yogurt dressing; 125Kč). Appetizers 75-130Kč. Burgers 110-135Kč. Entrees 120-195Kč. Open M-F 11am-1am, Sa 2pm-1am, Su 2pm-midnight. Cash only. ❷

Noi, Újezd 19 (☎257 311 411; www.noirestaurant.cz). Ⓜ A: Malostranská. From the metro, take the tram to Újezd. High-end restaurant reminiscent of a stylish lounge with interior decor chosen and arranged according to zen principles. Yuppies of all palates enjoy a mix of traditional and original Thai dishes classified according to a spiciness scale. The Noi noodle (fried rice noodles vermicelli with seafood, broccoli, carrot, mushroom, and sauce; 280Kč) is a house specialty. Appetizers 90Kč. Entrees 180-290Kč. Open daily 11am-1am. Reservations recommended. AmEx/D/MC/V. ❷

Trattoria Amedeo, Újezd 20 (☎257 312 523). Ⓜ A: Malostranská. From the metro, take the tram to the Újezd stop. Reasonably priced Italian food and stylishly patterned walls attract a constant crowd of students and other young people to the small dining area. The menu covers all the basics, but manages to sneak in a few surprises, like the Venezia pizza (cream, chicken, asparagus, mozzarella, and blue cheese; 139Kč) and the *gnocchi mafioso* (beef sirloin with spicy tomato sauce; 149Kč). ISIC card holders love the buy-1-get-1-free pizza deal (before 5pm). Salads 129-189Kč. Pasta 119-149Kč. Pizza 109-139Kč. Steak 139-199Kč. Wheelchair-accessible. Open daily 11:30am-11pm. Cash only. ❷

Café Savoy, Vítězná 5 (☎257 311 562; www.ambi.cz). Ⓜ A: Malostranská. From the metro, take the tram to the Újezd stop; the restaurant is at the corner of Újezd and Vítězná. Upscale restaurant disguised as an upscale cafe with marble tabletops, chandeliers, and servers with vests and bowties. Though most of the menu is probably off-limits for budget travelers, a few reasonably priced gems, like the omelette with Gruyére cheese (148Kč) and the Frankfurter Savoy (124Kč) remain for those who care to look. Small menus 128-198Kč. Entrees 168-285Kč. Coffee 65Kč. Tea 45-78Kč. Wheelchair-accessible. Open M-F 8am-10:30pm, Sa-Su 9am-10:30pm. AmEx/D/MC/V. ❸

Malý Buddha, Úvoz 46 (☎220 513 894; www.malybuddha.cz). Trams 12, 20, 22, 91, Malostranské náměstí tram stop. From the tram, head west on Malostranské náměstí, which will become Nerudova, and then eventually Úvoz; the restaurant will be on your right. Various East Asian dishes served in a candlelit setting surrounded by Tibetan prayer flags and depictions of the Buddha to set your wandering soul at ease. Specialties include Tibetan fried rice (126Kč) and prawns with mushrooms and bamboo shoots (220Kč). Vegetarian options 70-169Kč. Entrees 136-250Kč. Meditation M 7pm-8pm. Open Tu-Su noon-10:30pm. Cash only. ❸

Cantina, Újezd 38 (☎257 317 173). Ⓜ A: Malostranská. From the metro, take the tram to Újezd. Large portions of passable Tex-Mex food. The service is prompt and the atmosphere is colorful and friendly. Come hungry so you can start off with the Sopa Azteca (50Kč), a house specialty. Appetizers 50-95Kč. Enchiladas 160-179Kč. Fajitas 219-309Kč. Entrees 159-245Kč. Wheelchair-accessible. Open daily 11am-11pm. Cash only. ❸

Jurldica Baroque Restaurant, Karmelitská 19 (☎257 199 263; www.juridicaclub.cz). Trams 12, 20, 22, 91, Hellichova tram stop. From the tram, head north on Karmelitská. Pairs Baroque opulence with fairly cheap prices. The leather benches, mirrors, and chandelier will make you feel like you're spending more money than you actually are. House specials include braised beef with cream sauce and cranberry (125Kč) and traditional schnitzel (165Kč). Be sure to leave room for some homemade plum brandy with ice cream (95Kč). Appetizers 85-95Kč. Entrees 125-225Kč. Daily menu 109Kč. Open daily 11am-11pm. Cash only. ❷

Pivnice U Švejků, Újezd 22 (☎257 313 244; www.usvejku.cz). Ⓜ A: Malostranská. From the metro, take the tram to Újezd. Another Švejk-themed restaurant, decorated with marionettes and paintings of an enthusiastic soldier. Typical Czech fare includes the hearty Peasant Plate (roasted pork, pork neck, roasted meat hash, cabbage, potato, and dumplings; 168Kč). Standard wooden benches and tables remind you that you're supposed to be in an authentic Czech pub, and after 7pm, an accordion player is on-hand to dispel any lingering doubt. Soups 35Kč. Vegetarian options 118-138Kč. Entrees 148-199Kč. Open daily 11am-midnight. Cash only. ❷

U Sedmi Švábů, Jánský Vršek 14 (☎257 531 455; www.svabove.cz). From the tram, head west on Malostranské náměstí, which will become Nerudova, turn left onto Jánský Vršek. Medieval-themed tourist trap with more gimmicks than dishes. If the serving wenches and suits of armor don't convince you that someone is trying too hard, maybe the occasional firebreathers, dancers, or lute players will. The menu, said to contain many 15th- and 16th-century recipes, includes fried camembert with cranberry (150Kč) and "the Knight's scrag end" (smoked meat with horseradish, mustard, and sour *gherkin;* 170Kč). Appetizers 65-85Kč. Entrees 150-390Kč. Open daily 11am-1pm. MC/V. ❸

Restaurace Nostitz, Nosticova 2a (☎257 007 681; www.nostitz.cz). Trams 12, 20, 22, 91, Hellichova tram stop. From the tram, walk south down Újezd and make a left on Hellichova, the restaurant is in the Sokol Organization complex. Located in a former summer palace used by the Jesuits, now popular with local families and guests from Hostel Sokol (p. 156). The decor is simple, the service friendly, and the food hearty. Specials include the chicken breast stuffed with cream cheese and topped with red pepper sauce (189Kč) and the roasted rabbit larded with bacon (229Kč). Salads 89-179Kč. Pasta 149-179Kč. Entrees 169-359Kč. Wheelchair-accessible. Open daily 11am-midnight. AmEx/D/MC/V. ❸

CAFES

🏠 **Kavárna v Sedmém Nebi,** Zborovská 68 (☎257 318 110). Trams 6, 9, 12, 20, 22, 91, Újezd tram stop. From the tram, take Vítězná toward the river, then turn right on Zborovská. Bustling cafe and popular hangout for artists, intellectuals, and those who just like the smell of cloves. Manages to keep the feel of a neighborhood establishment just off Malá Strana's main drag. A selection of tasty sandwiches (75-90Kč) keeps intense conversations well-fueled all through the afternoon. Tea 25Kč. Espresso 29Kč. Beer 38Kč. Salads 75-95Kč. Free Wi-Fi. Open M-F 10am-1am, Sa noon-1am, Su noon-midnight. Cash only. ❶

John and George Café and Restaurant, Velkopřevorské náměstí 4 (☎257 217 736; www.johngeorge.cz). Trams 12, 20, 22, 91, Malostranské náměstí tram stop. From the tram, take Mostecká toward the river and then make a right on Velkopřevorské náměstí; the restaurant is behind the Lennon Wall. Great cafe in the garden of the Velkopřevorský palác. Locals and foreigners (often from the nearby French embassy) dig the assortment of healthy menu options, including the Fit breakfast (yogurt, fruit, homemade muesli, and juice; 90Kč) and hummus with Arabic bread (110Kč). Tea 55-65Kč. Espresso 55Kč. Salads 130-155Kč. Pasta 148-165Kč. Entrees 130-190Kč. Free Wi-Fi. Wheelchair-accessible. Open daily 11am-11pm. Cash only. ❷

Dobrá Trafika, Újezd 37 (☎257 320 188; www.dobratrafika.cz). Ⓜ A: Malostranská. From the metro, take the tram to Újezd. Small, relaxed coffeehouse with pillows and wooden furniture. Peruse the extensive tea menu, complete with lots of herbal and rooibos options (42-57Kč). Creative mixed drinks like the "Happy House" and "Blueberry Hill" (42Kč) help you find your thrills in the intimate, dimly lit back room. Espresso from 27Kč. Fruit shakes 55Kč. Wheelchair-accessible. Open M-F 7:30am-11pm, Sa-Su 9am-11pm. Cash only. ❶

Café Kafíčko, Míšeňská 10 (☎724 151 795). Ⓜ A: Malostranská. From the metro, walk south on U lužického semináře and then turn right on Míšeňská. A popular hangout for area expats, this small, comfortable cafe feels much farther away from the throngs than it actually is. Surrounded by burlap and hanging plants, you can expect your tea (50Kč) to come served in a large pot, with a candle to keep it warm and a cookie for dipping. Coffee and espresso 38Kč. Beer 30Kč. Open daily 10am-10pm. Cash only. ❶

HRADČANY

U Císařů, Loretánská 5 (☎220 518 484; www.ucisaru.cz). Trams 22, 91, Brusnice tram stop. From the tram, take U Brusnice south and then turn left on Loretánská. Fine Czech dining in a 13th-century cellar complete with crossed swords and a boar's head. The kitchen has served the likes of George H.W. Bush, Margaret Thatcher, and Lech Wałęsa. Finally, a goulash worth splurging on (340Kč). Other specialties include roast duck in honey and ginger (420Kč) and pork sirloin stuffed with carrots and celery (440Kč). Appetizers 210-230Kč. Entrees 340-550Kč. No dress code per se, but you'd probably feel awkward in jeans and a T-shirt. Open daily 9am-1am. Reservations recommended. AmEx/MC/V. ❺

Restaurace Nad Úvozem, Loretánská 15 (☎220 511 532). Trams 22, 91, Brusnice tram stop. From the tram, take U Brusnice south and then turn left on Loretánská. Turn and go down the stairs toward Úvoz; the entrance will be on your left. Tricky to find but worth the search—the view of Petřín Hill and the surrounding area is one of the best you can have while dining in the city. The atmosphere is friendly and casual, and you might even spot a real Czech person eating here on occasion. The menu majors in traditional Czech, with an emphasis in skewers (169Kč). The Balkan sirloin skewer (chicken, pork, bacon, and onion) may not make you popular in crowded rooms. Entrees 159-279Kč. Daily menus 179Kč. Open daily 11am-11pm. Cash only. ❸

Hotel Loreta Cafe Restaurant, Loretánské náměstí 8 (☎233 310 510; www.hotelloreta.cz). Trams 22, 91, Brusnice tram stop. From the tram, take U Brusnice south, turn right on Loretánská, and then right again on Loretánské náměstí. Reasonably priced and reasonably tasty. Just off the historic (read: old) and peaceful (read: boring) Loreta Square. Like most restaurants in the area, this one caters mainly to tourists. The outdoor seating is as nice as any. Most of the menu is probably too rich for traveler's blood; stick to the baguettes (100-150Kč) unless you're starving. Entrees 175-225Kč. Daily menu 239Kč. Wheelchair-accessible. Open daily 11am-11:30pm. AmEx/D/MC/V. ❷

ŽIŽKOV

Spirit Bar, Dalimilova 2 (☎724 133 433; www.spiritbar.cz). Trams 5, 9, 26, Husinecká tram stop. From the tram stop, take Seifertova east and veer left on Blahníkova, then make a right at Dalimilova. A no-frills Czech pub and grill with decent food at reasonable prices. The special salad (chicken, shrimp, parmesan on a bed of lettuce, tomato, crouton, and cucumber; 110Kč) may not be all that special, but it's pretty tasty. Appetizers 55-90Kč. Pasta 95Kč. Vegetarian dishes 65-85Kč. Entrees 110-132Kč. Open M-F 11am-2am, Sa-Su 4pm-2am. Cash only. ❷

Geronimo, Milíčova 3 (☎603 293 107). Trams 5, 9, 26, Lipanská tram stop. From the tram, take Seifertova west and then make a right onto Milíčova; the restaurant will be on your right. Standard grill fare as well as a couple of surprising seafood options, including sushi and scallops (which must be ordered 1 day in advance; 160Kč) and grilled squid with cherry tomatoes and lime (195Kč). Salads 85-135Kč. Homemade gnocchi 115-130Kč. Entrees 120-290Kč. F and Sa live music. Open daily noon-1am. Cash only. ❸

Amores Perros, Kubelíkova 33 (☎222 733 980; www.amoresperros.cz). Ⓜ A: Jiřího z Poděbrad. From the metro, cross diagonally through the park and then take Milešovská; Kubelíkova is on the other side of the Žižkov tower park. Enjoy as close an approximation to Mexican food as you're likely to find in Central Europe while surrounded by cacti and stuffed iguanas. A mix of locals and tourists enjoy sipping Coronas (76Kč) on the corner while dining on Cajun burritos (155Kč). Pasta 99-134Kč. Entrees 140-265Kč. Open M-Th and Sa 11am-midnight, F 11am-1am. MC/V. ❷

CAFES

Cafe Pavlač, Víta Nejedlého 3 (☎222 721 731; www.cafepavlac.cz). Trams 5, 9, 26, Husinecká tram stop. From the tram stop, take Seifertova east, then make a right onto Víta Nejedlého. A clean, modern coffeeshop and cafe frequented by trendy students. Also includes a gallery of local art. A great place to pick up an international student with whom to discuss post-modernism all night; while you're pretending to listen you can enjoy a brie and cranberry sandwich (70Kč) or a tasty chocolate crepe (57Kč). Sandwiches 60-90Kč. Pasta 85-138Kč. Free Wi-Fi. Open M-F 10am-11pm, Sa noon-midnight, Su noon-11pm. Cash only. ❶

VINOHRADY

▩ **Pizzeria Grosseto,** Francouzská 2 (☎224 252 778; www.grosseto.cz), on the corner of Náměstí Míru and Francouzská. Ⓜ A: Náměstí Míru. One of the area's more affordable upscale Italian places with a lovely view of the St. Ludmila Church and the surrounding park. The clientele may not be the youngest or the coolest, but the delicious *gnocchi al pomodoro* (165Kč) and *penne al salmone* (139Kč) make the excursion worthwhile. Appetizers 155-193Kč. Pizza 115-198Kč. Pasta 135-189Kč. Open daily 11:30am-11pm. D/MC/V. ❷

Radost FX Cafe, Bělehradská 120 (☎224 254 776; www.radostfx.cz). Ⓜ C: I.P. Pavlova. The early morning, vegetable-loving alter ego of the super hip nightclub downstairs. The menu makes brunch sound sexy with section headers like "Foreplay" and "Between the Sheets." Highlights include the "Avocado Dream Triangle" (grilled tortilla with olive oil, avocado, cucumber, arugula, and balkan cheese; 195Kč) and the fresh spinach and smoked tofu sandwich (160Kč). Su brunch. Wheelchair-accessible. Open daily 11am-midnight. Cash only. ❷

Vinárna U Palečka, Nitranská 22 (☎224 250 626). Ⓜ A: Jiřího z Poděbrad. From the metro, take Nitranská heading south; the restaurant will be on your left. A typical Czech bistro that serves a mixture of local families and tourists at some of the most reasonable prices you can hope to find in the area. Wine racks and exposed masonry give you the feeling of being in a wine cellar. Entrees include the "Old Prague Meat Mixture" (sirloin, bacon, mushrooms, and edam cheese; 180Kč), as well as some chicken and pork dishes with more appealing names. Appetizers 60-120Kč. Soups 30Kč. Entrees 140-260Kč. Open daily 11am-midnight. Cash only. ❸

Aromi, Mánesova 78 (☎222 713 222; www.aromi.cz). Ⓜ A: Jiřího z Poděbrad. From the metro, head north on Slavikova and then turn right on Mánesova; the restaurant is at the end of the block on your left. Of all the highly regarded and expensive restaurants in Vinohrady, Aromi is the most highly regarded and one of the most expensive. Expect decadent Italian specials like sautéed octopus over chickpea mousse (345Kč) and braised veal neck (415Kč). Appetizers 195-365Kč. Entrees 325-695Kč. No dress code posted, but you'll probably feel out of place in anything less than business casual. Open M-Sa noon-11pm, Su noon-10pm. Reservations recommended. AmEx/D/MC/V. ❺

Banditos Restaurant & Bar, Melanouvá 2 (☎224 941 096; www.banditosrestaurant.cz). Ⓜ C: I.P. Pavlova. From the metro, walk west down Ječná and make a left on Melanouvá; the restaurant is on your left. A mix of Mexican and American grill fare. Options range from the tasty Bourbon Street steak with Jack Daniels sauce (285Kč) to the eyebrow-raising shark tacos (185Kč). Though, surrounded by English speakers and skeletons wearing sombreros, you might wonder why you came all the way to Central Europe to eat burgers and burritos (170-255Kč). Breakfast served until 6pm appeals to Americans who believe the rest of the world should operate according to their native time zone. Appetizers 85-150Kč. Pasta 170-195Kč. Steaks 275-620Kč. Open daily 9am-12:30am. Cash only. ❸

Restaurace U Neklana, Neklanova 18 (☎224 916 051). Albertov Tram Station, trams 7, 18, and 24. From the tram station, walk down Svobodova going west, then cross under the overpass, making a left onto Vnislavova, and veer right on Neklnova. This out-of-the-way place makes no pretense of authenticity. Patrons eat hearty, inexpensive Czech food while listening to Czech Top 40 radio or watching television. Potato soup in a bread bowl 68Kč. Salads 45-119Kč. Entrees 125-169Kč. Open daily 11am-midnight. Cash only. ❷

Restaurant Mozaika, Nitranská 13 (☎224 253 011; www.restaurantmosaika.cz). Ⓜ A: Jiřího z Poděbrad. From the metro, take Nitranská heading south; the restaurant will be on your right. Spotless white table cloths and decor make you feel like you're eating at a rich acquaintance's house where you feel uncomfortable touching anything. One of their specialties is the "Tournedos Charolais" (foie gras souffle, shallot in port wine, and light veal au jus; 378Kč). Appetizers 89-114Kč. Salads 128-154Kč. Pasta 129-169Kč. Entrees 274-378Kč. Reservations recommended. AmEx/D/MC/V. ❹

Ambiente Mánesova, Mánesova 59 (☎222 727 851; www.ambi.cz). Ⓜ A: Jiřího z Poděbrad. From the metro, take Mánesova west; the restaurant is on your right. This upscale, American-style grill serves food on large, clean white plates in a bright yellow interior. You can even choose your own breed of cow for its various steak and rib options (228-455Kč). Handy diagrams help in case you can't distinguish between Angus and Hereford beef. Sports-deprived American tourists can savor the BBQ wings (175-178Kč) while watching televised professionals toss the ball around. Salads 135-165Kč. Open M-F 11am-midnight, Sa-Su noon-midnight. AmEx/D/MC/V. ❷

CAFES

▨ **Čajovna Pod Stromem Čajovým,** Mánesova 55 (☎776 236 314). Ⓜ A: Jiřího z Poděbrad. From the metro station take Mánesova west; the teahouse is on your right. There's no better place to catch up on your Kafka or check your e-mail than in the no-shoes area of this vaguely Near Eastern-themed teahouse. Peruse a (non-English) menu of more than 100 varieties of tea from all over the world. Consider the delicious pita with edam cheese (50Kč) or one of their couscous dishes (74-88Kč). Open daily 10am-11pm. Cash only. ❶

Kavárna Medúza, Belgická 17 (☎222 515 107). Ⓜ A: náměstí Míru. Walk down Rumunská and turn left at Belgická. A laid back coffeehouse where Vinohrady's 20-somethings chill in permanently reclined chairs. The menu contains a wide variety of tasty dishes like feta-and-potato-filled dumplings with fried onion (3 pcs 59Kč, 6 pcs 118Kč). Tea 33-46Kč. Coffee 33-50Kč. Salads 74-108Kč. Open M-F 10am-1am, Sa-Su noon-midnight. Cash only. ❶

HOLEŠOVICE

▨ **La Crêperie,** Janovského 4 (☎220 878 040; www.lacreperie.cz). Ⓜ C: Vltavská. From the metro, take Antoninská west and at the 5-way intersection turn left onto Janovského; the restaurant is on your left. A young and cool staff serves their young and cool customers delicious crepes and galettes in a pleasantly francophilic atmosphere. Some of the more appetizing galettes include one with mushroom, cream, chicken, and two cheeses (145Kč) and one with smoked ham, cheese, egg, and potatoes with garlic butter (125Kč). Galettes 105-145Kč. Crepes 35-85Kč. Open daily 9am-11pm. Cash only. ❷

▨ **Fraktal,** Šmeralova 1 (☎777 794 094; www.fraktalbar.cz). Ⓜ C: Nádraží Holešovice. From the metro, take the tram to Letenské náměstí; the restaurant is at the corner of Šmeralova and Letenské náměstí. Delicious, hearty portions of American and Mexican food and all manner of unconventional seating, including high leather benches and a tree-stump table that appears to be reserved for hobbits. Locals appreciate the funky atmosphere while expats are happy for a taste of home. Expect standbys like the trusty chicken chimichanga (175Kč), alongside pleasant surprises like the goat cheese and pistachio burger with chili mayonnaise (185Kč). Appetizers 55-80Kč. Entrees 130-295Kč. Outdoor seating available. Open daily 11am-midnight. Cash only. ❷

Lucky Luciano, Dělnická 28 (☎220 875 900; www.luckyluciano.cz). ⓂC: Nádraží Holešovice. From the metro, take the tram to Dělnická, walk to the corner of Dělnická, and turn left. Another gangster-themed Italian place that distinguishes itself from its competition with a colorful brick oven and dishes named for notable gangsters and gangbusters, such as the Don Vito pizza (cream, mozzarella, salmon, shrimp, spinach, and lemon; 150Kč) and the Eliot Ness (pork steak with olives and roquefort sauce; 180Kč). Those who know how good it feels to be a gangster can challenge would-be drive-bys in the ample outdoor seating. Salads 115-190Kč. Pizzas 105-155Kč. Specialties 165-210Kč. Wheelchair-accessible. Open M-F 11am-11pm, Sa-Su 11:30am-11pm. Cash only. ❷

Zlatá Kovadlina, Komunardů 36 (☎246 005 313; www.zlatakovadlina.com). ⓂC: Nádraží Holešovice. From the metro, take the tram to Dělnická, walk north on Komunardů; the restaurant is on your right. Every once in a while, two things are combined that you would never have expected, but when you see it you think, "Man, what a good idea." This is the sort of place that inspires such whispered awe. Heart-stopping Bohemian pub fare meets American-style bowling as hearty locals enjoy the cheese-stuffed pork with bacon and mushrooms (179Kč). Highlights from the appetizer section include haggis with onion (45Kč) and pickled sausage with paprika and onion (25Kč). Salads 79-129Kč. Entrees 129-219Kč. Bowling 300-360Kč. Open M-Th 11am-11pm, F 11am-midnight, Sa noon-midnight, Su noon-10pm. Cash only. ❷

První Holešovická Kavárna, Komunardů 30 (☎283 871 327; www.kavoska.cz). ⓂC: Nádraží Holešovice. From the metro, take the tram to Dělnická, walk north on Komunardů; the restaurant is on your right. The oldest restaurant in the area with a large, red dining area frequented by locals. The menu has everything you would expect from a Czech place as well as a couple of items you wouldn't, such as the Diavlo (spaghetti with sliced filet mignon, onion, garlic, and chili pepper; 155Kč) and the Mexican chicken with corn flakes and chili salsa (145Kč). Salad 135-155Kč. Entrees 135-185Kč. Open M-F 10:30am-midnight, Sa-Su 11:30am-midnight. MC/V. ❷

CAFES

Long Tale Cafe, Osadní 35 (☎266 310 701; www.longtalecafe.cz). ⓂC: Nádraží Holešovice. ⓂC: Nádraží Holešovice. From the metro, take the tram to U Průhonu, walk to the corner of U Průhonu, and turn left; at the end of the block, turn left on Osadní. A nice, out-of-the-way coffeeshop with courtyard seating where students and progressive-looking older people can listen to light jazz in peace. The fresh ginger lemonade (50Kč) and assortment of baguettes and panini (65-76Kč) give this place an edge over lesser coffeehouses. Tea 35Kč. Espresso drinks from 35Kč. Soups 40Kč. Salads 42Kč. Free Wi-Fi. Wheelchair-accessible. Open M-Th 9am-7pm, F 9am-10pm, Sa 10am-10pm, Su 10am-5pm. Cash only. ❶

DEJVICE

Pivnice Bruska, Dejvická 20 (☎224 322 946; www.restaurace-bruska.com). ⓂA: Hradčanská. From the metro, walk north on Bubenečská and then turn left on Dejvická. Something of a neighborhood landmark that locals have largely managed to keep to themselves. The wooden furniture, brick floor, and wooden ceiling beams all signal a typical Czech pub, but the menu contains several surprises for those who can read Czech or find a server to translate. Highlights include kangaroo with cranberry sauce and vegetables (143Kč) and pork stuffed with bacon (189Kč). Salads 70-125Kč. Entrees 120-190Kč. Free Wi-Fi. Open M-Sa 11am-11:30pm, Su 11:30am-10pm. Cash only. ❷

PRAGUE

Haveli, Dejvická 6 (☎233 344 800; www.haveli.cz). ⓂA: Hradčanská. From the metro, walk north on Bubenečská and then turn left on Dejvická. Authentic Indian food with a price to match. Dine in yet another brick cellar, albeit this time surrounded by portraits of Indian people rather than Czechs or Italians. Vegetarians with money to burn will appreciate the wealth of options, including Bharwan Aloo (stuffed potatoes with cottage cheese, cashew nuts, and raisins cooked in tandoor; 145Kč). Those with fewer inhibitions may spring for the Raunaq-e-Seekh (lamb with coriander, tomato, and onion 325Kč). Appetizers 70-160Kč. Vegetarian dishes 145-225Kč. Entrees 235-330Kč. Open M-Sa 11am-11pm, Su noon-10pm. AmEx/D/MC/V. ❸

Perpetuum, Na Hutích 9 (☎602 666 550; www.restauraceperpetuum.cz). ⓂA: Dejvická. From the metro, walk through the traffic circle and veer right onto Dejvická, then turn left on Na Hutích. High-end restaurant that serves only home-bred duck and contains various duck effigies of the wooden and rubber variety scattered throughout. We couldn't make this stuff up. Specialties include duck with stuffing and apple (280Kč) and home-made duck ravioli with tomato sauce, cinnamon, and pumpernickel (190Kč). For starters, try the strong duck broth with quail egg and celery (85Kč). Appetizers 130-180Kč. Entrees 260-420Kč. Open M-Sa 11:30am-11pm. AmEx/D/MC/V. ❹

U Cedru, Národní obrany 27 (☎224 312 386). ⓂA: Dejvická. From the metro, walk through the traffic circle onto Československé armády and then make a right onto Národní obrany. On nice days, the outdoor seating offers a fantastic view of downtown Dejvice. Though usually only in the price range of well-to-do older residents, even the occasional student is willing to shell out for some *shawarma* (265Kč); but be warned, whatever your definition of *shawarma* includes, they still charge for pita. Appetizers 85-150Kč. Entrees 265-295Kč. Open daily 11am-11pm. AmEx/D/MC/V. ❸

Sakura, Náměstí Svobody 1 (☎774 785 077; www.sushisakura.cz). ⓂA: Dejvická. From the metro, walk through the traffic circle onto Československé armády and then veer left onto Náměstí Svobody. Professionals and tourists dine on expensive, though occasionally surprising sushi. Some of the more unusual rolls include pumpkin and egg (100Kč). Specialties include the Buddha Tamago (cucumber, sesame, pumpkin, egg, and caviar; 100Kč) and the Dragon (batter, cucumber, eel, caviar, sakura sauce; 240Kč). The sleek bar interior is partially undermined by the enormous stuffed animals that occupy one corner of the dining area. Maki 100-140Kč. Trays 150-790Kč. Nigiri sushi 75-150Kč. AmEx/D/MC/V. ❸

Argument Restaurant-Cafe, Bubenečská 19 (☎220 510 427; www.argument-restaurant.cz). ⓂA: Hradčanská. From the metro, walk up Bubenečská; the restaurant is on your left. Stylish, white-walled interior with comfortable benches and chairs. Trendy locals and visitors dine on unclassifiable dishes surrounded by purely decorative bookshelves and charts of various insects. The chili goulash in a bread bowl (195Kč) is particularly well-liked. The less adventurous will still appreciate the hearty chicken caesar salad (175Kč). Appetizers 85-220Kč. Entrees 195-360Kč. Open daily 11:30am-11:30pm. AmEx/D/MC/V. ❸

CAFES

Mazurka, Bubenečská 13 (☎224 316 291). ⓂA: Hradčanská. From the metro, walk up Bubenečská; the cafe is on your left. Small, simple cafe and coffeehouse that covers the basics. The cold desserts and local art on the wall serve as fleeting distractions, and the small white formica tables provide ample space for a laptop. If nothing else, it's a good place to get on the internet to find someplace more exciting to go. Espresso drinks 55Kč. Tea 29Kč. Cold desserts 16-60Kč. Free Wi-Fi. Open M-F 9am-10pm, Sa-Su noon-10pm. Cash only. ❶

◉ SIGHTS

If you visit Prague during the summer months, you will be viewing the histori-cal sites around **Prague Castle** and **Staroměstské náměstí** with thousands of other people trying to cram into the same tightly packed spaces as you. The tours of many of the historic buildings are often long and dry. The numerous towers in the Old Town area offer more or less the same view of the city, yet each trip up could cost you up to 100Kč. It will be loud. It will be unpleasant. You might get your wallet stolen. It doesn't have to be like this. You'll miss the crowds and save a lot of money if you do your Old Town sightseeing at night. You won't get to see the interiors of the buildings, but for most part that's no great loss. The entire Old Town, and especially the **Charles Bridge**--virtually impassable during the day--are lit up beautifully at night. Once you get away from Staroměstské náměstí, your options start to open up. **Nové Město** is home to the **Emauzy Monas-tery**and **Vyšehrad**, two of the city's most beautiful and overlooked historic sights. To the east, **Žižkov** has its share of large structures, including the ubiquitous **TV Tower** and the always impressive **Jan Žižka Statue**.

Aside from historical sites, Prague also has lots to offer in way of museums. If you're going to spend a lot of money on sightseeing, you should really get to a few museums at the very least; the city's numerous art museums are some of its best treasures. These museums are generally smaller, focusing on a specific artist, movement, or style. The largest art museum around is the fantastic but often overlooked **Veletržní Palace**. The museum is reason enough to make the trek over to **Holešovice**. If you need another reason, **Letná Park** is a great place to relax, and the view from the **Metronome** is one of the best (free) views you can get of the city on a clear day.

NOVÉ MĚSTO

DANCING HOUSE. Designed by Vlado Milunić and Canadian architect Frank Gehry (of Guggenheim-Bilbao fame), the gently swaying Tančící dům (Danc-ing House) at the corner of Resslova and Rašínovo nábřeží was a great source of controversy in its early days. Though former president Václav Havel sup-ported the building's construction, many locals thought the building had no place among the area's neo-Baroque and Art Nouveau architecture. In the years following its construction, however, the building was known affectionately by Americans as "Fred and Ginger" and irreverently by some Czechs as "The Drunken House." Visitors will have to admire it from outside, however, as the building is closed to non-tenants. (*Záhořanského 6. ⓜB: Karlovo náměstí. As you walk down Resslova toward the river, the building is on the left.*)

FRANTIŠEK PALACKÝ MONUMENT. Made by Stanislav Socharda, this complex sculpture depicts the prominent Czech historian and politician, František Palacký. One of the fathers of Czech nationalism, Palacký's image is carved in stone, shown seated while all around him the dramatic and grotesque forms of angels and demons wage war for reasons still unclear. (*ⓜB: Karlovo náměstí. Exit the metro station at the escalator nearest the river, the monument is right next to the escalator.*)

NEW TOWN HALL. Built in the 14th century, Novoměstská radnice (New Town Hall) served as the administrative center of Nové Město for nearly 400 years. Constantly renovated and rebuilt, the hall is something of an architectural hodgepodge, with the distinctly Renaissance-style south wing set against the medieval ▨**Outlook Tower**. In 1419 the hall was also the site of the first and lesser known (though more fatal) of the Prague defenestrations, when a mob of Hussites threw the town councilors out the window and then beat the survivors to death. Nowadays, the second and third floor of the building house a much more benign, rotating art gallery. If you have time, you should definitely climb to the top of the Outlook Tower. Though the walk involves eight rickety, wooden staircases, the views of the city from the top are unbeatable. Also check out the enormous bell hanging in one of the lower levels of the tower. *(Karlovo náměstí 23. ⓂB: Karlovo náměstí. From the metro station, turn left and look for the enormous tower. Open Tu-Su 10am-8pm.)*

EMAUZY. Built by Holy Roman Emperor Charles IV and the former home of Jan Hus, the Emauzy Monastery has a long and storied history. It was occupied by several monastic orders over the centuries, served as a tavern at one point, and survived heavy damage from an Allied air raid during WWII. These days the monastery is much quieter, except for the occasional service in the chapel. The chapel itself is beautifully adorned, but the monastery's real treasures are in the cloister itself. Take a slow walk around the cloister and pay attention—on the walls and ceiling, the remains of dozens of beautiful 14th-century murals are still visible. A guide to the murals is available at the entrance. *(Vyšehradská 49. ⓂB: Karlovo náměstí. From the park, follow the brown signs to the monastery down Vyšehradská. Open M-F 11am-3pm. 30Kč, 20Kč for students.)*

CHARLES UNIVERSITY BOTANICAL GARDENS. Surrounded by an ancient wall, the Botanicka Zahrada University Karlovy (Charles University Botanical Gardens) contain thousands of varieties of flowers and trees. When the weather is nice, there are few better ways to spend an afternoon in the city than relaxing on a bench in the botanical gardens. The gardens are situated on a steep slope, however, so be prepared to hike a little to get to the top. *(Benátská 2. ⓂB: Karlovo náměstí. From the metro, follow Vyšehradská south until it becomes Na Slupi; though the address is on Benátská, the actual entrance is across the street from Na Slupi 17.)*

WENCESLAS SQUARE. More a commercial boulevard than a square, Václavské náměstí (Wenceslas Square) owes its name to the statue of 10th-century Czech ruler and patron **Saint Wenceslas** (Václav) that stands in front of the National Museum. At his feet smaller statues of the country's other patron saints kneel in solemn prayer, including those depicting St. Agnes, St. Adalbert (Vojtěch), St. Ludmila, and St. Prokop. The sculptor, Josef Václav Myslbek, took 25 years to complete the series of statues. The inscription under St. Wenceslas reads, "Do not let us and our descendants perish." While Wenceslas' ancestors may not have perished, their sense of reverence may have somewhat diminished. Today, the square is lined with overpriced restaurants, department stores, American fast food joints. The area is particularly dangerous in the evening. Traces of its rich history remain, however: a former publishing house turned luxury hotel, the **Melantrich Building** once served as a platform for speakers to address the crowds gathered in the square during the **Velvet Revolution.** One of the Revolution's iconic moments came when Alexander Dubček and Václav Havel appeared together on its balcony. *(Václavské náměstí 36. ⓂA or B: Můstek or ⓂA or C: Muzeum.)*

OUR LADY OF THE SNOWS. When construction began in 1347, Kostel Panny Marie Sněžně (Our Lady of the Snows) was meant to surpass even St. Vitus Cathedral in size. Unfortunately, the untimely **Hussite Rebellion** interrupted construction. By the time someone had the chance to finish the church in 1603, the enormous amount of repairs that needed to be done prevented the church from achieving its intended size. Inside, dozens of ornate sculptures and statues line the sanctuary's Gothic walls. The church is still a popular place for prayer during the day; visitors are asked to remain silent. In other parts of the building,

Adventure in Europe?
Do it by rail

With a Eurail Global or Select Pass you zoom fast from country to country, from city centre to city centre. So you can soak up hip street scenes. Shop till you drop. Explore the nightlife and meet cool people.

Why wait? Go to www.adventure-europe.com or contact your local travel agent now!

a rotating gallery displays the work of local artists. *(Jungmannovo náměstí 18. ⓜA or B: Můstek. From the metro, walk up Wenceslas Sq. and then turn left on Jungmannovo náměstí; the entrance to the church is behind the statue. Open daily 6am-7:30pm.)*

CHARLES SQUARE. Charles IV wanted a park built for New Town that would rival the picturesque Old Town Square, though for many years Karlovo náměstí (Charles Square) was little more than an enormous mud pile and occasional cattle stomping ground. In the late 19th century, the area was transformed into a park filled with trees and fountains. Statues of prominent Czech writers and scientists are scattered throughout the park. The park, which is Prague's largest, is a popular place to relax during the day, though visitors would be well-advised to avoid the area after dark. Across the street, the **Faůstuv dům** (Faust house) is known for the sordid stories of its tenants, but visitors will need to imagine them from afar, as the building is closed to the public. *(ⓜB. Karlovo náměstí. Park open daily from dawn to dusk.)*

FRANCISCAN GARDEN AND VELVET REVOLUTION MEMORIAL. Originally built with the founding of New Town in 1348 and later seized and opened to the public by the Communist regime, the Františkánské zahrady (Franciscan Garden) provides a semblance of calm only a few steps away from Wenceslas Sq. The tiny clothing boutique in the center of the garden does slightly spoil the atmosphere. Down the street on Národní, a plaque under the arcades and across from the Black Theatre memorializes the citizens beaten by police in the 1989 protest; it depicts several hands reaching out, with the simple inscription 17.11.1989, the date of the protests. Visitors regularly leave flowers in or near the outstretched hands in acts of remembrance and honor. *(ⓜA or B: Můstek. Enter through the arch to the left of Jungmannova and Národní, behind the statue. Open daily from mid-Apr. to mid-Sept. 7am-10pm; from mid-Sept. to mid-Oct. 7am-8pm, from mid-Oct. to mid-Apr. 8am-7pm. Free.)*

SAINTS CYRIL AND METHODIUS CHURCH. Originally built during the 18th century, Kostel sv. Cyrila a Metodeje (Saints Cyril and Methodius Church) famously served as the hiding place of a pair of Czech paratroopers during the Nazi occupation of Bohemia. The two soldiers assassinated the ruthless Nazi-appointed governor Reinhard Heydrich and hid in the church's crypts where they managed to ward off their Nazi pursuers in a protracted firefight. The crypts now serve as a museum memorializing both the victims of the German occupation and the organized Czech resistance during WWII. Bullet holes from the firefight can still be seen in the walls of the crypt itself. *(Resslova 9. ⓜB: Karlovo náměstí. From the metro, walk down Resslova toward the river, the church will be on your right. Open Tu-Su 10am-4pm. 60Kč, students 30Kč.)*

STARÉ MĚSTO

CHARLES BRIDGE. Thronged with tourists and the hawkers who feed on them, the Charles Bridge (Karlův Most) is Prague's most treasured landmark. Those seeking to avoid the crowds should visit late at night when the bridge is illuminated. If you can get around the vendors selling 5min. caricatures and cheap jewelry, you might be able to appreciate the 30 Baroque replica statues that line the bridge (the originals are safe and sound in the Lapidary). The defensive towers on each side offer splendid views. The Old Town Bridge Tower, itself a beautiful Gothic building, was used to defend against the Swedish invasion in 1630. Five stars and a cross mark the spot where, according to legend, St. Jan Nepomuck was tossed over the side of the bridge for concealing the queen's extramarital secrets from a suspicious King Wenceslas IV in the 14th century; it has become local tradition to make a wish at the place on the bridge where

ESTORING" THE CZECH REPUBLIC

At the Charles Bridge, a 600-ear-old and 500-yard-long tourist magnet, an exhibit details the restoration of its tower's facade and statues. There I realized that the Czech definition of "restoration" is strikingly similar to my definition of "replacement." The statues was appreciating were mere replicas of the originals, which were kept underground somewhere for heir protection.

When I visited Karlstejn Castle, learned that I was not walking on he original floors, but rather 19th century imitations. Later, I learned hat the crown jewels I was admiring were actually just heavily-projected replicas.

I have become convinced that here is a second Czech Republic underneath the one that you and think we're enjoying. There are probably in-the-know tourists who pay exorbitant amounts to tour he "real" Czech Republic, which imagine is a vast underground complex full of statues and medieval floorboards that you and I can only appreciate by cheap proxy. I'm not sure how one would go about inding one of these tours. I don't hink it's the sort of thing they put on the internet.

And, in case you were wondering, the woolly mammoth at the National Museum isn't real either.

- Justin Keenan

he was thrown over. (Ⓜ*A: Malostranská or Staroměstská. Tower open daily 10am-10pm. Last entry 30min. before closing. Entry to tower 70Kč, students 50Kč.*)

OLD TOWN SQUARE. Staroměstské náměstí (Old Town Square) is the heart of Staré Město. The surrounding buildings—a mix of Gothic, Baroque, Art Nouveau, and even Cubist styles—would make your average architecture student giddy. In the center of the square stands the bronze statue of 15th-century theologian **Jan Hus,** whose burning at the stake in 1415 could be called the death that launched a thousand defenestrations. Nowadays, the square is filled with tourists of all flavors, snapping pictures, riding around in horse-drawn carriages, and gorging themselves on overpriced food in one of the dozen or so restaurants with seating on the square itself. For the discerning visitor, however, the square still offers its share of (occasionally bizarre) historical value. (Ⓜ*A: Staroměstská;* Ⓜ*A or B: Můstek.*)

OLD TOWN HALL. Composed of several different structural styles, the Staroměstské Radnice (Old Town Hall) has been missing a piece of its facade since the Nazis partially demolished it in the final days of WWII. A tour of the historical rooms inside will take you through various council chambers; the tour concludes in a basement photography exhibit. You can also see the old well and the prison pits where the names and dates of inmates from as early as 1605 are posted. While paying to climb to the top of the clock tower, as usual, the best things in life are free. The view from the top doesn't hold a candle to people-watching outside where people crowd every hour to watch the **astronomical clock** chime. On the hour, the windows open and a procession of apostles marches by 15th-century depictions of the four evils—a skeletal Death holding his hourglass and ringing a bell, a lute-playing Vanity, a corrupt Turk, and an avaricious Jew clutching his moneybags. After WWII, the Jew's horns and beard were removed and his name was changed to Greed. (*Exhibition hall open in summer M 10am-7pm, Tu-F 9am-7pm, Sa-Su 9am-6pm. Clock tower open M 11am-6pm, Tu-Su 9am-6pm; enter through 3rd fl. of Old Town Hall. Exhibition hall 100Kč, students 50Kč. Clock tower 100/50Kč.*)

TÝN CHURCH. The spires of **Chrám Matky Boží před Týnem** (Church of Our Lady Before Týn) rise above a mass of Baroque homes, though the careful observer will note that its spires are—in keeping with Gothic tradition—slightly different sizes. At night, the glowing towers are one of the most striking sights in the city. Even in an interior ornamented with gold, the altar stands out for its elaborate decor. Buried inside is astronomer **Tycho Brahe,** whose overindulgence at Emperor Rudolf's lavish dinner party in 1601 may have cost him his life. Since it was deemed improper to leave the table unless the emperor himself did so, Tycho had to remain in his chair until his bladder burst. He died 11 days later, though scholars believe mercury poisoning may have been the culprit. *(Open daily Apr.-Sept. 10am-8pm, Oct.-Mar. 10am-6pm. Mass Tu-F 5pm, Sa 8am, Su 9:30am and 9pm. Free.)*

SAINT JAMES'S CHURCH. Barely a surface in Kostel sv. Jakuba (St. James's Church) remains un-figured, un-marbleized, or unpainted. Located near Old Town Square, this church is home to an organ dating back to the early 18th century. Despite its interior splendor, the church has something of a macabre history. Inside the church is the tomb of Count Vratislav of Mitrovice. After his tomb was sealed, horrible sounds could be heard inside the church for days. When it finally occurred to someone to investigate, the count's body was found in a contorted position with claw marks on the inside of the tomb. Perhaps most striking is the mummified forearm that hangs to the left of the entrance. Legend has it that 500 years ago a thief tried to pilfer a gem from the Virgin Mary of Suffering, whereupon the figure sprang to life and yanked off his arm. *(Ⓜ︎B: Staroměstská. On Malá Štupartská, behind Týn Church. Open M-Sa 10am-noon and 2-3:45pm. Mass Su 8, 9, and 10:30am. Free.)*

KLEMENTINUM. Founded in 1232 and second only to Prague Castle in size, the Klementinum complex encompasses two hectares. Over the course of its 700-year history, it has served the needs of musicians, artists, scholars, and scientists alike. Unfortunately, most of the library is accessible only to card-holding patrons. The expensive and lengthy tour takes you through several of the building's most ornate rooms, including the heavily frescoed **Mirror Chapel,** which houses an organ regularly played by Mozart on his visits, and the **Baroque Library Hall,** which contains the library's oldest books and globes. From the Astronomical Tower, you can see the instruments used by Tycho Brahe and Johannes Kepler to make their measurements of the universe. *(Karlova 1. Ⓜ︎A: Staroměstská. Close to the Charles Bridge. ☎ 222 220 879; www.nkp.cz. Open 10am-8pm. Last tour 1hr. before closing. Tours every hr. Admission and tour 220Kč, students 140Kč. Cash only.)*

POWDER TOWER. Construction began on Prašná brána (the Powder Tower) in 1475 as an addition to the royal court, which was then located in Old Town Square. A few years later, however, the royal court moved and the tower was left unfinished for another 400 years. In the 18th century, it was used to store gunpowder (hence the name). Now the tower doesn't really guard or store anything except a few copies of paintings and the tourists looking at them. *(Ⓜ︎B: Náměstí Republiky. Open daily Apr.-Oct. 10am-6pm. Last entry 30min. before closing. 70Kč, students 50Kč.)*

MUNICIPAL HOUSE. Directly adjacent to the Powder Tower, the Obecní dům (Municipal House) is the most ornate Art Nouveau building in Prague. Built at the beginning of the 20th century, the building was the site of the proclamation of Czechoslovak independence in 1918. The interior was designed and decorated by a who's who list of early 20th-century Czech artists brought together by a sense of patriotic fervor. **Alfons Mucha's Hall** is one of the most beautiful, with its ornate ceiling supported by figures from the nation's history. The **Smetana Hall** is home to some of the biggest, and most expensive, classical concerts in Prague. *(Náměstí Republiky 5. Ⓜ︎B: Náměstí Republiky. ☎ 222 002 101; www.obecni-dum.cz. Open daily 10am-7pm. Tours every hr. 270Kč, students 220Kč. Casual dress expected for performances. AmEx/D/MC/V.)*

JOSEFOV

SYNAGOGUES

ⓜ*A: Staroměstská. Synagogues open M-F and Su Apr.-Oct. 9am-6pm; Nov.-Mar. 9am-4-:30pm. Closed Jewish holidays. Admission to all synagogues except Staronová 300Kč, students 200Kč. Staronová 200/140Kč. Combined tickets 480/320Kč. Men must cover their heads; yarmulke free. AmEx/MC/V.*

Four of the five synagogues in Josefov are administered by the Jewish Museum of Prague *(Židovské muzeum v Praze)*, which has ticket booths outside of each synagogue. Tickets are good for all of the synagogues (except the Old-New Synagogue) and also the Old Jewish Cemetery. The sights below (up to **Pinkas Synagogue**) are organized in the order our Let's Go researchers recommend you visit them, not necessarily in order of quality. Because of its separate ticketing system, **Old-New Synagogue** does not follow this particular visiting order and is thus included at the end.

OLD JEWISH CEMETERY (STARÝ ŽIDOVSKÝ HŘBITOV). The Old Jewish Cemetery stretches between the Pinkas Synagogue and the Ceremonial Hall. A winding path snakes through the uneven mounds covered with eroded and broken tombstones, jutting out of the ground at unexpected angles. Between the 14th and 18th centuries, the graves were dug in layers and over time, the earth settled and the stones from the lower layers were pushed to the surface, forcing many of the newer stones out of position and creating an indistinguishable mass of graves. The effect is slightly surreal. Rabbi Loew is buried by the wall opposite the entrance. His grave is easily recognized by the pebbles and coins placed on top of it. *(At the corner of Široká and Žatecká. Camera fee 40Kč.)*

KLAUSEN SYNAGOGUE (KLAUSOVÁ SYNAGOGA). Connected to the far more interesting Old Jewish Cemetery, the Klausen Synagogue was originally built in 1573, burned down a while later, rebuilt in 1604, and then reconstructed in the 1880s. The inside is dedicated to the role of the synagogue in Jewish life, that is, before it became a place to put old things. Next door, the **Ceremonial Hall** maintained by the Prague Burial Society rings in reality with an exhibit on disease and death in Judaism. *(On U starého hřbitova, between the Reservation Center and Ceremonial Hall.)*

MAISEL SYNAGOGUE (MAISELOVA SYNAGOGA). Like most old things in Prague, the Maisel Synagogue has been partially destroyed and subsequently rebuilt several times. While originally built in the Renaissance style, the synagogue is now a hodgepodge of Baroque and pseudo-Gothic elements. It contains artifacts from the history of Jews in Bohemia and Moravia up until the Jewish enlightenment. Some of the more interesting artifacts include the oldest tombstone from the Old Jewish Cemetery, as well as the robes of a 16th century Jewish visionary and martyr who was burned at the stake by the Inquisition. *(Maiselova, between Široká and Jáchymova.)*

SPANISH SYNAGOGUE (ŠPANĚLSKÁ SYNAGOGA). The Spanish Synagogue is easily the most richly decorated of the Josefov synagogues and one of the most stunning in Europe. Built in the Moorish-Byzantine style, the synagogue is covered from floor to ceiling with elaborate geometric patterns in beautiful reds, greens, and golds. The cupola is especially gorgeous. In fact, the interior of the synagogue itself overshadows the exhibit within, which details the history of the Jews in the Czech lands from the Jewish Enlightenment to the decades after WWII and contains probably the most impressive set of silver Torah pointers you're likely to in your lifetime. The synagogue also hosts classical concerts throughout the year. *(On the corner of Široká and Dušní. Wheelchair-accessible. Concerts about 700Kč.)*

PRAGUE

■PINKAS SYNAGOGUE (PINKASOVA SYNAGOGA). At the time of the Nazi take-over, there were 118,310 Jews living in the Prague ghetto, many of them refu-gees from the conquered territories. While a few managed to flee before the terror began, more than 92,000 remained in Prague. Of these remaining Jews, about 80,000 were deported to their deaths at Terezín or other concentration camps. The names of these victims are recorded on the otherwise bare walls of the nearly 500 year old Pinkas Synagogue. The names were originally added in the 1950s, but under the Communist regime they were whitewashed as part of ongoing efforts to reframe the victims of the Holocausts as anti-fascists. When Václav Havel was elected president in 1989, his first act was to have the names reinscribed on the synagogue walls. The second floor contains the haunting drawings of children from their time in Terezín. By far the most powerful of the synagogue visits, Pinkas should be reserved as the final stop of the tour. *(On Široká, between Žatecká and Listopadu 17. Men may wish to cover their heads. Yarmulkes 5Kč.)*

OLD-NEW SYNAGOGUE (STARONOVÁ SYNAGOGA). The oldest operating syna-gogue in Europe and one of the earliest Gothic structures in Prague, the rela-tively small Old-New Synagogue is still the center of Prague's Jewish community. The usual explanation for the name is that the synagogue was called the "New" synagogue when it was built in 1270 and took its present name when newer synagogues were built in the 16th century. However, a rumor persists that the synagogue was built with stones from the Temple in Jerusalem and that the name "Old-New" (*Alt-Neu* in German) is a mistranslation of the Hebrew "Al-Tnai," meaning "on condition," that the stones would be returned when the Temple in Jerusalem was rebuilt. Inside the synagogue, behind the iron gates hangs the remains of a flag flown by the congregation in 1357, when Charles IV first allowed the Jews to fly their own city flag. Nearby hangs the remnants of a red banner given to the Jews by the Holy Roman Emperor Ferdinand III for their part in the defense against the Swedes in 1648. According to legend, Rabbi Loew's famed Golem is stored in the attic of the synagogue should its powers ever be required again. Unfortunately, the attic is closed to the public. *(On the corner of Široká and Žatecká. Open in summer M-F and Su 9:30am-6pm. Services F and Sa at 8pm reserved for practic-ing members of the Jewish community. Men must cover their heads. Yarmulkes free.)*

OTHER SIGHTS. Though closed to the public, the **Jewish Town Hall** (Židovská rad-nice, Maiselova 18) is notable, if not for its architecture (standard Renaissance with a Baroque facade), than for its clock tower. The top clock displays the time in standard Roman numerals, while the lower face is marked with Hebrew numerals, and ticks counter-clockwise, according to Hebrew convention. *(Adja-cent to the Old-New Synagogue.)* Next to the Spanish Synagogue stands a statue of **■Franz Kafka,** astride an enormous figure that appears to be nothing more than a suit of clothes, as depicted in his story, "Description of a Struggle." At about 12 feet tall, the statue is nowhere near the scale of many of the city's other notable statues, but has quickly earned the attention of tourists and locals alike. *(On Dušní, at the corner of Žatecká, between the Spanish Synagogue and the Catholic church.)*

MALÁ STRANA

PETŘÍN HILL
This impossible-to-miss piece of the Prague skyline serves as a recreational area for Praguers and contains many of Malá Strana's landmarks.

PETŘÍNSKÁ ROZHLEDNA (PETŘÍN LOOKOUT TOWER). The most notable of Petřín's landmarks looks suspiciously like the Eiffel Tower. Built in 1891 for an exposition, the tower continues to provide tourists with postcard views of

Prague for a price. *(Open Apr.-Oct. 7am-10pm daily. Open Nov.-Mar. weekends 10am-5pm. Wheelchair-accessible. 100Kč, students 50Kč.)*

BLUDIŠTĚ (MIRROR LABYRINTH). Built for the same exposition as the Lookout Tower, this nearby labyrinth offers a brief, thoroughly unexciting romp through some mirrors and a few photo ops in a standard carnival-mirror room. For some reason, the building also contains a large diorama depicting the defense of the Charles Bridge against Swedish invaders. Save your money and get ice cream instead. *(Open May-Aug. daily 10am-10pm, Oct. daily 10am-6pm, Jan.-Mar. Sa-Su 10am-5pm, Apr.-Sept. daily 10am-7pm. 50Kč, students 40Kč.)*

ŠTEFÁNIKOVA HVĚZDÁRNA (ŠTEFÁNIK OBSERVATORY). The hill is also home to this observatory, which allows for great views of sun spots on clear days, and of stars, galaxies, and nebulae on clear nights. On a cloudy day, you can settle for an audiovisual program and a tour of the observatory, or you can save your money and come back when there's something worth seeing. *(☎ 257 320 504; www.observatory.cz. Open Apr.-Aug Tu-F 2-7pm and 9-11pm, Sa-Su 11am-7pm and 9-11pm. Check website for other hours. Wheelchair-accessible. 50Kč, students 35Kč. Audiovisual program 60/40Kč. Cash only.)*

A WALK WITHOUT YOUR WALLET. A trip to the hill need not also require a trip to the bank. The park itself is, as you might expect, pretty steep; you should expect any jaunt to the top to take at least 20 to 30 minutes. If that doesn't sound like fun to you, a **funicular** runs from the base of the hill to the top on a regular schedule, though on busy days you can expect a long line. *(Funicular uses public transportation tickets.)* However you reach the top, the **Rose Gardens** provide hundreds of beautiful rose varieties in spring and summer, and benches on which to admire such floral wonders.

Stretching from Strahov to Újezd through the park, the **Hunger Wall** was originally built by Charles IV in the 14th century during a period of intense famine as a way to employ many of the area's poor and starving. Though it appears to be a defensive wall, it actually serves no strategic purpose; consequently, the term "Hunger Wall" has entered Prague slang as a term for any useless and expensive public works project. The inner walkway of the wall, however, especially near the observatory, offers a priceless view of the city. Near the base of the hill, at the end of Vitězná, stands the **Memorial to the Victims of Communism,** a striking series of bronze figures showing a haunted, emaciated man who deteriorates the farther you go up the hill, until there's nothing left but a foot. A bronze strip running up the stairs shows the number of Czechs imprisoned, exiled, or killed under the Communist regime.

JOHN LENNON WALL. After Lennon's assassination, someone spray-painted a simple portrait of the artist on a Malá Strana wall. During the Communist period, the singer was an icon of love and freedom to the Czech people, and soon the wall exploded with portraits and lyrics from Beatles songs, along with grievances against the government. Though the original portrait of Lennon is long covered over (and some might say the original significance of the place along with it) people continue to write and draw all manner of political and personal messages across the Malá Strana landmark. *(Velkopřevorské náměstí. Trams 12, 20, 22, 91, Malostranské náměstí tram. From the tram, take Mostecká toward the river and then make a right on Velkopřevorské náměstí.)*

SAINT NICHOLAS'S CATHEDRAL. This Baroque landmark's massive dome can be seen all over Prague and is second only to Prague Castle in the Malá Strana skyline. Inside, you find yourself surrounded by more marble statues than you know what to do with. The statues supporting the beautifully frescoed dome are some of the best to be found in Prague. A handy guide is available at the entrance to tell you exactly what the hell you're looking at. Mozart regularly played on the cathedral's organ, which can still be heard at its frequent classical concerts. (*Malostranské náměstí 26. ⓂA: Malostranská. From the metro, take Letenská to Malostranské náměstí. ☎ 257 534 215. Open Nov.-Feb. 9am-4pm daily, Mar.-Oct. 9am-5pm daily. Last entry 15min. before closing. Concerts start around 6pm. Admission 70Kč, students 35Kč. Concerts 490/300Kč. Cash only.*)

WALLENSTEIN PALACE AND GARDENS. Duke Albrecht Wenzel von Wallenstein, who rose to prominence during the Thirty Years' War, originally intended for his Baroque palace to rival the nearby Prague Castle. However, the duke only got to live in his pleasure place for a year before Emperor Ferdinand II had him assassinated. Since WWII, the palace has housed various government offices and is currently the location of the Czech senate. A brief self-guided tour of the grounds takes you through several of the palace's most splendid rooms, including the **Main Hall,** which contains an enormous ceiling fresco of the late Duke depicted as Mars on a chariot. In a further gesture of hubris, the duke's chariot is pulled by four horses rather than the traditional three associated with the deity. Outside, the gardens contain immaculately manicured shrubbery, a fountain depicting Venus, and a family of peacocks. (*Vadštejnské náměstí 4. ⓂA: Malostranská. From the metro, take Klárov north and then turn left on Vadštejnské. ☎ 257 072 759. Palace open Sa-Su 10am-4pm. Gardens open June-Aug. M-F 7:30am-7pm, Sa-Su 10am-5pm. Last entry 30min. before closing. Gardens wheelchair-accessible. Free.*)

CHURCH OF OUR LADY VICTORIOUS. The oldest Baroque church, **Kostel Panny Marie Vítězné** (Church of Our Lady Victorious) in Prague has a marble theater as impressive as any other you're likely to find in the city, though its main draw is the famed **Infant Jesus of Prague,** a 47cm high wax statue from the 16th century with a seasonally rotating collection of robes and an alleged reputation for healing powers. Since coming into the church's possession in the 17th century, the statue has amassed quite a wardrobe, including a robe sewn by Mother Theresa herself. A portion of the wardrobe is on display in the church museum. (*Karmelitská 9. Trams 12, 20, 22, 91, Hellichova tram stop. From the tram, head north on Karmelitská. ☎ 257 533 646; www.pragjesu.info. Open M-Sa 8:30am-7pm, Su 8:30am-8pm. Museum open M-Sa 9:30am-5:30pm, Su 1-7pm. Free.*)

HRADČANY

PRAGUE CASTLE (PRAŽSKÝ HRAD)

Take tram #22 or 23 from the center, get off at "Pražský hrad," and go down U Prašného Mostu past the Royal Gardens and into the Second Courtyard. Or, hike up Nerudova. ☎ 224 373 368; www.hrad.cz. Open daily Apr.-Oct. 9am-5pm; Nov.-Mar. 9am-4pm. Castle grounds open Apr.-Oct. 5am-midnight; Nov.-Mar. 9am-midnight. Ticket office and info located opposite St. Vitus's Cathedral, inside the castle walls. Tickets come in 4 different flavors. The Long Tour (350Kč, students 175Kč) gets you everything, while the Short Tour (250/125Kč) covers the most important things. Tickets valid for 2 consecutive days.

One of the largest castles in the world, Pražský hrad (Prague Castle) has been the seat of the Bohemian government since its construction more than a millennium ago. After WWI, Czechoslovakia's first president, **Tomáš Masaryk,** invited Slovenian architect **Josip Plečnik** to rebuild his new residence after centuries of Hapsburg neglect. Plečnik not only restored the castle to its former majesty, but also added his own fountains and columns. During WWII, Reinhard Heydrich, the Nazi-appointed governor and notorious "Hangman of Prague," used the castle as his headquarters. Flaunting an old legend like his comrades in "Raiders of the Lost Ark," Heydrich wore the crown jewels that only rightful Bohemian kings were meant to wear. Though Heydrich's face didn't melt off, he was assassinated less than a year later, as per the film's legend. Arrive on the hour to catch the changing of the guard, complete with fanfare (daily from 5am-midnight).

⬛SAINT VITUS'S CATHEDRAL. The centerpiece of the castle complex and visible from all over Prague, St. Vitus's Cathedral (Katedrála sv. Víta) is an architectural masterpiece, complete with three magnificent towers and more flying buttresses than it knows what to do with. (No wonder it took 600 years to complete.) The cathedral, not surprisingly, is also the most popular attraction at Prague Castle. During tourist season, expect waits of 20-30min. just to get inside. Once you make it in, though, there's plenty to see. In the main church, precious stones and paintings telling the saint's story line the walls of **Saint Wenceslas Chapel** (Svatováclavská kaple). Don't miss the gorgeous **Mucha Window,** perhaps the cathedral's most beautiful. For a great view and a healthy hike, climb the 287 steps of the **Great South Tower.** Many of Prague's most important religious and political figures are buried here. To the right of the altar stands the silver **tomb of Saint Jan Nepomuck** of Charles Bridge fame. Nearby, a statue of an angel holds what is purportedly Jan's silvered tongue, somehow severed after he was thrown into the Vlatva by Charles IV. The tongue remains on display, though the story surrounding it has long since been proven false. Underground, the **Royal Crypt** (Královská hrobka) holds the tomb of Charles IV. The Bohemian crown jewels are kept in a room with seven locks, the keys to which are kept in the hands of seven different Czech leaders, both secular and religious.

OLD ROYAL PALACE. The Old Royal Palace (Starý královský palác), to the right of the cathedral, is one of the few Czech castles where visitors can wander largely unattended—probably because its mostly empty. The lengthy **Vladislav Hall** is the largest Gothic hall in the Czech Republic; it once hosted coronations and indoor jousting competitions. Upstairs in the Chancellery of Bohemia, a Protestant assembly found two Catholic governors guilty of religious persecution and threw them out the window during the 1618 Second Defenestration of Prague (see **Life and Times,** p. 139), though without paying for an audioguide you would have no way of knowing this, since what little information there is is in Czech.

ROYAL SUMMER PALACE AND ROYAL GARDENS. The Italian-designed Royal Summer Palace was built in the 16th century to provide entertainment for royals until it fell into the hands of Austrian army, whose stay necessitated extensive rebuilding. Near the entrance, the **Singing Fountain** uses a vibrating bronze plate to create its rhythmic and enchanting sound, though you have to squat down somewhat awkwardly to actually hear it. The surrounding Royal Gardens contain dozens of species of trees and shrubbery, and make for a relaxing stroll at any time of day. The garden is also home to an assortment of birds of prey, which a falconer displays from noon to 5pm daily.

SAINT GEORGE'S BASILICA AND CONVENT. Across from the Old Royal Palace stands St. George's Basilica (Bazilika sv. Jiří), a large, austere church built in AD 920, later burned down, reconstructed, occupied, and then reconstructred again in the Romanesque style you see today. In one of the adjoining rooms, the tomb and skeleton of St. Ludmila are displayed. The convent next door houses the **National Gallery of Bohemian Art,** which collects Bohemian art from the Gothic period through the 19th century and includes an impressive collection of landscape paintings. The work by **Anonín Mánes** is some of the museum's best. *(Open Tu-Su 10am-6pm. 100Kč, students 50Kč.)*

GOLDEN LANE AND DALIBOR TOWER. Originally used to house castle servants, the small dwellings that line crowded Golden Lane once housed the castle's alchemists, hence the present name. At other times it has been home to the castle's artillerymen and artisans. Franz Kafka worked for a time at a workspace at **#22**, a small blue house marked with a plaque. At the end of the street you'll come to the base of **Dalibor Tower**, which was a cannon tower until it was converted into a prison after a fire. Its most famous resident was the knight Dalibor, the subject of the old Czech adage "Necessity taught Dalibor how to play the fiddle" even though the actual fiddle was a torture instrument designed to make the knight change his tune, rather than a musical instrument. The tower exhibits a variety of torture and execution implements, including cages, racks, stocks, "Spanish boots," and a headsman's axe. *(To the right of the Basilica, follow Jiřská halfway down and take a right on Zlatá ulička, or "Golden Lane".)*

STRAHOV MONASTERY

Strahovské nádvoří 1. Tram 22, Pohořelec tram stop. From the tram, walk south and make a right on Dlabačov, then take a sharp left onto Strahovské nádvoří. ☎233 107 711; www.strahovskyklaster.cz. Open Tu-Su 9am-noon and 1-5pm. Last entry 15min. before closing. Admission to library 80Kč, students 50Kč. Gallery 60/30Kč. Audio tour 90/75Kč. Cash only.

Part pilgrimage site, part library, and part gallery, the Strahov Monastery (Strahovský klášter) has had a rough history; it was built in 1120, burned down in 1258, rebuilt and then blundered in turn by the Hussites, Swedes, and French. Since the fall of Communism, things seem to have quieted down. The renowned library contains thousands of volumes of philosophical, astronomical, mathematical, and historical knowledge, though your admission only entitles you to look from behind a barrier. In the anterior chamber, an 18th-century cabinet of curiosities contains the remains of dozens of species of crustacean and other sea fauna, including a crocodile, octopus, and hammerhead shark, as well as various shells, ceramics, and Hussite weaponry. Its most-prized artifact, however, is the remains of a dodo. A little ways up, the Strahov Gallery contains a large picture gallery with a mix of religious, classical, and secular subjects. If you want a great view that you don't have to pay for, walk down the dirt path at the foot of the monastery, there will be a sign that reads "Grand Panorama." The view from the top of the hill gives you a postcard view of Prague.

THE LOCAL STORY

BONE-CHILLING CHAPEL

In and around Prague, you'll find churches made of stone, brick, iron, glass—and one of bones. Kutná Hora, a small, picturesque village 1hr. from Prague (p. 205), is infamous for its ossuary, a chapel filled with artistic and religious creations made entirely from parts of human skeletons. The village earned its fame from silver mining in the 14th century. Its morbid side only came out when its graveyard gained a reputation as a sacred place to bury plague victims. Since the cemetery was overflowing with corpses, the Cistercian Order built a chapel to house the extra remains. In a fit of creativity (or possibly insanity), one monk began designing flowers from pelvises and crania. He never finished the ossuary, but the artist František Rint eventually completed the project in 1870, decorating the chapel from floor to ceiling with the bones of over 40,000 people.

Trains run from Hlavní nádraži in Prague to Kutná Hora (1½hr., 1 per hr., one-way 62Kč). The ossuary is a 1km walk from the station. Turn right out of the station, then take a left, and go left again on the highway. Continue for 500m and go right at the church; the ossuary is at the end of the road. ☎728 125 488; www.kostnice.cz. Open daily 8am-6pm.

LORETA. The Loreta complex consists of two chapels and a two-story, arcaded courtyard. The central **Santa Casa** contains a statue of the Lady of Loretta, holding what is purported to be a piece of Mary's house at Bethlehem. The site is considered the holiest place in the Czech Republic and is the traditional starting point of pilgrimages from the area. On the second floor, a small treasury contains several jewel-encrusted religious texts and an impressive collection of chalices. *(Loretánské námesti 7. Tram 22, Pohořelec tram stop. From the tram stop, walk south, turn left on Pohořelec, then left on Loretánské námesti. ☎ 220 516 740; www.loreta.cz. Open Tu-Su 9am-12:15pm and 1-4:30pm. 110Kč, students 90Kč. Cash only.)*

ŽIŽKOV AND VINOHRADY

VYŠEHRAD NATIONAL CULTURAL MONUMENT. A large castle complex overlooking the Vltava from a hill, Vyšehrad seems to play second fiddle to the larger and better known Prague Castle. Even the neo-Gothic spires of the **Church of Saint Peter and Saint Paul** look suspiciously similar to that of the Cathedral of St. Vitus. At the same time, Vyšehrad has many fine qualities of its own, and may be slightly less inundated with tourists if you're hoping for a quiet afternoon of historical immersion. Vyšehrad is famous for its views of the Vlatava and the surrounding area, so spend some time strolling the old ramparts. The area to the south of the complex, near the **Gothic Cellar,** contains one of the best views, with a vista of the ruins of the **Baths of Libuše,** where the visionary princess is said to have foreseen the creation of a marvelous city within the surrounding hills. The park at the top of the hill contains beautiful classical statuary. If you have time, take a stroll through the **Vyšehrad cemetery,** which contains the graves of prominent Czechs, including Antonín Dvořák, Karel Čapek, and Alfons Mucha among others. *(V Pevnosti 5B. Metro C: Vyšehrad. ☎ 241 410 348; www. praha-vysehrad.cz. Grounds open 24hr. Exhibitions open daily Apr.-Oct. 9:30am-6pm, Nov.-Mar. 9:30am-5pm. Wheelchair-accessible, though there are some steep hills. Entrance free; Gothic Cellar 30Kč, students 20Kč.)*

ŽIŽKOV TELEVISION TOWER. From a distance, the Žižkov TV Tower has looks like a Communist-era rocket that never left the launch pad. Its three enormous pillars certainly make it an unconventional-looking structure, especially rising out of the otherwise unimpressive Žižkov skyline. Like the Dancing House and other strikingly modern structures in Prague, the tower was initially met with great hostility during its construction in the mid 1980s, at least in part because some feared that the tower would eradicate area infants. After more than 20 years, however, people have grown to at least accept, if not totally embrace, its unusual architecture. In 2000, controversial Czech artist David Černý cast nine figures of babies—perhaps in reference to that earlier paranoia—and attached them to the tower, where they have been suspended ever since. The tower hosts an overpriced restaurant and three observation decks, allowing for impressive views of the city minus the hassle of walking up hundreds of stairs. The fee (150Kč, students 120Kč) might make the tower better appreciated from the outside. *(Mahlerovy sady 1. Metro A: Jiřího z Poděbrad. From the metro, cross diagonally through the park and then take Milešovská toward the enormous tower. ☎ 242 418 778; www. tower.cz. Observation deck open daily 10am-11:30pm. Cash only.)*

JAN ŽIŽKA STATUE AND NATIONAL MEMORIAL. In June 1420, Hussite general Jan Žižka repulsed an attack from King Sigismund of Germany and Hungary on Vítkov Hill, breaking the siege of Prague. The grateful citizens named the area after their savior, and in 1950, an enormous statue by Bohumil Kafka was erected on the hill to commemorate the great leader. At more than 30 feet high, the statue remains the largest equestrian statue in the world. Behind the statue stands the monolithic National Memorial, built in honor of the Czechoslovak legionnaires who secured the independence of the former Czechoslovakia. Under Communism, the building was made into a mausoleum to hold the remains of Klement Gottwald and other Communist leaders. Unfortunately, the National Memorial is currently closed for renovation: the dead Communists have been moved and the entire complex has been turned into a modern historical museum, scheduled to open in the fall or winter of 2009. Though you can't get very close, the statue is still impressive and worth making the trip uphill. The surrounding park is a popular place for dog walkers and picnics. *(Husinecká tram stop, trams 5, 9, 26. From the tram stop, follow Husinecká, then turn left on Jeronýmova and walk up the hill.)*

HOLEŠOVICE AND DEJVICE

LETNÁ PARK. On a plateau overlooking the Vltava, Letná Park provides a nice escape from the bustle of Prague proper. On a nice day, thousands can be found picnicking or otherwise lounging on the benches and green spaces. The park also includes several recreational areas for children, including the oldest functioning carousel in Europe. Near the center of the park, the **Letná beer garden** is one of the most popular in Prague. (Open daily 11am-1am. Beer 25Kč. Cash only.) Though the park is mostly recreational now, it has a distinctly political past. In 1955, the world's largest statue of Joseph Stalin was erected on a platform facing Old Town. The next year, however, came Khruschev's "Secret Speech" denouncing Stalin and his cult of personality, making the enormous statue something of an embarrassment for the Czech people. In 1962, the statue was demolished. In the early 1990s, the bomb shelter beneath the statue's plinth housed a pirate radio station and later a rock club, though today, the doors have unfortunately been closed. In 1991, an enormous **metronome** was erected on the sight. The remains of the monument are now covered in layers of graffiti, and the area behind the metronome is a popular destination for skateboarders year-round. *(Metro A: Staroměstská. From the metro, walk north along the river and cross at Čechův most.)*

PRAGUE ZOO. A popular destination for locals, the Prague Zoo stretches over 160 acres on the bank of the Vlatva and contains more than 500 species. The modern enclosures often make use of natural boundaries like creeks or rocks rather than the bars and concrete walls of more traditional zoos. Several large, enclosed areas allow you to get as

FROM THE ROAD

THE CHANGING TIMES

In the early 1950s, Prague's Letenské sady (Letná Park), was chosen to be the site of the world's largest monument to Joseph Stalin, though neither the dictator nor the monument's architect lived to see its completion. The statue depicted the Soviet leader surrounded by peasants, soldiers, workers, and intellectuals, symbolizing the way he supposedly unified the Soviet state, though by the time of its unveiling, many were disenchanted with the ex-leader. As if to add insult to injury, Krushchev's denunciation of Stalin came only a few years after the statue's completion. Deeming it too big to dismantle, the Czech authorities demolished the statue in 1962.

Walking up to the base of the statue, I expected to find a pristine park with no trace of its Soviet past. What I found instead was a bunch of bright, vibrant graffiti. Even the enormous bronze bowls that once flanked the monument were covered in elaborate tags. Also, at some point, skateboarders realized that the grandiose granite steps and blocks were perfect for grinding. I found dozens of kids of all ages popping kickflips and shooting videos all over the base. To top it off, several pairs of shoes dangled from the power line connected to the metronome that has been installed in the monument's stead.

- Justin Keenan

close as possible to the exotic bird species within. A handy, elevated platform gives you a great view of the elephant, hippo, and stork enclosures and provides the unique opportunity of reenacting the opening scene of the Lion King, if you can stand the judgments which inevitably exude from the surrounding jumble of humans and animals. A tram (20Kč) takes you to the upper level with splendid panoramic views of the surrounding area. The zoo is world-renowned for its successful breeding programs involving gorillas, big cats, and wild horses. (*Metro C: Nádraží Holešovice. From the metro station, catch bus 112 to Zoologická Zahrada.* ☎ *266 112 111; www.zoopraha.cz. Last entry 1hr before closing. Wheelchair-accessible. Open daily Jun-Aug. 9am-7pm, Sept.-Oct. and Apr.-May 9am-6pm, Nov.-Feb. 9am-4pm and Mar. 9am-5pm. 150Kč, students and seniors 100Kč. AmEx/D/MC/V.*)

🏛 MUSEUMS AND GALLERIES

🖼**MUCHA MUSEUM.** Devoted to the work of Alfons Mucha, the Czechs' most celebrated artist and an Art Nouveau pioneer, the museum divides his body of work into easily digested segments. His graphic design work, particularly his many posters featuring "la divine" Sarah Bernhardt, remains the most impressive. A lengthy and amusingly over-the-top video gives the painter's biography and discusses the lengths to which he went to create his masterpiece, the Slav Epic. While closer in size to a large gallery than a museum proper, the posters alone are worth the price of admission. (*Panská 7.* Ⓜ*A or B: Můstek. Walk up Václavské náměstí toward the St. Wenceslas statue. Go left on Jindřišská and left again on Panská.* ☎ *221 451 333; www.mucha.cz. Open daily 10am-6pm. 120Kč, students 60Kč. AmEx/MC/V.*)

🖼**MUSEUM OF CZECH CUBISM.** Appropriately located inside the **House of the Black Madonna** (U Černé Matky Boží), itself a masterpiece of cubist architecture, the Museum of Czech Cubism contains three floors of work from various painters, sculptors, designers, and architects. The Museum demonstrates how Czech Cubism permeated all areas of the fine arts during its heyday (even areas where it maybe shouldn't have, such as home furniture). The works from Emil Filla and Bohumil Kubista are particularly noteworthy. (*Ovocný trh 19.* Ⓜ*B: Náměstí Republiky.* ☎ *224 301 803; www.ngprague.cz. Open daily 10am-6pm. Wheelchair-accessible. 100Kč, 50Kč for students, 50Kč after 4pm. Cash only.*)

🖼**FRANZ KAFKA MUSEUM.** This fantastic museum eschews the stuffy display case approach to museums with a series of original and occasionally bizarre multimedia exhibits. The first half of the museum attempts to examine the role of Prague in the author's life, using pictures and diary entries that prepare you for the museum's more exciting and more unconventional second half. Its latter portion contains a combination of multimedia displays, haunting music, and a seemingly endless corridor of filing cabinets to evoke the feelings of isolation and dread so important to the author's work. (*Cihelná 2b.* Ⓜ*A: Malostranská. Go down Klárov toward the river, turn right on U. Luzické Semináré and left on Cilhená.* ☎ *257 535 507; www.kafkamuseum.cz. Open daily 10am-6pm. 120Kč, students 60Kč. MC/V.*)

🖼**VELETRŽNÍ PALACE.** Those searching for a more conventional palace may be confused by the rectangular, distinctly Modernist building that looks like it ought to contain offices rather than priceless works of art. The flagship (and largest) collection of Prague's dispersed National Gallery, the Veletržní Palace houses three full floors devoted to its impressive permanent collections of 20th- and 21st-century art, while the ground floor and mezzanine contain rotating galleries of contemporary art. While Picasso, Kilmt, Warhol, and others make occasional appearances, the vast majority of artists represented are Czech, with an emphasis placed on the ways in which Czech artists have sought to engage with and distinguish themselves from international art movements. The gallery devoted to the Czech Cubists is the perfect follow-up for those who didn't get their fill at the House of the Black Madonna. There's no better way to spend a rainy Prague afternoon than getting lost in the museum's massive collections. *(Dukelských hrdinů 45. ⓜC: Vltavská. From the metro, take Antonínská west and turn right onto Dukelských hrdinů. ☎ 224 301 090; www.ngprague.cz. Open Tu-Su 10am-6pm. Last entry 30min. before closing. Free 1st W of every month 3-6pm. Wheelchair-accessible. 200Kč, students and seniors 100Kč. AmEx/D/MC/V.)*

▧**MUSEUM OF MINIATURES.** Devoted to the work of Siberian artist Anatolij Koněnko, the museum's forty exhibits all require either a magnifying glass or a microscope to view and could be carried in a purse, if they weren't bolted to the table. The collection features everything from miniature reproductions of works by Leonardo DaVinci, Matisse, and Dali to portraits of John Lennon and Václav Havel on poppy seeds. Some of the more exciting pieces include a menagerie on the wing of a mosquito and a caravan of camels passing through the eye of a needle, though the museum's greatest treasure is a 0.9mm x 0.9mm book containing the text of a Chekhov story along with illustrations. *(Strahovské nádvoří 11. ☎ 233 352 371. Tram 22, Pohořelec tram stop. From the tram, walk south, make a right on Dlabačov, and then make a sharp left onto Strahovské nádvoří. Wheelchair-accessible. Open daily 10am-5pm. 50Kč, students 30Kč. D/MC/V.)*

MUSEUM KAMPA. Located on the picturesque Kampa island in a converted former flour mill, the Kampa Museum contains one of the best collections of contemporary art in Prague. The museum owes its existence to a pair of collectors who smuggled the work of persecuted or marginalized artists out of Soviet Czechoslovakia during the Cold War. Thanks to their efforts, the museum has impressive collections of some of the Czech Republic's most important artists. The two large galleries devoted to František Kupka and Otto Gutfreund are some of the museum's finest. *(U Sovových mlýnů 2. ⓜA: Malostranská. From the metro, take the tram to the Újezd stop, walk north on Újezd, turn right on Říční, and then follow it to Kampa Island. ☎ 257 286 147; www.museumkampa.cz. Open daily 10am-6pm. Last entry 30min. before closing. Wheelchair-accessible. 220Kč, students 110Kč. Cash only.)*

NATIONAL MUSEUM. Situated at the top of Wenceslas Sq. and housed in a massive 19th-century building, the Národní Muzeum (National Museum) is unmistakable. A shining example of Neo-Renaissance architecture, its interior is full of vaulted ceilings and ornate marble staircases. The museum is divided into a series of enormous wings devoted variously to mineralogy, anthropology, prehistory, zoology, and paleontology. Highlights include five enormous halls of precious (and occasionally radioactive) stones and a complete whale skeleton suspended from the ceiling. The real showpiece is the ▧**Pantheon**—a gorgeous room which contains statues and busts of famous Czech politicians, writers, composers, scientists, and religious figures. The cupola depicts the firmament supported by angels and is surrounded by murals representing Inspiration, Knowledge, Right, and Art. Be warned: the basement exhibit, oddly titled "Europe as the Cradle of Scientific Obstetrics," seems amusing until you see the videos of live births that play on loop. Regular classical music concerts are held on the immaculate grand staircase. *(Václavské náměstí 68. ⓜA or C: Muzeum. ☎ 224 497 111; www.nm.cz. Open M-Tu and Th-F 10am-6pm, W 10am-8pm, Sa 10am-7pm, Su 11am-7pm. Last entry 30min. before closing. 150Kč, students 100Kč. Free first M of every month from 10am-7pm, closed the following Tu. Audio tours 200Kč, students 100Kč. Classical music tickets 500Kč, students 400Kč, seniors 450Kč. AmEx/MC/V.)*

CZECH MUSEUM OF MUSIC. A former Baroque church now serves as the home for the České muzeum hudby (Czech Museum of Music) and its collections. The ground floor typically houses an array of rotating exhibitions, but the museum's real treasure is its impressive collection of historic and unusual instruments. Some of the more interesting artifacts include a set of quarter-tone pianos and clarinets, several unusually shaped upright pianos, and a collection of folk instruments like bagpipes and hurdy gurdys. Many of the instruments (though not always the most exciting-looking ones) can be listened to on headphone stations throughout the museum. *(Karmelitská 2/4. Trams 12, 20, 22, 91, Hellichova tram stop. The museum is directly across the street from the tram stop. ☎ 257 257 735; www.nm.cz. Open M 1pm-6pm, W 10am-8pm, Th 10am-6pm, F 9am-6pm, Sa-Su 10am-6pm. Last entry 30min. before closing. Wheelchair-accessible. 100Kč, students 50Kč. Photo fee 40Kč. Cash only.)*

ANTONÍN DVOŘÁK MUSEUM. Situated in an 18th-century baroque townhouse, the **Antonín Dvořák Museum** houses thousands of artifacts from the composer's life and work as well as reproductions of his desk and study. The collections of sheet music manuscripts and correspondence are beautiful and fascinating, though often illegible. The grounds themselves make for a pleasant afternoon stroll. On Tuesdays and Fridays from April to October, the museum hosts performances of Dvořák's music, complete with period costumes. *(Ke Karlovu 20. ⓜC: I.P. Pavlova. From the metro, take Jecna toward the river and then turn left on Ke Karlovu; the museum will be on your left. ☎ 224 918 013; www.nm.cz. Open Tu-Su 10am-5:30pm, closed 1:30-2pm for lunch. 50Kč, students and seniors 25Kč. Guided tours 500Kč. Fee for taking photographs and filming 30Kč. AmEx/MC/V.)*

CITY GALLERY PRAGUE. With seven locations throughout greater Prague, the City Gallery (Galerie Hlavního Města Prahy) offers an impressive variety of permanent and rotating collections. The **Dům U Zlatého prstenu** (House of the Golden Ring) has a massive collection of Czech art that spans three floors and serves as an introduction to the work and import of 11 Czech artists from the latter half of the 20th century. Each artist gets his or her own gallery space, giving the museum a disparate feel, though common themes, such as reactions to the perceived decline of the 1970s and 1980s, help unify the mix of painters, printmakers, and sculptors. *(Týnská 6. ⓜA: Staroměstská. Behind and to the left of Týn Church. ☎ 222 327 677; www.citygalleryprague.cz. The building itself has an elevator, though some of the passages may be too narrow for wheelchairs. Open Tu-Su 10am-8pm. 120Kč, students 60Kč. Cash only.)*

MUSEUM OF ◙COMMUNISM. Located above a McDonald's and next to a casino, this gallery attempts to explore the dream, reality, and nightmare of life under Communism in Czechoslovakia through a mix of audiovisual aids and artifacts from daily life. The museum truly outdoes itself in its elementary-school-style poster board displays. Unfortunately, the museum's gift shop and publicity posters have a much better sense of humor than the museum itself. *(Na Příkopě 10. ⓜA: Můstek. ☎ 224 212 966; www.museumofcommunism.com. Open daily 9am-9pm. 180Kč, students 140Kč. Cash only.)*

PRAGUE TOY MUSEUM. Two floors and seven exhibition rooms are barely enough to contain this comprehensive collection of toys, that once belonged to the cartoonist and filmmaker Ivan Steiger. This collection includes everything from 19th-century Bohemian toys made from wood and tin to a finger that once belonged to a robot in *Terminator 2: Judgment Day*. The second floor, occupied almost entirely by Barbie dolls, is less a monument to toys than a monument to one man's obsession. *(Jiřská 4. ☎ 224 372 294. ⓜA: Malostranská. From the metro, take walk north on Klárov and then turn left onto Staré zámecké schody; the museum is in the courtyard to the right, on the 2nd and 3rd floors. Open daily 9:30am-5:30pm. 70Kč. Cash only.)*

🎵 ENTERTAINMENT

For information on Prague's concerts and performances, consult *The Prague Post, Threshold, Do mesta-Downtown,* or *The Pill* (all free at many cafes and restaurants). Most performances start at 7 or 8pm and offer rush tickets 30min. before curtain. The majority of Prague's theaters close in July and August. Late spring and early summer usually bring an array of regular and one-off festivals. The **Prague Spring International Music Festival** (☎257 312 547; www.prague-spring. net), which runs from mid-May to early June, has weathered six decades of political and artistic turmoil yet continues to draw musicians from around the world. Every year a number of Czech and international composers and musicians debut material. Leonard Bernstein made his international debut at the festival in 1946-7. June brings all things avant-garde with the **Prague Fringe Festival** (☎224 935 183; www.praguefringe.com), featuring dancers, comedians, performance artists, and—everyone's favorite—mimes in a different venue every day. That same month, the **Prague Writers' Festival** (☎224 241 312; www.pwf.cz) brings renowned writers of all languages together for a week-long discussion covering current topics in literature and culture. At this series of public readings, rountables, and panel discussions, audience participation is welcome. Most readings are subtitled in Czech and English. Now entering its sixth year, the **United Islands of Prague** (☎257 325 041; www.unitedislands.cz) attracts more than 100 bands and a crowd of eager backpackers from across the globe. The free and open festival spans several days and multiple islands on both sides of the Vltava. For tickets to the city's shows, try **Bohemia Ticket International,** Malé náměstí 13, next to Čedok. (☎224 227 832; www.ticketsbti.cz. Open M-F 9am-5pm, Sa 9am-1pm.)

National Theater, Národní 2 (☎224 224 351; www.nationaltheatre.cz). ⓂB: Národní třída. From the metro, take Spálená north and then turn left on Národní. The place to go if you want to look like you know anything about Czech opera, ballet, or drama. The building itself is a neo-Renaissance masterpiece, topped by chariot-driven angels with an interior inspired by the work of Josef Mánes. Tickets 800-1200Kč. No dress code per-se, though you'll probably look out of place in anything less than a cocktail dress for women or dress shirt and sweater for men. Box office open M-F 10am-5:30pm, Sa-Su 10am-12:30pm. AmEx/D/MC/V.

Image Theater, Pařížská 4 (☎222 329 191; www.imagetheatre.cz). ⓂA: Staroměstská. From the metro, take Široká east, and then turn right on Pařížská. A fusion of music, pantomime, dance, and blacklight performed entirely without words. Rest assured that the native Czechs in the audience are just as confused by the strange, though strangely compelling, performances as you. Tickets 480Kč. Box office open daily 9am-8pm. MC/V.

National Marionette Theater, Žatecká 1 (☎224 819 322; www.mozart.cz). ⓂA: Staroměstská. From the metro, take Valentinská east and then turn right on Žatecká. The best place to see why marionette shops are such a big deal in Prague. Little-to-no spoken dialogue makes these performances ideal for travelers and the hard of hearing. The theater has also staged more than 3000 performances of its greatest hit, a hilarious rendition of Don Giovanni complete with period costumes, perfect for children and the short of attention. Tickets 590Kč. Box office open daily 10am-6pm. MC/V.

Municipal House, Náměstí Republiky 5 (☎222 002 101; www.obecni-dum.cz). ⓂB: Náměstí Republiky. Prague's grandest (or most ostentatious, depending on your preferences) Art Nouveau building stages some of the city's premier classical performances, with odd ballet thrown in for good measure. Look and feel fancy escorting your date to seats in the multi-storied, multi-statued Smetana Hall. Tickets 700-1300Kč. Casual dress expected for performances. Box office open daily 10am-7pm. AmEx/MC/V.

START: Futura Gallery.

FINISH: Žižkov Television Tower.

DURATION: 2½-4hr.

WHEN TO GO: late morning or early afternoon.

CHUMMING WITH ČERNÝ

The undisputed L'enfant terrible of Czech art, David Černý first made a name for himself while still an art student, when he and several friends painted an entire tank—part of the former Monument to Soviet Tank Crews—bright pink, much to the amusement or chagrin of most of Prague. His subsequent works continue to leave a mark on Prague both physically and psychically. His signature irreverence has made him enormously popular with young people in the Czech Republic and farther afield, though many of the parents and grandparents of those same young people don't understand why this man can't leave the city's buildings and monuments alone.

Černý's recent claim to international fame came from his controversial piece "Entropa," which was commissioned to represent the 27 member states of the European Union in celebration of the Czech Republic's temporary presidency of the Council of the EU. See **Going Entropic over Entropa** on p. 146. What a prankster.

1. FUTURA GALLERY. The Futura Gallery is owned by a non-profit group devoted to presenting contemporary art. In the courtyard of this otherwise unassuming building, you can find two figures named Klaus and Knizak, both of whom appear to be coming out of the wall, back ends first. Stick your face in the rather gaping rear end of one of the statues and you can see a video of two Czech politicians spooning slop to one another while Queen's "We Are the Champions" plays on loop.

2. MUSEUM KAMPA. While the Kampa is certainly worth your money, you don't even have to go inside to see replicas of Černý's famous baby sculptures hanging around outside. Consider it a teaser for your eventual trek to the Žižkov Tower. You might also notice that the babies don't have any faces. We don't know what to make of this, either.

3. PISSING MEN. In front of the Kafka Museum, you'll notice a sculpture of two Czech men who appear to be—ahem—relieving themselves inside an oddly shaped basin. Depending on how your geography is, you might realize that the basin is in the outline of the Czech Republic. Small motors inside the statues cause their torsos and other parts to turn and move around realistically. While this might seem like an unnecessary detail, it's used to great effect. The motors move the parts of the statue in such a way that the streams of water are actually rewriting famous quotes from prominent Czech leaders and thinkers.

4. HANGING OUT. After you finish in Mala Strana, cross one of the bridges and head over to the intersection of Husova and Betlémské náměstí. Look up, and you'll see a statue of someone who looks a lot like Sigmund Freud hanging from a rather phallic beam just over the street. We leave the interpretation up to you.

5. SAINT WENCESLAS BEATING A DEAD HORSE. Downstairs in the Lucerna building you can find one of New Town's hottest clubs. Upstairs, in front of the old theater, you can find suspended overhead a very stubborn-looking Saint Wenceslas riding a very dead and very upside-down horse. The depiction of the Good King seems to be an exact copy of the more

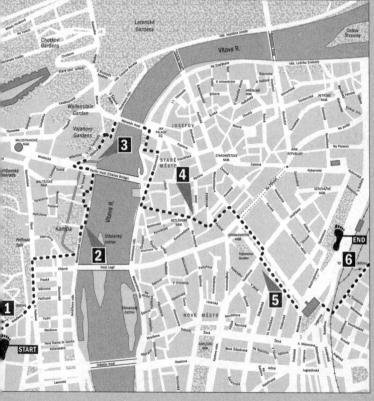

...mous statue found at the top of nearby Wenceslas Square. Subtle cultural and historical ...ommentary? Meaningless rubbish? Is there a difference?

. ŽIŽKOV TELEVISION TOWER. Here we find Černý's most famous work. When the Žižkov ...wer was originally proposed in the 1970s, there was a great public debate over whether or ...ot the radio waves emanating from the tower would be strong enough to harm people living ... the area. Most notably, there were exaggerated claims that the presence of the tower ...ould be harmful to the area's young children. Though the debate was largely forgot-...n after the tower's completion, the memory may have inspired Černý. Originally ...stalled in 1994 as a temporary exhibit, the babies proved so popular that they ...ere installed permanently a few years later. After you've seen your fill of David ...erný, you can eat your fill of overpriced food at the top of the tower. Or not. ...u've already seen the best part.

Velvets and Plastics

When Frank Zappa was invited to Prague in 1990 by Václav Havel, Czechoslovakia's first post-Communist president, many saw it as the climactic end to decades of cultural repression. But emerging from his plane on that cold January day, Zappa was stunned to find a throng of adoring fans awaiting his arrival, many of them more intimately familiar with his music than he could ever have imagined.

Universe, the most influential underground Czech rock act of the 20th century, picked up their guitars and rewrote the rules of music, politics, and dissent. Banned by the authorities and forced to practice and play in friends' basements and abandoned buildings, The Plastics drew heavily from the repertoire of disaffected, nihilistic American musical subcultures (most notably, the psychotropic Berkeley scene of Zappa and Captain Beefheart, and the sexually and sonically deviant New York City scene of The Fugs and The Velvet Underground). According to their charismatic manager, Ivan Jirous, it was precisely this sound that expressed the agony and angst of living in a shallow, materialistic society—which, ironically enough, was an attitude that resonated perfectly with the post big-bit Czech youth, fed up with the fear-stricken conformity of 1970s Czechoslovakia.

"...the Plastic People picked up their guitars and rewrote the rules of music, politics, and dissent."

The Czech audience had been eagerly following the developments of Western rock music since its first swaggering steps onto the global arena. Despite their best efforts, the Communist authorities of the 1960s Czechoslovak Socialist Republic were powerless to halt the influx of the Western sound, streaming across the border in the form of pirated radio signals and bootlegged vinyl. Almost overnight, every Czech teenager was parroting the Southern drawl of Elvis Presley and Fats Domino, crooning "yeah yeah yeah," and dancing the twist. Just as dapper youngsters had prowled the vast network of Prague nightclubs during WWII, shimmying to jazz in defiance of the Nazis, so, too, did the "big-bit" (big beat) generation living under Communism seize on the subculture of their supposed Capitalist enemies.

But the euphoria of the big-bit generation was short-lived. The Soviet invasion of August 1968 was followed by a period of "normalization," which meant a crackdown not just on outright political dissent, but also on the insubordinate attitude that rock music fostered. Czech big-bit acts were silenced and prohibited from touring if they did not fit the saccharine standards of the Communist cultural police: i.e., no long hair, no English lyrics, no suggestive or strange performances, no deviant behavior of any kind.

It was in this puritanical environment that the The Plastic People of the

But the "tune in, drop out" mantra emanating from the West took on a deeper political shade on the other side of the Iron Curtain. When The Plastics were finally arrested and put on trial in 1976, it was none other than Václav Havel, the most prominent dissident in the country, who came to their rescue, building a massive campaign around their cause. In Czechoslovakia, a Zappa-esque riff or the lyrics to "Sweet Jane" acquired enough political heft to spawn first a government crackdown, then the widely-circulated "Charter 77" on human rights, and, finally, Havel's enormously influential political essay and virtual template on East and Central European dissent, The Power of the Powerless. Talk about a fan base.

When Zappa arrived in Prague at the end of the Cold War, then, he was not simply signaling a new phase in Czech cultural development. He was fulfilling a promise heard by Czechs in the Western records they loved, a promise The Plastics refused to break, even through the darkest days of repressive Communist rule. This was the promise of rock—that no matter who gets you down, the music can pick you right back up again. No matter whose flag flies atop the Prague Castle, there'll always be room for the banner of the defiant, independent artist. All the rest is history.

Maryana Pinchuk *earned a Bachelor of Arts from Tulane University, where she studied English, Russian, and French literature. She is now pursuing a PhD program in Slavic Languages and Literature at Harvard.*

Laterna Magicka, Národní 2 (☎224 931 482; www.laterna.cz). ⓂB: Národní třída. From the metro, take Spálená north, and then turn left on Národní. Shows consist of actors performing a mix of pantomime and ballet in front of enormous screens playing a conglomeration of video art and something reminiscent of a regrettable acid trip. Throw in clowns with cartoon-like costumes and you sort of have an idea of what's going on. The theater seems to recognize that words wouldn't help the performance make any more sense, so they generally dispense with spoken parts entirely. Performances take place in the Magic Lantern building, the enormous alien spaceship that appears to have touched down next to the National Theater. Tickets 680Kč. Wheelchair-accessible. Box office open M-Sa 10am-8pm. AmEx/D/MC/V.

Rudolfinum, Alšovo nábřeží 12 (☎227 059 111; www.czechphilharmonic.cz). ⓂA: Staroměstská. Prague's most elaborate Neo-Renaissance structure. Now home to the Czech Philharmonic Orchestra, the building once housed the Czechoslovak Parliament. Dvořák Hall, the finest performance space in the Czech Republic, pays tribute to the only Czech composer most people can name. Tickets from 520Kč. Casual dress expected. Box office open Tu-Su 10am-6pm. AmEx/D/MC/V.

🐾 NIGHTLIFE

You can't stay in a Prague hostel without seeing at least a dozen fliers for the city's various pub crawls. Though these are certainly a good way to get drunk with a lot of English-speaking strangers, the drinks will be overpriced and the bars forgettable. The city's true gems don't put themselves on the pub crawl lists, precisely because they strive to be bars where people want to stay longer than a half an hour. Good, old-fashioned pubs are scattered throughout the city, serving a variety of brews. **Gambrinus** and **Kozel** are popular brands, though **Pilsner Urquell** is by far and away the preferred Prague beer. **Staropramen** is usually looked down upon by discerning pub-goers. Several restaurant-pubs, most notably **Pivovarský Dům,** produce their own specialty brews.

Once you make it to the pub, you usually don't have to flag down the server. They assume that if you're in the pub then you want beer, and subsequent rounds will usually appear without explicit requests. The server will keep track of your drinks by adding tick marks to a small strip of paper on your table. At the end of the night, your table will be charged according to the tick marks. Best not to draw on this piece of paper when you get bored or take it for a bookmark, however perfect the shape may be. Your server will not be amused.

For those who view drinking primarily as a prelude to dancing, Prague has plenty of clubs to suit any taste or tolerance. In the past few years, the city has been making strides toward becoming a major European clubbing destination, opening several enormous venues in an effort to attract some of the world's best DJs. Many of these clubs also double as live music venues on certain nights. Some of the biggest clubs post event calendars throughout the city. At the city's dedicated music venues, you can expect to find lots of punk and ska acts, as well as "revival" (read: cover) bands. Those who are more interested in wearing sweaters than getting sweaty may want to check out some of the city's renowned jazz clubs. Though cover charges and drinks will usually be higher than at most places, these clubs attract a surprisingly wide range of local and international talent.

Staré Město is something of a one-stop shop for every conceivable manifestation of nightlife. Expect expensive drinks, stags, and pub crawls. Once you've figured out what kind of scene you're into, head elsewhere. With more bars per capita than anywhere else in the world, and far away from the pub crawls,

Žižkov is the undisputed king of places to get triggity-trashed in Prague. The community of locals and expats can be a little disdainful toward the crowds of tourists that take over other parts of the city, but they are surprisingly welcoming to out-of-towners who've caught wind of their favorite spots. While the area has its share of regular pubs, it really shines as the home of Prague's best cocktail bars. Places like **Hapu** and **Blind Eye** serve a variety of delicious and devastating drinks that you'd be hard-pressed to find anywhere else. Nearby Vinohrady has a less-active pub scene, but several good wine bars when looking for a classy evening out. It also contains the majority of Prague's gay bars. All of them distribute *Amigo* (90Kč; www.amigo.cz), a thorough English-language guide to gay life in the Czech Republic. (Check www.praguegayguide.net or www.praguesaints.cz for a list of attractions and resources.) If you want to stay closer to the center of town, Malá Strana has a good mix of bars and live music venues, all along Újezd and Karmelitská. Nové Město has several of the city's better music venues in close proximity, though you may have to deal with spillage from the area around Wenceslas Square.

NOVÉ MĚSTO

Vagon Music Pub and Club, Národní třída 25 (☎221 085 599; www.vagon.cz). ⓂB: Národní třída. Near the station down a flight of stairs. A favorite haunt of local musicians with spiked haircuts, this club is always friendly and never too crowded, despite what its punk-rock image may suggest. Local acts play fast and hard while their fans dance frantically in the intimate concert area. Seating and foosball tables give sweaty moshers a place to cool down. Beer 26Kč. Cover 100Kč. Open M-Sa 7pm-5am, Su 7pm-1am.

Lucerna, Vodičkova 36 (☎224 216 972; www.lucerna.cz). ⓂA or B: Můstek. From the metro, walk up Václavsté náměstí toward the National Museum. Turn right on Štěpánská; the giant neon Lucerna marquis is hard to miss. A music bar in the basement of the beautiful and historic Lucerna Palace building. Amusing drinks with politically incorrect names like the "Pearl Harbor" (Havana rum, pineapple, and melon). Monthly music acts electrify the normally relaxed atmosphere. Beer 36Kč. 80s and 90s night Sa. Cover 50-75Kč for live music. Open M-Sa 10am-1am, Su 10am-11pm. Cash only.

Radost FX, Bělehradská 120 (☎224 254 776; www.radostfx.cz). ⓂC: I.P. Pavlova. Internationally renowned DJs spin the latest hits in an industrial-chic setting. Regular theme nights, including the always-packed R&B night, keep the action from getting stale. The observation deck provides a place to survey the room when you don't feel like diving in. Creative drinks like "Frozen Sex with an Alien" (140Kč) will broaden your clubbing horizons. Beer 35Kč. Mixed drinks 120Kč. Cover from 250Kč. Open Th-Sa 10pm-5am.

Club Nebe, Křemencova 10 (☎224 930 343; www.nebepraha.cz). ⓂB: Karlovo náměstí. From the metro, walk north on Karlovo náměstí, take a left at Myslíkova and then a right on Křemencova. Offers a classier, less tourist-ridden nightlife option right across the street from U Fleků. A popular spot for discerning internationals with the feel of a designer air raid shelter. DJs blast a variety of R&B and house music during the week, while Su is reserved for more low-key jams complemented by the occasional trick-happy bartender. More than 100 mixed drinks, including the "Suffering Bastard" (rum, triple sec, and almond; 115Kč). Beer 45Kč. Open M and Su 6pm-2am, Tu-Th 6pm-4am, F-Sa 6pm-5am. Cash only.

Reduta Jazz Club, Národní 20 (☎224 933 486; www.redutajazzclub.cz). ⓂB: Národní třída. From the metro, walk north on Spálená and then turn right on Národní; the club shares an entrance with Rock Cafe. A Prague landmark and favorite haunt of former president Havel, who made a point to bring Bill Clinton here on his visit to the city. It is also a favorite spot of local students and NPR-contributing American tourists, as well as their international equivalents. Beer 50Kč. Cover 300Kč. Open daily 9pm-midnight. Cash only.

Friends, Bartolomejská 11 (☎224 236 272; www.friends-prague.cz). ⓂB: Národní třída. From the station, turn right, head down Na Perštýně, and take a left on Bartolomejská. A welcoming atmosphere define this fun, low-key, GLBT-friendly club. Regular theme nights and DJs, as well as an ample supply of disco balls, add a little spice to the mix. Even on a slow night, the bartender can still get you a "blowjob" (Bailey's, Kahlua, and cream; 80Kč). The monthly lesbian party is one of the most popular GLBT events in Prague. Women and straight customers welcome but rare. Karaoke Tu is a local favorite. Beer 35Kč. Mixed drinks 75-115Kč. Open daily 6pm-4am. Cash only.

Karlovy Lázně, Novotného lávka 1 (☎222 220 502; www.karlovylazne.cz), next to the Charles Bridge. A massive tourist magnet that purports to be the largest dance club in Central Europe. Each of its 5 sweaty floors caters to a different style, though an industrial and futuristic decor runs throughout. Some of the more nonsensical accoutrements include a vat-turned-private seating area on the 1st floor, massive laser-eyed statue on the 3rd floor, and a replica of Elvis gyrating behind an artificial waterfall. Free internet terminals mean you can send regrettable emails before you even leave the dance floor. Shots 50-85Kč. Beer 40Kč. Cover 120Kč, 50Kč before 10pm and after 4am. Open daily 9pm-5am.

Molotow Coctail Bar, Karlovo náměstí 31 (☎603 251 275; www.molotow.cz). ⓂB: Karlovo náměstí. From the metro, walk to the other side of the park and turn left on Karlovo náměstí; the bar is on the right. Not your typical Prague basement bar, Molotow distinguishes itself with its home-infused liquors like vanilla vodka and rum with rose petals. Bartenders sporting white lab coats lend their experimental concoctions an air of legitimacy; if you stay around long enough they may even put on a fireshow for you. DJs periodically bring Latin or techno beats to the small adjoining dance floor. Otherwise, expect club remixes of "Blinded by the Light" and "Eye of the Tiger." Mixed drinks 80-129Kč. Happy hour 6pm-9pm. 18+. Open Tu-Th 6pm-2am, F-Sa 6pm-4am. Cash only.

Rocky o'Reilly's, Štěpánská 32 (☎732 473 481; www.rockyoreillys.cz). ⓂA or B: Můstek. From the metro, walk up Václavsté náměstí toward the National Museum, then turn right on Štěpánská; there are signs for the bar on most streetlights. A raucous Irish pub run by real Irishmen. Expect lads dancing on tables and impromptu conga lines on the weekends. Things remain remarkably friendly despite the rowdiness. The website has a live webcam so your friends at home can watch you make an ass of yourself in real time. Wings, shrimp, ribs, and other typical American bar fare at American bar prices (245-335Kč). Beer 60Kč. Open daily 10am-late. Kitchen open until 11pm. AmEx/MC/V.

Rock Cafe, Národní 20 (☎224 933 947; www.rockcafe.cz). ⓂB: Národní třída. From the metro, walk north on Spálená and then turn right on Národní; the bar shares an entrance with Reduta Jazz Club. Caters to the 18-25 crowd with angsty art on the walls and heavy metal on the stereo. Expect loud drinkers with lots of piercings. Periodic live music mostly consists of cover bands. Beer 33Kč. Open M-Sa 10am-3am, Su 7pm-3am. Cash only.

STARÉ MĚSTO

Harley's, Dlouhá 18 (☎227 195 195; www.harleys.cz). ⓂB: Náměstí Republiky. From the metro, walk north on Revoluční and then make a left on Dlouhá. A bar for travelers with a love for Harley Davidsons and Jack Daniels. The rough and tough exterior belies a surprisingly sophisticated bar, offering over 200 drink options. For Epicureans, Cuban cigars and Havana Rum are an added draw. Not surprisingly, the Prague chapter of the Hell's Angels are fans and occasionally stop by. Rock and dance DJs nightly. Beer 55Kč. Mixed drinks 100-130Kč. Open daily 7pm-6am. Cash only.

Roxy, Dlouhá 33 (☎224 826 363; www.roxy.cz). ⓂB: Náměstí Republiky. Same building as the **Travellers' Hostel** (p. 156). Hip music venue and club located in a historic building. Especially popular with young skateboarders and those experimenting with facial hair for the first time. Techno and house DJs attempt to get the young people off the rows of comfy couches and onto the massive dance floor, some nights more success-fully than others. From the balcony you can play pool or watch all the action. Beer 33Kč. Shots 60-80Kč. Cover Tu and Th-Sa 100-350Kč. Open daily 10pm-late.

Bombay Cocktail Bar, Dlouhá 13 (☎222 328 400). ⓜB: Náměstí Republiky. From the metro, walk north on Revoluční and then make a left on Dlouhá. Unashamed to be a tourist bar with a large (if unexciting) drink menu and nightly DJs who spin the same overplayed songs. Mixed drinks 115-145Kč. Open M-W and Su 7pm-4am, Th 7pm-5am, F-Sa 7pm-6am. Cash only.

M1 Lounge, Masná 1 (☎227 195 235; www.m1lounge.com). ⓜB: Náměstí Republiky. From the metro, walk north on Revoluční and make a left on Dlouhá; follow the street down to the square and make a hard left onto Masná. To misquote Baudelaire, "the greatest trick M1 ever played was convincing tourists that it was an ultra-exclusive club." Neon-filled with plush purple benches and TVs embedded in the tables for people who are impressed by that sort of thing. Nightly DJs pack the small dance floor with standard club music. Beer 50Kč. Mixed drinks 125-165Kč. No athletic wear. 100Kč cover for guys. Open M-Th and Su 7pm-3am, F-Sa 7pm-5am. Cash only.

MALÁ STRANA

▨ **Klub Újezd,** Újezd 18 (☎257 570 873; www.klubujezd.cz). ⓜA: Malostranská. From the metro, take the tram to the Újezd stop. Local gathering place for young Czech artists, poets, and punks. 3 levels provide slight variations on the same theme. The paintings, drawings, and collages that line the walls run the gamut from amusing to confusing to alarming. On warm summer nights, the ground floor opens up and the party spills onto the sidewalk. Weekend DJs spin a mix of punk, ska, and old school hip hop. Beer 35Kč. Shots 30-120Kč. Wheelchair-accessible. Open daily 2pm-4am. Cash only.

U Malého Glena Jazz & Blues Club, Karmelitská 23 (☎257 531 717; www.malyglen. cz). Trams 12, 20, 22, 91, Hellichova tram stop. From the tram stop, head north on Karmelitská. Low-key jazz and blues venue that draws a crowd with its great combina-tion of drinks, food, and live music. The upstairs feels like a typical American bar, with a few creative dishes like the "New Wave Nicoise" (greens, tuna, potato, hardboiled eggs, green beans, red peppers, onion, and tarragon dressing; 145Kč) and mixed drinks like the notorious "duck fart" (Kahlua, Carolans, and whiskey; 69Kč). Downstairs, an intimate club setting hosts some of the best jazz acts from greater Prague every weeknight. Beer from 30Kč. Mixed drinks 59-149Kč. Burgers 155-185Kč. Salads 105-145Kč. Blues M and W. Cover usually 200Kč. Open M-F 10am-2am, Sa-Su 10am-3am. Kitchen open daily 10am-midnight. AmEx/MC/V.

PopoCafePetl Music Club, Újezd 19 (☎602 277 226; www.popcafepetl.cz). ⓜA: Malostranská. From the metro, take the tram to Újezd. Big brother to the Nové Město cafe, drawing the same cool, young crowd into a small, brick basement venue decorated with posters and old LPs. An assortment of acoustic, rock, folk, and world music acts keep the atmosphere (and to some extent the crowd) constantly changing, though regu-lar events like 80s and 90s, latino, or gypsy night each have their own dedicated follow-ing. Beer 29Kč. Mixed drinks 69-149Kč. Cover 60-100Kč. Open daily 6pm-2am. MC/V.

Shadow Cafe, Újezd 16 (☎774 742 369; www.shadowazyl.cz). ⓜA: Malostranská. From the metro, take the tram to Újezd. Small, stylish bar where patrons can relax in near-total darkness at almost any time of day. The money saved on electricity keeps the cost of drinks at levels students will appreciate. The grotesque black and white figures that occupy huge stretches of wall are some of the coolest around. "Apple Pie" (Morgan spiced rum, apple, and cinnamon) 55Kč. Beer from 19Kč. Shots 35-100Kč. Mixed drinks 45-125Kč. Wheelchair-accessible. Open M-F 2pm-1am, Sa-Su 4pm-1am. Cash only.

Klub 007 Strahov, Koleje ČVUT, Blok 7, Chaloupeckého 7 (☎775 260 071; www. klub007strahov.cz). Trams 15, 22, 23, 25, Malovanka tram stop. From the tram, take

Vaničkova and then turn left on Chaloupeckého; the club is in the basement of Blok 7. Small, dark joint popular with students and the skinny jeans crowd. The English graffiti on the walls will make you feel like you're back home. Young rockers crowd the dance floor when a mix of local and touring punk, indie, hardcore, and ska acts take the stage. Beer 23Kč. Shots 25-50Kč. Cover varies, usually 100Kč. Open M-Th and Su 7pm-midnight, F-Sa 7pm-1am. Cash only.

Hell's Bells Rockin' Pub, Na Bělidle 27 (☎723 184 760; rockinpub.hellsbells.cz). Ⓜ️B: Anděl. From the metro, take Nádražní north and then turn right onto Na Bělidle. Simple pub decorated with flames and skeletons caters to Prague's KISS aficionados. The loud music may make asking that goth chick about her favorite Iron Maiden album more difficult than expected. Beer 22Kč. Open M-F 3pm-3am, Sa 5pm-3am, Su 5pm-midnight. Cash only.

ŽIŽKOV

🔲 **Hapu,** Orlická 8 (☎775 109 331). Ⓜ️A: Flora. From the metro, walk west on Vinohradská and then make a right on Orlická. Something of a bartender's bar, this inconspicuous little place serves some of the most creative and best-mixed cocktails in Prague. The extensive and constantly changing mixed drink menu includes a ½-dozen members of the Collins drink family as well as more suspect options like "Alien Secretion" (120Kč). Beer 35Kč. Mixed drinks 80-140Kč. Open daily 6pm-2am. Cash only.

🔲 **Blind Eye,** Vlkova 26 (www.blindeye.cz). Trams 5, 9, 26, Husinecká tram stop. From the tram, walk east on Seifertova, then make a right on Krásova; the bar is at the corner. Named after the one-eyed Jan Žižka who lends his name to the entire neighborhood. Small, dark, rowdy, but much-loved by area expats and well-informed travelers. Regular DJs and live rock shows in an intimate atmosphere. A wide assortment of drinks you couldn't describe to your mother, including "Sex with the Bartender" (150Kč) and the appropriately named "Adios, Motherf***er" (195Kč). Beer 22Kč. Most mixed drinks 60-100Kč. Karaoke M night. Wheelchair-accessible. Open 7pm-late. Cash only.

Bukowski's, Bořivojova 86 (☎774 539 689). Trams 5, 9, 26, Husinecká tram stop. From the tram, take Seifertova east, make a right onto Víta Nejedlého and then another right onto Bořivojova. A designer bar with a literary flourish. Prides itself on using high quality beer (30Kč) and liquors for its signature mixed drinks like "the Naked Lunch" and "the Dorian Gray." A relaxed atmosphere and stylish crowd make this a good place to get respectably sauced. Those who find themselves

IN SEARCH OF THE ORIGINAL MOTHERF***ER

The Žižkov bar scene is tight-knit community of locals and expats. Whenever I leave a bar in the area, I'm invariably sent to deliver a message from one bartender to the next. Usually it's as innocuous as a "Tell the guy with the ugly mustache that I say hey!", though sometimes the messages contain a little more vitriol.

While visiting one bar, I was struck by the special drink menu, which included such gems as "Sex with the Bartender," "Žižkov Liberatör," and my personal favorite, the "Adios Motherf***er." The bartender told me the latter was his signature drink. Later that evening, I was at another bar and mentioned the earlier encounter. The bartender's eyes grew wide and he told me that he had invented the drink and the other bartender had stolen it. Later, yet a third bartender claimed the same.

By the end of the evening, I didn't know who to believe. I dropped into my last bar and asked the bartender, half-jokingly, if this was also the home of the "Adios Motherf***er." The bartender scrunched up his face and said, "You know, everyone argues about who invented that drink and they raise a lot of hell over it, but I'm pretty sure it's just a Long Island Iced Tea."

- *Justin Keenan*

slipping past respectability can slow down with a smoothie (75Kč). Mixed drinks 80-100Kč. Open daily 7pm-3am. Cash only.

Palác Akropolis, Kubeliková 27 (☎296 330 912; www.palacakropolis.cz). ⓂA: Jiřího z Poděbrad. From the metro, cross diagonally through the park and then take Milešovská; Kubelíkova is on the other side of the Žižkov tower park. Situated in a pre-WWII theater, this entertainment complex has become a landmark in the Žižkov area. The bar and cafe upstairs serve a mix of expats, local artists, and intellectuals, while the multi-level club downstairs contains 2 bars, each with its own nightly DJ and a clientele that changes according to the music. Reggae night Su is always well attended. The space also hosts concerts and regularly collaborates with a group of performance artists. Beer 25Kč. Cover F and Sa 30Kč. Cafe open daily 11am-1am. Cash only.

VINOHRADY

Radost FX, Bělehradská 120 (☎224 254 776; www.radostfx.cz). ⓂC: I.P. Pavlova. Internationally renowned DJs spin the latest hits in an industrial-chic setting. Regular theme nights, including the always-packed R&B night, keep the action from getting stale. The observation deck provides a place to survey the room when you don't feel like diving in. Creative drinks like Frozen Sex with an Alien (140Kč) will broaden your clubbing horizons. Beer 35Kč. Mixed drinks 120Kč. Cover from 250Kč. Open Th-Sa 10pm-5am.

The Saints, Polská 32 (☎222 250 326; www.praguesaints.cz). ⓂA: Jiřího z Poděbrad. From the metro, take Slavíkova north and then turn left onto Polská. Main basement bar where Prague's GLBT tourists and English speakers of all ages meet and chat. This small, cozy space plays a light, indie soundtrack. Beer 26Kč. Wine (40Kč). Things get a little louder during the themed Quiz Night on the last Su of every month. Women and straight customers welcome but uncommon. Shots 60-120Kč. Open daily 7pm-4am. Cash only.

Valentino, Vinohradská 40 (☎222 513 491; www.club-valentino.cz). ⓂA: Náměstí Míru. From the metro, walk east on Korunní, then turn left on Sázavská and left on Vinohradská. The Czech Republic's largest gay club draws a mixed crowd to its 4 bars and 3 levels. The 1st level and terrace contain a bar and lounge area. The further down you go the more exciting things get. The 2nd level cultivates a permanent disco style, while the lowest level, open only on weekends, hosts techno and house DJs in a dark, crowded atmosphere where anything can happen. Female customers common, straight customers not so much. Beer from 19Kč. Shots 40-78Kč. Open daily 11am-late. Cash only.

Vinárna Vinečko, Lodynská 135/2 (☎222 511 035; www.vineckopraha.cz). ⓂA: Námesti Miru. Head west on Rumunská and turn left on Lodynská. A classy wine bar in the heart of the Vinohrady district brimming with thirsty locals and expats. Enjoy a glass of one of many wines (small glass 30-38Kč, full glass 75-95Kč) over a salad (85-105Kč). Sidewalk seating is the perfect place to sample a cheese plate (54-165Kč). Wheelchair-accessible. Open M-F noon-midnight, Sa-Su 2pm-midnight. AmEx/D/MC/V.

Piano Bar, Milešovská 10 (☎224 252 049; www.latimerieclub.cz). ⓂA: Jiřího z Poděbrad. From the metro, take Vinohradská east, then turn left on námesti Jiřího z Poděbrad, which becomes Milešovská. A popular hangout for gay locals and the occasional female friend. Decor features colorful lights and random housewares stuck to the walls. A good place for a low-key evening, but you'll need to brush up on your Czech before you approach anyone. Beer from 23Kč. Shots 37-67Kč. Open daily 5pm-late. Cash only.

Latimerie Club Cafe, Slezská 74 (☎224 252 049; www.latimerieclub.cz). ⓂA: Jiřího z Poděbrad. From the metro, take náměstí Jiřího z Poděbrad south and then left on Slezská; the bar is on the corner of Slezská and Nitranská. A small, GLBT-friendly place with a nautical motif and a slightly older crowd. Spontaneous dancing is not uncommon. Beer from 35Kč. Mixed drinks from 80Kč. DJs every Sa and occasional video parties keep things interesting on the weekends. 18+. Open daily 4pm-late. Cash only.

HOLESOVICE

Cross Club, Plynární 23 (☎736 535 053; www.crossclub.cz). ⓂC: Nádraží Holešovice. From the metro, take Verbenského east and then turn right onto Argentinská and right onto Plynární. An impossible-to-categorize mix of bar, cafe, club, and rock venue. DJs and live acts of all stripes encourage people to get out of their comfort zones. The best part, though, may be the club itself, with its awesome, if bizarre, sense of aesthetics. Chill out in the bungalow-esque bar area before descending into the always-crowded techno-industrial-themed downstairs, lit by all manner of glowing, flashing, and spinning contraptions. Beer 20Kč. Shots 50-100Kč. Mixed drinks 85-95Kč. Cover varies, usually 75-100Kč. Open daily 4pm-late. Cash only.

SaSaZu, Bubenské nábřeží 306 (☎284 097 444; www.sasazu.com). ⓂC: Vltavská. From the metro, take the tram to Pražská tržnice; the club is inside the market, in the warehouse with the red roof. One of the biggest and most exclusive clubs in Prague, bringing world-renowned DJs to its renovated warehouse that can accommodate up to 2000 people. The massive dance floor is a tempest of sweat and sex while the surrounding couches and tables offer some respite for those who can't handle the action. The 80s and 90s theme nights have recently become fixtures in the Prague nightlife scene. Beer 50Kč. Shots 75-150Kč. No streetwear. Cover 200-300Kč. Open daily 10pm-6am. Cash only.

Mecca, U Průhonu 3 (☎602 711 225; www.mecca.cz). ⓂC: Nádraží Holešovice. From the metro, take the tram to U Průhonu, walk to the corner of U Průhonu, and turn left. The place to see and be seen in Prague for locals and tourists who go to clubs for that reason. The main lounge and dance floor attempt to offset the tackiness of dozens of discoballs with an equally ludicrous number of chandeliers. If the drinks and sweaty, crowded dance floor don't disorient you, the strobe lights and fog machine probably will. Live DJs nightly. Beer and wine 49Kč. Shots 69-149Kč. Cover 190Kč. Open M, W, Sa 11pm-6am. AmEx/D/MC/V.

⚑ DAYTRIPS FROM PRAGUE

KARLŠTEJN
Take the Beroun train (88Kč) from Prague's Hlavní nádraží station, which runs every hour. Once you get to the Karlštejn station, walk 2km to get to the castle itself; just follow the signs marked "Hrad." ☎311 681 617; www.hrad-karlstejn.cz. Open Tu-Su Nov.-Mar. 9am-3pm, Apr. and Oct. 9am-4pm, May-Jun. and Sept. 9am-5pm, July-Aug. 9am-6pm. AmEx/MC/V.

Built in 1348, the majestic Karlštejn castle was occasionally home to Bohemian kings and Holy Roman Emperors, but was used mostly to store crown jewels and holy relics. Twenty-two kings called this castle home, from Charles IV in 1348 to Ferdinand I in 1836. A guided tour (50 min.; 250Kč, students and children 150Kč) takes you through most of the castle, including **Knights' Hall,** which contains the original cabinets used by knights to store their armor. In the **Castle Treasury,** one can see a 2000-year-old carved opal as well as momentos like pieces of St. Wenceslas's armor and a crocodile skull once believed to be the head of the dragon decapitated by St. George. The view from the parapets after the tour offers a gorgeous view of the Czech countryside. A second, longer tour which includes the Great Tower and the Chapel of the Holy Cross is also available, though reservations must be made in advance.

The town itself hugs the spiral pathway up to the castle's base. For a small fee, horse-drawn carriages are available to take you to the top in style. Street vendors sell Czech garnet, tacky t-shirts, and replicas of Communist-era uniforms. More than half a dozen restaurants line the ascent, selling traditional Czech food as well as hamburgers and french fries. The closest to the castle itself, **Restaurace U Adama,** Karlštejn 61, has an array of delicious, inexpensive menus (80-118Kč) and good beer (19Kč). If you're lucky, one of the owner's cats might join you for lunch on the outdoor patio. (☎775 361 008; www.restauraceuadama.cz. Cash only.)

If you have the time, you should consider hiking through the beautiful **Český kras** protected area. Trails to the **Svatý Jan Pod Skalou** (St. John Under a Rock) monastery leave from the marked area near the castle walls, though the actual hike is closer to 12km rather than the 8km posted. The sparsely traveled and sometimes poorly marked trail traverses streams, forests, and steep hills. It is not recommended for the inexperienced or unprepared. With proper equipment and grit, however, the hike offers some of the best views of the Czech landscape around. The monastery itself contains five rooms carved out of a cave; come early, it closes at 4pm. After your stay at the monastery, make your way to Beroun, and catch the train back to Prague. Accommodations and restaurants are available near the monastery for those who want to extend their stay, or miss the last train.

KŘIVOKLÁT

Trains (174Kč) from Prague's Hlavní nádraží station run every hour. You'll want to take the Beroun train and then transfer to the Rakovník train and get off at the Křivoklát stop. Once you get off at the station, you'll need to walk about ½km to the castle itself, it should be clearly visible once you cross the creek. ☎313 558 440; www.kri-voklat.cz. Open Jan.-Mar. M-F 10am-3pm; Apr. and Oct. Tu-Sa 9am-4pm; May-June and Sept. Tu-Sa 9am-5pm; July-Aug. Tu-Sa 9am-6pm; Nov.-Dec. Sa-Su 10am-3pm. Last tour begins at closing hour. AmEx/D/MC/V.

In many ways, Křivoklát is Karlštejn's less-accomplished younger sibling. The castle and the town itself are significantly smaller than their better known counterparts. The upside is, of course, that Křivoklát and its town are less touristy than Karlštejn. The downside is that there just isn't as much to do once you get there. For what it's worth, Křivoklát offers a wide variety of tours (70-150Kč, 50/90Kč for students, 35-120min) that are long enough to cover all the interesting things, but not so long as to bore you to death. The best tour for time and money is the 50min. tour of the castle interiors. *(100/70Kč. English translation of tour, complete guided tours in English 150/105Kč per person. Must be booked in advance.)*

The castle was built in the 13th century by Wenceslas I, on the site of a popular royal hunting lodge. Unfortunately, the master builder must have misplaced his bevel, because the castle is not entirely even—hence one possible derivation of the name Křivoklát from "crooked surface." In the 17th century, the castle became the residence of the noble Furstenberg family until it was sold to the Czechoslovak state in 1929. The castle is still full of many of its original furnishings, including the **chapel,** one of best-preserved Gothic rooms in Europe, containing a beautiful altar surrounded by statues of saints. The **museum and library** of the Furstenberg family contains, among other things, a vast number of portraits and what was once the third largest library in the Czech Republic, not to mention an impressive collection of sleighs, pole-axes, and dueling pistols. The best part of the tour comes at the end when you visit the **prison cells** still containing various torture implements such as the stocks, an iron maiden, and several "cages of shame" from which alcoholics, dishonest craftsmen, and loose women would be dangled for public ridicule.

The surrounding village contains little more than a couple of nearly-identical restaurants and a hotel. The restaurant át **Hotel Sýkora** (☎313 558 114; www.hotel-sykora.krivoklatsko.com) offers cheap beer (18Kč) and a variety of reasonably-priced dishes, though you'll need to be able to read either German or Czech to make much sense of it. *(Entrees 105-140. Steaks 240-305. Open daily 11am-11pm. Cash only.)* For the outdoorsy types, a variety of (at least three or four) hiking trails begin from the base of the castle and spread out into the surrounding countryside.

TEREZÍN (THERESIENSTADT)

Bus from Nádraží Holešovice (45min., 16 per day, 174Kč roundtrip) to the Terezín LT stop. The Ghetto Museum and Magdeburg Barracks are in the town; the Small Fortress, cemetery, and crematorium are about ½km back down the road. Follow the large signs. The tourist office is at náměstí ČSA 179. ☎416 782 616; www.pamatnik-terezin.cz. Open Apr.-Oct. daily 8am-6pm, Nov.-Mar. daily 8am-4:30pm. Barracks and museum open Nov.- Mar. daily 8am-5:30pm; Apr.-Oct. daily 8am-6pm. Admission to Small Fortress or Ghetto Museum 160Kč, students 130Kč. Combined admission 200/150Kč. Cash only.

The fortress town at Terezín (Theresienstadt) was built in the 1780s by Franz Josef II to safeguard his empire's northern frontier. In 1940, Hitler's Gestapo set up a prison in the small fortress, and a year later the town became a concentration camp. Over the course of the war, the camp served as a way station for more than 140,000 Jews awaiting transport farther east. Hitler also tried to turn the camp into a propaganda tool, touting it as a resort with clean, modern facilities. The large park that dominates the town square was built to create the illusion of aesthetic and athletic opportunities for residents, yet, except for the occasional publicity stunt, no Jews were allowed near it. In reality, overcrowding, malnourishment, and plotted executions killed over 30,000 people in the camp, while another 85,000 were transported to camps farther east. The town was re-populated after the war, though its streets still feel uncomfortably empty. As fascinating a place as it is, it's not somewhere you feel compelled to linger.

The **Ghetto Museum,** located in a former school to the left of the bus stop, places Terezín in the wider context of the Holocaust and WWII by showcasing personal artifacts from the camp's victims. The passports and childrens' drawings are certainly haunting, but the recorded accounts of survivors are the most striking. The nearby **Magdeburg Barracks** contain exhibits on art, theater, and literature in the camp, as well as a replica of a prison dormitory.

Across the river, the **Small Fortress** was used as a Gestapo prison. The ticket booth distributes self-guided tours of the grounds. You can go in almost any of the buildings, most of which are now empty except for a telling piece of furniture or two. The dormitories are empty except for the enormous wooden frames where upwards of 100 people used to be crammed every night. In the "barbershop," you can still see the sinks and mirrors placed on the walls to give Red Cross inspectors the illusion that the prisoners were being well cared for. The showers and delousing facilities next door will give you a much better idea of what hygiene in the camp truly consisted of. On your way to the Death Tunnel and execution grounds, notice the swimming pool to your right; it was built by camp inmates for the families of the camp guards. Bizarrely, the former officers' mess is now a small cafe, serving the most uncomfortable snacks you will ever eat. Outside the fortress walls lie the **cemetery** and **crematorium.** The nearby **columbarium** was used to store the ashes of those cremated at the camp, until the end of the war when the fleeing Nazis buried some of them and tossed the rest into the Ohře River. Men should cover their heads before entering.

KUTNÁ HORA

Trains (172Kč) from Prague's Hlavní nádraží station run every 2hr. The ossuary is about 1km from the train station. From the train station, turn right, then left, then right again on the highway. After about 500m, turn right at the church. The ossuary is at the end of the road. From the train station, you can also take a bus to the center of town (10Kč). ☎606 647 996; www.kostnice.cz. Open M-Sa 8am-6pm. 50Kč, students 30Kč.

Kutná Hora was once the second most important town in Bohemia thanks to its silver mines, which brought vast amounts of wealth to the region. Now, it's mostly (in)famous for the nearby **ossuary,** a chapel decorated with the bones of 40,000 people. Plagues and wars left the village cemetery overflowing with bodies. The Cistercian Order built a charnel house to hold the extra remains until one monk in a fit of divine inspiration (or possible insanity) began designing flowers from crania and pelvic bones. He never finished the ossuary, but the artist František Rint completed the project in 1870. Creations like a chandelier containing at least one of each bone in the human body, and a representation of the town crest are chilling sights, though the influx of camera-toting tourists makes the site less creepy than it might otherwise be.

Though the ossuary is undoubtedly the town's main attraction, those who want to spend a day in something more closely resembling a real Czech town will find a lot to appreciate in the city center, a UNESCO World Heritage Site. At the far end of town, the **Church of Saint Barbara** was meant to be a monumental testament to the town's wealth and power when work began in 1388. The decline in production from the town's silver mines forced the design to be scaled back and construction of the church was delayed for nearly five centuries. The church's circus-tent-like exterior and ample supply of flying buttresses are hard to miss, and the stained-glass and stone interior are satisfyingly impressive despite the reduced scale. (Open daily 9am-6pm. Wheelchair-accessible. 50Kč, students 30Kč. Cash only.)

For those with slightly more heretical tastes, the nearby **Alchemy Museum** offers a brief, entertaining diversion. Though the gothic cellar with replica bellows, alembics, and various other alchemical equipment is interesting, the wonderfully eccentric Englishman who gives a freewheeling, digressive tour is most definitely the highlight. (☎327 511 259; www.alchemy.cz. Open daily 10am-5pm. 50Kč, students 30Kč. Cash only.) Near the center of town, the **Plague Column,** decorated with various saints and what appear to be buboes growing along the shaft, recalls the losses the town faced during the Black Death, and the source of much of the ossuary's construction material. Those looking for a bite to eat should consider **Pivnice Dačický ❸**, Rakova 8, a medieval pub and restaurant that serves a wide selection of wild game including wild boar and deer (239Kč) and hearty goulash (299Kč). The restaurant also serves an assortment of homemade lagers (15Kč). Finish with a treat from the special section of alchemical cuisine, including various dishes wrapped in gold foil (we kid you not). (☎327 512 248; www.dacicky.com. Appetizers 39-115Kč. Soups 39-99Kč. Entrees 109-245Kč. Open daily 11am-11pm. MC/V.)

BUDAPEST

This particular stretch of the Danube has been home to one settlement or another since the time of the Roman Empire, when it was a now-defunct town called Aquincum, capital of the also-defunct province Lower Pannonia. The Magyars arrived on the scene in the middle of the AD ninth century, led by seven chieftains who didn't take lip about their headgear. All was not smooth sailing, though, as the towns of Buda, Óbuda, and Pest were ravaged by the Mongols in the 13th century and later incorporated into the Ottoman Empire. In 1873, Buda and Pest joined forces to become, conveniently enough, Budapest. (Óbuda joined, too, but got left out of the name game.) For its 1896 millennial celebration, the city decided it was time to become a major world hub, and to that end constructed a subway system (the first in continental Europe), a world-class opera house, and many, many statues. The 20th century was incredibly painful for Budapest, and for Hungary as a whole, as the nation endured successive occupation by two totalitarian regimes. In the 1960s, Budapest was known as "the happiest barrack" due to its idiosyncratic brand of Communism (and perhaps also to the large number of statues erected during the period). After the collapse of Communism many of these statues became politically problematic. The always resilient people of Budapest took this as an opportunity to erect even more new statues, while quietly shuffling the old ones outside of town.

FACTS AND FIGURES

YEAR FOUNDED: 1873

YEAR HUNGARY SAID "PEACE OUT" TO THE SOVIET UNION: 1989

METRO AREA POPULATION: 1,708,000

AS A PERCENTAGE OF HUNGARY'S POPULATION: 17%

OFFICIAL CURRENCY: the Forint (Ft)

NUMBER OF STUDENTS: 38,523

TOTAL AREA: 525 sq. km

NUMBER OF DISTRICTS: 23

LARGEST DISTRICT: XXVI Rákosmente

AVERAGE ANNUAL PRECIPITATION: 24 in.

HIGHEST ELEVATION IN BUDAPEST: János Hill at 1729 ft.

RELIGIOUS MAJORITY: Roman Catholic, 46%

NUMBER OF ISLANDS IN THE DANUBE: seven; Shipyard Island, Margaret Island, Csepel Island, Palotai-sziget, Népsziget, Háros-sziget, and Molnár-sziget

Modern Budapest looks and feels like a major city, one that is refreshingly unconcerned with milking you for your nice, stable foreign currency. This is not to say that Budapest does not have plenty of lovely things to see and do—it does. But it's not a city that bends over backward to accommodate tourists (it has larger things on its mind). Thus far, it hasn't developed as large or tight-knit of an expatriate community as that of nearby Prague. You probably won't have much trouble being understood in English (Budapesters learned long ago that expecting foreigners to pick up Hungarian is a lost cause), though you may have difficulty finding native English speakers who've been in the city for longer than a weekend. Budapest hasn't made the same effort to market its mystique as other former Soviet cities. This means that sometimes the streets are dirty. Sometimes there are homeless people begging near metro stops. At night, there are parts of town that you should avoid. In short, everything you know about large cities applies to Budapest.

NEIGHBORHOODS OF BUDAPEST

Buda and Pest are separated by the **Danube River** (Duna), and the city preserves the distinctive character of each side. On the west bank, **Buda** has winding streets, a hilltop citadel, and great vistas of the more interesting side of the city. Down the north slope of **Várhegy** (Castle Hill) is **Moszkva tér,** Buda's tram and local bus hub. To the south, **Gellért Hegy** (Gellért Hill) has some of the city's nicest green spaces as well as its own hilltop fortifications. To the north, **Óbuda** exists, and that's about all that's relevant about it.

On the eastern bank, **Pest** is home to the majority of the city's nightlife and culture. For your convenience, the city has six bridges to help misguided tourists get back to Pest as fast as possible. **Széchenyi Lánchíd** (Chain Bridge) is the oldest means of crossing the Danube. **Erzsébet híd** (Elizabeth Bridge) is beautiful, but a history of corruption during its construction means that it now runs almost directly into the side of Gellért Hill, much to the dismay of drivers. **Szabadság híd** (Liberty Bridge) is remarkable only because it was built, along with everything else in the city, for the 1986 millennial.

The city's commercial center is Pest's northern half of the fifth district, **Lipótváros,** right on the eastern shores of the Danube. Here you can find the beautiful Gothic **Parliament,** as well as **Szent István Bazilika** (St. Stephen's Basilica). Metro lines converge in Pest at **Deák tér,** next to the main international bus terminal at **Erzsébet tér.** Two blocks west toward the river lies **Vörösmarty tér** and the pedestrian shopping zone **Váci utca.** From the center of the city, follow **Andrássy út** into the heart of hip and active **Terézváros,** which features some of the city's best cafes and restaurants. From there, follow the **Nagykörút** (Grand Boulevard) south to **Erzsébetváros,** once the city's Jewish Ghetto and now the heart of its nightlife, especially around snaking **Dob utca.** Farther south, you will come to the highly residential, occasionally mob-run parts of **Józsefváros** and **Ferencváros.** Stick to the areas inside the Grand Boulevard and you'll find lots of dining and drinking options, especially along **Ráday utca.**

Budapest addresses begin with a Roman numeral representing one of the city's 23 districts. Central Buda is I; central Pest is V. A **map** is essential for Budapest's confusing streets; pick one up at any tourist office or hostel. Maps from *CitySpy* (www.cityspy.com) are generally accurate and come with many solid recommendations for under-the-radar establishments.

PEST

THE BELVÁROS (INNER CITY)

The Belváros has traditionally been the commercial center of Budapest. Many businesses have their offices around the congested **Váci utca.** Fortunately, there's a lot more to the Inner City than overpriced shopping: it is also home to several classy coffee shops, a good variety of restaurants, and some of the nicest green spaces in the downtown. The **Grand Market,** a must for any visitor to the city, is also located in the Belváros. There you'll find row after row of market stalls in a beautifully restored, turn-of-the-century interior.

The area past **Ferenc körút** went neglected for years. Recently, efforts have been made to reinvigorate the area by relocating the **Ludwig Museum** (p. 259) and the **National Theatre Concert Hall (p. 246)** to an otherwise depressed area by the Danube. Whether the efforts are a sincere attempt at urban renewal or a disingenuous way of putting modern art where it belongs has yet to be seen.

LIPÓTVÁROS

The closest thing Budapest has to a real tourist district, Lipótváros is technically composed of two neighborhoods: government center (V) and classy Újlipótváros (XIII). It is home to some of the city's major attractions, including the **Parliament, Saint Stephen's Basilica,** and historic **Liberty Square (see Sights, p. 245).** Most of Budapest's embassies and major government buildings are also located in Lipótváros. Everywhere you look, you'll find tiny parks and green spaces, often just large enough for a single bench, tree, and statue of someone you'll have no hope of recognizing. Nightlife pickings in Lipótváros are slim, but you will be able to find some good places to eat, and a couple of boutique hostels, if you're into that sort of thing.

ERZSÉBETVÁROS

Named for the beloved wife of Emperor Franz Joseph, Erzsébetváros has been the center of Jewish life in Budapest for more than 150 years. During WWII, 80,000 Jews were imprisoned in the ghetto here. Between the destruction of the Jewish community and neglect of the city under Communism, the area was largely unpopulated throughout the second half of the 20th century. In recent years, it has undergone a cultural revival. The **Great Synagogue** (p. 248) has finally been restored, and many of the districts abandoned buildings have been turned into cultural centers or ruin pubs, making the district Budapest's most popular nightlife destination. Erzsébetváros is also home to kosher delis and some decent accommodations; just be careful in the streets around the train station, which can get a little dicey at night.

TERÉZVÁROS

The city's sixth district seems to have a disproportionate share of Budapest's best streets, restaurants, hostels, and museums. **Andrássy út** makes for a lovely walk at any time of day. Some of Budapest's best restaurants surround **Liszt Ferenc tér** and

THE INSIDER'S CITY

THE BEST OF BUDAPEST

Not everyone has the luxury of spending weeks on end in Budapest. Luckily, we've hand-picked the city's best sights, museums, restaurants, and nightlife so that you can get a sense of Budapest and hit most major sights, even if you're here for just a few days. No matter how long your stay, be sure to check out:

The House of Terror (p. 258), which chronicles the terror tactics of the Nazis and the Soviets, will give you a sense of the tragedies Hungary has endured over the past century.

Memento Park, (p. 257). Don't miss Budapest's most oppressive Soviet statuary—it's all been moved to this park on the outskirts of town.

Giero, (p. 237**).** Before you leave, be sure to experience real home cooking accompanied by real gypsy music at this true hole-in-the-wall in Terézváros.

1000 Tea, (p. 232). Budapest's best teahouse is perhaps the only reason to visit touristy **Váci utca.**

Great Market Hall, (p. 246). Your one-stop shop for produce, knives, and stacking George W. Bush dolls—all under the roof of a beautifully restored turn-of-the-century edifice.

Gödör Klub, (p. 265). The best underground venue in Budapest that's actually underground.

Kiraly Baths, (p. 254). Thanks to the Ottomans, you'll always have a place to unwind, even if you find yourself besieged. If you must limit yourself to one bath complex during your whirlwind tour of Budapest, make it the Kiraly Baths.

Pál-völgyi Caves, (p. 257). Eat a light breakfast: you'll need all the room you can to finish the Sandwich of Death. The caves are the perfect excursion for the truly ambitious outdoorsperson who has had it up to here with city life. Climb an echoey, chilly 220m down to sea-level.

Hummus Bar, (p. 235). One bit of this delicious, authentic hummus and you'll wonder why the Austro-Hungarian Empire ever asked the Ottomans to leave.

Millennium Monument. Built for the millennial celebration in 1896, this impressive monument hearkens back to an age when men were men and hats were 3 ft. tall. While you're at it, take a look at **Heroes' Square** or catch one of the major concerts or festivals held in the shadows of the seven chieftains.

Corvintető, (p. 269). Your last night in Budapest will be best spent taking in the sunrise with the city's other young revelers from the roof of this hip club in the eighth district. Forget that early flight or train ride—after all, when's the next time you'll be in Budapest?

Jókai tér. At night, the streets are filled with people on their way to and from the area's late-night cafes and bars. Street performers are also common, though the real spectacle is the **opera house,** which takes on an ethereal glow that's mesmerizing on a warm summer night. If you're lucky enough to find a hostel in the area, you'll never be at a loss for things to do and see.

JÓZSEFVÁROS

Józsefváros can get a little rough-and-tumble at night once you head past the Grand Boulevard, where the neighborhood becomes the red light district. But with the many hostels, pubs, and clubs as well as a large student population from the university nearby, there's really no reason to venture farther afield.

FERENCVÁROS

Ferencváros is in the midst of a cultural renewal. Though it's still a little run-down in some places, the recent additions of Budapest's **National Theater Concert Hall (p. 246)** and **Palace of the Arts** have attracted all kinds of artists and intellectuals to the neighborhood. With the artsy fartsy types came the independent and secondhand shops, which are now scattered throughout the area. Many of the best clubs have recently been closed or demolished, but you'll still find some pretty good nightlife in the area. **Ráday utca** offers a selection of cafes and restaurants that rivals that of **Váci utca** in the Belváros.

THE VÁROSLIGET (CITY PARK)

Originally an ox meadow, Budapest's City Park received a major overhaul in preparation for the 1896 millennial celebration. Located northeast of Heroes' Sq., the park is dominated by an enormous artifical pond. When the park isn't being renovated during the summer, you can sometimes rent a rowboat to spend a few hours out on the water. During the winter, rent a pair of skates when the pond turns into Central Europe's largest ice-skating rink. The park itself is a popular recreational area for locals, with great bike paths, spaces for picnicking, and even outdoor table tennis boards. The park's main road is closed to automobiles on weekends. *Let's Go* recommends a visit to one of the neighborhood's many impressive museums, followed by a stroll in the park, and a splurge on a nice dinner out in one of the area's many fancy restaurants.

BUDA

VÁRHEGY (CASTLE HILL), **CENTRAL BUDA, AND THE VÍZIVÁROS** (WATERTOWN)

Some will tell you that the best part about Buda is the view of Pest. The area is mostly a tourist zone, with many expensive restaurants and accommodations, and a couple of good museums. Though it may lack the affordable dining and lodging options of its eastern neighbor, Buda does sport its share of sights, including beautiful panoramic views of Pest and the Danube. The palatial grounds of Várhegy, sporting several fountains and statues, make for a good stroll even if you don't get to wear an awesome 19th-century costume. A **funicular** (800Ft) is available to take you to the top of the hill, but the wait is inevitably longer than the ride. A better way to get to the hill is to take the stone stairs to the right of the funicular and the tunnel. When you get to the split, take the left side to get a fantastic view of Pest from atop the tunnel. After you've gotten your pictures, take the stairs up to the palace itself.

Buda's Víziváros has long been a privileged piece of Hungarian real estate. During the Ottoman occupation, the Turks made their homes in the area, supposedly planting roses all over the hillside, hence the modern name for the Rózsadomb (literally "Rose Hill") neighborhood. Today, the area is home to many prominent Hungarian politicians, including the former prime minister.

GELLÉRT HEGY (GELLÉRT HILL)

After the coronation of King Stephen, the first Christian Hungarian monarch, in AD 1001, the Pope sent Bishop Gellért to convert the Magyars. After those unconvinced by the bishop's message hurled him to his death, the hill he was thrown from was named Gellérthegy in his honor. Today, Gellért Hegy is home to embassies and ambassadors, pricey real estate, several baths, and forested parkland. The hill's many winding pathways contain some of the best views of the winding Danube and Pest that you're likely to find.

ÓBUDA

Óbuda was one of the original three towns to unite to form Budapest. Though it was slighted during the naming process, it more than makes up for it with an awesome Roman amphitheater, many beautiful old churches, and plenty of museums (see **Sights, (p. 245)** and **Museums, (p. 258)**). Otherwise, Óbuda is mostly a residential area, with blocks and blocks of upscale apartment buildings. Without any metro stops, it's not terribly pedestrian friendly, either.

MARGIT-SZIGET (MARGARET ISLAND)

The earliest records mentioning the large island stuck in the middle of the Danube refer to it as Nyulak szigete (the Island of the Rabbits), and indeed it was a popular hunting ground among nobles for many years. Now its offerings are a little more universal—you might literally say pedestrian, as no motor vehicles are allowed on the island, except for a single bus line which ferries people from one end to the other. The island provides Budapest's residents with just about every kind of recreational activity available. Walking along the main road, don't be surprised if you have to jump out of the way to avoid a group of intense-looking cyclists. Runners love the 5km running track following the island's perimeter. For those less into exerting themselves, the island also has every kind of vehicle rental you could possibly need (and several that are unnecessary in most circumstances). **Bicycle rentals** are available at the southern end of the island (450Ft per 30min., 650 per hr., 1500 per day), while two-person "walk bicycles" and electric carts can be found at the northern end of the island (walk bicycles 1680Ft per 30min., 2680 per hr.; electric carts 2900/4300Ft). Be advised: these alternative modes of transportation go very poorly with a few drinks from the island's **outdoor pubs,** which draw crowds of locals and tourists to the southern half of the island on summer nights. Don't miss the island's two UNESCO world-heritage sites, the **Music Fountain** (Zenélő szökőkút) and the **water tower (p. 256).**

☑ LET'S GO PICKS

BEST FORMER UKRAINIAN FREIGHTER IN WHICH TO GET DRUNK: A38 (p. 269) on the Buda side of Petőfi Bridge.

BEST FORMERLY STATE-OWNED DEPARTMENT STORE ON WHICH TO GET DRUNK: Corvintető (p. 269), a stylish club in the eighth.

BEST GOVERNMENT BUILDING THAT LOOKS MORE LIKE A CHURCH: apparently nobody told the **Parliament (p. 247)** about separation of Church and State.

MOST REGAL HEADGEAR: the seven chieftains of the **Millennium Monument** in Heroes' Square.

BEST MUSEUM WHERE YOU CAN'T UNDERSTAND A WORD: one of our favorite museums in Budapest, the **Museum of Literature Petőfi (p. 261)**, is unfortunately entirely in Hungarian.

BEST MUSEUM THAT'S ALMOST TOO FAR AWAY TO VISIT: the **Ludwig Museum (p. 259)** has the best collection of 20th- and 21st-century Hungarian art.

BEST PLACE TO PLAY CHESS WITH HAIRY OLD MEN: the **Széchenyi baths (p. 250)** in the Varosliget is one of Europe's largest and most luxurious bath complexes. Incidentally, it's also one of our favorite places for a game of chess with a hairy old man.

MOST STATUES OF DEFIANT WORKERS: Memento Park (p. 257).

BEST HOLE IN THE GROUND: ☑**Gödör Klub (p. 265)**, a failed National Concert Hall turned hip concrete club-cum-cultural-center.

BEST PUN: ☑**Marquis de Salade (p. 237)** in Terézváros.

GRIMMEST MUSEUM: the **House of Terror (p. 258).**

PERHAPS THE ONLY RESTAURANT IN BUDAPEST WHERE LARD IS NOT THE MAIN INGREDIENT: Okay, maybe it's not the *only* place, but we like ☑**Hummus Bar (p. 235).**

LIFE AND TIMES

HISTORY

IT AIN'T EASY BEING A VASSAL STATE. It was in roughly AD 1 that the **Celts** plopped down on the shores of the Danube at the site of modern-day Budapest. Unfortunately, this was a little too close to the **Romans** for comfort (some 500 miles, but who's counting?). Over the next hundred years, the Romans swooped in, took the city off the Celts' hands. They then renamed it Aquincum, introduced Christianity, and built a few roads and baths (as Romans are wont to do). The **Huns** arrived on the scene in the AD fourth century and the **Great Age of Migrations** began. What did this mean for your average proto-Hungarian city on the Danube? From the time of the first Hun incursions until the AD ninth century, Budapest was settled by no fewer than 10 distinct groups, among them the **Goths** and the **Slavs.** Finally, the Magyars came along to clean up the mess.

MEET THE MAGYARS. Under the leadership of **Árpád,** the Magyar tribes swept through Bulgaria and Hungary, spilling the blood of previous settlers, under the blessing of the Byzantine emperor, **Leo VI.** The Magyars would hold down the fort, so to speak, until the 16th century.

WAR AND MORE WAR. Estimates place the Hungarian death toll from the Mongol invasion of 1241 at a staggering two million. But those aggressive Magyars just couldn't get enough: war with the Tartars, Lithuanians, Venetians, and Ottomans ravaged Hungary for centuries. The **Ottomans** occupied Buda and Pest in 1541, and built mosques left and right until the Hapsburgs finally got their act together and snatched up the city in 1686.

HAPSBURGIAN HUNGARY. The early Hapsburg rulers, such as Charles III and Maria Theresa, were met with significant challenges from Prussia and the early part of the 18th century was filled with such belt-tightening measures as Protestant repression, appeasement of nobles, and harsh economic decline. Enlightenment ruler Joseph II tried to undo some of the damage when he ascended the throne in 1780. He granted the Patent of Toleration in 1781, replaced Latin with German as the official language, and freed Hungary's serfs. Needless to say, the nobles were displeased.

TALKIN'·'BOUT A REVOLUTION. The French Revolution had aftershocks throughout Europe, and dissatisfaction mounted as the "Enlightened" Hapsburgs failed to respond. The situation erupted into the Revolution of 1848, which unseated the Hapsburgs and established the **First Republic of Hungary,** a young nation supported primarily by Slovaks, Germans, and the Jewish community, all of whom had languished under a sluggish and unresponsive monarchy.

DEMOCRATIC REPUBLICS ARE SO 1866. Under the leadership of Prime Minister **Lajos Batthyány,** the Hungarian government democratized with the passage of the **April Laws,** only to be thrown into war with neighboring Austria and the government of Franz Joseph shortly thereafter. The behemoth Russian Empire marched into Buda on the side of the Austrians in 1849 and executed the leaders of the Hungarian army. In 1867, Hungary came under Austrian control and Austria-Hungary was reinstated.

In 1873, under this regime, Buda, Pest, and nearby Óbuda were officially merged into the metropolis of Budapest, which grew into the cultural, economic, and political hub that it is today. The earlier compromise with Hungarian nobility granted the newly minted Budapest status as one of two national capitals under the Hapsburgian monarchy, second in regional influence only to the other capital, Vienna. Industrialization and urbanization modernized the economy. In 1910 the city had grown from the 17th to the eighth largest city in Europe; Budapest had gone from a refractor of the Western tradition to a cultural bastion in its own right. Before the outbreak of WWI, the city presided over a Hungarian Kingdom that was three times its modern size, its influence felt as far west as Italy.

THE WORLD WARS. During WWI, Hungary remained united with Austria and defended against Russia and Italy, at a Hungarian toll of over 600,000 fatalities. The war ended with the collapse of Austria-Hungary and the beginning of the **Hungarian Soviet Republic** in 1919. The young republic was quickly squashed, and its leader, **Béla Kun,** was sent into exile. In 1920 the **Treaty of Trianon** dismembered Hungary, gutting the nation's economy and transforming Budapest into an unwieldy, overlarge capital without a country to support it.

After the oppression and failure of the Soviet Republic, the people of Budapest and Hungary were skeptical of leftist movements and of the Soviet Union. The Great Depression was the nail in the leftist coffin: the 1930s and 40s saw the rise of radical groups such as the **Arrow Cross Fascists.** Hungary entered WWII on the side of the Germans, going down with the ship and falling into the hands of the Soviet Union in 1945. The Communist leaders of 1919 returned, and **Mátyás Rákosi** imposed Stalinist rule over Budapest.

NOT SO FAST, SOVIET INVADERS. Hungary didn't exactly bend over backwards to accommodate the Soviets. Rákosi's successor, **Imre Nagy,** worked against full state suppression of anti-Communists and the media, and in 1956, the **Hungarian Revolution** broke out. Peaceful protests in the streets of Budapest, which had before led to random arrests, starvation, oppression, and the massacre of thousands, boiled over into a powerful uprising. The nation temporarily withdrew from the **Warsaw Pact,** but the Soviet Union retaliated with force, and the revolt was crushed, though not before hundreds of thousands escaped the open borders.

LET THEM EAT GOULASH. The authoritarian, Soviet-elected **János Kádár** took over Hungary and led ruthless attacks against the revolutionaries. He hoped to eliminate his enemies and create "the happiest barrack" within the Eastern Bloc. As a happy coincidence, Hungary's successful industrialization and high standard of living made it a real-life happier Communism, known affectionately as **Goulash Communism.**

AND THEN THERE WAS CAPITALISM. Kádár's rule came to an end in 1988, and the Soviet presence dissolved soon thereafter. With its capital in Budapest, Hungary began full free market liberalization, and in 1997, with a whopping 85% of the national electorate, voted to join NATO, which it did two years later in 1999. It moved on to successfully join the EU in 2004.

Budapest's modern government has been led by the Alliance of Free Democrats' candidate, Mayor **Gábor Demszky,** since 1990. The city itself is home to the democratic government of Hungary, a single-parliament democracy dominated largely by the **Hungarian Socialist Party** and the center-right coalition **Fidesz-KNDP.** Its current prime minister, **Gordon Bajnai,** came to power after 2006 protests in Budapest that led to the deposition of the elected minister **Ferenc Gyurcsány,** who was revealed to have lied to win the election.

PEOPLE AND CULTURE

LANGUAGE

As its name would imply, the official language of Hungary is Hungarian *(Magyar)*. The preponderance of English (roughly 22% of Hungarians speak it), means that a quick *"beszél Angolul"* (BEH-sayl ON-go-lool; do you speak English?) may be more useful than your pocket dictionary.

DEMOGRAPHICS

With a population of over 1.7 million as of 2008, Budapest is the largest urban area in Central and Eastern Europe. While roughly 91% of Budapest's population identifies themselves as Magyar descendants, the other 9% are a testament to the city's turbulent history and the constant changing hands between ruling powers. Germans, Slovaks, Greeks, Romanians, Chinese, Ukrainians, Poles, and others are all part of Budapest's minority melting pot.

With respect to religion, Budapest proves more of an anomaly. While a substantial portion of its population (roughly 46%) identifies as **Roman-Catholic,** the real story here is the lack of religion: despite housing such religious landmarks as St. Stephen's Basilica, Matthias Church, and Dohány Street Synagogue (the largest synagogue in Europe), a whopping 21% of Budapest's citizens describe themselves as atheists.

THE ARTS

ARCHITECTURE

Budapest's architectural tradition has been colored by its conquerors. Classicism, introduced by the Romans in the AD first century, can be seen in the arches, vaults, and domes of structures such as **Contra Aquincum,** an old Roman fortress, and the **amphitheater** in Pest. During the 12th century, the Gothic craze took hold. For a glimpse at this style, check out the delicate ornamentation of the flying buttresses, pointed arches, and ribbed vaults the **Buda Castle (p. 249)** or the **Church of Saint Elizabeth of the House of Arpad**.

The Ottoman invasion brought with it Turkish bath houses; examples include the **Király (p. 219)** and **Rudas**. The builders of these thermal bath complexes mastered both the control of light and shadow in the arabesque interiors and the effortless-looking domes perched on top. This paved the way for Budapest's the **Moorish Revivalist** tradition, an ornamental style drawn from Ottoman Turkey and Moorish Andalusia that took root in the mid-19th century.

Bauhaus architecture, imported from Walter Gropius's school in Weimar Germany, held particular sway over Budapest in the modern era. The style shunned ornamental architecture of the past and embraced functionality as the guiding aesthetic principle. Residential buildings, theaters, and churches (such as the **Heart of Jesus Church** in the eighth and second districts stand as monuments to the movement.

Luminaries of modern Hungarian design include the creator of the world's most famous puzzle, **Ernő Rubik,** who was born in Budapest in 1944. A graduate of Budapest's Technical University and a professor at the Budapest College of Applied Arts, Rubik has spent his whole life in Hungary developing software and puzzles at his Rubik Studios. **Imre Makovecz,** born in Budapest in 1935 and also a graduate of Rubik's alma mater, has been a leading figure in **Organic architecture,** a movement that represents Hungary's modern artistic trend toward embracing its Magyar roots. Makovecz is best known as an architectural theorist who championed a style similar to that of Frank Lloyd Wright, which emphasized working with nature rather than against it. He has also been a sharp critic of Communism and the utilitarian, uniform style of the Bauhaus. His politics, as well as his architecture, represented a turn towards **Nationalist Romanticism,** the elevation of nature and cultural roots seen across modern Hungarian art.

LITERATURE

Hungary's literary tradition begins after the Magyars made a switch to the Latin script following their conversion to Christianity in the 11th century. Poetry flourished in this early period. The Renaissance tradition saw the publication of Hungary's first book, the **Chronica Hungarorum.** This give way to warrior and love poetry and eventually spiraled into an age Enlightenment literature that was in keeping with the European trend.

In the 19th century, poetry flourished alongside revolution. **János Arany,** best known for his darkly satirical epic poetry, made a name for himself as the

BUDAPEST

"Shakespeare of ballads." Before his death in Budapest in 1882, he translated three of Shakespeare's works into Hungarian. The so-called poet of the 1848 revolution, who would later become Hungary's national poet and the writer of its national anthem, was **Sándor Petőfi.** His statue stands in Buda, a testament to a revolutionary fervor that inspired similar movements world-wide in the 20th century. Be sure to check out the **Museum of Literature Petőfi** (p. 261), where you'll find exhibits on Petőfi's work and his intellectual and artistic circles.

The early 20th century was marked by critical philosophical and political texts born out of the Marxist tradition. **György Lukács** wrote some of the critical foundations of the Western Marxist political tradition during the interwar period, as well as a wealth of literary criticism. His 1938 "Realism in the Balance" argues that realistic portrayal in fiction is the only way to actually create valuable literature that can comment on social reality. He later served as Hungary's Minister of Culture after the Revolution of 1956. Lessons of Lukács's realism appear in the works of **Arthur Koestler,** whose *Darkness at Noon* (1940) was a semi-autobiographical (and thoroughly realist) portrayal of the Communist party. A journalist by trade, Koestler was, apart from this, a controversial figure: he dabbled in paranormal science and was both a staunch opponent of Darwinism and a vocal proponent of voluntary euthanasia.

As for contemporary fiction, Budapest's most well-known writer, **Kertész Imre,** survived the concentration camps and made a career for himself first as a translator of Nietzsche, Wittgenstein, and several dramatic works. In 2002, he won the Nobel Prize in Literature for works such as *Fatelessness (Sorstalanság)*, a stark work that describes the tribulations of a 14-year-old Hungarian Jew during his imprisonment at Auschwitz.

MUSIC

Hungary has rich traditions in both folk and classical music. The traditional Gregorian chant was imported from the west in the 11th century. This led to the evolution of medieval and Renaissance music along Western lines, with a heavy emphasis on the use of the organ and the lute. In the 19th century, the Western path gave way to a more uniquely Hungarian folk music. First came the rise of **verbunkos,** a military type of folk music used as a recruitment tool during the 18th century. Then came several flavors of Magyar music, among them the **czardas** (*verbunkos* with modified tempo) and the **Nóta.**

In the realms of classical music, two artists stand out in particular. **Franz Liszt,** though not born in Budapest, was uniquely attached to the city as a result of its Music Academy, which was later renamed in his honor. The composer and musician inspired what as known as **Lisztomania** in the mid-1800s: his fans would fight over handkerchiefs and his other personal effects as though they were the rarest of jewels. Primarily a virtuoso pianist, Liszt transcribed and composed plenty of original music, and also invented the **symphonic poem,** a short orchestral piece meant to evoke the image of a literary subject. Other pieces, such as his *Hungarian Rhapsodies*, abandoned classical experimentation and instead elevated the Gypsy folk music of Hungary. His *Bagatelle sans Tonalité* explored the cacophonous aspect of atonal music, a radical departure from earlier classical traditions.

Béla Bartók, the creator of ethnomusicology (the study of cultural elements of music), was a disciple of Liszt and a significant force in the integration of Magyar peasant music into Hungary's classical tradition. In 1908, he traveled into the countryside, discovered this pentatonic and pastoral music, and began to integrate it into his own work. Over 40 years after his death, his body was returned to Hungary for his funeral; he was buried in Budapest's Farkasréti Cemetery.

VISUAL ARTS

Throughout its history, Hungarian art has been informed by its folk traditions. Magyar art, for instance, is known for its black pottery and fine embroidery. Made of the same black clay used to brew one of the nation's finest wine, *Egri Bikavér* (literally Bull's Blood), **black pottery** is a utilitarian art whose firing process turns it charcoal black. Black pottery vessels are often used to carry water or cook traditional meals, and are thus an artistic relic of the Magyars' nomadic past. Over the past few centuries, the process has been diluted as modern pieces have lost the traditional technique and the old process. Magyar **embroidery** commonly adorns tablecloths, clothing, and even traditional wall hangings. Its style varies regionally and typically incorporates Baroque, Persian, and Renaissance elements of ornamentation that consist of flowers, birds, spirals, and peacock's feathers.

In the realm of painting, **Victor Vasarely,** born in 1906, is considered the father of **Op-art.** His canvases were often infused with illusion that required the viewer to reason through abstract tableaus that appear to move or warp. A museum of Vasarely's collected work opened in Budapest in 1987 (see **Vasarely Múzeum, p. 261**). Other famous Hungarian artists include photographer **Gyula Halasz** (better known as Brassaï) and the film-maker **Béla Lugosi,** best known for his 1931 *Dracula.*

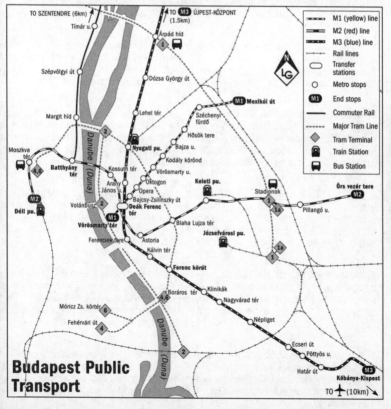

Budapest Public Transport

YOU SEEM A BIT OCCUPIED

For a country at the intersection of three civilizations—Western Europe, Eastern Europe, an the Middle East—it's remarkable that Hungary has managed to retain a distinct identity. At th same time, the marks of the region's former empires have left their traces on Budapest's phys cal and cultural landscape. The Ottomans were the original uninvited guests, building mosque and luxurious baths all over the Buda side of the Danube for 150 years. After soundly trounci the Ottomans, the Austrian Hapsburgs absorbed the entire Kingdom of Hungary, and, despi the Hungarians' best efforts, maintained control until WWI. After WWII, the Communists rebu a largely leveled Budapest in their own image, complete with squat apartment buildings an monumental statues. While the occupations themselves were never welcome, the influences th came with them have helped to shape Budapest into a modern, cosmopolitan city.

1. TOMB OF GÜL BABA AND ROSE HILL. The death of Suleiman the Magnificent's poe in-residence and comrade at the walls of Buda Castle cast a dark shadow over the Ottoman victory celebrations. His ornate and octagonal tomb, however, is a fitting tribute. The nearby ro gardens that give Rose Hill its name were said to have first been planted by the Ottomans duri their stay in Buda's most desirable neighborhood (p. 254).

2. KIRÁLY BATHS. The city's only siege-proof baths are a testament to Ottoman forward-thinki and Epicureanism. Soak in the spirit of the Ottomans as you relax in the thermal baths benea 500-year-old domes. Experiencing history has never felt so relaxing; just make sure you're going the right gender-specific day (women only M, W; men only Tu, Th-Sa; both Su; p. 254).

3. HISTORICAL MUSEUM OF BUDAPEST. Located in the Buda Palace, which has its housed more than its share of foreign regimes, the Historical Museum contains numerous ar facts from the city's not-so-welcome guests, including Turkish plates and silverware and dress replicating the latest Vienna fashions. You'll also find artifacts dating from the original imperia ists, the Romans, and their settlement at Aquincum (p. 261).

4. CITADELLA. This structure was designed and built by the Hapsburgs after the failed revol tion of 1848 as a reminder to the Hungarian people of who wore the pants along the Danub Even after Budapest became a dual-capital, it took the Austrians until 1897 to vacate th Citadella, which remained vacant until World War II, when it was turned into an air-raid shelte Skip the lame exhibit inside, but soak in the fantastic view of Pest.

5. CHAIN BRIDGE. Double back to cross the Széchenyi Lánchíd (Széchenyi Chain Bridge the first permanent Bridge across the Danube in Budapest. At the time of its construction, th bridge was the longest in the world and considered an architectural marvel. Though built und the Hapsburgs, the bridge became a symbol of growing Hungarian national consciousness. Ju don't believe that myth about the lions not having any tongues (p. 253).

6. HUNGARIAN STATE OPERA HOUSE. Despite Emperor Franz Joseph's stipulation that th new opera house in Budapest must be smaller than his beloved opera house at Vienna, th Hungarian-designed and built opera house is one of the city's greatest cultural treasures. Eve better, cheap student tickets let you have a taste of European culture at its best at a fraction the price you'd pay elsewhere (p. 249).

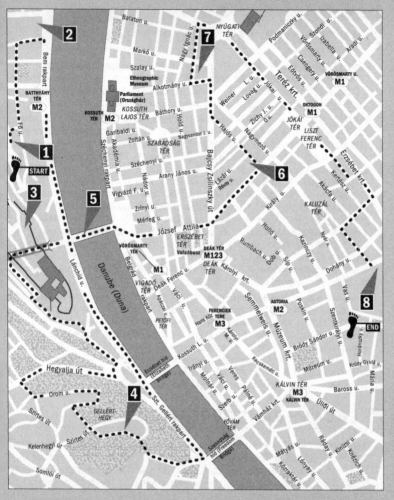

7. HUMMUS BAR. While the Turks have been gone for more than 300 years, their culinary influence thankfully remains, though it's largely confined to nonstop gyro stands (here usually called *Török gyorsétterem* or "Turkish fast food"). For those willing to look, the tiny Hummus Bar serves some of the best mashed chickpeas this side of Istanbul. If you can find a volume of Gül Baba's collected poems, there's no better place to get acquainted with them than on the softly padded upper floor of this popular Erzsébetváros eatery (p. 235).

8. CORVINTETŐ. If there's one thing the Hungarians are good at, it's turning abandoned buildings into places to drink. Budapest's youth live it up on top of an ugly, gray Communist-era building where most of their parents will remember waiting in long lines to buy light bulbs and underwear. The service elevator is the oldest in Hungary, and offers the truly impatient a chance to start drinking before they even get to the roof, thanks to a handy in-elevator cooler. If you have the fortune to be here on a warm summer night, grab a good seat and wait for the sunrise (p. 269).

▣ INTERCITY TRANSPORTATION

Flights: Ferihegy Airport (BUD; ☎01 296 9696). **Malév** (Hungarian Airlines; ☎01 235 3888) flies to major cities. To the center, take bus #93 (20min., every 15min. 4:55am-11:20pm, 270Ft), then ⓜ3 to Kőbánya-Kispest (15min. to Deák tér, in downtown Budapest). Airport Minibus (☎01 296 8555) goes to hostels (2990Ft).

Trains: The major stations, **Keleti Pályaudvar, Nyugati Pályaudvar,** and **Déli Pályaudvar,** are also Metro stops (☎40 49 49 49). Most **international trains** arrive at Keleti station, but some from Prague go to Nyugati station. For schedules, check www.mav.hu, part of which is in English. To: **Berlin** (12-13hr., 4 per day, 15,800Ft); **Bucharest, ROM** (14hr., 5 per day, 23,600Ft); **Prague** (7-8hr., 5 per day, 16,300Ft); **Vienna, AUT** (3hr., 17 per day, 3600Ft); **Warsaw, POL** (11hr., 2 per day, 18,500Ft). The daily Orient Express stops on its way from **Paris, FRA** to **Istanbul, TUR.** Trains run to most major destinations in Hungary. Purchase tickets at an **International Ticket Office** (Keleti station open daily 8am-7pm; Nyugati station open M-Sa 5am-9pm; info desk 24hr.). Or try **MÁV Hungarian Railways,** VI, Andrássy út 35. (☎01 461 5500. Branches at all stations. Open Apr.-Sept. M-F 9am-6pm, Oct.-Mar. M-F 9am-5pm. Say *"diák"* for student or under 26 discounts.) The **HÉV commuter railway** station is at Batthyány tér, opposite Parliament. Trains head to **Szentendre** (45min., every 15min. 5am-9pm, 460Ft). Purchase tickets at the station for transport beyond the city limits.

Buses: Buses to international and some domestic destinations leave from the **Népliget station,** X, Üllői út 131. (ⓜ3: Népliget. ☎01 382 0888. Ticket window open M-F 6am-9pm, Sa-Su 6am-4pm.) To **Berlin** (14hr., 6 per week, 19,900Ft), **Prague** (8hr., 6 per week, 11,900Ft), and **Vienna, AUT** (3½hr., 5 per day, 5900Ft). Buses going east of Budapest leave from **Népstadion station,** XIV, Hungária körút 46-48. (ⓜ2: Népstadion. ☎01 252 4498. Open M-F 6am-6pm, Sa-Su 6am-4pm.) Buses to the **Danube Bend** and parts of the Uplands depart outside Árpád híd metro station on the ⓜ3 line. (☎01 329 1450. Cashier open 6am-8pm.) Check www.volanbusz.hu for schedules.

▣ LOCAL TRANSPORTATION

Commuter Railway: The **HÉV** station is across the river from Parliament, 1 Metro stop past the Danube in Buda at Batthyány tér. On the list of stops, those within the city limits are displayed in a different color. For these stops, a regular metro ticket will suffice. Purchase tickets at the counter to travel beyond the city limits. Békásmegyer is the final stop within the city limits.

Public Transportation: Subways, buses, and **trams** are convenient. The subways and trams run every few minutes. Buses are generally on-time and some run 24hr.; schedules are posted at stops. **Budapest Public Transport (BKV;** ☎ 80 40 66 86; www.bkv. hu) has info in Hungarian and an English website. The **metro** has 3 lines: M1 (yellow), M2 (red), and M3 (blue). **M1** runs west to east from downtown Pest past City Park along Andrássy út. **M2** runs west to east and connects Deli Train Station in Buda with Keleti Train Station in Pest along Rákóczi út. **M3** runs north to south through Pest and provides a transfer bus to the airport from the southern terminus (Kőbánya-Kispest). A 4th metro line is currently under construction that will connect southern Buda to northeastern Pest, though it is not expected to open until 2012. The metro runs 4:30am-11:30pm. Most buses and trams stop running at 11pm. Single-fare tickets for public transport (one-way on 1 line; 300Ft) are sold in metro stations, in Trafik shops, and by sidewalk vendors at tram stops. Punch them in the orange boxes at the gate of the metro or on buses and trams; punch a new ticket when you change lines, or face a fine of 5000Ft from the undercover ticket inspectors. Day pass 1550Ft, 3-day 3850Ft, 1-week 4600Ft, 2-week 6200Ft, 1-month 9400Ft.

Night transit: After you've missed the last tram, transportation is available in the form of night (É) buses which run midnight-5am along major routes: #7É and 78É follow the Ⓜ2 route; #6É follows the 4/6 tram line; #14É and 50É follow the Ⓜ3 route.

Taxis: The Budapest public transit system is pretty efficient, so you will rarely need a cab. Beware of scams; ask how much the ride will cost and always check for yellow license plates and a running meter. Base fares are always 300Ft, with an additional 350Ft per km and 70Ft per min. waiting. **Tele5Taxi** (☎01 555 5555) is 230Ft per km by phone, 240Ft per km on the street. To the airport: 4600Ft from Pest and 5100Ft from Buda. Also try **Főtaxi** (☎01 222 2222), 225Ft per km by phone, 240Ft per km on the street or **6x6 Taxi**(☎01 666 6666), 229Ft per km by phone, 240Ft per km on the street. To the airport: 4600Ft from Pest and 5100Ft from Buda.

Car Rental: You'll need to get a certified translation of your American driver's license to drive in Hungary. Car rentals are available from several reliable agencies, though most will only rent to those over 21 (and several only to those over 25). Credit card required. **Avis,** Szabadság tér 7 (☎01 318 4240). Cars from 7900Ft per day. Drivers must be 21 and have had a license for at least 1 year. Open M-Sa 7am-6pm, Su 8am-6pm. AmEx/MC/V. **Budget,** I, Krisztina krt. 41-43 (☎01 214 0420; www.budget.hu). Cars from 7500Ft per day. Drivers must be 21. Open M-F 8am-8pm, Sa-Su 8am-6pm. AmEx/MC/V.

Bike Rental: Yellow Zebra Bikes, V, Sütő utca 2 and VI, Lázár utca 16 (☎01 266 8777), rents a wide variety of bikes at four different price levels. Also provides bike tours. Bikes 1500-2500Ft for all-day rental. Open Nov.-Mar. daily 10am-6:30pm, Apr-Oct 9:30am-7pm. MC/V.

DON'T STRESS YOURSELF ÚT. In keeping with the general incomprehensibility of the Hungarian language, street names may often get confusing. Here's a quick run-down. *Út* is different than *utca* (the former means road and the latter means street), though you'll see them abbreviated variably. *Tér* is different than *tere* (both, however, refer to some type of square). *Körút* is often abbreviated "krt" and stands on its own, meaning boulevard.

⑦ PRACTICAL INFORMATION

TOURIST AND FINANCIAL SERVICES

Tourist Offices: Tourinform, V, Sütő u. 2 (☎01 438 8080; www.hungary.com). Ⓜ1, 2, or 3: Deák tér. Off Deák tér behind McDonald's. Open daily 8am-8pm. **Vista Travel Center,** Andrássy út 1 (☎01 429 9751; incoming@vista.hu). Arranges tours and accommodations. Open M-F 9am-6:30pm, Sa 9am-2:30pm. Both offices sell the **Budapest Card** (Budapest Kártya), which provides discounts, unlimited public transportation, and admission to most museums (2-day card 6300Ft, 3-day 7500Ft). A great deal, except when museums are closed on Mondays.

Embassies and Consulates: See **Essentials,** p. 7.

Currency Exchange: Banks have the best rates. **Citibank,** V, Vörösmarty tér 4 (☎01 374 5000). Ⓜ1: Vörösmarty tér. Cashes traveler's checks for no commission and provides MC/V cash advances. Bring your passport. Open M-Th 9am-5pm, F 9am-4pm.

LOCAL SERVICES

Luggage Storage: Lockers at all 3 train stations. 150-600Ft.

English-Language Bookstore: Libri Könyvpalota, VII, Rákóczi út. 12 (☎01 267 4843). Ⓜ2: Astoria. The best choice in the city, this multilevel bookstore has 1 fl. of up-to-date English titles. Open M-F 10am-7:30pm, Sa 10am-3pm. MC/V. **Treehugger Dan's,** VI, Csengery utca 48 (☎01 322 0774; www.treehugger.hu). Ⓜ1: Vörösmarty utca. Massive selection of secondhand English books with a hip, laid-back, and adamantly fair-trade coffee shop. Open M-F 10am-6pm, Sa 10am-5pm. Cash only.

GLBT Resources: GayGuide.net Budapest (☎06 30 93 23 334; www.budapest. gayguide.net). Posts an online guide and runs a hotline (daily 4-8pm) with info and a reservation service for GLBT-friendly lodgings. **Na Vegre!** (www.navegre.hu). Publishes an up-to-date guide to gay nightlife. Available at any gay bar.

EMERGENCY AND COMMUNICATIONS

Tourist Police: V, Sütő utca 2 (☎01 438 8080). Ⓜ1, 2, or 3: Deák tér. Inside the Tourinform office. Open 24hr. Beware of impostors demdanding to see your passport.

Pharmacies: Look for green signs labeled Apotheke, Gyógyszertár, or Pharmacie. Minimal after-hours service fees apply. **II,** Frankel Leó út 22 (☎01 212 4406). AmEx/MC/V. **VI,** Teréz körút 41 (☎01 311 4439). Open M-F 8am-8pm, Sa 8am-2pm. **VII,** Rákóczi út 39 (☎314 3695). Open M-F 7:30am-9pm, Sa 7:30am-2pm.

Medical Services: Falck (SOS) KFT, II, Kapy út 49/b (☎01 275 1535). Ambulance service US$120. **American Clinic,** I, Hattyú utca. 14 (☎01 224 9090; www.americanclinics. com). Open for appointments M-F 8am-8pm, Sa 8am-2pm. 24hr. **emergency** call line ☎01 224 9090. The US embassy (p. 7) maintains a list of English-speaking doctors.

Telephones: Cards are sold at kiosks and metro stations. 50-unit card 800Ft, 120-unit card 1800Ft. Domestic operator and info ☎198. International operator ☎190, info 199.

Internet: Cybercafes are everywhere, but they can be expensive and long waits are common. Most coffee shops and cafes have free Wi-Fi. Try **Ami Internet Coffee,** V, Váci utca. 40 (☎01 267 1644; www.amicoffee.hu). Ⓜ3: Ferenciek tér. 200Ft per 15min., 700Ft per hr. Open daily 9am-2am.

Post Office: V, Városház utca 18 (☎01 318 4811). **Poste Restante** (Postán Mar) in office around the right side of the building. Open M-F 8am-8pm, Sa 8am-2pm. Branches at Nyugati station; VI, Teréz körút. 105/107; Keleti station; VIII, Baross tér 11/c; and elsewhere. Open M-F 7am-8pm, Sa 8am-2pm. **Postal Code:** Depends on the district—postal codes are 1XX2, where XX is the district number (1052 for post office listed above).

⌂ ⛺ ACCOMMODATIONS AND CAMPING

Budapest's hostels are centers for the backpacker social scene, and their common rooms can be as exciting as many bars and clubs. Book ahead in July and August when tourists flood the city. If you book a room, call or e-mail the night before to confirm: many hostels require such a confirmation as a rule, but some have been known to "misplace" reservations booked far in advance. Many hostels are run by the **Hungarian Youth Hostels Association (HI),** which operates from an office in Keleti station. Representatives wearing Hostelling International shirts—and legions of competitors—accost travelers as they get off the train. Beware that they may provide inaccurate descriptions of other accommodations in order to sell their own. Private rooms are more expensive than hostels, but they offer peace, quiet, and private showers. Arrive early, bring cash, and haggle. ■**Best Hotel Service,** V, Sütő utca 2, arranges apartment, hostel, and hotel

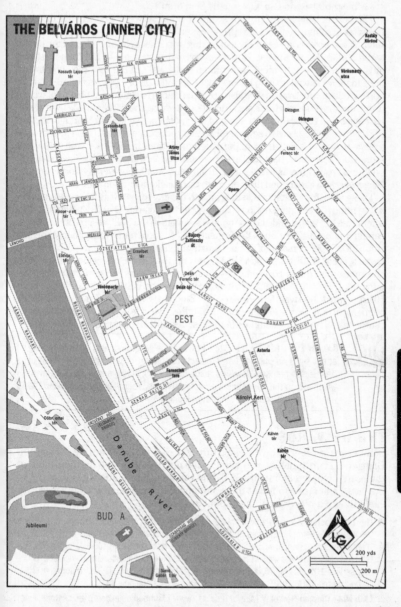

THE BELVÁROS (INNER CITY)

BUDAPEST

reservations (7000Ft and up). Take ⓜ1, 2, or 3 to Deák tér. (☎01 318 4848; www.besthotelservice.hu. Open daily 8am-8pm.)

The best hostels in the city are evenly divided between Pest's major districts. **Lipótváros** has many respectable options especially in the streets around **Szent István körút.** These hostels are centrally located between the areas of Buda and the dining and nightlife deeper in Pest. Hostels in **Terézváros** are some of the friendliest and most social in the city. Most are within a short walk of the best restaurants and bars: ideal for travellers who believe that the best part of a place's culture is at the bottom of a bottle. **Erzsébetváros** also provides places to sleep right next to places to drink, but most hostels there are strict about keeping the party outside their walls. **Józsefváros** and **Ferencváros** host some of the most laid-back hostels in the city, and offer convenient access to several museums and students bars. Good luck finding a place to stay in **Buda**—most of the accommodations in the area come with a few more stars than most backpackers are comfortable with, though a few gems can be found around the **Gellért Hill** area. In July and August, university dorms around **Móricz Zsigmond körtér** open their doors to backpackers and tourists.

Those who, for whatever reason, came to the city to get away from it all can find a few removed camping options. **Zugligeti "Niche" Camping ❶,** XII, Zugligeti út 101, offers free hot water and and communal showers in the hills west of Buda. (www.campingniche.hu. Take bus #158 from above Moszkva tér to Laszállóhely, the last stop. 1800Ft per person; 1500Ft per small tent; 2000Ft per large tent. Cash only.) **Camping Római ❶,** III, Szentendrei út 189, just north of Buda, offers modern facilities and more than a few conveniences, including a grocery store, park, and swimming pool. (☎388 7167. ⓜ2: Batthyány tér. Take the HÉV to Római Fürdő; walk 100m toward the river. Laundry 1000Ft. Electricity included. Campsites 5000Ft per person; bungalows 3500Ft; cars 5000Ft. Reserve at least 1 month in advance as campsites fill up during summer. 3% tourist tax. 10% HI discount. MC/V.)

> **BY THE NUMBERS.** While Budapest is generally pretty good at putting street signs on buildings at intersections, the art of putting signs in front of businesses manages to elude restaurants, bars, clubs, and hostels, many of which are on the upper floors of older buildings. Your best bet is to follow the number on the address, rather than looking for a sign.

THE BELVÁROS

Sometimes it feels like you can't throw a rock without hitting a hostel in District V. Unfortunately, you wouldn't really be able to tell because most of them are completely unmarked. While the inner city's hostels lack many of the extra amenities found at the accommodations in nearby Lipotváros, you can still find a place to suit just about any taste.

The Loft Hostel, V, Veres Pálné utca 19 (☎01 328 0916; www.lofthostel.hu). ⓜ3: Kálvin tér. From the metro, Kecskeméti út west, turn left onto Szerb utca, and then right onto Veres Pálné. Perfect for people who enjoy a relaxed, social atmosphere. Rustic-looking beams and slanted ceilings. All the wall art is by staff members or former guests. Linens included. Laundry service 1000Ft. Free Wi-Fi. Reception 24hr. 8-bed dorms 3600Ft; 6-bed dorms 4000Ft; 4-bed dorms 4500. 300Ft rate increase on weekends. Cash only. ❷

11th Hour Cinema Hostel, V, Magyar utca 11 (www.11thhourhostel.com). ⓜ2: Astoria. From the metro, take Kossuth Lajos west and turn left on Magyar út. Spacious dorms with large windows for the claustrophobic and Vitamin D-deprived. Grab a movie from the massive DVD collection, fire up the projector, and get your swerve on without even having to leave the hos-

BUDAPEST

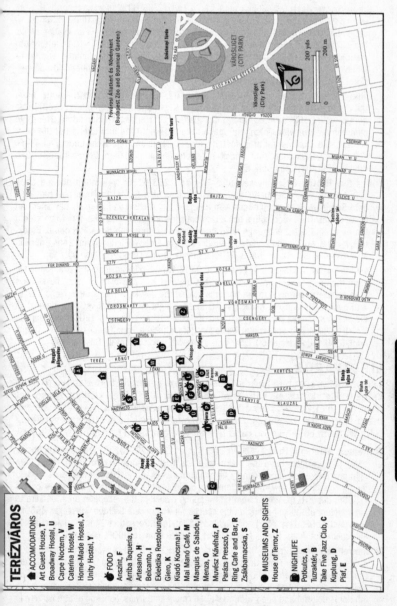

TERÉZVÁROS

▲ ACCOMMODATIONS
Art Guest House, **T**
Broadway Hostel, **U**
Carpe Noctem, **V**
Caterina Hostel, **W**
Home-Made Hostel, **X**
Unity Hostel, **Y**

● FOOD
Anszint, **F**
Arriba Taqueria, **G**
Artesano, **H**
Belcanto, **I**
Eklektika Restolounge, **J**
Giero, **K**
Kiadó Kocsmai, **L**
Mai Manó Café, **M**
Marquis de Salade, **N**
Menza, **O**
Muvész Kávéház, **P**
Parázs Presszó, **Q**
Ring Cafe and Bar, **R**
Zsákbamacska, **S**

● MUSEUMS AND SIGHTS
House of Terror, **Z**

▯ NIGHTLIFE
Potkulcs, **A**
Tuzraktér, **B**
Take Five Jazz Club, **C**
Kuplung, **D**
Piaf, **E**

tel. Linens and towel included. Internet and Wi-Fi. Reception 24hr. Check-out 11am. Dorms 1900-3500Ft; singles 6000-12,000Ft; doubles 5100-7500Ft. Cash only. ❷

Green Bridge Hostel, V, Molnár utca 22-24 (☎01 266 6922; www.greenbridgehostel.com). Ⓜ3: Ferenciek tere. From the metro, take Károlyi Mihály utca, turn right on Irányi utca, and left on Molnár utca. Colorful walls and no bunks make this an inviting place. The outgoing and social types will appreciate its proximity to Váci, while the environmentally-conscious will dig its commitment to sustainability. Free internet and Wi-Fi. Wheelchair-accessible. Reception 24hr. Check-out 11am. Reserve ahead in summer. Dorms 1400-2700Ft. Cash only. ❶

Ginkgo Hostel, V, Szép utca 5 (☎01 266 6107; www.ginkgo.hu). Ⓜ2: Astoria. From the metro, take Kossuth Lajos utca toward the river and then turn left on Szép. Large dorms with graffiti-covered doors, chandeliers, and Alfons Mucha prints. The large common area provides plenty of space to relax, even if the furniture is not the most comfortable. Continental breakfast included. Lockers and linens included. Free Wi-Fi. Key deposit. Reception 24hr. Check-in flexible. Check-out 10am. Dorms from 3500Ft; doubles 5500Ft. Cash only. ❷

Red Bus Hostel, V, Semmelweis utca 14 (☎01 266 0136; www.redbusbudapest.hu). Ⓜ2: Astoria. From the metro, take Kossuth Lajos utca toward the river and turn right onto Semmelweis. A small hostel with a large guest kitchen and sparsely furnished but clean dorms. The 2-bed suites come with couches and cupboards. Be sure to check out the excellent English-language used bookstore next door with the same name. Breakfast, lockers, and linens included. Laundry 1500Ft. Free Wi-Fi. Reception 24hr. Check-in 11am. Check-out 10am. Dorms 4100Ft; private rooms 10,500Ft. Cash only. ❸

Domino Hostel, V, Váci utca 77 (☎01 235 0492; www.dominohostel.com). Ⓜ3: Kálvin tér. From the metro, take Vámház körút toward the river and turn right on Váci; the address is Váci, but the entrance to the hostel is around the corner at Havas utca. Large interior with basic beds and not much else. Its location right on Váci puts you in middle of all the action that most people try to avoid. Breakfast 1000Ft. Laundry 1200Ft. Key deposit 2700Ft. Wheelchair-accessible. Reception 24hr. Check-in 2pm. Check-out 10am. Dorms from 4600Ft; doubles 8400Ft. 10% discount with valid student ID. Cash only. ❸

LIPÓTVÁROS

The old apartment buildings in Lipótváros are generally better suited to hole-in-the-wall style hostels with small dorms and little if any common space. Yet what they lack in size, they often make up for in amenities. Several hostels in the area appear to be engaged in a sort of quality arms race, offering everything from widescreen televisions and free bicycle rentals to free shots of Palinka.

Aventura Boutique Hostel, XIII, Visegrádi utca 12 (☎239 0782; www.aventurahostel.com). Ⓜ3: Nyugati. From the metro, take Szent István körút toward the river and turn right on Visegrádi. A super-friendly, helpful staff makes you feel comfortable in 4 themed rooms. The amply pillowed India dorm has colorful linens and curtains as well as lockers (1500Ft deposit) fashioned from old weapons crates. In the reception area, be sure to get a picture of yourself sitting on the couch that was once a bathtub. Massages 4500Ft. Breakfast 450Ft. Free Wi-Fi and high speed internet. Reception 24hr. Flexible check-in and check-out times. Dorms from 3300Ft; doubles from 10,900Ft. Cash only. ❷

Central Backpack King, V, Október 6 utca 15 (☎200 7184; www.centralbpk.hu). Ⓜ1: Bajcsy-Zsilinszky út. From the metro, take József Attila utca toward the river and then turn right on Október 6 ut. Upon arriving, you'll be greeted by the enthusiastic staff as well as a complimentary shot of Palinka from the manager's grandmother's village. The interior is colorful and lined with rugs of all colors and styles. Fun, social atmosphere in the center of Lipótváros means you'll never be at a loss for people to go out with. If you don't feel like going out, you can hang out in the always bustling common room, complete with a widescreen TV and movies to watch with the other bored kids. Free lockers. Linens included. Free Wi-Fi. Minimum stay of 2 nights. Reception 24hr. Check-in 2pm. Check-out 11am. Dorms from 4000Ft; doubles 8000Ft per person. Cash only. ❸

Riverside Hostel, V, Szent István krt 15 (☎302 6341; www.riversidehostelbudapest. com). Ⓜ3: Nyugati. From the metro, take Szent István körút toward the river; the hostel will be on your left. One of the most archetypical hostels you'll ever see. The staff is friendly, the rooms are clean, the baths are shared, and the decor is reasonably eclectic, with colored walls and paper lanterns. A few of the private rooms come with TVs. Lockers 1000Ft deposit. Linens and towels included. Laundry 1000Ft. Wi-Fi. Bike rental 1000Ft per 3hr., 2000Ft per 24hr. Reception 8am-11pm. Check-in 11am. Check-out 10am. Dorms from 2200Ft; doubles from 9500Ft. Cash only. ❶

The Groove Hostel, XIII, Szent István krt 16(☎786 8038; www.groovehostel.hu). Ⓜ3: Nyugati. From the metro, take Szent István körút toward the river; the hostel will be on your right. A young, laid back hostel for young, laid back people. Every available nook and cranny has been turned into a social space with couches, beanbags, or plush cubes, and the whole place has an enjoyable ad-hoc feel to it, especially the TV "room" above the reception desk. Consider yourself lucky if you manage to score the massive private double. Free lockers. Linens included. Wi-Fi. Reception 24hr. Flexible check-in and check-out times. Dorms from 4500Ft; double from 7700Ft. Cash only. ❸

Adoro Hostel and Garibaldi Guesthouse, V, Garibaldi utca 5 (☎302 3456;www. adorohostelbudapest.com and www.garibaldiguesthouse.hu). Ⓜ2: Kossuth Lajos tér. From the metro, take Akademia utca south and then turn left on Garibaldi. The warm and welcoming staff will make you feel like you're visiting your loving, eccentric country grandparents. Dorm beds range in size from typical bunk to comfortable to superfluous. One of the dorms features a terrace with a great view of the Danube. For weary travelers who need to feel a little more pampered, private suites are suitably luxurious. Each of the suites is decorated in its own style, though a large wooden duck seems to be a consistent feature. Linens included. Internet access and Wi-Fi. Reception 24hr. Check-in noon. Check-out 10am. Dorms from 3600Ft; lofts from 5000Ft; suites from 6000Ft per person. Cash only. ❷

East Side Hostel, V, Falk Miksa utca 24-26 (☎574 0224). Ⓜ3: Nyugati. From the metro, take Szent István körút toward the river and then turn left on Falk Miksa. Look for the sneaker spray-painted gold outside the entrance. Its location close to Parliament and the Ministry of Defense means you will be very protected in a state of emergency. This small hostel may not look like much, but it has a funky touch. The staff occasionally cooks a free breakfast or dinner if guests are around. Great view of the Danube from the terrace. Linens included. Free Wi-Fi. Free bike rentals. Reception 9am-11pm. Check-in noon. Check-out 11am. Dorms from 1800Ft; doubles 8000Ft. Cash only. ❶

ERZSÉBETVÁROS

Accommodations in the Jewish quarter are often not less luxurious than those in the nearby sixth district. If you want to sleep near the party, expect standard bunks and common rooms that range from boring to okay. Also, don't expect the staff to appreciate you trying to bring the party home with you—these are generally places in which to sleep, not to socialize.

🔲 10 Beds, Erzsébet körút 15 (☎20 933 5965). Ⓜ2: Blaha Lujza tér. From the metro, take Erzsébet körút north for a block and a half; the hostel is on your right. A super laid-back attitude characterizes this small, intimate hostel where long-term guests sometimes become quasi-staff members. Aside from the bunk beds, the place feels more like a good friend's apartment. The friendly staff is full of recommendations and the owner frequently takes people out for trips to the baths or pubs. Free laundry service is just icing on the cake. Lockers and linens included. Free Wi-Fi. Reception 24hr. Dorms from 3000Ft. Cash only. ❷

Thumbs Up Hostel, VII, Kertész utca 18 (☎30 318 4443; www.thumbsuphostel.com). Ⓜ2: Blaha Lujza tér. From the metro, take Erzsébet körút north and then veer left at the 1st intersection; the hostel is near the corner of Kertész and Wesselényi. Mid-sized hostel with basic bunks across 2 10-bed dorms and a common room furnished with plenty of sofas and a bowl chair. A large flatscreen TV and DVD collection gives you something to do if you don't feel like going out. Breakfast included. Lockers and linens included. Towel rental 300Ft. Laundry 2000Ft. Free Wi-Fi. Reception 24hr. Check-out 11am. Quiet after 10pm. Dorms from 4800Ft. Cash only. ❸

Yep! Hostel, VII, Wesselényi utca 13 (☎01 785 5115). Ⓜ2: Astoria. From the metro, take Rákóczi út east, turn left on Kazinczy utca, and then turn left at Wesselényi. Manages to fit a remarkable amount of stuff into a relatively small space; almost every inch is occupied by a couch, table, chair, or bed. A welcome shot of *pálinka* helps you overcome any reservations you may have about getting close to your dormmates. The tipi-looking beds in the dorms are a whimsical touch. Lockers, linens, and towels included. Laundry 1700Ft. Free Wi-Fi. Reception 24hr. Check-out noon. 8-bed dorms from 3000Ft; 4-bed dorms from 3500Ft; doubles from 8000Ft. Cash only. ❷

Adagio Hostel, VII, Erzsébet körút 25-27(☎01 951 4138). Ⓜ2: Blaha Lujza tér. From the metro, take Erzsébet körút north for 3 blocks; the hostel is on the right by the corner with Wesselényi. A bargain on one of Pest's busiest streets, with a common area furnished with matching furniture and plants. Ideal for people tired of the typical, hodgepodge hostel aesthetic. The dorms themselves come with the same bunks you've seen everywhere else as well as large windows so everyone on Erzsébet can watch you dress in the morning. Free Wi-Fi. Laundry 2000Ft. Reception 24hr. Check-out 10am. 10-bed dorms from 3000Ft; 4-bed dorms from 3800Ft; doubles from 9000Ft. Cash only. ❷

Peppermint Hostel, Dohány utca 47 (☎01 851 5510). Ⓜ2: Blaha Lujza tér. From the metro, take Erzsébet körút north and then make a sharp left at Dohány; the hostel is on your left. Typical dorms will suit most while well-furnished, spacious doubles appeal to travelers looking to treat themselves while on a budget. Lockers and linens included. Free Wi-Fi. 2 night min. stay. Reception 24hr. Check-out noon. Dorms from 3500Ft; doubles 6000Ft per person. Cash only. ❷

Big Fish Hostel, VII Kertész utca 20 (☎01 786 2131; www.bigfishbudapest.hu). Ⓜ2: Blaha Lujza tér. From the metro, take Erzsébet körút north and then veer left at the 1st intersection; the hostel is near the corner of Kertész and Wesselényi. Welcomes weary travelers with a shot of *pálinka* and a larger tub than any human being could possibly need. The bunked dorms and atmosphere are nothing to write home about, though the location close to many of the area's clubs and bars should provide ample material. Locker deposit 500Ft. Linens included. Laundry 1500Ft. Free Wi-Fi. Reception 24hr. Check-out 11am. Dorms from 4200Ft; doubles from 5600Ft per person. Cash only. ❸

TERÉZVÁROS

Some of the best hostels in Budapest can be found near Oktogon. These hostels tend to be well-furnished and their staff friendly and eager to help. For travelers who prefer to be left to their own devices, there are several more basic options that lack the character of places like Home-Made and Carpe Noctem, but which are still relatively close to the area's restaurants and nightlife.

▨ **Home-Made Hostel,** VI, Teréz körút 22 (☎01 302 2103; www.homemadehostel.com). Ⓜ1: Oktogon. From the metro, take Teréz körút east from Oktogon; the hostel is on your left. An intimate hostel where the staff makes you feel right at home. Bond with your roommates over a homemade Hungarian dinner twice weekly. The bunkless dorms, decorated with antique TVs, radios, and rugs, make you feel like you're stepping into a

1950s Hungarian apartment. Locker deposit 1000Ft. Towels and linens included. Laundry 1000Ft. Free internet and Wi-Fi. Scooter rental available. Reception 24hr. Dorms from 3800Ft; doubles 12,000-15,000Ft. Cash only. ❷

Carpe Noctem, VI, Szobi utca 5 (☎20 365 8749; www.carpenoctemhostel.com). Ⓜ3: Nygati pályaudvar. From the metro, take Teréz körút east from the train station and turn left onto Szobi. Budapest's most reputable party hostel with plenty of social space. After checking in, you'll be treated to a 30min. crash course on what to do and where to drink in Budapest. Groups go out nightly and return in early morning. The dorms themselves are standard bunk affairs and furnishings mostly consist of bean bags, which allow for portable chilling. Best for those looking to meet people and have a great time they'll never remember. Towels, linens, and lockers included. Laundry 1500Ft. Free internet and Wi-Fi. Reception 24hr. Dorms 4200Ft. No groups larger than 4. Cash only. ❸

Art Guest House, VI, Podmaniczky utca 19 (☎302 3739). Ⓜ3: Nyugati. From the metro, take Teréz körút east and turn right on Podmaniczky. Great for people who want a break from the bustling party atmosphere of some larger places without sacrificing the convenient location. The hostel itself may be small, but the rooms are comfortable and come with large baths. The kitchen is also surprisingly large and well stocked for such a small place. Lockers and linens included. Wi-Fi intermittent, but high-speed internet always available on the free terminal. Reception 24hr. Check-in 1pm. Check-out 10am. Dorms 4400-5000Ft; doubles 12,200-12,800Ft. Cash only. ❸

Unity Hostel, VI Kiraly utca 60 (☎01 413 7377; www.unityhostel.com). Ⓜ1: Oktogon. From the metro, take Teréz körút west from Oktogon and turn right on Kiraly. A quiet, low-key hostel that offers relief from the area's more social options, with a strict quiet hours policy. For people who want to be close to the action but want to leave the action outside at the end of the night. Musicians from the renowned music academy across the street serenade guests on the lovely terrace of the private double. Continental breakfast included. Free goulash periodically. Linens included. Laundry 2500Ft. Free internet and Wi-Fi. Reception 24hr. Check-out 10am. Quiet after 10pm. Dorms 3800Ft; doubles 6000Ft per person. Cash only. ❷

Broadway Hostel, VI, Ó utca 24-26 (☎01 688 1662; www.broadwayhostel.hu). Ⓜ1: Opera. From the metro, take Hajós ut past the opera house and turn right onto Ó utca; the restaurant is on the left. Billed as an alternative to traditional backpacking hostels. Cell-like double bunk situations and curtain partitions limit privacy and leg room, while a closet-sized double hardly feels like an improvement over the dorms. An inner courtyard with hammocks provides a laid-back escape from the interior. Linens included. 1500Ft deposit for key and locker. Free Wi-Fi. Internet 275Ft per 30min. Reception 24hr. Check-in 2pm. Check-out 10:30am. Dorms 3900Ft; doubles 11,100Ft. Cash only. ❷

Caterina Hostel, VI, Teréz körút 30 (☎01 269 5990; www.caterinahostel.hu). Ⓜ1: Oktogon. From the metro, take Teréz körút east from Oktogon; the hostel is on your left. Plain-Jane hostel centrally located within Terézvaros and devoid of decoration, with (most of) the amenities you've come to expect, except for Wi-Fi. Ideal for those who have no interest in socializing or in being exceptionally comfortable. Breakfast included. Linens included. Laundry 1500Ft. Free internet. Reception 24hr. Check-out 10am. Dorms 2700Ft; triples 3800Ft per person. Cash only. ❶

JÓZSEFVÁROS AND FERENCVÁROS

The districts to the south of Pest are clustered near the Great Market Hall. With a few exceptions, they tend to be smaller, more intimate places. Those looking for hardcore party hostels are advised to consider a place closer to downtown.

Budapest Bubble, VIII, Bródy Sándor utca 2 (☎266 9532; budapestbubble@gmail.com). Ⓜ3: Kálvin tér. From the metro, take Múzeum körút north and turn right on Bródy Sándor. An intimate, inviting hostel near the National Museum with young, local hosts

BUDAPEST

who are quick to provide information on the city. Multiple common areas, decorated with Fritz Lang posters and the occasional hookah, make you feel like you're in a sophisticated film studies major's dorm. Most evenings, the staff leads a group out to some of the area's best undiscovered bars and clubs. Free internet and Wi-Fi. Linens included. Reception 24hr. Dorms 2800-3700Ft; doubles 10,000-12,000Ft. Cash only. ❷

Lavender Circus, VIII, Múzeum körút 37 (☎618 4536; www.lavendercircus.com). Ⓜ3: Kálvin tér. From the metro, take Múzeum körút north. More a budget guest house than a hostel, with a retro bric-a-brac decor for those who tire of more pedestrian hostel aesthetics. In addition to a large bed, couch, and recliner, every room comes equipped with an antique phone, radio, or typewriter, some more functional than others. Paintings, sculptures, and collages, all created by the owner, line the walls, shelves, and stairs leading up to the guest house. Free internet and Wi-Fi. Reception 24hr. Doubles 5600-6200Ft. ❹

Goat Hostel, IX, Vámház körút 15 (☎01 210 3512). Ⓜ3: Kálvin tér. From the metro, take Vámház toward the river. Comfortable, pastel-colored rooms and a great staff set this otherwise simple hostel apart. That, and the psychedelic goat pictures all over the common room. Dorms come in several flavors, including bunked for those who don't care, and huge-windowed for those who enjoy sunbathing indoors. A great option for people who want to relax rather than party. Breakfast included. Lockers and linens included. Laundry service 850Ft. Free internet and Wi-Fi. Reception 24hr. Check-out 11am. Dorms 3600-4200Ft. Cash only. ❸

Casa de la Musica, VIII, Vas utca 16 (☎938 8888; www.casadelamusica.hu). Ⓜ2: Astoria. From the metro, take Rákóczi út east and turn right on Vas. New place attempting to bring some Latin American spice to the Hungarian hostel scene. During the summer months, the multi-functional terrace serves breakfast in the morning and drinks in the evening, when it's not busy as a swimming pool. The rooms have basic bunks with bathrooms (or "water blocks" as the owner calls them). Free Wi-Fi. Key and locker deposit 1400Ft. Reception 24hr. Check-in 1pm. Check-out 11am. Dorms 2800Ft; doubles from 10,000Ft. Cash only. ❶

GELLÉRT HEGY

Affordable accommodations are sparse on the Buda side of the river. The area around Castle Hill is home to expensive guest houses and designer hotels, which will be of little interest to most student travelers. Your best bet, if you absolutely have to stay in Buda, is in the area around Gellért Hill, which offers university dorms and a few smaller, comfortable options.

▧ **Backpack Guesthouse**, XI, Takács Menyhért utca 33 (☎01 385 8946; www.backpackersbudapest.hu), 12min. from central Pest. From Ferenciek tere, take bus #7 or 7a toward Buda. Get off at Tétényi utca, then backtrack and turn left to go under the bridge. Take another left on Hamzsabégi út and continue to the 3rd right. The 49E night bus runs here after trams stop. A relaxed, earthy hideaway with an attentive staff and fantastic Mongolian garden. The mix of Hindu and Bob Marley murals on the walls tell you everything you need to know about the social scene. Rarely has a place this far away been so worth the trip. Laundry 1800Ft. Free internet and Wi-Fi. Reception 24hr. Yurts in garden 3000Ft; 7- to 12-bed dorms 3800Ft; 4- to 6-bed dorms 4500Ft; doubles 11,000Ft. AmEx/MC/V. ❷

Buda Base, Döbrentei utca 16 (☎20 543 7481; www.budabase.com). Döbrentei tér tram stop, trams 18,19. From the tram stop, head south toward the square. A small, friendly hostel at the base of Gellért Hill. Red partitions and comfortable chairs add some color to the otherwise standard dorms. The common room and kitchen provide a cozy place to watch TV or chat late into the night. Those tired of cramped shower stalls will appreciate the spacious baths. Lockers and linens included. Free internet and Wi-Fi. Reception 24hr. Dorms 2750-3300Ft; double 8200-10,950Ft. Cash only. ❷

Martos Hostel, XI, Stoczek utca 5-7 (☎01 209 4883; hotel.martos.bme.hu). Petőfi híd, budai hídfő, trams 4, 6. From the tram stop, walk north along the river and turn left on Bertalan Lajos utca, then left on Stoczek utca. College dorms of various sizes, ideal for students and people who wish they still were. Every suite comes with a sink and shower, though you'll have to walk down the hall to find the toilets. Decor is usually limited to whatever the previous semester's occupants left behind. Some have balconies with views of the other institutional-looking dorms. Linens included. Free Wi-Fi. Wheelchair-accessible. Reception 24hr. Check-in flexible. Check-out 10am. Open July-Aug. Rooms 3800-5600Ft. Cash only. ❸

◻ FOOD

Hungarian food is hearty and generally spicier than most food in continental Europe, owing largely to an unnatural enthusiasm for **paprika,** which is considered an indispensable ingredient in most soups and entrees. Other essential ingredients include onions and lard. This type of cooking is not for the weak of stomach (or heart). **Goulash** is common, and typically comes in a more soup-like form than its Czech counterpart. **Főzelék,** a thick and delicious stew consisting of paprika, potatoes, tomatoes, and whatever else is lying around, is a staple in many households and restaurants. Also typical of Hungarian cuisine are various cold fruit soups, often made from cherries or strawberries.

Restaurants in **Buda** and the area around **Parliament** and **Saint Stephen's Basilica** cater mainly to wealthy tourists. The cafes on **Castle Hill** and almost any place facing the Danube are especially overpriced. If you need to invent a reason to go to **Óbuda,** pick a better one than the restaurants, which are uniformly expensive and stuffy. **Terézváros** and **Erzsébetváros** offer the best variety and value for money. Fancier restaurants and cafes may be found around **Liszt Ferenc tér** and along **Andrássy út. Ráday utca,** way down in Ferencváros, also has plenty of decent options if you don't mind spending a while scoping out menus. Ethnic restaurants populate the upper floor of **Mammut Plaza,** just outside the Moszkva tér metro in Buda and **West End Plaza,** near the Nyugati metro in Pest. For a light meal, stick to cafes, which serve soups and sandwiches at reasonable prices.

Servers at Hungarian restaurants are usually friendly and happy to offer suggestions. Often times they will be standing outside the front door to greet you as you come in, but if you don't see anyone feel free to seat yourself. Good service is usually prompt and you won't wait long for your food, even on busy nights. It's common for people to have coffee or espresso after dinner. Your check will not be brought until you ask for it. At many fancier restaurants the service charge is often irritatingly included in the bill, whether you thought the service was worth it or not; if there are any, these charges are usually indicated at the bottom of the menu and run anywhere from 10 to 18%. If one is not included, a 10% tip is customary. Give the money directly to the server; do not leave it on the table. If you need it, the server will usually provide change on the spot.

Cafeterias with *"Önkiszolgáló Étterem"* signs serve cheap food (entrees 300-500Ft). Many restaurants will claim to have gypsy folk music—rarely is it authentic. In these situations, the musicians will approach you and ask if they may play a song. What they won't tell you is that you're expected to pay for it. If you don't want to pay, kindly reject the offer; otherwise, expect to be committed to a 1000Ft tip.

Combination gyro and pizza stands are extremely common around the Grand Boulevard and offer the best value after a long night at the bars. Budapest has few supermarkets, but corner markets, many open 24hr.—the signs will usually say "non stop"—stock the basics. The king of them all, ▉**Grand Market Hall**, IX, Fövam tér 1/3, next to Szabadság híd (⑩3: Kálvin tér), has acres of stalls, where you can find produce, baked goods, and traditional folk costumes all in one place.

THE BELVÁROS

Váci utca has its share of expensive restaurants, but be careful—only a few of them are actually worth the price tag. More affordable options with less exhausting atmospheres are often just a few side streets over.

Kárpátia, V, Ferenciek tere 7-8 (☎317 3596; www.karpatia.hu). ⑩3: Ferenciek tere. One of Budapest's oldest restaurants. Immaculate Baroque interior, with red, gold, and green patterns covering the vaulted ceiling. Serves a mix of traditional and contemporary Hungarian cuisine. Expect dishes like chicken breast stuffed with goose liver (4400Ft) and the epic venison filet with balsamic strawberries and maize polenta with black truffles (6900Ft). With appetizers the price of entrees at other places, it's probably out of the budget range for most students, but it will do for a last-night-in-town splurge. Appetizers 1900-2900Ft. Entrees 3400-6900Ft. Wheelchair-accessible. Reservations recommended. Open daily 11am-11pm. MC/V. ❺

Bangkok Thai Restaurant, V, Só utca 3 (☎965 5510; www.thairestaurant.hu). ⑩3: Kálvin tér. From the metro, take Vámház toward the river, turn right on Veres Pálné, and then left on Só. A celebrated Thai restaurant that houses one of Budapest's largest Buddha shrines in the basement. Generous helpings of traditional Thai, including a wide selection of squid (2690Ft). Vegetarians who've somehow survived in Budapest will appreciate the break from pickles and potatoes. Soups 950-2490Ft. Entrees 1790-2690Ft. Lunch menus 1300-1600Ft. Open daily noon-11pm. MC/V. ❸

Fatál, V, Váci utca 67 (☎266 2607). ⑩3: Kálvin tér. From the metro, take Vámház toward the river and then turn right on Váci. Enormous portions of delicious Hungarian cuisine served in pots and pans in a cool, basement setting. Unfortunately, every other tourist on Váci will be attracted to the same stained-glass decorations and stop to investigate. The roasted beef in venison sauce is a crowd-pleaser (2990Ft). Salads 760-980Ft. Entrees 2100-2790Ft. Hungarian specialties 2960-4590Ft. Wheelchair-accessible. Open daily noon-midnight. MC/V. ❹

Babel, V, Váci utca 83 (☎388 2143; www.babeldelicate.hu). ⑩3: Kálvin tere. From the metro, take Vámház toward the river and turn right on Váci. Bills itself as a "delicate" restaurant, serving small portions of expensive, exotic fare in a stylish interior. Specialties include calf brain-and-mushroom wontons (1590Ft) and pigeon breast in duck foie gras sauce (3990Ft). The 5-course Hungarian menu (10,500Ft) lets you sample many tiny, artfully prepared dishes you will never see again. Unfortunately, its location in the middle of the tourist zone means it'll never be as cool or classy as it wants to be. Wheelchair-accessible. Open M-Sa noon-midnight. Reservations recommended. AmEx/MC/V. ❺

Bar-Bár , V, Haris Köz 1 (☎318 3334). ⑩3: Ferenciek tér. From the metro, take Petőfi Sándor west and then turn left on Haris Köz. Inexpensive and tasty sandwiches draw the cheap and the hungry to a tiny side street near Váci. Enjoy creative, if shamelessly unhealthy options like the "seasoned ranch ranger" (720Ft) or the fried fish and fried cheese "favorite of the Vikings" (720Ft). Sandwiches 590-850Ft. Salads 780Ft. Entrees 980-1850Ft. Open M-F 9am-6pm, Sa 9am-2pm. Cash only. ❶

CAFES

▉ **1000 Tea,** V, Váci utca 65 (☎337 8217; www.1000tea.hu). ⑩3: Kálvin tér. From the metro, take Vámház toward the river and turn right on Váci. Japanese-style teahouse located in a tranquil courtyard just off Váci. One thousand teas may be stretching it, though the menu is certainly impressive, containing every tea you could imagine. Wear your cleanest pair of socks so you can enjoy your tea in the no shoes area. The indulgent may spring for tea served in traditional kung fu style (1200Ft), while bold 2-somes should consider one of the tea samplers (1400Ft). Teas 400-950Ft. Wheelchair-accessible. Open M-Sa noon-11pm, Su 1-11pm. Cash only. ❶

Cafe Alibi, V, Egyetem tér 4 (☎317 4209; cafealibi.hu). ⓜ3: Kálvin tér. From the metro, take Kecskeméti utca west and turn left on Egyetem tér. Scales and vintage-looking French advertisements line the walls of this small, quaint coffee shop. Sidle up to the remarkably long black leather bench and take a look at some of the more surprising menu options, including a gorgonzola apple salad (1590Ft) or the Popeye sandwich (spinach, tuna, and tomato; 1390Ft). Finish your visit with a tasty real-fruit smoothie (490Ft). Coffee 550Ft. Espresso drinks from 520Ft. Tea 490Ft. Salads 1090-1690Ft. Sandwiches 1090-1250Ft. Open M-F 8am-2am, Sa 9am-9pm, Su 9am-1am. AmEx/MC/V. ❶

Gerbeaud, V, Vörösmarty tér 7 (☎429 9000; www.gerbeaud.hu). ⓜ1: Vörösmarty tér. Hungary's most famous cafe and confectionary has been serving delicious layer cakes (750-770Ft) and ice cream sundaes (1700-1800Ft) for 150 years. The interior has been restored to its turn-of-the-century splendor, complete with chandeliers and draperies. While surrounded by flocks of sightseers shelling out twice what you would at another confectionary, you might find yourself wondering: at what price is tradition? Coffee 700Ft. Sandwiches 1650-3050Ft. Open daily 9am-9pm. AmEx/MC/V. ❸

Centrál Kávéház, V, Károlyi Mihály utca 9 (☎266 2110; www.centralkavehaz.hu). ⓜ3: Ferenciek tere. From the metro, take Károlyi Mihály east. The area's other high-end cafe has leather benches and marble tables almost as opulent as Gerbeaud's but with more reasonable prices and fewer tourists. Some of their more substantial dishes include the Danube salad (chicken, ripe cow cheese, vegetables, and seasoned mayonnaise; 2600Ft) and tagliatelle with black shellfish (2400Ft). Salads, sandwiches, and pasta 1800-2600Ft. Entrees 2300-3900Ft. Wine 500-1100Ft. Open daily 7am-midnight. AmEx/MC/V. ❹

LIPÓTVÁROS

The area near the river offers some of the most diverse dining options in the city. Lipótváros caters to a mix of local professionals and tourists; you can eat as poorly or as well as you'd like without having to walk too far out of your way.

▧ **Café Kör**, V, Sas utca 17 (☎311 0053; www.cafekor.com). ⓜ1: Bajcsy-Zsilinszky út. From the metro, take József Attila west and turn right on Sas. Cool, classy

ON THE FINER POINTS OF GOULASH

For the uninitiated, goulash holds something of the mystique of cafeteria mystery meat. Its exact contents are at first obscured by the dark red paprika used liberally in its preparation. Your first few bites are always hesitant, as if you expect to find bits of old shoe leather rather than beef floating amongst the onions, potatoes, and who knows what else.

Once these initial fears have been abated, you can begin to explore goulash's rich varieties. Like the related pörkölt and paprikas, goulash (in Hungarian, gulyás, pronounced goo-yash) was originally made by cattlemen who needed something simple, hearty, and tasty to nosh on out in the country. The basic ingredients are chunks of meat (usually beef), paprika, and water. Vegetables (most often potato, tomato, carrot, and peppers) are common, but unnecessary.

In Hungary, the dish is most often served as a watery soup, with chunks of beef and potato all floating around together. Occasionally, though, you'll find it served thick, almost like a sauce, over a bed of pasta. In some parts of the Czech Republic, the dish has a more stew-like consistency, with beer added to round out the flavor and dark bread with which to clean the plate. In Germany, expect to find lots of potatoes and a tomato-based broth.

dining caters mainly to professionals and tourists, though there are plenty of options that frugal backpackers will appreciate. Surrounded by nicely dressed servers and a simple, elegant interior, you'll trick yourself into thinking you're spending more than you actually are. Dishes like honeydew melon wrapped in prosciutto (1690Ft) set this place apart from the area's other boutique cafes. Salads 930-1890Ft. Entrees 1560-4290Ft. Wheelchair-accessible. Open daily 10am-10pm. Cash only. ❹

Trófea Grill Étterem, XIII, Visegrádi utca 50A (☎270 0366; www.trofeagrill.com). Ⓜ3: Nyugati. From the metro, take Szent István körút toward the river and then turn right on Visegrádi. Upscale all-you-can-eat, traditional Hungarian buffet. The large, wooden dining area is lined with the skulls of the species you'll be enjoying. Some of the more exciting specialties from the 100-dish menu include lamb hoof with Italian pasta, duck steak in cognac with grilled mushroom pie, and quail egg salad. All-you-can-drink beer, wine, champagne, and fountain drinks included in price, but we had you at "all-you-can-eat traditional Hungarian buffet," didn't we? Buffet 3400Ft M-F lunch; 3800Ft M-Th dinner; 4600Ft F dinner and all day Sa-Su. Free Wi-Fi. Wheelchair-accessible. Open M-F noon-midnight, Sa 11:30am-midnight, Su 11:30am-8:30pm. Reservations recommended. MC/V. ❺

Kashmir, V, Arany János utca 13 (☎354 1806; www.kashmiretterem.hu). Ⓜ3: Arany János utca. Follow the strong smell of curry. Choose chicken, beef, or pork, and then one of seven sauces or seasonings, including standbys like tikka masala and vindaloo. Vegetarians also have something to look forward to in the specialty paneer badam pasandaa (2190Ft). The interior is classy and simple, with comfy white benches strewn with pillows. Appetizers 990-1390Ft. Curry dishes 2190-2790Ft. Vegetarian entrees 1390-2190Ft. Open M-Sa noon-3pm, 5-11pm. Reservations recommended. MC/V. ❸

Csarnok Vendéglő, V, Hold utca 11 (☎269 4906). Ⓜ3: Arany János. From the metro, take Bank utca west and then turn right onto Hold utca. A typical Hungarian restaurant with wooden furniture, matching checkered tablecloths, and curtains—no pretensions whatsoever. The amiable staff caters to an older local crowd with delicious and affordable Hungarian fare. The entrees consist mostly of steaks and roasts (gypsy roast; 1250Ft). Start your meal off with a meat soup and quail egg (470Ft). Soups 450-980Ft. Salads 1200-1400Ft. Entrees 1150-2850Ft. Wheelchair-accessible. Open daily 11am-11pm. Cash only. ❷

Trattoria Pomo D'Oro, V, Arany János utca 9 (☎302 6473; www.pomodorobudapest. cz). Ⓜ3: Arany János. From the metro, walk west toward the river; the restaurant is on the right. Classy Italian served in a bustling but not abrasive atmosphere. Replicas of classical paintings and statuettes of religious figures fill every nook and cranny of the brick interior. Unique dishes like the "priest strangler" (homemade noodles in tomato ragout flambéed with parmesan; 2290Ft) make other area Italian places look like they aren't even trying. The penne with vodka sauce and bacon (1990Ft) is also a favorite. Appetizers 1490-2350Ft. Pasta 1990-3290Ft. Entrees 1750-5590Ft. Open M-F 11am-midnight, Sa-Su noon-midnight. AmEx/D/MC/V. ❹

Momotaro, V, Széchenyi utca 16 (☎269 3802). Ⓜ3: Arany János. From the metro, take Bank utca west; the restaurant is on the right. Finally, someone in Central Europe gets Chinese food right. Enjoy a mix of traditional Chinese and Japanese dishes in a simple wooden interior with a bar made to look like a pagoda. Ideal for a quick lunch while sightseeing near Parliament or St. Stephen's. The beef with oyster sauce (1600Ft) is a specialty, though they also serve the old standby—sweet and sour chicken (1500Ft)—for people who crave food court Chinese more than the real thing. Ramen 1500-3000Ft. Entrees 1500-3000Ft. Open daily 11am-10pm. Cash only. ❸

Lui & Lei Ristorante, V, Széchenyi utca 14 (☎312 1405; www.luiandlei.com). Ⓜ3: Arany János. From the metro, take Bank utca west; the restaurant is on the right. Upscale Italian wine bar and restaurant, catering mostly to tourists and upper crust locals. If you're lucky, you'll be able to nab the outdoor white leather bench when the weather's nice. If not, no worries: there are plenty more leather benches downstairs. Specialties include roast duck breast (2900Ft) and monkfish in bisque sauce (4700Ft). Appetizers 1700-3400. Pasta 1750-3500. Entrees 2600-5900. Open daily 11am-midnight. Reservations recommended. MC/V. ❹

Govinda Vegetarian Restaurant, V, Vigyázó Ferenc utca 4 (☎269 1625). Ⓜ3: Arany János. From the metro, take Arany János toward the river, turn left on Nádor, and make a right on Vigyázó Ferenc. Budapest's young, alternative, and lard-weary enjoy buffet-style Indian food. You can either buy an entire plate or pick and choose individual items. The stone-walled basement makes the place seem like a great place to plot a revolution. Samosas 230Ft. Pakoras 140Ft. Rice from 180Ft. Plates 1550-1850Ft. Student menu 760Ft. Open M-Sa noon-9pm. Cash only. ❷

Iguana Bar & Grill, V, Zoltán utca 16 (☎331 4352; www.iguana.hu). Ⓜ2: Kossuth Lajos tér. From the metro, take Kossuth Lajos tér east, turn right on Nádor, and then left on Zoltán. Those jonesing for a Mexican dinner they won't regret the next day can finally get their fix. During the summer, bask like a lizard in the outdoor seating with all of your Hungarian friends. Appetizers 490-2250Ft. Burritos 1990-2190Ft. Entrees 1790-2390Ft. Wheelchair-accessible. Open daily 11:30am-midnight. AmEx/MC/V. ❸

Firkász, XIII, Tátra utca 18 (☎450 1118). Ⓜ3: Nyugati. From the metro, take Szent István toward the river and then turn right on Tátra. The name refers to journalists who scribble in their notebooks, a motif echoed by the newspaper-covered walls and typewriters throughout the interior. Unfortunately, the food is nothing to stop the presses about. Expect run-of-the-mill Hungarian dishes like Kiev-style chicken (2190Ft) and veal paprika (2490Ft). While tourists take over in the evenings and on weekends, locals still show up for the lunch buffet. Don't bother with a tip: the 15% service charge is included in the bill. Salads 1690-1990Ft. Vegetarian dishes 990-1490Ft. Entrees 2190-4690Ft. Open M-Th and Su noon-midnight, F-Sa noon-2am. Cash only. ❹

CAFES

Cafe Kafka, V, Sas utca 9 (☎266 1242; www.kafkakavezo.hu). Ⓜ1: Bajcsy-Zsilinszky út. From the metro, take József Attila west and then turn right on Sas. Everything you could possibly want in a cafe: outdoor seating, Wi-Fi, reasonably priced sandwiches, and unnecessary literary references. 2 floors and sidewalk seating give the antisocial neurotic too much to choose from. Forget that coffee nonsense and drink wine like a real destitute Hungarian intellectual. The beef stew with gnocchi (1580Ft) is more substantial than standard cafe fare. Salads 1190-2090Ft. Sandwiches 890Ft. White wine from 550Ft. Red wine from 650Ft. Wheelchair-accessible. Open M-F 10am-11pm, Sa-Su 10:30am-11pm. MC/V. ❶

Európa Kávéház, V, Szent István körút 7-9 (☎312 2362; www.europakavehaz.hu). Ⓜ3: Nyugati. From the metro, take Szent István körút toward the river; the cafe is on your left. Large, bustling cafe with fake marble countertops and red imitation-leather benches. Not the best place to have a quiet conversation, though an extensive cake and dessert menu encourages patrons to hang around a little longer than they otherwise might. Free Wi-Fi. Espresso from 350Ft. Tea from 400Ft. Canapés 1100-1300Ft. Cake 490Ft. Wheelchair-accessible. Open daily 9am-11pm. Cash only. ❶

ERZSÉBETVÁROS

While most people think of Erzsébetváros as a place to drink rather than eat, the district contains a surprising variety of cuisines and price ranges. Vegetarians will especially appreciate the Indian and Mediterranean dishes here. **Klauzál Square** has a number of cafes and kosher delis nearby.

▧ **Hummus Bar,** VII, Kertész utca 39 (☎01 321 7477). Ⓜ1: Oktogon. From the metro, take Teréz körút south, turn right at Király, and then left at Kertész. One of Budapest's true gems—

a closet-sized place serving some of the city's best vegetarian and vegan food. Large plates of delicious and artfully presented hummus (800Ft) are delivered to you as you relax on the floor cushions upstairs. Another location at Alkotmány utca 20 just down the street from Parliament. *Phool* 900Ft. Pita 70-250Ft. Open daily noon-11pm. Cash only. ❶

Kőleves Restobar, VII, Kazinczy utca 35 (☎01 322 1011; www.koleves.com). Ⓜ2: Astoria. From the metro, take Károly körút north and then turn right on Dob utca; the restaurant is at the corner of Dob and Kazinczy. Haunt of expats, students, and artists, this colorful place turns into a lively hangout most evenings. The decor is a mix of vibrant local art, while the lighting fixtures appear as a bouquet of wineglasses. The seasonal menu contains many creative dishes, though the main draw is the soup selection, which includes gazpacho (650Ft) and the old standby goulash (650Ft). Soups 550-650Ft. Salads 560-1680Ft. Entrees 1950-2850Ft. Vegetarian options 1350-2250Ft. Open daily noon-1am. AmEx/MC/V. ❸

Shalimar, VII, Dob utca 50 (☎01 352 0297; www.shalimar.hu). Ⓜ1: Oktogon. From the metro, take Teréz körút south for 3 blocks and turn right at Dob utca. Budapest's best Indian food served in a classy, candlelit atmosphere. Large mirrors and ample shrines lining the walls mean that Shiva (destroyer!) will always be watching as you try to spy on other tables. Plenty of delicious vegetarian dishes like spicy mashed eggplant *baigan bhurta* (1420Ft) will even tempt carnivores. Reasonably prices lunch menus bring in many discerning professionals during the day. Lunch menus 1100-1300Ft. Vegetarian options 1050-1750Ft. Vindaloo 2140-2450Ft. Entrees 2140-4150Ft. Open daily noon-4pm and 6pm-midnight. Reservations recommended. MC/V. ❸

Cream Restaurant and Music Pub, VII, Dohány utca 28 (☎01 413 6997). Ⓜ2: Astoria. From the metro, take Rákóczi út east and turn left on Kazinczy; the cafe is at the corner of Kazinczy and Dohány. 2-level restaurant that accomplishes the rare feat of appearing fancy without also appearing obnoxious. The cream-colored walls create a relaxing atmosphere in which you can chill out while dining on gizzard stew with rice (1550Ft) or lazily sampling one of the menu's 8 types of pickles (350-420Ft). In the evening, the brick cellar pub next door brings a variety of live acts. Salads 1340-1550Ft. Entrees 1900-3400Ft. Open daily 11am-midnight. Reservations recommended. Cash only. ❸

CAFES

▦ **Bar Ladino,** VII, Dob utca 53 (☎30 874 3733; www.ladino.hu). Ⓜ1: Oktogon. From the metro, take Teréz körút east for 3 blocks and turn right on Dob utca. Named for the near-extinct language of exiled Spanish Jews, Bar Ladino provides good food and great service in a cool atmosphere. During the day, the cafe is home to students and young people as well as a few dedicated groups of elderly card players. The western style breakfast menu, served until 5pm, clearly has thrifty and hungover backpackers and expats in mind. At night, the cafe transforms into a popular but not overcrowded bar for cool people who want to hang out in a building that hasn't yet been condemned. Breakfast served M-F 9am-5pm, 490-790Ft. Salads 990-1690Ft. Entrees 990-2490Ft. Beer from 290Ft. Wine from 270Ft. Shots 390-700Ft. Open M-W and Su 9am-1:30am, Th 9am-2:30am, F-Sa 9am-3:30am. Cash only. ❷

Nelson Cafe, VII, Dohány utca 12 (☎01 411 1804; www.nelsoncafe.hu). Ⓜ2: Astoria. From the metro, take Károly körút north and turn right at the synagogue; the cafe is on the left just past the synagogue. A relaxing neighborhood cafe with big chairs and vintage posters on the walls. Despite its laid-back appearance, details like a marble-topped bar and unusually elaborate tea presentation (complete with lemon squeezers) show this place to be slightly fancier than you'd expect. The buffalo chicken sandwich (1290Ft) provides a great midday recharge. Coffee 330Ft. Tea 490Ft. Salads 480-540Ft. Sandwiches 990-1450Ft. Entrees 890-1890Ft. Wheelchair-accessible. Open M-F 7am-midnight, Sa 10am-midnight, Su 10am-10pm. MC/V. ❶

Noir et l'or, VII, Király utca 17 (☎01 413 0236; www.noiretlor.hu). Ⓜ1, 2, or 3: Deák Ferenc tér. From the metro, take Király north; the restaurant is near the intersection of Király and Káldy Gyula. Sexy, stylish cafe and restaurant where glowing orange lights add depth to the otherwise flat black and white interior. The menu is primarily colonial French cuisine with occasional Mediterranean or Hungarian influences. The chicken breast marinated in feta cheese (2570Ft) might be worth ironing that button-down shirt in the bottom of your backpack. Appetizers 2000-3050Ft. Soups 950-1100Ft. Salads 600-950Ft. Entrees 2100-4650Ft. Wheelchair-accessible. Open daily 11am-midnight. Reservations recommended. AmEx/MC/V. ❶

TERÉZVÁROS

Oktogon has several American fast-food chains and numerous gelato stands (expect a scoop to cost around 150Ft). Cafes, bars, and restaurants surround **Liszt Ferenc tér** and **Jókai tér.** The classier, more expensive places are on the Liszt Ferenc side. **Andrássy** is lined with restaurants and cafes of all price ranges and quality levels, though many of the fancier places are clustered near the Opera House. Many of the cafes pull double-duty as bars or lounges come nightfall.

▨ **Marquis de Salade,** VI, Hajós utca 43 (☎01 302-4086; www.marquisdesalade. hu). Ⓜ3: Arany János út. From the metro, take Bajcsy-Zsilinszky út north and then make a sharp right onto Hajós. Azerbaijani restaurant with the occasional Russian dish (or pun) thrown in for good measure. Relax on soft benches surrounded by pillows, bottles, and draperies as you browse an impressive salad selection. People who hated Shari Lewis as a kid might appreciate the menu's many lamb dishes, including grape leaves stuffed with minced lamb (2700Ft) and grilled lamb liver and heart (3400Ft). You can't go wrong with the original Marquis de Salade (chicken breast with grapefruit, shrimp, and fresh vegetables in a grapefruit dressing; 2500Ft). Salads 1300-2500Ft. Vegetarian options 2600-2800Ft. Entrees 2500-3900Ft. Not wheelchair-accessible. Open daily noon-1am. Cash only. ❺

▨ **Giero,** Paulay Ede utca 56. Ⓜ1: Oktogon. From the metro, take Andrássy út west, turn left on Ferenc ter, and then right onto Paulay Ede; the restaurant will be on your right. With no website, telephone number, or menu, this family-run basement-cellar restaurant is about as hole-in-the-wall as it gets. When you come down, you will be seated on a wooden bench and a kindly woman will ask if you'd like a glass of red wine (600Ft) with your dinner. After a while, a plate of delicious home-cooked food will appear in front of you. With the family's children around and occasionally playing gypsy folk music, you'll feel like you've been invited into someone's home. As a guest, you don't have a lot of say over what dinner is, though you rest assured: it will probably be delicious. Dinner 1800Ft. Live music occasionally. Not wheelchair accessible. Open daily noon-late. Cash only. ❷

Parázs Presszó, VI, Szobi utca 4 (☎01 950 3770; www.parazspresszo.com). Ⓜ3: Nyugati pályaudvar. From the metro, take Teréz körút and then turn left on Szobi. An unlikely Hungarian-Thai fusion prepared by a husband and wife team. Comfy floor cushions, couches, and chairs ensure that everyone's seating preferences are accommodated. Especially popular with students and backpackers from nearby hostels. The fried camembert with blueberry jam and jasmine rice (1580Ft) is a specialty. Appetizers 680-1350Ft. Soups 750-1100Ft. Entrees 1580-2350Ft. Vegetarian options 750-1750Ft. Not wheelchair-accessible. Open daily noon-midnight. Cash only. ❷

Menza, VI, Liszt Ferenc tér 2 (☎01 413 1482; www.menza.co.hu). Ⓜ2: Oktogon. From the metro, take Andrássy út west and then turn left onto Liszt Ferenc tér; the restaurant is at the corner with Paulay Ede utca. Reminiscent of Communist-era *menza* (canteens) this elegant eatery's decor combines modern chic with retro R&B jams and more wood paneling than you can shake a station wagon at. A favorite of ex-pats and tourists alike. Menu includes all manner of excellent Hungarian and international dishes, including the popular rolled veal with parma ham (1990Ft). Finish off with Hungarian cottage cheese dumplings with sour cream and strawberry sauce (890Ft). Salads 1390-1690Ft. Pasta 1290-1990Ft. Entrees 1890-3990Ft. Open daily 10am-1am. AmEx/MC/V. ❸

Artesano, Ó utca 24-26 (☎01 688 1696; www.artesano.hu). Ⓜ1: Opera. From the metro, Take Hajós utca past the opera house and then turn left onto Ó utca; the restaurant is on the right. Tucked away on unassuming Ó street, this stylish tapas bar is a favorite of classy locals and discerning expats. Spend the evening sampling a variety of creative original and Spanish-inspired dishes, such as king prawn wrapped in ham (1690Ft) or Spanish pancakes (480Ft). Tapas 400-1690Ft. Paella 1800Ft. Seafood 2100Ft. Wheelchair-accessible. Open M-Sa noon-midnight. Cash only. ❸

Zsákbamacska, Lovag utca 3(☎01 354 1810; zsakbamacska.hu). Ⓜ3: Arany János utca. From the metro, take Bajcsy-Zsilinszky út north, then make a sharp right onto Nagymező utca, and then turn left onto Lovag utca. Decent Hungarian food and friendly service in a brick cellar minus the stereotypical gypsy music soundtrack and walls covered in farming implements. What it lacks in authenticity it makes up for in drawings of cats. Try the crispy knuckle with Jóasszony ragout (2550Ft) or the heart-stopping fried wild hog larded with bacon (2950Ft). Appetizers 1350-2350Ft. Soups 750-1150Ft. Salads 550-950Ft. Entrees 1950-4550Ft. Vegetarian entrees 1550-2150Ft. Wheelchair-accessible. Open M-F 5pm-midnight, Sa-Su noon-midnight. MC/V. ❹

Arriba Taqueria, Teréz körút 25 (☎01 374 0057; www.arriba.hu). Ⓜ1: Oktogon. From the metro, take Teréz körút west; the restaurant will be on your right. A funky, colorful taqueria with a hipster-friendly soundtrack that serves surprisingly passable Mexican food to anyone and everyone. The furnishings are limited to a few plain tables, while the decor consists mostly of colorful murals, including one that features an angel lifting an enormous, radiant taco above his head with the words "Gracias a Dios por crear el taco!" A nice, cold Horchata (sweet rice milk with cinnamon; 450Ft) is great any time of day. Tacos 400-550Ft. Quesadillas 1050-1350Ft. Burritos 1120-1490Ft. Mexican beer 950Ft. Wheelchair-accessible. Free Wi-Fi. Open daily 11am-midnight. MC/V. ❷

Belcanto, Dalszínház utca 8 (☎01 269 2786; www.belcanto.hu). Ⓜ1: Opera. From the metro, take Andrássy toward downtown and then turn right at Dalszínház, which runs alongside the opera house. One of Budapest's fanciest restaurants, and probably out of the budget for most student backpackers. Timely travelers may be able to afford high-class Hungarian cuisine in the elegant and high-ceilinged interior if they show up between noon and 3pm, when all dishes are ▨**50% off.** Unfortunately, it may be hard to tell how much you're saving, since prices aren't listed on the menu. (They are available online.) Appetizers 3200-5200Ft. Pasta 3200-3500Ft. Entrees 4900-6200Ft. Salon orchestra Th-Sa 8-10pm. Not wheelchair-accessible. No dress code, but try to look sharp. Open M-Sa noon-3pm and 5pm-midnight. Reservations recommended. AmEx/MC/V. ❺

Abszint, Andrássy út 34 (☎01 332 4993; www.abszint.hu). Ⓜ1: Opera. From the metro, take Andrássy toward Oktogon; the restaurant will be on your left. Super classy restaurant and cafe serving a slightly older, more dignified clientele, who appreciate the vague but pervasive French theme and the small but diverse menu. Probably best reserved for romantic, pre-Opera dinners. Entrees include lamb with tatziki and hummus (2590Ft) and "vadas" beef with bread dumplings (2390Ft). Appetizers 990-1890Ft. Soups 790-1190Ft. Pasta and salads 1590-2190Ft. Entrees 2190-3490Ft. Wine from 500Ft. Wheelchair-accessible. Open daily 11am-11:30pm. AmEx/MC/V. ❹

CAFES

▨ **Ring Cafe and Bar,** Andrássy út 38 (☎01 331 5790; www.ringcafe.hu). Ⓜ2: Oktogon. From the metro, take Andrássy toward downtown; the cafe will be on your right. The best cafe for people-watching on historic and picturesque Andrássy and one of the best places in Budapest to find an affordable Western-style breakfast. The sleek and highly reflective interior provides a stylish escape during erratic summer showers. If you show up or stick around late enough, you can watch as the cafe transforms into an equally stylish street side bar. In the evenings, the delicious red-wine-paprika ragout of beef with mushroom gnocchi (1690Ft) is the best Hungarian dish you'll have that won't make you want to see your cardiologist afterward. Breakfast until noon 780-850Ft. Sandwiches 1090-1340Ft. Entrees 1190-1690Ft. Beer from 360Ft. Shots 650-1250Ft. Wheelchair-accessible. Open M-Th 8am-midnight, F 8am-1am, Sa 10am-1am, Su 10am-6pm. Cash only. ❷

🏨 **Kiadó Kocsma!,** VI, Jókai tér 3 (☎01 331 1955), in Pest, next to Cafe Alhambra. ⓜ1: Oktogon. From the metro, take Andrássy toward downtown and then turn right onto Jókai tér; the cafe will be on your left. From the outside it appears to be just a hipper-than-average bar, with a young alternative-looking crowd, Tibetan prayer flags, and nice terrace seating. And when you get a little hungry, take a look at the paper menu, and discover to your great delight that they also serve delicious light meals, including gnocchi with smoked salmon (1500Ft). Pasta 1350-1500Ft. Entrees 1650-2600Ft. Beer from 280Ft. Tea and coffee from 250Ft. Shots 360-630Ft. Mixed drinks 900-1800Ft. Open M-F 10am-1am, Sa-Su noon-1am. MC/V. ❸

Mai Manó Café, Nagymező utca 20 (☎01 269 5642). ⓜ2: Opera. From the metro, take Andrássy út toward Oktogon and then turn left onto Nagymező út. Small streetside cafe with a vague Middle Eastern aesthetic and plenty of throw pillows. Despite its laid-back appearance during the day, by evening it is a popular haunt of writers, artists, and performers from the nearby opera house. If you want to go Hungarian stargazing, find a place to sit before the performance ends, otherwise you may find yourself trying to steal a glimpse from across the street. Also serves a selection of specialty coffee drinks, including the appropriately pretentious "trendi coffee" (coffee with strawberry syrup and whipped cream; 600Ft). Coffee from 390Ft. Beer from 420Ft. Cocktails 690-1800Ft. Wheelchair-accessible. Open daily 10am-1am. Cash only. ❶

Eklektika Restolounge, Nagymező utca 30 (☎226 1226; eklektika.hu). ⓜ1: Oktogon. From the metro, take Andrássy toward downtown and then turn right onto Nagymező. Gay-friendly cafe that cultivates a stylish but welcoming atmosphere where Budapest's artists and intellectuals gather to lounge on comfy couches and discuss analytic philosophy. When you want to inject yourself into the discourse, try making an observation about the abstract art that lines the walls. A standard selection of mixed drinks (1400-1900Ft) makes those long summer afternoons slide into evening. Appetizers 990Ft. Soups 690-1190Ft. Salads 490-1200Ft. Pasta 1490Ft. Entrees 1290-2390Ft. Wheelchair-accessible. Open daily noon-midnight. Cash only. ❸

Művész Kávéház, Andrássy út 29 (☎343 3544; www.muveszkavehaz.hu). ⓜ2: Opera. With the opera house less than a gold pocket watch's throw away, it's no surprise this upscale cafe is a favorite of Budapest's upper crust and wealthy tourists who couldn't walk 150ft to find someplace better and cheaper. Nicely-dressed waiters, leather benches, chandeliers, and classical music encourage otherwise unacceptable behavior, like calling one another "dahling." Pre-opera entrees include Burgundy beef cheek (2690Ft) and Tuscan chicken (2290Ft). Sandwiches 990-1690Ft. Entrees 1690-2690Ft. Coffee 450Ft. Wine 790Ft. Wheelchair-accessible. Open daily 9am-11pm. MC/V. ❸

JÓZSEFVÁROS

🏨 **Sirius Klub,** VIII, Bródy Sándor utca 13 (☎266 1708; www.sirius-se.hu). ⓜ3: Kálvin tér. From the metro, take Múzeum körút north and turn right on Bródy Sándor; the teahouse is across the street from Vendéglő Háry. While "klub" may be a horrible misnomer, this super-cool but super-unpretentious teahouse serves great tea at reasonable prices. Relax in the massive shoeless area surrounded by floor cushions and Tibetan prayer flags—your tea will be served to you through a small window connected to the main seating area. 75

BUDAPEST

varieties of tea available, including a few you've probably never seen before, like banan-arama rooibos. Tea 570Ft. Cookies 250Ft. Open noon-10pm daily. Cash only. ❶

Bécsiszelet, VIII, Üllői út 16/a (☎267 4937). Ⓜ3: Kálvin tér. From the metro, take Üllői east. People don't come for the decor, but for the generous portions of typical Hungarian fare, which come in "regular" and "gigantic." The turkey stuffed with chicken liver (1190Ft) is a specialty. The gigantic wiener schnitzel (2290Ft) is perhaps best reserved for the truly ambitious. Soups 290-470Ft. Entrees 990-1250Ft. Specialties 1090-2290Ft. Open M-Sa 11am-11pm, Su 11am-10pm. Cash only. ❷

Vendéglö Háry, VIII, Bródy Sándor utca 30/a (☎338 4878). Ⓜ3: Kálvin tér. From the metro, take Múzeum körút north and turn right on Bródy Sándor; the restaurant is across the street from Sirius Klub. A giant boar head implores you to take a seat at the bottom of the steps. Dine in yet another candlelit cellar surrounded by English speakers. Favorites include pork chop stuffed with sausage and cheese (1600Ft) and venison ragout in red wine sauce (2300Ft). Live dulcimer music on weekends brings a light, ethereal sort of noise. Appetizers 950-2250Ft. Entrees 1550-3100. Vegetarian dishes 1050-1750Ft. Open daily 11am-10pm. Cash only. ❸

Múzeum Café and Restaurant, VIII, Múzeum körút 12 (☎338 4221; www.muzeumkave-haz.hu). Ⓜ3: Kálvin tér. From the metro, head north; the cafe is 1 block past the National Museum. The fancy drapes, crisp tablecloths, and other plush furnishings of this cafe and restaurant seem to have been designed more for the museum's benefactors than anyone else. The mural on the wall was painted by a 19th-century Hungarian master. Consider something from the extensive fish menu, like the pan fried trout with almonds and garlic (3300Ft). If you can figure out what vacuum-cooked veal shank (3400Ft) is, let us know. Appetizers 1900-3700Ft. Soups 800-1300Ft. Entrees 2700-5400Ft. Wheelchair-accessible. Open M-Sa noon-midnight. Reservations recommended. AmEx/MC/V. ❹

FERENCVÁROS

The area is home to some of the best and most varied cafes to be found in Budapest, perfect for a light meal in the middle of a hefty day of sightseeing. If you can't find something you like on Ráday út, then your gastronomical situation in Budapest is basically hopeless.

Pink Cadillac Pizzeria, IX, Ráday utca 22 (☎216 1412; www.pinkcadillac.hu). Ⓜ3: Kálvin tér. From the metro, take Kálvin tér toward the river and turn left on Ráday. One of Budapest's best pizza joints. Hefty pizza menu (including several vegetarian options) and standard Italian fare. Some of their specialties include the *"pirata," "dolce vita,"* and the massive signature "pink caddy" (mushroom, ham, salami, olives; 2860Ft). The decor includes some vintage advertisements as well as the front of the eponymous pink cadillac, sticking out of the wall with headlights on. Pizza 750-2860Ft. Pasta 1140-1900Ft. Wheelchair-accessible. Open 11am-1am daily. AmEx/D/MC/V. ❸

Pata Negra, IX, Kálvin tér 8 (☎215 5616; www.patanegra.hu). Ⓜ3: Kálvin tér. Across the street from the metro stop. Ideal for people whose definition of spicy encompasses more than paprika. While the small interior certainly earns its style points, the giant hunks of meat behind the bar let you know they take their tapas seriously. Tapas range from the banal (Catalan bread; 350Ft) to the exotic (crispy fried baby squid; 950Ft). White wine from 690Ft. Red wine from 750Ft. Entrees 840-1300Ft. Tapas 350-1950Ft. Open M-W 11am-midnight, Th-F 11am-1am, Sa noon-1am, Su noon-midnight. Cash only. ❷

Berliner Söröző, IX, Ráday utca 5 (☎217 6757; www.berliner.hu). Ⓜ3: Kálvin tér. From the metro, take Kálvin tér toward the river and turn left on Ráday. Typical Central European pub atmosphere, with a dark, brick cellar where you can drink away memories of your own misspent summers. Traditional Hungarian fare, including breaded turkey breast with almond and peaches (1680Ft), as well as the tasty but questionably named crunchy roast pig (1980Ft). Traditional Belgian drafts (from 400Ft). Appetizers 1120-2150Ft. Salads 360-400Ft. Entrees 1680-3250Ft. Open M-Sa noon-1am. Cash only. ❸

Soul Café, IX, Ráday utca 11-13 (☎217 6986; www.soulcafe.hu). Ⓜ3: Kálvin tér. From the metro, take Kálvin tér toward the river and turn left on Ráday. One of Ráday's classier cafes, complete with big wooden chairs and gold walls. A demure, low-lit atmosphere for people too cool for a bright summer's day. Expect a mix of reasonably priced and reasonably fancy salads and sandwiches during the day, such as the chicken baguette with bacon and honey mustard dressing (950Ft). In the evening, you can find more substantive fare, like the chicken paprika with gnocchi (1850Ft). Appetizers 940-2190Ft. Sandwiches (served til 6pm) 950Ft. Entrees 1990-4390Ft. Wi-Fi. Wheelchair-accessible. Open daily noon-1am. Cash only. ❸

Zoë Café, IX, Ráday utca 20 (☎210 1786; www.zoecafe.hu). Ⓜ3: Kálvin tér. From the metro stop, take Kálvin tér toward the river and turn left on Ráday. Attracts a younger, sexier crowd that enjoys wearing sunglasses inside its stylish 2-level red and black interior. Those who like to pretend they're clubbing at all hours of the day will also appreciate the R&B beats that play continuously. The gnocchi with veal (1980Ft) gives people with more reasonable sensibilities a reason to stop by as well. Soups 780-980Ft. Salads 1180-1380Ft. Pasta 1620-1890Ft. Appetizers 890-2180Ft. Entrees 1980-3580Ft. Wheelchair-accessible. Open daily noon-1am. Cash only. ❸

CAFES

Jaffa Café, IX, Ráday utca 39 (☎219 5285; www.jaffakavehaz.hu). Ⓜ3: Kálvin tér. From the metro, take Kálvin tér toward the river and turn left on Ráday. Surprisingly low-key in spite of the radioactive orange walls. Farther down on Ráday than many visitors are willing to wander means a more relaxed atmosphere than you might otherwise expect. Young professionals and young slackers both appreciate the reasonably priced drinks and food. The chicken ragout with potato dumplings (1890Ft) is a favorite. Coffee 290Ft. Tea 400Ft. Salads 990-1790Ft. Entrees 1790-2190Ft. Vegetarian options 1590-1690Ft. Wi-Fi. Wheelchair-accessible. Open M-Th 10am-1am, F 10am-2am, Sa noon-2am, Su 2pm-midnight. Cash only. ❸

Calvin Café, IX, Kálvin tér 8 (☎215 1215; www.calvincafe.hu). Ⓜ3: Kálvin tér. Across the street from the metro. A small cafe that would have a great view of Kálvin tér if it weren't perennially under construction. A dimly lit interior filled with leather benches makes for a comfortable place to enjoy a light, tasty meal with thrifty locals. Occasional acoustic acts give dinner a folksy feel. Look at the menu board for the current selection of salads and sandwiches. Pasta 480-680Ft. Salads 520-780Ft. Entrees 640-780Ft. Open M-Sa 10am-midnight, Su noon-midnight. Cash only. ❶

Chili Bar, IX, Tompa utca 7 (☎216 1637). Ⓜ3: Ferenc körút. From the metro, take Ferenc körút south and turn left on Tompa. Unpretentious Spanish-themed bar with comfy couches and an entire section of the menu devoted to dishes with chili peppers (580-1780Ft). Chili con carne (1380Ft) and chili-smothered nachos (1120Ft) are great when you don't plan on sitting anywhere near someone you have to impress for a while. Sandwiches 1280Ft. Salads 1440-1780Ft. Entrees 1680-3280Ft. Wheelchair-accessible. Open M-F 10am-midnight, Sa noon-midnight. Cash only. ❸

THE VAROSLIGET

Dining in or near City Park is an expensive endeavor. Most of the museums in the area have small cafes or gelato stands out front that charge predictably ludicrous prices. Almost every restaurant in the area claims a half dozen actors and at least one member of the royal family as satisfied guests. They also tend to assume their service is pretty great, sticking you with an automatic service charge of 10-20% on the bill. Getting something small from one of the area cafes might be your best bet until you can get back to Oktogon.

Gundel Étterem, XIV, Állatkerti út 2 (☎603 2480; www.gundel.hu). Állatkerti körút 6-12. ⓜ1: Hősök tere. From the metro, walk through Heroes' Square and then turn left; the restaurant is right next to the zoo. The only area restaurant classy enough for both the Queen of England and Pope John Paul II to have graced it with their presence. Most of the menu is well outside a backpacker's budget, but getting to sit in the elegant interior with well-to-do tourists might be worth the splurge. The best deal to be had is the 3-course lunch menu (3800Ft), which comes with a glass of house wine. Sandwiches 1990-2190Ft. Salads 3190-3790Ft. Entrees 3980-6200Ft. Wheelchair-accessible. Open daily noon-4pm and 6:30-midnight. Reservations required. AmEx/D/MC/V. ❺

Robinson Restaurant, XIV, Városligeti tó. (☎663 6871). Állatkerti krt. 6-12. ⓜ1: Hősök tere. From the metro, walk through Heroes' Sq. and then turn left; the restaurant is in the park across from the zoo. Certainly commands one of the more interesting locations in Budapest atop an artificial pond in the middle of City Park. Serves a mix of Hungarian and international dishes. Grilled goose liver (2790Ft) is the house specialty. Soups 1200-1400Ft. Entrees 1900-5890Ft. Wheelchair-accessible. Open daily noon-4pm, 6pm-midnight. Reservations recommended. AmEx/D/MC/V. ❹

Baraka, XIV, Andrássy út 111 (☎483 1355). ⓜ1: Bajza utca. Walk toward Heroes' Sq.; the restaurant is on the right. One of Budapest's most celebrated restaurants, on the ground fl. of a former historic hotel. The exterior overlooks the beautiful blvd. and Heroes' Sq., while the interior has the feel of a sleek New York lounge. Start off with the Thai-marinated salmon tataki in coconut crust (1800Ft). The 5-spice duck breast (4900Ft) is one of the chef's specialties. Appetizers 1500-1900Ft. Entrees 2400-6200Ft. Wheelchair-accessible. Open M-Sa noon-3pm and 6-11pm, Su noon-3pm. Reservations strongly recommended. AmEx/D/MC/V. ❺

Bagolyvár Étterem, XIV, Állatkerti út 2 (☎468-3110; www.bagolyvar.com). Állatkerti körút 6-12. ⓜ1: Hősök tere. From the metro, walk through Heroes' Sq. and then turn left; the restaurant is right next to the zoo. Vine-covered exterior prepares you for the elegance inside. High-end Hungarian cuisine proudly prepared by generations of Hungarian mothers and grandmothers. The small menu changes daily, though specialties like the rump steak (2350Ft) and the goose liver (4390Ft) are mainstays. Strictly for the wealthy. Prices? If you have to ask, you can't afford it. But seriously: appetizers 660-930Ft; entrees 1880-4390Ft. Reservations required. Open daily noon-11pm. AmEx/D/MC/V. ❹

CAFES

▨ **Cafe Kara**, XIV, Andrássy út 130 (☎269 4135; www.cafekara.hu). ⓜ1: Hősök tere. At the corner of Andrássy and Heroes' Square. A favorite of young Hungarians and backpackers, this Turkish cafe serves some of the tastiest and most reasonably priced food in the area. The toasted turkey and cheese sandwiches (950Ft) are perfect after a day of walking around the park. When you've finished with your coffee and hummus, you can wind down with a waterpipe and a variety of fruity tobacco flavors (pipe and tobacco; 1300Ft) as well as a few more unconventional varieties like cola and Red Bull. Turkish coffee 360Ft. Salads 900-1500Ft. Sandwiches 950-1500Ft. Bellydancing F-Sa 8pm. Open daily 10am-10pm. Cash only. ❷

Hősök Tere Cafe, XIV, Dózsa György 96 (☎354 1087; cafeheroessquare.com). ⓜ1: Hősök tere. From the metro, walk through Heroes' Sq. and turn left; the cafe is on the corner across from the Museum of Fine Arts. Small, clean cafe with comfy chairs and marble-top tables. In addition to the regular coffee drinks, the cafe has an extensive dessert, ice cream, and smoothie menu. Ba-ba Juice (smoothie with banana, peach, milk, honey, and cinnamon) 790Ft. Espresso from 430Ft. Baguettes 590Ft. Ice cream 690-950Ft. Open M-W and Su 9am-9pm, Th-Sa 9am-10pm. Cash only. ❶

BUDA

Some residents will tell you that dining in Buda is reserved for wealthy locals and unwitting tourists. While this is mostly true, the other side of the river does have a few gems that even the most miserly backpacker will appreciate. Most of the restaurants in central Buda cater to people with money to burn. Expect fancy waiters and rotating menus with lots of game entrees. Those looking for a light meal will have a slightly easier time finding cafes and coffee houses, though be warned, those around **Castle Hill** are overpriced. If you want the real deal, you'll need to head farther south into **Gellért Hill.** The lower parts of Gellért Hill, especially near the **Móricz Zsigmond körtér** tram stop, are home to cheap Chinese and gyro joints as well as several American fast food chains.

■ **Nagyi Palacsintazoja,** II, Hattyú utca 16 (☎01 212 4866) ⓜ2: Moszkva tér. From the metro, walk toward the river; at the big intersection veer right on Hattyú utca. Tiny, no-frills eatery dishes out small but tasty sweet and savory crepes piled with toppings like cheese, fruit, or chocolate sauce. A favorite of locals and tourists by day; a mix of surly youth and drunken tourists by night. After a raucous night partying, there are few better ways to avoid sleep than watching the sunrise over Parliament while noshing on a marzipan-stuffed crepe (180Ft). Another location is at Batthyány tér 5. Sweet crepes 130-640Ft. Savory crepes 240-620Ft. Open 24hr. Cash only. ❶

Aranyszarvas Bisztró, Szarvas tér 1 (☎01 375-6451; www.aranyszarvas.hu). Döbrentei tér tram stop, trams 18,19. From the tram stop, take Döbrentei tér away from the river, turn right onto Attila út, and then veer left; the restaurant is on the corner. Located in a former coffeehouse where many of the 18th century's most renowned literary luminaries gathered to reinvigorate the Hungarian language and invent modern Serbian. For years, this renowned Buda landmark was the only restaurant in Budapest that served game. Nearly 40 years later, venison, boar, and pheasant are still the only game in town. A weekly menu keeps the food from getting as stale as that pun. The black, white, and gold interior is appropriately classy given the location's pedigree. Appetizers 1850-3580Ft. Soups 950-1050Ft. Entrees 1550-3250Ft. Open daily noon-11pm. Reservations recommended. MC/V. ❸

Tabáni Terasz, I, Apród utca 10 (☎01 201 1086; www.tabaniterasz.hu). Döbrentei tér tram stop, trams 18,19. From the tram stop, take Döbrentei tér away from the river, turn right onto Attila út, and then veer right onto Apród utca. Upscale, traditional Hungarian fare served in a timeless yet relaxed atmosphere. While the old-fashioned portraits give the yellow interior a hint of class, in spring and summer most opt for 1 of the 2 outdoor terraces. The servers are friendly and happy to talk you through the menu, which includes specialties like the popular veal paprika stew with egg dumplings (2950Ft). Appetizers 1100-2980Ft. Soups 860-980Ft. Pasta 2100-2900Ft. Entrees 2500-4600Ft. Open daily noon-midnight. Reservations recommended. AmEx/MC/V. ❹

Menta Terasz, Margit körút 14 (☎20 316 7403; www.mentaterasz.hu). Margit hid tram stop, trams 4, 6. From the tram stop, take Margit körút away from the river and turn left to stay on Margit körút when the road becomes Margit utca; the restaurant is on the left. Elegant restaurant and lounge with an interior decorated with elaborate, Ottoman-style patterns. During the summer, the large garden is great for dinner after a day of schlepping around Castle Hill. Budapest's young and stylish enjoy dishes like the grilled monkfish (2690Ft) or the sour cream gnocchi with forest mushrooms (2100Ft). Appetizers 850-2200Ft. Soups 790-1650Ft. Vegetarian entrees 1290-2100Ft. Entrees 1990-6500Ft. Wheelchair-accessible. Open M-W and Su 11am-2am, Th-Sa 11am-4am. Reservations recommended. MC/V. ❸

Seoul House, Fő utca 8 (☎01 201 7452). Lánchíd tram stop, tram 19. From the tram stop, cross the street, take Jégverem utca to the corner, and then turn left on Fő utca. Korean barbecue served in a sleek, low-lit setting with bamboo screens. Specialties include sliced and broiled ox tongue (3000Ft) and barbecue spare ribs (3100Ft). Soup 500-1400Ft. Entrees 2300-3900Ft. Open M-Sa noon-11pm. Cash only. ❹

Csalogány 26, Csalogány utca 26 (☎01 201 7892; www.csalogany26.hu). Ⓜ2: Batthyány tér. From the metro, take Fő utca north and then turn left onto Csalogány utca; the restaurant is on the left. Small streetside restaurant that serves fancy food in a no-frills interior. Take your mind off the lack of decor by watching your delicious food prepared on a closed-circuit TV. Street side seating fills up quickly during the summer. The menu changes regularly, but is usually a pleasant mix of Hungarian, French, and Italian cuisines. Appetizers 1200-1800Ft. Entrees 3200-4000Ft. Open Tu-Sa noon-3pm, 7pm-midnight. Kitchen closes at 10pm. Reservations recommended. Cash only. ❺

Margitkert Étterem, Margit utca 15 (☎01 326 0860; www.margitkert.com). Margit hid tram stop, trams 4,6. From the tram stop, take Margit körút away from the river and then keep walking straight until it turns into Margit utca; the restaurant is on the right, across from the park. A traditional Hungarian restaurant that tries pretty hard to remind you that you're in a traditional Hungarian place. Primarily a haunt for bourgeois locals and wealthy foreigners. Enjoy tasty dishes like rolled filet mignon of pork with prunes and plum sauce (1860Ft) and appreciate that the same costumed gypsy musicians bothering you have also bothered more than their share of distinguished European statesmen. Appetizers 1180-1680Ft. Soups 490-630Ft. Entrees 1600-2690Ft. Wheelchair-accessible. Open daily noon-midnight. AmEx/MC/V. ❸

CAFES

▣ **Cafe Marvelosa,** Lánchíd utca 13 (☎01 201 9221; www.marvelosa.eu). Ybl Miklós tér tram stop, tram 19. Across the street from the tram stop. Lovely street side cafe with its share of literary and artistic pretension. Students and intellectuals gather to work on their laptops while enjoying dishes named after 19th-century artists and poets. Try the popular "Renoir" (orange, walnut, and duck salad with apple; 2850Ft) and the "Ady" (barbecue chicken with salad, honey, and chili dressing; 2390Ft). Street side seating offers a great view of the Chain Bridge. Espresso 400Ft. Tea 650Ft. Appetizers 1490-1850Ft. Salads 1890-2850Ft. Entrees 1950-2890Ft. Wheelchair-accessible. Open daily 9am-10pm. Cash only. ❸

Teaerdő Teaház, Lágymányosi utca 7 (☎01 784 5474; www.teaerdo.hu). Móricz Zsigmond körtér tram stop, trams 18, 19, 47 49. From the tram stop, take Bartók Béla út toward the river and then turn right on Lágymányosi utca. Fancy tea and ice cream sundaes make strange bedfellows in this minimalist, zen atmosphere. Sip luxurious teas on floor mats surrounded by sleek black furniture. After you've warmed your wandering soul, indulge in a decadent ice cream dessert, like the amaretto ice cream sundae (vanilla ice cream, kiwi, oranges, amaretto, melon, and whipped cream; 980Ft). Tea from 500Ft. Sundaes 940-1490Ft. Open M-F noon-10pm, Sa 2-10pm, Su 5-10pm. Cash only. ❶

Platán, I, Döbrentei tér 2 (☎20 361 2287). Döbrentei tér tram stop, trams 18,19. From the tram stop, head south toward the square. Small cafe near the base of Gellért Hill provides backpackers with a quiet, inexpensive place to relax after a day of sightseeing. In the summer, the terrace affords a charming view of the Liberation Monument and Erzsébet Bridge. A selection of baguettes (750Ft) won't substitute for a meal, but they may hold you over until you get back to Pest. Espresso 310Ft. Tea 350Ft. Beer from 320Ft. Wi-Fi. Open daily 10am-midnight. Cash only. ❶

ÓBUDA AND MARGIT-SZIGET

If you find yourself depleted by a day of wandering Óbuda without seeing much, rest assured that there are some establishments where you can buy food. Your options range from "sort of fancy" to "pretty fancy." The only people who really trek all the way out here for food are people who already live on the

Buda side, which means that they have money to burn that a student traveler might not. If you really need to eat, consider ordering something at one of the beer gardens on Margaret Island.

Kéhli Restaurant, III, Mókus utca 22 (☎01 368 0613; www.kehli.hu). Árpád híd (Szentlélek tér) tram stop. From the tram stop, head down the stairs and go south on Lajos utca, turn right at Óbudai, and left at Mókus. One of the most celebrated of Óbuda's expensive restaurants, Kéhli has been family-run since the 19th century. During the summer months sit in the garden while gypsy musicians serenade you for tips. The menu is mostly Hungarian specialties, including Gyuri Nádas' turkey-breast-miracle with mushroom fantasies (2590Ft) and their signature steaming hot-pot of marrow bone (1980Ft), which appeals to someone somewhere. Appetizers 690-890Ft. Soups 1490-2190Ft. Entrees 1990-4490Ft. Wheelchair-accessible. Open daily noon-midnight. AmEx/MC/V. ❹

Kisbuda Gyöngye, III, Kenyeres utca 34 (☎01 368 6402). Selmeci utca tram stop. From the tram stop, take Bécsi north and then turn right on Kenyeres. One of Budapest's most celebrated restaurants is lavishly decorated with turn of the century antiques for when you want to feel like you're eating at your rich grandmother's house. Far enough away that only dedicated gourmets will likely be interested in making the trip. Specialties include morel mushrooms with truffle cream and tagliatelle (2980Ft) or turkey steak in honey with potato puree (2780Ft). Appetizers 1980-3380Ft. Soups 1280Ft. Salads 1280-2680Ft. Entrees 2680-4740Ft. Open Tu-Sa noon-midnight. Reservations recommended. AmEx/MC/V. ❹

Új Sipos Halászkert, III, Fő tér 6 (☎01 388 8745; www.ujsipos.hu). Flórián tér tram stop. From the tram stop, take Tavasz utca toward the river and then turn left at Hídfő utca, which will lead to the square. Located right on Óbuda's quaint (read: boring) main square, where you can remind yourself how far you walked. The food (mostly seafood offerings) is good, and the interior simple and tasteful, with wooden furniture and some old photographs on the walls. Highlights from the menu include paprika catfish (2890Ft) and breaded and deep-fried chicken breast with liver (2390Ft). Appetizers 1590-2990Ft. Entrees 1990-4490Ft. Open daily noon-midnight. MC/V. ❹

Mókus Sörkert, Mókus utca 1-3 (☎70 332 7108; www.mokussorkert.hu). Árpád híd (Szentlélek tér) tram stop. From the tram stop, head down the stairs and go south on Lajos utca, turn right at Óbudai, and then left at Mókus. A more laid-back alternative to some of the area's oppressively fancy restaurants. The exterior, which appears to be made mostly of plywood, isn't much to look at, but you won't care when you're lounging in the outdoor terrace with area businesspeople looking for a (relatively) inexpensive lunch. The trotter in Bakerin style is a specialty (1790Ft) as is the turkey breast with smoked cheese (1490Ft). Appetizers 790-1990Ft. Entrees 1290-2590Ft. Wheelchair-accessible. Open daily 11am-midnight. MC/V. ❷

◎ SIGHTS

Many of Budapest's most picturesque features can be found close to the Danube. The views from Castle Hill, especially near **Fisherman's Bastion,** will make pleasing backgrounds for your scrapbook. The grounds of the **Royal Palace** provide a nice (free) stroll if you don't mind the masses of other tourists who will be there during the summer months. While shots of **Parliament** and the **Royal Palace** may make the best postcards, some of the city's greatest treasures will require you to dive deeper into the higher numbered districts.

In 1896, Hungary's millennial birthday bash prompted the construction of Budapest's most prominent sights. Among the works commissioned by the Hapsburgs were **Hősök tér** (Heroes' Square), **Szabadság híd** (Liberty Bridge),

Vajdahunyad Vár (Vajdahunyad Castle), and continental Europe's first metro system. Slightly grayer because of age, war, and occupation, these monuments attest to the optimism of a capital on the verge of its Golden Age. All of these beautiful sights can be found along **Andrássy út,** which provides more nationalist eye candy per block than any other part of the city. See the sights with a variety of themed itineraries from **Absolute Walking and Biking Tours.** (☎01 211 8861; www.absolutetours.com. 3½hr. tours 4000Ft, students 3500ft. Specialized tours 4000-7000Ft.) Budapest's museums range from the daring and cutting-edge to the terribly dull. One thing they do all have in common: they're closed on Mondays.

THE BELVÁROS

The Belváros has traditionally been the commercial center of Budapest. Many businesses have their offices around the congested Váci utca. Fortunately, there's a lot more to the Inner City than overpriced shopping. The area past Ferenc korut went neglected for many years. Recently, efforts have been made to reinvigorate the area by relocating the Ludwig Museum and the National Theatre Concert Hall to an otherwise depressed area by the Danube. Whether the efforts are a sincere attempt at urban renewal or a disingenuous way of putting modern art in its place has yet to be seen.

◼GREAT MARKET HALL (KÖZPONTI VÁSÁRCSARNOK). Built in 1894 and opened in 1897, Budapest's Great Market Hall was built to imitate the great indoor markets of major Western European cities, though from within you might think it was built to emulate their train stations. The building itself is worth the trip, with beautiful arched windows and a colorfully tiled roof. The massive interior comprises two floors and a basement brimming with fresh meats and produce. On the ground floor you'll find row after row of crowded produce stalls. Keep your fingers to yourself: many stalls post signs forbidding customers from handling the produce. On the second floor, you can find an assortment of bars, food stands, and stalls hawking leather goods, Hungarian folk costumes, and Soviet-era Astrakhan hats. Haggling for these treasures is encouraged. In the basement you'll find fish and pickle-mongers. Anything you find stuffed with cabbage—be it pickle, *gherkin,* pearl onion, or paprika—is likely to be a Hungarian specialty. (*Váci utca and Vámház körút.* Ⓜ3: Kálvin tér. From the metro, take Vámház toward the river. Open M 6am-5pm, Tu-F 6am-6pm, Sa 6am-2pm.)

◼ERZSÉBET TÉR. Once the site of Budapest's **International Bus Station,** Erzsébet tér was more recently the site of a political and architectural maelstrom. An overeager administration planned to construct the new **National Theatre Concert Hall** against the wishes of much of the city, and even began digging the foundation before they found themselves out of office. The beginnings of the foundation were left, and residents began referring to the enormous hole in the middle of downtown as *"gödör"* (the pothole). Fortunately, an ambitious urban renewal project has turned the area into one of the city's best-loved parks, with open green spaces, a long staircase dotted with tables and chairs, and a reflecting pool. The multi-function **Gödör Klub** now hosts art shows and live music in the former foundation. The area is also a popular destination for area skate punks, who have covered some parts of the area in spray paint and worn down much of the limestone architecture. There's no better place in the city to spend a summer afternoon relaxing with a book and a cold drink. After dark, you can unwind with hundreds of Budapest's young and fashionable while music from Gödör drifts up into the night. (Ⓜ1,2, or 3: Deák tér.)

FASHION STREET (VÁCI UTCA). Stretching from Vörösmarty tér to the Great Market Hall, Váci utca was once the exclusive shopping area of Budapest's rich and famous. The pedestrian-only avenue still retains some of the exclusive designer boutiques that made it famous, though in recent years it has also become a major tourist attraction. The upside, if you can call it that, is that you can now buy an alligator-skin handbag and a coffee mug that says "Hungry in Budapest" in the same 500 ft. stretch. The area is home to an assortment of restaurants and cafes, some as fancy as they look, and empties out at closing time. The lack of nightlife options along the street means the only people you're likely to encounter after dark are lost tourists and runners for area brothels.

LIPÓTVÁROS

The closest thing Budapest has to a real tourist center, Lipótváros contains the city's two major attractions, as well as most of its embassies and major government buildings. Everywhere you look you'll find tiny parks and green spaces, often just large enough for a single bench, tree, and statue of someone you'll have no hope of recognizing.

PARLIAMENT. "The motherland does not have a house," lamented Hungarian poet Mihály Vörösmarty in 1846. In response to the growing sense of Hungarian nationalism during the period, the palatial Gothic **Hungarian Parliament Building** (Országház) looks more like a cathedral than a seat of government. The building is the largest in Hungary and towers at 96m, a number symbolizing the date of Hungary's millennial anniversary. The building once required more electricity than the rest of the city combined to supply power to its 692 rooms. The gold and marble interior is breathtaking, and now contains the original **Holy Crown of Hungary**. The informative tour leads through the enormous cupola room where statues of the nation's founders stand several meters tall. The frescoes that line the ceiling above the beautiful staircase are especially pristine. Nearby **Lajos Kossuth Square** (Kossuth Lajos tér) gives the crowds of tourists waiting for their tours a place to mill around. The abstract **Memorial to the 1956 Revolution** is an imposing granite monolith appearing to melt away. The impressive **Kossuth memorial** was renovated by the Communists, who found the original statue too pessimistic. The former leader now points his finger toward a brighter future and also the damn kids he wants off his lawn. (Ⓜ2: Kossuth tér. ☎01 441 4000. English-language tours daily 10am, noon, 2pm; buy tickets early, as they often sell out during the summer.

THE LOCAL STORY

HOLE LOT OF TROUBLE

After the International Bus Station moved to the eastern part of the city, its former location at Erzsébet tér (Elizabeth Square) was left an unsightly parking lot. In 1996, the liberal government designated the site for the heretofore homeless National Theater. Unfortunately, a study determined that the building would block the fresh air from the Danube from reaching the inner city, something the city's chain-smoking artistic types probably hadn't considered.

Unconvinced, the administration commenced construction of the building's foundation despite mounting public concern. In the next election, the conservative opposition played to the growing pro-fresh air constituency and won. Once the new government had taken power, however, it found itself at a loss for what to do about the enormous hole next to the one of the city's most heavily-trafficked areas. The foundation, nicknamed the "National Hole" by nonplussed citizens, became a national embarrassment. In 2000, however, a contest was held to decide the fate of the hole. The winning team transformed the former parking lot into a park, and converted the hole into a cultural center and live music venue, the much-beloved **Gödör Klub**. Today, the square is a vibrant social center that proves fresh air and culture aren't necessarily mutually exclusive.

You can also ask permission from the guard to buy a ticket from the office at Gate X. Ticket office opens at 8am. Entrance with mandatory tour 2820Ft, students 1410Ft. Free with EU passport.)

SAINT STEPHEN'S BASILICA (SZ. ISTVÁN BAZILIKA). The Neo-Renaissance facade of the city's largest church immediately strikes you the first time you see it, and subsequent visits only reveal more layers of detail. The building was seriously damaged during the Siege of Budapest in WWII, though thankfully most of it has been restored. The magnificent red-and-green marble and gilded interior attracts throngs of tourists and worshippers. Regular classical concerts are occasions to hear and appreciate Hungary's largest and most richly decorated organ. The **Panorama Tower,** Budapest's highest vantage point, offers an amazing 360° view of the city. The museum's most macabre treasure is St. Stephen's mummified right hand, removed from his body by a priest and hidden in the countryside until it was stolen during WWII and subsequently returned. A 100Ft donation dropped in the box will illuminate it for two minutes. *(V. ⓂDeák tér. Church open daily 7am-7pm, Chapel May-Oct. M-Sa 9am-5pm, Su 1-5pm, Nov.-Apr. M-Sa 10am-4pm, Mass M-Sa 8am and 6pm, Su 8, 9, 10am, noon, 6, 7:30pm. Free. Tower open daily Apr.-Oct. M-Sa 10am-6pm. 500Ft, students 400Ft. Elevator available to top of tower. Cash only.)*

LIBERTY SQUARE. Built on the site of a former prison facility meant to tame the "rebellious" Hungarians, the square is now a green space with benches and a cafe. It also contains the only remaining Soviet monument in Budapest proper, a massive **obelisk** commemorating the Russian soldiers who liberated the city from the Germans during WWII. While the rest of the park's statues were moved outside the city after the fall of Communism, the Russian government asked that the obelisk remain to commemorate the Soviet soldiers buried under it. Ironically, the red star-topped monument now stands directly across from the American embassy. On one side of the street, the beautiful **Hungarian Television** (Magyar Televízió, often abbreviated MTV) building was the site of political turmoil in 2006 when protestors attempted to storm the building and demand the Prime Minister's resignation. Nearby, the **Hungarian National Bank** (Magyar Nemzeti Bank) has an elegant facade and a rather boring exhibit on the history of money inside. Amaze no one as you lift a gold brick worth approximately 60 million forints. *(Szabadság tér 8-9. Ⓜ3: Arany János. From the metro, take Bank utca west. ☎ 428 2752; english.mnb.hu. Bank open M-W and F 9am-4pm, Th 9am-6pm. Wheelchair-accessible. Free.)*

ERZSÉBETVÁROS

Named for the beloved wife of Emperor Franz Joseph, Erzsébetváros has been the center of Jewish life in Budapest for more than 150 years. During WWII, 80,000 Jews were imprisoned in the ghetto here. Between the destruction of the Jewish community and neglect of the city under Communism, the area was largely unpopulated throughout the second half of the 20th century. In recent years, however, it has undergone a cultural revival. The Great Synagogue has finally been restored, and many of the district's abandoned buildings have been turned into cultural centers or ruin pubs, making the district into Budapest's most popular nightlife destination.

GREAT SYNAGOGUE AND JEWISH MUSEUM. The largest synagogue in Europe and the second-largest in the world, 'Pest's Great Synagogue (Zsinagóga) was built in 1859 and heavily damaged during WWII, when the Nazis used it as a radio base during the Siege of Budapest. Restoration began in 1990 and is only now being completed. The synagogue was built in the Moorish Revival style, with two towering onion domes visible from all around. Designed to seat 3000 across its multiple levels, the interior is richly adorned with geometric patterns and chandeliers. Next to the synagogue is the last ghetto established during WWII. More than 80,000 Jews were imprisoned there and 10,000 died in the final months of the war. Today, the 2500 people whose bodies could not be identified are buried in the garden. The **Tree of Life**, an enormous metal tree in the form of a weeping willow, remembers those murdered during the Holocaust. Each leaf bears the name of a Hungarian family whose members perished. Next to it, four granite memorials honor "Righteous Gentiles" who risked their lives to aid Jewish victims during the Holocaust. The English-language guides are informative and engaging. Next door, the **Jewish Museum** (Zsidó Múzeum), built on the birthplace of Zionist Theodor Herzl, displays artifacts from the heyday of Judaism in Budapest. The permanent collection commemorates Hungarian Holocaust victims, while the upper level contains temporary exhibits. *(VII. At the corner of Dohány utca and Wesselényi utca M2: Astoria. ☎ 70 533 5696; www.greatsynagogue.hu. Open May-Oct. M-Th 10am-5pm, F and Su 10am-2pm; Nov.-Apr. M-Th 10am-3pm, F and Su 10am-1pm. Services F 6pm. Admissions usually start at 10:30am. Covered shoulders required. Men must cover their heads inside the synagogue; yarmulkes available at the entrance. Admission to Museum included with entrance to the Great Synagogue. Tours M-Th 10:30am-3:30pm every 30min., F and Su 10:30, 11:30am, 12:30pm. 1400Ft, students 750Ft. Tours 1900Ft/1600Ft.)*

KLAUZÁL TÉR. The tiny green center of the Jewish quarter is surrounded by kosher delis as well as many open-air cafes and restaurants that make it a nice retreat during the hot summer days. At the **Kárász House** (Klauzál tér 5), you can see the balcony where Lajos Kossuth, one of Hungary's great statesmen, delivered his last speech before going into exile. *(M2: Blaha Lujza tér. From the metro, take Rákóczi west and turn right on Nagy Diófa utca, which will take you right to the square.)*

TERÉZVÁROS

The city's sixth district seems to have a disproportionate share of Budapest's best streets, restaurants, hostels, and museums. **Andrássy út** makes for a lovely walk at any time of day. At night, the streets are filled with people on their way to and from the area's great late night cafes and bars. Street performers are also common, though the real spectacle is the opera house, which takes on an ethereal glow that's mesmerizing on a warm summer night. If you're lucky enough to find accommodations in the area, you'll never be at a loss for things to do and see.

ANDRÁSSY ÚT. Hungary's grandest boulevard, Andrássy út extends from Erzsébet tér northeast to **Heroes' Square** (Hősök tér). Its elegant gardens and balconies, laid out in 1872 and renovated after the fall of the Iron Curtain in 1989, recall the grandeur of Budapest's Golden Age. While the metro runs directly under the boulevard, it would be a shame to miss the walk, which takes you past rows of UNESCO-preserved buildings. At the intersection with Felsőerdősor utca, **Kodály körönd** is surrounded by beautifully painted buildings and statues of three of Hungary's greatest Ottoman-killers as well as a poet who celebrated the anti-Ottoman exploits of the other three when he wasn't writing erotic poetry.

BUDAPEST NYUGATI PÁLYAUDVAR (BUDAPEST WESTERN RAILWAY STATION). This railway station is smaller than its eastern cousin, though it has the advantage of being in a neighborhood you'll actually want to visit. The building was designed and built by the Eiffel Co., though notably less phallic than the company's Parisian masterpiece. The station itself is a beautiful Baroque construction with perhaps the most lavish McDonald's you'll ever see connected to it. *(M1: Nyugati pályaudvar. At the intersection of Teréz körút, Szent István körút, Váci út, and Bajcsy-Zsilinszky út.)*

MAGYAR ÁLLAMI OPERAHÁZ (HUNGARIAN STATE OPERA HOUSE). This opera house was built between 1875 and 1884 and largely funded by Austro-Hungarian Emperor Franz Joseph, who financed the building's construction on the condition that it would not be larger than Austria's own great opera house. The builders assented, though they built arguably the more beautiful opera house, which caused Franz Joseph to storm out of the inaugural performance in a rage. (He never returned.) His box has remained empty to all but the most important guests; even Queen Elizabeth II wasn't allowed to use it, though somehow Madonna and Antonio Banderas managed to snag a seat. The interior is built in a neo-Renaissance style, complete with scenes from classical mythology. The guided tours are informative and filled with amusing anecdotes about the building's history, including the smoking corridor that was once so thick with cigar smoke that aristocratic teens could make out in plain view of their hawk-eyed parents. *(Andrássy út 22. ⓜ1: Opera. ☎01 332 8197; www.opera.hu. 1hr. tours daily in 6 languages 3 and 4pm. 2800Ft, students 1400Ft. MC/V.)*

THE OKTOGON. One of the largest intersections in Budapest, where beautiful Andrássy út meets the Grand Boulevard. The name comes from the four large buildings which were designed by famed Hungarian architect, **Antal Szkalnitzky,** who wanted each building to represent a different architectural style. Around the intersection you can find a number of American fast-food joints, in addition to Hungarian cafes and restaurants. In the summer, you can't walk 20 ft. without hitting an ice cream stand of some kind.

THE VAROSLIGET

Originally an ox meadow, Budapest's City Park (Városliget) received a major overhaul in preparation for the 1896 millennial celebration. Located northeast of Heroes' Sq., the park is dominated by an enormous artifical pond. When the park isn't being renovated during the summer, you can rent a rowboat to spend a few hours out on the water. During the winter, rent a pair of skates as the pond turns into Central Europe's largest ice-skating rink. The park itself is a popular recreational area for locals, with great bike paths, spaces for picnicking, and even outdoor table tennis boards. The park's main road is closed to automobiles on weekends.

HEROES' SQUARE. At the Heroes' Sq. end of Andrássy út, the 🔲**Millennium Monument** commemorates Hungary's heroes. Built for the city's millennial celebration, the sweeping structure dominates the square. The pillar in the center is topped by the Archangel Gabriel, presenting the Hungarian crown to St. Stephen. At its base are equestrian statues of the seven chieftans said to be the leaders of the Magyar tribes that settled the Carpathian Basin. The pillar and the surrounding structures contain statues of other national heroes: it's a veritable hit parade of awesome hats through the ages. During the summer, concerts and other events are often held in the square.

🔲**SZÉCHENYI BATHS** (SZÉCHENYI-GYÓGYFÜRDŐ). Statues and fountain adorn the Neo-Baroque exterior of the biggest and one of the most luxurious bath complexes in Europe. A popular destination for locals and tourists alike, you could spend an entire day just relaxing in the swimming pool. Those looking to exercise their minds while their bodies unwind can challenge older intellectuals to a game of chess. Be warned, however: the games are often intense and don't be surprised if you find yourself surrounded by eager spectators. After your embarrassing defeat, swim away in shame and treat yourself to a consolation massage. The complex's 12 pools and three thermal baths mean you can probably avoid everyone who saw you lose. *(Állatkerti körút 11. ⓜ1: Széchenyi Fürdő. ☎363 3210; www.szechenyibath.com. Open daily 6am-10pm. Not wheelchair-accessible. Bring your own bathing suit and towel. Swimming pool 2500Ft per 2hr., 2800Ft per day. Thermal tub tickets 1500Ft per day. Massages from 2000Ft. Cash only.)*

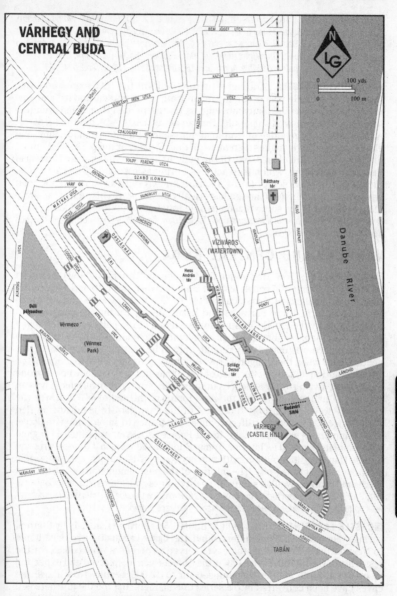

VÁRHEGY AND CENTRAL BUDA

REM JOSEF UTCA

KACSA UTCA

VITÉZ UTCA

VÁRSÁNDY IBEN UTCA

MARGIT KÖRÚT

FAZEKAS UTCA

CSALOGÁNY UTCA

TOLDY FERENC UTCA

DONÁTI UTCA

Bátthany tér

SZABÓ ILONKA

VÁRF OK

OSTROM

HUNFALVY UTCA

MÁTRAY UTCA

LOVAS UTCA

TÁNCSICS

VIZIVÁROS (WATERTOWN)

ORSZÁGHÁZ

FORTUNA

LOVAS UTCA

ÚRI

Hess András tér

LOVAS

Déli pályaudvar

ATTILA UTCA

Vérmező

(Vérmez Park)

TÁRNOK UTCA

HUNYADI JÁNOS U

HUNYADI JÁNOS U

PÁLOSA

PONTY

FŐ U

Szilágy Dezso tér

KRISZTINA KÖRÚT

SZT. GYÖRGY

LÁNCHID

LÁNCHID UTCA

Budavári Sikló

Danube River

BUDAI ALSÓ RAKPART

ISKOLA

ALAGÚT UTCA

ATTILA ÚT

GELLÉRTHEGY

VÁRHEGY (CASTLE HILL)

ALKOTÁS UTCA

NÁPRAY UTCA

MÉSZÁROS UTCA

UTCA

VÁRALJA

TABÁN

KRISZTINA KÖRÚT

ATTILA ÚT

0   100 yds

0   100 m

BUDAPEST

BUDAPEST ZOO AND BOTANICAL GARDEN. One of Central Europe's best zoos, the Budapest Zoo and Botanical Garden contains all the animals you would expect to see, though it distinguishes itself by encouraging patrons to get as close to the animals as possible. Numerous enclosures allow you to get up close and personal with exotic birds and flying foxes, and for 300Ft you can even feed the elephants yourself. *(Állatkerti körút 6-12. ⓜ1: Hősök tere. From the metro, walk through Heroes' Sq. and then turn left. ☎273 4900; www.zoobudapest.com. Open Jan.-Dec. M-F 9am-4pm, Sa-Su 9am-4:30pm; Mar. and Oct. M-F 9am-5pm, Sa-Su 9am-5:30pm; Apr. and Sept. 9am-5:30pm, Sa-Su 9am-6pm; May-Aug. 9am-6:30pm, Sa-Su 9am-7pm. Last entry 1hr. before closing. Wheelchair-accessible. Admission 1850Ft, students 1290Ft. AmEx/MC/V.)*

VAJDAHUNYAD CASTLE. Another structure built for the 1896 exposition, this Frankenstein castle was originally made from wood and cardboard and was meant to showcase the many movements represented in Hungarian architecture. The castle proved so popular that an actual castle was built in its place. A fascinating hodgepodge of Gothic, Renaissance, Baroque, and Romanesque elements, the castle makes a great stroll during a day at the park. While most of the buildings are closed, one of the main halls now contains the **Museum of Hungarian Agriculture**, which is exactly as boring as it sounds. The castle also includes a hooded sculpture of a scribe known only as Anonymous, who wrote a comprehensive (though historically innaccurate) history of the early Magyar peoples. For some reason people touch his quill for good luck. *(In City Park. ☎142 0573. Agricultural museum open Tu-Su 10am-5pm. Wheelchair-accessible. Grounds free; museum 200Ft. Cash only.)*

VÁRHEGY AND CENTRAL BUDA

▨ROYAL PALACE. Towering above the Danube on Várhegy, the Castle District has had something of a rough history. Built between the 12th and 14th centuries, the original castle was occupied by the Ottoman invaders, during which time it was turned into barracks and left to decay. During the campaign to retake Buda by the allied Christian forces, much of the palace was destroyed by heavy artillery bombardment. It wasn't until the middle of the 18th century that the palace was completely rebuilt, only to be destroyed again less than a century later when the Hungarian revolutionary army laid siege to it during the 1848 revolution. In the last decades of the 19th century, the palace became one of the most lavish royal residences in the world. For the Hungarians, it was an emblem of national pride. For the Axis forces at the end of WWII, it was the best place to stage a last-ditch defense of the city against the advancing Red Army. Once again, heavy artillery reduced the palace to smoldering wreckage. The Communists saw the ruined Royal Palace as a symbol of the old regime and completely gutted its interior. Today Buda Castle version 4.0 closely resembles its Hapsburg incarnation, with flowery courtyards, statues, and panoramic views of the rest of the city. The interior of the palace now houses the **National Széchényi Library** as well as some of the city's finest museums. *(Szent György tér 2. ⓜ1, 2, or 3: Deák tér. From the metro, take bus #16 across the Danube. Or, from ⓜ2: Moszkva tér, walk up to the hill on Várfok u. "Becsi kapu" marks the castle entrance.)*

▨CASTLE LABYRINTHS (BUDAVÁRI LABIRINTUS). Formed naturally by thermal springs that extend 1200m underground, the **Castle Labyrinths** were once home to Neanderthals. For a time, the caves served as personal wine cellars for the residents of Castle Hill. In the 1930s, the tunnels were connected and expanded to create a bomb shelter that housed up to 10,000 people. Nowadays, the caves have been converted into a series of chambers that toe the line between museum and haunted house. The caves are divided into several themed sections filled with decorations of dubious authenticity, including pseudo-cave paintings and statues. Most memorable, perhaps, is a fountain of red wine that the wise are advised not to drink and the foolish are likely to splatter on their clothes. The final stretch of labyrinth, named the **Labyrinth of Another World,** is a bizarre mix of social and self-reflexive critique centered around "artifacts" like enormous stone coke bottles from a species of man called "Homo Consumes." The best time to visit the labyrinths is between 6 and 7:30pm, when they turn out the lights and hand out woefully and comically ineffective oil lamps. Children under 14 and people with heart conditions are advised not to take part in the spooky festivities. *(2 entrances, 1 at Úri utca 9 and 2nd at Lovas út 4/a. ☎1 212 0207; www.labirintus.com. Open daily 9:30am-7:30pm. Wheelchair-accessible through Lovas út entrance. 2000Ft, students 1500Ft. Cash only.)*

MATTHIAS CHURCH (MÁTYÁS TEMPLOM). The colorful roof of **Matthias Church** on Castle Hill is one of Budapest's most photographed sights. The church was converted to a mosque in 1541. One hundred and forty five years later, the Hapsburgs defeated the Turks, sacked the city, and then reconverted the building, in that order. The church's decorations reflect its mixed heritage. Inside, intricate geometric patterns line the walls alongside murals by famed painter **Károly Lotz,** who also decorated the ceiling of the state opera house. Facing the altar, turn left and you can find the **tombs** of King Béla III and his first wife, the only tombs in the church to survive the Ottoman occupation; in 1967 archeologists stripped the bodies of their royal jewelery to be included in the National Museum. Ascend the spiral steps to view the exhibits of the **Museum of Ecclesiastical Art,** where you'll find plenty of gold and a replica of the Hungarian crown, complete with a crooked cross. *(I, Szentháromság tér 2. www.matyas-templom.hu. Open M-F 9am-5pm, Sa 9am-2:30pm, Su 1-5pm. High mass daily 7, 8:30am, 6pm; Su and holidays also 10am and noon. Church and museum 750Ft, students 500Ft.)*

FISHERMAN'S BASTION (HALÁSZBÁSTYA). Named for the fisherman's guild that was charged with defending that stretch of Castle Hill during the Middle Ages, **Fisherman's Bastion** is, despite its parapets and towers, a purely decorative structure. **Frigyes Schulek,** the same architect who restored Matthias Church, designed the bastion as a mix of neo-Gothic and neo-Romanesque elements that harmonize with the surrounding structures. The seven towers represent the seven Magyar chiefs who first settled Hungary in 896. The views from the top offer sweeping of the Parliament and St. Stephen's Basilica. At night, the view of Pest all lit-up is fantastic. *(I, Szentháromság tér, near Matthias Church. 300Ft during the day, free at night. Cash only.)*

SZÉCHENYI CHAIN BRIDGE (SZÉCHENYI LÁNCHÍD). Built in 1849, the Széchenyi Chain Bridge was the first permanent bridge across the Danube in Budapest and one of the longest bridges in the world. At the time of its construction, it was a sensation in Budapest, its imperious structure symbolizing Hungary's national awakening. During WWII, the chain bridge (along with every other bridge in the city) was destroyed by the retreating Axis forces, and had to be rebuilt. A pair of noble-looking lions flanks either end of the abutments. A popular myth states that the sculptor forgot to give the lions tongues and that the public's merciless mocking caused him to throw himself into the Danube. In reality, the tongues are just hard to see from below. At the Buda end of the bridge you can see the **Zero Kilometer Stone** that marks the place from which all Hungarian highways are measured.

THE VÍZIVÁROS

Buda's Víziváros has long been a privileged piece of Hungarian real estate. During the Ottoman occupation, the Turks made their homes in the area, supposedly planting roses all over the hillside, hence the modern name for the Rózsadomb (literally "Rose Hill") neighborhood. Today, the area is home to many prominent Hungarian politicians, including the former prime minister.

▓KIRALY BATHS (KIRALY FÜRDÓ). Construction began on the monumental Kiraly Baths by order of the Pasha of Buda in 1565. Unlike most of the area baths, the Kiraly baths are not connected directly to the thermal springs, instead taking water from another nearby bath. The Pasha ordered them built far from the springs so that bathing could continue even during an inevitable siege by Christian forces. Renovated and rebuilt after damage from WWII, the Kiraly baths, perhaps more than any other in the city, evoke the spirit of the old Turkish baths with their crescent-topped domes and octagonal bath surrounded by pillars. (*Fő utca 82-84. Margit hid tram stop, trams 4, 6. From the tram stop, take south Frankel Leó utca; it will become Fő utca. ☎01 202 3688; www.spasbudapest.com. Open daily M and W 8am-7pm (women only), Tu, Th-Sa 9am-8pm (men only), Su 9am-8pm. Bathing suit rental available. 2100Ft. Thermal tub 1200Ft. Cash only.*)

GÜL BABA'S TOMB (GÜL BABA TÜRBESI). Gül Baba was a Turkish dervish poet who accompanied Suleiman the Magnificent in his many campaigns against Europe. The stories of his death conflict—some accounts maintain that he died on the first day of celebration after the Ottoman victory, while others say that he died fighting at the castle walls. Either way, his death was significant enough for Suleiman himself to serve as one of Baba's coffin bearers. Soon afterward, a beautiful octagonal tomb was erected overlooking the city from Rose Hill. The tomb is the northernmost site of pilgrimage in the Islamic faith. The entire complex is beautiful and the tomb itself is covered in rich tapestries. The site, currently undergoing renovation, is now administered by the Turkish government. (*II, Mecset utca 14. Margit hid tram stop, trams 4, 6. From the tram stop, take Margit körút away from the river and then turn right on Mecset utca; the tomb is up the hill on the left.*)

GELLÉRT HEGY

▓LIBERTY MONUMENT (SZABADSÁG SZOBOR). Visible from all over the city, Budapest's **Liberty Monument** has a complicated history. One story goes that the figure was originally designed to hold a propeller by the order of Regent Horthy, Hungary's right-wing leader during the interwar period. Before anyone got around to building the statue, however, the Soviets had "liberated" a then-grateful Budapest, which replaced the propeller with a palm leaf and dedicated the statue to their Soviet heroes. After half a century of Communist rule, the citizens of Budapest no longer felt like they had been liberated, and, in 1989, the statue of a Soviet soldier was relocated from the base of the monument to **Memento Park** (see p. 257). The monument was rededicated to everyone who has ever fought for Hungary's freedom and success. (*XI, Gellért Hill. The monument is at the top of the hill, near the Citadella.*)

HOTEL GELLÉRT AND GELLÉRT BATHS. Located at the base of the hill, the world-famous Hotel Gellért was built in the Vienna Secession style and incorporates gorgeous elements of the then-emerging Art Nouveau. While the hotel itself is probably beyond most student budgets, the equally famous adjoining baths are certainly not. Probably the most popular of the Buda baths for tourists, the Gellért Baths feature a richly tiled interior with statues and columns surrounding the main bath. Outside, an enormous sitting bath is popular with visitors of all ages. (*Szent Gellért tér 1. Szent Gellért tér tram stop. ☎01 466 6166; www.spasbudapest.com. Open M-F 6am-7pm, Sa 6am-10pm, Su 6am-8pm. Last entry 1hr. before closing. Bathing suit and towel rental available. Admission with locker 3500Ft. Cash only. For hotel info ☎01 889 5500; www.danubiushotels.com.*)

THE CITADELLA. This structure was originally built by the gloating Hapsburgs after the failed 1848 revolution to remind Hungarians who was in charge. The angled walls occupy most of the hill's plateau and must have provided the Hapsburg soldiers garrisoned there with great views of the city that resented them. During WWII, the interior was converted into a massive, three-level air raid shelter, which served as one of the strong points for the German and Hungarian forces during the bloody **Siege of Budapest.** Today, the Citadella is home to a luxury hotel and expensive restaurant. The former air raid shelter contains an overpriced museum filled with wax figures depicting scenes from the war, which range from not very to quite interesting. During the summer, the surrounding area is swamped with food vendors and souvenir stands. If you can, go at night to take in the view in relative peace. *(XI, Citadella Sétány 1. ☎01 279 1963; www.citadella.hu. Museum open May-Sept. daily 9am-8pm; Oct.-Apr. daily 9am-5pm. 1200Ft. Cash only.)*

STATUE OF SAINT GELLÉRT. Overlooking Pest and Erzsébet Bridge, the statue of St. Gellért was originally commissioned by Emperor Franz Joseph. St. Gellért was a Venetian bishop who was sent to Hungary by the Pope after St. Stephen's coronation to convert the largely pagan peoples there. During the course of his missionary work, he also found time to personally educate St. Emeric, the son of St. Stephen. As a token of their gratitude for Gellért and his work, a group of people took him to the top of the hill and rolled him back down in a spike-lined barrel. The statue is surrounded by lovely marble columns and depicts the saint raising a cross to the sky while an impudent pagan clambers at his feet.

CAVE CHURCH (SZIKLATEMPLOM). Allegedly the abode of a holy, if hermetic, monk, the **Cave Church** was expanded by the Paulite order in the 1920s and 30s from the original cave into the complex you see today. Under the Communist regime, the entire order was arrested and imprisoned and the church was walled up with concrete for nearly 40 years. Today, the church is an active site for tourists and pilgrims. The interior of the church is certainly interesting, but don't expect to be occupied for much more than a short while. While tourists aren't allowed inside the church during services, the music played inside takes on a strange but compelling echo. *(XI, Gellért Hill. Szent Gellért tér tram stop, trams 18,19, 47, 49. From the tram stop, walk toward the hill, you should see the cross that marks the entrance to the church. Open daily 10-11am, noon-5pm, and 6:30-8pm. Shoulders and midriffs should be covered. Free.)*

MARGIT-SZIGET

The earliest records mentioning the large island stuck in the middle of the Danube refer to it as the **Island of the Rabbits** (Nyulak szigete), and indeed it was a popular hunting ground among nobles for many years. Now the island's offerings are a little more universal—you might literally say pedestrian, as no motor vehicles are allowed, except for a single bus line that ferries people from one end to the other. The island provides Budapest's residents with just about every kind of recreational activity available. Walking along the main road, don't be surprised if you have to jump out of the way to avoid a group of intense-looking cyclists. Runners love the 5km running track following the island's perimeter. For those less interested in exerting themselves, the island also has every kind of vehicle rental you could possibly need (and several that are unnecessary under all circumstances). Bicycle rentals are available at the southern end of the island (450Ft per 30min., 650Ft per hr., 1500Ft per day), while two-person "walk bicycles" and electric carts can be found at the northern end (walk bicycles 1680Ft per 30min., 2680Ft per hr.; electric carts 2900/4300Ft). Be advised: these alternative modes of transportation go very poorly with a few drinks from the island's outdoor pubs, which draw crowds of locals and tourists to the southern half of the island on summer nights.

RUINS. Though it may be hard to imagine now, there *was* once a time when the island was used for something besides outdoor drinking. For several centuries, Margaret Island was *the* place to be cloistered in Budapest. The Franciscans were the first on the scene, building their priory in the 13th century only to have it destroyed under the Ottomans in the 16th century. King Béla IV built a convent during the height of the Mongol invasion in the 13th century. At that time, he vowed to send his daughter, Margaret, to the convent if he ever had the chance to rebuild the country after the Mongol assault, though nobody seemed to have consulted Margaret on this arrangement. When the Mongols were finally beaten back, the king made good on his vow, and sent his then 11-year-old daughter to become a nun. While taking orders may not have done much for Margaret's social life, at least it guaranteed her a kind of immortality when the island was renamed after her death. Today, you can still see the ruins of both structures. Princess Margaret is buried on the site of the old nave. Taking the main road from the Margit Bridge entrance, you'll pass the Franciscan priory first, on your left, between the Hajós Alfréd Swimming Pool and the Palatinus Baths. The convent is farther along, on your right near the water tower.

PALATINUS STRANDFÜRDŐ (PALATINUS BATHS). The baths opened in 1921 and immediately became a favorite of the city's residents. Since then, constant improvements and additions have turned the former stretch of beach into a sprawling complex with enormous fountains, waterslides, and jets across three large pools, all fed by the thermal springs underground. The thermal pools are a little less harrowing than their Turkish counterparts, staying at a manageable 36°C to keep the pruning down. On weekends in the summer the pools are packed with local families and children. *(From the Árpád Bridge entrance, take Soó Rezső sétány south; the baths are on your right. ☎ 01 340 4505; www.spasbudapest.com. Open in summer daily 9am-8pm. Admission with lockers weekdays 2100Ft, weekends 2400Ft. On weekdays from 5-8pm, 1200Ft. Cash only.)*

HAJÓS ALFRÉD SPORTUSZODA (HAJÓS ALFRÉD SWIMMING POOL). During the day, hundreds of locals come to play and relax in one of the biggest pools in Hungary, designed by the country's first Olympic medalist. Many lanes are heavily used by water polo and swimming clubs, including the Hungarian national team, especially in the early afternoon. While lanes are always reserved for lappers, the best time to go is early in the morning before 8 or 9am. If you know what good lane etiquette is, you should observe it. If not, you should probably try a different pool. During the winter, the steam rising off the naturally thermally heated water is a sight to see. *(From the Margit Bridge entrance, take the main road and turn left at the 1st road past the athletic complex. ☎ 01 340 4946. Open M-F 6am-4pm, Sa-Su 6am-6pm. Cash desk closes 1hr. before pool. Parking available. Bring your own towel. Caps required in the 25m pool, but not the 50m. Single use 1500Ft. Hair dryers take 20Ft coins. Cash only.)*

ZENÉLŐ SZÖKŐKÚT (MUSIC FOUNTAIN). Built in 1936, the Music Fountain consists of multiple jets of water which are choreographed to music pouring from nearby speakers. Even if you can't make out the music, the sight of the jets pulsing and changing is mesmerizing. A favorite of local park-goers, Music Fountain attracts visitors who love to set up picnics and hookahs in the shaded area nearby. At night, colored lights add a whole other dimension to the show. While the sight of the enormous central jet is certainly impressive, perhaps someone should tell UNESCO that the island's beloved musical fountain is actually just a copy of an older fountain built by a Transylvanian handyman. *(From the Margit Bridge entrance, take the main road north; the fountain is just past the statue.)*

WATER TOWER. Originally built in 1911, this Art Nouveau structure dominates the center of the island. It is currently protected by UNESCO, though this hasn't stopped a beer garden from sprouting around its base. You can pay to go up to the top of the tower, which affords a nice enough view of the rest of the island and both banks of the Danube, but it's prettier from the outside. *(From the Árpád Bridge entrance, take Soó Rezső sétány south and turn left at the road by the tower. ☎01 239 0920. Open daily 10am-5pm. 300Ft, students 200Ft. Cash only.)*

OUTER BUDA

▧MEMENTO PARK (SZOBORPARK). While in the rest of the former Soviet republics people were happily dismantling and demolishing the symbols of their hated regimes, the monument-loving people of Budapest decided it might be worth their while to keep theirs around, even if they didn't want them anywhere near the city itself. Forty of these statues now reside a bus ride away in **Memento Park** (25min.) as a testament to a bygone political and artistic period. At the gates to the park you can see an authentic replica of the infamous Stalin statue that was torn down during the 1956 revolution so that only the dictator's boots remained. The remains of the statue became a symbol of the revolution. Other notable statues include a striking metallic mass of bayonet-wielding soldiers charging past a podium as well as the deranged-looking Soviet soldier that used to stand at the base of the **Liberty Monument,** clutching his Soviet flag and machine-gun. An indoor exhibition shows unnerving clips from old secret police training videos. If you pay attention, you may even learn a thing or two about how to hide secret messages in crushed soda cans. *(XXII, at the corner of Balatoni út and Szabadkai utca. Take express bus #7 from Keleti station. to Etele tér, then take the yellow Volán bus from terminal #7 bound for Diosd-Érd, get off at Memento Park. You'll need to buy a separate ticket from the Volánbusz ticket office. There is also a white direct bus from Deák tér (Ⓜ1, 2, or 3) every day at 11am (and also at 3pm during July and Aug.) for 3950Ft, students 2450Ft; includes price of admission and return ticket. www.mementopark.hu. Open daily 10am-dusk. Wheelchair-accessible. 1500Ft, students 1000Ft. AmEx/MC/V.)*

▧PÁL-VÖLGYI AND MÁTYÁS CAVES. Budapest is famous for its thermal baths, but few people know that the heated water that eats up entire afternoons has also spent hundreds of thousands of years eating through the limestone hills beneath the city. The result: more than 100km of caves directly below many of Budapest's residential areas. The second longest of Hungary's cave systems, the Pál-völgyi and Mátyás Caves offer the unskilled numerous spelunking opportunities. The no-climbing walking tours are informative and interesting without asking you to do anything more stressful than climb a short ladder. These walks descend 30m below the surface, where you'll see many dripstones and even the occasional 40-million-year-old fossil. Many people bring a sweater, though during the hot summer, nothing feels better than descending into the caves, which keep cool at 50°F all year long. Those looking for something a little more challenging should consider taking on **The Sandwich of Death.** *(Bus #86 from Batthyány tér to Kolosy tér; backtrack up the street and take the 1st right to reach the bus station. From there, catch bus #65 to get to the caves. ☎01 325 9505; www.caving.hu. Open Tu-Sa 10am-4pm. Tours every 1hr. Bring a sweater. 1050Ft, students 785. Tours also in Szemlőhegy Cave 1350Ft, students 900Ft. English tours available, call ahead for times. MC/V.)*

AQUINCUM RUINS. Long before the mighty Magyars settled the Carpathian basin, the Roman Empire had a thriving settlement of 40,000 inhabitants. The ruins of this ancient settlement can be seen all over the northern Buda side. The **Military Amphitheater** at the corner of Lajos utca and Pacsirtamező utca in Óbuda is especially awesome. The largest collection of ruins can be found at the **Aquincumi Múzeum,** just north of Budapest proper. The museum itself includes thousands of artifacts from the town, including pottery, bricks, and jewelry. Upstairs, an exhibit recreates parts of the proconsul's palace as well

THE SANDWICH OF DEATH

The descent into the Matyas Caves, situated in the depths of the Buda Hills, is met by overwhelming darkness and absolute silence. The air is so cold—hovering at a chilly 10°C—that you would be able to see your breath as clearly as a bellowing chimney—that is, if you could see.

What brings travelers into the silent depths is the opportunity to partake in caving, the unforgettable experience of snaking through the underground labyrinthine caves. Yet what draws visitors to these particular caves is the "Sandwich of Death," the finale of the journey. Equipped only with a helmet and flashlight, spelunkers venture through the path that descends 220m to sea level and back up again, inching past heart-stopping 40m drops and squeezing through crevices barely large enough to fit your helmet. The climactic sandwich isn't quite as dangerous as it sounds—it's a 12m stomach-crawl through two slabs of limestone.

Caving is not for the claustrophobic. That said, the experience certainly isn't only for the rough-and-ready. Guides judge the skill level of their groups and choose the difficulty of the path accordingly.

Follow directions to the Pál-Völgyi Caves (p. 257). Call ahead (☎28 49 69) to reserve a spot and check tour times. 2100Ft.

as the famed Aquincum organ. Outside, you can explore more than an acre of ruins, including the workshops of various craft guilds. When in the former Roman Empire, do as the former Roman citizens did and spend an afternoon hanging around the former thermal baths. *(Szentendrei út 135. From Batthyány tér, take the HÉV seven stops to Aquincum, then get off and backtrack about ½km; the ruins and museum are on your left. ☎01 250 1650; www.aquincum.hu. Museum open May 1-Oct. 1 10am-6pm; Apr. 16-May 1 and Oct. Tu-Sa 10am-5pm. Park open Apr. 16-Oct 31. 9am-dusk. Wheelchair-accessible. 1300Ft, students 500Ft. Cash only.)*

🏛 MUSEUMS AND GALLERIES

Budapest's museums range from the daring and cutting-edge to the terribly dull. One thing they do all have in common: they're closed on Mondays. The grounds of the Royal Palace contain the **National Gallery** and several other lesser museums. If **Óbuda** has anything besides old people, it's museums, many of them very small and devoted to a specific artist or movement. Alone, they're not that interesting, but combined they might make a decent afternoon. Two of the city's best art museums can be found across from one another at City Park. If you plan on doing a lot of sightseeing, consider picking up a Budapest Card from one of the tourist offices: it will get you free or discounted admission to many of the city's museums and other attractions (2-day card 6300Ft, 3-day 7500Ft).

◪TERROR HÁZA (HOUSE OF TERROR). The only thing that distinguishes this otherwise unassuming building from the others along Budapest's most beautiful boulevard is the museum's name, printed in giant block letters extending into the sky. First used by the Hungarian Arrowcross Party as their headquarters and called the "House of Loyalty," hundreds were beaten and killed in the cellar. After the Communist takeover, the building was transformed into the office of the secret police. Now a striking museum, the House of Terror uses video and audio presentations to tell the story of life under two totalitarian systems that differed in their ideological particulars but that both dehumanized and terrorized their victims. Telephones and radio headsets throughout the building play a mix of radio broadcasts and propaganda from the age of terror. A large tank with a pool of water surrounded by portraits of victims occupies the lobby. Under Communist control, the complex was expanded until the basement became an underground labyrinth of dank cells and torture rooms, many of which have been restored. The cells contain portraits of those once imprisoned in them. *(VI. Andrássy út 60. Ⓜ1: Vörösmarty tér. ☎01 374 2600; www.terrorhaza.hu. Open Tu-F 10am-6pm and Sa-Su 10am-7:30pm. 1500Ft, students 750Ft. Audioguides 1300Ft. AmEx/MC/V.)*

█**IPARMŰVÉSZETI MÚZEUM** (MUSEUM OF APPLIED ARTS). This collection includes exquisite pieces of tableware, furniture, and metalwork as well as a few more exciting oddities, ranging from Tiffany glass to an astronomical clock that once belonged to Emperor Maximilian II. The display case of unusually elaborate keys is one of the best among the medley of trinkets. Excellent temporary exhibits highlight specific crafts, from architecture to Oriental rugs and clocks. Built for the 1896 millennium, the Art Nouveau edifice, patriotically entitled "To the East, Hungarian!" ("Keletre magyar!"), is perhaps the most lovingly crafted piece of all. *(IX. Üllői út 33-37. Ⓜ3: Ferenc körút ☎01 456 5100; www.imm.hu. Open W and F-Su 10am-6pm, Th 10am-10pm, Tu 2-6pm. Open house Th 6-10pm. Permanent collection 1000Ft, students 500Ft. Combined ticket 2500/1250Ft. Cash only. Group tours available.)*

LUDVIG MÚZEUM (LUDWIG MUSEUM). Located on the outskirts of the city in the hypermodern Palace of the Arts, the Ludwig Museum ("LuMú") fills its three floors of gallery space with at least two rotating exhibitions in addition to its permanent collection. The collection focuses largely on 20th- and 21st-century Hungarian painting and sculpture, though international masters like Picasso make cameo appearances. The museum also dedicates a significant amount of space to American pop art, with contributions from Andy Warhol, Robert Rauschenberg, Jasper Johns, Roy Lichtenstein, and others. *(Komor Marcell utca 1. Take tram #4 or 6 to Boráros tér, then take the HÉV commuter rail 1 stop to Lágymányosi híd. ☎01 555 3444; www.ludwigmuseum.hu. Open Tu-Su 10am-8pm. Free last Su of the month to visitors under 26. Permanent collection 700Ft. Combined ticket for all exhibitions 1300Ft. MC/V.)*

MAGYAR NEMZETI GALÉRIA (HUNGARIAN NATIONAL GALLERY). The halls of Buda Castle now house the world's largest collection of Hungarian fine arts. Spread across three floors and divided by historical period, the permanent collection traces the development of Hungarian painting and sculpture from the Gothic period to the second half of the 20th century. The collections of painters like **Gyárfás Jenő** and **Károly Lotz** are some of the museum's best, though it's the sculptures that frequently steal the show. In the 20th-century galleries, look for pieces by the impressionist Béla Czóbel. The basement of the museum contains the crypt of the Hapsburg palantines, though admission can only be obtained through prior arrangement with a guide. *(Buda Palace, wings A, B, C, and D. ☎01 356 0049; www.mng.hu. Open Tu-Su 10am-6pm. Last entry 30min before closing. Wheelchair accessible. Admission 900Ft, Hapsburg crypt 600Ft. MC/V.)*

SZÉPMŰVÉSZETI MÚZEUM (MUSEUM OF FINE ARTS). Built to look like a worn temple from antiquity, this building's exterior is as much a work of art as the collections it houses. The museum's main focus is a large collection of Italian and Renaissance pieces. Many of Europe's artistic luminaries can be found here, running the gamut from Giotto and Bruegel to Monet and Rodin. An excellent collection of Dutch work appears on the top floor. The basement juxtaposes the modern art collection with an awe-inspiring Egyptian collection focusing on all things mummified. Some of the striking pieces include mummified hawks, cats, and alligators. One of museum's prized pieces, a magic wand that looks something like a boomerang, was once used to protect children and expectant mothers from harm. *(Ⓜ1: Hősök tere. From the metro, walk toward Heroes' Sq.; the museum is on the left. ☎01 469 7100; www.szepmuveszeti.hu. Open Tu-Su 10am-6pm. Ticket booth open Tu-Su 10am-5pm. Wheelchair-accessible. 1400Ft, students 700Ft. AmEx/MC/V.)*

GIVING BACK

HABITAT FOR HUNGARY

Habitat Global Villagers, a branch of Habitat for Humanity, leads volunteers on brief trips to various, less-touristed Hungarian regions. Travelers spend anywhere from 10-20 days in a host village, constructing houses for low-income families and immersing themselves in the local culture. In 2008, HGV organized two volunteer excursions to the village of Szarvas, about 120 miles southeast of Budapest, to build homes for struggling residents.

No previous construction experience is required; HGV group leaders ask only that you bring your enthusiasm. In addition to volunteering, participants are also scheduled for several days of sightseeing time to explore Budapest. Costs vary depending upon the length of the volunteer project, and all prices include lodging, food, ground transportation, travel medical insurance, orientation materials, and a small donation to the local village.

All projects led by experienced Habitat for Humanity group leaders. The website, www.habitat.hu, has updated information about upcoming volunteer trips. For more information, interested parties can contact the host office in Budapest at Podmaniczky u. 91 (☎354 1084; habitat@habitat. hu). 2008 prices ranged from $1,500-$2,000, plus the cost of round-trip airfare to Budapest.

MŰCSARNOK (ART HALL). The Art Hall attempts to challenge aesthetic conventions with its temporary exhibitions. Designed primarily for young people and students, the museum attempts to engage viewers with an array of contemporary paintings, photographs, sculptures, and installations. Interactive and multimedia pieces are some of the museum's trademarks. Depending on your sensibilities, it could be the best or worst time you've ever had in an art museum. (Ⓜ1: Hősök tere. From the metro, walk toward Heroes' Sq.; the museum is on the right, directly across Heroes' Sq. ☎01 460 7000; www.mucsarnok.hu. Open Tu-W and F-Su 10am-6pm, Th noon-8pm. Last entry 30min. before closing. 1200Ft, students 600Ft. AmEx/MC/V.)

HOLOCAUST MEMORIAL CENTER. This museum gives a powerful account of Hungary's involvement in the Holocaust by examining the tragedy not chronologically, but by the increasingly brutal methods of dehumanization that were inflicted on the Nazis' victims. The exhibit begins with the deprivation of rights and ends with the state of stripping away even the individual's sense of dignity. Audiovisual aids supplement personal artifacts. The most striking moment is emerging from the exhibit into a former synagogue, restored to its pre-war appearance but left hauntingly empty. (IX, Páva utca 39. Ⓜ3: Ferenc körút. From the metro, take Üllői út east and then turn right on Páva utca. ☎01 455 3333; www. hdke.hu. Open Tu-Su 10am-6pm. Free.)

NEMZETI MÚZEUM (NATIONAL MUSEUM). This Neoclassical landmark proves that museums can be just as much a part of history as the collections they house. During the revolution of 1848, Sándor Petőfi read his famous *Twelve Points* from the museum's steps, helping to cement its place as a symbol of Hungarian national identity. The ground floor houses an exhibit on the history of the area from Neolithic times until the arrival of the Magyar tribes. The area around the main staircase is lavishly decorated with murals depicting scenes from Hungarian history. The second floor (first floor to Europeans) contains the majority of the permanent exhibition, which traces the history of the Hungarian state from its formation through the end of the 20th century, mostly with English captions. Boys with short attention spans will appreciate the sheer number of swords, guns, and suits of armor. The cinema, which shows vintage newsreels from the 1930s and 40s, is great even if you can't understand much. (Múzeum körút. 14/16. Ⓜ3: Kálvin tér. ☎204 397 325; www. mng.hu. Open Tu-Su 10am-6pm. Last entry 30min before closing. 1040Ft, students 520Ft. MC/V.)

GYÖRGY RATH MUSEUM. Situated near Andrássy út, in the former villa of the first director of the **Museum of Applied Arts** (p. 259), this collection of art is one Hungary's best. Some of the treasures include exquisite bronze and gilded brass figures of Hindu bodhisattvas as well as a recreation of a 19th-century Chinese reception room. The surrounding grounds include the beautiful Moon Gate as well as other pieces of sculpture and gardening. Unfortunately, much of the historic grounds and the collections inside were destroyed during WWII and reconstruction is only partially complete. *(VI. Varosligeti fasor 12. ⓜ1: Kodály körönd. From the metro, take Felso Erdosor utca east and then turn left on Varosligeti fasor. ☎01 342 3912; www.hoppmuzeum.hu. Open Tu-Su 10am-6pm. 600Ft, students 300Ft. AmEx/MC/V.)*

PETŐFI IRODALMI MÚZEUM (MUSEUM OF LITERATURE PETŐFI). Located in the **Károlyi Palace,** a lovely Neoclassical palace once home to one of Pest's most important aristocratic families, the museum's relatively small permanent collection is dedicated to the life and work of the poet and revolutionary **Sándor Petőfi.** The museum's permanent and temporary exhibits examine Petőfi and other Hungarian literary giants by placing them in the context of related artistic movements in painting, sculpture, photography, and music. Unfortunately, everything's in Hungarian, though English audioguides are available for the permanent collection. *(Károlyi Mihály utca 16. ⓜ3: Ferenciek tér. ☎01 473 2441; www.pim. hu. Open Tu-Su 10am-6pm. 480Ft. English audio guide 980Ft. Cash only.)*

HISTORICAL MUSEUM OF BUDAPEST. Situated in the southernmost wing of the palace, the museum traces the rise of Buda and Pest from the prehistoric settlements though the unification and emergence as a modern European capital. Exhibits trace the history of the Romans in Budapest and the influence of the Ottomans on the city and its culture. It may not be the most exciting museum you've ever visited, though there are a few gems, such as the massive, gold-plated guestbook from the 1896 millennial celebration. Those who just can't get enough Hungarian sculpture should check out the ground floor, which contains a large collection from the medieval and Gothic periods. *(Buda Palace, wing E. ☎01 487 8800; www.btm.hu. Open Tu-Sa 10am-8pm. Last entry 30min. before closing. Wheelchair-accessible. 1300Ft, students 650Ft. MC/V.)*

VASARELY MÚZEUM. A museum dedicated almost entirely to **Victor Vasarely,** the French-Hungarian Op Art pioneer. Spread across two floors, the museum traces Vasarely's work chronologically, starting with his art school sketches and proceeding to his dabbling in abstract expressionism. The final highlight is Vasarely's fascination with geometric forms and optical illusions, which anticipated the rise of Op Art and computer generated art by decades. A rotating gallery of contemporary art confirms Vasarely's continued relevance. *(III, Szentlélek tér 6. From the tram stop, take the stairs down and head north toward Szentlélek tér; the entrance to the museum is behind the semicircle where the buses park. ☎01 388 7551; www.vasarely.tvn. hu. Open Tu-Su 10am-5:30pm. 800Ft, students 400Ft. Cash only.)*

NÉPRAJZI MÚZEUM (ETHNOGRAPHIC MUSEUM). This former home of the Ministry of Justice now houses a museum dedicated to Hungary's folk heritage. The permanent collection contains thousands of artifacts, mostly from the 19th century, covering every aspect of Hungarian life, from the home to the farm and from the cradle to the grave. The colorful and richly decorated costumes that line almost every room are easily the main draw. The other parts of the museum house temporary, occasionally politically incorrect exhibits about various non-Hungarian cultures. *(Kossuth L. tér 12. ⓜ2: Kossuth tér. Across the street from Parliament. ☎01 473 2441; www.neprajz.hu. Wheelchair-accessible. Open Tu-Su 10am-6pm. 800Ft, students 400Ft. Cash only.)*

KASSÁK MÚZEUM. A very small and very experimental art museum in the center of the otherwise unremarkable Óbuda. The museum might make for a nice post-lunch walk, but don't expect it to provide hours of distraction. (*III, Fő tér 1. Árpád híd (Szentlélek tér) tram stop. From the tram stop, take the stairs down and head north into Fő tér; the museum is through the arcade and straight ahead. ☎ 01 368 7021. Open W-Su 10am-5pm. 300Ft, students 150Ft.*)

MUSEUM OF MILITARY HISTORY. Located in the former municipal army barracks, the Museum of Military History may not be the most creative or best-organized museum, though it does contain a large share of artifacts from every stage of Hungarian military history. The hallways and stairwells are lined with propaganda posters spanning multiple conflicts and historical periods. WWI hogs the lion's share of exhibition space, with models of trenches and cannons. In addition to the standard collection of guns and swords, personal artifacts such as prosthetic limbs and letters written from POW camps attempt to show the less Romantic side of war. (*I, Tóth Árpád sétány 40. ☎ 01 356 9522; www.militaria.hu. Open Tu-Su 10am-6pm. 700Ft, students 350Ft. Cash only.*)

🎵 ENTERTAINMENT

Pesti Est, Budapest Program, Budapest Panorama, and *Budapest in Your Pocket* are the best English-language entertainment guides; pick them up at tourist offices, hotels, and many restaurants and bars. The Style section of the *Budapest Sun* (www.budapestsun.com; 300Ft) has film reviews and a 10-day calendar. The often entertaining and occasionally ascerbic *Pestiside* (Pestiside.hu) covers nightlife and cultural events. For event tickets, check **Ticket Express Hungary,** Andrássy út 18 (☎01 303 0999; www.tex.hu; open M-F 10am-6:30pm) or **Jegymester** (www.jegymester.hu). The box office at the **Palace of Arts** (☎01 555 3001; www.mupa.hu; open M-F 1pm-6pm, Sa-Su 10am-6pm) has tickets for many of the city's venues. Most of the city's major theaters are closed from July to September.

▪ **State Opera House** (Magyar Állami Operaház), VI, Andrássy út 22 (☎01 353 0170; www.opera.hu). Ⓜ1: Opera. One of Europe's grandest opera houses is a must-see for classical music lovers. The building is gorgeous. (Yeah? Because classical music lovers will love the music; building-enthusiasts will love the building.) Hosts some of the continent's finest operas, ballets, and classical performances. While some tickets sell out a year in advance, rush tickets at a fraction of the normal price are sometimes available 1hr. before the performance. Tickets 1000-9000Ft. Wheelchair-accessible. Box office open M-Sa 11am-7pm, Su 4-7pm. Closes at 5pm on non-performance days. Call for show schedules, or check the poster at the gates. AmEx/MC/V.

▪ **National Theatre** (Nemzeti Színház), IX, Bajor Gizi park 1 (☎01 476 6868; www.nemzetiszinhaz.hu). Millenniumi Kulturális Központ tram stop; trams 2, 24. The new home of Budapest's National Theatre is an architectural marvel, surrounded by sculptures and a partially submerged facade that serves as a memorial to the old National Theatre, which was blown up in order to expand the subway. The venue offers the best of Hungarian theater as well as works by Shakespeare and Shaw. Tickets 1200-4000Ft. Wheelchair-accessible. Box office open M-F 10am-6pm, Sa-Su 2-6pm. AmEx/MC/V.

National Concert Hall at the Palace of Arts (Művészetek Palotája), IX, Komor Marcell utca 1 (☎01 555 3001; www.mupa.hu). Millenniumi Kulturális Központ tram stop; trams 2,24. Located in the same massive arts complex as the Ludwig Museum, the National Concert Hall is one of Hungary's best venues. Performances range from opera and classical to contemporary jazz and world music. Standing room student tickets (200Ft) are available 1hr. before all performances. Tickets 3900-9300Ft. Wheelchair-accessible. Box office open M-F 1-6pm, Sa-Su 10am-6pm, on performance nights open until end of the final event. AmEx/MC/V.

The Comedy Theater (Vígszínház XIII), Szent István körút 14 (☎01 329 2340; www.pestiszinhaz.hu). Ⓜ3: Nyugati pályaudvar. Located near the Danube on the Grand Boulevard, the Vígszínház is one of Budapest's most ornate theaters, built as one of the "new-standard theaters" that sprung up across Central Europe at the end of the 19th century. As its name suggests, the theater specializes in comedy of all varieties, from Shakespearean classics to modern musicals. Tickets 1500Ft-4800Ft. Box office open daily 11am-7pm. MC/V.

National Dance Theatre (Nemzetí Táncszínház), I, Színház utca 1-3 (☎01 201 4407; www.dancetheatre.hu). On Castle Hill, just north of the royal palace. The only 18th-century theater building in Hungary that's still a theater has been home to many key events in Hungarian cultural history. The first Hungarian-language play was performed here in 1790, and many of classical music's luminaries, including Beethoven, played here. Today the theater is home to Budapest's dance performances, which encompasses ballet, modern dance, and folk. Tickets 2500Ft. Box office open M-Th 10am-6pm, F 10am-5pm. AmEx/MC/V.

🅺 NIGHTLIFE

In Budapest, many consider their evening to have been dull if they make it home before sunrise. Most pubs and bars are busy until 4am at least and more club-like venues are often alive past 5am. The party may be raging inside, but the streets are almost always quiet and eerily empty. This is because the city maintains very strict noise laws that can spell death for any club that gets more than the occasional complaint from neighbors. Most clubs, especially the elusive **ruin pubs,** employ bouncers to stand outside mostly for the purpose of keeping the noise to a minimum. In the case of the ruin pubs, these bouncers are often the best way to find the place. The city's most happening districts for young people are almost always **Erzsébetváros** and **Terézváros.** Here you can find (with some patience and a sharp eye or ear) most of the city's better-known ruin pubs like **Szimpla Kert** and **Kuplung.** Many of these clubs pull double- or triple-duty as music clubs or concert venues, bringing in DJs or live acts several times a week. The upscale cafes near **Ferencz Liszt tér** (Ⓜ2: Oktogon) attract the city's hippest 20- and 30-somethings. The Pest shore of the Danube around **Belgrád rakpart** contains many fancy tourist and hotel bars.

DRINK, DON'T CLINK

Woe be to any unknowing backpackers who celebrate their first night in Budapest by clinking their beer glasses together.

Inspired by the revolutions sweeping Europe, a group of Hungarian generals rose up against the Hapsburgs in the name of liberty and democracy. Russia and Austria, no fans of the minorities living within the borders of their empires, teamed up to crush the rebellion.

The ostentatiously named Austrian general, Julius Freiherr von Haynau, ordered the execution of the 13 Hungarian generals. As the story goes, the Austrian generals toasted Hungary's defeat at the execution by cheering and loudly clinking their beer glasses together.

In memory of the "13 Martyrs of Arad" and the ideals they stood for, the Hungarian people vowed not to clink their beer glasses for 150 years. Most Hungarians, especially older ones, don't seem to care that the moratorium expired more than 10 years ago.

So when you're out with those new Hungarian friends you made at the hostel, think twice before thrusting your beer glass toward your companions—you may be toasting something else entirely.

If there's one thing Hungarians love more than drinking late, it's drinking late *outside*. In late spring, you'll often hear expats asking one another when the **kerts** are supposed to open. These outdoor venues, Hungarian for "garden" are some of the city's most popular nighttime destinations during the summer. **Margaret Island** is home to several of the most popular for students and backpackers, while slightly fancier establishments can be found in Buda near the **Petőfi Bridge.**

NIGHTLIFE SCAM. The US Embassy advises against patronizing certain establishments around **Váci utca** and **Saint Stephen's Basilica.** In one common iteration of the scam, foreign men walking around the area will be stopped by two women who claim to need directions or a lighter. After a brief exchange, the women will ask the victim if he would like to accompany them to a famous bar or club. The menus typically don't list prices, but when the bill arrives, accompanied by imposing thugs, the price of each drink turns out to be astronomical. If the victim claims to have no cash, he will be directed to an ATM in the bar. Always check prices before ordering at unfamiliar places, and try to keep cash and credit cards concealed. For a current list of establishments with numerous complaints on record, visit the US embassy website at hungary.usembassy.gov/tourist_advisory.html. If you believe you have been the victim of a scam, call the police. Budapest maintains a special **tourist police service** with English language operators at ☎01 438 8080. Keep your receipts and complain formally at the Consumer Bureau.

Unlike it's pilsner-swigging neighbors, Hungary has never really been a beer country. You can certainly find decent beer on tap anywhere, but to experience nightlife like a real Hungarian, you're going to need to find an appreciation for *bor* (wine), the traditional everyman drink in these parts. Hungary has been producing quality wine at least since Roman times and today has more than a half-dozen world-class wine growing regions, including the famous **Tokaj** region, which is so dear to Hungarians that they mention it in their national anthem. At many restaurants and bars, a decent glass of red wine will often be cheaper than beer or water. Even red wine is usually served chilled here. A popular if occasionally reviled drink that originated as a cheap way for teenagers to budget alcohol is red wine mixed with Coke, called **"Vörösboros Kola,"** or more commonly **"VBK."** Every visitor should try it at least once, even if the bartender gives you a slightly confused look when you try to order it in English. Hungary also produces a unique variety of double-distilled fruit brandy called **pálinka,** most commonly made from plums, apricots, or pears. When raising a glass of *pálinka*, be sure to say *"Egészségedre!"* (literally "cheers to your health!") and *never* clink your glass. Few things will at best annoy or at worst offend your newfound Hungarian friends quite like the clinking of beer glasses. To Hungarians, this calls to mind the crushing defeat of nationalists at the hands of Hapsburg monarchists, who gleefully toasted the impending execution of the revolutionary leaders with excessive glass clinking.

With so much going on you'll probably want to pick up a guide to help navigate the city's nightlife. The Budapest *FUNZINE* and *Pesti Est* are the most reliable guides to everything loud, funky, and cheap in the area. Both guides are free and can be picked up at any bar. GLBT visitors should check out *Na Végre!* ("About time!"), a free gay guide to the city's nightlife, available at any gay bar in an English edition.

BELVÁROS

▣ **Gödör Klub,** V, Erzsébet tér, (☎01 201 3868; www.godorklub.hu). Ⓜ1,2, or 3: Deák tér. What was once Budapest's biggest embarassment is now one of its most popular hangouts. The conspicuously bare concrete walls give you the sense that the club, situated in the former foundation of what was supposed to be the new National Concert Hall, is still unfinished. On the weekends you can hardly move in the crowded concert area, where rock, jazz, world, techno, or folk music envelop the audience. Once you're ready to settle down, try to grab one of the tables on the long staircase that leads to the basement area, or take a spot on one of the benches or retaining walls. During the week the cultural center maintains an extensive activities calendar, which includes pilates classes. Beer from 350Ft. Shots 200-800Ft. Open M-Th and Su 10am-2am, F-Sa 10am-4am. Cash only.

Csendes, V, Ferenczy István utca 5 (www.kiscsendes.hu). Ⓜ2: Astoria. From the metro, take Múzeum körút toward the National Museum and then turn right on Ferenczy István utca; the bar will be on your left. A favorite of local artists and intellectuals right across the street from the university. The aesthetic, if you can call it that, seems to be that of a deranged child's bedroom. The walls are drawn on and covered with picture frames, mannequins, and a bicycle. From the ceiling you can find a ½-dozen kinds of chandeliers and a precariously secured TV. Kudos to you if you can find a matching set of chairs and table. Beer from 250Ft. Shots 275-790Ft. Mixed drinks 880-1150Ft. MC/V.

Fregatt, V, Molnár utca 26 (☎01 318 9997). Ⓜ3: Kálvin tér. From the metro, take Vámház toward the river, turn right on Váci, left on Havas, and then right on Molnár. One of the 1st pubs to open in Budapest in the 1980s, Fregatt was once among the best places to drink in town. The crowds have thinned over the years, however, and what was once a lively, raucous British-style pub is now a much more subdued place to knock back a few beers or shoot some pool. The interior is decorated like an old Man o' War, complete with a mermaid figurehead on the corner of the bar. Beer from 300Ft. Open M-F 4pm-1am, Sa 5pm-1am. Cash only.

Capella Cafe, V, Belgrád rakpart 23 (☎70 328 6775; www.capellacafe.hu). Trams 2, 2a, Március 15 tér. Budapest's first gay discotheque can often draw a crowd to its 3 levels even midweek. Downstairs, themed dance rooms, each with varying music to satisfy most musical tastes, though it's the regular drag shows that keep the place packed. The upstairs is a laid-back bar with balcony seating so you can watch the action downstairs while staying out of the fray. Attracts a mix of gay, lesbian, and straight patrons. Beer 600Ft. Wine 600Ft. Shots 900Ft. Mixed drinks 1300Ft. Cover W-Sa usually 1000Ft. Open daily M-Sa 10am-5am. Cash only.

LIPÓTVÁROS

Beckett's Irish Pub, V, Bajcsy-Zsilinszky út 72 (☎311 1035; www.becketts.hu). Ⓜ3: Nyugati. From the metro, walk south; the pub will be on your right. The only Irish pub in Budapest that is owned and operated by an actual Irishman. Draws a healthy mix of locals, expats, and a few tourists with its traditional Irish grub and open atmosphere. The beef and Guinness pie (2550Ft) fills you up so you can hold your liquor. 8 plasma TVs show the latest World Cup or American sports action. The fall and winter bring live music in the form of Oasis cover bands. Salads 900-1900Ft. Sandwiches 950-1950Ft. Beer from 650Ft. Shots from 450Ft. 10% discount with student ID. Wheelchair-accessible. Open M-Th and Su noon-midnight, F-Sa noon-2am. Kitchen open until midnight. AmEx/D/MC/V.

Le Cafe M, V, Nagysándor József utca 3 (☎ 01 312 1436; www.lecafem.com). Ⓜ3: Arany János utca. From the metro, take Bajcsy-Zsilinszky út north and then turn left on Nagysándor József utca. Stylish and small gay bar in the heart of the 5th district that caters to a crowd looking for a slightly more demure evening. A healthy mix of locals and tourists share drinks and subdued conversation surrounded by brick walls, leather booths, and atmospheric lighting. Though anyone is welcome, the bar is frequented almost exclusively by gay men. Beer from 450Ft. Shots 300-850Ft. Mixed drinks 990-1990Ft. Open M-F 4pm-4am, Sa-Su 6pm-4am. MC/V.

Cafe Negro, V , Szent István tér 11 (☎302 0136). Ⓜ1: Bajcsy-Zsilinszky út. From the metro, take József Attila west, turn right on Sas, and then right into the courtyard. This bar and lounge holds itself in high esteem, as evidenced by the sleek black interior and reflective silver behind the bar. During the day, tourists and people who wear sunglasses indoors enjoy overpriced mojitos (1500Ft). Regular DJs play the latest club and dance hits. Mixed drinks 1500-2000Ft. Wheelchair-accessible. Open daily 11am-4am. Cash only.

ERZSÉBETVÁROS

🔲 **Szimpla Kert,** VII, Kazinczy utca 14 (☎01 352 4198 ; www.szimpla.hu). Ⓜ2: Astoria. From the metro, take Rákóczi út east and then turn left on Kazinczy. Budapest's original and perhaps best-loved ruin pub is also one of the largest, sporting 5 bars scattered across 2 floors. Most people prefer to relax in the open-air courtyard where old bathtubs and sedans have been turned into choice seating. Strange self-distributed films play on massive projection screens throughout the interior. When you want to escape to someplace more solitary, you can duck away into any of a number of bizarrely decorated rooms where the cream of the city's artists, hipsters, expats, and students are likely to be lounging until the wee hours. Sip one of the bar's 16 varieties of *pálinka* (900Ft). Beer from 350Ft. Shots 600-800Ft. Mixed drinks 1400-2000Ft. Wheelchair-accessible. Open daily noon-3am. Cash only.

🔲 **Mumus,** VII, Dob utca 18. Ⓜ2: Astoria. From the metro, take Károly körút north and then turn right onto Dob utca. What Mumus lacks in contact info and conspicuous signage it makes up for in atmosphere. Unlike many of the area's ruin pubs, which have expanded and are now competing with one another for "Most Nonsensical Decor," Mumus remains a very simple, personal bar for those who like to go off the grid of Budapest nightlife. You won't find loud music or dancing, but you will find laid-back students, artists, and backpackers relaxing at tables made from old oil drums while enjoying some of the cheapest drinks in town. Beer from 250Ft. Shots 250-450Ft. Wine from 200Ft. Open M-Sa 3pm-3am, Su 4pm-midnight. Cash only.

Vittula, VII, Kertész utca 4 (☎20 527 7069; www.vittula.hu). Ⓜ2: Blaha Lujza tér. From the metro, take Erzsébet körút north, turn left after 1 block, and then make an immediate right onto Kertész. Small, friendly neighborhood bar in a brick cellar decorated with a mix of graffiti and Asian-influenced murals. Low drink prices, an unpretentious atmosphere, and an unabashed hatred of Coldplay. Occasional DJs bring some noise to the lower level. Not the most bumpin' place in the 7th district, but a good retreat when the throngs overwhelm. Beer from 340Ft. Shots 430-600Ft. Open M-Sa 6pm-late. Cash only.

Ellató, Klauzal tér 1-2. Ⓜ2: Blaha Lujza tér. From the metro, take Rákóczi west and then turn right on Nagy Diófa utca, which takes you right to the sq.; the bar is on the right. A brick bar that masquerades as a restaurant during the day and attracts a more cosmopolitan clientele than many area nightspots. Expect to find intellectuals discussing political philosophy over drinks and lots and lots of cigarettes. Popular dishes include the *strapachka* noodles with sheep curd cheese, bacon, and sour cream (1120Ft). Soups 550-850Ft. Salads 400-900Ft. Entrees 1100-1320Ft. Beer from 210Ft. Shots 290-520Ft. Open M-Sa 2pm-2am, Su 4pm-midnight. Cash only.

Szoda, VII, Wesselényi utca 18 (☎70 389 6463; www.szoda.com). Ⓜ2: Astoria. From the metro, take Rákóczi east, and then turn left on Kazinczy; the bar is near the corner of Kazinczy and Wesselényi. Once one of the 7th district's most popular nightspots, Szoda now cultivates a more low-key, lounge-like atmosphere than the more standard pubs nearby. Bathed in red light, with the ceiling covered in life-sized manga comics, the place could never be accused of having a "derivative aesthetic." Unfortunately, it's often empty even on the weekends, despite the efforts of occasional DJs downstairs. Beer 300Ft. Shots 350-600Ft. Open M-F 9am-5am, Sa-Su 2pm-5am. Cash only.

Minyon Bar and Cafe, VII, Király körút 8 (☎01 878 2016). Ⓜ1, 2, or 3: Deák Ferenc tér. From the metro, take Király north; the restaurant is on the left. One of Budapest's more happening lounge-cafes. Large, comfortable chairs and a spacious interior make for relaxed eating and drinking (but mostly drinking). By day, the city's 20-30-something professionals enjoy expensive specialties like pressed guinea fowl with roasted apple (3300Ft). By night, those same businessmen loosen their ties as nightly DJs play a distinctly chill mix of lounge and jazz music from 6pm-10pm before switching to more dance oriented club hits. Appetizers 950-2400Ft. Entrees 2400-3600Ft. Beer from 360Ft. Shots 820-1600Ft. Wheelchair-accessible. Open M-Tu and Su noon-midnight, W-Sa noon-4am. MC/V.

TERÉZVÁROS

🔲 **Pótkulcs,** VI, Csengery utca 65/b (☎01 269 1050; www.potkulcs.hu). Ⓜ1: Vörösmarty utca. From the metro, take Vörösmarty toward the train station and turn left at Szondi; the bar is on the corner of Csengery and Szondi. One of Budapest's most difficult-to-find ruin pubs, but well worth the effort. The terrace is full of greenery and surrounded by the old brick of a former apartment building. Every Tu a Hungarian folk band inspires spontaneous dancing in the main room. Don't be surprised if you have to move because people have started to use your table as a dance floor. The expansive, inexpensive drink list (which includes honey *pálinka*) gives you ample reason to stick around. Beer from 450Ft. Wine from 190Ft. Shots from 500Ft. Live folk, rock, or gypsy music most nights. Terrace wheelchair-accessible. Open daily 5pm-2am at least. Cash only.

Tűzraktér, VI, Hegedű utca 3 (www.tuzrakter.hu). Ⓜ1: Oktogon. From the metro, take Teréz körút south 2 blocks, turn left on Király, and then right on Hegedű. A 3-story high mural of a girl riding a bicycle greets you at the entrance to this cultural center situated in an old high school; Tűzraktér also happens to be one of the best pubs around. If you get there during business hours, take a look around the galleries, where artists freely exhibit their work. At night, occasional house and techno DJs bid the lounging clientele to dance with varying degrees of success. Beer from 230Ft. Shots 280-800Ft. Bar open daily 3pm-2am. Cash only.

Instant, VI, Nagymező utca 38 (www.instant.co.hu). Ⓜ1: Opera. From the metro, take Andrássy toward Oktogon and turn left on Nagymező. Prime example of a ruin pub gone legit. Most of the charm of a stony, vine-covered

A CITY IN RUINS

So you've met up with a few locals who tell you that they know a great place to go for an evening in Budapest.

You follow them down some of the seventh district's worst-lit alleyways to a graffiti-covered building that doesn't look like it's been happening since boy bands were popular. Your guides open a door with no signage and beckon for you to follow.

After passing through a long hall you find yourself in a colorful courtyard, filled with young people seated around picnic tables. To one side, a DJ plays music from the rusted chassis of an old Trabi.

You've just been initiated into the underground world of Budapest nightlife.

These bars (called *romkocsma* in Hungarian, literally "ruin pub") began appearing in the late 1990s, when a group of enterprising friends set up an unlicensed bar for their friends in the courtyard of one of the area's many abandoned buildings.

The original plan was for the bar to remain open only until the condemned building was demolished. However, the place became so popular that the owners got a license and became **Szimpla,** Budapest's original ruin pub.

Since then, the ruin pub has blossomed into a Budapest institution. Their crowds are generally a mix of students, artists, and expats who are attracted to the unique atmosphere and cheap drinks.

Their decor is almost always a sort of ruined chic--the more dissonant and distressed your furniture, the better. Many of the old stone and brick walls are covered in graffiti or elaborate murals.

While some of the bigger and better known places like Szimpla or Kuplung are now legitimate businesses with licenses and permanent locations, many of the area's bars still operate on the old model, closing when their building is torn down and re-opening wherever their owners can find a place.

These places can be frustrating for travelers to find: they open and close without notice, and they've no signage to speak of. All you can hear from the outside is the muffled roar of chatter inside. There may also be a bouncer outside to help keep the noise off the street: nothing will shut a ruin pub down more quickly than noise complaints from the neighbors.

If you're lucky enough to find one of these places, you'll be treated to an experience that most of Budapest's visitors never get to see.

courtyard, but with a roof to keep the party going no matter the weather. In addition to the main level, 2 fl. above and a basement below provide a dozen or more small rooms to retreat to if you want a more private experience and aren't afraid of getting lost. Attracts a slightly older, more unassuming crowd than some of the other bars in the area. Beer from 270Ft. Wheelchair-accessible. Open daily 6pm-2am. Cash only.

Take Five Jazz Club, VI, Paulay Ede utca 2 (☎30 986 8856; www.take5.hu). Ⓜ1: Bajcsy-Zsilinszky út. From the metro, take Bajcsy-Zsilinszky út south; the club is at the corner with Paulay Ede. In only a few years, this club has established itself as Budapest's premier jazz venue, bringing renowned national and international acts to a long, narrow brick cellar. Expect artists, intellectuals, and people who wear a lot of black to appear more into the music than you find necessary. Come early if you want to get a good seat close to the stage. Also expect the drinks to be more expensive than elsewhere, though you didn't come to the jazz club to get plastered, did you? Beer from 450Ft. 1000Ft cover. Open W-Sa 6pm-2am, music starts at 9pm. Cash only.

Kuplung, VI, Király körút 46 (☎30 636 8208; www.kuplung.net). Ⓜ1: Opera. From the metro, take Hajos away from the opera house and continue on Vasvári Pál utca after Hajos ends. Turn left on Király; the club will be on your right. A ruin pub in 2 acts. 1st act: a large courtyard with graffiti, greenery, and a fountain, where various young and friendly people chat amiably into the night. 2nd act: through a small door a large, forbidding warehouse, where DJs spin from the chassis of an old car while the skeleton of a large sea beast hangs menacingly from the ceiling. Unfortunately, the club may have more space than it knows what to do with, as one part is often completely empty even on weekends. Beer from 300Ft. Shots 350-800Ft. Wheelchair-accessible. Open daily 2pm-4am. Cash only.

Piaf, VI, Nagymező utca 25 (☎01 312 3823). Ⓜ1: Opera. From the metro, take Andrássy toward Oktogon and then turn left on Nagymező. Named for the French singer, this popular destination might as well be called "Jekyll and Hyde." The upper level cultivates a trashy-chic feel with red velvet to spare. Here the more sophisticated half of the clientele cavorts over fancy mixed drinks while a resident piano player keeps the jazz coming. Downstairs, however, a cross-section of Budapest's alternative scene drifts onto the dance floor. Cover 800Ft; includes 1 beer. Beer from 350Ft. Shots 600-1200Ft. Open daily 10pm-6am. Cash only.

JÓZSEFVÁROS AND FERENCVÁROS

Corvintető, VIII, Blaha Lujza tér 1-2 (☎772 2984; www.corvinteto.hu). Ⓜ2: Blaha Lujza tér. From the metro, walk toward the Corvin building; the entrance to the club is along Somogyi Béla út, up the stairs. Don't be misled by the graffiti-covered tile stairs—this club situated on top of a former state-owned department store is one of the most stylish places to party in Budapest. Regular DJs and live acts are a popular draw in the red-lit and vaguely Japanese-themed lounge area, though the coolest place is undoubtedly on the roof, where Budapest's youth spend summer nights above the city and beneath the stars. If you play your cards right, the backdrop could make for the most romantic drunken hookup to be had in Budapest. Beer from 320Ft. Shots 600-900Ft. Open daily 6pm-5am. Cash only.

Könyvtár (The Library), VIII, Múzeum krt 4 (☎509 0189; www.konyvtarklub.hu). Ⓜ2: Astoria. From the metro, walk toward the university; the club is through the gate and down the stairs to the left. A favorite of students, who appreciate being able to tell their mothers that they're spending their weekends in the library. The (literally) underground club brings a variety of live acts throughout the year, although during the summer the action is in the outdoor garden, where students and even a few older types enjoy student-rate drinks under glowing paper lanterns. Beer from 320Ft. Shots 500-800Ft. Wine from 560Ft. Open M-F 7pm-3:30am and Sa 6pm-3:30am. Cash only.

Cökxpôn, IX, Soroksári út 8-10 (www.cokxponambient.hu). Boráros tér tram stop, trams 4, 6. From the tram stop, walk to the corner of Soroksári út and Lilliom utca. Bar and cafe run by the sinister-sounding Cökxpôn Ambient Society, a group of local artists and musicians dedicated to cross-genre arts and chilling out. Young hippies, musicians, and students lounge around on floor cushions and uneven benches while listening to music that might put others to sleep. Regular live acts and DJs play a mix of electronic and experimental music in the shoeless concert area in the next room. Beer from 250Ft. Shots 280-700Ft. Wine from 220Ft. Cover for live acts varies. Open M-W and Su 6pm-midnight, Th 6pm-2am, F-Sa 6pm-4am. Cash only.

Monyó Café, IX, Kálvin tér 7 (☎216 5500). Ⓜ3: Kálvin tér. The bar is between Ráday út and Lónya út. A quality local bar unfortunately obscured by the near-constant construction around the square. Friendly, unpretentious atmosphere. Standard barstools are replaced by swings which is a great novelty at first but may become more of a liability as the evening (and your judgment) wears on. Occasional DJs spin tunes that the drunkest people in the room will dance to. Beer 400Ft. Mixed drinks 900-1000Ft. Wheelchair-accessible. Open M-W noon-midnight, Th-F noon-2am, Sa 4pm-2am. Cash only.

BUDA

A38, XI, Near Petöfi Bridge, Buda side (☎01 464 3940; www.a38.hu). Petöfi híd, budai hídfő tram stop, trams 4,6. From the tram stop, go down the stairs and head toward the river; the club is on the large boat docked next to the road. Of all the clubs in Budapest situated inside abandoned things that were not meant to be clubs, A38 is perhaps the most improbable. Originally a Ukrainian freighter, the ship is now permanently docked on the Buda side of the Danube. The top deck has a relaxing bar that's open during the summer, while the former cargo hold now houses regular DJs and live acts. Unfortunately, the quality of the evening very much depends on the quality of the act, and some nights even the small lounge at the back of the dance floor is largely empty, though you can kill a few minutes just looking at the old equipment still lying around. Beer from 450Ft. Mixed drinks 1100-1850Ft. Open M-Sa 11am-midnight. Cover around 500Ft. Cash only.

Zöld Pardon, XI, Goldmann György tér (☎01 279 1880; www.zp.hu). Petöfi híd, budai hídfő tram stop, trams 4,6. A large beer garden billing itself as a summer-long party, with nightly DJs and live acts while 3 large screens flash occasionally trippy, often nonsensi-cal designs. Attracts a large crowd nightly to its 4 bars (one elevated above the dance floor on a mock island) and two stages, one for hip hop and one for more rock- and pop-oriented live music (all of it Hungarian). While the music is hit-or-miss, the crowd is always up for dancing along the riverside. Cover 300Ft. Beer from 350Ft. Mixed drinks from 1000Ft. Wheelchair-accessible. Open daily Apr.-Oct. 11am-5am. Cash only.

Cafe del Rio, XI, Goldmann György tér (☎30 297 2158; www.rio.hu). Petőfi híd, budai hídfő tram stop, trams 4,6. Buda's other outdoor summer venue caters to a more exclusive crowd than nearby Zöld Pardon. Palm trees, armchairs, and spotlights make you feel like a South American crime lord whose island is getting raided by the feds. Every evening, local hip hop and electronic DJs shepherd hordes of young, style-conscious clubbers into large white tents where they grind the night away to the latest beats. Beer from 350Ft. Mixed drinks 1500-2100Ft. Wheelchair-accessible. Open daily Apr.-Sept. 6pm-5am. AmEx/MC/V.

MARGIT-SZIGET

Margit-sziget's nightlife options are open May through September.

Cha Cha Cha Terasz, XIII, Margit-sziget (☎01 329 2788; www.chachacha.hu). From the Margit Bridge entrance, take the main road and turn left at the entrance to the athletic complex; the garden is on your left. The summer retreat of a popular Terézváros club brings a slightly more alternative crowd than the island's other gardens. The relaxed atmosphere combined with comfy outdoor couches make it feel like your scruffy friend with the enormous supply of liquor moved his furniture into the backyard for the sum-mer and invited everyone over. Nightly DJs get the party started as soon as they whisk through the door. Unfortunately, there is a charge for bathrooms (100Ft) which most people circumvent by using nearby trees. Most shots 350-700Ft, though some high-end drinks go for 3500Ft. Beer from 350Ft. Open daily 11am-late. Cash only.

Holdudvar, XIII, Margit-sziget (☎01 236 0155; www.holdudvar.net). From the Margit Bridge entrance, take the main road; the garden will be on your right, across from the Hajós Alfréd Swimming Pool. Ball-like orange lanterns and a large, distressed-looking deer mark the entrance to the largest and classiest of the island gardens, which also serves some of the best food to be found on the island, such as homemade gnocchi with ham "dried in the wind" (1700Ft). By day, the garden is full of families and tour-ists. By night, a mix of students, hostel groups, and locals descend on the dance floor manned by nightly DJs. Beer from 400Ft. Most shots 790-1400Ft. Appetizers 1700-2500Ft. Pasta 1700-2900Ft. Entrees 1500-4500Ft. Film screenings on the open-air cinema Su 9pm. Wheelchair accessible. Open daily 11am-5am. MC/V.

Sziget Klub Terasz, XIII, Margit-sziget (☎20 203 7488; www.szigetklubterasz.hu). From the Margit Bridge entrance, take the main road; the garden will be on your left just past the bus stop. More commonly known as "the other one," this small summer garden lacks much of the atmosphere of its larger rivals. To its credit, the large, multi-tiered terrace sports some nice river views and on nights when the other gardens are packed to capac-ity you can often find a space here. Travelers may appreciate the small menu of budget-friendly grill options during the day, including gingered chicken breast with peach and chili (1150Ft). Beer from 350Ft. Shots 700-900Ft. Mixed drinks 650-900Ft. Appetizers and salads 850-1500Ft. Entrees 1150-1500Ft. Open daily 11am-late. Cash only.

✾ FESTIVALS

Budapest Spring Festival (www.fesztivalvaros.hu), Mar. 19-Apr. 5 in 2010. Showcases Hungary's premier musicians, dancers, and actors across 10 of the city's best venues.

Sziget Festival (www.sziget.hu), in August. Óbudai Island hosts Central Europe's largest rock festival. In recent years, the sweaty, week-long festival has also become something of an experiment in alternative lifestyles, reminiscent of America's Burning Man festival. Non-camping tickets 32,600Ft; camping tickets 40,700Ft.

Formula 1 Hungarian Grand Prix (☎01 317 2811; www.hungaroring.hu), in August. Racing enthusiasts flock to the suburb of Mogyoró.

◪ DAYTRIPS FROM BUDAPEST

Just north of the city, the mighty Danube makes a 90° turn to the west. This region, known as the Danube Bend (Dunakanyar) is home to breathtaking scenery and several terminally quaint towns. Regular boat rides from Budapest allow you to take in all of the scenery and make stops at some of the more popular towns along the way. While Szentendre and Esztergom are perhaps less representative of small town life in Hunagary than they would have you believe, the fresh air and beautiful views of the Danube, especially from Esztergom's Basilica, are worth the trip alone.

SZENTENDRE

HÉV trains go to Szentendre (45min., 3 per hr., 480Ft) from Budapest's Batthyány tér station. Buses run from Szentendre to Budapest's Árpád híd metro station (30min., 1-3 per hr., 280Ft), Esztergom (1hr., 1 per hr., 660Ft), and Visegrád (45min., 1 per hr., 375Ft). Boats (☎01 484 4000) leave from the pier below Vigadó tér (1½hr., 2 per day, 2000Ft). The train and bus stations are 10min. from Fő tér; descend the stairs past the HÉV tracks and through the underpass up Kossuth utca. At the fork, bear right on Dumtsa Jenő utca. From the ferry station, turn left on Czóbel sétány and left on Dunakorzó utca. Tourinform, Dumtsa Jenő út. 22, is between the center and the stations. ☎02 631 7965. Open from mid-Mar. to Oct. daily 9:30am-1pm and 1:30-4:30pm; from Nov. to mid-Mar. M-F 9:30am-1pm and 1:30-4:30pm. In summer, a huge festival sweeps through town, bringing concerts, meat grilling booths, and other lively festivities to the town and the riverbanks. Check www.szentendreprogram.hu for details. Usually runs from late June to late Aug.

FROM THE ROAD

HOW NOT TO IMPRESS GIRLS IN BUDAPEST

During my first week in Budapest, I asked someone from my hostel what the most surprising thing about Hungarians was, and without missing a beat, she told me "at bars, people mix red wine and coke." I filed this away in my database of "quirky things about Hungarians." A few weeks later, my visiting friend asked me the same question, and I responded the same way. His eyes lit up. "We have to try that right now," he said.

I took him out to one of my favorite ruin pubs. We ran up to the bar like anxious schoolchildren to the ice cream truck and asked for two red wines with coke. The female bartender looked at us curiously for a moment, so my friend repeated our order, a little more slowly. She turned to the other bartender, who said something to her in Hungarian. A moment later, she produced two tall glasses with neon-colored straws. At our table we took a few hesitant sips. "It's not bad," my friend said. I agreed. After a moment, though, my friend looked around, and I saw his smile fade a little. I asked him what was the matter and he told me to look around. Then I realized: almost every woman in the bar was drinking red wine with coke. We quickly and silently finished our drinks and then ordered a round of beers.

- Justin Keenan

To see a quaint approximation of Hungary's rural past without straying far from Budapest, head north to relaxing Szentendre (pop. 23,000), known for its cobblestone streets and art collections. The city does a remarkable job of supporting more than a dozen small art museums and galleries. During the summer, the streets are packed with tourists, especially on weekends, so try to go early in the day during the week to see the town at its best. The center of town is Fő tér, where you can catch a tour of the town on a horse-drawn carriage (15min. 3000Ft per hr., 15,000Ft), complete with a stoic townsperson in traditional dress. The city is best surveyed from **Church Hill** (Templomdomb), above the town center. Once you've gotten your requisite photographs, check out the 13th-century **Parish Church of Saint John,** one of the few surviving medieval churches in Hungary. (Open Tu-Su 10am-4pm. Services Su 7am. Free.)

To the left of the church, the **Czóbel Museum,** Templom tér 1, exhibits work by noted artist Béla Czóbel, including his bikini-clad *Venus of Szentendre.* Admission includes access to the adjoining exhibit of works by the Szentendre Artists' Colony. (☎26 310 244 . Open W-Su 10am-6pm. English captions. 500Ft, students 300Ft. Cash only.) Of the city's other art museums, the popular **Kovács Margit Museum,** Vastagh György utca 1, off Görög utca, is one of the best, displaying a large collection of whimsical ceramic sculptures by the celebrated 20th-century Hungarian artist. (Open June-Aug. Tu-Su 9am-7pm, Sept.-May Tu-Su 9am-5pm. 700Ft, students 350Ft.)

By far the town's strangest museum is the ⬛**Szamos Marzipan Museum and Confectionery,** Dumtsa Jenő utca 12, where you can find, among other things, a life-size replica of the Hungarian crown jewels, scenes from the Wizard of Oz, and a 160cm long replica of the Hungarian parliament, all made from marzipan. The real "thriller," though, is undoubtedly the 80kg white-chocolate statue of Michael Jackson. On your way out, it's hard to resist getting at least a little something from the confectionery or the adjoining cafe. (☎01 412 626; www. szamosmarcipan.hu. Open daily May-Oct. 10am-7pm; Nov.-Apr. 10am-6pm. 400Ft.) The **Nemzeti Bormúzeum** (National Wine Museum), Bogdányi utca 10, consists of little more than a cellar with some displays set up to elaborate on Hungary's various wine regions. The museum tour is available with a wine tasting course, which features eight Hungarian wines as well as Hungarian appetizers. During the hot, sticky summer, the mercifully cool wine cellar is worth the trip alone. (www.bor-kor.hu. Open daily 10am-10pm. Exhibit 200Ft, tasting and English-language tour 2200Ft.) Those craving more substantial sustenance may want to check out **Cafe Christine,** Görög utca 6. Enjoy reasonably priced tourist food right by the Danube. In the summer, the small cafe opens up onto the sidewalk with plenty of seating and shade from a mix of umbrellas and trees. Those with little regard for their arteries will spring for the deep fried pork medallion (2100Ft) stuffed with ewe cheese. (☎20 369 7008; www. cafechristine.hu. Open daily 8am-11:30pm. MC/V.)

If the charm of Szentendre leaves you so overwhelmed that you just can't leave, consider staying the night at **Ilona Panzió ❹,** Rákóczi Ferenc utca 11, which rents simply furnished but comfortable rooms with baths. In the summer, breakfast is served on the outdoor terrace, surrounded by hanging plants. (☎026 313 599; www.ilonapanzio.hu. Breakfast included. Call ahead. Singles from 5800Ft; doubles from 8000Ft. Cash only.) Two kilometers north of the center, along the main waterside road, **Pap-szigeti Camping ❷** maintains its own island on the Danube near a small, popular beach. The campsite maintains more than a hundred sites for caravan and tent camping, as well as several bungalows on stilts with their own kitchen, shower, and toilet. (☎026 310 697;

www.pap-sziget.hu. Call ahead. Open May-Oct 15. Tent sites 3500Ft; 2-person caravan 4700Ft; 2-person bungalows 11,100Ft. Cash only.)

ESZTERGOM

Trains run from Budapest's Nyugati station (1½hr., 22 per day, 700Ft). The train station is about a 15min. walk from town. Facing away from the train station, go left on the main street. Follow the street around the bend to the left and turn right at Kis János Vezerezredes út. Buses run from Szentendre (1½hr., 1 per hr., 500Ft) and Visegrad (45min., 1 per hr., 350Ft). From the bus station, walk by Simor János út toward the market. The most spectacular way to get there is by MAHART ferry (☎ 484 4013; www. mahartpassnave.hu) leave the pier at Gőzhajó utca on Primas Sziget Island for Budapest (5hr., 6 per day, 2985Ft). Grantours, Széchenyi tér 25, at the edge of Rákóczi tér, assists tourists. ☎033 41 70 52; grantour@mail.holop.hu. Open July-Aug. M-F 8am-6pm, Sa 9am-noon; Sept.-June M-F 8am-4pm.

A millennium of religious history has made Esztergom a major religious and tourist destination. The birthplace of Saint-King Stephen was also the site of the first royal court of Hungary and its capital from the 10th to the 13th century. Its most striking feature, however, is doubtless the magnificent **Basilica of Esztergom,** a hilltop cathedral now the seat of the Hungarian Catholic Church. This Neoclassical cathedral, built on the site of an 11th-century cathedral, commands a majestic view of the Danube Bend. While approaching the basilica from the train station, look for the ridge to your right with the small church on top. The winding ridgebacks of the centuries-old walls are a long walk, but the view of the basilica and the town from the outlook is worth it.

There are several sites of interest within the basilica itself. The nave lacks much of the ornamentation of other cathedrals, which gives it a sense of quiet grandeur. The organ, adorned with a few angelic statues, is one of the largest in Hungary. To one side, you can find the reliquary containing the millenia-old skull of **Saint Stephen,** founder of the Kingdom of Hungary. The beautiful **Bakócz Chapel,** to the left of the nave, is the only surviving chapel from the Middle Ages. The builders of the cathedral disassembled the chapel into 1600 pieces and reincorporated it into the new church while preserving its original form. (☎33 40 23 54; www.bazilika-esztergom.hu. Open Mar.-Oct. Tu-Su 9am-4:30pm; Nov.-Dec. Tu-F 9am-4:30pm, Sa-Su 10am-3:30pm. Chapel free.) The cathedral **treasury** houses icons, textiles, and more relics than it knows what to do with, including the skull of St. Adalbert, the tooth of King-Saint Ladislaus, and the humerus of St. Gyllent, among others. The upper floor contains some exquisite shepherd's crooks and gold-adorned horns from the 16th century, as well as the better part of the cathedral's priestly wardrobe. (700Ft.) The sign at the entrance to the cathedral's **cupola** (400Ft) cautions against "persons having agoraphobia" visiting the cupola. While the translators may have gotten their phobias mixed up, the hike up more than 400 stairs, mostly in tightly wound spiral staircases, should probably be reserved for the healthy and the patient. Mercy on groups who meet another large group going the opposite direction. Still, the climb is worth whatever trials and tribulations you may have to undergo—the view from the top is one of the best you'll ever see. On clear days, you can see the beautiful pine-covered peaks of the Slovak Low Tatras. Guarded by two enormous statues, the church **crypt** contains the remains of Hungary's archbishops. The tomb of Csernoch János, to the left of the main crypt, is especially beautiful, with a bronze angel embracing the priest's marble effigy (200Ft).

Around the basilica, you can see the ruins of the castle where St. Stephen was born, which once dominated the same hilltop. A **museum** now occupies the former ruins, showcasing many artifacts from the medieval and Renaissance periods. Some areas allow you to look through the glass floor into the excavation site below. The views from the castle walls offer some great views of the basilica and the Danube. The lapidarium is strictly for the architecturally inclined, containing fragments of the castle's doorframes, parapets, and columns. (☎033 415 986. Open Tu-Su 10am-4:45pm. 840Ft.)

For a bite to eat near the base of the cathedral, try **Csülök Csárda ❷**, Batthyány út 9, where you can find traditional Hungarian fare in a picnic-like atmosphere. Dishes range from the questionable (smoked ox tongue; 1390Ft) to the politically incorrect (trout with crosus made in the "goodwife" style; 2190Ft). Every meal is better when it starts with some crispy goose cracklings (790Ft). Judging from the restaurant's sign, the ghost from the Ghostbusters logo is a regular patron. (☎363 341 2420; www.csulokcsarda.hu. Appetizers 790-1390Ft. Entrees 1690-3890Ft. Open July-Aug. M-F 8am-5pm, Sa 9am-noon; Sept.-June M-F 8am-4pm. Cash only.)

APPENDIX

CLIMATE

AVG. TEMP. (LOW/ HIGH), PRECIP.	JANUARY			APRIL			JULY			OCTOBER		
	°C	°F	mm	°C	°F	mm	°C	°F	mm	°C	°F	mm
Berlin	-3/2	26/35	43	4/13	39/55	43	13/23	55/73	53	6/13	42/55	36
Budapest	-3/2	27/36	39	7/17	44/62	47	16/28	62/82	50	8/16	46/61	47
Prague	-4/2	26/35	24	4/13	38/56	38	13/24	56/75	66	5/13	41/55	31

To convert from degrees Fahrenheit to degrees Celsius, subtract 32 and multiply by 5/9. To convert from Celsius to Fahrenheit, multiply by 9/5 and add 32.

°CELSIUS	-5	0	5	10	15	20	25	30	35	40
°FAHRENHEIT	23	32	41	50	59	68	77	86	95	104

MEASUREMENTS

Like the rest of the rational world, Berlin, Budapest, and Prague all use the metric system. The basic unit of length is the meter (m), which is divided into 100 centimeters (cm) or 1000 millimeters (mm). One thousand meters make up one kilometer (km). Fluids are measured in liters (L), each divided into 1000 milliliters (mL). A liter of pure water weighs one kilogram (kg), or 1000 grams (g). One metric ton is 1000kg.

MEASUREMENT CONVERSIONS	
1 inch (in.) = 25.4mm	1 millimeter (mm) = 0.039 in.
1 foot (ft.) = 0.305m	1 meter (m) = 3.28 ft.
1 yard (yd.) = 0.914m	1 meter (m) = 1.094 yd.
1 mile (mi.) = 1.609km	1 kilometer (km) = 0.621 mi.
1 ounce (oz.) = 28.35g	1 gram (g) = 0.035 oz.
1 pound (lb.) = 0.454kg	1 kilogram (kg) = 2.205 lb.
1 fluid ounce (fl. oz.) = 29.57mL	1 milliliter (mL) = 0.034 fl. oz.
1 gallon (gal.) = 3.785L	1 liter (L) = 0.264 gal.

LANGUAGE

GERMAN (DEUTSCH)

I can understand German as well as the maniac that invented it, but I talk it best through an interpreter. - Mark Twain

Most Germans speak at least basic English, but you will encounter many that don't. Preface any questions with a polite *Sprechen Sie Englisch?* (Do you speak English?) When out at restaurants, bars, and attractions, a simple *Bitte* (please) and *Danke* (thank you) go a long way. Even if your command of German is shaky, most Germans will appreciate your effort.

PRONUNCIATION

With a little bit of effort, you can make yourself easily understood in German. German pronunciation, for the most part, is consistent with spelling. There are no silent letters, and all nouns are capitalized.

German vowels and diphthongs also differ from their English counterparts. An **umlaut** over a letter (e.g., ü) makes the pronunciation longer and more rounded. An umlaut is sometimes replaced by an "e" following the vowel, so that "schön" becomes "schoen." Germans are generally very forgiving toward foreigners who butcher their mother tongue; there is, however, one important exception: place names. If you learn nothing else in German, learn to pronounce the names of cities properly. Berlin is "bare-LEEN," Hamburg is "HAHM-boorg," Munich is "MEUWN-shen," and Bayreuth is "BUY-royt."

Different pronunciations for certain letters and diphthongs are listed below. German also has one consonant that does not exist in English: the "ß," which is alternately referred to as the *scharfes S* (sharp S) or the *Ess-tset*. It is shorthand for a double-s, and is pronounced just like an "ss" in English. The letter appears only in lower case and shows up in two of the most important German words for travelers: Straße, "street," which is pronounced "SHTRAH-sseh" and abbreviated "Str."; and Schloß, "castle," pronounced "SHLOSS." The "ß" is currently being phased out by the German government in accordance with other German-speaking countries and replaced with "ss" in an effort to standardize spelling.

PHONETIC UNIT	PRONUNCIATION	PHONETIC UNIT	PRONUNCIATION
a	AH, as in "father"	j	Y, as in "young"
e	EH, as in "bet"	k	K, as in "kelp"
i	IH, as in "wind"	r	gutteral RH, like French
o	OH, as in "oh"	s	Z, as in "zone"
u	OO, as in "fondue"	v	F, as in "fantasy"
au	OW, as in "cow"	w	V, as in "vacuum"
ie	EE, as in "thief"	z	TS, as in "cats"
ei	EYE, as in "wine"	ch	K, as in "loch"
eu	OI, as in "boil"	qu	KV, as in "kvetch"
ä	similar to the E in "bet"	sch	SH, as in "shot"
ö	similar to the E in "perm"	st/sp	SHT/SHP, as in "spiel"
ü	close to the EU in "blue"	th	T, as in "time"

PHRASEBOOK

The following phrasebook is meant to provide only the most rudimentary phrases you will need in your travels. Nothing can replace a full-fledged phrasebook or a pocket-sized English-German dictionary. German features both an informal and formal form of address; in the tables below, the polite form follows the familiar form in parentheses. In German, all nouns can take any one of three genders: masculine (taking the article **der;** pronounced DARE), feminine (**die;** pronounced DEE), and neuter (**das;** pronounced DAHSS). All plural nouns also take the *die* article, regardless of their gender in the singular.

ENGLISH	GERMAN	PRONUNCIATION
Hello!/Hi!	Hallo!/Tag!	Hahllo!/Tahk!
Goodbye!/Bye!	Auf Wiedersehen!/Tschüss!	Owf VEE-der-zain!/Chuess!
Yes.	Ja.	Yah.
No.	Nein.	Nine.
Sorry!	Es tut mir leid!	Ess toot meer lite!

EMERGENCY

ENGLISH	GERMAN	PRONUNCIATION
Go away!	Geh weg!	Gay veck!
Help!	Hilfe!	HILL-fuh!
Call the police!	Ruf die Polizei!	Roof dee Pol-ee-TSEI!
Get a doctor!	Hol einen Arzt!	Hole EIN-en Ahrtst!

GREETINGS

ENGLISH	GERMAN	ENGLISH	GERMAN
Good morning.	Guten Morgen.	My name is...	Ich heiße...
Good afternoon.	Guten Tag.	What is your name?	Wie heißt du (heißen Sie)?
Good evening.	Guten Abend.	Where are you from?	Woher kommst du (kommen Sie)?
Good night.	Guten Nacht.	How are you?	Wie geht's (geht es Ihnen)?
Excuse me./Sorry.	Enthschuldigung/Sorry.	I'm well.	Es geht mir good.
Could you please help me?	Kannst du (Können Sie) mir helfen, bitte?	Do you speak English?	Sprichst du (Sprechen Sie) Englisch?
How old are you?	Wie alt bist du (sind Sie)?	I don't speak German.	Ich spreche kein Deutsch.

USEFUL PHRASES

ENGLISH	GERMAN	ENGLISH	GERMAN
Thank you (very much).	Danke (schön).	Please.	Bitte.
What?	Was?	No, thanks.	Nein, danke.
When (what time)?	Wann?	I don't care.	Es ist mir egal.
Why?	Warum?	No problem.	Kein problem.
Where is...?	Wo ist...?	I don't understand.	Ich verstehe nicht.
I'm from...	Ich komme aus...	Please speak slowly.	Sprechen Sie bitte langsam.
America/USA	Amerika/den USA	Please repeat.	Bitte wiederholen Sie.
Australia	Australien	Pardon? What was that?	Wie, bitte?
Canada	Kanada	How do you say that in German?	Wie sagt man das auf Deutsch?
Great Britain	Großbritannien	What does that mean?	Was bedeutet das?
Ireland	Irland	I want...	Ich möchte...
New Zealand	Neuseeland	I'm looking for...	Ich suche...
My (...) is broken.	Meine (...) ist kaputt!	I need...	Ich brauche...
I'm not feeling well.	Mir ist schlecht.	How much does that cost?	Wieviel kostet das?
I need a doctor.	Ich brauche einen Arzt.	I don't know.	Ich weiß nicht.
Leave me alone!	Laß mich in Ruhe!	Where is the toilet?	Wo ist die Toilette?

ENGLISH	GERMAN	ENGLISH	GERMAN
I'll call the police.	Ich rufe die Polizei.	I have potato salad in my Lederhosen.	Ich habe Kartoffelsalat in meinen Lederhosen.
Okay.	Alles klar.	I am a university student (male/female).	Ich bin Student (m)/ Studentin (f).
Maybe.	Vielleicht.	Are there student discounts?	Gibt es Studentenermäs-sigungen?
Too bad.	Schade.	How's the weather today?	Wie ist das Wetter heute?

CARDINAL NUMBERS										
0	1	2	3	4	5	6	7	8	9	10
null	eins	zwei	drei	vier	fünf	sechs	sieben	acht	neun	zehn
11	12	20	30	40	50	60	70	80	90	100
elf	zwölf	zwanzig	dreißig	vierzig	fünfzig	sechzig	siebzig	achtzig	neunzig	hundert

ORDINAL NUMBERS					
1st	erste	5th	fünfte	9th	neunte
2nd	zweite	6th	sechste	10th	zehnte
3rd	dritte	7th	siebte	20th	zwanzigste
4th	vierte	8th	achte	100th	hunderte

DIRECTIONS AND TRANSPORTATION			
(to the) right	rechts	(to the) left	links
straight ahead	geradeaus	Where is...?	Wo ist...?
next to	neben	opposite	gegenüber
How do I find...?	Wie finde ich...?	It's nearby.	Es ist in der Nähe.
How do I get to...?	Wie komme ich nach...?	Is that far from here?	Ist es weit weg?
one-way trip	einfache Fahrt	round-trip	hin und zurück
Where is this train going?	Wohin fährt das Zug?	When does the train leave?	Wann fährt der Zug ab?

ACCOMMODATIONS			
Rooms available	Zimmer frei	I would like a room...	Ich möchte ein Zimmer...
No vacancies	besetzt	...with sink.	...mit Waschbecken.
Are there any vacancies?	Gibt es ein Zimmer frei?	...with shower.	...mit Dusche.
Single room	Einzelzimmer	...with a toilet.	...mit WC.
Double room	Doppelzimmer	...with a bathtub.	...mit Badewanne.
Dormitory-style room	Mehrbettzimmer/ Schlafsaal	nonsmoker	Nichtraucher
Do you have anything cheaper?	Haben Sie etwas Bil-ligeres?	At what time?	Um wieviel Uhr?

TIME AND HOURS			
open	geöffnet	closed	geschlossen
morning	Morgen	opening hours	Öffnungszeiten
afternoon	Nachmittag	today	heute
night	Nacht	yesterday	gestern
evening	Abend	tomorrow	morgen
What time is it?	Wie spät ist es?	break time, rest day	Ruhepause, Ruhetag
It's (seven) o'clock.	Es ist (sieben) Uhr.	At what time?	Um wieviel Uhr?

OUT TO LUNCH			
bread	Brot	water	Wasser
roll	Brötchen	tap water	Leitungswasser
jelly	Marmelade	juice	Saft

meat	Fleisch	beer	Bier
beef	Rindfleisch	wine	Wein
pork	Schweinfleisch	coffee	Kaffee
chicken	Huhn	tea	Tee
sausage	Wurst	soup	Suppe
cheese	Käse	potatoes	Kartoffeln
fruit	Obst	milk	Milch
vegetables	Gemüse	sauce	Soße
cabbage	Kohl	french fries	Pommes frites
I would like to order...	Ich hätte gern...	Another beer, please.	Noch ein Bier, bitte.
It tastes good.	Es schmeckt gut.	It tastes awful.	Es schmeckt widerlich.
I'm a vegetarian.	Ich bin Vegetarier (m)/ Vegetarierin (f)	I'm a vegan.	Ich bin Veganer (m)/ Veganerin (f).
Service included.	Bedienung inklusiv.	Daily special	Tageskarte
Check, please.	Rechnung, bitte.	Give me a Nutella sandwich.	Geben Sie mir ein Nutellabrötchen.

OPPOSITES ATTRACT

together	zusammen	alone	allein/e
good	gut	bad	schlecht
happy	glücklich	sad	traurig
big	groß	small	klein
young	jung	old	alt
full	voll	empty	leer
warm	warm	cool	kühl
safe	sicher, ungefährlich	dangerous	gefährlich
alive	lebendig	dead	tot
special	besonders	simply	einfach
more	mehr	less	weniger
before	vor	after	nach
pretty	schön	ugly	häßlich

RIDICULOUS(LY) USEFUL PHRASES

Here's looking at you, kid.	Schau mich in die Augen, Kleines.	Many thanks for the pleasure ride in your patrol car.	Vielen Dank für den Ausritt in Ihrem Streifenwagen.
May I buy you a drink, darling?	Darf ich dir ein Getränk kaufen, Liebling?	I'm hung over.	Ich habe einen Kater.
Cheers!	Prost!	There is a disturbance in the force.	Es gibt eine Störung in der Kraft.
You're delicious.	Du bist lecker.	Inconceivable!	Quatsch!
That's cool.	Das ist ja geil/crass.	Hasta la vista, baby.	Bis später, Baby.

APPENDIX

GLOSSARY

ab/fahren: to depart
die Abfahrt: departure
das Abteil: train compartment
Achtung: beware
die Altstadt: old town, historic center
das Amt: bureau, office
an/kommen: to arrive
die Ankunft: arrival
die Apotheke: pharmacy
die Arbeit: work
der Ausgang: exit
die Auskunft: information
die Ausstellung: exhibition
die Ausweis: ID
das Auto: car
die Autobahn: highway
der Autobus: bus
das Bad: bath, spa
das Bahn: railway
der Bahnhof: train station
der Bahnsteig: train platform
der Berg: mountain, hill
die Bibliothek: library
die Brücke: bridge
der Brunnen: fountain, well
der Bundestag: parliament
die Burg: fortress, castle
der Busbahnhof: bus station
die Damen: ladies (restroom)
das Denkmal: memorial
die Dusche: shower
der Dom: cathedral
das Dorf: village
eklig: disgusting

die Einbahnstraße: one-way street
der Eingang: entrance
ein/steigen: board
der Eintritt: admission
der Fahrplan: timetable
das Fahrrad: bicycle
der Fahrschein: train/bus ticket
die Festung: fortress
der Flohmarkt: flea market
der Flughafen: airport
der Fluß: river
das Fremdenverkehrsamt: tourist office
die Fußgängerzone: pedestrian zone
das Gasthaus: guest house
die Gedenkstätte: memorial
geil: cool (or horny)
das Gleis: track
der Hafen: harbor
der Hauptbahnhof: main train station
der Hof: court, courtyard
die Innenstadt: city center
die Insel: island
die Jugendherberge: youth hostel
die Karte: ticket
das Kino: cinema
die Kirche: church
das Krankenhaus: hospital
das Kreuz: cross, crucifix
die Kunst: art
der Kurort: spa/resort
die Kurverwaltung: resort tourist office

das Land: German state/province
die Lesbe: lesbian (n.)
der Markt: market
der Marktplatz: market square
das Meer: sea
das Münster: cathedral
das Museum: museum
der Notausgang: emergency exit
der Notfall: emergency
der Notruf: emergency hotline
der Paß: passport
der Platz: square, plaza
die Polizei: police
das Postamt: post office
die Quittung: receipt
das Rathaus: town hall
die Rechnung: bill, check
das Reisezentrum: travel office in train stations
die S-Bahn: commuter rail
das Schiff: ship
das Schloß: castle
der See: lake
die Stadt: city
der Strand: beach
die Straße: street
die Tankstelle: gas/petrol station
das Tor: gate
die U-Bahn: subway
die Vorsicht: caution
der Wald: forest
das W.C.: bathroom
wandern: to hike
der Wanderweg: hiking trail
der Weg: road, way
die Zeitung: newspaper
der Zug: train

CHA-CHA-CHA-CZECH IT OUT

Cut from the same cloth as many Slavic languages (though cleverly severing the ties of using the Cyrilic alphabet as the Russians do), Czech (Česky) is the official language of the Czech Republic and you will likely encounter it at least once on your journey to Prague. Basic Czech could take years of practice, but don't despair—a basic understanding of the pronunciation, some elementary phrases, and a healthy dose of courage will get you from A to B.

PRONUNCIATION

There are no two ways about it: Czech pronunciation is tough for the average English speaker. If a word appears vowel-less, try not to panic. In Czech, the stress falls on the first syllable, though an accent (á, é, í, ó, or ú) lengthens a vowel. The table below covers the basics of Czech pronunciation.

PHONETIC UNIT	PRONUNCIATION	PHONETIC UNIT	PRONUNCIATION
c	TS, as in "gets"	ř	ZH, close to the -ge sound in "luggage"
ě	YE, close to "yet"	w	V, as in "very" or "Vaclav"
j	Y, as in "young"	Milan Kundera; Václav Havel	MEE-lahn KOON-dehr-ah; VAHTS-lahv HAH-vel

PHRASEBOOK

ENGLISH	CZECH	PRONUNCIATION
Hello	Dobrý den (formal)	DOH-bree dehn
Yes/No	Ano/ne	AH-noh/neh
Please/you're welcome	Prosím	PROH-seem
Thank You	Děkuji	DYEH-koo-yee
Goodbye	Nashledanou	NAS-kleh-dah-noh
Good morning	Dobré ráno	DOH-breh RAH-noh
Good evening	Dobrý večer	DOH-breh VEH
Good night	Dobrou noc	DOH-broh NOHTS
Sorry/excuse me	Promiňte	PROH-meen-teh
Do you speak English?	Mluví anglicky?	MLOO-veet-eh ahng-GLEET-skee
I don't speak Czech.	Nemluvím Česky.	NEH-mloo-veem CHESS-kee
I don't understand.	Nerozumím.	NEH-rohz-oo-meem
Please write it down.	Mohl byste to napsat?	MO-huhl BI-ste to NAP-sat
When?	Kdy?	gdee

TRAVELING		
Where is...?	Kde je...?	gdeh yeh
...the bathroom?	...koupelna?	KOH-pehl-nah
...the nearest telephone booth?	...nejbližší telefonní budka?	NEY-bleezh-shnee TEH-leh-foh-nee BOOT-kah
...the center of town?	...centrum města?	TSEN-troom MYEHST-steh
toilet	W.C.	VEE-TSEE
left	vlevo	VLEH-voh
right	vpravo	VPRAH-voh
straight ahead	přímo	PRZHEE-moh
Do you have a vacancy?	Máte volný pokoj?	MAH-teh VOL-nee POH-koy
I'd like a room.	Prosím pokoj.	proh-SEEM PO-koy
single room	jednolůžkový pokoj	YEHD-noh-loozh-koh-vee POH-koy
double room	dvoulůžkový pokoj	DVOH-loozh-ko-vee POH-koy

APPENDIX

reservation	rezervace	REH-zer-vah-tseh
luggage	zavadla	ZAH-vahd-lah
station	nádraží	NAH-drah-zhee
train	vlak	vlahk
bus	autobus	OW-toh-boos
bus station	autobusové nádražé	PW-toh-boo-sohv-eh NAH-drazh-eh
airport	letiště	LEH-teesh-tyeh
I want a ticket to...	Chtěl bych jízdenku do...	khytel bikh YEEZ-den-koo DOH
ticket	lístek	LEES-tek
round-trip	zpáteční	SPAH-tehch-nyee
one-way	jedním směrem	YED-neem SMNYE-rem
How much does this cost?	Kolik to stojí?	KOH-leek STOH-yee
How long does the trip take?	Jak dlouho ta cesta trva?	yahk DLOH-ho tah TSE-stah TER-vah
departure	odjezd	OHD-yehzd
arrival	příjezd	PREE-yehzd
square	náměstí	NAH-myeh-stee
passport	cestovní pas	TSEH-stohv-nee pahs
bank	banka	BAHN-kah
exchange	směnárna	smyeh-NAHR-nah
post office	pošta	POSH-tah
stamp	známka	ZNAHM-kah
airmail	letecky	LEH-tehts-kee

DAYS OF THE WEEK		
Monday	pondělí	POHN-dyeh-lee
Tuesday	úterý	OO-teh-ree
Wednesday	středa	STRZHEH-dah
Thursday	čtvrtek	CHTVER-tehk
Friday	pátek	PAH-tehk
Saturday	sobota	SOH-boh-tah
Sunday	neděle	NEH-dyeh-leh
today	dnes	dnehs
tomorrow	zítra	ZEE-trah
day	den	dehn
week	týden	tee-dehn
morning	ráno	RAH-noh
afternoon	odpoledne	OHD-pohl-ehd-neh
evening	večer	VEH-chehr

OUT TO LUNCH		
breakfast	snídaně	SNEE-dahn-yeh
lunch	oběd	OHB-yed
dinner	večeře	VEH-cher-zheh
market	trh	terh
grocery	potraviny	POH-trah-vee-nee
menu	listek/menu	LEES-tehk/meh-noo
I'd like to order...	Prosím...	proh-SEEM
bread	chléb	khlep
vegetables	zelenina	ZEH-leh-nee-nah
meat	maso	MAH-soh
coffee	káva	KAH-vah

milk	mléko	MLEH-koh
hot	teplý	TEHP-leeh
cold	studený	STOO-deh-nee
beer	pivo	PEE-voh
Cheers!	Na zdraví!	nah-ZDRAH-vee
I don't eat...	Nejím maso...	NEH-yeem MAH-soh
I'm allergic.	Jsem alergický.	ysehm AH-lehr-gits-kee
Check, please.	Paragon, prosím.	PAH-rah-gohn proh-SEEM

EMERGENCY		
Help!	Pomoc!	POH-mots
Go away.	Prosím odejděte.	pro-SEEM ODEH-dyeh-teh
police	policie	POH-leets-ee-yeh
doctor	doktor	DOHK-tohr
hospital	nemocnice	NEH-mo-tsnyi-tseh

THE UNIVERSAL LANGUAGE		
I love you.	Miluji tě.	MEE-loo-yee tyeh

CARDINAL NUMBERS		
one	jedna	YEHD-na
two	dvě	dvye
three	tři	trzhee
four	čtyři	CHTEER-zhee
five	pět	pyet
six	šest	shest
seven	sedm	SEH-doom
eight	osm	OH-suhm
nine	devět	DE-vyet
ten	deset	DE-set

HUNGARIAN (MAGYAR)

If you thought Czech was hard, hang onto your hat. Hungarian is a Uralic language, which means it's basically unrelated to most others in Europe. We've tried to keep it simple in the tables that follow. Just remember that as with Czech, stress falls on the first syllable of each word. After consonants, especially g, l, or n, the y is not pronounced but serves to soften the letter it follows.

PHRASEBOOK

ENGLISH	HUNGARIAN	PRONUNCIATION
Hello	Szervusz (polite)/Szia (informal)/ Hello	SAYHR-voose/see-ya/Hello
Yes/No	Igen/nem	EE-gehn/nehm
Please/you're welcome	Kérem	KAY-rehm
Thank You	Köszönöm	KUH-suh-nuhm
Goodbye	Viszontlátásra	VEE-sohnt-laht-ah-shrah
Good morning	Jó reggelt	YAW RAHg-gailt
Good evening	Jó estét	YAW EHSH-teht
Good night	Jó éjszakát	YAW AY-sah-kaht
Sorry/excuse me	Elnézést	EHL-nay-zaysht
Do you speak English?	Beszél angolul?	BESS-ayl AHN-gawl-ool

I don't speak Hungarian.	Nem tudok (jól) magyarul.	nehm TOO-dawk (yawl) MAW-jyah-rool
I don't understand.	Nem értem.	nem AYR-tem
Please write it down.	Kérem, írja fel.	KAY-rem, EER-yuh fel
When?	Mikor	MEE-kohr

TRAVELING		
Where is...?	Hol van...?	haul vahn
...the bathroom?	...a W. C.?	ah VAY-tsay
...the nearest telephone booth?	...a legközelebbi telefonfülke?	ah LEHG-kawz-ehl-ehb-ee teh-leh-FAWN-FOOHL-keh
...the center of town?	...a városközpont?	ah VAH-rosh-kohz-pohnt
toilet	W.C.	VAH-tsay
left	bal	bohl
right	jobb	yawb
straight ahead	egyenesen	EHDJ-ehn-ehshen
Do you have a vacancy?	Van üres szoba?	vahn oo-REHSH SAH-bah
I'd like a room.	Szeretnék egy szobát	seh-reht-naik ehj SAW-baht
single room	egyágyas	EHD-ahd-awsh
double room	kétágyas szoba	keht-AHGAHS soh-bah
reservation	helyfoglalás	HEY-fohg-lah-DASH
luggage	csomag	CHOH-mahg
airport	repülőtér	rep-oo-loo-TAYR
train	vonat	VAW-noht
bus	autóbusz	AU-OO-toh-boos
bus station	buszmegálló	boos-mehg-AH-loh
I want a ticket.	Szeretnékegy jegyet.	sehr-eht-nayk-ehj yehj-at
ticket	jegyet	YEHD-eht
round-trip	oda-vissza	AW-doh-VEES-soh
one-way	csak oda	chohk AW-doh
How much does this cost?	Mennyibe kerül?	MEHN-yee-beh KEH-rool
departure	indulás	IN-dool-ahsh
arrival	érkezés	ayr-keh-zaysh
square	tér	tehr
passport	az útlevelemet	ahz oot-leh-veh-leh-meht
bank	bank	bohnk
exchange	pénzaváltó	pehn-zah-VAHL-toh
post office	posta	PAWSH-tah
stamp	bélyeg	BAY-yeg
airmail	légiposta	LAY-ghee-PAWSH-tah

DAYS OF THE WEEK		
Monday	hétfő	hayte-phuuh
Tuesday	kedd	kehd
Wednesday	szerda	SEHR-dah
Thursday	csütörtök	choo-ter-tek
Friday	péntek	payne-tek
Saturday	szombat	SAWM-baht
Sunday	vasárnap	VAHSH-ahr-nahp
today	ma	mah
tomorrow	holnap	HAWL-nahp
day	nap	nahp
week	hét	hayht

morning	reggel	REHG-gehl
afternoon	délután	deh-lu-taan
evening	este	EHS-te

OUT TO LUNCH		
breakfast	reggeli	REHG-gehl-ee
lunch	ebéd	EHB-ayd
dinner	vacsora	VAWCH-oh-rah
market	piac	PEE-ohts
grocery	élelmiszerbolt	AY-lehl-meh-sehr-bawlt
I'd like to order...	kérek	KAY-rehk
vegetables	zöldségek	ZUHLD-seh-gehk
meat	húst	hoosht
coffee	kávé	KAA-vay
milk	tej	tay
hot	meleg	MEE-lehg
cold	hideg	HEE-dehg
beer	sör	shurr
Cheers!	Egészségedre!	ehg-eh-SHEHG-eh-dreh
I don't eat...	Nem eszem...	nem eh-sem
I'm allergic.	Allergia's vagyok.	ah-lehr-ghee-ahsh vah-jawk
Check, please.	A számlát, kérem.	uh SAHM-lot KAY-rehm

EMERGENCY		
Go away.	Távozzék.	TAH-vawz-zayk
police	rendőrség	REHN-doer-shayg
doctor	kórház	KAWR-haaz
hospital	orvos	AWR-vahsh

THE UNIVERSAL LANGUAGE		
I love you.	Szeretleu.	sehr-EHT-lyuh

CARDINAL NUMBERS		
one	egy	ehj
two	kettő	KEHT-tuh
three	három	HAH-rohm
four	négy	naydj
five	öt	uht
six	hat	hawt
seven	hét	hayt
eight	nyolc	nyawltz
nine	kilenc	KEE-lehntz
ten	tíz	teehz

APPENDIX

INDEX

MAP INDEX

MAP LEGEND

▪ Sight/Service	✈ Airport	⛪ Convent/Monastery	℞ Pharmacy
🏠 Accommodation	⊓ Arch/Gate	⚓ Ferry Landing	✛ Police
⛺ Camping	$ Bank	(347) Highway Sign	✉ Post Office
🍎 Food	⛱ Beach	⊞ Hospital	🎿 Skiing
☕ Cafe	🚌 Bus Station	💻 Internet Cafe	✡ Synagogue
🏛 Museum	◎ Capital City	📖 Library	☎ Telephone Office
● Sight	♜ Castle	Ⓜ M Metro Station	☗ Theater
🍺 Bar/Pub	⚑ Church	▲ Mountain	🛈 Tourist Office
★ Nightlife	Consulate/Embassy	Mosque	🚉 Train

Park		Water	⋯ Pedestrian Zone	LG The Let's Go compass always points NORTH.
			▥ Stairs	

HELPING LET'S GO. If you want to share your discoveries, suggestions, or corrections, please drop us a line. We appreciate every piece of correspondence, whether a postcard, a 10-page email, or a coconut. Visit Let's Go at **http://www.letsgo.com,** or send email to:

  feedback@letsgo.com, subject: "Let's Go Berlin, Prague & Budapest"

Address mail to:

  Let's Go Berlin, Prague & Budapest, 67 Mount Auburn St., Cambridge, MA 02138, USA

In addition to the invaluable travel advice our readers share with us, many are kind enough to offer their services as researchers or editors. Unfortunately, our charter enables us to employ only currently enrolled Harvard students.

Maps by Let's Go copyright © 2010 by Let's Go, Inc.

Distributed by Publishers Group West.
Printed in Canada by Friesens Corp.

ISBN-13: 978-1-59880-306-8
ISBN-10: 1-59880-306-9
First edition
10 9 8 7 6 5 4 3 2 1

Let's Go Berlin, Prague & Budapest is written by Let's Go Publications, 67 Mount Auburn St., Cambridge, MA 02138, USA.

Let's Go® and the LG logo are trademarks of Let's Go, Inc.